NOVELS
for Students

Advisors

Jayne M. Burton is a teacher of English, a member of the Delta Kappa Gamma International Society for Key Women Educators, and currently a master's degree candidate in the Interdisciplinary Study of Curriculum and Instruction and English at Angelo State University.

Tom Shilts is the youth librarian at the Okemos branch of Capital Area District Library in Okemos, Michigan. He holds an MSLS degree from Clarion University of Pennsylvania and an MA in U.S. History from the University of North Dakota.

Amy Spade Silverman has taught at independent schools in California, Texas, Michigan, and New York. She holds a bachelor of arts degree from the University of Michigan and a master of fine arts degree from the University of Houston. She is a member of the National Council of Teachers of English and Teachers and Writers. She is an exam reader for Advanced Placement Literature and Composition. She is also a poet, published in *North American Review*, *Nimrod*, and *Michigan Quarterly Review*, among others.

NOVELS

for Students

**Presenting Analysis, Context, and Criticism
on Commonly Studied Novels**

VOLUME 45

Sara Constantakis, Project Editor

Foreword by Anne Devereaux Jordan

GALE
CENGAGE Learning®

Detroit • New York • San Francisco • New Haven, Conn • Waterville, Maine • London

GALE
CENGAGE Learning®

Novels for Students, Volume 45

Project Editor: Sara Constantakis

Rights Acquisition and Management:
  Margaret Chamberlain-Gaston

Composition: Evi Abou-El-Seoud

Manufacturing: Rhonda Dover

Imaging: John Watkins

Product Design: Pamela A. E. Galbreath,
  Jennifer Wahi

Digital Content Production: Allie Semperger

For product information and technology assistance, contact us at
Gale Customer Support, 1-800-877-4253.
For permission to use material from this text or product,
submit all requests online at **www.cengage.com/permissions.**
Further permissions questions can be emailed to
permissionrequest@cengage.com

While every effort has been made to ensure the reliability of the information presented in this publication, Gale, a part of Cengage Learning, does not guarantee the accuracy of the data contained herein. Gale accepts no payment for listing; and inclusion in the publication of any organization, agency, institution, publication, service, or individual does not imply endorsement of the editors or publisher. Errors brought to the attention of the publisher and verified to the satisfaction of the publisher will be corrected in future editions.

Gale
27500 Drake Rd.
Farmington Hills, MI, 48331-3535

ISBN-13: 978-1-4144-9488-3
ISBN-10: 1-4144-9488-2

ISSN 1094-3552

This title is also available as an e-book.
ISBN-13: 978-1-4144-9274-2
ISBN-10: 1-4144-9274-X
Contact your Gale, a part of Cengage Learning sales representative for ordering information.

Printed in Mexico
1 2 3 4 5 6 7 18 17 16 15 14

Table of Contents

The Informed Dialogue:
Interacting with Literature

When we pick up a book, we usually do so with the anticipation of pleasure. We hope that by entering the time and place of the novel and sharing the thoughts and actions of the characters, we will find enjoyment. Unfortunately, this is often not the case; we are disappointed. But we should ask, has the author failed us, or have we failed the author?

We establish a dialogue with the author, the book, and with ourselves when we read. Consciously and unconsciously, we ask questions: "Why did the author write this book?" "Why did the author choose that time, place, or character?" "How did the author achieve that effect?" "Why did the character act that way?" "Would I act in the same way?" The answers we receive depend upon how much information about literature in general and about that book specifically we ourselves bring to our reading.

Young children have limited life and literary experiences. Being young, children frequently do not know how to go about exploring a book, nor sometimes, even know the questions to ask of a book. The books they read help them answer questions, the author often coming right out and *telling* young readers the things they are learning or are expected to learn. The perennial classic, *The Little Engine That Could,* tells its readers that, among other things, it is good to help others and brings happiness:

> "Hurray, hurray," cried the funny little clown and all the dolls and toys. "The good little boys and girls in the city will be happy because you helped us, kind, Little Blue Engine."

In picture books, messages are often blatant and simple, the dialogue between the author and reader one-sided. Young children are concerned with the end result of a book—the enjoyment gained, the lesson learned—rather than with how that result was obtained. As we grow older and read further, however, we question more. We come to expect that the world within the book will closely mirror the concerns of our world, and that the author will *show* these through the events, descriptions, and conversations within the story, rather than *telling* of them. We are now expected to do the interpreting, carry on our share of the dialogue with the book and author, and glean not only the author's message, but comprehend how that message and the overall affect of the book were achieved. Sometimes, however, we need help to do these things. *Novels for Students* provides that help.

A novel is made up of many parts interacting to create a coherent whole. In reading a novel, the more obvious features can be easily spotted— theme, characters, plot—but we may overlook the more subtle elements that greatly influence how the novel is perceived by the reader: viewpoint, mood and tone, symbolism, or the use of humor. By focusing on both the obvious and more subtle literary elements within a novel, *Novels for Students* aids readers in both analyzing for message and in determining how and why that message is communicated. In the discussion on Harper Lee's *To Kill a Mockingbird* (Vol. 2), for example, the mockingbird as a symbol of innocence is dealt with, among other things, as is the importance of Lee's use of humor which "enlivens a serious plot, adds depth to the characterization, and creates a sense of familiarity and universality." The reader comes to understand the internal elements of each novel discussed—as well as the external influences that help shape it.

"The desire to write greatly," Harold Bloom of Yale University says, "is the desire to be elsewhere, in a time and place of one's own, in an originality that must compound with inheritance, with an anxiety of influence." A writer seeks to create a unique world within a story, but although it is unique, it is not disconnected from our own world. It speaks to us *because* of what the writer brings to the writing from our world: how he or she was raised and educated; his or her likes and dislikes; the events occurring in the real world at the time of the writing, and while the author was growing up. When we know what an author has brought to his or her work, we gain a greater insight into both the "originality" (the world of the book), and the things that "compound" it. This insight enables us to question that created world and find answers more readily. By informing ourselves, we are able to establish a more effective dialogue with both book and author.

Novels for Students, in addition to providing a plot summary and descriptive list of characters—to remind readers of what they have read—also explores the external influences that shaped each book. Each entry includes a discussion of the author's background, and the historical context in which the novel was written. It is vital to know, for instance, that when Ray Bradbury was writing *Fahrenheit 451* (Vol. 1), the threat of Nazi domination had recently ended in Europe, and the McCarthy hearings were taking place in Washington, D.C. This information goes far in answering the question, "Why did he write a story of oppressive government control and book burning?" Similarly, it is important to know that Harper Lee, author of *To Kill a Mockingbird,* was born and raised in

Monroeville, Alabama, and that her father was a lawyer. Readers can now see why she chose the south as a setting for her novel—it is the place with which she was most familiar—and start to comprehend her characters and their actions.

Novels for Students helps readers find the answers they seek when they establish a dialogue with a particular novel. It also aids in the posing of questions by providing the opinions and interpretations of various critics and reviewers, broadening that dialogue. Some reviewers of *To Kill A Mockingbird,* for example, "faulted the novel's climax as melodramatic." This statement leads readers to ask, "Is it, indeed, melodramatic?" "If not, why did some reviewers see it as such?" "If it is, why did Lee choose to make it melodramatic?" "Is melodrama ever justified?" By being spurred to ask these questions, readers not only learn more about the book and its writer, but about the nature of writing itself.

The literature included for discussion in *Novels for Students* has been chosen because it has something vital to say to us. *Of Mice and Men, Catch-22, The Joy Luck Club, My Antonia, A Separate Peace* and the other novels here speak of life and modern sensibility. In addition to their individual, specific messages of prejudice, power, love or hate, living and dying, however, they and all great literature also share a common intent. They force us to *think*—about life, literature, and about others, not just about ourselves. They pry us from the narrow confines of our minds and thrust us outward to confront the world of books and the larger, real world we all share. *Novels for Students* helps us in this confrontation by providing the means of enriching our conversation with literature and the world, by creating an *informed* dialogue, one that brings true pleasure to the personal act of reading.

Sources

Harold Bloom, *The Western Canon, The Books and School of the Ages,* Riverhead Books, 1994.

Watty Piper, *The Little Engine That Could,* Platt & Munk, 1930.

Anne Devereaux Jordan
Senior Editor, TALL (Teaching and Learning Literature)

Introduction

Purpose of the Book

The purpose of *Novels for Students* (*NfS*) is to provide readers with a guide to understanding, enjoying, and studying novels by giving them easy access to information about the work. Part of Gale's "For Students" Literature line, *NfS* is specifically designed to meet the curricular needs of high school and undergraduate college students and their teachers, as well as the interests of general readers and researchers considering specific novels. While each volume contains entries on "classic" novels frequently studied in classrooms, there are also entries containing hard-to-find information on contemporary novels, including works by multicultural, international, and women novelists. Entries profiling film versions of novels not only diversify the study of novels but support alternate learning styles, media literacy, and film studies curricula as well.

The information covered in each entry includes an introduction to the novel and the novel's author; a plot summary, to help readers unravel and understand the events in a novel; descriptions of important characters, including explanation of a given character's role in the novel as well as discussion about that character's relationship to other characters in the novel; analysis of important themes in the novel; and an explanation of important literary techniques and movements as they are demonstrated in the novel.

In addition to this material, which helps the readers analyze the novel itself, students are also provided with important information on the literary and historical background informing each work. This includes a historical context essay, a box comparing the time or place the novel was written to modern Western culture, a critical essay, and excerpts from critical essays on the novel. A unique feature of *NfS* is a specially commissioned critical essay on each novel, targeted toward the student reader.

The "literature to film" entries on novels vary slightly in form, providing background on film technique and comparison to the original, literary version of the work. These entries open with an introduction to the film, which leads directly into the plot summary. The summary highlights plot changes from the novel, key cinematic moments, and/or examples of key film techniques. As in standard entries, there are character profiles (noting omissions or additions, and identifying the actors), analysis of themes and how they are illustrated in the film, and an explanation of the cinematic style and structure of the film. A cultural context section notes any time period or setting differences from that of the original work, as well as cultural differences between the time in which the original work was written and the time in which the film adaptation was made. A film entry concludes with a critical overview and critical essays on the film.

To further help today's student in studying and enjoying each novel or film, information on media adaptations is provided (if available), as well as suggestions for works of fiction, nonfiction, or film on similar themes and topics. Classroom aids include ideas for research papers and lists of critical and reference sources that provide additional material on the novel. Film entries also highlight signature film techniques demonstrated, and suggest media literacy activities and prompts to use during or after viewing a film.

Selection Criteria

The titles for each volume of *NfS* are selected by surveying numerous sources on notable literary works and analyzing course curricula for various schools, school districts, and states. Some of the sources surveyed include: high school and undergraduate literature anthologies and textbooks; lists of award-winners, and recommended titles, including the Young Adult Library Services Association (YALSA) list of best books for young adults. Films are selected both for the literary importance of the original work and the merits of the adaptation (including official awards and widespread public recognition).

Input solicited from our expert advisory board—consisting of educators and librarians—guides us to maintain a mix of "classic" and contemporary literary works, a mix of challenging and engaging works (including genre titles that are commonly studied) appropriate for different age levels, and a mix of international, multicultural and women authors. These advisors also consult on each volume's entry list, advising on which titles are most studied, most appropriate, and meet the broadest interests across secondary (grades 7–12) curricula and undergraduate literature studies.

How Each Entry Is Organized

Each entry, or chapter, in *NfS* focuses on one novel. Each entry heading lists the full name of the novel, the author's name, and the date of the novel's publication. The following elements are contained in each entry:

Introduction: a brief overview of the novel which provides information about its first appearance, its literary standing, any controversies surrounding the work, and major conflicts or themes within the work. Film entries identify the original novel and provide understanding of the film's reception and reputation, along with that of the director.

Author Biography: in novel entries, this section includes basic facts about the author's life, and focuses on events and times in the author's life that inspired the novel in question.

Plot Summary: a factual description of the major events in the novel. Lengthy summaries are broken down with subheads. Plot summaries of films are used to uncover plot differences from the original novel, and to note the use of certain film angles or other techniques.

Characters: an alphabetical listing of major characters in the novel. Each character name is followed by a brief to an extensive description of the character's role in the novel, as well as discussion of the character's actions, relationships, and possible motivation. In film entries, omissions or changes to the cast of characters of the film adaptation are mentioned here, and the actors' names— and any awards they may have received— are also included.

Characters are listed alphabetically by last name. If a character is unnamed—for instance, the narrator in *Invisible Man*—the character is listed as "The Narrator" and alphabetized as "Narrator." If a character's first name is the only one given, the name will appear alphabetically by that name.

Variant names are also included for each character. Thus, the full name "Jean Louise Finch" would head the listing for the narrator of *To Kill a Mockingbird*, but listed in a separate cross-reference would be the nickname "Scout Finch."

Themes: a thorough overview of how the major topics, themes, and issues are addressed within the novel. Each theme discussed appears in a separate subhead. While the key themes often remain the same or similar when a novel is adapted into a film, film entries demonstrate how the themes are conveyed cinematically, along with any changes in the portrayal of the themes.

Style: this section addresses important style elements of the novel, such as setting, point of view, and narration; important literary devices used, such as imagery, foreshadowing, symbolism; and, if applicable, genres to which the work might have belonged, such as Gothicism or Romanticism. Literary terms are explained within the entry but can also be found in the Glossary. Film entries cover how the director conveyed the meaning, message, and mood of the work using film in comparison to the author's use of language, literary device, etc., in the original work.

Historical Context: in novel entries, this section outlines the social, political, and cultural climate in which the author lived and the novel was created. This section may include descriptions of related historical events, pertinent aspects of daily life in the culture, and the artistic and literary sensibilities of the time in which the work was written. If the novel is a historical work, information regarding the time in which the novel is set is also included. Each section is broken down with helpful subheads. Film entries contain a similar Cultural Context section because the film adaptation might explore an entirely different time period or culture than the original work, and may also be influenced by the traditions and views of a time period much different than that of the original author.

Critical Overview: this section provides background on the critical reputation of the novel or film, including bannings or any other public controversies surrounding the work. For older works, this section includes a history of how the novel or film was first received and how perceptions of it may have changed over the years; for more recent novels, direct quotes from early reviews may also be included.

Criticism: an essay commissioned by *NfS* which specifically deals with the novel or film and is written specifically for the student audience, as well as excerpts from previously published criticism on the work (if available).

Sources: an alphabetical list of critical material used in compiling the entry, with full bibliographical information.

Further Reading: an alphabetical list of other critical sources which may prove useful for the student. It includes full bibliographical information and a brief annotation.

Suggested Search Terms: a list of search terms and phrases to jumpstart students' further information seeking. Terms include not just titles and author names but also terms and

topics related to the historical and literary context of the works.

In addition, each novel entry contains the following highlighted sections, set apart from the main text as sidebars:

Media Adaptations: if available, a list of audiobooks and important film and television adaptations of the novel, including source information. The list also includes stage adaptations, musical adaptations, etc.

Topics for Further Study: a list of potential study questions or research topics dealing with the novel. This section includes questions related to other disciplines the student may be studying, such as American history, world history, science, math, government, business, geography, economics, psychology, etc.

Compare and Contrast: an "at-a-glance" comparison of the cultural and historical differences between the author's time and culture and late twentieth century or early twenty-first century Western culture. This box includes pertinent parallels between the major scientific, political, and cultural movements of the time or place the novel was written, the time or place the novel was set (if a historical work), and modern Western culture. Works written after the mid-1970s may not have this box.

What Do I Read Next?: a list of works that might give a reader points of entry into a classic work (e.g., YA or multicultural titles) and/or complement the featured novel or serve as a contrast to it. This includes works by the same author and others, works from various genres, YA works, and works from various cultures and eras.

The film entries provide sidebars more targeted to the study of film, including:

Film Technique: a listing and explanation of four to six key techniques used in the film, including shot styles, use of transitions, lighting, sound or music, etc.

Read, Watch, Write: media literacy prompts and/or suggestions for viewing log prompts.

What Do I See Next?: a list of films based on the same or similar works or of films similar in directing style, technique, etc.

Other Features

NfS includes "The Informed Dialogue: Interacting with Literature," a foreword by Anne Devereaux

Jordan, Senior Editor for *Teaching and Learning Literature* (*TALL*), and a founder of the Children's Literature Association. This essay provides an enlightening look at how readers interact with literature and how *Novels for Students* can help teachers show students how to enrich their own reading experiences.

A Cumulative Author/Title Index lists the authors and titles covered in each volume of the *NfS* series.

A Cumulative Nationality/Ethnicity Index breaks down the authors and titles covered in each volume of the *NfS* series by nationality and ethnicity.

A Subject/Theme Index, specific to each volume, provides easy reference for users who may be studying a particular subject or theme rather than a single work. Significant subjects, from events to broad themes, are included.

Each entry may include illustrations, including photo of the author, stills from film adaptations, maps, and/or photos of key historical events, if available.

Citing Novels for Students

When writing papers, students who quote directly from any volume of *NfS* may use the following general forms. These examples are based on MLA style; teachers may request that students adhere to a different style, so the following examples may be adapted as needed.

When citing text from *NfS* that is not attributed to a particular author (i.e., the Themes, Style, Historical Context sections, etc.), the following format should be used in the bibliography section:

> "*Monkey Wrench Gang.*" *Novels for Students*. Ed. Sara Constantakis. Vol. 43. Detroit: Gale, Cengage Learning, 2013. 157–193. Print.

When quoting the specially commissioned essay from *NfS* (usually the first piece under the "Criticism" subhead), the following format should be used:

> Holmes, Michael Allen. Critical Essay on "*The Monkey Wrench Gang.*" *Novels for Students*. Ed. Sara Constantakis. Vol. 43. Detroit: Gale, Cengage Learning, 2013. 173–78. Print.

When quoting a journal or newspaper essay that is reprinted in a volume of *NfS*, the following form may be used:

> Bryant, Paul T. "Edward Abbey and Environmental Quixoticism." *Western American Literature* 24.1 (1989): 37–43. Rpt. in *Novels for Students*. Vol. 43. Ed. Sara Constantakis. Detroit: Gale, Cengage Learning, 2013. 189–92. Print.

When quoting material reprinted from a book that appears in a volume of *NfS*, the following form may be used:

> Norwick, Steve. "Nietzschean Themes in the Works of Edward Abbey." *Coyote in the Maze: Tracking Edward Abbey in a World of Words*. Ed. Peter Quigley. Salt Lake City; University of Utah Press, 1998. 184–205. Rpt. in *Novels for Students*. Vol. 43. Ed. Sara Constantakis. Detroit: Gale, Cengage Learning, 2013. 183–85. Print.

We Welcome Your Suggestions

The editorial staff of *Novels for Students* welcomes your comments and ideas. Readers who wish to suggest novels to appear in future volumes, or who have other suggestions, are cordially invited to contact the editor. You may contact the editor via e-mail at: **ForStudentsEditors@cengage.com.** Or write to the editor at:

Editor, *Novels for Students*

Gale

27500 Drake Road

Farmington Hills, MI 48331-3535

Literary Chronology

1818: Emily Brontë is born on July 30 in Thornton, Yorkshire, England.

1847: Emily Brontë's *Wuthering Heights* is published.

1848: Emily Brontë dies of tuberculosis on December 19 in Hawroth, Yorkshire, England.

1858: Charles Waddell Chesnutt is born on June 20 in Cleveland, Ohio.

1885: D. H. Lawrence is born on September 11 in Eastwood, England.

1900: Charles Waddell Chesnutt's *The House behind the Cedars* is published.

1904: Edna Ferber is born on August 15 in Kalamazoo, Michigan.

1904: Graham Greene is born on October 2 in Berkhamsted, England.

1907: James Ramsey Ullman is born on November 24 in New York, New York.

1913: D. H. Lawrence's *Sons and Lovers* is published.

1925: Edna Ferber is awarded the Pulitzer Prize for Fiction for *So Big*.

1930: Edna Ferber's *Cimarron* is published.

1930: D. H. Lawrence dies of complications from pleurisy and tuberculosis on March 2 in Vence, France.

1932: Charles Waddell Chesnutt dies of arteriosclerosis and hypertension on November 15 in Cleveland, Ohio.

1934: N. Scott Momaday is born on February 27 in Lawton, Oklahoma.

1937: Walter Dean Myers is born on August 12 in Martinsburg, West Virginia.

1939: The film *Wuthering Heights* is released.

1940: Greg Toland is awarded the Academy Award for Best Cinematography, Black and White, for *Wuthering Heights*.

1940: Bharati Mukherjee is born on July, 27 in Calcutta, India.

1941: Jerry Spinelli is born on February 1 in Norristown, Pennsylvania.

1946: Joyce McDonald is born on August 4 in San Francisco, California.

1948: Graham Green's *The Heart of the Matter is published.*

1954: James Ramsey Ullman's *Banner in the Sky* is published.

1954: Kazuo Ishiguro is born on November 8 in Nagasaki, Japan.

1957: Jane Hamilton is born on July 13 in Oak Park, Illinois.

1962: Tracy Chevalier is born on October 19 in Washington, DC.

1968: Edna Ferber dies of cancer on April 16 in New York, New York.

1969: N. Scott Momaday is awarded the Pulitzer Prize for Fiction for *House Made of Dawn*.

1969: N. Scott Momaday's *The Way to Rainy Mountain* is published.

1971: James Ramsey Ullman dies of cancer on June 20 in Boston, Massachusetts.

1991: Graham Greene dies of an unspecified blood disorder on April 3 in Vesey, Switzerland.

1994: Jane Hamilton's *Map of the World* is published.

1997: Joyce McDonald's *Swallowing Stones* is published.

1999: Tracy Chevalier's *Girl with a Pearl Earring* is published.

2000: Jerry Spinelli's *Stargirl* is published.

2002: Bharati Mukherjee's *Desirable Daughters* is published.

2005: Kazuo Ishiguro's *Never Let Me Go* is published.

2008: Walter Dean Myers's *Sunrise over Fallujah* is published.

2010: The film Never *Let Me Go* is released.

Acknowledgements

The editors wish to thank the copyright holders of the excerpted criticism included in this volume and the permissions managers of many book and magazine publishing companies for assisting us in securing reproduction rights. We are also grateful to the staffs of the Detroit Public Library, the Library of Congress, the University of Detroit Mercy Library, Wayne State University Purdy/Kresge Library Complex, and the University of Michigan Libraries for making their resources available to us. Following is a list of the copyright holders who have granted us permission to reproduce material in this volume of PfS. Every effort has been made to trace copyright, but if omissions have been made, please let us know.

COPYRIGHTED EXCERPTS IN NfS, VOLUME 45, WERE REPRODUCED FROM THE FOLLOWING PERIODICALS:

ALAN Review, Vol. 33, No. 2, Winter 2006. Copyright © 2006. All rights reserved. Reproduced by permission.—***Belles Lettres: A Review of Books by Women***, Vol. 10, No. 1, Fall 1994, p. 25. Copyright © 1994 by *Belles Lettres*. All rights reserved. Reproduced by permission.—***Booklist***, Vol. 94, No 4, October 15, 1997. Copyright © 1997 by American Library Association. All rights reserved. Reproduced by permission.—Kristin M. Jones, "Childhood's End: The Mortal Concerns of Mark Romanek's 'Never Let Me Go'," ***Film Comment***, Vol. 74, No. 10, September-October 2010. Copyright © 2010 Kristin M. Jones. All rights reserved. Reproduced by permission.—***Film Quarterly***, Vol. 65, No. 4, Summer 2012. Copyright © 2012 by *Film Quarterly*. All rights reserved. Reproduced by permission.—***Horn Book***, Vol. 76, No. 4, July 2000. Copyright © 2000 by The Horn Book, Inc. All rights reserved. Reproduced by permission.—***Journal of Adolescent & Adult Literacy***, Vol. 45, No. 2, October 2001. Copyright © 2001 by International Reading Association. All rights reserved. Reproduced by permission.—***Literator: Journal of Literary Criticism, Comparative Linguistics, and Literary Studies***, Vol. 32, No. 3, December 2011. Copyright © 2011 by African Online Scientific Information. All rights reserved. Reproduced by permission—***Mosaic***, Vol. 44, No. 2, June 2011. Copyright © 2011 by *Mosaic*. All rights reserved. Reproduced by permission.—***NWSA Journal*** (now *Feminist Formations*) 11:1 (1999), 30-34, 40. Copyright © 1999 *NWSA Journal*. Reprinted with permission of The Johns Hopkins University Press.—***Publishers Weekly***, Vol. 225, No. 16, April 21, 2008; Vol. 244, No. 39, September 22, 1997. Copyright © 1997, 2008 by PWxyz, LLC. All rights reserved. Reproduced by permission.—***School Library Journal***, Vol. 54, No. 4, April 2008. Copyright © 2008 by Library Journals LLC. All rights reserved. Reproduced by permission.—***Sewanee Review***, Vol. 109, No. 2,

Spring 2001. Reprinted with the permission of the editor and the author.—***Studies in Canadian Literature***, Vol. 29, No. 1, 2004. Copyright © 2004 by *Studies in Canadian Literature*. All rights reserved. Reproduced by permission.

COPYRIGHTED EXCERPTS IN NfS, VOLUME 45, WERE REPRODUCED FROM THE FOLLOWING BOOKS:

From ***Presenting Walter Dean Myers***, 1E. Copyright © 1991 Cengage Learning.—Brosh, Liora. From ***Screening Novel Women: From British Domestic Fiction to Film***. Palgrave Macmillan, 2008. Copyright © 2008 by Palgrave Macmillan. All rights reserved. Reproduced by permission.—Charles, Jim. From ***Reading, Learning, Teaching N. Scott Momaday***. Edited by P.L. Thomas. Peter Lang Publishing, 2007, pp. 53-60. Copyright © 2007 by Peter Lang Publishing. All rights reserved. Reproduced by permission.—Daly, McDonald. "Relationship and Class in 'Sons and Lovers'". From ***D.H. Lawrence's "Sons and Lovers": A Casebook***. Edited by John Worthen and Andrew Harrison, 2005, pp. 81-86. Copyright © Oxford University Press. All rights reserved. Reproduced by permission.—Haire-Sargeant, Lin. From ***Nineteenth Century Women at the Movies: Adapting Classic Women's Fiction to Film***. Edited by Barbara Tepa Lupack. Bowling State Green University Popular Press, 1999. Copyright © 1999 by Bowling State Green University Popular Press. All rights reserved. Reproduced by permission.—From ***Charles Chesnutt Reappraised: Essays on the First Major African American Fiction Writer***. Edited by David Garrett Izzo and Maria Orban. Copyright © 2009. Reproduced by permission of McFarland & Company, Inc., Box 611, Jefferson NC 28640. ww.mcfarlandpub.com.—Kenaga, Heidi. From ***Middlebrow Moderns: Popular American Women Writers of the 1920s***. Edited by Lisa Botshon and Meredith Goldsmith. Northeastern University Press, 2003, pp. 173-178.—Kroeber, Karl. From ***Make Believe in Film and Fiction: Visual vs. Verbal Storytelling***. Palgrave Macmillan, 2006. Copyright © 2006 by Palgrave Macmillan. All rights reserved. Reproduced by permission.—McWilliams, Dean. From ***Charles W. Chesnutt and the Fictions of Race***. University of Georgia Press, 2002. Copyright © 2002 by the University of Georgia Press. All rights reserved. Reproduced by permission.—Reprinted from ***Ancestral Voices: Conversations with N. Scott Momaday*** by Charles L. Woodard, by permission of the University of Nebraska Press. Copyright © 1989 by the University of Nebraska Press.—Murfin, Ross C. From ***Sons and Lovers: A Novel of Division and Desire: A Student's Companion to the Novel***. Copyright © Cengage Learning.—Newman, Judie. From ***Fictions of America: Narratives of Global Empire***. Routledge, 2007. Copyright © 2007 by Taylor and Francis. All rights reserved. Reproduced by permission.—Nyman, Jopi. From ***Home, Identity, and Mobility in Contemporary Diasporic Fiction***. Rodopi BV, 2009. Copyright © 2009 by Rodopi BV. All rights reserved. Reproduced by permission.—From ***Graham Greene: The Enemy Within*** by Michael Shelden. Copyright © Michael Shelden, 1994. Reprinted by permission of A.M. Heath & Co Ltd.—Turnell, Martin. From ***Graham Greene: A Critical Essay***. William B. Eerdmans, 1967. Copyright © 1967 William B. Eerdmans. All rights reserved. Reproduced by permission.—Watts, Eileen H. From ***Modern Jewish Women Writers in America***. Edited by Evelyn Avery. Palgrave Macmillan, 2007. Copyright © Palgrave MacMillan. All rights reserved. Reproduced by permission.—Wilson, Matthew. From ***Whiteness in the Novels of Charles W. Chesnutt***. University Press of Mississippi, 2004. Copyright © 2004 by University Press of Mississippi. All rights reserved. Reproduced by permission.

Contributors

Bryan Aubrey: Aubrey holds a PhD in English. Entry on *Cimarron*. Original essay on *Cimarron*.

Andrea Betts: Betts is a freelance writer specializing in literature. Entry on *Stargirl*. Original essay on *Stargirl*.

Rita M. Brown: Brown is an English professor. Entry on *A Map of the World*. Original essay on *A Map of the World*.

Catherine Dominic: Dominic is a novelist and a freelance writer and editor. Entry on *Sons and Lovers*. Original essay on *Sons and Lovers*

Kristen Sarlin Greenberg: Greenberg is a freelance writer and editor with a background in literature and philosophy. Entry on *Girl with a Pearl Earring*. Original essay on *Girl with a Pearl Earring*.

Michael Allen Holmes: Holmes is a writer with existential interests. Entries on *Banner in the Sky* and *The Way to Rainy Mountain*. Original essays on *Banner in the Sky* and *The Way to Rainy Mountain*.

David Kelly: Kelly is an instructor of creative writing and literature. Entry on *Never Let Me Go*. Original essay on *Never Let Me Go*.

Michael J. O'Neal: O'Neal holds a PhD in English. Entries on *The Heart of the Matter* and *The House behind the Cedars*. Original essays on *The Heart of the Matter* and *The House behind the Cedars*.

April Paris: Paris is a freelance writer with an extensive background writing literary and educational materials. Entry on *Desirable Daughters*. Original essay on *Desirable Daughters*.

Rachel Porter: Porter is a freelance writer and editor who holds a bachelor of arts in English literature. Entry on *Swallowing Stones*. Original essay on *Swallowing Stones*.

Bradley Skeen: Skeen is a classicist. Entry on *Wuthering Heights*. Original essay on *Wuthering Heights*.

Leah Tieger: Tieger is a freelance writer and editor. Entry on *Sunrise over Fallujah*. Original essay on *Sunrise over Fallujah*.

Banner in the Sky

JAMES RAMSEY ULLMAN

1954

The 1954 novel *Banner in the Sky* is a mountaineering adventure tale by James Ramsey Ullman that was named a Newbery Honor Book. The protagonist is sixteen-year-old Rudi Matt, who is supposed to spend his time washing dishes but would rather be exploring the heights of the Citadel, the "last unconquered summit of the Alps," which he dreams of one day climbing to the top. Although his mother and uncle try to restrain him, and in spite of—or perhaps because of—the fact that his father died fifteen years ago in an attempt on the Citadel's peak, Rudi feels compelled to do whatever he can toward completing his father's quest.

Ullman was a very popular author in the mid-twentieth century. His credentials as an amateur mountaineer who climbed peaks in the American and Canadian Rockies, the Teton Range, the Andes, and elsewhere lent an air of authority to both his nonfiction and fiction on mountain climbing. He was enlisted as the official historian of the first American ascent of Mount Everest. One of the summits he reached was the Matterhorn, the emblematic mountain on the border of Switzerland and Italy that was first climbed in 1865. As he relates in the author's note that opens *Banner in the Sky*, the first ascent of the Matterhorn was the inspiration for his fictional tale, which takes place in the same year in an essentially similar Swiss locale. Ullman's descriptions evoke with heart-stopping

Ullman climbed in the White Mountains in 1945.
(© Jerry Cook | Time & Life Pictures | Getty Images)

realism the vertiginous heights and life-or-death choices confronted by mountaineers who wish to make history.

AUTHOR BIOGRAPHY

Ullman was born into a well-off family in New York City on November 24, 1907. His academic credentials allowed him to enter Princeton University, where he became an amateur mountaineer at age twenty and enjoyed a chance to climb to the peak of the Matterhorn. He graduated in 1929 and embarked on a career that would revolve around the literary arts for the next four decades. Publishing his Princeton thesis on English poet Percy Bysshe Shelley in 1930 as *Mad Shelley*, he proceeded to work as a newspaper reporter and features writer for several years. He then served as a theatrical producer through the mid-1930s. Among the dozen plays he worked on was the Pulitzer Prize–winning *Men in White* (1933). In 1938, he became an executive of the Works Progress Administration's Federal Theater Project, and that year he published *The Other Side of the Mountain*, a travelogue on a South American voyage he took across the Andes and along the Amazon River, following the route of sixteenth-

century Spanish explorer Francisco de Orellana. Ullman married just after leaving Princeton, in 1930; he would have two sons, divorce his first wife in 1945, and marry three times over the course of his life.

Ullman's profession as an independent writer was secured with his 1941 publication of *High Conquest: The Story of Mountaineering*, which earned him a reputation as the leading American authority on the topic. Though he was rejected from combat service during World War II, in 1942–1943 he served as an ambulance driver for the American Field Service, as attached to the British Eighth Army in Africa; he became a lieutenant and was decorated with the African Star. He then published the best seller *The White Tower* (1945), about wartime mountaineering in the Swiss Alps. After editing an anthology of mountaineering stories, *Kingdom of Everest* (1947), beginning in 1950 he would publish five novels in just five years, including *Banner in the Sky* in 1954. His other writings draw heavily on his travels in South America, East Asia, the South Pacific, and elsewhere.

The first ascent of Mount Everest in 1953 would be a lasting inspiration for Ullman. He teamed up with Tenzing Norgay, the Sherpa who led Sir Edmund Hillary to the summit, in the writing of Tenzing's autobiography, *Tiger of the Snows* (1955). Although Ullman was denied a spot with the American expedition to K2 in 1953, his dream to reach the Himalayas was fulfilled in 1963, when he was invited to accompany the first American expedition to the summit of Everest. Ullman suffered an attack of thrombophlebitis that kept him from reaching the base camp, at just below 18,000 feet—Everest's peak elevation is 29,028 feet—but his intimate account of the expedition, with contributions from the participating climbers, was published as *Americans on Everest: The Official Account of the Ascent Led by Norman G. Dyhrenfurth* (1964). With some twenty titles to his credit, Ullman died at the age of sixty-three in Boston, Massachusetts, on June 20, 1971.

PLOT SUMMARY

Chapters 1–3

Banner in the Sky opens with a paragraph that frames the tale as one from a bygone era, about why the great Swiss peak called the Citadel is

MEDIA ADAPTATIONS

- *Banner in the Sky* was adapted to film by screenwriter Eleanore Griffin with the title *Third Man on the Mountain* (1959). Directed by Ken Annakin for Walt Disney Productions, the film features outdoor scenes shot in Zermatt, Switzerland—Ullman's model for the village of Kurtal—and on the Matterhorn, and Ullman himself makes an uncredited appearance as a tourist.

- Audiobook versions of *Banner in the Sky* have been produced by Newbery Award Records in 1972 (LP), read by Betty Brown Preston, and Crane Memorial Library in 1982 (cassette), read by Peter McEwan, with editions available in various libraries.

known to locals as "Rudi's Mountain." In 1865, Rudi, a hotel dishwasher in Kurtal, sneaks out on a summer morning to go climbing. The cook, Teo, grumbles but at heart approves. Rudi dreams of being the first to reach the peak of the Citadel. He has traversed its glaciers some fifty times and circled the peak five times, scouting. Today, he hears a voice; someone is stuck in a glacial crevasse.

The man is some twenty feet down and has lost his ice axe. He urges Rudi to return down the mountain for help, but Rudi fears the man will freeze. To reach him, Rudi ties his tops and pants to the end of his walking staff, lies on the ice, and holds on desperately while the man clambers out. He is John Winter, a famous mountaineer. Winter believes the Citadel can be climbed, as did Rudi's father—who died trying. Rudi agrees and shares his opinions. He asks Winter to tell no one about his being up there that day.

Back in town, Teo covers for Rudi, but his stories to the waitress and to Rudi's uncle, Franz Lerner, get crossed. Realizing Rudi skipped out, Franz is angry, but Teo defends the boy's interests. Franz goes to discuss with Rudi's mother, Ilse, the boy's planned future as a hotelier. When

Rudi returns, he is chastised. Winter then arrives to ask Franz to guide him up the Wunderhorn tomorrow, and he asks if Rudi might serve as porter. When Winter realizes Rudi has been found out, he tells how Rudi rescued him. Franz agrees to let Rudi come along this once.

Chapters 4–6

Rudi dreams of planting a red-shirt banner atop the Citadel. After his morning's work, Rudi is given a note instructing him to pick up new gear at Winter's expense. Satisfied to surprise his onlooking peers on their way out of town, Rudi endures what for him is a strenuous hike up to the Wunderhorn's Blausee Glacier and the fully occupied hut, where Rudi feels he belongs.

They set out before dawn toward the shoulder of the Wunderhorn, which offers a view of the southeast ridge of the Citadel—Winter's true interest there. He asks Franz about climbing the Citadel, but Franz refuses to consider it. Rudi decides to contribute by looking for a better way down. As he approaches a platform, a thin ledge crumbles from beneath his feet, leaving him isolated. Franz has to risk his life clambering over to retrieve him. They walk down in near silence.

Rain comes, and Winter heads to Geneva, intending to return a few days later. Dejected, Rudi washes dishes. But on his day off, Teo offers to instruct him. They head up the Felsberg, where Teo sends Rudi up one practice cliff after another. He masters knots and belays. Teo recounts the story of Josef Matt's death: he died helping an injured client. The crippled Teo instructs Rudi to guide him to the peak of the Felsberg, a feat that boosts Rudi's confidence and spirits. But back in Kurtal, the hotel waitress tells Rudi that Winter has left town for good.

Chapters 7–10

Franz tells Ilse that Winter is obsessed with the Citadel. Rudi is despondent. When Klaus happens upon him patching his father's red shirt and belittles him, Rudi starts a fight—and ends up on the ground with a bloody nose. Kurtal's guides are especially busy that week. Even the rarely used old hut below the Citadel's southeast ridge is occupied; Rudi figures that Winter must be there with a guide from Broli. Without sleeping, Rudi sneaks out of town at two in the morning, praying at the shrine to his father and collecting his staff on the way.

At the old hut, Rudi finds Winter and Emil Saxo. Rudi claims that his uncle approved of his departure. They plan to scale up to the Fortress, a foreboding wall on the Citadel's southeast ridge, at the base of which Josef Matt perished. They trudge up a glacier at forty- to fifty-degree angles, cross a snowbridge over the uppermost crevasse, climb through the icefall, and embark up a snowslope. There is an avalanche.

That day, Franz takes a client up the Felsberg, then returns to town to hear from Hans Andermass, who was in Broli, that Saxo and Winter are climbing the Citadel. Ilse reports that Rudi has been gone all day. From the Beau Site Hotel's telescope, Teo spots the Citadel climbers, including a third man. Knowing the third is Rudi, Franz curses him, but Teo toasts him. Led by Franz, the Kurtalers resolve to climb the Citadel the next day to stop the others.

In the deep snow, Rudi surfaces, as does Saxo, and they fish out Winter, whose head is injured. They go down to the old hut and eat, and the exhausted Rudi falls fast asleep. In the morning, Winter declares that he and Saxo need to return to Broli for food, while Rudi must return to Kurtal to persuade his uncle to join them. On the way back, Rudi heads not down the Blue Glacier but up the Citadel.

Chapters 11–13

Rudi climbs up past the snowslope onto the southeast ridge. With steep drops on either side, he climbs up over towers called *gendarmes*. For a moment he fears the mountain's rumored demons, but he calls on God and his father's spirit and is strengthened. At the Fortress, to the left he finds a cleft, an open chimney, just past a nearly sheer rock wall. He realizes it may be too late to continue but feels compelled to go up the chimney. At the top, he exults in being the first man to get so far—then realizes a snowstorm is coming on.

With a southerly wind and wet footing, the descent is treacherous. Rudi scrambles back down to the base of the Fortress, where a small cave—the one his father died in—gives shelter. He waits out the snow, feeling timelessness. But when the snow ends, dark is already falling. He eventually sleeps. In the misty night, the cave is spooky; he feels a spirit in the air. Realizing this is only his loving father's ghost, he loses his fear. In the morning, he starts to descend.

That day, Winter and Saxo reach the old hut to find six climbing packs. Saxo suspects ill will.

Franz and the others return, having failed to find Rudi all day. They think he must have fallen in a crevasse. Franz blames Saxo, and the men grow belligerent, but Winter intercedes. Rudi then arrives, exhilarated: he has found the key to the Fortress, the cleft he climbed up. Franz scolds him, but Teo and Winter defend him. Franz concedes that he, too, wants to scale the Citadel—as Winter and Saxo's rivals. But Winter insists that they cooperate, and the men accede. Winter, Saxo, Franz, and Rudi will head up the next day.

Chapters 14–16

They rise before dawn. While the four go up, three will follow the next day for support, while Teo will stay at the hut and cook, and a Tauglich brother will descend to Kurtal to report the historic attempt. At the southeast ridge, Winter orders Rudi to lead. At the Fortress, Saxo wants to go right, but Winter chooses Rudi's route. Carrying his staff, Rudi almost gets stuck in the chimney. With Saxo now leading, they reach a later steep pitch and follow Saxo's choice of route. Beneath a battlement below the mountain's shoulder, they pitch camp to sleep there.

Getting up in the dark again, they head up, with much trial and error. Winter is getting ill. At a tricky crack, Rudi slips and dangles and must be hauled up. At the top of the shoulder is a vertical outcropping called the Needle. Saxo and Franz try a cleft, but it is too narrow. Winter tries an outer route but fails near the top; Saxo and Franz also fail. Rudi volunteers to try the cleft, and he squeezes through, then helps the others up the outer route.

Atop the shoulder, late in the day, they remain two to three hours from the top. Though Winter cannot go on, Saxo wants to, but Franz shames him for considering leaving behind a client. They camp again. That night, Saxo advises that Winter is not recovering; they should go for the summit without him; but Franz refuses. Closer to morning, Rudi awakes to a sound: Saxo has left for the top. Rudi follows.

Chapters 17–19

Everyone in Kurtal tensely awaits, with guides manning the telescope. Two men are spotted near the top. Franz had deceived Ilse about Rudi's whereabouts, but she overhears the guides reveal that he is among the summiting party. She defers to Rudi's will and goes to the church. At the old hut, having failed to meet the summiting party the previous day, the three men head up again, and Teo joins them. That morning, Franz finds Saxo and Rudi missing. Winter insists they follow. Struggling up an icy pitch, they can see clear to the summit, with no sign of the others. At a catwalk ridge, they find Rudi's pack on the ground, with the staff and red shirt tucked inside. Winter takes the items.

Above all the others that day, Rudi catches up with Saxo at the catwalk ridge. Saxo tells Rudi to go back. He approaches the guide anyway, touching his arm, and Saxo wheels angrily but slips and falls down an embankment to a perilous ledge; his arm is broken. He tries but cannot climb back up. Saxo tells Rudi to continue, he has won, but Rudi climbs down to help. Even together they cannot go back up, but a long fault leads back down to their camp on the shoulder. With great effort, Rudi helps Saxo navigate the fault. Along the way, Rudi spots Franz and Winter near the summit, but he does not call out, to ensure they reach the top. Rudi and Saxo pass out by the camp.

The conquering party descends, the incapacitated Rudi and Saxo being lowered down. At the Fortress, Rudi slips—but is caught by Teo. The eight men together head back to the old hut. Before leaving for Broli, Saxo thanks Rudi and salutes Winter and Franz. The route back to Kurtal is like a parade, with cheering supporters up and down the path. In town there is a great party, and Ilse and Rudi are reunited. When Franz and Winter are hailed as the heroes, Winter declares that the Citadel is "*Rudi's mountain.*"

CHARACTERS

Hans Andermass
A Kurtaler, Hans Andermass returns from Broli to report that Winter and Emil Saxo are attempting the Citadel. Hans remains in town when the other Kurtalers head up after them, and later, speaking with Paul Tauglich, he unwittingly reveals to Ilse Matt that Rudi is among the summiting party.

Johann Feiniger
Johann Feiniger is another Kurtal guide. He is the first to see through the telescope two men nearing the peak of the Citadel.

Gretchen
The Beau Site Hotel waitress, Gretchen is not amused by Rudi's tendency to skip work to go climbing.

Toni Hassler
A young Kurtaler who sometimes works as a porter, Toni Hassler fills in at the hotel when Rudi goes climbing with Winter.

Herr Hempel
The heavyset owner of the Beau Site Hotel, Herr Hempel cluelessly hogs the telescope when Winter's party is climbing the Citadel.

Andreas Krickel
Andreas Krickel is a guide from Kurtal who supports the collective opinion that Broli guides are no good. He joins the supporting party when Winter's group attempts the summit.

Franz Lerner
Franz Lerner is the foremost guide in Kurtal and also Ilse Matt's brother and Rudi's uncle. Fully aware of his sister's grief and hardship in having lost her husband, Franz uses his authority to prevent Rudi from becoming a guide. But in supporting Ilse, he becomes blind to Rudi's innermost desires. Only when Teo and Winter speak up on Rudi's behalf does Franz begin to accept that Rudi must choose his own path in life. Though he resents and suspects Saxo as a guide from Kurtal's rival village, Franz goes along with Winter's insistence that they cooperate. His keen mountaineer's ethics will not allow him to leave Winter behind near the peak. On the descent after summiting, Franz proves the backbone of the party.

Frau Ilse Matt
Frau Ilse Matt, Rudi's mother, is still beset by grief from time to time fifteen years after the death of her husband. She is unwilling to let her only son suffer the same fate and so, with Franz's support, is forcing Rudi into the hotel business. When she eventually learns that Rudi is among the men trying to climb the Citadel, she finally accepts Rudi's incipient manhood and independence.

Josef Matt
The ghost of Rudi's father has lingered around the Citadel throughout Rudi's life. Josef died near the age of thirty when his client, Edward

Stephenson, was struck by a falling rock and was unable to descend from their attempt on the Citadel's peak. The two men stayed in a cave at the Fortress overnight and froze during a three-day storm. On the path up from Kurtal, at the edge of the forest is a shrine to Josef. Though the seemingly spiritual presence atop the Citadel is suspected to be demons, Rudi realizes, during his night at the Fortress, that the spirit is his father's and nothing to be feared.

Rudi Matt

Although he never really knew his father, who died when he was just one, the slender sixteen-year-old Rudi Matt is very much his father's son: exploring and climbing mountains seems to be in his blood, as there is nothing he would rather be doing. But in order to fulfill his need for mountain air, Rudi has to disobey his mother and uncle, who are trying to secure a mundane future for him in the hotel business, which is thriving in Kurtal. Fortunately for Rudi, Old Teo is on his side, giving him crucial instruction, as is Captain Winter after Rudi rescues him from the glacial crevasse. In the face of taunts from Klaus and doubts from his uncle Franz, Rudi overcomes his missteps on his first excursion with Winter to prove to his elders that he is strong, brave, and selfless enough to be a mountain guide. When Winter declares that the Citadel is Rudi's mountain more than any other's, Rudi becomes the pride of Kurtal.

Emil Saxo

Greatly despised by the Kurtalers, the Broli guide Emil Saxo has a gruff exterior and a low opinion of the cowardly guides from Kurtal. He consents to the cooperative attempt on the Citadel for Winter's sake, but near the peak, when Franz insists on remaining with the ailing Winter, Saxo prioritizes the summit instead and sneaks off before dawn. But his antipathy to Kurtalers does him in: when Rudi refuses to let him reach the peak alone, Saxo lashes out and in doing so topples down an embankment, breaking his arm. He manages to descend only with the support of Rudi and then Franz.

Sir Edward Stephenson

Stephenson was the Englishman who employed Josef Matt and Teo in his attempt on the Citadel in 1850. A falling rock broke his leg at the base of the Fortress, and he and Josef died there.

Paul and Peter Tauglich

Paul and Peter Tauglich are brothers who are both guides from Kurtal. When Winter's party attempts the Citadel's summit, Peter joins the supporting party, while Paul heads back to Kurtal to rouse the village.

Klaus Wesselhoft

The tall, powerful, eighteen-year-old Klaus Wesselhoft is an up-and-coming guide and the envy of Rudi Matt. Klaus calls Rudi "Angel-face" and "Plate-scraper" and bloodies his nose when he stands up for himself after Klaus taunts him for sewing. But Klaus is consigned to the supporting party when Winter leads his group of four men, including Rudi, up the Citadel.

Captain John Winter

An amiable man with great people skills, Captain John Winter is a famous mountaineer whose presence in Kurtal is widely known. Rudi is astonished to have saved his life after he fell down the crevasse. Winter's resulting allegiance to Rudi is made clear, as he pays for expensive gear for Rudi and makes every effort to get Rudi to climb with him. Though he starts coughing and sputtering after his head is struck during the avalanche, Winter proves the glue that holds the Citadel expedition together: he insists on teamwork between the Kurtal and Stoli rivals, and he is the one to plant Rudi's staff and Josef's red shirt as the banner proclaiming the conquest of the peak.

Teo Zurbriggen

The one survivor of the climb on which Josef Matt perished, Teo Zurbriggen was yet crippled by a fall on the way down: his left arm is half paralyzed, his shoulder is hunched up, and he walks with a limp. Now the fifty-five-year-old cook at the Beau Site Hotel, the weathered Old Teo supports Rudi's trips up to the Citadel by covering for him at work. When Rudi fears that his error on the Wunderhorn climb has ruined his hopes, Teo spends a day turning him into a master climber, even obliging him to help Teo reach the peak of the Felsberg—a great challenge. After cooking at the old hut to support the Citadel summiting effort, Teo insists on climbing up to meet Winter's party on the way down, and at the Fortress he joyfully receives the faltering Rudi.

TOPICS FOR FURTHER STUDY

- How might the ending of *Banner in the Sky* have played out differently? Starting with the point at which Rudi spots Saxo on the narrow ridge just below the Citadel's peak, write an alternate version of the remainder of the plot, imitating Ullman's prose style.

- Read Roland Smith's young-adult novel *Peak* (2008), about a fourteen-year-old named Peak Marcello whose long-lost father enlists him to join an expedition up Mount Everest, which would make Peak the youngest person ever to reach the summit. Write an essay comparing and contrasting *Peak* and *Banner in the Sky*, addressing the personalities of the teenage boys, their motivations, the roles their fathers play, the authors' literary approaches, and other qualities of interest.

- Watch the film *Third Man on the Mountain* (1959), the adaptation of *Banner in the Sky*. Write an essay in which you gauge the success of the adaptation, considering changes and consistencies with regard to character development, plot, emotional impact, morals, and so forth and expressing your overall opinion of the film.

- Create a travel brochure for the fictional village of Kurtal in the year 1865, just after the Citadel has been climbed. Consult *Banner in the Sky* and also, using print and online sources, conduct historical research to determine how tourists would arrive in the village, what amenities they could expect to find there, what sort of equipment they would need to bring or buy there, and so forth. Collect and include pictures that could represent Kurtal and the Citadel, use part of your brochure to celebrate the recent expedition to the peak, and mention the availability of the services of Kurtal's guides.

- Choose a significant mountain in North America, such as Iztaccíhuatl (Ixtacihuatl) or Mount McKinley, or elsewhere in the world, and write a research paper on the first attempts to climb to the peak.

THEMES

Freedom

The most pressing question in the early chapters of *Banner in the Sky* is that of Rudi's freedom. Technically, he has almost none: not only are his day-to-day activities determined by his mother and uncle—he must work at the hotel as a dishwasher, and he is not allowed to scale the mountains—but his future is predetermined as well, as he is slated for training in Zurich in hotel keeping. During the fortunate escape up the Citadel when Rudi makes the acquaintance of Captain Winter, the narration makes clear Rudi's attitude toward hotel work: "A few minutes before, he had been a prisoner. Now he was free." The same imagery recurs when he is back confined in the hotel kitchen: "What good did it do to have the world before him, when he couldn't get to it? When he was like a prisoner staring at it from behind the bars of a cell?" Despite Rudi's evident need for the freshest possible air, Franz is willfully blind to what freedom would mean to him. Franz's view is legitimate: Ilse, his sister, has already suffered greatly owing to the death of her husband, and she does not deserve to suffer doubly so, as she would if Rudi were to likewise die while mountaineering.

This is a well-explored circumstance in literature and film: what happens when a parent's fears curtail the freedom of the child. Typically, the child is the main protagonist and, in time, often by intently overstepping boundaries as an exercise of will and a means of argument, secures the needed freedom. Such is the case in Ullman's novel. It takes some convincing, accomplished mostly by Teo, but Ilse and Franz come around to the view that Rudi needs the chance to follow his dreams. Franz has in part justified dictating Rudi's life by stressing the boy's misbehavior, his deception and disobedience. But as Winter points out, "He was only doing what he *had* to do" to find self-fulfillment. Teo affirms, "There's also something you both owe to the boy, and that's the freedom to be himself." Rudi indeed undertakes risk—just what his mother has feared—but with proper guidance from Teo, he proves equal to the challenges and justifies his quest for personal freedom.

Masculinity

Addressed in critical ways throughout the tale are the perceived differences between boyhood and manhood. There are two layers to this theme. The primary layer is a sincere exploration of what it means for a boy to become a man. The age of sixteen is a difficult one with regard to classifying both males and females. Legally in America, one ceases to become a minor at age eighteen, which makes for a convenient marker of adulthood, but many people, depending on their experiences, will reach—or at least claim to have reached—an adult level of maturity before then. Through the beginning of the novel, Ullman explicitly refers to the sixteen-year-old Rudi as a boy. This occurs in the first two chapter titles—"A Boy and a Mountain" and "A Boy and a Man," the latter making the distinction between Rudi and Winter crystal clear—as well as in the running text, beginning with the first paragraph: "there lived in that valley a boy called Rudi Matt . . . ."

On this level the novel proceeds to treat how Rudi becomes a man, which involves such classical milestones as enduring oppressive comments and acts from older peers (Klaus taunts him and bloodies his nose); tests of physical strength (climbing up the Wunderhorn with a heavy pack, drawing Teo up the Felsberg); learning from immature mistakes (trying to descend the Wunderhorn on his own); and joining a community of adults (the men filling the Blausee Hut, then later Winter's summiting party). All of this is especially challenging for Rudi because of his slim stature—in a village and, more broadly, a perception-centered world in which physique is often equated with manliness—and his restrictive authority figures. He must overcome both his own limited size, which actually proves an asset in scaling the Citadel's shoulder, and limitations placed on him by others. Already by the

end of chapter 4, at the Blausee Hut, Rudi "was where he belonged. He was a man among men." But the matter is not entirely decided yet. In chapter 9, Franz calls Rudi "a crazy boy. . . . A wild fool of a boy," and even Old Teo, criticizing the Kurtal guides, counters by agreeing that Rudi is still "a boy. A sixteen-year-old boy, who alone among you is not afraid." And chapter 12 is titled "A Boy and a Ghost." But by chapter 14, Winter, Franz, Saxo, and even Rudi are denoted the "First of All Men" to pass the Fortress. In the end, a paragraph that complements the opening passage and brings closure to the novel affirms that this was the story of the conquest of the Citadel "and of how Rudi Matt . . . grew from a boy into a man."

There remains a secondary layer with regard to the theme of masculinity. Manhood, Ullman's novel expresses, cannot be construed as unreservedly positive, because various traits of the novel's men are distinctly negative. Klaus Wesselhoft, for one, uses his own advanced manhood as a pedestal from which to belittle others, especially Rudi; in a word, he is a bully. Klaus's opinions help point the reader in the opposite direction: Rudi should not, in fact, be perceived as unmasculine because he engages in a supposedly feminine act like sewing. Rather, his sewing represents a very mature sense of filial duty and morality, since he is patching, with his own two hands, the cherished red shirt that belonged to his father and which represents the father's selflessness in trying to save Edward Stephenson. The majority of the Kurtal guides also reflect a problem with masculinity, namely, that macho aggression is often, perhaps usually, counterproductive. The Kurtalers are quick to ridicule the men of Stoli, especially Emil Saxo, as loudmouthed, preening, and untrustworthy; and Saxo is quick to ridicule the Kurtalers. In other words, the men think of manhood as a contest, in which fellow competitors are to be quashed through ridicule. Franz and Saxo alike intend to approach the conquest of the Citadel as a contest that will have winners and losers. But Winter has a more mature approach in mind.

Cooperation

The approach to conquering the Citadel that Winter favors is one of cooperation. Winter makes a strong case for himself as the voice of morality in the tale when the men of Kurtal face off with Saxo in the old hut. The Kurtalers' overflowing masculinity threatens to upset the

Sixteen-year-old Rudi Matt climbs a mountain to complete the challenge that killed his father. *(© pchais /*
Shutterstock.com)

scene: "Their hands were clenched tight. Once again it appeared only a matter of seconds before fists would be flying." But Winter, evincing a supposedly less masculine but clearly wiser attitude, quells the collective anger by softly refuting the idea of a Broli-Kurtal contest: "'It won't be like that at all,' said John Winter. 'Because we are going together.'" Winter proceeds to make clear the immaturity that their machismo actually represents: "'What are you?' he asked. 'Men? Or children?.... Together we can do it, I tell you.... But separately, there's not a hope. Quarreling and competing—there's not a hope.'"

The Citadel is recognized as such an extraordinary challenge that it will take all their ingenuity, as well as collective peace of mind, to reach the top. Winter's words prove prescient two days later when Saxo, now possessed of the desire to be the one famous climber to reach the peak first, channels his macho competitive urges into an aggressive gesture toward Rudi—and this is his undoing, because it literally throws him off balance and leaves him toppling off the highest ridge. He is lucky not to die; and only

thanks to the cooperative efforts of Rudi and then Winter and Franz is he able to descend at all. The moral of the story is sealed when Saxo offers a hearty display of gratitude for what Rudi did for him. Through teamwork, Franz and Winter—as well as Rudi and even Saxo himself, in truth—deserve to be hailed by Saxo as the "conquerors of the Citadel!"

STYLE

Historical Fiction

The fictionalizing of history can be approached in several ways. One approach is to take what is known from the documented history of a person or time period and add imagined conversations and events that realistically could have happened. A more common approach, giving the author more leeway, is the use of a significant real-life event or era as a backdrop for a tale with fictional characters. Many wartime books—such as Leo Tolstoy's *War and Peace* (1869), treating France's 1812 invasion of Russia, and Ernest Hemingway's *For Whom the Bell Tolls* (1940), treating the Spanish Civil War—take this approach. Ullman goes one step further in his fictionalization in *Banner in the Sky*, as he relates in an "Author's Note" that functions as an acknowledgment: he has not entirely invented the circumstances but rather has directly drawn on the first ascent of the Matterhorn in 1865.

This note may strike some readers as unnecessarily preemptive; that is, it might be seen to lessen the novel's impact by classifying it as something less than the truth. Of course, any work of fiction can be a vessel of truth, regardless of how true to real events it is. With regard to the truth, Ullman's note to the reader is a very honorable one: he has no desire to deceive the reader and admits that he cannot take credit for the framework of his tale. And then he quite gracefully ushers the reader into the story with the reminder that it "*is* fiction" and "branches out on its own trail, to its own mountaintop." Ideally, these comments leave the reader in the perfect state of mind—having no doubts about the author's integrity, no reason to second-guess his possible sources—to approach the story openly and appreciate its adventures as well as the truth it conveys.

Storytelling

Beyond the author's note, Ullman employs another tactic that likely affects the reader's distance from the story at hand, whether positively or negatively. The author's note has already made the reader privy to the author's mind-set and creative debts in writing the novel. In a sense, this makes the story less pure, because the reader cannot plunge right into it without any consciousness of the existence of the author. Many authors benefit if their personality and thought processes are the furthest things from the reader's mind when immersed in the author's fiction; knowing which preceding fantasy authors J. K. Rowling drew plot points from does not make the Harry Potter series any better. Interestingly, having already informed the reader that he is telling a story, Ullman opens his novel with a paragraph that frames it as a story being told. In a sense, this actually places the novel back within history, saying that the long-ago events to be told happened in a certain year at a certain place. The reader knows this to be fiction, but the opening paragraph nonetheless lends the tale historical credence by affirming its realism.

As it happens, the opening passage partly gives away the tale: knowing the Citadel to be called by locals "Rudi's Mountain," the reader can expect that Rudi will in some way or another conquer the mountain. Most readers, perhaps, will thus expect Rudi to reach the Citadel's peak, even to be the first one there. As such, the unraveling of the plot at the end, when Rudi declines to make a dash for the peak in order to prioritize saving Saxo's life, may surprise the reader. From an expectation that Rudi will be a conqueror, the reader progresses to find that being a conqueror would mean being morally unsound. It would mean prioritizing an egotistic accomplishment over a man's life; and so Rudi proves a conqueror in a different sense, as the youthful, ethically innocent spirit of Winter's four-man expedition. The banner in the sky, Josef Matt's red shirt of selflessness atop Rudi Matt's hand-cut climbing staff, signifies this.

HISTORICAL CONTEXT

The Conquest of the Matterhorn

Ullman makes clear in the author's note that opens *Banner in the Sky* the historical reality he drew upon in writing his fictional story. The Matterhorn, standing 14,692 feet tall, was indeed one of the last, though not the very last, of the great peaks of the Alps to be climbed to the summit. In his landmark volume *Men and the Matterhorn*, Gaston Rébuffat cannot resist waxing poetic about the incomparable mountain, remarking,

> Each time you arrive at Zermatt or Breuil and raise your head at last to see the peak you have been dreaming about night and day, such is the magnetism of the mountain that you are struck to the very depth of your being.

He adds, "The other peaks are beautiful—the Matterhorn is a presence." When one views the mountain, Rébuffat declares, one cannot help but

> indulge in reverie about the great millenary earth tremors, the shocks and foldings, the convulsions, thrusts and collapses which threw up this mountain, symbol of the will, born of happy chance. . . . The miracle is permanent: emotion immediately takes over from aesthetic satisfaction: the fusion of beauty and inaccessibility is indissoluble.

The era of great Alpine ascents can be said to have begun in 1786 with the conquest of Mont

COMPARE & CONTRAST

- **1860s:** In 1865, the peak of the Matterhorn is reached for the first time by Englishman Edward Whymper's seven-man expedition. Four of those seven men perish in a tragic fall on the way down.

  1950s: The Matterhorn continues to challenge mountaineers who wish to make first ascents of sorts: the first winter ascent of the Furggen arête is made in 1952; the first winter ascent of the north face will be made in February 1962; the west face will be scaled directly in August 1962; and the first solo winter ascent of the north face will be made in 1965.

  Today: Competitive mountaineers approaching the Matterhorn may seek to log record times, such as the ascent and descent of the Hörnli Ridge in two hours and thirty-three minutes in 2007. Most climbers take seven to nine hours to accomplish this. Since 1865, over five hundred people have died trying to climb the Matterhorn, and presently about a dozen fatalities occur each year.

- **1860s:** The Alps are the focus of ambitious mountaineers, with the Matterhorn (1865), Aiguille Verte (1865), Gran Paradiso (1869), and Meije (1877) being among the last summits over 13,000 feet attained.

  1950s: The Himalayan and Karakoram peaks over 26,250 feet (8,000 meters) are what expert mountaineers most dream of climbing, with the ascents of Annapurna (1950) and Everest (1953) opening a wave of first ascents of the fourteen highest mountains, with the last made in 1964.

  Today: The greatest mountaineers are considered to be those who have climbed all fourteen of the world's 8,000-meter peaks, which only twenty-nine individuals have accomplished as of 2011. The feat is even greater if one reaches the peaks without supplemental oxygen.

- **1860s:** After climbing the Matterhorn in 1865 and other peaks through the decade, Edward Whymper produces in 1871 one of the first works of mountaineering literature, *Scrambles amongst the Alps in the Years 1860–69*. Through its straightforward recollections, this book captures the imaginations of generations of aspiring alpinists to come.

  1950s: James Ramsey Ullman, whose writing style is sincere and idealistic—and some say old-fashioned—is one of the foremost authors of mountaineering literature, as seen in his histories, like *The Age of Mountaineering* (1954), and fictions, including *Banner in the Sky*.

  Today: The most recent works of literature on real-life mountaineering exploits, like Jon Krakauer's *Into Thin Air* (1997), enhance the drama by focusing on the expedition members' differences of opinion and conflicts, which have become all the more frequent in the competitive modern era.

Blanc (15,771 ft.), in France. Through the subsequent decades, and especially in the 1850s and 1860s, first ascents were made with increasing frequency. Out of over 660 major peaks, some 300 were first climbed by Englishmen, including about a dozen intrepid men who made multiple first ascents. One of these men was Edward Whymper, whose interest in the Matterhorn was sparked in 1860, when he was just twenty years old. He had been commissioned to make sketches of the great Alpine peaks and, after first seeing the Matterhorn, came to greatly desire climbing what he considered "the most inaccessible of all the mountains" (cited in Rébuffat).

Whymper first approached the mountain from the Italian side, obtaining from near Breuil

Against his uncle and mother's wishes, Rudi goes out on the glacier. *(© Roberto Caucino | Shutterstock.com)*

the services of the expert and somewhat defiant guide Jean-Antoine Carrel. Mostly with Carrel, Whymper made seven attempts on the Matterhorn between 1861 and 1863. Carrel himself had dreamed of scaling the Matterhorn—known from the Italian side as Cervino—since his boyhood in the 1830s. As such, Carrel had not just a professional but a personal desire to fulfill in climbing the Matterhorn, and he was reluctant to help Whymper attain the summit because he knew his name would be secondary in the historical record. In several respects, Carrel suggests himself as the model for the novel's character of Emil Saxo. But in real life Whymper and Carrel, who both, Rébuffat notes, "wanted victory too much to contemplate losing it or sharing it," would not make the first ascent together.

WHYMPER'S EXPEDITION

By 1865, Whymper was determined to take an expedition all the way to the Matterhorn's peak. Historically, Zermatt, on the Swiss side, was not known for its hospitality. In the late eighteenth century the Alpine explorer Horace-Bénédict de Saussure, himself a Swiss, encountered a high level of provincial xenophobia when

he alighted in the village, finding it nearly impossible to persuade anyone to extend his party lodging for the night. The next time he approached the Matterhorn, de Saussure did so from the Italian side. Whymper went to the Italian side first on July 8, 1865, but Carrel was already engaged to attempt the Matterhorn beginning on July 11. Thus, after meeting up with the young Lord Francis Douglas, Whymper traveled to Zermatt, where Douglas hired the local guide Peter Taugwalder and his son, also named Peter, a porter. (These men are apparently commemorated in *Banner in the Sky* in the brothers Peter and Paul Tauglich.) More importantly, Whymper found Michel Croz, a renowned former guide of his from Chamonix, France, who was already planning to bring two Englishmen, the Reverend Charles Hudson and the young novice Douglas Hadow, up the mountain. All together, the team of seven began an ascent.

The attempt would prove historic, and also tragic. With the team led by Carrel simultaneously scaling the Matterhorn from the opposite side, Whymper's team was able to reach the top on the second day after leaving Zermatt. At the summit, they looked over to see Carrel's team just 1,000 feet below them. Tossing stones to get Carrel's attention, they actually induced his team to turn back. Extra company going down might have proved fortuitous (though they all might have gone back the way they came). As it happened, Croz led the Swiss descent—for which all seven men were roped together—in order to assist Hadow, literally placing his feet from one stance to the next. But at one precipitous point, as Croz turned to advance, Hadow slipped and fell into him, and both men tumbled off the cliffside, dragging Hudson and then Douglas with them. Between Douglas and the elder Peter Taugwalder, the rope broke; Whymper and the Taugwalders survived to complete the descent, while the other four men tumbled some 4,000 feet to their deaths.

As one can see, there were a number of intriguing aspects to the first ascent of the Matterhorn in 1865, easily worthy of fiction. What Ullman borrowed and what he did not merit consideration. Above all he drew on the stature and majesty of the Matterhorn itself, on humankind's perceptions of it, and on the role it played in history. The real-life story was one of implicit competition and, ultimately, tragic death. Instead of catering to the drama of rivalry, however, Ullman crafted a story in which the glory of competition is subordinated to the ideal of cooperation. And instead of recasting the 1865 tragedy—which only enhances the supernatural aura of the Matterhorn and which could have increased the visceral intensity of his book— Ullman, writing for younger audiences, wrote a strictly inspiring story in which, thanks to the virtues of the protagonists, life prevails for all.

CRITICAL OVERVIEW

While the comprehensive review publications *Booklist* and *Publishers Weekly* took note of the 1954 publication of *Banner in the Sky*, as a book aimed at young-adult readers, the novel did not receive a great deal of critical press. Reviewing the book in 1968, Brian Alderson of the London *Times* affirmed, "The realism in the descriptions of the climb provide a welcome interlude in the heady drama of the various personalities involved."

Ullman's broader reputation as a writer has been more widely discussed. In the 2003 article

"The Ethics of Mountaineering, Brought Low," Maurice Isserman points to Ullman as a writer of great moral integrity and communal idealism. Isserman notes that in Ullman's 1941 historical volume *High Conquest*, written as the nation was preparing for World War II, he drew on German mountaineering to criticize the ethos of the Nazi state. Later, Ullman hailed the 1953 ascent of Everest not as the accomplishment of a Briton who was assisted by a Sherpa, but as the cooperative accomplishment of a man from the East and a man from the West who stood as equals, as brothers, upon the summit. Isserman observes that "Ullman was the kind of writer whose readers felt they could contact and confide in him." After the first American team climbed Everest in 1963, with the official history written by Ullman, President John F. Kennedy presented the group with the Hubbard Medal and told Ullman, in Isserman's phrasing, "how much he admired his books."

In *Fatal Mountaineer: The High-Altitude Life and Death of Willi Unsoeld, American Himalayan Legend*, about one of the men on the first American Everest expedition, Robert Roper offers a few assessments of Ullman's writing, in particular regarding Ullman's book *Americans on Everest* and the associated film script. In Roper's opinion, like

> just about everything else written before the end of the sixties...both book and film hate to report bad news, and in fact, never knowingly attribute unworthy motives to any climber; by the same token, they love to find evidence of heroism, self-sacrifice, and team spirit in the complex story of the expedition.

In line with Roper's remarks, the reader may observe that, in *Banner in the Sky*, Saxo does take an anticommunal turn near the novel's end, but he is punished for his mistake, as if karmically, and his gratitude toward Rudi and the others appears to reflect a lesson learned. Roper adds that Ullman "remains largely uncynical, honoring selflessness and heroism wherever he finds them."

CRITICISM

Michael Allen Holmes

Holmes is a writer with existential interests. In the following essay, he examines what the character of Rudi Matt and the action of Banner in the Sky *suggest about the notions of virtue and destiny.*

WHAT DO I READ NEXT?

- A good Ullman novel to turn to after *Banner in the Sky* is *The White Tower* (1945), a best seller that brings men of a range of nationalities together to conquer a mountain during the global turmoil of World War II.

- In 1956, W. E. Bowman published *The Ascent of Rum Doodle*, a mountaineering classic that, rather than focusing on the visceral intensity and challenges of a climb, frames one as a comedic endeavor.

- James Salter's novel *Solo Faces* (1988) features a man who roofs churches as a profession but feels confined by flatland civilization and thus travels away to climb the Alps—where he happens to play a crucial role when other climbers are trapped during a storm.

- A best-selling book about an Everest expedition is Jon Krakauer's *Into Thin Air: A Personal Account of the Mount Everest Disaster* (1996), which records how a mountaineering ethic that had drifted away from cooperation and toward competition and individual glory contributed to a turn of events in which a dozen climbers died in a blizzard.

- The same Everest expedition described by Krakauer was treated from an opposing, often contradictory perspective by one of the members whom Krakauer singled out for blame, the Russian mountaineer Anatoli Boukreev, in *The Climb: Tragic Ambitions on Everest* (1997).

- In Geraldine McCaughrean's young-adult novel *The White Darkness* (2008), the heroine, Sym, joins her overambitious uncle on an ill-fated expedition to Antarctica and is left at her wit's end when she gets hopelessly lost.

- In the Swiss author Johanna Spyri's beloved novel *Heidi* (1880), an orphaned six-year-old girl is taken in by her grandfather, who lives in seclusion up in the high pastures of the Alps. Heidi and the friends she makes come to realize the healing powers of the alpine world.

An intriguing strain of thought in James Ramsey Ullman's novel *Banner in the Sky* concerns the notion of destiny. This notion can be approached from a number of different angles. Some of these are religious angles: whether called Allah, God, Jehovah, or any other moniker, a supreme being is believed by many to control or have deciding influence over the fates of humankind. Others believe in a supreme god, one who created or manifested the world, but conceive that this god does not intervene in daily affairs. In the twenty-first century, perhaps a majority of Americans, whether religious or not, subscribe to the notion of free will, believing that individual humans have the power to make choices and decisions and thus determine their own direction in life—though fate may nonetheless enter the picture in unexpected ways, such as through accidents and natural disasters. Ullman's novel makes a number of direct statements about fate, but the book's ultimate statement on the notion appears to be concealed within the final turn of events.

Rudi is portrayed from the beginning of the novel as a young man who is exceptionally in tune with his own self. While many people (especially in a twenty-first century rife with social media) find being alone uncomfortable, calling on a friend or flicking on a radio, television, or computer to fill any silences, Rudi is the exact opposite: he gladly climbs around the Citadel with no companions, in spite of the danger, and even "was not conscious of loneliness. He was too used to being alone for that." Being alone gives one plenty of time to ponder and review one's own impulsive thoughts and reflections, which often relate to one's present circumstances. For example, a person who has a fight with his or her parent and then goes on a solitary hike will likely pore over the details of the quarrel in minute detail, considering what brought it about, how it could have been solved more effectively, and perhaps how it could have been avoided altogether. In sum, without necessarily intending to, one will seek to improve one's circumstances by modifying one's attitude and responses—by improving oneself.

The ideal of constantly improving oneself, of honing one's virtue, is a hallmark of more than one Eastern philosophy, including Taoism. Proposing that there is a Tao, the Way, which one should follow to reach the highest spiritual state, Taoist thinkers also posit that the surest

> TO ACT SELFISHLY IN ORDER TO PLANT
> THE BANNER OF SELFLESSNESS WOULD BE AN
> INTOLERABLE CONTRADICTION."

way of attaining the Way is to perfect one's sense of virtue, one's capacity to think justly and do the right thing. People with the surest sense of virtue will be so attuned to notions of justice that they will not even need to reflect carefully on their actions; when a situation arises, they will quite naturally do what is most just, what is right. As an example, a firefighter need not think twice before running into a burning building to try to save someone: the firefighter has the training to enter such a hazardous situation and thus feels a responsibility to use that training to save lives whenever possible. On the other hand, if the firefighter recognizes that his or her own life would be seriously jeopardized by such an attempt, the firefighter will retreat and seek the next-best solution. Rational intelligence plays a role, but the intuitive response is the most virtuous one.

There is a Chinese term referring to the state that one reaches when one need not act consciously in order to act virtuously: *wu wei*, which can be translated as "inaction," "nonaction," or, more descriptively (if paradoxically), "actionless action." Burton Watson, in his introduction to his translation *Chuang Tzu: Basic Writings*, describes *wu wei* as signifying "a course of action that is not founded upon any purposeful motives of gain or striving"—that is, not upon any selfish motives. One acts, but not with ego-driven intentions. When one acts selflessly, one acts in harmony with the Tao, the Way.

Rudi can be seen as being in harmony with the Way in this sense. The reader is not given a great number of scenes by which to gauge his virtue directly. In fact, Franz sees him as lacking in virtue, believing that the boy should do as directed by his mother and uncle and humbly work as a dishwasher at the Beau Site Hotel. And Rudi has played truant from both school and church in order to climb. But Rudi is clearly reluctant to overburden the hotel cook, Teo, by skipping out on work: he gets a replacement

dishwasher when possible, and at the very end of the novel, he intends to leave the once-in-a-lifetime celebration of the first conquest of the Citadel in order to tend to the "thousand dirty dishes" he assumes must be piled up back in the hotel kitchen. Moreover, one need not always take orders to be virtuous. In many cases, refusing to take an order is the more virtuous choice, such as, say, if an interrogator instructs an assistant to torture a detainee. Rudi's basis for refusing Franz's orders is his own need for freedom. This is a need that the nineteenth-century transcendentalist Henry David Thoreau, author of "Civil Disobedience"—which inspired, among others, Mahatma Gandhi and Martin Luther King Jr.—would applaud as worthy.

Indirect evidence of Rudi's virtue can be found in his largely unconscious approach to his existence, which can rightly be called a reliance on actionless action. In several places the novel's narrator notes how Rudi does not consciously make a choice—as in, "I should do this for this reason"—but simply does whatever he happens to do. Regarding the choice he must make, during the first climb of the book, between two glaciers,

> just why he picked the Blue, rather than the Dornel, he could not have said. Later, thinking back to that day, he racked his memory for some sign, some motive or portent, that had been the reason for his choice. But he could never find one. He simply crossed the junction of the two ice-streams, bore left, and climbed on toward the south . . . and his destiny.

It is subsequently noted that "he was not going anywhere, specifically, but only climbing, watching, studying." When he approaches the shrine to his father while starting up the Citadel late in the night, "Why Rudi did what he did next"—lighting a match and touching his father's name—"he could not have said, except that he needed to do it."

These descriptions accord with Watson's further comments on actionless action:

> In such a state, all human actions become as spontaneous and mindless as those of the natural world. Man becomes one with Nature, or Heaven, as Chuang Tzu calls it, and merges himself with Tao, or the Way, the underlying unity that embraces man, Nature, and all that is in the universe.

Along these lines, the narrator of *Banner in the Sky* also remarks several times on Rudi's unity with whatever is around him. When he first collects his hand-cut climbing staff, "as he hefted it now in his hand, feeling its familiar weight and balance, it was no longer merely a stick, but a part of himself." When he sees a lammergeier up past the Fortress, "It whirled and swooped and glided,... a thing of soaring beauty, wild and free. And as Rudi watched, his heart soared too—up and up with the great bird... into the blue beyond."

All of this suggests that Rudi is tune with the universe, his self, and his destiny in a positive sense. In the text of *The Book of Chuang Tzu*, it is said that the wise man "will realize that action-less action is the best course. By non-action, he can rest in the real substance of his nature and destiny." But an alternate view is suggested by narration that frames Rudi's actions not as destiny but as compulsion. When he parts company with Winter and Saxo and then embarks up the Citadel alone, "what he was doing was not a result of conscious choice or decision; it was simply what he *had* to do." Climbing past the Fortress, "as high as any man had gone... was what he wanted; what he *had to have*." Rather than suggesting a connection with unconscious, selfless destiny, these lines suggest a connection with egotistic desire, a want framed as a need.

These comments about what Rudi wants or needs happen to anticipate the book's pinnacle of action, which occurs just below the summit of the Citadel. In the course of this climb, Rudi has evinced his own belief in how virtue can or should determine fate. Regarding the ailing Captain Winter, Rudi thinks, "He will make it.... He *must* make it. Because, of all of us, he most deserves to make it." This aligns with the Hindu concept of karma, whereby a person's actions (including in past lives) determine one's fate; in reductive terms, one with "good karma" will earn a good fate, one with "bad karma" a lesser fate. Rudi believes that Winter has earned himself a good fate. Rudi has also reinforced his unity with the world outside him, specifically his unity with his companions, his compassion for them, as expressed when they attacked the insurmountable Needle: "As each man in turn had made the attempt, he had hoped and striven with him, suffered and despaired with him, no less than if he had been climbing himself." Such a heightened sense of compassion is associated in Zen Buddhism with a high degree of personal enlightenment—analogously, of oneness with the Tao.

In light of these passages, the reader is likely to imagine that, if confronted with a difficult choice, Rudi will make the right one, the most virtuous one. Except there remains the one strand of egotistic desire, his almost single-minded determination to reach the top. This determination seems to be a primary motive when Rudi decides, after waking late in the night to find that Saxo has departed for the peak, to pursue him—to abandon the man to whom the guides on this venture supposedly must be loyal, Captain Winter. Franz makes clear his own stance on this issue: like Josef Matt before him, Franz believes that the guide must serve the client, the master, no matter what, and under no circumstances should leave the master behind to continue, even in the case of a potentially historic first ascent. Winter is sick, and Franz will not leave him. Saxo does not feel the same way, even though Winter employed Saxo foremost. Saxo wants to reach the top, and so he is trying. He can perhaps use the excuse that Franz alone can tend to Winter until he returns on the descent, but this is ethically hazy reasoning at best.

Rudi can use the same excuse—technically he is not even a guide—but rather than making a consciously immoral choice, he lets himself act unconsciously: "Without willing it—almost without knowing it—he was approaching his own tent." After gathering what is needed, "He did not pause. He did not hesitate. For the waking dream in which he now moved was even more powerful than the dream of sleep." The notion of haziness is made explicit in the description that follows:

> For one shuddering moment the force that gripped him seemed to loosen its hold. The coils of the dream fell away, his mind was clear, and, for the first time since he had awakened, he was aware of just what he was doing.

Thus, here again, the suggestion is that Rudi is acting not out of intuitive virtue but out of egotistic desire, the force gripping him, which places him in a sort of dream in which unvirtuous acts can be most easily carried out. Indeed, though Rudi realizes that his father would not have done what he is now doing, he continues: "The moment of clearness passed; the force, the compulsion returned. The consequences did not matter. Right and wrong did not matter." All that matters in his mind now is that he catch and pass Saxo and prove "victorious" on the summit. Rudi has slipped out of his ordinary virtuousness to allow himself to be driven by egotistic desire.

It is in this state of mind that Rudi is confronted with his next great choice. He catches up with Saxo on the catwalk ridge; Saxo, through his own unwise action, tumbles down the embankment to a ledge below, breaking his arm. What should Rudi do? Would it be just for him to continue to the top, leaving Saxo behind, as Saxo in fact directs him to do? The reader knows that Saxo is not the voice of reason: he is the voice of competition, the voice of hubris, excessive pride. And yet there would be justice in Rudi's leaving Saxo to head for the top. Even if Rudi did not feel that his earlier decision to pursue Saxo was virtuous, he could have felt that it was just: did Saxo deserve to be the first one to the top, rather than any of the other three? And though Rudi's own desire to be the first to the peak can be construed as egotistic, it can also be construed as symbolic, since the banner he wishes to plant there is his father's red shirt, which represents the selflessness Josef Matt displayed in keeping Edward Stephenson warm and staying by his side until both of their deaths.

The narration makes clear that this is the most significant decision of Rudi's young life: "Thought and emotion met, conflicted, tangled, and seemed almost to tear his mind to shreds." Rudi proceeds to wrestle with the morality of either evident choice, to ascend to the top or climb down and help Saxo. Returning to the hazy, dreamlike state he experienced earlier—the egotistic state—Rudi envisions himself at the top, even hears a voice urging him up. The voice suggests that in reaching the top, he would be his "father's son." Rudi could have easily heeded this voice; he could have allowed himself to call the voice destiny, act unconsciously, and continue upward. But by now he recognizes what this voice represents: egotistic desire and selfishness. To act selfishly in order to plant the banner of selflessness would be an intolerable contradiction. To be "*his father's son*," he knows, he must consciously make the selfless choice. He descends to help Saxo. In the end, there is justice in the fact that Winter takes up the red-shirt banner and plants it at the top, where it belongs. In the meantime, Rudi has demonstrated that what he has been following along is not simply destiny; he is not obliged to simply obey whatever a voice in his head happens to say, to do whatever he happens to be doing. Rather, he has been following virtue, he has been doing what feels like and indeed is the right thing—and his virtue is what determines his destiny.

Rudi uses his father's old red shirt to make a flag to plant at the end of his climb. (© Jiri 'Tashi' Vondracek / Shutterstock.com)

Source: Michael Allen Holmes, Critical Essay on *Banner in the Sky*, in *Novels for Students*, Gale, Cengage Learning, 2014.

CRITICISM

Leah Tieger

Tieger is a freelance writer and editor. In the following essay, she discusses destiny, morality, birthright, and the ghost of the father in Banner in the Sky.

Rudi Matt's desire to climb the Citadel in *Banner in the Sky* is a mixture of destiny and birthright. It is a means of honoring his father, who died in the same attempt. The fatherless boy has several father figures on his journey: his uncle Franz Lerner, Captain John Winter, and Teo Zurbriggen. The spirit of Rudi's father also guides him, appearing to the boy in chapter 12, "A Boy and a Ghost." Alone, trapped by a sudden snowstorm, Rudi is forced to retreat and take shelter in a cave. It is the very cave where his father froze to death. Rudi tries to avoid the same fate, and he must face the ghosts that haunt the Citadel. The mountain's spirits are led by the specter of Rudi's father, "a ghost with a red shirt." The terrified boy calls out to the spirit, and "then the strange thing happened: the incredible and wonderful thing." Rudi is no longer afraid. "His fear had vanished." The child realizes that his father "died proud and unafraid" because he gave his life for another.

The ghost of Josef Matt stays with Rudi and influences him from that point on, as he navigates the moral and ethical dilemmas that arise on his journey. In the end, Rudi chooses to honor his father's noble and self-sacrificing actions, which are more important than conquering the Citadel's summit. The boy fulfills his birthright and his father's legacy, not by reaching the mountain's peak, but by giving up his dreams for another. Where Josef gave his life to save Sir Edward Stephenson, Rudi risks his life to save Emil Saxo. Father and son give up their dream of conquering the Citadel for something more noble, keeping their moral code.

Destiny and birthright drive Rudi's actions. When he climbs, he is doing what he has "been born to do." The boys in Kurtal call Rudi "Angel-face," which symbolically pits him against the imposing mountain. Franz calls the Citadel an "evil" peak, a "killer," and the people of Kurtal believe that the mountain is inhabited by devils. If the mountain is evil, then it can only be conquered by good (an angel versus the devils). The boy senses the mountain's malevolent spirits on more than one occasion, but they do not appear after he senses his father's ghost. The closer Rudi is to his father and his actions, the closer he is to success, and the only way for Rudi to survive is by honoring his father's legacy.

Rudi's birthright is both a privilege and a responsibility. He inherits his natural climbing ability from his father, but he also inherits his father's sense of duty. Rudi's physical talents are accompanied by his father's heart and spirit, which center upon the duties of a guide, the duties his father lived and died by, the duties his uncle and Teo continue to live by. When Captain Winter hires Emil Saxo and Uncle Franz as his guides, this makes him their client, their *Herr*. Rudi's father gave his life to save his *Herr* on the citadel, and Uncle Franz insists that they cannot leave Winter and continue their

> BY HONORING HIS FATHER'S LEGACY AND HIS OWN BIRTHRIGHT, RUDI'S DREAM COMES TRUE, THOUGH NOT IN THE WAY HE HAD IMAGINED."

climb when the captain becomes too sick to proceed. Rudi knows his uncle is right, and he knows this "with a knowledge that was deeper than mere learning; that was part of his heritage, part of his blood and bone." This is the legacy of Rudi's father, not only the skill to climb, but the impulse to do the right thing.

This impulse is acknowledged and cultivated by Teo, the only man to survive the ill-fated expedition undertaken by Rudi's father. Teo is Rudi's mentor and the man who believes most in the boy. He teaches Rudi that climbing is more than putting one foot in front of the other. In chapter 6, "Master and Pupil," Teo tells Rudi that the boy nearly died on the Wunderhorn from a simple mistake because he was "thinking, not of others, but only of yourself." To become a guide like his father, Rudi must "help others." This is what made Rudi's father great, and Teo explains that Josef Matt "had a flame in him . . . not of the body but of the heart."

In chapter 16, "Darkness and Dawn," Rudi ignores this lesson. He leaves Captain Winter and Uncle Franz behind to find Saxo, overtake him, and claim the summit as his own. Rudi is conscious of the choice he has made, and he thinks of Teo's advice: *What would his father have done in such a situation? Not what he was doing.* That he knew." Rudi is so driven by his dream of conquering the Citadel that "right and wrong did not matter." He is too obsessed to honor his father, but he is given an opportunity to correct that misstep when he catches up to Saxo.

Rudi continues alone up the mountain, and he momentarily struggles with his decision. His "wave of guilt" is soon replaced by "pride and defiance." He knows that the expedition could not have made it this far without him. He is the one who found a route past the Fortress, and the only one small enough to get through the Needle. But when Rudi catches up to Saxo, he asks to be allowed to climb with him. They can share the summit together, he says. Saxo, however, is even more prideful than Rudi, who at least has some justification for feeling the way he does. In his pride, Saxo tries to shoo the boy away, losing his balance and nearly falling to his death.

Rudi knows that even though Saxo is to "blame" for his own injury, "the helping of another climber in trouble must always—*always*—take precedence over everything else." Thus, he corrects the mistake he made by leaving Captain Winter behind and dishonoring his father's legacy. He revives his father's moral code, one he would not have broken if Saxo hadn't left the group behind in the first place. The thought of Saxo stealing his and his father's claim on the mountain's peak becomes a literal nightmare that causes Rudi to momentarily forget morality. Although it is not clearly stated, the moral responsibility to save Saxo is greater than the moral responsibility to stay with Winter. When Rudi left the captain with his uncle, he was not in any immediate danger. Saxo, however, will die if Rudi abandons him.

As Rudi considers leaving Saxo behind, he realizes that leaving the others "had been wrong, and two wrongs did not make a right." On the one hand, Rudi believes that he has more of a responsibility to his *Herr* than he does to a fellow guide. Even Saxo tells the boy to leave him behind. The injured guide urges Rudi to reach the top of the mountain and achieve glory, to become "your father's son." This phrase brings Rudi to his senses, and he knows that he must save Saxo if he ever hopes to become "*his father's son.*" With these words, Rudi's desire to climb the mountain disappears, and "in its place was clearness." Rudi does not leave Saxo, and he gives up his dream of reaching the Citadel's peak in order to save his enemy. He not only acts in the spirit of his father's ethics, he goes above and beyond them.

Rudi's only regret is that he will never plant his father's flannel as a flag on top of the Citadel. He left his pack, his staff, and the flannel behind to help Saxo, and his most precious belongings are lost to him forever. When he spots Captain Winter and Uncle Franz scaling the mountain in the distance, all he has to do is call out to them. They will turn back to help him and Saxo. With one shout, Rudi could prevent the other men from taking his glory, creating an opportunity to achieve his dream on another expedition. The boy stays silent and continues down the mountain with Saxo. By doing so, he continues to live by his father's code. "'Yes, that is good, Uncle,' said the son of Josef Matt," when Winter and Franz return from the peak of the Citadel. "We are guides of Kurtal, and we got our *Herr* to the top."

By honoring his father's legacy and his own birthright, Rudi's dream comes true, though not in the way he had imagined. The red flannel that Rudi carried up the mountain is retrieved by Captain Winter, who picks it up and erects it on top of the mountain. The shirt that Josef Matt took from his back to keep his *Herr* warm flies like a flag at the peak of the Citadel, a symbol of the triumph that can only be achieved through self-sacrifice. In this manner, both Rudi and his father have succeeded, and even Captain Winters acknowledges this. When the entire village of Kurtal gathers to celebrate, Winter says that the mountain belongs not to him, but to Rudi.

Source: Leah Tieger, Critical Essay on *Banner in the Sky*, in *Novels for Students*, Gale, Cengage Learning, 2014.

SOURCES

Alderson, Brian, "Checklist," in *Times* (London, England), September 14, 1968, p. 21.

Chuang Tzu, *The Book of Chuang Tzu*, translated by Martin Palmer, with Elizabeth Breuilly, Chang Wai Ming, and Jay Ramsay, Arkana, 1996, p. 83.

"8000m Peaks," SummitPost.org, March 18, 2012, http://www.summitpost.org/8000m-peaks/171372 (accessed April 14, 2013).

Isserman, Maurice, "The Ethics of Mountaineering Brought Low," in *Chronicle of Higher Education*, Vol. 52, No. 35, May 5, 2006, pp. B15–B16.

"James Ramsey Ullman, American Novelist," in *Times* (London, England), June 22, 1971, p. 14.

Minton, Ryan, "Record Retour on the Matterhorn's Hornli Ridge," in *Alpinist*, September 20, 2007, http://www.alpinist.com/doc/web07f/newswire-matterhorn-hornli-ridge-record (accessed April 21, 2013).

Norman-Culp, Sheila, "Misadventures in Switzerland: How Not to Climb the Matterhorn," in *USA Today*, May 23, 2007, http://usatoday30.usatoday.com/travel/destinations/2007-05-23-climbing-the-matterhorn_N.htm (accessed April 21, 2013).

Rébuffat, Gaston, *Men and the Matterhorn*, translated by Eleanor Brockett, Oxford University Press, 1973, pp. 13–29, 34–42, 82–136, 184–90.

Roper, Robert, *Fatal Mountaineer: The High-Altitude Life and Death of Willi Unsoeld, American Himalayan Legend*, St. Martin's Press, 2002, pp. 152–58.

Shoumatoff, Nicholas, and Nina Shoumatoff, *The Alps: Europe's Mountain Heart*, University of Michigan Press, 2001, pp. 112–13, 143–44, 188–206, 212–13.

Ullman, James Ramsey, *Banner in the Sky*, Harper Trophy, 1988.

Ullman, James Ramsey, et al., *Americans on Everest: The Official Account of the Ascent Led by Norman G. Dyhrenfurth*, J. B. Lippincott, 1964, pp. 307–308.

"Ullman, James Ramsey (1907–1971)," in *Benet's Reader's Encyclopedia of American Literature*, Vol. 1, 1991, p. 1075.

Watson, Burton, trans., Introduction to *Chuang Tzu: Basic Writings*, Columbia University Press, 1996, p. 6.

FURTHER READING

Birmingham, David, *Switzerland: A Village History*, St. Martin's Press, 2000.

> The chapter "The Romance of the Alps" in this book by a British professor provides a comprehensive treatment of life in the rural Swiss borough of Château-d'Oex from a thousand years ago until the modern day. Birmingham discusses traditions, professions, and also the mountains.

Clark, Ronald W., *The Day the Rope Broke: The Story of the First Ascent of the Matterhorn*, Harcourt, Brace & World, 1965.

> Beyond Edward Whymper's own 1871 account of the tragic first ascent of the Matterhorn, which is included in *Scrambles amongst the Alps in the Years 1860–69*, Clark has provided a definitive full account of that climb, from the backgrounds of the cast of characters to the tragic denouement.

Pellegrini, Robert J., and Theodore R. Sarbin, *Between Fathers and Sons: Critical Incident Narratives in the Development of Men's Lives*, Psychology Press, 2002.

> This work of narrative psychology explores the nuances of a number of real-life relationships between father and son and how the son's worldview has been shaped by the father.

Simpson, Joe, *Touching the Void*, Jonathan Cape, 1988.

> In this book the author narrates what is recognized as one of the greatest mountaineering survival stories in history. During the descent after reaching the summit of Siula Grande in the Andes, Simpson broke his leg. At length his climbing mate, Simon Yates, was forced to cut the rope from which Simpson was suspended and, presuming his friend dead after a 150-foot fall, abandon him in a crevasse. But Simpson survived—just barely.

Wroth, Katherine, ed., *The Zen of Mountains and Climbing: Wit, Wisdom and Inspiration*, Skipstone, 2009.

> With a foreword by Ed Viesturs, who has climbed all fourteen of the world's 8,000-meter peaks, this book is an artful collection of quotes, including one by James Ramsey Ullman, that evoke the holistic beauty of mountain climbing.

SUGGESTED SEARCH TERMS

James Ramsey Ullman AND Banner in the Sky

James Ramsey Ullman AND mountaineering OR mountain climbing

James Ramsey Ullman AND Mount Everest

Third Man on the Mountain

Switzerland AND mountaineering

Matterhorn AND first ascent

Matterhorn AND literature

Alps AND literature

Banner in the Sky AND review

Cimarron

EDNA FERBER

1930

Cimarron, a novel with a western setting by Edna Ferber, was published in 1930. Like many of Ferber's novels, it was very popular and was made into a Hollywood film, one year after publication. The well-researched novel is set in Oklahoma and covers the period from 1889 through the 1920s. The two main characters, Yancey and Sabra Cravat, move from Wichita, Kansas, to Oklahoma a short while after the land run in 1889, when vast amounts of uninhabited land are there for the taking and free of charge. Small towns spring up overnight, and Yancey and Sabra settle in the fictional town of Osage, which is modeled on Guthrie, Oklahoma, in the north-central part of the state. Yancey starts a newspaper in Osage, and the story shows how the rough-and-ready town grows to maturity. The tale extends all the way to the discovery of oil in the new state and the resulting oil boom of the early twentieth century. Apart from being an entertaining story about the origin and early development of Oklahoma, *Cimarron* tackles important social and political issues of the time, including the treatment of Native Americans.

AUTHOR BIOGRAPHY

One of the most popular of twentieth-century female novelists, Edna Ferber was born on August 15, 1885, in Kalamazoo, Michigan, to

Edna Ferber (© *The Library of Congress*)

Jacob Charles and Julia Neumann Ferber. Her father was a Jewish immigrant from Hungary; her mother was a second-generation German Jew. Ferber grew up in Appleton, Wisconsin, where she graduated from high school and then became a reporter for the *Appleton Daily Crescent* and later, in Milwaukee, for the *Milwaukee Journal*. Returning to Appleton to live again with her family, she began her career as a novelist with the publication of *Dawn O'Hara: The Girl Who Laughed* (1911), based on her experiences as a journalist in Milwaukee. She quickly followed this with two collections of short stories, *Buttered Side Down* (1912) and *Roast Beef Medium* (1913), and several novels within five years, including *Fanny Herself* (1917), *The Girls* (1921), and *Gigolo* (1922).

In 1924, Ferber scored a big success with her novel *So Big*, which won the Pulitzer Prize in 1925. The novel is set in the Dutch community of a Chicago suburb. This success propelled Ferber to a highly productive decade. *Show*

Boat followed in 1926. The novel is about a floating theater that travels up and down the Mississippi River, from the 1880s to the 1920s, putting on shows for small towns. A collection of short stories, *Mother Knows Best* (1927), and the novel *Cimarron* (1930) soon followed. Ferber's novels were not only best sellers, but many of them were also adapted for other genres. *Show Boat* became a Broadway musical in 1927 and was made into a film, based on the musical, three times, in 1929, 1936, and 1951. *Cimarron* was made into an Academy Award–winning film in 1931, and a remake followed in 1960.

Ferber also wrote plays with George S. Kaufman. These include *The Royal Family* (1928), which was made into a film in 1930; *Dinner at Eight* (1932); and *The Land Is Bright* (1941). Other works by Ferber include *American Beauty* (1931), *They Brought Their Women* (short stories; 1933), *Come and Get It* (1935), *Nobody's in Town* (1938), *A Peculiar Treasure* (1939), *No Room at the Inn* (1941), *Saratoga Trunk* (1941), *Great Son* (1945), *One Basket* (1947), *Giant* (1952), *Ice Palace* (1958), and *A Kind of Magic* (1963). Of these, *Saratoga Trunk* and *Giant* were adapted for film, in 1945 and 1956, respectively. Ferber, who never married, died of cancer on April 16, 1968, in New York City.

PLOT SUMMARY

Chapters I–IV

Cimarron begins in Wichita, Kansas, in May 1889 at the home of Lewis Venable; his wife, Felice; and their family, who moved from Mississippi to Kansas two decades earlier. The family is eating dinner. Family members present at the table include the Venables' daughter, Sabra; her husband, Yancey Cravat; and their four-year-old son, Cim. Yancey is a great talker and is holding forth about his most recent adventure, when he went to the Indian Territory, which would later become part of Oklahoma, and took part in the land run there. Millions of acres of uninhabited land had been made available for those who were willing to take their chances and grab what they could.

Yancey relates how thousands of people came for the run from places like Texas, Arkansas, Colorado, and Missouri. Conditions were rough as they all assembled at the border.

MEDIA ADAPTATIONS

- *Cimarron* was made into a film in 1931 by RKO Radio Pictures, and it won three Academy Awards. Another version was released by Metro-Goldwyn-Mayer, starring Glenn Ford and Maria Schnell, in 1960.

At midday, soldiers fired their muskets, and the run began. Yancey was on horseback, as followed by a young woman on a thoroughbred. He got within fifty yards of the land he wanted to claim but then stopped to help the girl, whose horse had fallen and was dying. The woman took advantage of his generosity, stealing his horse and claiming the land he had set his sights on. As he tells his tale, Yancey says he did not want the farmland anyway and would rather be in a town. He says he plans to go back to one of the towns that sprang up overnight and practice law and start a newspaper there. He intends to take Sabra and Cim with him. The family is shocked, but Yancey insists, and Sabra says she is determined to go with him.

Sabra says farewell to Mother Bridget, who runs the mission school she attended as a child, and then she, Yancey, and Cim depart on two wagons. Later, they discover that their little black servant, six-year-old Isaiah, is a stowaway on the wagon, so he goes to the Indian Territory with them.

Chapters V–VIII

During the journey Yancey enthralls his son with stories about the Indians and how they were cheated out of their land by the white people. Yancey is very sympathetic to the Indian plight, although Sabra is not. Sabra has a scare when Cim goes missing for a while, but she finds him being cared for by a group of men, whom she later discovers are outlaws led by a man named the Kid.

They arrive in Osage and stay in a rooming house. The town seems to be made up entirely of wooden shacks and dried mud. Sabra hates it

all—the place, the people, the food. Yancey, who gets to know everyone quickly, tries to reassure her. He wants to get out the first issue of his newspaper, the *Oklahoma Wigwam*, within two weeks. He promises to identify the man who killed the previous newspaper editor, Pegler. A group of three men tries to scare Yancey by shooting his sombrero off, but Yancey takes it all in stride.

They rent a four-room house and attach a two-room cabin to it. The house serves as law office, newspaper office, and printing shop, as well as a home. The practical Sabra does a great deal to help set things up, including in the print shop, assisted by Jesse Rickey. Yancey seems more interested in finding out who killed Pegler.

A delegation of citizens asks Yancey to conduct a religious service the following Sunday morning. There is no church, so the service is to be held in a large gambling tent. On that day, it seems that almost everyone in the town comes to the service, including the Indians.

Chapters IX–XII

The service starts with everyone singing a song they all know, even though it is not a hymn. Then Yancey orders a collection, and they raise $133.55 to go toward buying a church organ. He begins his sermon with a quotation from Proverbs, then announces that he is about to name Pegler's killer. At that moment he drops his Bible on purpose and stoops to pick it up. There is a gunshot, and as quick as a flash Yancey returns fire, killing a man named Lon Yountis, who already had a bad reputation and is now revealed to be the murderer.

The first issue of the newspaper comes out, and Sabra starts to play a bigger role in producing it. She also takes the lead in developing community activities for the women of the town, including the formation of a culture club. But she is shocked when a young woman she admires, Mrs. Evergreen Waltz, is killed by her much-older husband when he discovers she has a lover.

In June 1890, Sabra gives birth to a baby girl, Donna. Yancey rescues Sol Levy, a Jewish man who is being tormented by some of the men in the town. Yancey invites him to dinner at their home and promises he will protect him.

Several years pass. After nearly four years in Osage, Sabra has come to enjoy life there, and the brief trip she makes back to her old home in

Wichita is not a successful one. Sabra finds that she no longer gets along with her mother and does not accept her authority.

Chapters XIII–XVII

When Sabra returns to Osage, she discovers that Yancey has become the town hero for killing the outlaw, the Kid, whose gang was attempting to rob the bank. There is a lot of reward money available, but Yancey refuses it all, saying that he does not take money for killing a man.

Yancey grows restless and moody, losing interest in the newspaper. Sabra takes on more and more of the responsibilities in producing it. In 1893, Yancey wants to uproot his family and take them on a new land run, since the Cherokee Strip is opening for white settlement. Yancey wants to claim 160 acres and start a ranch. Sabra says no. In September, Yancey departs on his own for the run. He disappears for five years.

In the meantime, Sabra gets on with her life in Osage, running the newspaper efficiently and being a prominent figure in the town's social life. The town is booming, and Dixie Lee, the owner of the town brothel, who is a shrewd businesswoman, is thriving. Sabra dislikes her, condemning her as immoral.

Sabra's Osage Indian household assistant, Arita Red Feather, gives birth to a baby. The father is Isaiah, who is now a young man. The Osage Indians do not permit intermarriage, and on the orders of the tribal leaders, Arita Red Feather and Isaiah are killed in a gruesome manner.

In 1898, war breaks out between the United States and Spain, and the city of Osage is on fire with patriotic fervor. After his five-year absence, Yancey returns, wearing the uniform of the Oklahoma Rough Riders. He gives no explanation of where he has been, but later that evening he tells the gathered townspeople that he spent two years in Alaska during the gold rush, though he has returned with very little gold. Yancey leaves the next day on his way to the Philippines to join the war, but not before he has successfully defended Dixie Lee, who is in court on a disorderly conduct charge.

Chapters XVIII–XXI

Several years later, Yancey returns from the war a hero. The newspaper continues to flourish, and new technology is introduced. Yancey takes up the cause of combining Oklahoma Territory with Indian Territory to make up the single state of Oklahoma. Sol Levy runs for mayor of Osage, supported by Yancey, but he loses. The town continues to grow, and Sabra designs and builds a new, bigger house. She hires an Indian girl, Ruby Big Elk, as a house servant. To Sabra's irritation, Ruby starts to teach Cim to speak Osage. Cim has adopted his father's attitude of sympathy to all things Indian. Sabra discovers that Cim has been eating peyote, the hallucinogen from a cactus plant that the Indians use in religious rituals. She is furious with him, but Cim defends himself and the Indians.

Donna is sent to an eastern finishing school against Yancey's wishes. Cim hates working in the newspaper office and wants to be a geologist. One night Sabra finds him at the Osage Indian Reservation, where he has taken peyote as part of the Osage religious ceremony. The ceremony is nearly over, and Cim is asleep. Sabra and Sol Levy, who took her out there, put him in the buggy and drive home. Sabra also knows that night that Yancey has left home once again.

Oklahoma becomes a state, and at about that time huge oil deposits are found there. Thousands of ordinary people become rich overnight. Donna returns from the East Coast, but mother and daughter do not get along well. Donna plans to pursue Tracy Wyatt, a middle-aged, newly oil-rich resident of Osage, simply because he is rich. He is currently married, but that does not deter Donna.

Sometime after the discovery of oil, Yancey returns home with the startling news that the largest amounts of oil in the state have been discovered under the barren soil of the Osage Indian Reservation, where two thousand Osage live. The impoverished Indians there will now be rich.

Cim returns home from Colorado, where he has been studying geology. He finds himself being consulted by many people about oil. Yancey and Sabra acquire no oil wealth, but their newspaper becomes highly influential throughout the Southwest. The newly rich Osage Indians buy luxury cars and flaunt their wealth around town. Sabra is shocked when Donna announces that she is to marry Tracy Wyatt, who is divorcing his wife.

Chapters XXII–XXV

About 1910, Sabra, who has never liked Indians, is shocked to learn from Big Elk that his daughter, Ruby Big Elk, has married Cim. Yancey, however, is pleased with the match. At the dinner given in honor of the newlyweds, Sabra can barely bring herself to eat anything.

Nearly two decades later, in the late 1920s, Osage has grown enormously owing to its oil wealth and now has skyscrapers and luxury hotels. Sabra has become a congresswoman. Cim and Ruby have a daughter, Felice, who is a state tennis champion, and a son, Yancey. Donna is still married to the hugely wealthy Tracy Wyatt. Sabra rarely visits her. Yancey has been gone for well over a decade, and Sabra has had no news of him for five years. She knows that he fought in World War I and was listed as missing. She now believes he is dead.

In Congress, Sabra introduces a bill for more protection for the Osages and calls for the abolition of the Indian reservations, since that would help Indian development. A top-quality Polish sculptor named Krbecek creates a statue that embodies the Oklahoma pioneer. The statue shows Yancey Cravat leading an Indian.

In her capacity as congresswoman, Sabra starts a campaign against the poor conditions that prevail in the state's newest oil towns. With a delegation of twenty important people, she visits the town of Bowlegs and shows the delegation around the town. There is a commotion, and Sabra learns that a man has just acted quickly in order to save the town from a potentially devastating explosion at the oil rig. The man has been injured and is dying. No one quite knows who he is, but some call him old Yance. Sabra knows immediately it is Yancey, and she rushes to his side. They manage to say good-bye to each other before Yancey dies.

CHARACTERS

Big Elk

Big Elk is the tribal chief of the Osages and the father of Ruby Big Elk. He is a proud man who refuses to speak English. He is friends with Yancey. Big Elk and his family become wealthy during the oil boom.

Mrs. Big Elk

Mrs. Big Elk is about thirty years younger than her husband, Big Elk. Unlike her husband, she speaks English, having attended a mission school, but she does not care to speak it correctly.

Ruby Big Elk

Ruby Big Elk is an Indian girl hired as household help by Sabra. She marries Cimarron Cravat and is the mother of Yancey and Felice.

Cimarron Cravat

Cimarron Cravat, known as Cim, is the son of Yancey and Sabra Cravat. He is four years old when the family moves to Oklahoma. As a young man he has no aptitude for the newspaper business and goes to Colorado to study geology. He has learned from his father to be sympathetic to the Indian cause, and when he returns home he marries Ruby Big Elk, to his mother's disgust but his father's pleasure. Cim and Ruby have two children, Felice and Yancey.

Donna Cravat

See Donna Wyatt

Felice Cravat

Felice Cravat is the daughter of Cim and Ruby Cravat. She is strong and athletic and becomes a state tennis champion.

Sabra Cravat

Sabra is Yancey Cravat's wife. She is twenty-one years old when the story begins. She was married at sixteen and has a four-year-old son, Cim. She is pleased to accompany her husband to Oklahoma, since this will enable her to escape the dominating influence of her mother. However, when she arrives in Osage she hates the rough living and the unfamiliar people. She eventually settles down and comes to enjoy life in the new town, organizing social clubs for the ladies. She also plays a large practical role in running the newspaper that Yancey sets up. Her relations with the townspeople are warm, except in the case of Dixie Lee, owner of the town brothel, who offends Sabra's strong sense of morality.

When Yancey deserts her for five years following the land run of 1893, Sabra, now with two children to care for, adapts well to her new situation. She runs the newspaper herself and writes some hard-hitting editorials. When Yancey finally returns, she is overjoyed to see him and does not question why he has been away for so long. She eventually gets used to his frequent absences and continues to flourish in her own right. She is an independent, strong-minded woman who becomes one of the most respected figures in Osage. In the 1920s she is elected to Congress and gains a reputation for her extensive knowledge of the state.

One of Sabra's less attractive traits is her dislike of Indians, and she is bitterly disappointed when her son marries an Indian woman. She is also disappointed with the shallow, materialistic attitude of her daughter, and she does not approve of her marriage either. Despite these family disappointments, Sabra has a highly successful life as one of Oklahoma's pioneer women.

Yancey Cravat (the Elder)

Yancey Cravat is the husband of Sabra. He is a dashing, romantic, chivalrous, adventurous, charming, impulsive man about whom many stories are told. When he married Sabra, he was the editor of the Wichita *Wigwam*, a newspaper, and he was also a lawyer. He has high ideas and is very supportive of Indians, believing that the US government cheated them out of their rights. Many people believe that he has Choctaw Indian blood in him, but this is never established for sure. When he first arrives in Osage with Sabra and four-year-old Cim, Yancey expends a great amount of effort in establishing the newspaper there. He quickly makes many friends and enemies, and he kills in self-defense the man who killed the previous newspaper editor, Pegler. He also kills the area's most notorious outlaw, the Kid. He is offered the position of governor of Oklahoma Territory, but he is not interested in such a position because he has a very low opinion of all politicians.

Yancey is better at starting projects than continuing with them once they have been set up, and after a while he grows bored and restless in Osage. He tries but fails to get Sabra to go with him on a second land run to the Cherokee Strip in 1893. Yancey ends up going on his own, and he disappears for five years. He returns home, and it transpires that for two of those missing five years he was in Alaska, as part of the gold rush. Yancey departs again almost immediately to fight in the Spanish-American War as a member of the Oklahoma Rough Riders. He comes home as a war hero. For a while he takes up the cause of the Indians, arguing for Oklahoma Territory to be combined with Indian Territory as a single state. He even travels to Washington, DC, to lobby for the cause. Once again he is touted as the next governor of the Oklahoma Territory, but he

deliberately scuttles his chances by penning a fiery editorial in the *Oklahoma Wigwam* arguing that the Indians in the United States should be allowed to live wherever they please.

A few years later Yancey disappears again. It transpires that he fought in World War I and was listed as missing. Sabra believes he is dead. But Yancey finally turns up again in the small town of Bowlegs, where he is killed in an accident as he saves the town from a likely explosion at the oil rig.

Yancey Cravat (the Younger)

The younger Yancey Cravat is the son of Cim and Ruby Cravat and the grandson of Yancey and Sabra Cravat. He becomes a good-looking young man who embraces his Indian heritage.

Cousin Jouett Goforth

Cousin Jouett Goforth is present at the Sunday dinner where Yancey tells of his trip to Oklahoma. He is visiting the family from Louisiana for the first time in fifteen years.

Grat Gotch

Grat Gotch is the owner of the gambling tent in Osage in which the first religious service is held.

Louie Hefner

Louie Hefner owns a furniture store and an undertaker's office in the pioneer days in Osage. He also serves as the town's coroner.

Isaiah

Isaiah is a young black boy who is a servant in the Cravat household in Wichita. He stows away on the wagons that are taking Yancey, Sabra, and Cim to Oklahoma. Isaiah is a very capable and willing boy, and he soon makes himself indispensable to the family, doing many chores as well as being a playmate for Cim and later Donna. Unfortunately, when he is a teenager, Isaiah fathers a child by Arita Red Feather, and he is killed by the Osages, who do not approve of mixed marriages.

The Kid

The Kid is a notorious outlaw who holds up trains and robs banks. He is shot dead by Yancey when he tries to rob the bank in Osage.

Krbecek

Krbecek is a noted Polish sculptor who creates the statue that honors the Oklahoma pioneers.

Pat Leary

Pat Leary is an Irish lawyer who comes to Osage after Yancey disappears in 1893. He is the prosecutor in the Dixie Lee case but fails to win a conviction. Later he becomes very wealthy through oil.

Dixie Lee

Dixie Lee owns the town brothel. She is also the woman who beat Yancey to claim land in the run of 1889. She is a successful businesswoman, and many of the men socialize at her establishment. At one point she is prosecuted for disorderly conduct, but Yancey Cravat defends her and ensures her acquittal. Dixie eventually moves to Oklahoma City and becomes a respectable citizen. She adopts a baby boy, but the child is taken from her when the women of Osage tell the authorities about Dixie's past. She dies six months later.

Sol Levy

Sol Levy is a Jew who lives in Osage and faces harassment and discrimination on account of his ethnicity. He starts out as a peddler but becomes successful with the Levy Mercantile Company and owns a lot of property. He also sets up a zoo. Yancey and Sabra befriend him, and when he is prosperous, he helps Sabra financially with the newspaper and also runs unsuccessfully for mayor. He remains a bachelor.

Cliff Means

Cliff Means is a fifteen-year-old boy who works as an assistant on the *Oklahoma Wigwam*, the Osage newspaper.

Estevan Miro

Estevan Miro is a Spaniard. Along with Pete Pitchlyn, he is known as a town gossip. He appears to know everything that is going on for miles around. He passes on to Yancey something he has heard: Yancey should stop investigating who killed Pegler or it will cost him his life.

Doc Nisbett

Doc Nisbett is the town doctor in the earliest days. He is originally from New England and managed to nab some prime land in Osage during the run of 1889. The Cravats plan to rent a house from him, but Sabra, knowing no better, asks that ten barrels of water be made available to them every day. That is far too much, so Doc declines to rent the house to them.

Pete Pitchlyn

Along with Estevan Miro, Pete Pitchlyn is a disreputable character and a town gossip. He used to be an Indian scout and is married to a Cherokee woman.

Arita Red Feather

Arita Red Feather is a fifteen-year-old girl who works as household help in the Cravat home when Donna is very young. She has a baby, fathered by Isaiah. The Osage Indians do not then allow such intermarriage, and the tribal elders order that she be killed.

Jesse Rickey

Jesse Rickey is a printer employed at the *Oklahoma Wigwam*. He is frequently drunk.

Don Valiant

Don Valiant is the doctor who delivers Sabra's second baby, Donna. He is a colorful figure who is also known for treating bandits.

Cousin Dabney Venable

Cousin Dabney Venable attends the Sunday dinner in Wichita where Yancey Cravat tells of his first visit to Oklahoma. He expresses some contempt for the region and makes some anti-Indian remarks.

Felice Venable

Felice Venable is Sabra's mother, who lives in Wichita, Kansas. She is married to Lewis Venable. Originally the family was from Mississippi, and Felice likes to cling to the elegant southern ways. She opposes Yancey and Sabra in their desire to move to Oklahoma. In later years, she does not enjoy a good relationship with her daughter.

Lewis Venable

Lewis Venable is Sabra's father. He is an aged, sick man with a gentle manner. He was wounded in the Civil War and has also suffered from malaria. He does not object to Sabra's going to Oklahoma with her husband, pointing out to his wife, Felice, that she came with him to Kansas twenty years earlier, against the wishes of her mother.

Evergreen Waltz

Evergreen Waltz is a gambler who earns a living playing cards. He kills his young wife when he finds out that she has a lover.

Mrs. Evergreen Waltz

Mrs. Evergreen Waltz is a young woman in Osage whom Sabra admires and wants to include in her social circle. Mrs. Waltz is shot by her husband because she has a lover. Sabra discovers that she used to be a prostitute.

Donna Wyatt

Donna Wyatt is the daughter of Yancey and Sabra Cravat. She is five years younger than her brother, Cim. When she is fifteen Donna is sent to a finishing school on the East Coast. When she returns, she talks like an easterner and is alienated from her mother. Materialistically minded, Donna decides she will marry the richest man in town, Tracy Wyatt, even though he is over thirty years older than she and is already married. Tracy falls in love with her and divorces his wife.

Tracy Wyatt

Tracy Wyatt operates the bus and dray line in Osage, but as a result of the oil boom he becomes immensely rich as head of the Wyatt Oil Company. Although he is in his early fifties, he divorces his wife and marries Donna Cravat, who is thirty years younger than he.

Mrs. Tracy Wyatt

Mrs. Tracy Wyatt is the first wife of Tracy Wyatt. She is a proud woman who claims to be able to trace her ancestry back to William Whipple, one of the signers of the Declaration of Independence. After her husband becomes wealthy, she wears expensive clothes from New York and becomes neurotic.

Lon Yountis

Lon Yountis is the man who killed the newspaper editor Pegler, before Yancey came to Osage. When Yancey tricks Yountis into taking a shot at him during the religious service, Yancey returns fire and kills him.

THEMES

Husband-Wife Relationships

Running through the novel is the long marriage of Yancey and Sabra, and the author uses the relationship of husband and wife to show the growth of Sabra as a character. In the early years of her marriage she is charmed by the dashing adventurer who is her husband. For his part, Yancey is very chivalrous and tender toward her, but he is also patronizing, regarding her as a "charming little fool." He does not take her abilities or her opinions seriously. There is no doubt that Sabra loves her husband, and she learns to play the role of frontier wife, looking after home and family, very well. But it does not take long in Oklahoma for her to realize that, unlike what she was taught to believe in her southern-style upbringing, men are not always right. She starts to become aware that Yancey is in fact wrong about lots of things and also that "he was enthralled by the dramatics of any plan he might conceive, but that he often was too impatient of its mechanics to carry it through to completion." At first she refuses to accept these heretical thoughts, but she gradually comes to recognize the truth.

It is Sabra, not Yancey, who is most responsible for making the newspaper a success, because she is the one who puts in the necessary day-to-day work over a period of years. Yancey sometimes stirs up excitement with his colorful and opinionated editorials, but he soon loses interest. Sabra is referred to as "Oklahoma's first feminist," and she comes into her own power most fully when Yancey disappears for five years. She becomes a force to be reckoned with in Osage and beyond, eventually even getting elected to Congress. When Yancey returns after his first five-year absence, Sabra seems to forgive his selfish behavior and is still in love with him. As time goes by, she adapts to his frequent absences and just gets on with her own life. She and Yancey remain, in their different ways, in love with each other, but each has a separate life. However, when Yancey is at home in Osage, even in the later years, such as when the oil boom comes, he insists on being in charge. When he wants to run an editorial in support of the Osage Indians, he tells her that she must kill the editorial she was planning and print his instead. When she protests that she is the editor, he marches her outside and points to the sign he erected when they first came to Osage, which identifies Yancey Cravat as the proprietor and editor of the newspaper. Sabra has no choice but to acquiesce.

United States History

The novel covers several decades in the history of Oklahoma, from 1889 to the late 1920s. Native Americans were an important component of this history, and issues regarding the Indians are a major part of the novelist's concern. Ferber's two main characters have diametrically opposed

TOPICS FOR FURTHER STUDY

- In *Cimarron*, Yancey Cravat joins the Rough Riders and goes to fight in the Spanish-American war with Teddy Roosevelt. Who was Roosevelt? Who were the Rough Riders? Give a class presentation starting with how the topic is introduced in the novel. Then describe Roosevelt and the Rough Riders and what they did in that war. For more information, consult the relevant sections of *Teddy Roosevelt: American Rough Rider* (2007), by John Garraty, a biography for young adults.

- Write a book review of *Cimarron* and post it to the website of one of the major booksellers, such as Amazon or Barnes & Noble. Also post it to a blog and invite comments from your classmates. Incorporate the thoughts of classmates and web reviewers into a paper detailing the variety of readers' critiques on the book.

- Write a character analysis of Yancey Cravat, making reference to the novel. What sort of man is he? Is he an admirable character, or is he seriously flawed? Do his virtues outweigh his faults?

- Watch either the 1931 or 1960 film version of *Cimarron*. With a small group of other students, prepare a class presentation in which you discuss the film, emphasizing how effective the film is in translating the novel to the screen. How does the movie differ from the book?

views on the matter. Yancey is a strong supporter of the Indians. He feels that they have suffered greatly from their treatment by the US government. Yancey makes sure that his son, Cimarron, knows the recent history of the Indians. He tells him of the Trail of Tears. This came about as a result of the Indian Removal Act of 1830, which forced the Indians who lived in southeastern United States as autonomous nations to move to the eastern

part of what would then be known as Indian Territory and would later become Oklahoma. The nations were the Cherokee, Creek, Seminole, Chickasaw, and Choctaw. The Cherokees called the march they were forced to take the Trail of Tears because many died of malnutrition, disease, and exhaustion. More than four thousand of the fifteen thousand Cherokees died.

Sabra, on the other hand, hates Indians. This is a prejudice that she appears to have inherited from her family. Her father, for example, refers to the Indians as "savages." Sabra sees them in a stereotypical manner and is exasperated by Yancey's sympathetic interest in them. "The sooner they're all dead the better. What good are they? Filthy, thieving, lazy things," she says, and she echoes these sentiments on many occasions. She dislikes seeing the Osage Indians in town, but, of course, Yancey is sympathetic to them and has also explained the tribe's history to Cimarron. The Osage were forced by the US government to move from Missouri to Kansas and then to their reservation in Oklahoma. They suffered hardship during this period, their population falling by 50 percent owing to scarcity of food and poor medical supplies, according to the website of the Osage Nation Reservation.

Furthermore, Cimarron explains to a visiting family member that the Osage were given a very bad deal in Oklahoma. Cimarron says, about the Osage Reservation, "it's all bare there, and nothing grows in that place—it's called the Bad Lands—unless you work and slave and the Osages they were used to hunting and fishing not farming, so they are just starving to death." Ferber's research appears to be accurate on this point. The Osage Nation website states that "for agricultural purposes, their new land was the poorest in the Indian Territory." The website points out, however, that later the Osage learned how to raise cattle, and their reservation, which was covered with bluestem grass, turned out to be the "best grazing in the entire country." Prominent later in the novel is the discovery of oil on the Osage Reservation and the subsequent wealth of the Osage Indians. Once again, Ferber accurately reflects history. Large quantities of oil were discovered on the reservation in 1894. Congress passed the Osage Allotment Act in 1906, under which all members of the Osage living on the reservation were allocated a share of its

The Cravats live in a town called Osage in Oklahoma Territory. *(© Philip Lange | Shutterstock.com)*

subsurface natural resources. Osage Indians became rich overnight (as the novel depicts), with royalties peaking in 1925.

Another major issue regarding the Indians is also presented in the novel. As the movement toward statehood gathers steam, Yancey campaigns for Indian Territory and Oklahoma Territory to be combined into one state. He is bitterly opposed by many whites, whose slogan is "The White Man's State for the White Man," and Sabra disagrees with him, too. Many Indians themselves want the Indian Territory to form a separate state. Although the novel does not pursue the issue in detail, the faction supported by Yancey succeeds, and the state of Oklahoma is created by combining the Indian and Oklahoma Territories.

STYLE

Historical Fiction

Ferber's novel belongs to the genre of historical fiction. Such novels are set in certain historical time periods and reflect the life of the times. They are usually well researched to ensure

accuracy. The characters are fictional but are placed at the center of real historical events. Actual historical characters may also appear or be referenced, as in this novel Theodore Roosevelt is mentioned. Yancey fights alongside him during the Spanish-American War and later visits him when Roosevelt is US president. Through such means the reader gets a picture of a past age and how it must have been experienced by people who lived at that time. Examples of historical novels are Sir Walter Scott's Waverley novels, beginning with *Waverley* (1814). Other famous historical novelists include Leo Tolstoy, James Fenimore Cooper, and James A. Michener.

Setting

The novel realistically creates its setting in pioneer Oklahoma with some long descriptive passages. For example, the book depicts Pawhuska Avenue, the main street in Osage in 1889, as an "absurdly wide street—surely fifty feet wide—in this little one-street town," in chapter VI. The author describes the houses with their "unpainted wood," the "wide-rutted red clay road," and the varied means of conveyance:

Tied to the crude hitching posts driven well into the ground were all sorts of vehicles: buckboards, crazy carts, dilapidated wagons, mule drawn; here and there a top buggy covered with the dust of the prairie; and everywhere, lording it, those four-footed kings without which life in this remote place could not have been sustained—horses of every size and type and color and degree.

There are many similarly vivid descriptions of life in Osage at the turn of the century and, in chapter XX, of how Oklahoman towns were transformed by the discovery of oil. The descriptions give authenticity to the historical setting and provide the reader with a realistic picture of what life was like in Oklahoma in those long-ago times.

HISTORICAL CONTEXT

The Oklahoma Land Runs of 1889 and 1893

In March 1889 the US government passed a bill that permitted white settlement on Indian lands. This opened up 1,887,796 acres, which amounted to 4 percent of the area that would later become the state of Oklahoma. People seeking portions of what was known as the Unassigned Lands were permitted to enter at noon on April 22, 1889. Anyone who entered before that time would not be allowed to claim any land. (Those who did were known as "sooners.") At the appointed time, soldiers fired pistols along the borders, which measured thirty miles east to west and fifty miles north to south, and the land run began. People traveled by a variety of means, including train, horseback (like Yancey and Dixie Lee in the novel), wagon, and buggy, as well as on foot (like Sol Levy). An estimated fifty thousand settlers made the run. One day later the population of Oklahoma City was more than twelve thousand, and Guthrie, on which the fictional town of Osage in *Cimarron* is modeled, numbered about ten thousand people.

For the first year there was no territorial government, and each town established its own government. In *Cimarron*, Ferber paints a romantic picture of Osage as rather like an outpost of the Wild West, in which men stroll the streets wearing their six-shooters and there is often a hint of violence in the air. Ferber did historical research for the novel, and this aspect

of it was influenced by *Hands Up! Stories of the Six-Gun Fighters of the Old Wild West*, a book by Fred E. Sutton and A. B. McDonald (1927). Later historians have offered a more sober view of what life was like in those very early days in the new settlements of Oklahoma. Edwin C. McReynolds, for example, in *Oklahoma: A History of the Sooner State*, noted that there was little violent crime or any other kind of crime amongst the pioneers. He attributed this to the character of the people:

> Conditions of settlement did not attract adventurers. People who came to Oklahoma seeking farm homes were not likely to resort to murder if some contestant appeared who laid claim to the same quarter section. Men who brought lumber into Guthrie or Stillwater and constructed shacks for sheltering a little stock of groceries bought with their savings were not given to shooting their way out of difficulties.

The land run of 1893 (which Yancey goes on alone in *Cimarron*) took place on September 16 and opened the Cherokee Outlet (called the Cherokee Strip in the novel). This was the largest of the four Oklahoma land runs, with one hundred thousand people involved. There were 6,361,000 acres of land available for white settlers.

The Oklahoma Oil Boom

In *Cimarron*, Osage is transformed by the discovery of oil, and Ferber presents an accurate portrait of how fortunes were made overnight as a result of it. The oil boom in Oklahoma began in 1899, in Bartlesville. In 1901, the Red Fork Field was discovered, and Tulsa became known as "the Oil Capital of the World," according to Kenny A. Franks in his entry "Petroleum" in the *Encyclopedia of Oklahoma History and Culture*. By 1905, the discovery of the Glenn Pool oil field made Oklahoma one of the nation's leading oil-producing states. In 1912, the Cushing Field was discovered in Cushing. Seven years later, Franks points out, the Cushing wells were producing 17 percent of all oil sold in the United States. From 1912 to 1919, they produced 3 percent of global output. In the 1920s, Oklahoma produced more oil than any other US state, with the industry being concentrated in the central and eastern regions.

COMPARE & CONTRAST

- **1890s–1900s:** As Oklahoma develops, different ideas for statehood are put forward. In 1905, representatives of the Five Civilized Tribes create a constitution for a state to be named Sequoyah, after the great Cherokee leader. Congress refuses to consider a separate Indian state, however.

  1910s–1920s: In 1924, the Indian Citizenship Act grants US citizenship to Native Americans. Indians in Oklahoma have been citizens with voting rights since the beginning of statehood.

  Today: There are thirty-nine Native American tribal governments in Oklahoma. Of all US states, Oklahoma has the second-largest Native American population. According to the 2010 US census, an estimated 259,809 Native Americans live in the state. This amounts to 7.1 percent of the state's population.

- **1890s–1900s:** Oklahoma opens to white settlement in 1889 and develops rapidly in the 1890s and beyond, becoming the forty-sixth US state in 1907.

  1910s–1920s: Oklahoma becomes prosperous through the oil industry as, in 1920, oil fields in Osage County begin major oil production.

  Today: The oil and natural gas industry is the most important industry in Oklahoma. In 2011, it contributes $61 billion into the state economy. This amounts to $1 of every $3 in the state economy. ·

- **1890s–1900s:** The movement for woman's suffrage gains momentum. Women in Utah (1895) and in Idaho (1896) gain the right to vote.

  1910s–1920s: Jeannette Rankin becomes the first woman to be elected to Congress, in 1916 in Montana. The Nineteenth Amendment, guaranteeing women the right to vote, becomes law in 1920. Later that year, Alice Robertson becomes the second woman to be elected to Congress and the first from Oklahoma.

  Today: In the 113th Congress, which began in January 2013, there are more women than ever before. Seventy-eight members of the House and twenty members of the Senate are women.

CRITICAL OVERVIEW

Cimarron was extremely popular with the larger book-reading public, but as Ferber reports in her autobiography *A Peculiar Treasure*, it was not so well received in Oklahoma. Ferber received "a flood of letters" from people in that state, ranging from "remonstrance to vilification" at her portrayal of life in early Oklahoma. She also notes that newspaper editorials in Oklahoma heavily criticized the novel. Although reviews elsewhere were positive, *Cimarron* has not been extensively discussed by later literary critics. Indeed, although Ferber might be considered a feminist writer—her portrayal of Sabra as a moving force in the history of Oklahoma being an example—J. E. Smyth notes in *Edna Ferber's Hollywood: American Fictions of Gender, Race, and History* that her work has not been as extensively studied or as highly rated as the work of other American female writers such as Kate Chopin, Edith Wharton, and Willa Cather.

Paula Reed mentions *Cimarron* in her essay on Ferber in the *Dictionary of Literary Biography*. Reed describes the novel as "possibly her best book. Certainly it contains her most subtly rendered depiction of differences between the sexes and between generations." Reed writes further:

The Oklahoma Land Rush began in 1893 with a shot from a starting gun. *(© Victorian Traditions / Shutterstock.com)*

Yancey is a variation of Ferber's typical male protagonist in that he is irresponsible and somewhat unrealistic in his handling of practical matters, deserting Sabra for years at a time out of sheer restlessness. His idealism, however, gives him positive moral value. Sabra's practicality and efficiency are tinged with a petty morality which needs the scope of Yancey's ideals to broaden into an enlightened ethic. Sabra represents security and civilization; Yancey, the progress which builds civilization yet challenges that security in the process.

In another *Dictionary of Literary Biography* volume, Steven P. Horowitz and Miriam J. Landsman draw attention to the incident in which Yancey rescues Sol Levy, the Jewish character, from some town bullies. The authors note that "Ferber's use of this scene suggests her resentment of Christians' antagonism toward Jews."

CRITICISM

Bryan Aubrey

Aubrey holds a PhD in English. In the following essay, he discusses Ferber's treatment of minorities in Cimarron.

In the mid-twentieth century, almost everyone knew about Edna Ferber, the famous writer whose novels were frequently adapted as successful Hollywood films. In the early twenty-first century, however, her name and reputation have faded. It is not unusual today to find literate people who have barely heard of her. Nevertheless, *Cimarron* was one of her most successful novels, and in the 1930s, the book-buying public eagerly devoured it as an entertaining yarn.

But is the novel something more than that? Ferber seemed to think so. Like any author would be, she was pleased with the success of her book, but she felt that it had been misunderstood by reviewers and general readers alike. She wrote in her autobiography, *A Peculiar Treasure*, that the novel was

> a malevolent picture of what is known as American womanhood and American sentimentality. It contains paragraphs and even chapters of satire and, I am afraid, bitterness, but I doubt that more than a dozen people ever knew this. All the critics and the hundreds and thousands of readers took *Cimarron* as a colorful romantic Western American novel.

WHAT DO I READ NEXT?

- *O Pioneers!* (1913), by Willa Cather, is the story of a pioneer woman in the Great Plains. A Swedish immigrant family struggles to make a living on a farm in Nebraska at the turn of the century. The main character is Alexandra Bergson, who inherits the farm from her father and eventually makes a success of it.

- Ferber's novel *Giant* (1952) was successful in its day and was made into a film in 1956, starring James Dean, Elizabeth Taylor, and Rock Hudson. The story takes place in Texas and presents a panoramic portrait of that state through the lives of a cattleman named Jordan "Bick" Benedict and three generations of his sons, up to the early 1950s.

- Like Ferber, James A. Michener (1907–1997) was a popular writer of well-researched historical fiction during the twentieth century. *Chesapeake: A Novel* (1978) is a family saga set in the Chesapeake Bay area from 1583 to 1978. It begins with a war between Indian tribes and goes all the way to the modern period, including the Watergate scandal that ended the presidency of Richard M. Nixon in 1974.

- *Out of the Dust* (1997), by Karen Hesse, is a novel told in verse. It is set in the Oklahoma dust bowl during the 1930s and is narrated by fourteen-year-old Billie Jo, who describes what it is like to experience years of frequent dust storms. Tragedies befall both her parents, and eventually Billie Jo escapes farther west. This novel was awarded the Newbery Medal in 1998.

- *Ghost Towns of Oklahoma* (1978), by John W. Morris, tells the fascinating story of 130 of the two thousand villages, towns, and cities that sprang up in Oklahoma, flourished for a while, and then died. Covering 150 years of the state's history, the book describes why the towns were built, what people did there, and why the towns failed.

- *Shell Shaker* (2001), by LeAnne Howe, alternates between two stories separated by two centuries. In one, a Choctaw family takes part in a war against the English in 1738; in the other, their descendants in Oklahoma fight an attempt by the Mafia to take over the Choctaw's casino. Howe is a member of the Cherokee Nation of Oklahoma. The book won an American Book Award in 2002 and was a finalist for the Oklahoma Book Award in 2003.

The satire Ferber refers to is, in fact, not difficult to spot. It can be seen, for example, in the petty concerns of the womenfolk of Osage, who are fascinated by accounts in the newspaper of what was served at the church supper or the costumes worn at a wedding. In one incident, Sabra presents a paper titled "Whither Oklahoma?" to the Culture Club she founded. It is well received by "Osage's twenty most exclusive ladies, who had scarcely heard a word of it, their minds being intent on Sabra's new dress."

The "malevolent picture" Ferber refers to, however, seems to consist of more than this

rather mild satire. It is quite possible that Ferber meant to include her main character, Sabra Cravat, in what the author thought of as her damning portrait of American womanhood. Although Sabra is without doubt a woman of determination and some achievement, she does have one glaring flaw in her otherwise admirable character. This flaw is so obvious that not a single reader is likely to miss it: her hostility and even hatred toward the Indians. For the twenty-first-century reader, this raises the important topic of Ferber's treatment of minorities in this novel.

> SINCE THE NOVEL IS TOLD MORE FROM SABRA'S POINT OF VIEW THAN YANCEY'S, MOST OF THE SCENES THAT DESCRIBE ACTUAL INDIANS OR DEPICT INCIDENTS IN WHICH THEY ARE INVOLVED ARE SEEN THROUGH SABRA'S HOSTILE EYES."

The most visible of the minorities in *Cimarron* are the Indians, but Ferber also includes the African American boy Isaiah and the Jew Sol Levy. In the case of Levy, Ferber is clearly on the side of the outsider. Levy is "the town Jew," and as such "he was a person apart." On one occasion Yancey has to physically rescue him from the town bullies. Although as the years go by Levy becomes a respected citizen, he rarely mingles with the townspeople other than for business. Yancey supports his bid to become mayor, but Levy never has a chance of succeeding; the town's elders also try to exclude him from the dinner given in honor of Sabra when she is elected congresswoman, and he is able to attend only because Sabra insists on it. But Levy is also presented as refusing to be beaten down by the discrimination he faces; he always has a tart response ready through which he upholds his dignity. When he is told, for example, that the dinner for Sabra is only for those who were on the land run in 1889, he says, "That's all right. I walked" (which he did). Passages such as this show where the author's sympathies lie.

Regarding Isaiah, who is the only African American character in the novel, Ferber also presents a sympathetic portrait. Isaiah is a capable, smart young boy who is loyal to the Cravats and acquires many useful skills. He meets a tragic end after he fathers a child with the Osage girl Arita Red Feather. Since the Osage Indians do not permit intermarriage with African Americans, in this case they do not allow either the father or the mother to live. At least in regard to intermarriage, Ferber was historically accurate. The Osages, as well as the Chickasaws, Cherokees, and Choctaws, banned intermarriage with African Americans. In some cases, according to Murray R. Wickett's *Contested Territory: Whites, Native Americans and African*

Americans in Oklahoma, 1865–1907, offenders were punished with a whipping, although there appears to be no record of a death penalty being applied in such cases. However, although Ferber's portrayal of Isaiah is a positive one, it is influenced by the contemporary attitudes toward race and the period she is writing about. In the early days of the family's arrival in Oklahoma, Isaiah, although he is otherwise treated well, does not sleep in the house with the family. Instead, he lives outside, surrounded by the refuse of empty tomato cans: "in a sort of shed-kennel . . . he slept there, like a faithful dog, for all day long he was about the house and the printing office, tireless, willing, invaluable." Just two paragraphs later, Isaiah is described as "industrious" and "lovable," as Sabra teaches him to read and write. He perches on a stool "like an intelligent monkey." Just as it never occurs to the Cravats that Isaiah perhaps deserves a little more than a dog kennel to sleep in, it does not seem to have occurred to Ferber, in spite of her eagerness to present Isaiah as a remarkably capable boy, that it might be patronizing and insulting to employ the similes quoted. Ferber's intended kindly treatment of a member of a minority race is thus laced with an unintended irony that might not have been quite so apparent upon publication in 1930 but stares the twenty-first-century reader in the face.

Regarding the third minority group, which is by far the most prominent in the novel, Ferber uses the Indians and the issues surrounding them to dramatize the conflicting attitudes of Sabra and Yancey. Yancey gives mini-lectures to Cim, Sabra, and anyone else who will listen (including those who read the editorial page of the *Oklahoma Wigwam*) about the injustices the Indians have suffered. He mixes well socially with Indians and also takes Cim to visit the Osage Reservation. He seems pleased when Cim marries an Indian girl. For the most part, though, Yancey is Ferber's vehicle for getting out the facts of what happened to the Indians in the past. Ferber is clearly on the side of the Indians, as she was with the Jewish character, Sol Levy. Yet paradoxically, she allows her heroine, the otherwise admirable Sabra, to nurse a virulent hatred of Indians, a hatred Sabra insists is "unconquerable." Sabra's hostility to Indians is a frequently recurring theme, and no expression of it is too extreme for her. When she finds out that Yancey has been telling young Cim about what the Indians

In a scene from the 1960 film version of Cimarron, *Dixie Lee (played by Anne Baxter) meets her former sweetheart, Yancey "Cimarron" Cravat (played by Glenn Ford) and his wife Sabra (played by Maria Schell) as they arrive at the turbulent starting line from where the great Oklahoma Land Rush of 1889 will be launched.* (© Archive Photos / Moviepix / Getty Images)

have suffered at the hands of the US government, she is determined to instill in him a different impression: "Indians are bad people," she tells him. "They take little boys from their mammas and never bring them back. They burn down people's houses, and hurt them. They're dirty and lazy, and they steal." Sabra thinks of Indians as "useless two-footed animals."

Since the novel is told more from Sabra's point of view than Yancey's, most of the scenes that describe actual Indians or depict incidents in which they are involved are seen through Sabra's hostile eyes. Even when Big Elk and his wife show up in impressive ceremonial regalia to invite Yancey and Sabra to the wedding dinner, the scene is presented through Sabra's experience of it, and it seems that all she can perceive

is the "dull black unsmiling eyes" of the Indians, which terrify her.

It seems likely, then, that Sabra's hatred of Indians is part of the "malevolent picture" of American womanhood that Ferber believed she had written. Sabra's views are undeniably ugly and expressed in language that utterly denies the humanity of the Indians. In this she is only expressing what she absorbed from her parents and her schooling. It seems that she never learned to grow beyond such crude views. But in the end, Ferber plays a cruel joke on her principal character (cruel in how it must seem to Sabra, that is). Desperate to shield Cim from all corrupting influences, she forbids him from even speaking to an Indian, only to discover later, when Cim is a young man, that not only does he talk to Indians, he actually marries one, too. (The Osages and the Five Civilized Tribes permitted intermarriage with whites, unlike with African Americans, and such intermarriage was extremely common, according to Wickett.) So Sabra, whether she likes it or not, must learn to live in a racially blended family, her son at home in Indian culture, her daughter-in-law an Indian, and her grandson, Yancey, strongly identifying with his Indian heritage. It is as if Ferber is saying to Sabra, and to the whites who so vehemently advocated "The White Man's State for the White Man," that they lost the argument, and it was a good thing that they did.

Although history does not regard *Cimarron* as a great novel, Ferber tried hard to deliver something that was more than romantic adventure in the Southwest. Her critique of the dominant white culture's attitude to other races is seriously meant, and while it is hammered home with some lack of subtlety, it can hardly be said to be a trivial concern.

Source: Bryan Aubrey, Critical Essay on *Cimarron*, in *Novels for Students*, Gale, Cengage Learning, 2014.

Eileen H. Watts

In the following excerpt, Watts examines Ferber as a Jewish writer.

... Edna Ferber lived to be 83 years old (she died of cancer in April 1968) and in that time produced a prodigious amount of work. Because she believed that humanitarian causes are congruent with Jewish causes, the moral, if not intellectual, superiority of oppressed people is a steady undercurrent in nearly all of her fiction, as are the commensurate ebb and flow of the oppressors' inhumanities. For example, the Emma McChesney stories collected in *Roast Beef, Medium* (1913), *Personality Plus* (1914), and *Emma McChesney and Co.* (1915) tackle the adventures of a divorced woman in a man's business. Similarly, the Pulitzer Prize–winning *So Big* (1924) dramatizes the physical and moral superiority of farm women, as the widowed Selina DeJong raises her son, Dirk, in High Prairie, outside Chicago. Amid the drama and romance of *Showboat* (1926), Ferber turned her attention to the cruelty of the South's miscegenation laws. *Cimarron* (1929) deals with the homesteaders of the 1889 Oklahoma land rush. Even here, her characters battle bigotry and racism against Jews and Native Americans, and she depicts women as the primary civilizing

forces on the frontier, as physically and socially capable as men, but morally stronger. In this novel women stake land claims, but, unlike men, are immune to wealth's corrupting influences. *Giant* (1950) is perhaps Ferber's most sustained treatment of racism. As sprawling as Texas itself, the novel chronicles the life of the oil baron Benedict, who becomes a giant in his wife's eyes for championing Mexicans who are being evicted from a seedy diner. Ferber also exposes the cruel living conditions of and absence of medical care for Mexican ranch hands in early twentieth-century Texas. Here too, portraits of strong, capable, humanitarian women dominate. Finally, *Ice Palace* (1958), also an account of the ways in which building enormous wealth eviscerates people's ethics, presented Ferber with the opportunity to unmask racism and prejudice against Eskimos and Chinese immigrants in Alaska. In all, she wrote 11 volumes of short stories, 12 novels, and 6 plays, 5 of which were written with George S. Kaufman, including *The Royal Family* (1928), *Dinner at Eight* (1932), and *Stage Door* (1936).

In her novels, however, Ferber gave free reign to Judaism and the evils of anti-Semitism only in *Fanny Herself*. Her only other fictional treatment of anti-Semitism in novels appears in *Cimarron* and *Great Son* (1944). Set during the Oklahoma land rush of 1889, *Cimarron* features "the town Jew." The shopkeeper Sol Levy is forced to drink whisky, is shot at repeatedly for sport, and assumes the gaunt appearance and approximate position of the crucified Christ. Levy is quickly rescued by the novel's hero, Yancy Cravat, who risks his life to do so. Although a minor character, Sol Levy in Oklahoma is a fictionalized version of Edna Ferber in Ottumwa, allowing Ferber to expose in print the degradation and abuse she endured as a little girl. Even the town madam, Dixie Lee, and her girls, tease Sol: "'Come on, Solly!... Why don't you smile? Don't you never have no fun? I bet you're rich. Jews is all rich.'... His deep-sunk eyes looked at them. Schicksas. 'Go on, get the hell out of here! You got your money, ain't you? Get, sheeny.'... He was the town Jew. He was a person apart. Sometimes the cowboys deviled him; or the saloon loungers and professional bad men. They looked upon him as fair game. He thought of them as savages" (*Cimarron*).

After rescuing Sol from the drunken cowboys, Yancy tells him, "This Oklahoma country's no place for you, Sol. It's too rough, too hard. You come of a race of dreamers," to which Sol later replies, "Those barbarians! My ancestors were studying the Talmud and writing the laws the civilized world now lives by when theirs were swinging from tree to tree." Of course, Sol builds his business into the Levy Mercantile Company, whose building sports the only penthouse in Oklahoma . . . .

. . . With the relatively minor exceptions then of *Cimarron*, *Great Son*, "No Room at the Inn" and, of course, *Fanny Herself*, Ferber's virtual divestiture of Judaism from her prolific output of fiction and drama, coupled incongruously with her vociferous defense of her Jewish identity, has its roots, no doubt, in Ottumwa. For example, when asked in 1912 by a *New York Sun* reporter to what she attributed her success, then founded on the exceedingly popular Emma McChesney tales, Ferber replied the (at the time) unprintable, "We - e - ell, I think if I've had any success it's because I was born a Jew" (*A Peculiar Treasure*, 189). Ferber believed that her gifts of "quick appraisal and decision" were Jewish traits, and saw Jewish artists such as Mendelssohn, Bernhardt, Heifetz, Rachmaninoff, Menuhin, Zimbalist, and Gershwin as Jews who turned 5,000 years of suffering and persecution into song (70). Arguably, Ferber has done the same by investing her fiction with what emerges as a Jewish sensibility, a sensitivity to the oppressed, a revulsion to bigotry. In fact, her description of the "Jew" applies equally to many of her characters, and, to an extent, to herself: "He has acquired great adaptability, nervous energy, ambition to succeed and a desire to be liked."

In *Fanny Herself*, Ferber forces the title character (named for Ferber's older sister, Fannie) to recognize her Jewish soul and permit its expression in the form of decidedly feminist sociopolitical cartoons that expose the inhumanity of sweatshops, the human cost of industrial efficiency, and the environmental cost of progress. Fanny herself is divided between the American Dream of being a financially successful textile buyer, who lies about her Jewish identity, and the humanitarian thrust of her Jewish soul, which compels her to identify with the poor, the oppressed, and the powerless. The novel chronicles this battle for Fanny's soul. Should she sell and assimilate it to the materialistic wealth of the American Dream? Or should she allow her soul to find its own voice in her art, and so define her? Ferber herself, armed with Fanny's soul, successfully divided her Jewishness from nearly all her fiction and drama, but remained fiercely proud of her race and its history. How she maintained the often-opposing roles of American, woman, writer, and Jew in the first half of the twentieth century is the subject of *Fanny Herself* and *A Peculiar Treasure*. In Fanny Brandeis, the 32-year-old Ferber created an alter ego that established the divisive issues she would tackle in future fiction and in her own life: the moral cost of chasing the American Dream, feminism, the relation of women to humanity, the artistic value of suffering, the spiritual and creative nature of a Jewish soul, and living as a Jew (or other minority) in America. Fanny ultimately overcomes the twin handicaps of being a Jew and a woman by redefining success in America in terms of serving the shared humanitarian imperatives of Jewish history and feminism . . . .

Source: Eileen H. Watts, "Edna Ferber, Jewish American Writer: Who Knew?," in *Modern Jewish Women Writers in America*, edited by Evelyn Avery, Palgrave Macmillan, 2007, pp. 42–44, 47–48.

Heidi Kenaga

In the following excerpt, Kenaga discusses the image of the pioneer woman and the fact that Ferber was one of the first women to write historical fiction about the American West.

. . . In late 1925, Edward C. Marland, president of an Oklahoma oil company, invited a number of nationally known sculptors to submit bronze models in competition for a monument called the "Pioneer Woman of the West." Within public discourse. his initiative was styled as both philanthropic venture and noble civic duty. Donating 2,000 acres and $300,000 to the project, Marland claimed—as if taking his lead from Emerson Hough—that such recognition was overdue: "Looking about our Western country in the last few years I saw monuments to Buffalo Bill, Kit Carson, and a dozen other pioneers. Great men, every one of them, and a fine tiring to honor their deeds. But what about the pioneer woman?" Cultural historian Kirk Savage has argued that sponsors of such monuments "worked hard to sustain the fiction that they were merely agents of a more universal collective whose shared memory the project embodied.... They had to summon the symbolic ... participation of a 'public' that the monument would represent." In subsequent years, such symbolic participation was still deemed crucial in securing the legitimacy of such public memorials. Early in 1927, Marland sent twelve three-foot models on a national tour, starting in New York, with subsequent exhibitions in Boston, Chicago, Washington, Kansas City, Oklahoma City, and other major cities. Marland noted that he sought "the opinion of the public as well as that of prominent art critics, publishers and directors of art museums" in making his decision. Thus, gallery visitors in all of the tour's locations were asked to vote for the best statue. At first, Marland told the sculptors that there were two requisite elements of the figure: a sunbonnet as headgear and an accompanying child, since the pioneer woman had carried "the seed of America's wealth" to the frontier. Later, the artists were given a freer hand; nonetheless, all but two of the models have sunbonnets, and only one does not depict a child. The eventual winner was Bryant Baker's statue of a sunbonneted woman, striding across the prairie, holding a male child by the hand and clutching a small bag and a Bible. Described as "pretty" and a "pleasant enough commercial piece," this figure is more idealized than the "gaunt and sad-faced" figure in a "ragged sunbonnet" described by Hough in *The Passing of the Frontier*. The inclusion of the Bible, as opposed to the gun or ax carried by five other figures, implies the significance of the pioneer woman in bearing Christianity and the codified knowledge associated with the East out to the West.

In order to encourage Oklahomans' participation in the Pioneer Woman dedication, Governor W. J. Holloway declared 22 April 1930 a statewide holiday. More importantly, "symbolic participation" by the American nation was fostered via an invention of the industrial age, radio, when NBC decided to broadcast the proceedings. As Savage notes, "the more widely the monument campaign appealed, the more enthusiasm it seemed to generate, the more convincingly its public would come to resemble the democratic vision of one people united by one memory." The radio audience heard speeches from Ponca City by Marland, Bryant Baker, Will Rogers, and Governor Holloway, and from Washington by President Herbert Hoover and Secretary of War

> THUS, FROM THE START OF THE NOVEL, FERBER FOREGROUNDS THE IMPORTANCE OF STORYTELLING AND MYTHMAKING TO THE INSTITUTIONS OF PIONEER CULTURE, OVERTLY POSITIONING MALE CONTROL OF THE NARRATIVE WHILE WOMEN (OR THE FEMINIZED VENABLE MEN) FORM AN ENTHRALLED BUT PASSIVE AUDIENCE."

Patrick Hurley (described as a "product of the pioneer woman of Oklahoma"). In his address, President Hoover noted that pioneer women "carried the refinement, the moral character and spiritual force into the West," while Secretary Hurley overtly acknowledged the tutorial uses of such monuments for the present day: "In the erection of this monument we pledge a reverence to the woman who has laid the foundation of the character of our community, State and nation.... Every citizen who passes this way and looks upon this memorial will be strengthened in the conviction that this State shall be kept worthy of the woman whom this bronze statue commemorates." Editorial response in the *New York Times* suggests that the sponsor of the Pioneer Woman monument had successfully devised a commemorative event with both national scope and unifying power: "The woman as pictured in this statue belongs not to Oklahoma alone. The rest of the country will see in her the form and features of the woman of every frontier from Maine to California."

Echoing Emerson Hough's lament about the historiographic neglect of the pioneer woman, Secretary Hurley concluded that this was "probably due to the fact that most of the pages of history are written by men about men." He did not, however, go so far as to suggest that more women should engage in the production of such pages. Given these specific historical and cultural contexts, Edna Ferber's address of the frontier heritage, particularly the pioneer woman, in *Cimarron* can be understood as an engagement with an existing tradition that until that time was almost entirely the province of male writers. Not surprisingly, Ferber's authorship of the Oklahoma story came under scrutiny. The film industry had found episodes in Western history not just lucrative but fungible properties as well, bartering the artifacts of national culture for social legitimacy and sanction. However, Ferber was not perceived in public discourse as an authoritative source for the dissemination of historical knowledge about the West—neither by birthright (she was female and Jewish) nor by personal history or experience (she was born in the Midwest). In addition, although Ferber was often described as a regional writer, she was much identified with New York life, particularly its literary and theatrical elites. In her autobiography, Ferber herself foregrounded this apparent incongruity in her account of the novel's origin. After a tour of Oklahoma, her long-time friend and journalist William Allen White regaled her with stories about the state's oil rush history. He urged her to write about it, but Ferber refused, recalling the "tough job" that writing *Show Boat* had been: "No, the story of Oklahoma is a man's job.... No more big open spaces for me. Let somebody else do the American-background stuff. Too hard work" (*Treasure* 325–26). Comparing this account of *Cimarron*'s genesis with the origin of *The Covered Wagon* reveals Ferber's liminal position within the field of Western literary production. An influential editor encourages the writer to pursue the topic, yet assumptions about gender and "authenticity" of authorship inform the exchange. White introduces Ferber to the "masculine West" (although having experienced the frontier as a tourist), and she replies in kind, as if the "gendered spaces" of the West require a male chronicler.

Ferber's personal correspondence suggests she may have had other qualms about the material than that offered in her autobiographical narrative. In May 1928, she decided to "have a tourist's look at this Oklahoma" herself, interviewing local inhabitants in smaller towns, doing research in Oklahoma City, and visiting the state's oil capital, Tulsa. In letters to her family, Ferber wrote of her despair in finding any "freshness" in the subject matter: "There's enough stuff, God knows, for a ten-volume novel. But some of it has been done, much of it is bad man, Indian, pioneer stuff that is an old story," particularly in the movies. Ferber found the Oklahoma historical materials like "an old fashioned western—the kind of thing I'd walk out on if they were doing it at the Harper or

Rivoli." However, Ferber hammered out a final draft within a year, and in late 1929 the first chapters appeared in *Woman's Home Companion*, a popular periodical with a predominantly female readership.

As popular Western fiction, *Cimarron* is a compelling case study to the extent that it appears to be the only successful epic Western written by a woman. Yet given the cultural context within which it was produced and circulated, it can also be read as a rather skillful critique of the relationship between gender and the dissemination of "authentic" historical knowledge about the West. A careful analysis of *Cimarron* indicates Ferber's implicit characterization of the male Western writer as historical fabulist. What she described as the improbable, "movie-like" quality of her research into Oklahoma's historical legacy resulted in a foregrounding of the imbrication of fact and fiction in the historical work, particularly in terms of the divergent and competing ways that men and women's experiences often figure in such a process. The foreword to the novel contains the following declaration:

> Only the more fantastic and improbable events contained in this book are true. There is no attempt to set down a literal history of Oklahoma. All the characters, the towns, and many of the happenings contained herein are imaginary.... In many cases material entirely true was discarded as unfit for use because it was so melodramatic, so absurd as to be too strange for the realm of fiction.... There was no Yancey Cravat—he is a blending of a number of dashing Oklahoma figures of a past and present day. There is no Sabra Cravat, but she exists in a score of bright-eyed, white-haired, intensely interesting women of sixty-five or thereabouts who told me many strange things as we talked and rocked on an Oklahoma front porch.

Ferber inverts the hierarchy between actual events and fiction so that the invented becomes acceptable as historical truth. Similarly, she inverts the hierarchy of gender in relation to the origins of the narrative. Yancey is clearly more abstract, distant, mythified, whereas Ferber more directly locates Sabra's origin in real Oklahoman women who witnessed the historical episodes detailed in the novel. We know that she interviewed men of the same age, but she chooses to acknowledge these women's contribution by citing their oral history as the dominant source. In the first two chapters,

Ferber sets up Yancey Cravat as something like a historiographic straw man, "a bizarre, glamorous, slightly mythical figure. No room seemed big enough for his gigantic frame; no chair but dwindled beneath the breadth of his shoulders.... Rumor, romantic, unsavory, fantastic, shifting and changing like clouds on a mountain peak, floated about the head of Yancey Cravat." His chief appeal lies in his oratorical style and incommensurate skills as a raconteur. Thus, the 1889 Oklahoma land rush that begins the novel is not narrated directly but rather presented via Yancey's recollection of its events for the benefit of Sabra's antebellum relatives, the aristocratic Venables from Mississippi now living in Wichita. He describes the panoramic rush for this rapt audience in a highly cinematic way: "Whole scenes, as he talked, seemed to be happening before his listeners' eyes." Although Yancey himself is enthralled with the recounting of such scenes, his actual participation in nearly all such episodes in *Cimarron*—including the two land rushes, the shootout with the Kid and his gang, and the Spanish-American War—are never directly described but rather are related second-hand. Thus, from the start of the novel, Ferber foregrounds the importance of storytelling and mythmaking to the institutions of pioneer culture, overtly positioning male control of the narrative while women (or the feminized Venable men) form an enthralled but passive audience....

Source: Heidi Kenaga, "Edna Ferber's *Cimarron*, Cultural Authority, and 1920s Western Historical Narratives," in *Middlebrow Moderns: Popular American Women Writers of the 1920s*, edited by Lisa Botshon and Meredith Goldsmith, Northeastern University Press, 2003, pp. 173–78.

SOURCES

"A Brief History of the Osage Nation," Osage Nation Historic Reservation website, 2006, http://www.osagetribe.com/historicpreservation/info_sub_page.aspx?subpage_id=14 (accessed March 23, 2013).

Camia, Catalina, "Record Number of Women in Congress Out to Change Tone," in *USA Today*, January 3, 2013, http://www.usatoday.com/story/news/politics/2013/01/03/women-congress-senate-record/1807657/ (accessed March 21, 2013).

"Chronology of Oklahoma Events," Oklahoma State University Library website, http://info.library.okstate. edu/content.php?pid=200114&sid=1728846 (accessed March 21, 2013).

Ferber, Edna, *Cimarron*, Grosset & Dunlap, 1930.

———, *A Peculiar Treasure*, Lancer Books, 1960, p. 302.

Franks, Kenny A., "Petroleum," in *Encyclopedia of Oklahoma History and Culture* website, Oklahoma Historical Society, http://digital.library.okstate.edu/encyclopedia/entries/P/PE023.html (accessed March 20, 2013).

Gilbert, Julie Goldsmith, *Ferber: A Biography*, Doubleday, 1978, pp. 358–62.

Horowitz, Steven P., and Miriam J. Landsman, "Edna Ferber," in *Dictionary of Literary Biography*, Vol. 28, *Twentieth-Century American-Jewish Fiction Writers*, edited by Daniel Walden, Gale Research, 1984, pp. 58–64.

Marks, Jay F., "Oil Industry Adds $61 Billion to Oklahoma Economy, Report Shows," in *NewsOK*, May 10, 2012, http://newsok.com/oil-industry-adds-61-billion-to-oklahoma-economy-report-shows/article/3674059 (accessed March 23, 2013).

McReynolds, Edwin C., *Oklahoma: A History of the Sooner State*, University of Oklahoma Press, 1954, pp. 288–92, 299–301.

McReynolds, Edwin C., Alice Marriott, and Estelle Faulconer, *Oklahoma: The Story of Its Past and Present*, rev. ed., University of Oklahoma Press, 1967, p. 288.

"Portrait of Oklahoma's First Congresswoman Dedicated," Oklahoma State Senate website, April 15, 2003, http://www.oksenate.gov/news/press_releases/press_releases_2003/pr20030415b.html (accessed March 23, 2013).

Reed, Paula, "Edna Ferber," in *Dictionary of Literary Biography*, Vol. 9, *American Novelists, 1910–1945*, edited by James J. Martine, Gale Research, 1981, pp. 306–13.

"Report of the Rural Population Workgroup," Oklahoma Department of Mental Health and Substance Abuse Service website, June 28, 2012, http://ok.gov/odmhsas/documents/Rural%20Population%20Workgroup%20Final%20Report.pdf (accessed March 23, 2013).

Smyth, J. E., *Edna Ferber's Hollywood: American Fictions of Gender, Race, and History*, University of Texas Press, 2010, pp. 9–10.

"The Trail of Tears," PBS website, http://www.pbs.org/wgbh/aia/part4/4h1567.html (accessed March 23, 2013).

"Tribes, Brief History," American Indian Cultural Center and Museum website, http://www.theamericanindiancenter.org/oklahoma-tribal-history (accessed March 23, 2013).

Wickett, Murray R., *Contested Territory: Whites, Native Americans and African Americans in Oklahoma, 1865–1907*, Louisiana State University Press, 2000, pp. 35–36.

FURTHER READING

Baird, W. David, and Danney Goble, *Oklahoma: A History*, University of Oklahoma Press, 2008.

> Hailed as the best single-volume history of Oklahoma for a general readership, this book tells the story of Oklahoma from its ancient communities up to the present day.

Baker, Terri M., and Connie Oliver Henshaw, eds., *Women Who Pioneered Oklahoma: Stories from the WPA Narratives*, University of Oklahoma Press, 2007.

> This book tells the stories, largely in their own words, of women who lived in Oklahoma in the pioneer days. White women and Native American women are included. The interviews were part of a Works Progress Administration project in the 1930s. Eleven thousand interviews were conducted.

Foreman, Grant, *Indian Removal: The Emigration of the Five Civilized Tribes of Indians*, University of Oklahoma Press, 1932.

> *Indian Removal* is the classic book about the removal of the Indians. It gives a day-by-day account of what happened on the Trail of Tears.

Shaughnessy, Mary Rose, *Women and Success in American Society in the Works of Edna Ferber*, Gordon Press, 1977.

> This is the only full-length critical work on Ferber's literary output. Shaughnessy emphasizes that Ferber was a feminist writer who created confident, independent female characters.

SUGGESTED SEARCH TERMS

Edna Ferber

Cimarron

Oklahoma history

Oklahoma AND oil and natural gas industry

Indian Territory

Oklahoma Territory

Osage Nation

Cherokee Nation

Trail of Tears

Spanish-American War

Rough Riders

historical fiction

Desirable Daughters

BHARATI MUKHERJEE
2002

Desirable Daughters is the first novel of a trilogy by Bharati Mukherjee. Published in 2002, the three-part novel explores the themes of traditional Hindu culture and assimilation as it weaves history with personal narrative. The novel follows the lives of three sisters of a wealthy Bengali family from Calcutta, India, and the secret that comes back to haunt them. The threat of a family scandal slowly takes on aspects of a mystery as the main character, Tara, finds herself swept up in a web of deceit that threatens her family while she searches for the truth about her sister. Ultimately, *Desirable Daughters* uses the mystery as a backdrop for Tara's exploration of her identity.

AUTHOR BIOGRAPHY

Bharati Mukherjee was born in Calcutta (now Kolkata), India, on July 27, 1940, while India was still a British colony. She was born into a wealthy Brahmin family, which is the highest Hindu caste. The family's ancestry is Bengali, meaning that they came from the Bengal districts. As Fakrul Alam explains in *Bharati Mukherjee*, "Their families had moved to Calcutta, as did many other educated, high-caste Hindus." Both of Mukherjee's parents were devoted to educating their three daughters, which was not common at the time, and her father encouraged her to pursue writing.

Bharati Mukherjee (© *Steve Russell / Toronto Star / Getty Images*)

In 1947, Mukherjee's father moved the family to London, where he could research his field as a chemist. India officially attained independence this year and entered a time of turmoil. The family returned to Calcutta in 1951. Mukherjee earned a BA at the University of Calcutta in 1959 and a master's in ancient Indian culture and English at the University of Baroda in 1961.

In 1961, Mukherjee joined the Iowa Writers' Workshop of the University of Iowa, where she attained an MFA in 1963. Her father had chosen a groom for her to marry after she graduated and returned to India; Mukherjee, however, met Canadian writer Clark Blaise at the writers' workshop, and they married in 1963. She informed her parents of the marriage after the fact because, in choosing her own husband, she had broken from the Hindu tradition of arranged marriage.

In 1966 the couple moved to Montreal, Quebec, where Mukherjee worked as a lecturer at McGill University. She gained her PhD from the University of Iowa in 1969. Her first novel, *The Tiger's Daughter*, was published in 1971, and she

became a naturalized Canadian in 1972. She published her second novel, *Wife*, in 1975. In 1978 Mukherjee was a full-time professor at McGill University, but she was not happy in Canada. She felt that racial discrimination was worse there than in the United States, and her family returned to America in 1980. Her experiences of Canadian discrimination are reflected in her 1985 short-story collection *Darkness*.

Mukherjee won a grant from the National Endowment for the Arts in 1986 and became a professor at the University of California at Berkeley in 1989, and as of the early 2010s, she was still teaching and writing there. *Desirable Daughters*, the first book of a trilogy, was published in 2002. The trilogy was continued and completed with *The Tree Bride* in 2004 and *Miss New India* in 2011. Mukherjee considers herself an American writer and is "a powerful member of the American literary scene," according to Erin Soderberg in *Voices from the Gaps*. Mukherjee continues to write novels and stories that reflect modern-day changes in both Indian and American culture.

PLOT SUMMARY

Desirable Daughters combines a morality play with a crime drama. The three-part story is told in the first person. The narrator, Tara Chatterjee, shifts between history, memory, and present events as she searches for the truth and her own identity.

Part One

1

The first chapter is set in italics as it begins with the history of Tara Lata, who shares the narrator's name. In 1879, five-year-old Tara Lata is going to marry a thirteen-year-old boy from a neighboring village, but he is bitten by a snake and dies the night of the ceremony. According to custom, she is considered cursed. Her father saves her from an unhappy life as a widow by marrying her to a tree.

Tara Chatterjee reveals that when she was growing up in Calcutta with her two sisters, her mother told her the story of the Tree Bride. Tara Lata lived in her father's home for seventy years, and she did not leave until shortly before her death. Tara Chatterjee visited the house in a search for her roots. Over the years, people have searched unsuccessfully for the tree where Tara Lata's father, Jai Krishna Gangooly, buried her gold dowry.

Jai Krishna's son by his ninth wife is Tara Chatterjee's grandfather, so she feels a connection to the Tree Bride. Tara reveals that she also had an arranged marriage, but she divorced after ten years. She ends the story of Tara Lata by explaining that Tara Lata only left the house when the British arrested her in 1944. She reportedly died of a heart attack shortly after the arrest.

2

Tara and her older sisters, Padma and Pavarti, were born in Calcutta, and the three of them share the same birthday. Tara remembers the city as a center of culture. By the time she is nineteen, Tara has completed both a BA and an MA. This is the age when her father informs her that she is going to marry Bishwapriya Chatterjee. The couple moves to America, where his friends call him Bish, which means "poison." Later, she comes to call him by the same name. They name their son Rabi, short for Rabindranath. Bish is a cocreator of an Internet bandwidth that his company provides called CHATTY. This makes him an extremely wealthy and

MEDIA ADAPTATIONS

- *Desirable Daughters* is available on CD and in MP3 format. Read by Deborah Kipp, the audiobook runs for 11 hours and 10 minutes and was released by CNIB in 2004.

- An audiocassette recording of *Desirable Daughters* is available through Public Library InterLink. Jacqui Bishop narrates this 2005 edition, which runs for 12 hours.

influential businessman in Silicon Valley. After the divorce, Tara moves to San Francisco with Rabi. Her boyfriend and former contractor, Andy, lives with them.

Tara recalls that her oldest sister, Padma, whom she calls Didi, meaning "sister," always wanted to be a performer. Her father, however, would not allow it. Didi had a Christian friend named Poppy Dey when she was a teenager. Poppy's brother, Ronald, was extremely handsome. As a child, Tara knew that Didi loved Ronald, but she also knew that Ronald was a Christian from a lower caste. His status made a marriage to Didi impossible.

One day, Tara returns home to find fifteen-year-old Rabi with a strange young man. The man claims that his name is Christopher Dey and he is the illegitimate son of Ronald and Didi. He says that Pavarti gave him Tara's address and asks for an introduction to Padma. Tara is suspicious, but Chris gives her a letter from Ronald Dey. Tara believes that it is possible Didi had a child, but she feels threatened by Chris.

Chris leaves, and Rabi takes his side, calling Didi cruel and selfish. He also accuses the three sisters of secretly hating each other. The chapter ends with Tara reading the letter. She is not sure what to believe.

3

Tara feels that she never knew her sisters. She relives her early years in America with Bish, when she was trying to fulfill expectations and hold on to tradition. She talks to Andy, who tells her to speak with Padma and asks her if she is certain Chris is not a scammer. Tara remembers Bish warning her that people would try to take advantage of her because of money.

4

Tara explains that Pavarti's marriage was not arranged. She married Auro out of love. He is a Brahmin she met while going to school in Boston. The marriage was scandalous because she chose her own husband and she married before her older sister, Padma. Pavarti now lives in a high-rise in Bombay. Didi is married to Harish Mehta, and they live in Mont Claire, New Jersey.

Tara calls Pavarti to confront her about Chris, but Pavarti is hysterical because her neighbors were robbed and murdered. Tara decides not to address the subject on her mind, which leaves her in a foul mood. Later, over dinner, she snaps at Andy about her house. He tells her that she needs to take care of her own problems, and she decides to call Pavarti again.

Tara calls Pavarti, asking why Pavarti gave Chris her address. Pavarti denies meeting Chris and tells her that he is a fraud. She warns Tara that it is easy to find information about people on the Internet. Afterward, the sisters have a normal, pleasant conversation.

Rabi returns home after spending a week in Amsterdam with his father, and Tara is happy again. Her happiness is overshadowed when she recalls that Didi was suddenly sent to a Swiss finishing school as a teenager. She remembers that Didi was not excited, and her mother cried as she helped her pack. Tara wonders if Didi had been pregnant.

She thinks back to the time she and Rabi stayed with Pavarti in Bombay when Rabi was ten. He asked to go to the beach below, where children were playing, because he was bored. He was warned that the people on the beach were all thieves and murderers. To alleviate his boredom, Rabi became attached to Pavarti's two dogs. But one night, Rabi walked into the kitchen and was badly bitten by one of the dogs. Pavarti told Tara that the kitchen is the dogs' domain at night, and protecting it is their nature.

Tara also recalls that when Pavarti overheard a plot to poison her dogs and rob her home, Pavarti's first thought was to save the dogs by taking them with her to complain to the manager. One dog is now dead, and the other has severe arthritis.

5

Andy takes Tara to a winery while Rabi is away with Bish. Tara compares Andy and Bish and decides that they are complete opposites.

When Tara returns, she has a message that the books she ordered for the school where she volunteers have arrived. When she goes to pick them up, she sees Rabi out with Chris. Rabi has cut school, and Tara is furious.

Tara remembers her early life in America with Bish. Left alone, she befriended Meena Melwani. The two would go out alone together, although it went against Indian custom to leave their children. Meena eventually left her husband for another woman.

Tara returns home and searches Rabi's room. When he arrives, she confronts him about leaving school with Chris. He lashes out at her, calling Pavarti a liar. Tara believes he never forgave Pavarti for the dog bite. When Andy comes home, he advises her to leave Rabi alone and to separate the past from the present.

Tara considers calling Didi, remembering how Didi said that her divorce from Bish shamed the family. Tara calls and leaves a message for Didi. Her sister never returns the call, but a pack of letters arrives from Pavarti.

6

In the first letter, Pavarti begs Tara to leave the past alone. In another, she recalls that their father discussed marriage with Ronald Dey's father, but the Deys refused him. Finally, she says that she will discuss the matter with Ronald when she sees him at a party. She ends by asking Tara to help find a bride in California for a relative.

7

Tara calls Pavarti, who informs her that Ronald Dey says that he never wrote Tara a letter and that Christopher is not his son. Tara looks Ronald up online and sends a letter to him through a courier. She tells Rabi that she wants to speak to Chris.

The next day, Chris finds Tara as she is leaving the grocery store and walks home with her. She feels threatened by him and pages Andy, who is waiting when they arrive. Andy tells Tara that she is needed on the phone and takes Chris for a walk. Tara talks to Didi, but Didi refuses to discuss the matter of Chris. Tara is not sure what to believe.

8

Ronald sends a reply to Tara acknowledging Chris as his son, but he describes him as tall and unable to speak Bengali. Tara is confused because Chris is short and speaks perfect Bengali.

9

Rabi and Andy make Tara promise to stop investigating Chris. She agrees but decides to go to the police anyway. She meets Sergeant Jasbir Singh Sidhu, who goes by Jack. Jack is a Sikh who specializes in crimes related to India. He agrees to look into the matter off the record, as he is concerned that the real Chris may have been murdered and replaced by an impostor.

10

Tara has to go meet with Rabi's teachers at a conference. She remembers Bish creating the Atherton School for Rabi. After the divorce, however, she placed him in a school that focused on the arts because of his innate talent for drawing.

On the way to the conference, Rabi tells Tara that he believes Chris is an impostor because he asked for Tara's social security number.

At the conference, Rabi's teachers are very happy with his progress. She discovers that Rabi has written a play about an Indian family. She visits the counselor, who gives her a letter from Rabi admitting that he is gay and the play is about him. Tara tells Rabi that she loves him.

When they arrive home, there is a message from Jack. Andy leaves Tara because she broke her promise to leave Chris alone. Jack tells Tara that the real Chris is over six feet tall according to his passport, and they are searching for him.

Part Two

11

Tara goes to visit Didi while Rabi is away with Bish. Didi is working for a business tycoon and television producer. She is already a television personality, and she tells Tara that she is involved in a new Indian soap opera and might have a part. She confesses that she was offered an important movie role when she was a teenager, but their father would not allow her to act.

The next morning, Didi tells Tara that her saris are out of date. They are out of date because Tara does not typically wear saris in California. Didi decides to give Tara a makeover and play matchmaker for her at a party.

12

While they are traveling on the train to New York, Didi tells Tara about the people she will meet at the party that night. Tara calls Jack and gives him Didi's phone number. Didi assumes that Jack is a boyfriend, and she refuses to listen to Tara after she says that Jack is a police officer.

13

After a haircut, Didi takes Tara to find some jewelry for the party and have tea. She tells Tara that she is going to introduce her to Danny Jagtiani, or DJ, her boss and the owner of much of the real estate in the area.

Jack calls during tea and tells Tara that he has pictures of suspects for her to examine to try to identify the impostor. Didi gives Tara DJ's fax number, not realizing what Jack wants to fax. Jack also tells Tara that Ronald is dead, possibly murdered. Tara tells Didi that Chris is in trouble, but Didi stops the fax from reaching DJ when she realizes what is being sent.

14

Didi and Tara make their way to DJ's office, where they discuss the party. Jack calls Tara to inform her that DJ's fax is not working. Tara realizes that Didi turned off the machine. DJ turns the machine on, and the picture of the man she knows as Chris appears. His name is Abbas Sattar Hai. A picture of the real Chris follows, and Tara recognizes Didi in his features.

Tara identifies Hai to Jack, and he tells her that he is a murderer associated with the Dagwood gang in Bombay. The gang has an interest in technology, which makes Tara, Bish, and Rabi potential targets. She calls Bish but cannot get through to him.

Tara has lunch with Didi and DJ. He informs Tara that he met Didi in New York when she was only nineteen. He credits her with helping him develop the persona necessary to become a successful businessman. He also explains that the party is an event where vendors sell merchandise to Indian women in New York who admire Didi's sense of style.

15

Tara and Didi are alone in a limo when Tara asks about Chris and the ten years Didi lived away from home. Didi is too afraid to discuss Chris, even with only the driver present. She does confess that she came to New York with a Parsi boy she met in London. She was in love with him, but realized he was gay when they moved to New York together. She remained with him until he died of AIDS. Tara reveals that Rabi is gay. Didi ends the conversation by explaining that DJ is gay and that he needs her as much as she needs him. She also says that her "mishap" will remain a secret.

At the party, Tara decides to have fun and help Didi sell the clothes and jewelry. Bish calls her back, and she tells him about Jack's suspicions. He tells her that he and Rabi will be in San Francisco in the morning.

16

Tara arrives home early the next morning and plans to keep Bish with her when he drops off Rabi. While Bish and Rabi nap, she makes Bish's favorite food. After cooking, she seduces Bish. That night, she and Bish are standing on the deck when Rabi joins them, claiming he heard voices. Tara is happy with her family for a moment before an explosion occurs in the house. Rabi jumps to the ground below, but Tara is stuck in flames until Bish grabs her and jumps. He is badly burned while saving her life.

17

Tara discovers that a bomb destroyed her house, and Andy is a suspect. Tara's life is now fodder for the media. The chapter is written to reflect news headlines. The real Christopher Dey's body washes ashore, and Andy is cleared of suspicion while the police search for Hai. Meanwhile, Bish's company has trouble in the stock market because of his injury. With her reputation ruined and her family in trouble, Tara follows Pavarti's advice to come home to India and her family.

Tara spends her days at the hospital with Bish before leaving for India. She remembers the story of the Tree Bride and decides that she has stories to tell.

Part Three

18

Tara is in Bombay discussing the story of the Tree Bride with Pavarti. By this time, Tara knows that Ronald Dey was murdered. She looks down and sees Rabi taking pictures on the beach he was warned to avoid. She hides this information from Auro and Pavarti. Although Auro is angry that Rabi is out late, he is pleased that Rabi has taken up photography because he believes it is more marketable

than painting. He tells Rabi that all painters are gay. When Rabi responds politely, Pavarti realizes the truth about him.

Tara's mother has Parkinson's disease and has refused to go see a specialist in San Francisco. She is dying, but she will not leave her husband.

19

Tara is drinking tea at her parents' home in Rishikesh with Rabi when she recalls how the house came to be. When she was a child, her father met a swami who told him that they would travel to Rishikesh together. Her father brought the entire family on the journey. When they arrived, her father heard the goddess Shaktu call on him to prepare for the third phase of life. He purchased a plot of land in Rishikesh after hearing the goddess speak. After Tara married, he sold his estate and moved to Rishikesh to focus on his spiritual journey. Her father is now happily teaching Rabi from the saints' lectures.

Tara tells her parents about her recent brush with death, and her father calls Hai an agent of Manasha, the snake goddess, who causes people to question their lives. This is the same goddess believed to be responsible for the death of the Tree Bride's original groom.

Rabi and Tara go through old books, and Rabi finds the story of Tara Lata's betrayal and death.

20

Tara takes Rabi to Tara Lata's home in Mishtigunj. She shifts the story back to 1943, when the Tree Bride is sixty-eight. The wounded are taken to her home after defying the British. She records the atrocities the people suffered for a reporter, who betrays her. The police blame her for leading an insurrection and take her from the house. She is later killed. As Tara and Rabi walk through the remains of the house, she is able to hear the events from the day of the arrest. Tara tells Rabi to remember the moment because it is a miracle.

CHARACTERS

Aurobindo "Auro" Banerji
Auro is Pavarti's husband. He works and lives in Bombay and is often moody because of his job. He does not approve of Rabi participating in the arts but is happier when Rabi takes up photography.

Pavarti Banerji

Pavarti is Tara's older sister and the middle Bhattacharjee sister. Pavarti marries Auro for love, creating a scandal by choosing her own husband and marrying before her older sister. She lives in an expensive high-rise apartment in Bombay, India. Tara is closer to Pavarti than to Didi, and the two younger sisters communicate weekly. Pavarti remembers more about Didi and the Dey family than does Tara. She confronts Ronald about Christopher at a party, but he denies having an illegitimate son.

"Daddy" Bhattacharjee

Tara's father, the head of the Bhattacharjee family, is financially successful in his youth. He is strict, but he provides for his daughters' education and futures. He moves to Rishikesh after Tara marries in order to pursue his spiritual journey.

"Mummy" Bhattacharjee

Tara's mother has Parkinson's disease. She lives in Rishikesh with her husband and refuses to move for better medical care.

Bishwapriya "Bish" Chatterjee

Bish is Tara's former husband and the father of Rabi. Bish is one of the creators of CHATTY, which is a technological bandwidth his company controls. He is extremely wealthy and influential. He is also very traditional. Bish is badly burned saving Tara the night that her house explodes. His health is compromised, which creates panic about the future of his company.

Rabindranath "Rabi" Chatterjee

Rabi is the son of Tara and Bish. He is a teenager who lives with his mother in San Francisco. He has a talent for art and attends a school focused on the arts. He is the first member of the family to meet the impostor Chris Dey. Rabi finds Christopher interesting and defends him at first. He lashes out against his mother and Hindu custom. Rabi later decides that Chris is not who he claims to be. He writes Tara a letter revealing that he is gay.

Rabi manages to jump to the ground before the fire from the explosion reaches the deck where he was standing with his parents. He accompanies his mother to India and reconnects with his family and culture.

Tara Chatterjee

Tara is the youngest of the Bhattacharjee sisters and a descendent of Jai Krishna Gangooly. Her father arranges her marriage to Bish when she is nineteen, and they move to Silicon Valley, in California, where she later gives birth to Rabi. Tara is lonely after her husband becomes successful, and she divorces Bish after ten years of marriage. She is living in San Francisco with Andy and Rabi when she investigates the claims of the purported Christopher Dey.

Andy leaves Tara because of her investigation, but Tara discovers that the Chris she knows is an impostor. She visits Didi to learn the truth of her sister's past. Tara soon learns that the real Chris is dead and the impostor is from an Indian gang with an interest in technology.

Tara returns home and reunites with Bish shortly before her house explodes. The explosion causes a media frenzy, and Tara's life is exposed. Tara decides that she has stories to tell. She returns home to India, where she researches the life of Tara Lata.

Christopher Dey

Christopher, or Chris, is the illegitimate son of Ronald Dey and Didi. He is murdered in California before he meets any members of his mother's family. Abbas Sattar Hai impersonates Chris to get close to Tara and Rabi.

Poppy Dey

Poppy was Didi's classmate at the convent school, and the two were very close as teenagers. Poppy is Ronald's younger sister.

Ronald Dey

Ronald Dey is a doctor in Bombay. He comes from a Christian family, and his sister was a classmate of Didi's. He reveals in a letter that he had a relationship when he was a teenager, and he is the father of Christopher Dey. Ronald is murdered in Bombay after replying to Tara's letter about Christopher.

Didi

Didi is a word that translates to "sister." It is what Tara calls her oldest sister, Padma. Didi was infatuated with Ronald Dey as a teenager and spent time at his house visiting his sister, Poppy. She has lived in London and New York for ten years and has little contact with her family. During this time, she lived with a gay man without her parents' knowledge. She never directly admits to being Christopher Dey's mother, but it is clear that she is. Didi lives in New Jersey with her husband, Harish Mehta. She is a local television personality and works closely with DJ.

DJ

Originally named Devanand Jagtiani, DJ changes his name to Danny after moving to America. He is a Sindhi from Bombay who became successful in real estate. His success in business continued, and he is now a producer. Didi calls him DJ, and the two work together in television production. Didi is devoted to DJ. She believes that they need each other. She also helps him sell her look at parties for wealthy Bengalis. DJ is gay, but he keeps this a closely guarded secret.

Jai Krishna Gangooly

Jai Krishna has a Western education but follows Hindu traditions, including an arranged marriage for his five-year-old daughter. After the groom is killed by snakebite, Jai Krishna chooses to marry her to a tree rather than see her live as a cursed widow. After the wedding to the tree, he chooses to go by his true family name, Gangopadhaya, rather than the westernized Gangooly. He buries Tara Lata's gold dowry beneath the tree, and it is never seen again.

Jai Krishna Gangopadhaya

See Jai Krishna Gangooly

Abbas Sattar Hai

Abbas Sattar Hai impersonates Christopher Dey and attempts to develop a relationship with Rabi. He is a member of the Dagwood gang from Bombay, India, and has a violent criminal record. He is the main suspect in the bombing that destroys Tara's house.

Jack

Sergeant Jasbir Singh Sidhu goes by Jack. He is a Sikh who works at the San Francisco Police Department, and he specializes in Indian affairs. He investigates the man claiming to be Christopher and discovers that he is an impostor. He suspects that Tara's family is in danger from the Dagwood gang. Bish knows Jack, and Jack is the one Bish calls after the explosion in Tara's house.

Danny Jagtiani

See DJ

Andrew Karolyi

Andy is a contractor and Tara's boyfriend at the beginning of the novel. He is a former biker and world traveler who follows the teachings of Buddhism. Andy leaves Tara after she breaks her promise to him and continues to investigate Christopher Dey. He becomes a suspect after Tara's house is bombed. He is released, but only after being vilified by the media.

Tara Lata

Tara Lata is the daughter of Jai Krishna Gangooly. Her father arranges her marriage when she is five, but the groom is bitten by a snake and dies on the way to the ceremony. To save her from being cursed as a widow, her father marries her to a tree. She remains in her father's home caring for people until she is sixty-eight. She is blamed for an insurrection and arrested by the British in 1943. She dies in police custody.

Harish Mehta

Harish is Didi's husband. He is older than she is, and he dotes on her. He is not Bengali and teases her about Bengali people. Harish works from home and relies on Didi's social connections and influence.

Padma Mehta

See Didi

Meena Melwani

Meena is Tara's friend, and they were close when Tara was married to Bish. They would go out shopping together. Meena eventually left her husband for another woman.

Sergeant Jasbir Singh Sidhu

See Jack

THEMES

Hinduism

The clash between Hindu tradition and Western culture dominates the landscape of *Desirable Daughters*. Tara explains that the expectations of caste and family of Hindu traditions determine whom they marry and their social circle. The novel begins with the child bride Tara Lata, who is married to a tree after her groom dies before the ceremony. A widow is considered cursed, and the wedding to the tree is necessary

TOPICS FOR FURTHER STUDY

- Read *Born Confused* (2002), by Tanuja Desai Hidier. This young-adult novel explores the life of Dimple, a teenage daughter of Indian immigrants who has trouble reconciling India and her life in America. Write a dialogue between Dimple and Rabi from Mukherjee's novel. How would they relate as the children of Indian immigrants? What advice would Dimple give to Rabi, and what advice would Rabi give to Dimple?

- Read *The Tree Bride* (2004), the sequel to *Desirable Daughters*, and write an essay that compares and contrasts the two novels. Explain how the sequel builds upon the themes and plot devices of the first. Also be sure to discuss how the sequel establishes new themes and plot devices.

- Research the history of India under colonial rule. Create a video or multimedia time line for this period, focusing on the movement for independence. Be sure to include the Quit India movement of World War II.

- Read Pam Muñoz Ryan's *Esperanza Rising* (2000). This young-adult novel tells the story of Esperanza, an upper-class girl from Mexico who moves to America and faces the stigmas and adjustments of living in a new country. Draft a one-act play with a classmate where an aged Esperanza meets a newlywed Tara. How would Esperanza assist Tara in her immigration experience? How do their immigration experiences differ? Perform the play with your partner in class, or record the performance and present it online.

- Research Hindu religion, art, and culture. Choose a topic, such as gods or marriage customs, and create a visual representation of the topic to present along with a paper on the subject. If you prefer, you may use an artistic medium such as drawing, painting, or sculpting or technology.

to preserve her status. Tara Lata lives her life serving others and is a role model of Hindu virtue.

Tara and her sisters both fulfill and defy the expectations placed on them by Hindu society and their families. Tara obeys her parents and follows through with her arranged marriage to Bish. She lives as a dutiful wife and mother for ten years. But she breaks with tradition and turns her back on Hindu culture when she divorces Bish and sees other men. After the divorce, she becomes more westernized in her dress and behavior.

By contrast, Pavarti breaks with Hindu culture and tradition by marrying for love and doing so before her older sister marries. This act of rebellion takes place in America, which shows the clash between Hindu tradition and American culture. Despite her scandalous marriage, however, Pavarti has a traditional Indian life in Bombay. She hosts her relatives and focuses on caring for her husband and family. She goes so far as to ask Tara to help her find a potential wife for a relative.

Didi, or Padma, breaks with tradition before either of her sisters. She has a romance with the Christian Ronald Dey, and she lives with a gay man in New York as a young woman. Unlike her sisters, however, Padma keeps all of her youthful indiscretions a secret, even from her family. As a married woman, Didi manages to become an influential television personality and Bengali role model in New Jersey. Unlike Tara, she chooses traditional Indian dress and focuses on traditional Hindu values in her public persona.

Assimilation

As a transplant to the United States, Tara is suspected of assimilation, which affects the way her family perceives her. Pavarti, for example, says of Auro in a letter to Tara, "Don't suggest he get on Prozac. We Indians don't run to psychiatrists for every problem." Anything that an Indian finds unusual about Tara is attributed to her living in America. For example, when she directly asks Ronald Dey in a letter if Chris is his son, he replies, "I surmise that the frankness of its phrasing is a consequence of your long residence in the United States." In many ways, Tara does assimilate. She assimilates when she leaves her husband and begins seeing other men. She also wears American clothing and sends her son to an artistic school.

Tara settles in San Francisco with her son. (© Alexander Demyanenko | Shutterstock.com)

Rabi is not the traditional Indian son. He reflects the culture in which he has been raised. Tara realizes that Pavarti does not approve of the way Rabi is raised: "To Auro and her, ten-year-old Rabi must have seemed a savage, a trust-fund American savage." Tara is not raising the perfect Hindu son in the perfect Indian family. To her sisters, Rabi is not fully Indian. He is too assimilated into American society.

Identity

Tara struggles with her identity throughout *Desirable Daughters*. She plays many roles over the course of her life. She is the dutiful daughter and wife before the divorce. Afterward, she is the westernized, independent woman from the American point of view; but she is a wanton female and family disgrace from the Hindu perspective. She is both an Indian and an American, and she blends each culture to create her identity. She is "tired of explaining India to Americans," but communication is not easier with her family. She explains, "We didn't have a language for divorce and depression, which meant we couldn't fit in concepts like powerlessness and disappointment." Her status as a divorced woman in Indian culture and as an exotic woman in America places her in the periphery of both worlds.

Rabi has his own identity crisis as Tara has hers. Rabi acts out in the first part of the novel. He resents his mother's family, and he sides with the impostor. His outbreaks of anger, however, come from his struggle to accept his identity. He fears that he will be a disappointment to his parents in admitting that he is gay. Once he reveals his identity to his mother, however, Rabi improves their relationship. He stops acting out and resenting his Indian relatives. By the end of the novel, Rabi enjoys exploring faith and the scriptures with his grandfather in India.

STYLE

Morality Play

Suzanne Ruta points out in her review of *Desirable Daughters* in the *Women's Review of Books* that the novel is "a mix-and-match morality play." While morality plays typically revolve around Christian themes, Mukherjee weaves elements of such themes into her novel. According to M. H. Abrams in *A Glossary of Literary Terms*, a morality play is a "quest for salvation, in which the crucial events are temptations, sinning, and the climactic confrontation with death." Tara faces the temptations of Western civilization and is judged as sinning in her relationships with different men and her pulling away from her family. She faces death in the explosion that destroys her home as she attempts to reconcile with Bish. This confrontation with death leads her back to her roots and the story of her namesake, Tara Lata. Her journey to India shows her the way to redemption.

Mystery

Desirable Daughters blends mystery with thriller. The term *mystery novel* is "used to designate a work in which mystery or terror plays a controlling part," according to William Harmon's *A Handbook to Literature*. Mukherjee begins the mystery when Christopher Dey appears at Tara's home, claiming to be her illegitimate nephew. Tara takes on the role of detective as she observes the young man and researches his claims.

Thriller

After Tara contacts Ronald Dey, the novel takes on aspects of a thriller, which is a subgenre in which people find themselves "in dangerous situations from which they must extricate themselves," according to Radenka Vidovic and David Hansen's "*Thrillers*—a Guide for Readers' Advisors." Through a series of revelations and two suspicious deaths, Tara finds that she and her family are the target of a gang from Bombay. The thriller framework ends with the explosion that destroys Tara's home and sends her on a mission of self-discovery.

HISTORICAL CONTEXT

Indian Independence

The story of Tara Lata coincides with the colonial period in India. India came completely under British rule in 1858. The Indian National Congress was established in 1885 and worked tirelessly toward the independence of India. The early part of the twentieth century saw the rise of leaders such as Mahatma Gandhi and the nonviolent resistance movement.

When the British entered World War II in 1939, they needed Indian support to win the war. The Indian people, however, were not happy about being involved in a war without being consulted first. To obtain cooperation, Sir Stafford Cripps was sent to India in 1942 with the offer of independence after the war in exchange for assistance. As the British Library website notes, "The Indian National Congress launched the 'Quit India' movement" in response. Many Indians began supporting Japan during the movement. Because of its opposition to the war, the Indian National Congress was declared illegal, and the participants were arrested.

The transition to independence became complicated after the congress was declared illegal. Clashes between the British and Indians increased, but those dedicated to independence became divided. As Patrick French points out in *India: A Portrait*, "Many felt that for all the talk of inclusiveness, the Congress leadership was made up largely of Hindus from the higher end of the caste system who would . . . undermine the security and status of Muslims." As a result, many Muslims wanted a separate state. India gained independence in 1947, and over the next year, thousands of people died from the violence caused by the partition of India and Pakistan.

Hindu Caste System

The Hindu caste system is an important element of *Desirable Daughters*. The caste system is part of the Vedic tradition and dates back thousands of years. The Vedas are holy books associated with Hinduism and were a part of an oral tradition before they were written down two thousand years ago. Karma and dharma are the two Vedic laws that guide the spiritual journey of Hindu followers. *Dharma* is the code of conduct that individuals must follow based on the scriptures. *Karma* determines how a person is reincarnated. The caste system is based on dharma and the conduct that was necessary for different trades.

According to tradition, people are born into a caste, and the only way to change one's caste is through reincarnation. Castes were originally based on four different occupations. While there are four main castes, there are actually thousands of subcastes or *jati*. The four original castes are Brahmin, Kshatriya, Vaishya, and Shudra. The Brahmin caste was the priestly

COMPARE & CONTRAST

- **1940s:** India is still under colonial rule at the beginning of the decade but gains independence in 1947. The unrest of the decade leads to a struggling economy.

  2000s: India is developing an open market and improving the economy after reforms in the 1990s. The country has its strongest financial growth in 2007, increasing the middle class.

  Today: India is an international power. Although growth has slowed over the past few years, the economic outlook for the country is positive.

- **1940s:** There is tension between Hindus and Muslims during the movement for independence. Pakistan is formed in 1947, the same year that India gains independence, and there are violent clashes between people. War between India and Pakistan occurs in 1948 over Kashmir.

  2000s: Military conflict between India and Pakistan again develops over Kashmir in

2001. A cease-fire occurs in 2004, and India begins to withdraw troops.

  Today: Tension between India and Pakistan remains high, but there is no military conflict. Violence by religious extremists remains a risk.

- **1940s:** The caste system influences the class structure in India. Reformers such as Mahatma Gandhi work to end the injustice that untouchables and lower castes face. The constitution does not include protection for untouchables and against discrimination based on caste until the 1950s.

  2000s: Discrimination based on caste is illegal. K. R. Narayanan is the first Dalit (the term applied to untouchables) president.

  Today: Laws are in place protecting people from discrimination based on caste. Caste and family, however, still play roles in society, and discrimination continues.

---

class, and the Kshatriyas were warriors and nobility. Vaishyas were farmers and artisans, and the Shudra were servants and tenant farmers. Those born outside the castes were untouchables, or pariahs. Marriage between castes was forbidden, and caste determined how people interacted and what occupations they held.

The British exploited the caste system to maintain control of India. They worked mainly with the Brahmin and Kshatriya castes, making the upper castes wealthier and creating further differences in class divide between the castes. As a result, "the caste structure had invaginated itself into the class structure evolved in colonial India," according to Ramkrishna Mukherjee in an *Economic and Political Weekly* article.

Movements to reform the caste system and protect the lower castes, untouchables in particular, date back to the early twentieth

century. After India was granted independence, the nation made laws to ensure opportunity for everyone. Caste, however, still plays a role in Hindu life and culture. As Bobbie Kalman points out in *India: The Culture*, "Although the caste system is now illegal in India, it still rules the lives of most people."

CRITICAL OVERVIEW

Critics have noted Mukherjee's evolution as a writer, and the author was aware of the shift. She described her first novel, *The Tiger's Daughter*, in an interview for *Atlantis* as "very British, still Edwardian in a sense . . . terribly mellifluous and ordered." Over time she embraced more complex storytelling, which earned her greater respect as an author. She reached public acclaim in 1988 with *The Middleman and Other Stories*,

The sisters are raised together in a wealthy Brahmin family, but while Tara assimilated into mainstream American culture, her older sisters hold onto Indian traditions by wearing saris and eating Indian food. (© Vladimir Sklyarov | Shutterstock.com)

for which she was awarded the National Book Critics Circle Award for Fiction. Although Mukherjee has been praised for her skill with words, her stories and characters have faced criticism, particularly from Indian Americans and South Asian critics. As Soderberg points out, she is "criticized for a tendency to overlook unavoidable barriers of caste, education, gender, race and history in her tales of survivors."

Mukherjee's novels and short stories have been praised and criticized over the years, and *Desirable Daughters* was no exception. For example, the *Publishers Weekly* review states, "Only a writer with mature vision, a sense of history and a long-nurtured observation of the Indo-American community could have created this absorbing tale of two rapidly changing cultures and the flash points where they intersect." Other critics were less enthusiastic about the novel. Ramlal Agarwal asserts in his *World Literature Today* review that the novel presents characters who "with no likeable qualities or strong personalities fail to impress the reader, notwithstanding Bharati Mukherjee's many felicities of language."

Mukherjee continued to be a galvanizing writer after publishing *Desirable Daughters*. Her 2011 novel *Miss New India*, for example, "fails to capture India's zeitgeist, or authentically voice the emerging small-town girl," according to Kishwar Desai's review in *India Today*. The *New York Times Book Review* assessment by Akash Kapur also notes the flaws of the book but states that "Mukherjee's writing can be evocative, even poetic." The criticism against Mukherjee has not diminished her literary influence. As Alam states, "we can conclude that Mukherjee has created original and valuable fiction about the immigrant experience in North America."

CRITICISM

April Paris

Paris is a freelance writer with an extensive background writing literary and educational materials. In the following essay, she argues that the characters in Desirable Daughters *who understand they*

WHAT DO I READ NEXT?

- Published in 2010, *The Kitchen House* is a historical novel by Kathleen Grissom set in the antebellum South. Lavinia, an Irish servant, works with the slaves of the kitchen house. Once she is accepted into the main house, she becomes, like Tara, torn between two worlds.

- Published in 2011, *India: A History; From the Earliest Civilisations to the Boom of the Twenty-First Century*, by John Keay, provides an overview of India's history and diverse culture, offering a helpful introduction to a rich and complex nation.

- *A Concise History of Modern India*, by Barbara Metcalf and Thomas Metcalf, was published in 2012. A third edition of the title, the book includes useful information about India in the twenty-first century.

- *A History of Prejudice: Race, Caste, and Difference in India and the United States*, by Gyanendra Pandey, compares the history of untouchables in India with that of African Americans. Published in 2013, the book explores issues of race and class in both countries.

- Kashmira Sheth's young-adult novel *Keeping Corner* explores the life of a child bride and widow in colonial India. Published in 2007, the novel suggests what Tara Lata's life would have been like if she had not become the Tree Bride.

- Stanley M. Stephen's 2010 volume *Bharati Mukherjee: A Study in Immigrant Sensibility* is a critical study that examines Mukherjee's exploration of the immigrant experience in her writing. The book is a useful source that showcases where Mukherjee falls within the landscape of Indian diaspora authors.

- Mukherjee's novel *Jasmine*, published in 1989, is the story of a seventeen-year-old widow in India who migrates to America. The novel explores the themes of identity, exile, and assimilation.

are not in control of their lives are able to transform their identities.

In her novel *Desirable Daughters*, Bharati Mukherjee uses the immigrant experience to explore the concepts of control, identity, and transformation. The characters Tara and Didi both immigrated from India to the United States, but each responds to her status as an immigrant differently. Only Tara is able to reconcile her Bengali, Hindu heritage with her life as an American and transform herself. As Jennifer Drake explains in a *Contemporary Literature* article, Mukherjee "rejects the hyphen and the acceptable stories it generates—stories about immigrants struggling between two incommensurable worlds, finally choosing one or the other."

The idea that you can choose to be affected by one culture and not the other creates a false sense of security and control. Tara is able to transform herself when she understands that this control does not exist and experiences the "fusion of opposites." This is a term Mukherjee used in her *Atlantis* interview with Francisco Collado Rodríguez. By embracing the positive together with the negative of each culture, Tara is able to create her own identity, which allows her to become an agent of change. As Mukherjee explained in her interview with Ameena Meer in *BOMB*, "I'm writing about an American immigrant group who are undergoing many transformations within themselves. And who, by their very presence, are changing the country."

Tara faces internal conflict as a woman who is both Indian and American. Throughout the novel, she feels the need to choose between her Indian heritage and the lifestyle she has as a single, American woman. This pressure to choose between two worlds is apparent when she visits Pavarti after her divorce. She understands that they consider her identity to be at risk: "Come back to India, our parents are getting old and weak and your child isn't American or Indian and if you stay there any longer, you won't be either." Tara, however, is not willing to give up her life in America.

By outward appearances, Tara is a modern, American woman who makes personal choices and has taken control of her own fate. There is, however, always the question of how much control she has over her own life and the life of her son. This question of control is not limited to Tara. It goes back to the story of her namesake,

> THE IDEA THAT YOU CAN CHOOSE TO BE AFFECTED BY ONE CULTURE AND NOT THE OTHER CREATES A FALSE SENSE OF SECURITY AND CONTROL. TARA IS ABLE TO TRANSFORM HERSELF WHEN SHE UNDERSTANDS THAT THIS CONTROL DOES NOT EXIST AND EXPERIENCES THE 'FUSION OF OPPOSITES.'"

Tara Lata, and Jai Krishna's attempt to control his fate and the fate of his daughter. When a tragedy causes a reversal of fortunes, his control is gone. Mukherjee explained in *Atlantis* that for Hindus, "there is no good and devil, . . . there is no differentiation between snake, human, and god, they are just appearance." Understanding this concept represents the fusion of opposites. Such understanding allows Jai Krishna to interpret his family's situation correctly and experience a personal transformation.

As a lawyer, Jai Krishna has an English education, but he is a devout Hindu who follows tradition. Although he is not an immigrant, he lives between two worlds. He interprets the signs and omens when selecting a groom for Tara Lata, and all of the necessary rituals are performed for the ceremony. He is confident that his daughter's marriage will be a success. This confidence that he is in control is shattered when the groom is bitten by a snake and dies on the way to the ceremony. Jai Krishna realizes that the snakebite is not a divine punishment sent because a ritual was not performed correctly. Rather, the snake was sent to teach him: "The snakebite had occurred to remind Jai Krishna . . . how precarious social order and fatherly self-confidence are." Although some see the snake as a sign of evil, its intervention results in a personal transformation for Jai Krishna, who experiences an increase of faith in the gods and embraces his Hindu identity by refusing to use the westernized version of his family name.

The snakebite also helps to shape Jai Krishna's daughter into a national hero. Because Tara Lata is considered cursed by Indian society, Jai Krishna makes the decision to marry her to a tree. As a result of this decision, Tara Lata grows

up to do great things. She gives aid during famine and supports the movement for independence by sheltering people in her home. Her life would have been very different had the snake not bitten her intended groom.

The same goddess responsible for the Tree Bride would later test the confidence of Jai Krishna's descendant. Tara describes the impostor Christopher as a snake who sneaks into her life. This impostor is a villain, but he is also a tool whose actions give Tara the opportunity to blend her heritage with her American life.

Tara begins her life in America by adhering to her upbringing and culture. Her point of view changes, however, after she becomes a mother and Bish becomes wealthy. Although she has the life that she expected, she discovers she is lonely and depressed. Her unhappiness leads her to an unthinkable decision for a Hindu. She chooses to divorce. The choice, however, costs her. She loses the company of the Indian wives who formerly composed her social circle. Her sister tells her that she disgraced the family name. Like Tara Lata, not having a husband makes Tara an outcast in her social circle, which only increases her loneliness.

After her divorce, Tara lives a westernized life. She is a wealthy, American divorcée with a live-in boyfriend and an active life in the San Francisco community. Tara's mother explains this shift away from heritage when she says, "You've moved away from us in your heart." Tara takes on this new identity and mistakenly assumes that her world is safe and secure. She does not believe that trouble from India will come to haunt her in America. The refusal to acknowledge risk and danger is repeated by different characters throughout the novel. As Mukherjee explained in her interview with Susan Ruta in the *Women's Review of Books*, "The tragedy for this group, for the family in the novel, is that continual and aggressive refusal to acknowledge that anything is wrong."

Tara learns that she does not have as much control as she believes once Hai enters her world. The fear of a family scandal, however, is paramount to Tara. She is dedicated to discovering if Didi had an illegitimate son, and she overlooks the warning signs that criminals are targeting her until she talks with Jack. Likewise, Andy, Rabi, and Bish all seem relatively unconcerned about the strange man claiming a family tie to Tara. Rabi believes that the man he knows as

Christopher Dey is an impostor, but he is not worried. He calmly tells Tara, "Ma, life's dangerous." Andy believes Tara should simply stop investigating Christopher and relax. Bish is comfortable with his security. All of their lives, however, are forever changed when a bomb destroys Tara's home.

With her life as fodder for the media and Bish's company in danger, Tara finds her reputation ruined in both Indian and American society. She has lost all control and begins to question her own identity, which leads her back to India. She surmises that Hai "seems a true agent sent to waken mortals, doesn't he? A form of Goddess Manasha, perhaps, the ever-opportunistic snake goddess who can slither into any space, over or under any barrier." The goddess calls "our self-protective little lives into question by injecting them with venom." Mukherjee explained in her interview with Rodríguez, "the real job of the god or hero, of the agent of goodness is to neutralize the venom; not to kill the snake." Tara remembers the saying "The only antidote for poison is poison." Bish, whose name means "poison," neutralizes the venom by saving Tara from the fire.

With the poison neutralized, Tara transforms the act of terror into an opportunity to reconnect with her heritage rather than focusing on revenge. She discovers more about Tara Lata and decides it is a story that needs to be told. As Mukherjee explained to Ruta, "the narrator suddenly realizes, 'This is my heritage in ways that I never understood, never cared about, and I have to make sense of it and put it down in writing.'" By investigating the story of Tara Lata, Tara takes the final step toward a fusion of opposites and reconciles her Indian heritage with her American life.

Unlike Tara, Didi never manages to blend her life in America with her Indian heritage. She remains separate, refusing any signs of assimilation. As a young woman, Didi is the first sister to break away from tradition. She falls in love with a Christian from the wrong caste and has an illegitimate child. She also lives with a gay man in New York. However, Didi rejects the ideas of rebellion and westernization once she is married. She concentrates on controlling her world by protecting her reputation.

Didi chooses tradition over Americanization, believing that the two are incompatible. Although she lives in New Jersey, Didi appears to be the perfect Hindu wife, without a hint of assimilation. She designs and dresses in fashionable saris and wears the traditional gold bangles. She socializes with other wealthy Indian immigrants to the United States. She refuses to blend into American society. Even the soap opera she is developing is focused on traditional values, avoiding "American stuff." She explains, "Just because bad things happen doesn't mean we have to show them on television." This statement reflects how Didi lives her life, in denial. She believes that she can control her world by rejecting the truth of reality.

As with Tara, Didi's world is threatened when Hai appears and claims to be her son, Christopher Dey. Didi, however, does not learn from the snakebite. She chooses to keep the rebellious part of her life a secret, hidden safely in the past. She falsely believes that secrecy will spare her any consequences. Even seeing a picture of her son and realizing that he is in danger does not weaken her resolve. Mukherjee explained to Ruta that Didi is unwilling to accept that "there are material consequences to that transgression. At the very last moment Tara acknowledges it, but the older sister never does."

Didi is unwilling to participate in the "fusion of opposites." She becomes a liar to herself and to those around her. Even after Tara's house is bombed and the true Christopher is found dead, she only says, "I'm glad you finally have something bigger to deal with than your silly little fantasy about me and Ronald Dey." The deaths of her son and former lover help ensure that her indiscretion will remain a secret, allowing her to continue her illusion of control.

Tara's and Didi's approaches to immigration show the two extremes, but each approach is an attempt at control. Didi refuses to participate in anything *American* in order to prevent any hint of assimilation. This allows her to maintain her status in Bengali society in America. Tara, however, lives a westernized life, which affects the way Indians and Americans see her. Each one has the opportunity to transform her identity and fuse her worlds together when Hai emerges, but only Tara is honest enough to embrace the lesson.

Source: April Paris, Critical Essay on *Desirable Daughters*, in *Novels for Students*, Gale, Cengage Learning, 2014.

The novel's intrigue begins when a young man approaches Tara, claiming to be her oldest sister's illegitimate child. *(© sita ram / Shutterstock.com)*

Jopi Nyman

In the following excerpt, Nyman discusses the tension between modernity and tradition in Desirable Daughters.

. . . Like Divakaruni's *The Mistress of Spices*, Mukherjee's novel thematizes the rupture between tradition and modernity in a postcolonial *and* American setting. The terms Tara uses in representing her own transformation are particularly interesting because they also voice what the sociologist Zygmunt Bauman has discussed in his book *Liquid Modernity* (2000). Bauman emphasizes that the traditional understanding of modernity as being structured upon the "solid" categories of machinery and ordered state-based politics needs to be revised to achieve a better understanding of the chaotic nature of the globalized world. According to Bauman, the contemporary destabilized society is bound to "'flow,' 'spill,' 'run out,' 'splash,' 'pour over,'

'leak,' 'flood,' 'spray,' 'drip,' 'seep,' 'ooze'; unlike solids it is not easily stopped" (2000: 2). Rather than based on solid machines and the controlling powers of the nation-state, the world described in Mukherjee's novel is one of cellphones and laptops, of electronic communications and transnational computer networks (like Bish's CHATTY), of power that is "*exterritorial*, no longer bound, not even slowed down, by the resistance of space" (2002: 11; emphasis original).

Indeed, the society described in Mukherjee's novel is one of constant flow, where flows of migrants—and transnational crime leagues—seek to enter the centres of the West, showing thus the global at work in the local. In so doing, they transform its space but also remain connected to other diasporic communities, unlike the paradigmatic immigrants and exiles of earlier discourses (cf. Kaplan 1996). This process with rapidly expanding flows of people

> IN ADDITION TO TARA'S RECONSTRUCTION OF HER IDENTITY, THE NOVEL SHOWS THAT THE LIFESTYLE OF THE THREE SISTERS AND THEIR SOCIAL GROUP HAS COME TO AN END AND IT MAY ONLY BE PERFORMED IN CONDITIONS OF DIASPORA, IN THE MANNER OF THE PARTY."

and commodities can be noted in Tara's description of the area of Jackson Heights in New York:

> It's still a shock, however, and kind of inspiration, to see the might of one's community on parade. The swagger is subtle, and perfectly Indian. Poky little storefronts for sweets and spices that look marginal at best are shipping tons of the hot mix out the back door, repackaged in French and Spanish, English, Hindi, Urdu, and any other language, for every Indian speciality store in North America. Every little storefront that looks no more impressive than it might have in India, dim, cluttered, badly painted, indifferently displayed, has an "office" somewhere in rear where a computer-savvy nephew expands the online client base by factors of several thousand. Travel agents, whose idea of decor is Scotch-taped Air India poster on the wall, issue dozens of India-bound tickets every hour, from every airport on the continent. (2002: 199–200)

The transformation of American space as a result of the flow of immigration can also be seen in Tara's description of her San Francisco, a multicultural landscape tended by global migrants all of whom do not share in her and her ex-husband's prosperity. Thus the novel shows how the United States is changing from a melting pot to a nation displaying the effects of contemporary globalization. Its "ethnically ambiguous" citizenry includes dislocated Palestinian families, not only older immigrants:

> Their names inspire me: Ib, Selim, Moh, Safid, Ali ... all the neighborhood services, except the laundries and the Japanese restaurant, are owned and staffed by crack-of-dawn rising, late-night closing Palestinians, whose shifting roster of uncles and cousins seems uniformly gifted in providing our needs and anticipating our desires. (2002: 25)

In such a world characterized by constant mobility and migrant labour, the maintenance of

traditional identity appears impossible. In pitting the traditional against the modern, the novel contrasts Tara's transformation with the fates of Bish and Didi. Her ex-husband and Silicon Valley magnate Bish is a traditionalist, who thinks that social changes should not be reflected in gender roles, marriage, and the family. Regardless of his crucial role in developing the world of electronic communications ("The system is called 'CHATTY' and without it, nothing in the modern world would work" [2002: 24]), he prefers the values of an imagined past to those of the contemporary USA, as can be seen in his view of the education of his son. Unable to find a British-style educational institution resembling the colonial school he once attended in Calcutta, he founds one in Atherton, San Mateo County, California to cater for the needs of nostalgic Asian millionaires worrying over the future of their children. Thus Rabi's first school is based, nostalgically, "on the English model, with a 'Commons' for lunch, prayers in the morning, Greek and Latin, and hard-fought sports whose rules, vocabularies, and passions were unreplicated anywhere on this continent, and perhaps any time in this century" (2002: 152). What Bish's fantasy of replicating a colonial British upbringing in the contemporary USA shows is how tradition seeks to resist modernity. Unfortunately it appears to become a mere performance like the "regimental schoolmasters" employed:

> Indian millionaires were the new monarchs of snob, and the old schoolmasters took note, spiking their vocabularies with Indo-Anglicisms of the 1920s ("Let's take a dekko, shall we?") and their lunches with "curries," that conveyed their sympathies with excessive turmeric that stained our children's shirts with bright yellow that no amount of bleach could wash out. (2002: 152)

The spaces of tradition function as attempts to recreate a fixed sense of identity for the imagined community of expatriate Indians whose members share the same values. Nevertheless, the novel reveals that such a project is impossible because of the different historical situatedness of the millionaires and their American-born children. For Bish, a son who expresses more interest in the arts than sports marks failure: "Bish could not tolerate a son who was not a perfect replica of himself; hardworking, respectful, brilliant. Soberly sociable. Effortlessly athletic" (2002: 154). Regardless of his father's aims, Rabi will not become a gentleman like him, as can be seen in his acquiring a homosexual identity which initially shocks his mother (and eventually also his father and all homophobic relatives).

A further example of the crisis of the traditional identity can be seen in Tara's eldest sister, the embittered Didi, who lives in a cold New Jersey apartment with her pathetic Punjabi husband Harish Mehta. Didi, a well-known public figure in the South Asian diasporic communities on the East Coast, runs a community channel television programme called "Namaskar, Probasi." For her, it has proved financially profitable to transform her Bengali identity into a commodity. This is shown in the novel when the two sisters attend a party intended for "la crème de la crème of Bengali New Jersey society" (2002: 187), a group consisting of well-to-do doctors, professors, businessmen, and their spouses. Didi, however, is not a mere guest at the party arranged by the Ghosals, but uses her appearance and name to sell her products as if they represented "the authentic India." For her the party is a fashion show, not a normal social occasion. What matters most is reputation and performance, not reality. Indeed, the novel reveals that with the help of her boss Danny Jagtiani (an Americanized character formerly known as Devanand Jagtiani), she has turned herself into a brand and sells elegant (and expensive) silk saris with the tag "*Padma Mehta Design, New York*" (2002: 196; emphasis original). Similarly, the expensive jewelry that Tara wears at the party is there on exhibition: by the end of the evening the necklaces and other accessories are sold to the dislocated New Jersey wives who want to acquire a version of Indian femininity, dress up in almost traditional clothing, and display jewels worth up to 10,000 dollars. In the words of Danny Jagtiani, "we throw these parties so that the community can sample these styles in saris and jewelry that they might be missing by being out of Bengal" (2002: 231). As is the case at Tupperware parties (and in Didi's kitchen Indian food does indeed go into these American plastic containers [see 2002: 182]), the social functions and relations of Didi's parties appear to be subordinated to economic profit. Indeed, as Tara manages to assist her sister in selling the products and performs her Indianness as if scripted, the evening results in almost 17,000 dollars. The economic discourse enters her report of interaction at the party:

And now a word from our sponsor. "Thank God, Didi showed me her fabulous sari collection!" I said. "I don't know what I would have done, arriving in the dead of night with all these parties coming up, and nothing to wear." It sounded to me like a badly designed television ad, two women in a kitchen comparing detergents, but in Bengali it came off as almost sincere. (2002: 233)

Whereas Bish considers tradition as a counterforce of modernity, Didi constructs Indianness as a form of purity rather than as hybridity. "She let me know she couldn't be seen with me in public ('My reputation, Tara') and couldn't introduce me to New Jersey Bengali society in my present bedraggled condition" (2002: 186), as the novel puts it. Yet Tara remains unable to accept entirely either way of relating to the tradition. Bish's attempt to reproduce the past in the present is no less problematic than Didi's performative version of tradition. Instead, her unuttered words to Didi show her homing desire located in the present, a way of using the past in countering a form of identity able to come to grips with the contemporary:

I don't blame Daddy and I don't blame Bish and Calcutta, and nuns might not have equipped me for San Francisco but they're all gone, that world is gone, we're here, we have to stop pretending, we have to stop living in a place that's changed on us while we've been away. I don't want to be a perfectly preserved bug trapped in amber, Didi. I can't deal with modern India, it's changed too much and too fast, and I don't want to live in a half-India kept on life-support. (2002: 184)

In contrast to Didi's attempt to escape history into a performance of Indianness, and Bish's attempt to reconstruct the tradition, Tara's words make it clear that no such space immune to historical change exists. In addition to Tara's reconstruction of her identity, the novel shows that the lifestyle of the three sisters and their social group has come to an end and it may only be performed in conditions of diaspora, in the manner of the party. Mrs. Ghosal makes the point explicit by pointing out that it is only at the parties that "the species" survives: "'The apparent survival anyway. We look to be thriving, don't we? Homo Bengalensis, subspecies, Hindu Calcuttan, subbreed, Ballygunge. In your case, Brahmin'" (2002: 245)....

Source: Jopi Nyman, "Transnational Travel in Bharati Mukherjee's *Desirable Daughters*," in *Home, Identity, and Mobility in Contemporary Diasporic Fiction*, Rodopi, 2009, pp. 206–11.

Judie Newman

In the following excerpt, Newman analyzes the connectedness between different characters' stories in Desirable Daughters.

... Mukherjee's model of relationships also builds notions of rebellion and revolt into the lines of descent and consent. Unknown to her sisters, Didi had given illegitimate birth to a son, Christopher, fathered by Ronald Dey, an Anglo-Indian Christian. Tara's attempts to excavate the story, verify or disprove the identity of the claimant, and engage in wholesale cheater detection, expose the lack of real connections between the apparently intimate family, in the context of the political contest between tradition and modernity. In the novel, the illegitimate child is doubly bastardised and twice rejected. As the illegitimate offspring of a Bengali Brahmin's eldest daughter, conceived in passion with an Anglo-Indian Christian, Chris Dey's existence goes unrecognised, his mother refusing ever to admit to his existence. His descent is utterly denied. Before the adult Chris can claim his heritage, his place is usurped by an interloper who kills him, steals his name and attempts to take his place in the family. By the time Tara establishes the existence of the illegitimate child, the real son is already at the bottom of San Francisco Bay. The claims of descent are not validated. The point of the novel is not to re-establish contact with a denied male line, but to focus on a sibship. Or rather, two sibships: the three sisters of the present and their distant relation, the Tree Bride, also one of a sibship of three. Mukherjee's plot sets up two models of connectedness: the global (embodied in both the apparent master of connectivity, Bish Chatterjee, the software genius, and the criminally networked 'Chris Dey') and the three sisters whose connections are traditional, intimate and lateral. In the action there is a continual tension between the two stories, alternately prioritised.

... Tara's own story is ostensibly that of an entirely untraditional Bengali-American who has rebelled against the enclosed life of an Indian wife, divorced her husband, and set up home with a lover in a multi-ethnic neighbourhood almost synonymous with revolt: the Haight. She has recently campaigned for a gay Chicano candidate, wears blue jeans and works in a school. If the Tree Bride's path is narrow and traditional, and her world circumscribed, Tara's is quite the reverse. Hers is emphatically a

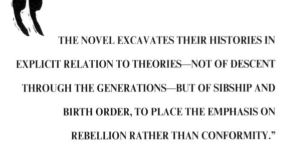

broadband world. As students at Stanford her husband Bish and his partner Chet Yee discovered a process for allowing computers to create their own time, instantaneously routing information to the least congested lines. As an architect of globalisation, Bish is none the less exceptionally traditional. 'A first son from an outstanding family' of Calcutta conservatives, Bish lives up to family expectations, becoming an engineering student in India 'because his father told him he would be an engineer.' Bish is part of the process of globalisation, the process by which people become increasingly interconnected across natural borders and continents. His mobile phone routing devices connect the whole world. Yet he is also the product of complete loyalty to tradition. As previously mentioned, Bish's discovery was prompted by a football game in which the players exploited the 'West Coast Offense,' a tactic in which short passing plays replace the running game, to control the ball—a process invented by Bill Walsh of the Cincinnati Bengals. The bandwidth system, called CHATTY, is 'about width, using the whole field, connecting in the flat, no interference, a billion short passes linked together.' It also exemplifies the method of Mukherjee's novel. In interview Mukherjee said that

> The aesthetic strategy of the book was using the width of the field—of history, geography, diaspora, gender, ethnicity, language—rather than the old-fashioned long, clean throw.

So what happens in the novel is that the reader is passed from story to story across a broad geographical and historical sweep; the narrative passes from one controller to another, at times appearing to be misdirected or displaced, with the story moving forward through changes of direction, side-passes, misdirections and feints. The straight trajectory of a story based on descent is replaced by a model which involves many side connections, sibships and horizontal or lateral moves. Connections are made through a process which also underlines the problems of connection. Arguably, through the connectedness of information, and the shrinking of space and time, all our histories intersect in the modern world. We can no longer move back onto the traditional narrow path; we are in the same time with interconnecting histories, and an awareness of time as space. Bish's discovery underlines the sense in the novel of a complex network of connections in which people are both receivers and senders across a very broad field, where routers are as important as roots. As Paul Harris argues,

> Narrative no longer seems to work by imposing the telos of plot on the contingencies of the world, but by sifting through dispersed bits of discrete input and rendering them intelligent and coherent.

The risk of loss of aesthetic value is a real one. In this vision, what differentiates the novel from a form of information farming? Cultural synthesising or programming does not facilitate cheater detection, the seeking of truth.

Bish's connectivity also has its darker side. On the one hand the mobile phone figures repeatedly as a security device. When 'Chris Dey' appears, Tara relies on the phone; she has both her lover and the police on her speed-dial. She uses the internet to locate Ronald Dey and check the intruder's claims. But 'Chris Dey' located her on the internet, and is himself part of a worldwide criminal network. Manuel Castells has highlighted the emergence of global crime, the networking of powerful criminal organisations across the planet, as a relatively new phenomenon; in his argument, criminal penetration of financial markets constitutes a critical element in a fragile, global economy, and an essential feature of the Information Age. While basing their management and production firmly in low-risk, controllable areas, such cartels habitually target areas of affluence, exploiting allegiances with other cartels, their 'business practices' closely following those of the network enterprise of the Information Age. Immigrant networks are often used to penetrate First World societies; contemporary cartels exploit cultural identity to hold their enterprise together. 'Criminal networks are probably in advance of multinational corporations in their decisive ability to combine cultural identity and

global business.' Mukherjee herself has good reason to be aware of the transnationality of crime. Her non-fiction work, *The Sorrow and the Terror*, explored diasporic fundamentalism, sleeper cells and cyber-terrorism. In a painstaking investigation of the 1985 Air India bombing in which a Khalistani (Sikh secessionist) group blew up a Canadian flight bound for India, killing 329 people, Mukherjee drew attention to the worldwide fundraising for terrorist activities in Sikh temples, and to the laxness of airport security. Before 9/11, she commented, the white establishment assumed that any violence would be exported back to immigrant homelands. What she learned (as she explained to Bill Moyers on PBS) was the strength of the terrorist fear of modernisation, particularly as it affected religion and women's willingness to follow religious rules. As a result of the book she found herself stalked and under death threat for two years, publicly denounced in Sikh temples in large American cities. In interview she described the sense of finding oneself scripted into other people's stories, as her heroine is.

> It wasn't until the World Trade Center was demolished that the average citizen began to realize how, like Tara, you can be living your life, immersed in your own personal conflicts—Should I go back to my husband? Why did my Hungarian lover leave me for someone else? *etcetera*—while unknowingly you are enmeshed in someone else's incredible fantasies.

Those who combine and select their own materials to form their own cultural syntheses enmesh others in the resultant scenarios, whether modern or traditional. Globalisation connects the Indian Dawood gang across the globe, threatening security and destroying identities. Fundamentalism can exploit the same networks and synergies. If traditionalism can be transposed into radical revolt (in the example of the Tree Bride), modern globalisation can do the reverse, hand-in-glove with the forces of coercive and fundamentalist tradition.

As the narrator, Tara is caught between different stories. On one level (as Dragana Obradovic has argued) she is faced with a variety of shared histories and has to reconfigure her own cultural space, becoming to some extent at least a cultural programmer, navigating a range of cultural territories. Just as technology may give us the sense of being in two worlds at the same time (in a chatroom, a real room, on a cell phone) so the novel gives the reader the bewildering sense of having jumped from one story to another, of being deflected, off-balance, led astray by another seductive linkage. Is the novel a story of America? Or India? Or the British empire? Of parents and children? Or of sisters? In a metaphor drawn from anti-earthquake technology (as practised by Andy, Tara's lover) the story concerns the problems of how, given the seismic shifts in people's lives, we can 'retrofit,' making for a secure structure, without embracing either rickety traditions or a simplistic fundamentalism, how we relate tradition and modernity in the new, networked world.

Tara's connection to the Tree Bride is not, therefore, a connection back to a secure, primordial identity, steeped in religious tradition, but to a rebel. She feels a profound connection to the Tree Bride, as a member of a sibship. 'She had two sisters, as do I. Perhaps we learned the same nursery rhyme. We are sisters three/as alike as three blossoms on one flowering tree.' To an external eye, Tara's sisters are very alike. All share a birthday (at intervals of three years); all have played the same roles in the same Gilbert and Sullivan operettas at the same convent school; all are exceptionally attractive. But the apparent homogeneity of the sibship is an illusion. The novel excavates their histories in explicit relation to theories—not of descent through the generations—but of sibship and birth order, to place the emphasis on rebellion rather than conformity. It is not for nothing that the Tree Bride, her father and Tara Chatterjee are all third children—or that dutiful Bish is a first son. What I want to suggest is that Mukherjee deliberately casts her discussion of the relation of tradition to modernity in the context not of vertical lines of descent and consent but in terms of sibships and lateral familial connections, a model which is suggestively related to a networked world . . . .

Source: Judie Newman, "Priority Narratives: Bharati Mukherjee's *Desirable Daughters*," in *Fictions of America: Narratives of Global Empire*, Routledge, 2007, pp. 153, 155–58.

Katherine Miller

In the following excerpt, Miller examines issues of identity in Desirable Daughters.

. . . In Mukherjee's texts, female identity is often linked to an imprisoning home. Although Nalini Iyer argues that Mukherjee's novels examine "the need for immigrants to construct for themselves a narrative of home" (29), in *Wife*,

Jasmine, and *The Holder of the World*, home is frequently associated with images of imprisonment. The title character of *Jasmine* moves away from defining herself solely by her community and home, referring to one place as a "fortress of Punjabiness" (148). Jasmine "shuttles between different identities" (Dayal 77), seeing America as a place where "nothing is rooted anymore. Everything was in motion" (*Jasmine* 152). This earlier novel, which validates the concept of a fluid identity linked to perpetual motion, ends with Jasmine, now called Jase, at the beginning of another identity transformation, fleeing to California with a new lover. Perhaps it is significant that Tara lives in San Francisco, almost as far west as one can travel in the continental United States.

The modern Tara begins her story with "*that most American of impulses or compulsions, a 'roots search.'*" She then describes her own childhood in Calcutta in the late fifties and early sixties with her two older sisters, Padma and Parvati. Named after goddesses, the "desirable daughters" of the title are, in Tara's words, "*sisters three . . . as like as blossoms on a tree.*" Using the metaphor of the family tree, Tara seems to imply that identity is essential, defined by one's home, community, and culture. She calls attention to this belief, noting that

> Bengali culture trains one to claim the father's birthplace, sight unseen, as his or her *desh*, her home. . . . When I speak of this to my American friends—the iron-clad identifiers of region, language, caste, and subcaste—they call me 'overdetermined' and of course they are right. When I tell them they should be thankful for their identity crises and feelings of alienation, I of course am right.

The opening story of the Tree Wife reaffirms the importance of region, language, and caste, specifically for a gendered identity. Tara Lata's father marries his daughter to a tree because he believes that this is the only way in which she can escape "*her true fate . . . a lifetime's virginity, a life without a husband to worship as god's proxy on earth, and thus, the despairing life of a woman doomed to be reincarnated.*" As a child, the modern Tara also feels bound by a world in which "every name declares your identity."

Focusing on "the conflation of home and self" (George 19), Rosemary George and other humanist geographers reiterate the "indivisibility of humans from their environment" (Rose 46). Tara, however, appears to have escaped from the constraints of a predetermined identity, an

> IN EARLIER NOVELS, MUKHERJEE EXPLORES THE LIVES OF WOMEN MARGINALIZED BY CASTE, CLASS, AND SOCIOECONOMIC POSITION. TARA AND HER SISTERS, ON THE OTHER HAND, ARE ECONOMICALLY AND SOCIALLY PRIVILEGED."

identity limited by constraints of community and culture. In her retrofitted American home, contained within the "rhetoric of modern San Francisco," Tara "feels not just invisible but *heroically* invisible, a border-crashing claimant of all people's legacies." Her overdetermined identity seemingly can be abandoned in the modern rhetoric of her new home. Yet, just a few pages later, Tara claims that she is "sick of feeling an alien." These contradictions held in tension within her life are challenged when a modern version of a snake appears.

Claiming that her family existed in Calcutta inside an "impenetrable bubble," Tara is shocked when the appearance of Chris Dey, supposedly her oldest sister's illegitimate child, challenges her perceptions of the past. Tara's son, Rabi (short for Rabindranath), brings Chris into the sanctuary of the house. Chris, who claims to be the son of Padma and a Christian doctor, betrays himself in several culturally specific ways—smoking a cigarette in front of an older woman, speaking a streetwise form of Bengali—as other than he seems. Although Tara claims to have lost what she calls her "Indian radar," she still uses social and cultural markers to structure her world. She tells a Sikh detective that Chris cannot be her nephew because he is "short, uneducated, rather crude, and Bengali-speaking" while acknowledging that her judgements sound "racist." In *Transnational Urbanisms* Michael Peter Smith claims that "individuals give meaning to their lives through the networks of communication in which they are involved and through which they constitute themselves [and] their identities." By challenging Tara's beliefs about her social network (i.e. her family and her community), Chris Dey also threatens her identity. His appearance in Tara's world leads her to question her assumptions about her past. Although she knew that her sister

was in love with Ronald Dey, Chris's purported father, Tara believed that "Ronald Dey was *not* possible," that "any violations of the codes, any breath of scandal, was unthinkable" for her family. The strict strictures of her Brahmin Bengali background still form Tara's beliefs, even within the rhetoric of her "retrofitted" American home.

Tara had thought that nothing could touch a Bengali Brahmin from Calcutta; Chris's presence destroys what she calls "that inherited confidence, the last treasure [she'd] smuggled out of India." As the opening story of Tara Lata demonstrates, no one can shut out the poisonous snake that destroys people's lives; homes can be invaded. The houses in the novel metaphorically illustrate the socioeconomic status of the characters. Tara's first home was a "nineteenth-century Raj-style fortress...set behind a wall topped with glass shards." Similarly, the house she shared with her husband, Bish, was in a gated community in Atherton, California. These fortress-style homes maintain the illusion of safety, a protected space for the privileged. In Bombay, Parvati and her husband live in a fifteenth-floor apartment of a high-rise overlooking the Arabian Sea. These homes correspond to what Rosemary George calls the "private sphere of patriarchal hierarchy, gendered self-identity, shelter, comfort, nurture, and protection." Speaking of the world of her childhood, Tara says, "The narrow world of the house and city felt as secure to me as it must have to Tara Lata in Mishtigunj." Rejecting her position as a married woman, in which she could live inside "a gated community, endlessly on display at dinners and openings," Tara divorces Bish, leaves the protected sphere, and moves with Rabi to San Francisco. Although she loves her family and her culture, Tara "walked away from the struggle to preserve them," searching for a "life apart from [her] husband's identity." After having her San Francisco house retrofitted by Andy, her "balding, red-bearded, former biker, former bad-boy, Hungarian Buddhist contractor/yoga instructor" and also her live-in lover, Tara claims to feel "totally at home."

By making these choices, Tara responds to the promise offered by American mobility and modern feminist idioms. In an article from *Burning Down the House*, K. Srilata discusses the figure of the New Woman, who expresses her agency "in terms of her public visibility, the clothes she wears, and her participation in the discourse of 'free choice' and its corollary, romantic love." Tara's rejection of protected space, her San Francisco image—which consists of old sneakers, shawls, and a "lank, California, retro-Beatnik haircut"—and her sexually adventurous lifestyle, which culminates with her love affair with Andy, the ultimate 'bad boy,' a former biker, seems to situate her as a New Woman. Discussing Andy and Bish's different approaches to love, Tara claims that Bish views love as "the residue of providing for parents and family, contributing to good causes and community charities, . . . and being recognized for hard work and honesty," while love for Andy means "having fun with someone, more fun with that person than with anyone else, over a longer haul." The differing definitions emphasize that Tara chooses between duty, family, and community, represented by Bish, and the appeals of "free choice" and "romantic love" as represented by Andy. Although she claims that she is not a "modern woman," Tara inhabits a world that her more traditional sisters criticize and reject. Even her name signifies her unique status: unlike Padma and Parvati, both named for Hindu goddesses, Tara is named for a goddess in Tibetan Buddhism, a goddess known as a "cheater of death" (Kinsley 167).

Mobility and modernity, however, do not free Tara from her community. Homi Bhabha argues that the "cultural construction of nationness [exists] as a form of social and textual affiliation." Despite her desire to escape the restrictions of her community, Tara remains constrained within it by the gender markers of wife and mother. For example, the detective she consults about Chris Dey's threats cautions her that she is a target because she is the wife of Bish Chatterjee. The detective, "Sgt. Jasbir 'Jack' Singh Sidhu, a tall Sikh with a trimmed beard and a thoroughly American manner and accent," points out to Tara that in "the eyes of Indians," Tara will always be linked to Bish. She cannot escape her identity as the ex-wife of a prominent and extraordinarily wealthy member of the Indian community, and therefore a target for the Indian underworld. Although Tara may aspire to invisibility within the rhetoric of a modern rootless life in San Francisco, she remains firmly embedded within the social and cultural identity assigned by her gender, caste, and economic status. Ideological determinants, those "iron-clad identifiers of region, language, [and] caste," cannot be easily abandoned.

Social and textual affiliations also define Tara's sisters' identities, even though, in Padma's case, she has also fled the family home and reconstructed her life. As the second sister, Parvati, writes, "[Padma] has always had a great capacity for starting over, for wiping her slate very clean." Rosemary George states that "wiping the slate clean" is characteristic of immigrant narratives, that "Forgetting the past, burning or burying it, creates the illusion of providing an escape route into the present that looks ahead rather than behind." Padma complicates Tara's quest for the truth about the past by denying the truth in Chris Dey's story and refusing to discuss the situation. Padma has escaped the gendered identity of daughter, wife, and mother: as a teenager she moved to Britain and then America, never returning to her parents' home; her marriage to a much older man seems a sham, designed to hide the fact that her closest emotional relationships are with homosexual male protectors. She rejects any claims from Chris Dey. Her husband, Harish Mehta, also "blotted out all that was inconvenient or didn't fit." This focus on the future marks these characters as "true American[s]." Padma is a typical Mukherjee heroine, shuttling between identities. Yet even though she speaks with hate about the past, she also tries "to lead a traditional Bengali life in New Jersey." When Tara visits Padma in New York, she initially sees her as possessing "a firm identity resisting all change," but upon closer examination Padma appears "fractured, like cracks under old glaze." The stress of maintaining the appearance of a traditional, Brahmin, female identity in New York leaves Padma concerned only with her reputation, unable to focus upon the emotional and social ramifications of her past actions. Tara uses the metaphor of "fault-lines" to analyze the distinctions in her family, separating the "forward-looking from the traditional and the adaptable from the brittle."

Tara also shuttles between identities. During the New York visit, Tara immediately slips into the role of "chhoto bon," the youngest sister, a role facilitated by the familiar clothing, language, and food of her past. Speaking Bengali with her sister, Tara thinks, "It was wonderful returning to my native language, rediscovering that mocking tone just shy of aggression. I liked the person I became when I spoke it." Later, at a jewelry party, she resolves to be "the good little sister, the pliable Loreto House girl" as she models her sister's sari designs with "an icy, walking-mannequin determination." Identity becomes a role that Tara performs.

Judith Butler's work on identity performance is useful here. Arguing that gender is "performative," Butler claims that "gender is always a doing, though not a doing by a subject who might be said to preexist the deed." Identity, however, is performed within social spaces. Barbara Gabriel notes that Butler's "revisioning constructs gender identity not only as a performative accomplishment but also as one bound by rigorous social sanctions." Claiming to be "too timid to feed [her] Ballygunge Park Road identity into the kitchen Garburetor," Tara defines its multiple layers, many of them determined by place of origin:

> That dusty identity is as fixed as any specimen in a lepidopterist's glass case, confidently labeled by father's religion (Hindu), caste (Brahmin), subcaste (Kulin), mother-tongue (Bengali), place of birth (Calcutta), formative region of ancestral origin (Mishtigunj, East Bengal), education (postgraduate and professional), and social attitudes (conservative).

Despite these definitions, she also claims to be "all things," a person who "thrive[s] on this invisibility." In Tara's polyvalent American society, the "dusty" identifying marks seem irrelevant. Yet, like the Tree Wife from the story, her fate remains tied to her identity.

Drifting between two lives and two identities leaves Tara vulnerable to threats, both as a modern woman who no longer lives behind the protection of fortress walls and as the former wife of a billionaire. In New York, she is chastised for "drifting between two lives" and told that she "mustn't let it go on any longer." Shortly after Chris invades her home, Tara phones Parvati and hears of another form of home invasion, the story of a neighbour who was murdered by thieves within the Bombay apartment complex. One of the thieves was Parvati's housekeeper. Tara's own house is eventually destroyed by a powerful bomb, presumably set by members of the Indian underworld associated with the false Chris Dey, a "chameleon" who assumed the identity of Tata's real nephew. Biddy Martin and Chandra Mohanty point out that "illusions of home are always undercut by the discovery of the hidden demographics of particular places." The demographics of both Tara and Parvati's homes establish the sisters as targets by the marginalized members of their societies. In earlier novels, Mukherjee explores the lives of women marginalized by caste, class, and socio-economic position. Tara and her sisters, on the other hand, are economically and socially privileged. Tara's marriage to Bish, the inventor of a computer bandwidth routing system, makes her "wealthy beyond counting." Acknowledging her privilege, Tara says that in Calcutta, she and her sisters were part of "a blessed, elite minority." Yet she also glosses over certain disparities. Her neighbourhood in San Francisco relies on the services of Palestinians, whose families are, as she says, "uniformly gifted in providing our needs and anticipating our desires." Her community identity remains structured by the social networks of her childhood; when she goes to the police station to investigate Chris Dey's background, she refuses to discuss her situation with a Bengali speaker because he is Muslim. Quoting bell hooks, Rosemary George highlights the concept that "recognizing one's spatial privilege" doesn't always produce "'counter-hegemonic cultural practices.'" The news of the discovery of the real Chris Dey's body is relegated to the last pages of newspapers splashed with headlines about the sensational story of Tara, Bish, and Andy, and the bombing of Tara's house. Despite the mobility of modern life, community networks continue to define Tara and her sisters' identities, keeping certain individuals on the outside . . . .

Source: Katherine Miller, "Mobility and Identity Construction in Bharati Mukherjee's *Desirable Daughters*: The Tree Wife and Her Rootless Namesake," in *Studies in Canadian Literature*, Vol. 29, No. 1, 2004, pp. 65–71.

SOURCES

Abrams, M. H., "Miracle Plays, Morality Plays, and Interludes," in *A Glossary of Literary Terms*, 7th ed., Harcourt Brace College Publishers, 1999, p. 166.

Agarwal, Ramlal, Review of *Desirable Daughters*, in *World Literature Today*, Vol. 77, Nos. 3/4, October–December 2003, pp. 86–87.

Alam, Fakrul, *Bharati Mukherjee*, Twayne Publishers, 1996, pp. 1, 147.

Desai, Kishwar, "Miss Old India," in *India Today*, May 6, 2011, http://indiatoday.intoday.in/story/kishwar-desai-reviews-bharati-mukherjee-book-title-miss-new-india/1/137300.html (accessed May 5, 2013).

Drake, Jennifer, "Looting American Culture: Bharati Mukherjee's Immigrant Narratives," in *Contemporary Literature*, Vol. 40, No. 1, Spring 1999, pp. 60–84.

French, Patrick, *India: A Portrait*, Alfred A. Knopf, 2011, p. 7.

Harmon, William, "Mystery Novel," in *A Handbook to Literature*, 9th ed., Prentice Hall, 2003, p. 325.

"Indian Independence: World War II," British Library website, http://www.bl.uk/reshelp/findhelpregion/asia/india/indianindependence/ww2/ (accessed May 5, 2013).

Kalman, Bobbie, *India: The Culture*, Crabtree Publishing, 2001, p. 7.

Kapur, Akash, "A Parable of the New India," in *New York Times Book Review*, July 3, 2011, p. 8, http://www.nytimes.com/2011/07/03/books/review/book-review-miss-new-india-by-bharati-mukherjee.html (accessed May 5, 2013).

Meer, Ameena, "Bharati Mukherjee," in *BOMB*, No. 29, Fall 1989, pp. 26–27.

Mukherjee, Bharati, *Desirable Daughters*, Hyperion, 2002.

Mukherjee, Ramkrishna, "Caste in Itself, Caste and Class, or Caste in Class," in *Economic and Political Weekly*, Vol. 34, No. 27, July 3–9, 1999, pp. 1759–61.

Review of *Desirable Daughters*, in *Publishers Weekly*, March 25, 2002, http://www.publishersweekly.com/978-0-7868-6598-7 (accessed May 5, 2013).

Rodríguez, Francisco Collado, "Naming Female Multiplicity: An Interview with Bharati Mukherjee," in *Atlantis*, Vol. 17, Nos. 1/2, November 1995, pp. 293–306.

Ruta, Suzanne, "Decoding the Language: Bharati Mukherjee Tells Suzanne Ruta Some of the Stories behind *Desirable Daughters*," in *Women's Review of Books*, Vol. 19, Nos. 10/11, July 2002, p. 13.

———, "Fairytale Princesses," in *Women's Review of Books*, Vol. 19, Nos. 10/11, July 2002, p. 12.

Soderberg, Erin, "Bharati Mukherjee," in *Voices from the Gaps*, University of Minnesota website, April 9, 1999, http://voices.cla.umn.edu/artistpages/mukherjee_bharati.php (accessed May 5, 2013).

Vidovic, Radenka, and David Hansen, "Thrillers—a Guide for Readers' Advisors," Nova Scotia Provincial Library website, https://www.library.ns.ca/files/thrillers_1.pdf (accessed May 5, 2013).

FURTHER READING

Cisneros, Sandra, *Caramelo; or, Puro Cuentro*, Knopf, 2002.

> Cisneros has created a work of fiction that explores the effects of migration on family dynamics. Lala Reyes, a Chicago native who spends her summer in Mexico with her grandparents, looks into her grandmother's past and discovers her heritage.

Dascalu, Cristina Emanuela, *Imaginary Homelands of Writers in Exile: Salman Rushdie, Bharati Mukherjee, and V. S. Naipaul*, Cambria Press, 2007.

> Dascalu analyzes the texts of the three authors, exploring how they react to living apart from their native lands. Dascalu identifies ideas regarding diaspora, migration, and exile within the authors' works.

Henderson, Carol E., *Culture and Customs of India*, Greenwood Press, 2002.

> Henderson's reference book explores the history and evolution of India's different social groups. Students will find it a useful overview of the complex cultural relationships that make up India's society.

Meola, Eric, *India: In Word and Image*, Welcome Enterprises, 2013.

> This collection contains poems, stories, and essays that date from classical India to the present day. Meola's photographs of the country allow students to see and appreciate the diversity of the landscape and people. Mukherjee has provided the introduction.

Rustomji-Kerns, Roshni, ed., *Living in America: Poetry and Fiction by South Asian American Writers*, Westview Press, 1995.

> This anthology showcases short stories and poems by influential authors of South Asian heritage. It includes biographical information and exposes students to a variety of themes and styles.

Venkatraman, Padma, *Climbing the Stairs*, Putnam's Sons, 2008.

> This young-adult novel tells the story of Vidya, a teenage girl in India during World War II. The child of a progressive father, Vidya sees her dreams of an education crumble when he is severely beaten by the British and they are forced to live with her traditionalist grandfather.

SUGGESTED SEARCH TERMS

Bharati Mukherjee

Bharati Mukherjee AND Desirable Daughters

Bharati Mukherjee AND biography

Bharati Mukherjee AND immigration literature

Bharati Mukherjee AND criticism

1940s AND India

India AND history

India AND colonialism

Hindu AND caste

Hindu AND culture

Girl with a Pearl Earring

TRACY CHEVALIER

1999

When Tracy Chevalier was twenty-two years old, she moved to London, England, from the United States, where she had been born, grown up, and gone to college. The experience of leaving her home country and settling in a completely new place undoubtedly had a profound effect on her. In an interview with Felicity Librie for the *Fiction Writers Review*, Chevalier explained that there is an "appealing universality" to stories about some-one out of his element and admits that her personal history has had an influence on her work: "Although I feel much more comfortable in England than I did at the beginning, I'm still aware of being an outsider. I think that gives me an edge."

Chevalier's 1999 novel *Girl with a Pearl Earring* is one of these fish-out-of-water stories. It portrays Griet, a sixteen-year-old girl who becomes house-maid to the great painter Johannes Vermeer and forms a complicated relationship with him while she struggles to get along with his wife, mother-in-law, children, and housekeeper. Through Griet's eyes, the reader sees a fascinating, detailed picture of Delft, Netherlands, in the 1660s and watches Vermeer create one of his masterpieces.

AUTHOR BIOGRAPHY

Chevalier was born in Washington, DC, on October 19, 1962, and lived in the DC area until she graduated from high school. Even as a

Tracy Chevalier (© *Jim Watson | AFP | Getty Images*)

small child, she thought she might become a writer. In her interview with Librie, Chevalier described herself as "one of those readaholics. I wasn't sporty, I was fat, I lay on my bed all day and read." As a teenager, she helped edit the school literary magazine. Although she was writing herself, she had a "typical teenage girl's loss of confidence, and I didn't think that I would be a very good writer, but I could work on other people's stuff."

After graduating from Oberlin College, in Ohio, with a bachelor's degree in English, she moved to London and worked as a reference book editor for several years before returning to school. She earned her master's degree in creative writing from the University of East Anglia. While studying, she began work on her first novel, *The Virgin Blue*, which was published in the United Kingdom in 1997. (It was released in the United States in 2003 after the success of *Girl with a Pearl Earring*.)

Chevalier is best known for *Girl with a Pearl Earring*, which was published in 1999. The novel had huge popular success, selling over four million copies and earning a Barnes & Noble Discover Award. The story was also adapted into a stage play and a major motion picture.

Chevalier's other works include *Falling Angels* (2001), *The Lady and the Unicorn* (2003), *Burning Bright* (2007), and *Remarkable Creatures* (2007). In the spring of 2013, Chevalier's novel *The Last Runaway* was published. It is another historical narrative, about a Quaker woman who becomes involved in the Underground Railroad.

Both *Burning Bright* and *Remarkable Creatures*, like *Girl with a Pearl Earring*, feature famous historical figures: poet William Blake and paleontologist Mary Anning, respectively. (Anning helped discover the first complete ichthyosaur fossil in the early nineteenth century.) Because Chevalier's novels are historical fiction, she relies heavily on research. In addition to research in libraries and online, she tries to immerse herself in the lives of her characters. On her author website, she explains, "For *Girl with a Pearl Earring* I took a painting class to get a feel for paint. I began looking for fossils on beaches where Mary Anning hunted in *Remarkable Creatures*. I am now making quilts by hand like Honor Bright in *The Last Runaway*."

As of 2013, Chevalier lives in a Victorian townhouse in London with her husband and son. She has dual American and British citizenship.

PLOT SUMMARY

1664

Girl with a Pearl Earring is told from the point of view of a first-person narrator: Griet, a poor girl who is forced to move into a stranger's house and work as a maid after an accident makes her father unable to work. Griet's employer is the famous artist Johannes Vermeer, and from the moment they meet, they have a connection. Griet feels very out of place in the house. She is in an unfamiliar neighborhood, and she finds some of the paintings in the house disturbing, especially those with Catholic themes.

Griet is responsible for doing the laundry and helping to look after Vermeer's many children, including mischievous Cornelia, who tries to cause trouble anywhere she can. Griet must also try to get along with the other women in the house, which proves to be no easy task. Vermeer's wife, Catharina, is a spoiled and difficult mistress. Being pregnant only increases her bad mood. Her mother, Maris Thins, is an intelligent woman who holds more real power in the household. The housekeeper, Tanneke, clearly resents

MEDIA ADAPTATIONS

- In 2004, Recorded Books released an unabridged audiobook of *Girl with a Pearl Earring*. The recording is narrated by Ruth Ann Phimister and has a running time of approximately 7½ hours.

- Lions Gate produced a film version of *Girl with a Pearl Earring* in 2004. The movie was directed by Peter Webber and stars Colin Firth as Vermeer and Scarlett Johansson as Griet. *American Artist* praises the film, pointing out that "almost every scene...is framed as if by Vermeer himself, from the natural light streaming through the windows to the subtle expressions on the faces of the actors."

Griet's presence and is suspicious and unfriendly. One of Griet's chores is to fetch meat from the butcher's stall, where she meets Pieter, the butcher's son, who takes an immediate liking to her.

Griet has Sundays off work, and she visits her parents at home or goes to see her brother, Frans, at the factory where he is apprenticed as a tile worker. Frans is unhappy with the work.

One of Griet's chores is to clean in Vermeer's studio, but she must be careful not to disturb anything. Being in the studio allows her to watch his creative process, and she is fascinated. One day Vermeer invites Griet to look into a camera obscura to show her how he uses it to plan his paintings. A camera obscura is a device sometimes used by artists to portray a scene with precise realism. The camera obscura consists of a box with a small hole in one side, which is sometimes fitted with a lens. The light passes through the hole into the box and projects an image of the surrounding scene on a screen. An artist might trace the image or simply examine the details of the scene and the effects of light to recreate them in his artwork.

The plague comes to Delft, and the neighborhood where Griet's family lives is quarantined.

Pieter asks around on Griet's behalf and learns that her younger sister, Agnes, is very ill. The next Sunday, Griet convinces Frans to go to church with her to pray.

Vermeer's patron, van Ruijven, comes to collect the latest painting he has commissioned— a portrait of his wife. Van Ruijven sees Griet and shows an inappropriate interest in her, but Maria Thins distracts him.

The quarantine is lifted, and Griet rushes home to see her family. Agnes has died, and Griet struggles with her grief. Frans "found it hard to visit" and begins to drift away from the family even more.

Catharina gives birth to a baby boy, and the preparations for the birth feast keep Griet and Tanneke more busy than ever, cleaning and cooking. At the party, while Griet is serving wine, van Ruijven sees her and suggests to Vermeer that he paint her.

1665

Griet begins to assist Vermeer more with his work, fetching materials from the apothecary and learning to grind pigments and mix paints. Vermeer begins a new painting of the baker's daughter and sometimes asks Griet to stand in when his model is not present so that he can see the effect of the light and the composition of the picture. Tanneke complains of having to share a room with the new baby's nurse, so she is moved to Griet's little room in the cellar, while Griet starts sleeping in the attic over the studio, immersing her even more in Vermeer's world. Cornelia suspects how involved Griet and her father are becoming, and she steals some of the paint pigment, throwing it onto Griet's apron to get her into trouble. Maria Thins intervenes, and Catharina does not find out that Griet is helping her husband.

Pieter increases his efforts to court Griet. He starts to attend services at the church Griet's family belongs to, and her parents invite him to Sunday dinner.

Vermeer begins a new portrait of van Ruijven's wife, and Griet sometimes stands in when Mrs. van Ruijven cannot be present. Griet changes the drape of the tablecloth that Vermeer has placed on the table where Mrs. van Ruijven will pose, and Vermeer approves. Catharina is unhappy that her jewels and jewelry box are being used for the painting and kept in the studio.

Cornelia steals the comb that Griet keeps hidden in her things. It belonged to Griet's grandmother. Cornelia is beaten, but Maria Thins warns Griet to be more careful; as a maid, Griet's position in the household is not secure. She takes the comb home to her mother. After this theft, Tanneke is kinder to Griet, Maria Thins seems to have more respect for her, and Catharina avoids her. Vermeer treats her no differently, but Griet wonders why she must go to such lengths to keep it a secret that she is helping him. She wishes that he would simply tell his wife the truth.

Van Ruijven and his wife come to collect the newest portrait, and again van Ruijven suggests the idea of a painting of Griet. Pieter later confirms that town gossip already says Griet is posing for Vermeer with van Ruijven. The idea makes Griet uncomfortable, but Vermeer finally gives in to his patron's request and plans to paint a portrait of Griet.

1666

While Vermeer begins to work on Griet's portrait, she is still responsible for household chores and helping to mix the paints. It takes a while to figure out how the portrait will look. Griet does not want to be painted doing the work of a maid. She also does not want to remove her cap and have her portrait taken with her head uncovered. Vermeer directs her to use some spare fabric and create a sort of head scarf.

Catharina is pregnant again. She is clumsy and self-absorbed. Griet worries that, even distracted by her pregnancy, Catharina will discover the painting.

Vermeer is dissatisfied with the progress of the painting. He knows that van Ruijven will be pleased, but he believes that it is not yet perfect. He decides that what the painting needs is the subtle glow of Catharina's pearl earrings. Griet resists wearing them, knowing it will ruin her if Catharina finds out. But finally she gives in and pierces her left ear.

Van Ruijven makes unwelcome advances, and Pieter comes to the house unannounced so that Griet has to make excuses and chase him away. Griet learns that her brother has run away from his apprenticeship.

When Griet finally sits for her portrait, Vermeer pushes the wire of the earring through her recently pierced earlobe, causing her pain. He insists that she must pierce the other ear and

wear both earrings, even if her right ear will not be visible in the painting, so she pierces her other earlobe as well.

Cornelia leads her mother to the studio, and Catharina sees the portrait of Griet. She is angry that Griet wore her earrings without her permission and jealous because her husband has never painted her portrait. She tries to damage the painting with a knife. Vermeer stops her, but he says nothing to defend Griet. Griet walks out of the house without another word.

1676

The final section of the book takes place more than ten years later. Griet is now married to Pieter, and they have two sons together. Griet works beside Pieter in the butcher stall and has found a kind of happiness in the way her life has turned out. The Vermeers buy their meat from another butcher from the moment Griet begins working beside Pieter, but Maertge, Vermeer's oldest child, sometimes sneaks away to talk to Griet, keeping her up to date about the family's news.

Tanneke comes into the stall one day, surprising Griet. She summons Griet to the Vermeer house. Vermeer has died, and he has left the pearl earrings to Griet. Catharina is angry and hurt, and Griet feels sorry for her. Griet sells the pearls and gives Pieter some of the money to repay the debt that the Vermeers owed him.

CHARACTERS

Agnes

Agnes is Griet's sister. She is about ten years old at the start of the novel. The sisters are clearly very fond of each other, because they have a hard time saying good-bye when Griet leaves to live with the Vermeers. When Griet hears that Agnes might be sick, she asks Pieter for help in getting information, and after that she feels like she owes him. This sets up the pattern of their relationship as a series of bargains or trades. When Agnes dies of the plague, Griet and her parents are heartbroken.

Frans (Griet's Brother)

Frans is Griet's brother. He no longer lives with the family because he is an apprentice at a Delft-ware tile factory. It is hard work, and he does not seem happy there. Griet tries to keep him as part of the family, but by the end of the story he has disappeared, abandoning his apprenticeship and his family.

Frans (Griet's Son)
One of Griet's sons is also named Frans. Griet names him after her brother, even though he has run away. This shows that family is important to Griet.

Griet
Griet is the first-person narrator of the novel. She is sixteen years old at the beginning of the story. Her parents arrange for her to work as a maid in the house of the artist Johannes Vermeer because they are having financial trouble. Vermeer is immediately intrigued by Griet because he notices the way she arranges the vegetables she is chopping for soup. He sees that she has an artistic eye for color. She in turn is fascinated by her master, by his paintings and his artistic process, and she risks the anger and jealousy of his wife to help him in his work and to learn about mixing paints. Griet always wears a cap or a head scarf to hide her hair, which is a metaphor for the way she hides the part of her self that is passionate and uncontrolled. She is afraid of this part of herself. In the end, Griet does what is expected of her and marries Pieter, the butcher's son, which ensures that her family will always have something to eat.

Griet's Mother
Griet's mother is a proud woman. She knows that the family cannot continue the way things have been going, but she is unwilling to take charity. She does her best to keep her family together and fed after her husband is blinded in an accident and can no longer work, but she does not have many options. She arranges for Griet to work as a maid and then encourages a marriage between Griet and the butcher's son, which will give the entire family some level of security. She does not like the arrangements she has to make for her daughter: when she tells Griet she is to leave the family home and work as a maid, Griet describes her mother as "hunching her shoulders as if against a winter chill, though it was summer and the kitchen was hot."

Jan (Griet's Father)
Jan is Griet's father. Before the story begins, he was blinded in an accident at the factory where he painted designs on Delftware tiles, so he cannot support the family anymore. He seems like a kind father. He tells Griet that he is sorry she has to work as a maid, and he listens to her attentively when she comes home for visits.

Jan (Griet's Son)
One of Griet's sons is named Jan, after Griet's father. Griet is affectionate to her children and clearly has found some degree of contentment with her life by the end of the story. Griet says that his birth "made me turn inward to my family," which made her fate "easier to accept."

Pieter the Father
Pieter the Father is the butcher to whom Griet is sent to buy meat for Vermeer's family. At first, Griet does not like him because he wears a blood-stained apron, whereas her family's butcher always wore a clean apron when dealing with customers. Griet earns his respect on the first visit to his stall when she refuses to accept meat that is not fresh. He sees that his son likes Griet and seems to encourage the match.

Pieter the Son
Pieter is the son of Pieter the butcher, from whom the Vermeer family buy their meat. From the first time he meets Griet, he is attracted to her. While he genuinely likes her, he knows the situation of her family and uses it to his advantage in courting her. By the end of the book, Pieter and Griet are married, and they seem to have a fairly strong marriage. Pieter does not press Griet for information about her time with Vermeer, although he knew something was going on and was jealous.

Tanneke
Tanneke is Vermeer's housekeeper, so she becomes Griet's boss, in effect, once Griet comes to work as a maid in the house. Tanneke is a difficult person to befriend. She seems suspicious and resentful of Griet from the very beginning. After a while, Griet is able to thaw Tanneke out a little, but in the end, Tanneke is loyal to her mistress, Catharina, and blames Griet for the baby that Catharina lost.

Maria Thins
Maria Thins is Vermeer's mother-in-law. She is an intelligent woman, and she sees that her daughter is petty and jealous. Maria Thins tries to protect Griet when van Ruijven starts to take an inappropriate interest in her. Understanding that Vermeer is a great artist and cannot be

rushed, Maria Thins disagrees with her daughter's urging him to work faster so that he can sell more paintings and earn more money.

Anton van Leeuwenhook

Anton van Leeuwenhook is a real historical figure. He was a scientist who worked with lenses in his research into microbiology and made improvements to the microscope. It seems likely that van Leeuwenhook and Vermeer were acquainted, and he was indeed executor of Vermeer's will, but there is no actual evidence to prove that van Leeuwenhook gave Vermeer a camera obscura.

Mrs. van Ruijven

Mrs. van Ruijven is the wife of Vermeer's patron. She sits for several portraits that van Ruijven commissions Vermeer to paint.

Pieter van Ruijven

The character of Pieter van Ruijven is also based on a real person. Van Ruijven was Vermeer's patron and commissioned many paintings from him. In the book, van Ruijven preys on young women, and Maria Thins tries to protect Griet from him.

Aleydis Vermeer

Aleydis is Vermeer's fourth child. She is about four years old at the beginning of the story.

Beatrix Vermeer

Beatrix is Vermeer's seventh child. She is born after the main action of the book, and Griet meets her when she returns to the house after Vermeer's death. There is another girl born after her, but her name is not revealed.

Catharina Vermeer

Catharina is Vermeer's wife and, in name at least, the mistress of the house. In truth, Maria Thins, Catharina's mother, keeps control of much that goes on in the household. Catharina is a jealous and petty woman. She does not like that Griet is allowed to enter Vermeer's studio when she herself is forbidden to do so.

Cornelia Vermeer

Cornelia is Vermeer's third child. She is a troublemaker, doing her best to make Griet angry and to get her into trouble. On her first day in the Vermeer household, Griet slaps Cornelia when she laughs at an order, hoping it will teach her a lesson, but it seems to turn Cornelia against her even more.

Franciscus Vermeer

Franciscus is Vermeer's sixth child. He is born during the course of the story. When Catharina is pregnant with Franciscus, she is more unpleasant and self-centered than ever, but after his birth she is pleased with herself, and the family throws a large party.

Johannes Vermeer

The character Johannes Vermeer is based on the historical figure, although not much is known about the real-life Vermeer. The character is a generally good man. He is an affectionate father, though because of social roles of the day he does not have all that much to do with his children. He is tolerant of his wife's bad temper. When Vermeer first meets Griet, he is drawn to her because of her vegetable color wheel—he sees that she has an artist's eye and recruits her to help with his work.

Johannes Vermeer (the Son)

Johannes is Vermeer's fifth child. He is the youngest in the family at the start of the book (though more children are born later). As an infant not yet able to walk, Johannes is cared for by his older sisters.

Lisbeth Vermeer

Lisbeth is Vermeer's second child.

Maertge Vermeer

Maertge is Vermeer's oldest child. Perhaps because she is close to the age of Griet's sister, Agnes, Griet takes to her, and they become friends. Maertge is responsible and tends to her younger siblings. Even after Griet leaves the house, Maertge visits her at Pieter's butcher stall and keeps in touch.

THEMES

Family

The theme of family is central to *Girl with a Pearl Earring*. The entire plot turns on the fact that Griet must leave her family and go to work in the house of another family. Griet does not like leaving her family; everything about her new life, from meeting new people to having to shop at a new butcher stall, is more difficult for her

TOPICS FOR FURTHER STUDY

- Research Vermeer's paintings using both traditional and online resources. Put together a collection of paintings that represent Vermeer's life's work, including still lifes, portraits, and landscapes. Create a PowerPoint presentation of the images, and set it to period music. Share the presentation with your class, including brief commentary in which you explain why you selected those particular paintings.

- Choose an important figure from the seventeenth century—another artist, a musician, or a significant figure in politics or exploration. Research the life of your chosen person, and then write a short story as Chevalier wrote *Girl with a Pearl Earring*, imagining what happens around an important event in the person's life.

- In her young-adult novel *Buddha Boy* (2003), Kathe Koja tells the story of the friendship between average kid Justin and a wildly talented, artistic boy called "Buddha Boy" because of his interest in Buddhism. (His Buddhist teacher names him Jinsen.) Although this novel takes place in a very different time and place than *Girl with a Pearl Earring*, both stories deal with issues of social hierarchies, and each book develops a relationship between dissimilar characters. Read *Buddha Boy*, and write an essay comparing the thoughts and reactions of Griet, as she gets to know Vermeer, and Justin, as he learns more about Jinsen.

- In *Burning Bright* (2007), Chevalier creates a fictional story about another historical figure, poet William Blake. Read the novel and compare the relationship of Jem and Blake with that of Griet and Vermeer. Write a scene where Jem meets Griet, and perform the dialogue with one of your classmates.

because she feels isolated from her home. She finds it hard to say good-bye to her sister, and she often visits her brother on her day off from work, trying to keep him connected to the family though he must live where he is apprenticed.

Griet has a tile that she tucks away as a keepsake. It was painted by her father and is decorated with a picture of Griet and her brother. When the troublemaker Cornelia breaks the tile, Griet is unhappy because the broken tile only reinforces her fear that her family is drifting apart.

Ultimately Griet's belief in the importance of family forces her into a life she most likely would not have chosen for herself. She marries Pieter in order to protect and provide for her parents. However, it is also Griet's reliance on family that helps her. Once she accepts her fate, she manages to find contentment. She knows she has a purpose, and she loves her children. The fact that Griet names her sons after her father and brother, even though her brother has disappeared, also highlights the importance of family in Griet's mind.

Control

Simply looking at one of Vermeer's paintings gives a hint about one of the major themes of *Girl with a Pearl Earring*: control. Vermeer's paintings are carefully composed, masterfully executed works of art. It is impossible to imagine, seeing the attention to detail that plainly went into these works, that Vermeer worked in a slapdash manner. He must have been meticulous and controlled, much as Chevalier portrays him: carefully considering where each item would be placed in a still life and trying various backgrounds and costumes for a portrait, not settling for anything less than perfection.

Griet also illustrates the theme of control. She always wears a cap to cover her hair, and even when Vermeer asks her to remove it when she sits for the painting, the idea makes her uncomfortable. Griet's hair is wild and uncontrolled. She wears a cap to tame it and to hide that part of herself from the world. At one point, Pieter says to Griet, "I never know what you're thinking.... You're so calm and quiet.... But there are things inside you. I see them sometimes, hiding in your eyes." Her immediate response is to touch her cap, "checking with my fingers for stray hairs" because she does not want Pieter to see that side of her.

When Vermeer interrupts Griet while she is preparing herself for a sitting, he sees her hair and

The Vermeer painting, The Girl with the Wine Glass, *displays the same treatments of light and composition that are important in* Girl with a Pearl Earring. *(© Oleg Golovnev | Shutterstock.com)*

cannot seem to take his eyes off her. After he has seen her hair, he adds the tiniest glimpse of it in the painting—just a shadow that hints at its dark, rich color. This small addition to the painting brings to mind the earlier scene where Griet changes the drape of the tablecloth in a carefully arranged scene for a portrait of van Ruijven's wife. Vermeer does not get angry at Griet for making the change but asks her why she did it. "There needs to be some disorder in the scene," Griet explains. Like the disarranged tablecloth, the glimpse of a strand of hair and the loose end of the fabric from the head wrap provide a bit of messiness and realism to the painting. The contrast provided by these hints of disorder highlights the controlled composition of the rest of the painting, just as the knowledge of Griet's wild hair and the passionate nature it represents makes her usual calm composure and obedience more remarkable.

STYLE

First-Person Narrator

Girl with a Pearl Earring is told from the perspective of a first-person narrator. This means that the narrator is one of the characters in the action of the story and that she refers to herself as "I." This is in contrast to an omniscient narrator, who can see everything that happens in the story and has knowledge of the thoughts and motivations of all of the characters.

Because the story is told by Griet, the reader only sees the action from her point of view. She cannot know what other characters are thinking or why they act the way they do, and she cannot know about events that occur when she is not present. Also, what she experiences is affected by her emotions. She might misunderstand or misrepresent what happens. Therefore, the reader must be constantly aware while reading that she might not be a completely reliable source of information.

Figurative Language

Figurative language is a tool used by writers to create a certain mood, portray how a character feels, or give information about a situation without explicit explanation. Chevalier's use of figurative language, such as similes, metaphors, and imagery, creates more interesting and graceful prose and prompts an emotional response in the reader. For example, Chevalier could have written that when Vermeer smiled, it made Griet feel happy and energetic. However, Chevalier uses a simile: "When he smiled his face was like an open window." A *simile* is a figure of speech that compares two different things with a linking word such as *like* or *as*. This sentence brings to the reader's mind the image of sunlight streaming in, or perhaps the sensation of a refreshing spring breeze chasing away darkness and stale air. Other similes occur in the very first scene of the novel, drawing direct comparisons between the characters and household furnishings. When Griet's future employers first visit her home, Catharina's voice is described as being as "bright as polished brass," and Vermeer's is "low and dark like the wood of the table." Just a couple of lines later, Chevalier employs a metaphor: "My mother's voice—a cooking pot, a flagon—approached from the front room." A *metaphor* differs from a simile in that the two things are described in terms of an identity between them rather than a comparison.

Such references to domestic furnishings, incorporated into figurative language of one kind or another, recur frequently in the novel, as do references to domestic chores. These references come naturally to Griet when she wants to explain or illustrate something. One example is that of needlework. Griet describes how, when she was growing up and met new people, she still felt at home because family and neighbors were always present, and she describes this process with a simile: "the new was woven in with the old, like the darning in a sock." The reference to needlework is implied later in a similar context when Griet explains why she tried to convince her brother to visit home with her; she was "hoping to knit our family together again."

Chevalier also uses some striking imagery. *Imagery* in literature is the use of descriptive language to give the reader a mental image that evokes a specific response. When Griet hears the Vermeers talking in the other room, she thinks, "They were the kind of voices we heard rarely in our house. I could hear rich carpets in their voices, books and pearls and fur." Obviously it is not possible for Griet to literally hear these objects in a person's voice, but the luxurious images make it clear that the people whose voices she is overhearing are wealthy and possibly more educated than she is herself. In contrast, in the metaphor quoted above, Griet's mother's voice is identified with common, plain things that could be found in any home. This use of figurative language highlights the social and economic difference between Griet's family and Vermeer's, which is an important theme of the book.

Chevalier uses some images repeatedly to reinforce their meaning. There are numerous recurring water images, for instance. Griet says that hearing Vermeer's "voice made me feel as if I were walking along the edge of a canal and unsure of my steps." When Pieter worries about Griet's family during the time of plague, she explains that "his concern made me feel as if I had just stepped off a boat and the ground was wobbling under my feet." Also, as Cornelia stands at the threshold of her father's studio, knowing that she is forbidden to enter, Griet describes her as "looking as if she were standing at the edge of a puddle and tempted to step in it." The unpredictable, uneven movement of water reflects the uncertainty of the characters in these situations.

Chevalier also employs a prominent symbol, in the form of a domestic object. A *symbol* is an object that in addition to its literal meaning signifies something else. It has a significance wider than itself. The symbol is the Delftware tile that Griet treasures. Delftware tiles served both functional and decorative purposes in homes at the time, surrounding fireplaces and lining walls, and this particular tile becomes even more important to Griet because her father painted it, portraying her and her brother. When Cornelia breaks the tile, it brings home to Griet the feeling that her family is breaking up and that her home will never be the same. The tile is therefore a symbol of the comforts of home and family.

HISTORICAL CONTEXT

Delftware

In *Girl with a Pearl Earring*, Griet's father is an artist who paints images on ceramic, a product that is known today as "Delftware." Although the name is sometimes applied to similar ceramics made in England and Ireland, true Delftware comes only from Delft, the city in the Netherlands that gave it its name.

Until the late sixteenth century, only the very wealthy could afford any kind of ceramics for their homes. In the early seventeenth century, Chinese porcelain became popular, and local craftsmen began to imitate the style. Some of the earliest attempts at imitation were made in Delft from the middle of the seventeenth century, and the city remained an important producer of ceramics for the next two hundred years. Soon, artists began to use Dutch scenes rather than copying Asian themes.

Delftware is made from a mixture of clay that is fired in a kiln and painted with a tin glaze. Artists then add the traditional images by hand. Although the pictures do not have to be in blue, this color has become traditional and most popular. At the end of the eighteenth century, Delftware was starting to be produced in greater numbers. Quality began to decline, and along with it, the popularity of Delftware faded. In the late nineteenth century, Joost Thooft took over at De Pordeleyne Fles, the only remaining factory producing Delftware, and turned the business around. Delftware once again became popular with collectors, and it remains so now. Today, one can tour factories where Delftware is still made, and tourists can paint their own pieces, mimicking the Delftware style.

COMPARE
&
CONTRAST

- **1660s:** An outbreak of the black death, or the bubonic plague, in northern Europe kills thousands of people, although the death rates do not come close to those in the mid-1300s, when approximately 35 percent of the population died. Those infected with the plague usually die within four days of showing the first symptoms of illness, and the disease is highly infectious. Although there are laws about quarantines, they do little to stem the contagion.

  1990s: The plague is no longer a major threat, although there are several deaths from the disease in the United States during the 1990s. In 1994, fourteen cases are reported in the United States. Worldwide, in 1997 there are 5,419 cases of bubonic plague, septicaemic plague, and pneumonic plague.

  Today: Modern cases of plague are rare, although there are some infections in the western United States and more commonly in parts of Asia and Africa. The bacteria that causes the plague is eliminated by antibiotics, but without treatment an infection can cause serious illness or death.

- **1660s:** The Netherlands contributes to global exploration and colonization in the late sixteenth and early seventeenth centuries. Dutch captain Willem Jansz is the first European to catch sight of Australia, and Henry Hudson's explorations of the Hudson River in 1609 lead to the formation of the Dutch West India Company and the foundation of the New Netherland colony in 1624. It is trade, however, that makes the Netherlands a major world power. Dutch merchants are famous for being practical and levelheaded, and in general the Dutch venture into the New World only when the potential profit is worth the risk. They prefer to make their fortunes transporting the goods of others rather than make discoveries simply for the glory.

  1990s: The Dutch economy is among the strongest in Europe, largely because of the continued success of Dutch merchants. The Netherlands has a healthy trade surplus,

meaning that the value of the country's exports exceeds the cost of what it must import. There is also income from the country's serving as an important transportation hub for Europe and globally.

Today: Although the Dutch economy suffers slightly during the financial crisis of 2009, there is quick recovery. Unemployment never rises above 7 percent, and the Netherlands remains a world economic power.

- **1660s:** The Netherlands has a long tradition of religious toleration. In the late sixteenth and early seventeenth centuries, Calvinism (the central idea of which is predestination, or the belief that God arbitrarily marks some for salvation and others for damnation) becomes the predominant religion among the Dutch. Although other religions are still tolerated, only Calvinist ministers are supported by the state, and non-Calvinists cannot hold public office. Religious minorities throughout Europe immigrate to the Netherlands for religious freedom. By 1650, approximately one-third of the population is Catholic, and Amsterdam has a sizable Jewish community.

  1990s: The Netherlands has no official religion. Throughout the twentieth century, religion has become less influential in political matters. In the 1980s and 1990s, Dutch policies become very liberal regarding many issues that are often influenced by people's religious beliefs, such as abortion and euthanasia. In fact, Dutch liberal views become so widespread that the Netherlands becomes the first country to legalize same-sex marriage in 2001.

  Today: The Dutch still enjoy complete religious freedom. Almost a third of the Dutch population is Roman Catholic, and approximately 20 percent is Protestant (mostly Dutch Reformed and Calvinist). About 42 percent of Dutch citizens do not affiliate themselves with any organized religion. The Netherlands has become one of the most secularized countries in the world.

The Golden Age of Dutch Painting

Because Vermeer and his art are of central importance to *Girl with a Pearl Earring*, it is useful to have an idea of Vermeer's place in Dutch art and the influence that Dutch painters had on European art in general. Perhaps the first important contribution of Dutch artists was the expert use of oil paints. Although the medium was used in northern Europe as early as the twelfth century, it was the masterful work of fifteenth-century Dutch artists, such as Jan van Eyck and Rogier van der Weyden, that made the artistic world take notice. Their paintings showed the versatility of oil paint in creating works of startling realism and vibrant color. Van Eyck and van der Weyden also contributed to the changes in subject matter. Although many artists still concentrated on religious scenes, more and more painters chose scenes from day-to-day life, still lifes, and landscapes. These secular subjects became commonplace by the time Vermeer was painting in the seventeenth century.

Perhaps the best-known artist of Holland's golden age is Rembrandt van Rijn, who began using only his given name in imitation of Renaissance masters like Michelangelo. Rembrandt's work shows strict realism. He was an artist who painted from direct observation— meaning he painted exactly what he saw. He was hugely successful during his lifetime. He had several pupils and assistants, owned an extensive art collection, and lived as a wealthy gentleman.

Frans Hals, though less well known than Rembrandt, is another great Dutch artist of the period. Many later realist and impressionist painters cited Hals as an influence because of his bold brushwork. Hals's style is notable in that his portraits captured his subjects' distinct personalities. To a modern viewer, this might seem an obvious requirement for a portrait, but at the time, it was assumed that a portrait would portray the sitter as a representative of a certain class: the person's social position would be clear from his or her clothing and setting. In this context, Hals's highly individualized portraits were almost revolutionary.

Although now Vermeer is considered to be one of the Dutch masters along with Hals and Rembrandt, he was not very well known until the late nineteenth century. He was not nearly as successful as Hals and Rembrandt and

Modern Delft retains many aspects of its historic past. (© alysta | Shutterstock.com)

produced a relatively small number of paintings—perhaps forty-five altogether (and several of them have been lost), compared to some artists who created hundreds of pictures. Also, no one knows who taught Vermeer, and he himself seemed not to have had any students, which might have lessened his influence in the art world.

As portrayed in Chevalier's novel, Vermeer did indeed experiment with the camera obscura, but its importance to his work has likely been exaggerated in popular culture. Vermeer's paintings show his interest in the effects of light and the importance of balanced composition. In the technical aspects of Vermeer's work, artists see great talent and careful attention to detail.

CRITICAL OVERVIEW

Girl with a Pearl Earring enjoyed an overwhelmingly positive reaction from readers. After an initial printing of 17,500 copies, the book sold so well that eventually over four million copies were sold. The book's popularity spawned a movie adaptation that earned three Academy Award nominations. Some of the reviews the book received, however, do not reflect this popular success.

Barbara Hoffert, in her review of *Girl with a Pearl Earring* in *Library Journal*, comments that Chevalier writes a bit too "plainly" and that although "the artist's coaxing of the reluctant sitter is delicately rendered . . . otherwise this text fails to ignite." Ron Charles, in his *Christian Science Monitor* review, believes that Chevalier goes too far in the opposite direction: her style is too "self-consciously rich. Her poor, illiterate narrator sounds at times as though she's earned a master's degree in creative writing, as the author has." A *Publishers Weekly* review of *Girl with a Pearl Earring* also criticizes Chevalier's use of some plot "devices" that "threaten to rob the narrative of its credibility," such as the great artist Vermeer accepting the suggestions of his housemaid regarding how to improve his painting.

In contrast, other critics admire Chevalier's style. For example, Deborah Carter in *Bookmarks* describes *Girl with a Pearl Earring* as "beautifully written" and calls the book "historical fiction at its finest." A review in *Atlantic Monthly* also praises the novel as "a fine story, which is exceptionally well told," and points out Griet as "a memorable character."

In spite of the widely varied opinions about Chevalier's writing, there seemed to be agreement about her ability to bring life to her historical setting. In *Publishers Weekly*, the reviewer writes that the novel "presents a marvelously textured picture of 17th-century Delft." The *Atlantic Monthly* review commends Chevalier's talent in "creating the feel of a society with sharp divisions of status and creed." Sheila Barry, in *School Library Journal*, also praises Chevalier's attention to detail, explaining that "everyday chores are described so completely that readers will feel Griet's raw, chapped hands."

Perhaps the review of the novel in *Publishers Weekly* best sums up the reaction to *Girl with a Pearl Earring*: in spite of its flaws, "this is a completely absorbing story with enough historical authenticity and artistic intuition to mark Chevalier as a talented newcomer to the literary scene."

CRITICISM

Kristen Sarlin Greenberg

Greenberg is a freelance writer and editor with a background in literature and philosophy. In the following essay, she examines Griet's relationships with Vermeer and Pieter in Girl with a Pearl Earring *from a feminist perspective.*

In *Girl with a Pearl Earring*, Tracy Chevalier sets up a juxtaposition between two very different relationships. First, there is Pieter's interest in Griet—not exactly an arranged marriage, but one that is encouraged by her mother and economically convenient for her family. Then, there is Griet's complicated relationship with Vermeer, which is part master and servant, part master and apprentice, and part romance. At first glance, Griet's courtship with Pieter seems to be the more superficial connection, but examining the novel's events through the perspective of feminist literary criticism reveals that the situation is more complicated than it appears.

When Griet and Vermeer first meet, the connection between them is instantaneous. She is cutting up vegetables for soup and has arranged them by color like slices in a pie. Vermeer notices her arrangement and asks her about it. He sees immediately that she understands color like an artist. They have a true meeting of the minds. She is fascinated by his creative process, watching him set up the tableau for each painting and eager to learn how to help him by grinding pigments and mixing paints. He in turn seems to revel in her interest in his work. He listens to her opinions and says in surprise when she rearranges the tablecloth, "I had not thought I would learn something from a maid." It seems unlikely that a housemaid would understand more about the composition of paintings than Vermeer, who by this point in his life was an experienced painter, but the effect for the story is what is important: they learn from each other, share ideas, and inspire each other.

Griet gives Vermeer what his wife, Catharina, cannot give him. She does not appreciate his work in the slightest. She only wants him to work more quickly so that he can sell more paintings to maintain the lifestyle she wants, with furs and jewels. Even Vermeer's mother-in-law understands that for him to rush his work would ruin him—his paintings are remarkable because of the painstaking care he puts into them. Catharina, however, does not even understand enough

WHAT DO I READ NEXT?

- In *Vermeer and the Delft School* (2001), Walter Liedtke, Michiel C. Plomp, and Axel Ruger outline the history of Delft from the thirteenth century through Vermeer's time. The book includes hundreds of photos displaying the rich accomplishments of the artists and craftsmen of the city, including paintings, statues, architecture, Delftware, glassware, and sketches. The particular focus on the city in the seventeenth century makes the book especially interesting to readers of *Girl with a Pearl Earring*.

- Charlotte Brontë's 1847 classic *Jane Eyre* shares many themes with *Girl with a Pearl Earring*. Much like Griet, Brontë's heroine comes to an unfamiliar household as a servant and develops a complex relationship with the master of the house.

- *Vermeer: A View of Delft* (2002), by Anthony Bailey, is a meticulously researched biography of the artist. Bailey's well-written book recreates both Vermeer's professional and domestic lives and analyzes the elements of his artistic genius.

- Ching Yeung Russell's *Child Bride* (1999) tells the story of Ying, a girl who runs away when her family tries to force her into an arranged marriage. Like *Girl with a Pearl Earring*, Russell's novel recreates the atmosphere and culture of another time and place with well-researched detail and portrays a young heroine struggling to find her place in a restrictive society.

- *The Last Runaway* (2013), Chevalier's most recent historical novel, takes place in 1850. The book follows the journey of Honor Bright, a young Quaker woman, as she leaves England to find a new life in America. Honor settles in Ohio and is drawn into helping runaway slaves through the Underground Railroad.

- *Book of a Thousand Days* (2007), a young-adult fantasy novel by Shannon Hale, describes the imprisonment of Lady Saren, who is being punished for refusing to submit to an arranged marriage. The story is told from the perspective of Saren's maid, Dashti. Where Saren is fearful and reliant on her maid, Dashti is practical and optimistic.

---

about art to grasp her husband's genius. Vermeer turns to Griet to find someone who truly sees his work for what it is. They have a genuine connection.

In contrast to this immediate rapport between Griet and Vermeer is the relationship Griet has with Pieter. The two young people are clearly attracted to one another, for she "could not keep from blushing" when "his eyes came to rest on me like a butterfly on a flower." Pieter wants to kiss Griet and be close to her, but the physical intimacy they share seems less significant than the meaningful intellectual connection Griet shares with Vermeer. Indeed, sometimes when Griet is with Pieter, she has to remember herself in Vermeer's studio to feel "something like pleasure."

Adding to the mixed feelings Griet has about Pieter is the fact of his profession. Because his father is a butcher, and Pieter is in line to inherit his father's business, he is quite a catch, in economic terms. Griet's father was blinded in an accident in the tile factory where he used to work and therefore can no longer support his family. Griet's mother arranged for her to work as a maid because of the family's financial worries, and marrying Pieter would ensure that they always have plenty of food. Although Griet does seem to have some attraction to and fondness for Pieter, she feels forced into the marriage, which is, in a sense, a financial transaction. Later, after they are married, Pieter teases her about the debt the Vermeers never repaid to the butcher stall after Griet left their house in

> THE SETTING OF *GIRL WITH A PEARL EARRING*,
> IN A TIME LONG AGO WHEN MEN HAD MORE
> POWER AND INDEPENDENCE THAN WOMEN, IS IDEAL
> FOR A FEMINIST READING OF THE STORY, LOOKING AT
> HOW THE FEMALE CHARACTERS ARE LIMITED
> BY SOCIAL RESTRAINTS THAT OPPRESS THEM
> PSYCHOLOGICALLY, SOCIALLY, AND FINANCIALLY."

disgrace and began working beside Pieter. He never asked them for the money and says, "It's the price I have paid for you." He is joking, but the truth remains that Griet agreed to marry Pieter because it would provide herself and her family with financial security.

It might seem that Griet's relationship with Vermeer is more attractive to her than being sold into marriage with Pieter. However, looking more closely at what happens from the perspective of feminist literary criticism puts a different spin on things. Feminist criticism examines the ways in which our culture and society have been dominated by men. The setting of *Girl with a Pearl Earring*, in a time long ago when men had more power and independence than women, is ideal for a feminist reading of the story, looking at how the female characters are limited by social restraints that oppress them psychologically, socially, and financially. Women were not free to make their own choices and instead had to bow to the wishes of their parents or their husbands. There were very few professions in which women could earn their keep, making them reliant on the men in their lives to furnish their basic needs, and women were generally not allowed the same level of education as men.

If one looks at Griet's situation from a feminist point of view, one sees that her relationship with Vermeer, so immediate and seemingly romantic, is at heart grossly unequal. Griet is a poor girl, a servant without any power. She takes on all of the risk for their clandestine meetings, hurrying to finish all of her household chores and still have time to mix paints for him. Griet knows that Catharina will be furious, and even Maria Thins, who acts to keep Griet from van Ruijven's

advances, would not be able to protect her if Catharina were to learn the extent of Griet's relationship with Vermeer. She would be fired, turned out into the street in disgrace, and no longer be able to earn money to feed her family.

Vermeer, however, risks only his wife's anger. He has all of the power in his relationship with Griet and bears none of the responsibility. The lack of equality in their relationship is highlighted by the fact that Griet does not refer to him by name. She calls him "Master"— or even just "him" or "he," as if there is no other man who matters. The closer Griet becomes to Vermeer, the less power she has: when she moves her things to the attic room and begins sleeping there, Catharina still holds the key to the door, and Griet "did not like being locked in at night."

Pieter sees the unfairness inherent in Griet's relationship with Vermeer, and though he is prompted in part by jealousy, he does try to warn her. "You are but a maid. . . . You have little power over what happens to you," he says. "If your master did want to paint a picture of you and van Ruijven, do you really think you could say no?" Griet cannot argue with Pieter, because she sees that he is right. She is upset with him though, and she "tartly" responds, "Thank you for reminding me of how helpless I am." Pieter continues, assuring Griet that she would not be so helpless if she married him: "We would run our own business, earn our own money, rule our own lives." Griet still resists, and if she were to marry Pieter, by the traditions of the day she would still have to look to him as her lord and master, but by saying this, Pieter is promising to make her as much his equal partner as possible. Marrying Pieter would indeed give Griet more independence and control than if she were to stay in her imbalanced relationship with Vermeer.

After this confrontation with Pieter, Griet starts to understand that he is right. When Vermeer enters the room while Griet is preparing to model for the painting, he sees her hair, which she has tried to keep hidden from him. Griet feels that once "he had seen me revealed, I no longer felt I had something precious to hide and keep to myself." He steals that secret from her and includes a hint of her hair in his painting without her permission. Pieter, however, allows Griet to keep some of her secrets: when he sees on their wedding night that her ears have been pierced, he says nothing. The truth of her unequal relationship with Vermeer is driven home for Griet on

Delft is famous for blue-painted china. (© r.martens | Shutterstock.com)

the day when Catharina finally sees the portrait and forces Griet to leave the house. Griet looks at Vermeer, knowing "it was for the last time." She says, "In his eyes I thought I could see regret," but he does nothing. He is unwilling to take any risks or even put forth a minimal effort to help her.

A feminist reading of the book also forces the reader to feel something for perhaps the least sympathetic character in the book: Catharina. In a time of arranged marriage, Catharina and Vermeer are a perfect example of a couple who are not well matched. As discussed above, she does not understand him, and he clearly does not respect her. She is not an equal who can appreciate his work, much less offer any kind of contribution. When Catharina sees the portrait her husband painted of Griet, she asks, "Why... have you never painted me?" For Vermeer, family life is completely separate from his artistic inner life, and Catharina can have no part in it.

Even Griet sees why Catharina would be upset, explaining, "She was not happy about my being in the attic—it meant I was closer to him, to the place she was not allowed in but where I could wander freely." Even after Catharina has been cruel to her, Griet understands that "it must have been hard for a wife to accept such an arrangement." Perhaps if Catharina had been allowed more education and greater experience in the outside world, she might have been more of an equal partner for her husband. Instead, she can only be a wife nagging him to work more quickly to earn more money to feed their growing brood of children. The social constraints put on women have made a happy marriage between them impossible.

A feminist reading of *Girl with a Pearl Earring* turns the most obvious interpretation of the novel on its head. The feminist perspective allows the reader to feel sympathy for the book's least likable character and makes the romance with Vermeer seem less attractive than the solid marriage Griet builds with Pieter, a relationship between equals—or at least as close to equals as the time period will allow.

Griet has as much independence in her life as she can hope for. Indeed, on the very last page of the book, Griet sells the pearl earrings, which Vermeer leaves to her in his will, and repays Pieter the fifteen guilders owed to him. She is able to feel truly "free."

Source: Kristen Sarlin Greenberg, Critical Essay on *Girl with a Pearl Earring*, in *Novels for Students*, Gale, Cengage Learning, 2014.

Pauline Morel

In the following excerpt, Morel examines the importance of the camera obscura in Girl with a Pearl Earring.

. . . For over a hundred years, art historians have been suggesting that Vermeer occasionally used the camera obscura, the predecessor of the photographic camera. Following several optical inventions of the sixteenth century, such as the silver-backed looking glass, the microscope, and the refracting telescope, the camera obscura (or "dark room") is an optical device with a pinhole or lens on one side that projects an inverted image on its far wall, bringing some parts of a composition into focus while blurring others, as well as intensifying colours. Philip Steadman, in *Vermeer's Camera: Uncovering the Truth Behind the Masterpieces*, controversially suggests that Vermeer's use of the device was much more extensive than is commonly believed, and in so doing he points to the fact that Vermeer "seems to reproduce in paint some idiosyncrasies of optical images and 'out-of-focus' effects that would not be visible to the naked eye." Steadman argues that Vermeer's "special technique" was intimately linked with "his special vision and his preoccupations with the effects of light." Svetlana Alpers, in *The Art of Describing: Dutch Art in the Seventeenth Century*, insists that "in the case of Vermeer, everything from spatial organization to the rendering of objects and the use of pigment—in short, much of what we think of as his distinctive style—has been at some time attributed to the camera obscura." Alpers analyzes the scopic regime of Dutch seventeenth-century art, based on the camera obscura, as an "art of describing." According to Alpers, "if we want historical precedence for the photographic image it is in the rich mixture of seeing, knowing, and picturing that manifested itself in seventeenth-century images." Van Leeuwenhoek—naturalist, optical inventor, and Vermeer's friend—was, in Alpers's terms,

> HOWEVER INVISIBLE SHE ATTEMPTS TO MAKE HERSELF—THROUGH HER IMPERCEPTIBLE WORK, SPOTLESS APRON, OR HABIT OF WEARING HER CAP TO HIDE HER FACE AND HAIR—GRIET WILL NOT REMAIN STATIC."

"amazingly the first, and for a while the only, man in Europe to pursue the study of what was seen in microscopic lenses." Alpers attributes the renewed interest in Vermeer and Frans Hals and their compatriots in the 1860s, shortly after the invention of the camera, to their use of the camera obscura; it may not be by chance that there is indeed a renewed interest today, in our world of exacerbated ocularcentrism, though we could attribute this also to stillness, possessiveness, fragility, or other qualities that the paintings equally exemplify.

The ocularcentrism of Dutch seventeenth-century culture is evident in *Girl with a Pearl Earring*. Although the novel is a popular romanticization of Vermeer's creation, it is invaluable for critical discussion on the subject of the gaze because the narrative is object-centred, not only in that it tells a (fictionalized) story of the title painting, but also because it is structured around a number of circular objects that are related to the eye: the pearl often present in Vermeer's paintings, which reflects the white of the eye; the lens of the camera obscura; Griet's circle of vegetables arranged according to their different hues; the fallen knife spinning in circles, with which Catharina attempts to stab at the eye of Griet's image in the painting; and the circle of tiles with the eight-pointed star in the middle, at the centre of the Market Square, to which Griet runs when she must make a decision. *Girl with a Pearl Earring*, as an art-historical novel, further centres on what Svetlana Alpers, and Michael Barandall before her, have called "Dutch visual culture" (Alpers xxv) in its concerns with domestic space, visual delight, craftsmanship, and an essentially descriptive mode, or "natural vision."

. . . The camera obscura epitomizes the interior/exterior topography that is recurrent in the book. Vermeer's "black box" enables the user to discover things that are obscured, kept secret, hidden from ordinary sight. It replicates other boxes or chambers in which valuable secret objects are hidden and searched for by desiring eyes, such a Griet's trunk, in which she hides her few valuable objects (her favourite comb and tile); or Catharina's jewellery box containing the pearls that fascinate Griet; or the recurring images of the shell or oyster that holds the pearl. Griet's grinding and washing of colours for Vermeer, while hidden away in the attic, and the portrait the painter makes of her are further examples of deeds or objects kept hidden and secret in closed spaces. Griet's hair is one corporeal secret that remains veiled until later in the novel, although both Vermeer and her future husband Pieter urge her to remove her cap. In all instances, the secrets contained in the jewellery box, or in the locked rooms and trunk, cause trouble and disruption in the household when they are unlocked and discovered. Like Pandora's box, the objects promote theft (the comb), vandalism (the tile), and passion or jealousy (the painting of Griet wearing the pearls). Some secret objects in the novel can also be exchanged, and are therefore mercantilized. The pearls Griet inherits of Vermeer at the end of the novel are exchanged for currency, the painting is purchased by Van Ruijven, and after his death it changes hands but remains in his family, just as the camera obscura is borrowed from Van Leeuwenhoek in exchange for the opportunity to see the master's work in progress: "Van Leeuwenhoek arrived with his camera obscura while I was in the attic. 'You will have to get one of your own someday,' I heard him say in his deep voice. 'Though I admit it gives me the opportunity to see what you're painting. Where is the model?'"

Cornelia and her mother Catharina are important characters in relation to this interior/exterior topography replicated in the camera obscura. Like many of the male characters, Cornelia, a Pandora figure, is bent on bringing the inside out. She seeks in several instances to penetrate locked up or forbidden spaces in order to bring the secrets there discovered out in the open, with the intent of causing Griet's demise. She penetrates Griet's quarters twice: once to steal her comb and make the household believe it is a comb Griet stole from Catharina; and a second time to enter Griet's room in the attic and steal a piece of the colour Griet is secretly grinding there. She also marks Griet's apron with the colour in an attempt to bring her secret activities as Vermeer's

assistant out in the open. Her desire to see and to know, to investigate and to violate something secret, stems from an intent to cause disruption, out of envy and spite. Catharina has and abuses the power to lock up and enclose, with her repeated and compulsive pregnancies and her habit of visibly and audibly carrying around all the keys to the house, through which she attempts to enforce her position as mistress of the household. She finally even succeeds in locking Griet in her attic room every night, thereby reinforcing Griet's position as "secret object" that she indeed assumes once she starts posing for Vermeer.

Vermeer's paintings capture stilled moments, usually representing "solitary women going about their domestic tasks—pouring milk, reading letters, weighing gold, putting on a necklace" (Chevalier, "Interview," *Book Browse*). This captured moment can be likened to the image captured in the camera obscura. When asked about the role of the camera obscura in the novel, Chevalier explains that it "reminds us that in order to see clearly you have to focus, shut out the world and look at one corner of a room. That is what Vermeer's paintings do—they reveal the world in a room. That is also what the novel tries to do—it is deliberately narrow and focused, and in it is a whole world" ("Interview," *Book Browse*). Seen through the camera obscura, the image is distanced, stilled, defamiliarized, captured. The stilled arrangement of objects in the corner of Vermeer's studio is twice stilled when captured in the camera obscura. In a similar way, Griet is twice removed in the novel: once from her family home, and again from the Vermeers'. She is twice "captured": once by Vermeer, whom she works for, learns from, and poses for, and a second time by Pieter, whom she finally marries and works with at the Meat Hall. Griet's life both with her family and with the Vermeers is regulated by stillness. In the studio, she is to clean without leaving a trace of her passage. She learned this skill at her own home, where, because her father was blind, every object had to be in its place. As Richard Eder explains, "In their world or workshop, respectively, blind people and painters both require objects to remain in place; the former because they cannot see, the latter because seeing is so searching and particular." By posing for Vermeer and being reproduced as image both in his painting and in the camera obscura, Griet herself runs the risk of becoming a commodity or fetish, a captured, stilled object. When he discovers that Griet is posing for Vermeer, van

Leeuwenhoek—significantly a "naturalist"—warns her to "remain herself" and not to let herself become "trapped" in the process:

> "His eyes are worth a room full of gold. But sometimes he sees the world only as he wants it to be, not as it is. He does not understand the consequences for others of his point of view. He thinks only of himself and his work, not of you. You must take care then . . ."
>
> "Take care to do what, sir?" I whispered.
>
> "Take care to remain yourself."
>
> I lifted my chin to him. "To remain a maid, sir?"
>
> "That is not what I mean. The women in his paintings—he traps them in his world. You can get lost there."

However invisible she attempts to make herself—through her imperceptible work, spotless apron, or habit of wearing her cap to hide her face and hair—Griet will not remain static. As Chevalier notes, "I thought that an outsider has an ability to look at something afresh and stirs up stuff. What could have been quite a static household ends up not being static because of her arrival" ("Interview by Gavin J. Grant"). Also, however she might attempt to avoid the gaze, Griet is under scrutiny throughout the entire narrative. Her most striking feature is her wide eyes, which are continually commented on by the characters Vermeer, van Ruijven, and Pieter the son. Van Ruijven calls her "the wide-eyed maid." The first time Vermeer speaks to Griet, to show her the camera obscura after she has started her duties as his maid, he remarks, "Your eyes are very wide," to which she replies, "So I have been told, sir." Wide eyes have traditionally been a sign of innocence, and the men who are constantly calling attention to her wide eyes seem bent on having her lose that innocence. Elkins, in *The Object Stares Back: On the Nature of Seeing*, indeed claims that looking is far from innocent when he writes, "Looking immediately activates desire, possession, violence, displeasure, pain, force, ambition, power, obligation, gratitude, longing [. . .] there seems to be no end to what seeing is, to how it is tangled with living and acting. But there is no such thing as just looking." He goes on to state, "Seeing is irrational, inconsistent, and undependable. It is immensely troubled, cousin to blindness and sexuality, and caught up in the threads of the unconscious. [. . .] It is entangled in the passions—jealousy, violence, possessiveness, and it is soaked in affect—in pleasure and displeasure, and in pain. Ultimately, seeing alters the thing that is seen and transforms the seer. Seeing is metamorphosis, not mechanism." . . .

Source: Pauline Morel, "'Look at Me': The Camera Obscura and the Apprenticeship of the Gaze in Tracy Chevalier's *Girl with a Pearl Earring*," in *Mosaic*, Vol. 44, No. 2, June 2011, pp. 68–69, 72–75.

Cushing Strout
In the following review, Strout praises Chevalier's skill in creating drama in a story with minimal action.

Merging fictional and historical characters seemed innovative in 1975 to many reviewers of E. L. Doctorow's *Ragtime*. Nowadays, in movies, in books, and in plays, the merger is so common that the essential question is not whether it is done at all, but whether it is done with respect for historical consciousness or instead turns a poetic license into a blank check to be executed according to the writer's fancy. Tracy Chevalier in her novel *Girl with a Pearl Earring* is a fine example of the most intelligent way of fictionalizing history. She focuses primarily on a fictional minor figure through whose eyes we see the historical person; takes account of what is historically known about the time and place; and invents an interesting, credible, and moving story about the fictional person without letting it diminish the achievements of the actual person. These are demanding conditions that are seldom met in contemporary culture, but I think that the author meets them all with eloquence and insight in her story of a maid to Johannes Vermeer in the Dutch Republic of the seventeenth century.

The novel makes use of historical knowledge about the house of his mother-in-law in which he and his family lived; his prosperous wife's relatives; class differences between masters and servants; Protestant/Catholic tensions in Delft; Vermeer's way of working; his major patron, Pieter van Ruijven; and his friend and executor, the microscopist Antonie van Leeuwenhoek. Making him a friend is the novelist's freedom of turning a plausible possibility into a fact, but her most brilliant invention is to imagine a particular identity for the figure in one of Vermeer's most popular paintings. That choice is highly appropriate. Vermeer's paintings of women set them in a room, and the figures have a close relationship to the objects around them.

These paintings induce us to see the women in a specific context and to appreciate their light, shape, and color in terms of that context. There are two exceptions in which the women have only a solid black background with no context. In one of them, *Portrait of a Young Woman* (or *Head of a Girl*), she looks as if she were sitting for a portrait, as one of Vermeer's daughters may have done, according to the suggestion of John Michael Montias in his minutely researched and judiciously analyzed account, *Vermeer and His Milieu: A Web of Social History* (1989). By contrast *The Girl with a Pearl Earring* is not static: she is looking over her shoulder directly at the spectator, as if she has just turned to answer a question or respond to her name, and her lips are parted expectantly. As the maid, Griet, who in the novel sits for the painting, says about it: "I seemed to be waiting for something I did not think would ever happen." That remark tells us about the maid's own character, but it also says something true about the compelling figure in the frame on the wall. Its immediacy, when you see it at the Mauritshuis in The Hague, is more arresting than any reproduction can quite prepare you for.

To find drama in a story that has its high point in a person being made the subject of a painting might seem difficult. It takes a Jamesian kind of imagination to invent one, and it has to be congruent with the remarkable tranquility of Vermeer's paintings which, even when they are about women in action—whether they are pouring milk, playing a musical instrument, making lace, fitting a necklace, holding a balance, or writing or reading a letter—are never melodramatic.

Even his magnificently lighted *View of Delft*, done on a surprisingly large scale, portrays the city as if it were frozen in time. The little human figures in the lower left-hand corner of the painting are as still as the buildings. Actually the bustling city underwent many social, political, and military changes in Vermeer's lifetime, including an explosion in powder magazines that devastated most of the northeast of town. It killed the painter Carel Fabritius, whose contribution to Dutch painting, as Arthur K. Wheelock, Jr., observes in his splendid collection, *Jan Vermeer* (1981), was to pay attention to the close interaction of figure and environment, a tradition on which Vermeer drew in his own work. Perhaps Vermeer's civic portrait is not really as timeless as it appears, however, for the Treaty of Münster in 1648 legally recognized the new republic that had defeated Spain; and the event promoted a civic pride that increased artistic interest in making monumental paintings of civic life. Vermeer was a member of a company of civic guards, and his radiant painting of Delft is his celebration of the city.

Vermeer's paintings are rarely anecdotal, but Tracy Chevalier has to take concrete time seriously, for she has a story to tell about her invented maid. The novel is set very solidly in the city's historical reality, taking account of religious and class differences. Vermeer converted from Protestantism to Catholicism when he married the daughter of a devout Catholic family, and the couple lived in the house of his wealthy Catholic mother-in-law, who had separated from her abusive husband more than a decade earlier. The fictional maid is compelled to work as a maid because her father, a tile painter, has been blinded by a kiln explosion. When she moves into Vermeer's family, she is made very uncomfortable as a Protestant by seeing a Catholic painting of a crucifixion scene. She is always aware of her lowly place as a maid, condemned to being overworked in doing the laundry, the cleaning, and often the buying of fish and meat. What distinguishes her, however, is a native sense of color and shape that gives her (as the painter recognizes) a kinship with the man whose work and presence stimulate her imagination.

The appropriately muted action of the plot shows her gradually becoming closer to Vermeer as she dusts his studio without disturbing anything and helps him in buying and grinding some of the ingredients for his paints. Eventually she is moved from the cellar to the attic just above his studio, and to her amazement he shows her how the camera obscura works. It is one of the tools he sometimes used to learn more about the look of light, shapes, and colors. Traditionally novels and films include the erotic possibilities in the master/servant relationship. Chevalier treats them with uncommon subtlety and restraint.

Griet and her master always keep their socially defined distance, but the intensity of her interest in him makes the moment when he asks her to take up the pose that we see in his picture a highly erotic one. When she loosens her hair in his presence, the moment is sexually charged; but the tension is released for her when she lets her boyfriend embrace her in an alley more intimately than he ever has been permitted earlier. When her master asks her to open her mouth as she poses for him, she feels as if he had been with them in the alley. No other paintings of single women by Vermeer could have made this interpretation at all plausible. (Sex is not entirely absent from his work—e.g. *The Procuress*; but it is never otherwise explicit.)

The special intelligence of this novel is to make us see that the most fundamental link between this master and his servant is her intuitive feeling for aesthetic matters of light, color, and shape. She believes strongly that her master's painting of her demands for its formal completeness the spot of light that an earring would provide; and he comes to the same conclusion on his own. Yet the earrings belong to the painter's wife; it would be unsuitable for a maid to wear them. Griet, moreover, in order to please her master, has to pierce her own ears painfully so that she can wear them. When he leaves them to her in his will, vexing his jealous wife, who has to carry out the directive, Griet pawns them, using most of the money to help pay her husband's debts. But she holds back a few coins, which are never to be spent or seen, as a remembrance of her intense experience of sitting for a man who was not only her master but a master of art, who saw in her something of his own aesthetic sensibility. That she never gets to see the finished painting is a poignant touch.

The maid appeals to us by virtue of her realistic sense of herself and her world as well as by her imaginative capacities. Dutch painting in the Golden Age seems itself to be a remarkable fusion of realism and imagination, so Griet is a thoroughly appropriate heroine. In principle it would be possible to imagine many different plots in which the girl with the pearl earrings might figure.

It is the great merit of Tracy Chevalier's novel that, after reading her version of the story behind the picture, I cannot imagine another one that would be as credible and poignant.

The dustjacket refers to "the young woman who was the inspiration behind one of Vermeer's finest paintings." There is, of course, no *was* about it. The flap should have said: "who is imagined to have been . . ." Because we have no idea in fact who sat for the picture, history has left an opening for the novelist. Clio, the muse of history who appears in Vermeer's unusually allegorical picture, *The Art of Painting*, must be silent about the young girl's identity. The novel that tells her story is not meant to be a contribution to the history of art. It is instead an admirable contribution to the continuing history of our response to Vermeer's painting. His eloquence has provoked hers.

Source: Cushing Strout, "Fact, Fiction, and Vermeer," in *Sewanee Review*, Vol. 109, No. 2, Spring 2001, pp. lxvi–lxix.

SOURCES

Ainsworth, Maryan W., "Early Netherlandish Painting," Metropolitan Museum of Art website, http://www.metmuseum.org/toah/hd/enet/hd_enet.htm (accessed May 5, 2013).

Almond, Kyle, "Same-Sex Marriage: Who Will Legalize It Next?" in *CNN World*, April 23, 2013, http://www.cnn.com/2013/04/04/world/same-sex-marriage-next-country (accessed May 7, 2013).

Barry, Sheila, Review of *Girl with a Pearl Earring*, in *School Library Journal*, Vol. 46, No. 6, June 2000, p. 173.

Berry, Gail, "'Ring around a Rosie': A Brief History of the Bubonic Plague," in *HealthDecide*, August 21, 2012, http://healthdecide.orcahealth.com/2012/08/21/ring-around-a-rosie/ (accessed May 5, 2013).

Carter, Deborah, "Summer Reading for Older Students," in *Bookmarks*, May–June 2008, pp. 12–13.

Charles, Ron, "Classic Review: *Girl with a Pearl Earring*," in *Christian Science Monitor*, January 16, 2011.

Chevalier, Tracy, *Girl with a Pearl Earring*, Dutton, 1999.

"Delftware: Tradition in Blue and White," I Amsterdam, http://www.iamsterdam.com/en-GB/experience/what-to-do/shopping/Typically-Dutch/Delftware-pottery (accessed May 6, 2013).

"Feminist Criticism (1960s–present)," Purdue Online Writing Lab website, http://owl.english.purdue.edu/owl/resource/722/11/ (accessed May 6, 2013).

"History: Delftware," Delft website, http://www.delft.nl/delften/Tourists/History_of_Delft/Delftware/History_Delftware (accessed May 6, 2013).

Hoffert, Barbara, Review of *Girl with a Pearl Earring*, in *Library Journal*, Vol. 124, No. 17, October 15, 1999, p. 103.

"Hudson, Henry," in *Colonial America Reference Library*, Vol. 3, *Biographies*, edited by Peggy Saari and Julie L. Carnagie, UXL, 2000, pp. 138–43.

Jones, Susan, "Painting in Oil in the Low Countries and Its Spread to Southern Europe," Metropolitan Museum of Art website, http://www.metmuseum.org/toah/hd/optg/hd_optg.htm (accessed May 5, 2013).

Karam, P. Andrew, "Dutch Exploration and Colonization," in *Science and Its Times*, Vol. 3, *1450 to 1699*, edited by Neil Schlager and Josh Lauer, The Gale Group, 2001, pp. 9–12.

Knight, Judson, "Willem Jansz," in *Science and Its Times*, Vol. 3, *1450 to 1699*, edited by Neil Schlager and Josh Lauer, The Gale Group, 2001, p. 87.

Lagassé, Paul, "Delftware," in *The Columbia Encyclopedia*, 6th ed., Columbia University Press, 2000.

Librie, Felicity, "Many Voices: An Interview with Tracy Chevalier," in *Fiction Writers Review*, January 6, 2011, http://fictionwritersreview.com/interviews/many-voices-an-interview-with-tracy-chevalier (accessed May 4, 2013).

Liedtke, Walter, "Frans Hals (1582/83–1666)," Metropolitan Museum of Art website, http://www.metmuseum.org/toah/hd/hals/hd_hals.htm (accessed May 5, 2013).

———, "Johannes Vermeer (1632–1675)," Metropolitan Museum of Art website, http://www.metmuseum.org/toah/hd/verm/hd_verm.htm (accessed May 5, 2013).

———, "Rembrandt van Rijn (1606–1669): Paintings," Metropolitan Museum of Art website, http://www.metmuseum.org/toah/hd/rmbt/hd_rmbt.htm (accessed May 5, 2013).

Lindemann, Mary, *Medicine and Society in Early Modern Europe*, Cambridge University Press, 2010, pp. 64–65.

Maryles, Daisy, "A Pearl Worth a Million," in *Publishers Weekly*, Vol. 248, No. 37, September 10, 2001, p. 19.

"Netherlands: Economy," *CIA: The World Factbook*, https://www.cia.gov/library/publications/the-world-factbook/geos/nl.html (accessed May 5, 2013).

"Netherlands: People and Society," *CIA: The World Factbook*, https://www.cia.gov/library/publications/the-world-factbook/geos/nl.html (accessed May 5, 2013).

"Plague," Centers for Disease Control and Prevention website, http://www.cdc.gov/plague/ (accessed May 7, 2013).

Review of *Girl with a Pearl Earring*, in *Atlantic Monthly*, Vol. 283, No. 2, February 2000, p. 106.

Review of *Girl with a Pearl Earring*, in *Publishers Weekly*, Vol. 246, No. 41, October 11, 1999, p. 52.

Review of *The Virgin Blue*, in *Publishers Weekly*, Vol. 250, No. 25, June 23, 2003, p. 48.

"Risk of Death from Plague Today and in History," in *Bandolier*, 2007, http://www.medicine.ox.ac.uk/bandolier/booth/risk/plague.html (accessed May 24, 2013).

Sommerville, J. P., "Dutch Religious and Intellectual History: Calvinism and Toleration in the Netherlands," University of Wisconsin–Madison Department of History website, http://faculty.history.wisc.edu/sommerville/351/351-082.htm (accessed May 4, 2013).

"Tracy Chevalier," British Council website, http://literature.britishcouncil.org/tracy-chevalier (accessed May 4, 2013).

"Tracy Chevalier: About Me," Tracy Chevalier website, http://www.tchevalier.com/index.php/about (accessed May 4, 2013).

"Tracy Chevalier: Frequently Asked Questions," Tracy Chevalier website, http://www.tchevalier.com/index.php/faqs (accessed May 4, 2013).

"Vermeer Nominated for Three Oscars," in *American Artist*, Vol. 68, No. 742, May 2004, p. 8.

FURTHER READING

Ames, Glenn J., *The Globe Encompassed: The Age of European Discovery (1500 to 1700)*, Pearson, 2007.

> The seventeenth century was a time of exploration. In this comprehensive volume, Ames outlines the causes and major events of global discovery and colonization. The book includes primary sources that provide interesting contemporary points of view.

Brooks, Geraldine, *Year of Wonders: A Novel of the Plague*, Viking, 2001.

> The terrifying contagion of the plague is an important element in the plot of *Girl with a Pearl Earring*. In *Year of Wonders*, Brooks portrays the trials of a small English town ravaged and isolated by the disease. The novel was inspired by the true story of the town of Eyam, which lived for a year under a self-imposed quarantine when struck by the plague in 1665.

Chevalier, Tracy, *Falling Angels: A Novel*, Dutton, 2001.

> In *Falling Angels*, Chevalier once again brings the past to life, this time portraying the lives of two English families in the first years of the twentieth century. This novel's first-person narration is split among the points of view of a dozen different characters.

Villa, Renzo, *Vermeer: The Complete Works*, Silvana Editoriale, 2013.

> Villa's volume reproduces all of Vermeer's thirty-four known paintings, including close-ups that show the painstaking attention to detail and incredible realism that make Vermeer's work remarkable.

SUGGESTED SEARCH TERMS

Tracy Chevalier AND Girl with a Pearl Earring

Tracy Chevalier AND historical fiction

Johannes Vermeer

Johannes Vermeer AND Girl with a Pearl Earring

Johannes Vermeer AND Delft

Johannes Vermeer AND Pieter van Ruijven

Frans Hals

Rembrandt

van Leeuwenhook AND camera obscura

Delft AND china

The Heart of the Matter

GRAHAM GREENE

1948

The Heart of the Matter, first published in 1948, is a novel by British author Graham Greene. Considered by many critics to be a masterpiece of twentieth-century literature, the novel is set in an unnamed British colonial outpost in West Africa during World War II. The setting is based on Greene's experience as a British intelligence agent in Sierra Leone during the war, although he insisted that the novel's setting is fictional and that his characters are not to be identified with anyone he encountered there.

The Heart of the Matter encompasses a wide range of concerns: war, espionage, love, adultery, pity, and betrayal. The enigmatic protagonist, Major Henry Scobie, is a deputy police commissioner responsible for security in the colony. He is also a Catholic who faces a life-altering moral crisis that arises from his relationships with his unhappy wife, Louise, and his mistress, Helen. Scobie commits acts that leave him deeply ashamed. His adultery and ultimate fate, as well as the visit of one of the characters to a brothel, might render *The Heart of the Matter* suitable primarily for more mature readers.

The novel became an international best seller. Within three years it sold nearly three hundred thousand copies in Great Britain, and it won the 1948 James Tait Black Memorial Prize for Fiction. The novel, however, was controversial, for many readers concluded that its moral vision conflicted with the teachings of the

Graham Greene (© AP Images; | Alexis Duclos)

Catholic Church, and for a time it was actually banned in Catholic Ireland.

The Heart of the Matter is available online at the Internet Archive website at http://archive. org/stream/heartofthematter031009mbp/heartof thematter031009mbp_djvu.txt.

AUTHOR BIOGRAPHY

Henry Graham Greene (who never used his actual first name) was born on October 2, 1904, in Berkhamsted, a historic town in Hertfordshire, England. He was one of six children born to Charles Henry Greene, a housemaster and senior teacher at Berkhamsted School, and Marion R. Greene, a first cousin to nineteenth-century author Robert Louis Stevenson. Greene had a troubled childhood: he was bullied at school, he tried to commit suicide, he ran away from home, and at age fifteen, he was taken to London for psychotherapy. In London, he developed a love of writing and literature after his therapist introduced him to a literary set that included poems by Walter de la Mare. In London, he met the poet Ezra Pound and novelist Gertrude Stein, who became mentors.

After graduating from high school in 1922, Greene enrolled in Balliol College at Oxford University, where he dabbled briefly in Communist politics. During his college years, he frequently suffered from bouts of depression, and he associated little with fellow students. He was even known to play Russian roulette with a pistol. He graduated in 1925 with a degree in history and began his writing career as an unpaid intern at the *Nottingham Journal*. Later he took a position at the London *Times*. In 1926, he converted from the Anglican (Protestant) faith to Catholicism as a result of his correspondence with Vivien Dayrell-Browning, whom he married the following year. The couple had a son and a daughter. They separated amicably in 1948, although they never divorced. Greene later had relationships with other women, as he had prior to his separation from Vivien. One was with his own goddaughter.

Greene published his first novel, *The Man Within*, in 1929, but his first successful book was *Stamboul Train* (1932), published in the United States as *Orient Express*. The 1930s were a productive time for Greene. During the decade he published several books, including *Brighton Rock* (1938), and wrote what many critics regard as his major novel, *The Power and the Glory* (1940). During the 1930s he was also a respected film and book critic for the *Spectator* and for the weekly magazine *Night and Day*, which he founded.

After the outbreak of World War II, Greene worked for the Ministry of Information in London. He then joined the Secret Intelligence Service (commonly known as MI6) and served as an intelligence officer in the African nation of Sierra Leone, which provided him with background material for *The Heart of the Matter* (1948). During the war, he published *The Ministry of Fear* (1943). Later in the war he worked in London for British counterintelligence (under the infamous double agent Kim Philby). In 1949, he cowrote (with Carol Reed) a film, *The Third Man*, which was based on a novella that he later published.

In 1955, Greene published *The Quiet American*, an antiwar novel that prefigured American entanglement in Southeast Asia. The novel was based on his experience in the early 1950s as a war correspondent for the London *Times* and the French magazine *Le Figaro*. The novel attracted the attention of US intelligence authorities, who placed him under almost constant surveillance for the rest of his life. Greene's expressed admiration for such figures as Fidel Castro in Cuba and Ho Chi Minh in Vietnam added to the perception that he still had Communist leanings. Later novels include *Our Man in Havana* (1958), *A Burnt-Out Case* (1960), *The Comedians* (1966), *The Honorary Consul* (1973), *The Human Factor* (1978, a *New York Times* best seller for six months), and *Monsignor Quixote* (1982). His last novel was *The Tenth Man* (1985), and his last published work during his lifetime was the short story "The Last Word" (1988).

Greene's health began to decline in 1990, so he and his longtime companion, Yvonne Cloetta, moved from his home in France to Vevey, Switzerland, where he could be closer to his daughter. He died of an unspecified blood disorder on April 3, 1991, in Vevey. To the consternation of his many admirers, Greene never won the Nobel Prize in Literature, although in compensation, his books sold a total of twenty million copies worldwide, and many were turned into films.

MEDIA ADAPTATIONS

- A film adaptation of *The Heart of the Matter* was released by London Films in 1953. The film, directed by George More O'Farrell, stars Trevor Howard as Scobie, Elizabeth Allan as Louise, and Maria Schell as Helen. Running time is 105 minutes. The production is available on DVD as part of *The Graham Greene Collection*, released by PAL.

- In 1983, a television adaptation of the novel was produced by Tele-München in Germany. The production starred Jack Hedley as Scobie and was directed by Marco Leto.

- An unabridged audio version of *The Heart of the Matter*, read by Joseph Porter, was released by Blackstone Audio in 2002. Running time is 11 hours and 30 minutes.

- Another unabridged audio version of the novel is read by British actor Michael Kitchen. It was released by BBC Audiobooks in 2009 and is available as an MP3 download. Running time is just over 10 hours.

PLOT SUMMARY

Book One

PART ONE

Book One introduces Major Henry Scobie, who has served for some fifteen years as a policeman in British West Africa and has just been passed over for promotion to commissioner. Following the outbreak of World War II, he is responsible for security. He is married to Louise, a lover of literature and poetry who is desperately unhappy and solitary. Scobie no longer loves her, and their lives were made still unhappier by the death of their only child, a daughter, three years earlier. Louise is a devout Catholic, as is Scobie, who converted to Catholicism. Louise is upset about Scobie's failure to win promotion, believing that if he had done so, she could have satisfied her own personal ambition to win acceptance from the colony's other British residents. She hates her life and believes that she would be happier if she

could escape to South Africa and Scobie, having been passed over, would decide to retire and join her. Scobie feels responsible for her unhappiness.

A new inspector, Wilson, has arrived. Wilson is socially awkward and, like Louise, a lover of poetry, although he hides his interest, fearing that his colleagues would ridicule him. He and Louise meet at a party and form a friendship, although Wilson mistakenly believes that Louise loves him. Wilson has a roommate named Harris, a cable censor.

Scobie encounters Yusef, a Syrian who operates several shops but in fact is involved with the black market. The two discuss Tallit, Yusef's main competitor, and the immense difficulty Scobie continues to face in locating black-market diamonds in the ships that arrive in port.

Scobie tries to borrow money from the bank to send Louise to South Africa, but the banker refuses to grant the loan because of the poor state of Scobie's finances. A Portuguese ship, the *Esperança*, arrives in port. As the police search the ship and examine the passports of the passengers, Scobie meets with the captain. A disgruntled steward passes a note for Scobie to one of his men, revealing that the captain has letters concealed in his bathroom. Scobie locates a letter addressed to a woman in Germany, Britain's enemy in the war. The captain claims the letter is addressed to his daughter, but Scobie confiscates it because it might contain German codes or other clandestine information. The captain begs Scobie to forget the matter and, when he learns that Scobie, like him, is a Catholic, offers him a bribe of a hundred pounds. Scobie turns down the bribe, but he takes the letter (along with others that were found) and, breaking the rules, opens it and reads it. He concludes that the letter is unimportant and burns it rather than sending it on to higher authorities.

PART TWO

Wilson and Harris discuss Wilson's relationships with Tallit and Louise. Wilson has his palm read by an Indian, who seems to know everything about Wilson's longings. Wilson has dinner with Tallit and his family at their home, where he meets Father Rank, the local priest. Rank notes the difficulty of locating smuggled diamonds. Harris passes the time by making a game of killing cockroaches. When Wilson returns home, Harris invites him to take part in the game, but the two quarrel about the rules of the game. Louise and Wilson enjoy an outing together and discuss their shared love of literature.

PART THREE

Scobie is summoned to Bamba, an inland town, to investigate the suicide of Pemberton, a local police inspector. Pemberton, who hanged himself, left behind a note suggesting that he committed suicide because he was unable to repay a large loan. Scobie later has a dream that he is in Pemberton's situation. He even dreams that he writes a similar note. When he wakes up, he concludes that he could never commit suicide, believing that nothing is worth the eternal damnation that suicide would merit. Scobie at once suspects that the loan was from Yusef and questions him about the matter. Yusef denies having made the loan but warns Scobie that the British authorities have dispatched a new inspector to look for smuggled

diamonds. Yusef lends Scobie the money he needs to send Louise to South Africa. An ocean liner arrives, and Louise departs for South Africa. Wilson meets them at the pier and tries to interfere with their parting.

Book Two

PART ONE

The survivors of a shipwreck begin to arrive at the port after having spent forty days in life-boats at sea. Scobie tries to comfort one young girl by pretending to be her father, who was killed in the wreck, but he fails, and she dies. One of the survivors is Helen Rolt, a nineteen-year-old woman who is clinging to a postage stamp album. Helen had married before the ship left its original port, but her husband died in the wreck. She is now a widow, with a wedding ring that is too big for her shrunken finger. Scobie is attracted to her, even though she is not especially pretty, for she reminds him of his daughter. Soon he begins a passionate affair with her, knowing full well that he is committing the mortal sin of adultery. Scobie tries to break off his connection with Yusef, although he will continue to pay interest on the loan.

PART TWO

Wilson receives information about potential diamond smuggling. His efforts to investigate take him to a brothel, where he is reluctant to have sex with one of the girls. A woman, however, refuses to allow him to leave and demands money from him. Reluctantly, he pays the money and appears to employ the girl.

PART THREE

Father Rank seems to suspect that Scobie is having an affair, but in the absence of firm knowledge, he can only obliquely warn Scobie about the danger to his soul. Scobie hears from Louise: she is returning to the colony. Scobie writes a love letter to Helen that falls into Yusef's possession. Yusef uses the letter to blackmail Scobie into shipping a package of diamonds for him on the *Esperança*, thus avoiding interference by the authorities.

Book Three

PART ONE

After Louise returns, Scobie tries to hide his love affair with Helen from her, but he is unable to give Helen up, even after Father Rank tells him in the confessional that he cannot grant absolution unless the affair is over. To please his wife, Scobie attends mass with her and receives communion. Scobie knows that it is a grave sin for a Catholic to take communion—the body and blood of Christ, according to Catholic doctrine—while in a state of mortal sin.

Yusef's servant delivers a "gift" to Scobie. Scobie's servant, Ali, witnesses the delivery. Shortly afterward, Ali is killed by a group of teenage thieves called wharf rats. Scobie had begun to question Ali's loyalty to him, and he hinted as much to Yusef. The narration suggests that Yusef was responsible for Ali's murder, but Scobie blames himself. He sees the image of God in Ali's body at the wharf.

PART TWO

Scobie is now desperate. He wants to free everyone, even God, from himself. He also wants to ensure that Louise can collect his life insurance, so he fakes the symptoms of angina, a heart ailment. Thus, although he kills himself by ingesting pills, his death will, he hopes, appear to be from natural causes.

PART THREE

Wilson and Louise meet and discuss Scobie's suicide. Louise, it turns out, knows that her husband committed suicide and that he was having an affair with Helen. Wilson again fails in his efforts to interest Louise in a romantic relationship. Helen moves on to an affair with Bagster, one of the shipwreck survivors, and in a final conversation with Father Rank, she tries to achieve understanding of Scobie's actions.

CHARACTERS

Ali

Ali is Scobie's long-time African servant. Early on, Scobie reflects on Ali's dedication in staying with him for fifteen years, but later he comes to suspect Ali's loyalty. Ali is later killed by "wharf rats" on the city's quays, possibly on Yusef's orders, although Scobie feels primarily responsible.

Bagster

Bagster, one of the survivors of the shipwreck, is identified as a flight lieutenant. He is immediately attracted to Helen Rolt, and after Scobie's suicide, it appears that Helen moves on to an affair with Bagster.

Father Clay

Father Clay is a mission priest at the inland town where Pemberton commits suicide. His principal function is to serve as the voice of the Catholic Church on the issue of suicide.

Harris

Harris is Wilson's housemate. He is initially identified as an accountant for the U.A.C., or United African Company, a trade enterprise, but he later states that his job is that of cable censor. He passes the time by making a game out of killing the cockroaches that appear each night in his quarters.

"Dicky" Pemberton

Pemberton is an inspector in the inland town of Bamba whose suicide Scobie is sent to investigate. He has committed suicide because he was unable to repay a large debt, presumably to Yusef.

Perrot

Perrot, a French Huguenot, is the district commissioner. He is present on the dock when the shipwreck survivors arrive. Because of his French heritage, his role is to fill in background on Vichy French control of adjacent African territories, which he refers to as "France."

Father Rank

Father Rank is the local Catholic priest and Scobie's confessor. He has been in the colony for twenty-two years. He urges Scobie to break off his affair with Helen and refuses to give absolution to Scobie when he confesses his affair.

Helen Rolt

After forty days stranded in lifeboats at sea, the survivors of a shipwreck begin to arrive at the colony. One is Helen, a nineteen-year-old woman who arrives holding on to a postage stamp album. The postage stamp album is a possession that enables her to cling to memories associated with individual stamps, especially her memories of her father, who gave her the album.

Before the ship left its original port, she was married. Her husband was killed in the wreck, so she is now a widow. Scobie is drawn to her in part because she reminds him of his daughter. Soon he begins a passionate affair with her. After Scobie's death, Helen moves on to an affair with another man.

Catherine Scobie

Catherine never appears in the novel, because three years before she died at school at the age of nine. Her death is one of the major factors contributing to the Scobies' unhappiness and frustration with their lives and to Henry Scobie's profound sense of waste and failure.

Major Henry Scobie

Scobie is the deputy police commissioner in the capital of an unnamed British West African colony during World War II. In many respects, he is an ordinary man who tries to do his job conscientiously. He has been in the colony for fifteen years and does not want to leave or retire, even after he is passed over for promotion to the post of commissioner. At the same time, he feels that his fifteen years in the colony have been a waste. He is married to Louise, but what he feels for her is less love and more pity and a sense of responsibility, for Louise is unhappy, and Scobie believes her unhappiness is his fault. It is this sense of pity for others that ultimately is his undoing.

Scobie is a convert to Catholicism, and he is devout in his religious beliefs, so when he begins to have an affair with Helen Rolt and refuses to break it off, he understands that he is living in mortal sin. His sin is made worse after Louise returns to the colony and, to please her, he goes to mass and takes communion, a grave sin for a Catholic already living in a state of sin. He writes a letter to Helen that falls into the hands of Yusef. Yusef uses the letter to blackmail Scobie into allowing him to smuggle a shipment of diamonds out of the colony. Ultimately, Scobie feels responsible for the death of Ali, a young servant who has been with him for years. In a state of despair, he commits suicide, trying, unsuccessfully, to make his death appear to be the result of angina so that Louise can collect his life insurance.

Louise Scobie

Louise is Henry's devout Catholic wife. She is profoundly unhappy living in the colony in Africa. She feels that she has no friends, and she is disappointed when she learns that her husband has been passed over for promotion to commissioner. She believes that she would be happier living in South Africa, and for a time she leaves. After she returns unexpectedly, her husband tries to keep his affair with Helen secret, although the reader learns that Louise knew about the affair all along. Louise is a lover of literature and poetry, interests she shares with Wilson. She and Wilson form a friendship that Wilson mistakes for love.

Tallit

Tallit is a Syrian and a Catholic. He is Yusef's main competitor in the black-market trade. Yusef previously fooled Tallit with fake diamonds, still a sore spot with Tallit.

Edward Wilson

Wilson is a new inspector who spies on the actions of Major Scobie. He secretly indulges a love of literature, which he hides from his colleagues, fearing their ridicule. He shares this interest with Louise and mistakes her friendship with him for love. He wants to have an affair with her, but she does not go along with his wishes.

Yusef

Yusef, a Muslim, is a Syrian black marketeer. He is representative of a class of scoundrels and opportunists who take advantage of wartime chaos through illegal activities. Throughout the novel, he denies any knowledge of diamond smuggling, yet when a letter in which Scobie expresses his love for Helen falls into his hands, he uses the letter to blackmail Scobie into allowing him to smuggle a cache of diamonds out of the colony.

THEMES

Moral Ambiguity

In the course of the novel, Scobie faces situations that require him to make choices that are morally ambiguous. For example, Scobie feels utterly responsible for the misery of his wife, Louise. Although he does not love her, he does not hate her either, so when she expresses the wish to move to South Africa, where she believes she will be happier, Scobie is willing to scrape up the money needed to send her. He tries to borrow money from a bank, but the banker turns him down because of his precarious finances, and the reader learns that he has very little money in the bank. Later, when the captain of the *Esperança*

TOPICS FOR FURTHER STUDY

- R. M. Ballantyne was a Scottish writer of fiction for younger readers. His 1857 adventure novel *The Coral Island* was one of the first books Greene remembered reading as a child. Read the novel, then write a report speculating on how the novel might have influenced Greene in his writing career.

- Greene has often been called a "Catholic novelist" (although he disliked the characterization) because several of his novels, including *The Heart of the Matter*, deal with moral and religious themes revolving around Catholic characters. One of Greene's Oxford schoolmates, Evelyn Waugh, is also regarded as a Catholic novelist. Read one of Waugh's novels (a popular one is *Brideshead Revisited*, published in 1945), then imagine a dialogue between the two authors about religion and literature. With a willing classmate, perform your dialogue for your class.

- Many critics, along with Greene himself, regard him as very much a cinematic writer, and many of his novels were adapted for film (some more than once), among them *This Gun for Hire, The Ministry of Fear, Brighton Rock, The Power and the Glory* (under the title *The Fugitive*), *The End of the Affair, Our Man in Havana, Travels with My Aunt, The Human Factor*, and *The Honorary Consul*. Locate a film version of one of Greene's novels. Develop an oral report for your class in which you describe what it means to be a cinematic writer and explain how Greene uses cinematic techniques in *The Heart of the Matter*.

- Conduct Internet research on the history of British colonialism in Africa and elsewhere during the twentieth century. What colonies did Britain hold? What was the nature of British colonial administration? What became of Britain's colonies in the postwar era? Prepare a chart addressing these questions, and share it with your classmates on your social networking site or in a Power-Point presentation.

- Yulisa Amadu Maddy (a Sierra Leonean) and Donnarae MacCann are the editors of *African Images in Juvenile Literature: Commentaries on Neocolonialist Fiction* (1996). Look through this book, and based on what you learn, prepare an oral report on the accuracy and fairness of Greene's depiction of West Africa in *The Heart of the Matter*.

- During World War II, Greene worked for Britain's Ministry of Information and as an intelligence agent for the Secret Intelligence Service, or MI6. What function did these organizations play during the war? In a written report, explain how Greene may have used these wartime experiences in *The Heart of the Matter*.

- Greene's novels often present their characters with moral dilemmas. So, too, does Terry Trueman's 2003 young-adult novel *Inside Out*, which examines the complexities people deal with when they face moral dilemmas. Read the novel, then write a report in which you discuss how Trueman and Greene each deal with moral complexity.

---

offers him a bribe, he still has moral fiber enough to turn the bribe down, but ultimately he weakens. He has a passionate affair with Helen, and when Yusef finds out about the affair through a letter Scobie wrote to Helen, he submits to the Syrian's blackmail by allowing a shipment of smuggled diamonds out of port. However, Scobie is by no means a bad man. Quite the contrary, he is depicted as an essentially good man who loves God but is overwhelmed by his own loneliness, desperation, and pity for others.

Suicide

The Heart of the Matter takes up the theme of suicide, examining it principally within a Catholic context. In traditional Catholic teaching, suicide is the ultimate unforgivable sin; it is a mortal sin, which condemns the sinner to hell, and it is unforgivable for the obvious reason that the sinner is no longer around to ask God for forgiveness. Scobie, however, is a man whose life has collapsed. He lost his daughter, Catherine, when she was just nine years old. He is passed over for the post of commissioner of police in the colony, where he has served for fifteen years that he has come to conclude were wasted. He no longer loves his wife, and he is not convinced that she loves him, given his failures and her desire to escape the colony. He commits adultery, but he takes communion while still in a state of sin—yet another mortal sin for Catholics. He finally submits to Yusef's blackmail. His beloved servant, Ali, is killed, and Scobie blames himself. He tries to hide his affair with Helen from Louise, but the reader learns that she knew about the affair all along. He concludes that the only way to separate himself from the people he has hurt is through suicide. He fakes a case of angina so that his death will appear to be the result of natural causes; in this way Louise can collect his life insurance. He then kills himself with pills. The fact that he committed suicide comes out, so his suicide is a final failure in his life. Scobie's suicide is foreshadowed by the suicide of Pemberton, an inspector who has apparently incurred a debt from Yusef he cannot repay.

British Colonialism

The Heart of the Matter is set in the context of twentieth-century European colonialism. During these years, Britain maintained four colonies that were collectively called British West Africa: Sierra Leone, the Gold Coast, the Gambia, and Nigeria. The British maintained other colonies in Africa as well, such as Rhodesia (now Zimbabwe). The French held neighboring colonies collectively called French West Africa; these colonies fell under the control of the Vichy government, that is, the French puppet government that collaborated with the Nazis after the Nazi invasion of France. Thus, they were perceived as a looming threat by the Britons in West Africa. Belgium, too, maintained African colonies, Italy seized nations in North Africa after Benito Mussolini assumed power, and

Germany had taken part in the so-called scramble for Africa in the nineteenth century. In 1950, still only four African nations were independent.

Greene, however, does not offer discussions of the evils of colonialism. Rather, in characteristic fashion, he comments on colonialism obliquely, through small details. For example, when Scobie is dealing with a local young woman who is lodging a complaint, he reflects that "fifteen years ago he would not have noticed her beauty...she would have been indistinguishable from her fellows—a black." Scobie wins some approval from the reader for having altered his view and become willing to see the local people as individuals. However, his initial attitude, which was to see the local people as just "blacks," is indicative of the colonial attitude maintained by most of the other Britons living there.

Religion

The Heart of the Matter is one of several "Catholic novels" Greene wrote; the others are *The Power and the Glory*, *The End of the Affair*, and *A Burnt-Out Case*. These novels share an interest in Catholic themes and feature Catholic characters. This literary interest in Catholicism was an outgrowth of the author's own conversion to Catholicism in the 1920s. Louise is a devout Catholic. Scobie is a convert to Catholicism, but his devotion is deep as well. Louise chides her husband for not going to mass often enough. Scobie has an affair with Helen, which he refuses to give up despite the counsel of his confessor, Father Rank. After Louise unexpectedly returns to the colony, Scobie, to appease her, attends mass and takes communion.

In Catholic doctrine, an adulterer who does not end the affair and seek forgiveness is living in a state of mortal sin. Further, receiving the Eucharist while in a state of mortal sin is itself another mortal sin. Scobie's sense of his own sinfulness causes him to commit the ultimate mortal sin in Catholic doctrine, suicide. Scobie, however, agonizes over his actions, seeing them in the context of his religious beliefs and his efforts to determine whether sin is justified when the sinner feels that the sin may shield another from hurt.

The Heart of the Matter is divided into three "books," and each book is divided into three "parts." It is quite possible that Greene wanted

Louise, depressed because of the death of her child, the husband who does not love her, and her lack of friends, wants to leave her home and go to South Africa. (© Oleg Golovnev / Shutterstock.com)

the structure of the book, with its emphasis on three groups of three, to reflect the trinity, the theological belief that God consists of three persons (Father, Son, and Holy Spirit), which is particularly important in Catholic doctrine.

STYLE

Point of View

The point of view Greene adopted in *The Heart of the Matter* would be referred to technically as limited omniscient. *Omniscient narration* refers to a story narrated in the grammatical third person, where characters are referred to as "he," "she," and "they." In contrast is first-person narration, where the narrator is a character and refers to him- or herself as "I" and "me." The word *omniscient* is derived from the Latin and means "all knowing," suggesting that omniscient

narration allows the narrative voice to move freely in time and space and in particular to enter the minds of the characters, re-creating their thoughts and perceptions. However, some writers of fiction choose to limit this access to the thoughts and perceptions of a single character. In *The Heart of the Matter* that character is, of course, Scobie. The bulk of the novel re-creates his thoughts, feelings, attitudes, and reactions, for they are the focus of the book.

Greene is not absolutely consistent about his use of limited omniscient narration. At times, he allows himself access to the minds of other characters. The first scene of the novel, for example, when Wilson and Harris survey the city from a balcony and watch Scobie come into view, is written principally from Wilson's point of view. The relationship between Louise and Wilson is sometimes narrated from Wilson's perspective, and sometimes the narration adopts

Louise's perspective on events. In general, however, the story is about Scobie, so his perspective is the one the narration usually takes.

Setting

The setting of *The Heart of the Matter* is a fictional West African British colony during World War II; the colony is not named, although most readers identify it with Sierra Leone, where Greene spent part of the war as an intelligence officer. The setting becomes an important part of the moral and ethical backdrop of the novel. Early on, for example, Scobie looks into a complaint made by a young woman about her landlady. Given the desperate poverty of many Africans, it is commonplace for a lodger to rent a shack, then put up partitions and rent out the rooms. The owner of the shack would eventually object, enter the shack, tear down the partitions, and in the process perhaps seize the tenant's belongings. Scobie notes that the police officer who investigates such an incident will often take bribes, or "dashes." Scobie used to investigate these incidents with a high sense of responsibility, but over time he came to understand that "guilt and innocence were as relative as the wealth." The inclusion of this type of incident early in the novel prepares the reader for the sense of moral ambiguity and relativism that will play an important role in Scobie's dissolution. In a setting where seemingly everyone is on the take or bending the rules, Scobie's moral absolutism stands out in starker relief.

Also important to the setting are the harbor and the wharf. Numerous ships anchor in the harbor, and Scobie is in part responsible for ensuring that these ships are not smuggling contraband goods or information to the enemy. The wharf attracts young thieves and other disreputable characters, like those who kill Ali.

Symbolism

The Heart of the Matter does not rely on large, overarching symbols, but it does make use of smaller symbols in ways that enhance the novel. One example can be found early in the novel. Scobie arrives at his office at the police station, which is described in a symbolic way: "a table, two kitchen chairs, a cupboard, some rusty handcuffs hanging on a nail like an old hat, a filing cabinet." The reader is told that "to Scobie it was home." The narration goes on to say that "other men slowly build up the sense of home by accumulation." Scobie, in contrast, "built his home by a process of reduction." Greene frequently makes use of this kind of symbolic detail: the rusty handcuffs suggest that Scobie himself is a captive, someone who is imprisoned by the circumstances of his own life: a failed marriage, a dead child, an unfulfilling job, and a lack of money. His captivity has been a long one, for the handcuffs are rusty. The sense of reduction that characterizes his office is indicative of the way his life has shrunk to a state of meaninglessness and despair. His final act of getting rid of the detritus of his life will be his suicide.

HISTORICAL CONTEXT

World War II in Africa

The Heart of the Matter makes limited reference to the events of World War II, yet the war provides the historical backdrop for the novel. Major Scobie has been assigned the task of maintaining security in the colony in light of the events taking place in Europe and Africa as Britain and its allies (including its colonies) resist the aggression of Nazi Germany and Fascist Italy. Greene never identifies by name the colony in which the novel is set. Mention, though, is made that the colony is adjacent to territory held by the collaborationist Vichy French government.

After France fell to the Germans in 1940, Italy saw an opportunity to attack British holdings in Egypt, Sudan, and Kenya. By March 1941, the Germans, led by General Erwin Rommel, had driven the British out of Libya into Egypt. Further, the Germans and Italians were attacking Britain's Mediterranean Sea bases, so it was difficult for ships to resupply British forces in the Middle East. The alternative was to sail around the southern tip of Africa, but such a voyage took far too long. To meet the crisis, the British developed a 3700-mile air route from its colony in the Gold Coast (Sierra Leone's near neighbor) to Egypt over the Sahara.

As Britain fought the Axis powers in the early stages of World War II, it relied heavily on its dominions, colonies, and protectorates for manpower and resources. Oddly, Sierra Leone comprised both a colony and a protectorate, as Harris notes in the novel's first chapter. The colony, with its own administration and laws,

COMPARE
&
CONTRAST

- **1940s:** After a century and a half, Sierra Leone, with its capital at the settlement of Freetown, remains a British Crown colony and protectorate, first established as a haven for escaped and freed North American slaves.

  Today: Sierra Leone, which achieved independence in 1961, continues to recover from a devastating ten-year civil war that ended in 2002 only after British and United Nations intervention.

- **1940s:** Britain's colonies in West Africa— Sierra Leone, the Gambia, the Gold Coast (now Ghana), and Nigeria, collectively called British West Africa—function as staging posts and military bases during World War II.

  Today: Britain's African colonies, as well as those of other European nations, have been independent since the 1960s.

- **1940s:** Greene, Evelyn Waugh, G. K. Chesterton, and Thomas Merton are among many British converts to Catholicism, forming a class of prominent Catholic intellectuals whose religious beliefs are sometimes controversial in Anglican England.

  Today: Catholics, once a tiny underground minority that historically was persecuted, now represent about 8 percent of the population of England and Wales and attract little notice for their religious beliefs.

- **1940s:** Africa, including Sierra Leone, is the scene of an active diamond smuggling operation during World War II and beyond, as diamonds are valuable not only as gemstones but also for industrial purposes.

  Today: Sierra Leone has an active diamond-mining sector, although it tends to be conducted on a small scale by individuals who rarely if ever rise out of poverty through the stones they find.

---

encompassed the original settlement: Freetown and the peninsula on which it is located, along with nearby islands. The protectorate consisted of outlying territories that surrounded Freetown. The distinction between colony and protectorate, however, was blurry. A colony was clearly under the legal control of the colonizer and enjoyed no independence. Protectorates, on the other hand, historically retained their autonomy as sovereign states, but in exchange for certain obligations (provision of natural resources, payment of taxes), they enjoyed the protection of the nations that administered their affairs. During the Second World War, the protectorate portion of Sierra Leone was treated much like a colony.

Sierra Leone, along with Britain's other West African colonies, provided Britain with raw materials such as bauxite, the ore that contains aluminum, which was essential for aircraft production. Additionally, Britain recruited some 200,000 troops from its West African colonies, and Britain's Royal Air Force recruited 10,000 West Africans for ground duty. These men, who constructed airfields, harbors, and roads, were essential, for they were able to withstand the region's punishing heat and malaria attacks, often in contrast to their British overseers.

Freetown played a prominent role in Britain's efforts during the war. It functioned as a convoy station, and at the peak of Freetown's wartime activity, as many as two hundred military and cargo vessels could be at anchor in the harbor at any one time; it is little wonder that Scobie's efforts to detect smuggling were like a search for the proverbial needle in a haystack. More generally, the city was highly militarized, with installations, officers, and troops. The population of the city doubled during a period

Helen is one of the survivors of a shipwreck who spent forty harrowing days at sea in a lifeboat before reaching land. (© Ensuper | shutterstock.com)

of less than two years after the outbreak of war, with thousands of men arriving to work on construction sites and on the docks, dragging in their wake wharf rats (young thieves, like those who kill Ali), smugglers, black marketers (like Yusef), and other unsavory characters.

To gain the consent of Sierra Leoneans to their wartime demands, British authorities employed propaganda, punishments, and threats. Much of Britain's success in winning support in Sierra Leone and the other West African colonies (and its colonies throughout the world) stemmed from the success of the propaganda efforts Greene took part in as an employee of the Ministry of Information. This propaganda, designed to shore up support against a common, dreaded enemy, had the ironic effect of bolstering a sense of nationalism in the West African colonies, so that within a decade after the war, they were agitating for independence. They won that independence in the early 1960s.

During World War II, diamonds were not just a luxury good. Diamonds were essential for converting industry in Britain and the United States to wartime production. Only diamonds were hard enough to allow industry to produce

the precision parts needed for the weapons of war. Boosting the value of diamonds was the fact that the world's diamond supply, emanating largely from Africa, was under the monopolistic control of De Beers, a cartel based in Luxembourg that today is still the major player in the diamond business. De Beers would not accede to Allied requests to provide stockpiles of diamonds, fearing that doing so would drive down prices. Thus, with prices propped up by a limited supply, a smuggling trade developed in South Africa and Sierra Leone, with millions of pounds' worth of diamonds smuggled out of Africa to Europe (especially Germany), the Middle East, and the United States each year.

CRITICAL OVERVIEW

Numerous reviewers in 1948 responded to *The Heart of the Matter* with applause. A contributor to *Kirkus Reviews*, for example, called it "a novel of considerable seriousness and stature." The reviewer went on to write that the novel has "a variety of virtues," among them its "drama," its "satiric subtlety," and "its relentless portrayal of a man destroyed by the strength of his conscience."

In a review in the *New York Times*, William Du Bois enthused:

> Mr. Greene (as a well-earned public knows) is a profound moralist with a technique to match his purpose. From first page to last, this record of one man's breakdown on a heat-drugged fever-coast makes its point as a crystal clear allegory—and as an engrossing novel.

Despite the success the novel enjoyed when it was published, it was vilified by no less a figure than George Orwell, author of the classic novel *1984*. In a review in the *New Yorker* magazine, Orwell called the novel's plot "ridiculous." He stated that Scobie's motives "do not adequately explain his actions," adding that the book is filled with "psychological absurdities." Orwell also believed that the novel's setting in Africa is unnecessary for the book's theme and therefore "gives it an air of triviality." Orwell questioned Greene's attitude toward Catholicism in the novel, writing that "it is impossible not to feel a sort of snobbishness in Mr. Greene's attitude, both here and in his other books written from an explicitly Catholic standpoint." In Orwell's view, what he calls the "cult of the sanctified sinner" featured in Greene's novels—that is, the belief that sinners, especially Catholic sinners, are somehow holier because they face greater temptations—is "frivolous."

Peter M. Sinclair, in an essay in *Renascence: Essays on Values in Literature*, disagrees, noting that "Greene does not prescribe moral behavior, nor does he necessarily make an epistemological inquiry into the nature of sin, but he speaks of good and evil as aesthetic categories in the context of fiction." Sinclair went on to write:

> Greene's novels never present anything systematic, and critics who attempt to make Greene's fiction fit within a theological system lose sight of the more human experience of despair that he presents. He claimed that if he did not make faith indeterminate—if he did not place Catholic concerns into existential contexts—he would "produce only advertising brochures setting out in attractive terms the advantages of Church membership."

Disagreeing with Orwell, too, is Henry J. Donaghy. In *Graham Greene: An Introduction to His Writings*, Donaghy comments favorably on the role of the novel's setting:

> Still another device used effectively is setting. The novel opens with Wilson on the balcony of the Bedford Hotel, looking out over the sloping tin roofs to the sea.... We see the quay, the ships, the prostitutes fighting for the sailors... as Scobie comes into view.

Donaghy went on to conclude: "It is a place of primitive passion that the white man likes to think he stands above.... [Scobie] somehow imagines the setting accords him a privilege not accorded others."

Also implicitly disagreeing with Orwell is a recent reviewer, Robert Coles. Writing in the *New Oxford Review*, Coles comments on the novel's African setting, seeing Scobie as "a representative of a smug, corrupt, exploitative colonial world—its mainstay, actually: the small-time official who does the daily dirty work." Coles added that "such a world [Greene] surely knew, even then, was on its last legs. Indeed, much of this novel exposes the dreary moral stupidity of that very world." For Cole, Scobie's suicide is emblematic of the death of colonialism.

Readers in the twenty-first century have continued to respond with enthusiasm to *The Heart of the Matter*. In 2005, *Time* magazine cited the book as one of its "All-*Time* 100 Novels." In describing the novel, Richard Lacayo

wrote of Greene, "no one could parse moral dilemmas with quite his eye for the subtle ways that Satan persuades the righteous." Author Aimee Liu, in an essay on *The Heart of the Matter* in the *Los Angeles Review of Books*, comments appreciatively on Greene's effective use of detail:

> The facts in Greene's fiction resonate not just historically, but also philosophically and theologically. Political exigencies within the narrative become prisms for personal choice. Layers of power and official status vibrate with the moral uncertainties that rank and title can't quite conceal. Information serves both a literal and a metaphoric purpose, as Greene's interpretation distills from his wartime experience the deeper truth of what he called "the human situation."

CRITICISM

Michael J. O'Neal

O'Neal holds a PhD in English. In the following essay, he examines the thematic use of setting in The Heart of the Matter.

In his 1948 review of *The Heart of the Matter* for the *New Yorker* magazine, George Orwell faulted Graham Greene's decision to set his book in Africa, writing, "The fact that the book is set in Africa while the action takes place almost entirely inside a tiny white community gives it an air of triviality." Orwell's dismissal is wide of the mark. For in fact, the African setting plays a crucial role in the novel.

For starters, Orwell is incorrect in his use of the phrase "almost entirely." While much of the novel is indeed set within the white community, much of it is not. Crucial scenes take place in the harbor and aboard the Portuguese ship, on the wharves, at the home of Tallit, and in the inland town of Bamba, among other places.

Beyond that, Greene makes clear the importance of the colonial setting in a crucial passage in Book One. Scobie is having a conversation with Yusef about rice shipments and the inability of locals to get rice at the controlled price. Yusef responds: "I've heard, Major Scobie, that they can't get their share of the free distribution unless they tip the policeman at the gate." The narration then comments:

> It was quite true. There was a retort in this colony to every accusation. There was always

WHAT DO I READ NEXT?

- *The Power and the Glory* (1940) is perhaps Greene's most famous and widely read novel. It tells the story of an unnamed fugitive in Mexico who is being pursued by an unnamed policeman. It raises profound questions about the nature of sin and salvation.

- Greene distinguished his serious novels from what he called "entertainments," or novels that he considered lighter fare. During a six-week period he wrote a novel of international intrigue, *The Confidential Agent* (1939), which he called an entertainment on the book's title page.

- *Men at Arms* (1952) is the first volume of Evelyn Waugh's World War II trilogy about war, religion, and politics. (The other two volumes are *Officers and Gentlemen* and *The End of the Battle*.) The protagonist is Guy Crouchback, a thirty-five-year-old divorced Catholic who joins the Royal Corps of Halberdiers, where he meets Apthorpe, an eccentric African.

- Nadine Gordimer is a Nobel Prize–winning novelist and short-story writer from South Africa whose work has been compared with Greene's because of its themes of race, love, and morality. Her 1979 novel *Burger's Daughter* tells the story of a daughter of Communists who tries to analyze her relationship with her antiapartheid father and is drawn into political activism.

- *The Oxford History of the British Empire: The Twentieth Century* (2001), edited by Judith M. Brown and William Roger Louis, is the fourth volume in the publisher's series about the history of the British Empire. It provides a comprehensive account of Britain's colonial activities during the twentieth century.

- Readers interested in Britain's Secret Intelligence Service, which counted Greene among its employees in World War II, will find Keith Jeffery's *The Secret History of MI6: 1909–1949* (2011) informative and comprehensive.

- Young adults for generations have enjoyed J. R. R. Tolkien's fantasy trilogy *The Lord of the Rings*, consisting of *The Fellowship of the Ring* (1954), *The Two Towers* (1954), and *The Return of the King* (1955). Tolkien, like Greene, was a Catholic, and he claimed that his Catholic faith informed his conception of *The Lord of the Rings*.

- Readers interested in African diamond smuggling and efforts to stop it will find *The Diamond Smugglers* (1957), a nonfiction book by Ian Fleming (of James Bond, agent 007, fame), informative.

- Biyi Bandele's *The King's Rifle* (2009) is a coming-of-age novel about a young West African soldier who fights in World War II.

- William Boyd's *A Good Man in Africa* (1982) is a comic novel about a British official in a fictional African country during the decline of colonialism.

- *Mister Johnson* (1939), by British author Joyce Cary, is based on his personal experiences in Africa. The novel, though comic in many places, is ultimately a tragic story of a young African man in Nigeria who runs afoul of the colonial administration

---

a blacker corruption elsewhere to be pointed at. The scandalmongers of the secretariat fulfilled a useful purpose—they kept alive the idea that no one was to be trusted. That was better than complacence.

Scobie goes on to reflect:

Why, he wondered, ... do I love this place so much? Is it because here human nature hasn't had time to disguise itself? Nobody here could

> SCOBIE IS PART OF A COLONIAL
> ADMINISTRATION THAT BELIEVES ITSELF TO BE
> BENEFICENT, BRINGING CIVILIZATION TO THE DARKER
> PARTS OF THE WORLD, BUT THE TRUE DARKNESS
> EXISTS WITHIN HIS OWN HEART AND SOUL."

ever talk about a heaven on earth. Heaven remained rigidly in its proper place on the other side of death, and on this side flourished the injustices, the cruelties, the meanness that elsewhere people so cleverly hushed up.

Scobie further reflects that "here you could love human beings nearly as God loved them, knowing the worst: you didn't love a pose, a pretty dress, a sentiment artfully assumed." These passages can be read to contain "the heart of the matter" in brief. The atmosphere that surrounds Scobie is one of corruption, bribes, distrust, meanness, injustice, and suspicion—an atmosphere that is intensified by the war and by the efforts of the colonists to cover it up with "a pose, a pretty dress" as they go about their normal business.

Although the war does not play a particularly active part in the novel, it serves as a crucial backdrop, for Scobie is trying to negotiate human relations and make moral decisions in the context of a threatening, hostile world, one that could collapse at any moment—as in a sense it does when the survivors of the shipwreck, among them Helen, arrive in the harbor after having been torpedoed by a German submarine. This atmosphere is further intensified by the presence of such characters as Wilson, who was sent to the colony essentially to spy on Scobie and report on his activities. Additionally, the diamond smuggling trade would likely have been less active were it not for the war. Throughout the novel, blackmail, murder, suicide, bribes, brothels, feverish passions, warfare, and sin create a world that seemingly dooms an essentially good man like Scobie to despair.

The importance of the setting extends beyond these factors, for Greene could have achieved the same ends in, for example, London's East End, with its own docks, wharves, thievery,

and corruption. By selecting an African setting, Greene pays a distinct nod of recognition to Joseph Conrad's short novel *Heart of Darkness*. In that novel, a narrator named Marlow travels down Africa's Congo River to find an ivory agent, Kurtz, who has plummeted into madness. Conrad uses the voyage into the "heart" of Africa to explore such issues as racism, colonialism, and savagery versus civilization. It is no accident that both writers used the word *heart* in their titles, for both novels are essentially about the human heart, about what the passage quoted above calls "human nature."

Greene examines that heart in the context of his Catholicism. Traditional lore invites Catholics to imagine the soul of a person who is in a state of grace as a blank, white canvas. Small sins, or venial sins, are isolated stains on the canvas. But the soul of a person living in a state of mortal sin is conceived of as entirely black. The words *white* and *black* are not intended to have racial connotations; they are simply a reflection of the age-old associations of whiteness (or light) with purity, innocence, and goodness, and of blackness (or darkness) with evil, corruption, and guilt. Scobie, in traditional Catholic teaching, is in a state of mortal sin, first, because of his adulterous affair with Helen, and second, by taking Holy Communion while still in a state of mortal sin because of his failure to renounce Helen and receive absolution from Father Rank; his soul is doubly tainted, and it becomes triply and irrevocably tainted when he commits suicide. He becomes a tragic figure because of the corrosion that overtakes his spirit. His life is a shambles. He is overwhelmed by his sense of pity and responsibility. Yet he is a civilized person, not a "savage." Scobie is part of a colonial administration that believes itself to be beneficent, bringing civilization to the darker parts of the world, but the true darkness exists within his own heart and soul.

At the same time, Scobie recognizes the futility of the colonial administration. He feels that his fifteen years in the colony have been a waste. He does not appear to have many friends among the Britons in the colony. He never enjoys any amusement, never truly takes part in community activities. He is isolated by his own loneliness, despair, and determination to take responsibility for the unhappiness and discontentment of the people in his life. In this context, the novel takes on a muted, darkened feeling. Everyone is a failure in some way. Fever, death, shipwreck, invasion, suicide, murder, and corruption are pervasive, despite a veneer of civilization: the social gatherings, the dress codes, the presence of the Catholic Church and its servants, the legal codes that govern the colony, and the efforts of Britain and its allies, including its colonies, to resist the evils of fascism.

The sense of civilization as a veneer runs throughout the novel. An example is provided by Wilson's visit to the brothel, where the woman who appears to be the madam blocks his efforts to leave and demands payment from him, even though he has not used the services of any of the girls. Wilson feels threatened by the corruption and feverish heat of the brothel that surround him, where the shiny surface of civilization is peeled away to show what festers underneath. Yusef provides yet another example. He operates a number of shops and on the surface appears to be a simple merchant. In fact, however, he exploits the political situation and, in particular, the weaknesses and vulnerabilities of others for his own gain. Like Satan in the desert, he tempts Christ in the figure of Scobie, except that Scobie, unlike Christ, succumbs.

The trappings of polite society in Britain's African colony fail to stamp out the "blacker corruption" that can always be pointed at, along with the distrust that people feel when they are removed from their settled, familiar surroundings and placed in an environment where they do not know the rules and where local people are forced to get by in any way they can. In this regard, Louise has an important role to play. She is unhappy in the colony. She feels isolated and alone. She claims to have no friends. She maintains a veneer of civilization through her interest in literature and her books of poetry.

However, Louise is lacking in fiber. She believes that the only way to achieve happiness is to leave the colony and remove herself to South Africa, which at the time had a much larger and more firmly entrenched Western community. She is unable to endure the heart of darkness, and so she leaves. Pemberton is overwhelmed by the heart of darkness, so he leaves at the end of a rope. Scobie, too, is unable to endure the heart of darkness, particularly the darkness of his own heart, so he leaves in the only way he knows how. He finds salvation, perhaps, "in its proper place on the other side of death."

Scobie's Catholic faith makes him believe his suicide will condemn him to damnation. (© James Steidl | Shutterstock.com)

Source: Michael J. O'Neal, Critical Essay on *Heart of the Matter*, in *Novels for Students*, Gale, Cengage Learning, 2014.

Michael Shelden

In the following excerpt, Shelden describes Scobie in The Heart of the Matter *as defiant and "determined to break the rules."*

… This situation is reflected in the novel that he began writing in the mid-1940s, *The Heart of the Matter*. Major Scobie, the assistant commissioner of police in Sierra Leone, is married to a woman he no longer loves. After many years of marriage, he has nothing left to share with her except misery. Louise Scobie wants to believe that their marriage will survive, not because she loves him but because she has no way to survive on her own. She constantly reminds him of how much she depends on him and complains of how lonely she feels. Unwilling to let him go, she tries to keep up appearances, calling him "darling" and using her childish nickname for him, Ticki. But he hates to hear such things and resents all her efforts to be kind. Everything about her annoys him—the way she talks, the odd dresses she wears, the clutter of her collection of little objects in their home. In a moment of candid reflection, Louise admits that she is fighting a losing battle, but she places most of the blame on her husband. Scobie, she says, is incapable of loving anyone, not even himself.

They have had only one child, but the girl died in England when she was three. The news of the girl's death reaches Scobie in a manner that recalls Greene's experience with his father's death. One telegram announces that the girl is ill, the second that she is dead. When the two messages reach Scobie in reverse order, he does not know what to think. Accepting her death is hard enough, but being left in doubt by the second message is the worst part. It seems that his whole life has been dogged by such pointless suffering. As a result he has come to expect the worst, and to be wary of any human ties. If he had his life to live over again, he tells himself, he would live it alone.

The only thing that keeps Scobie from abandoning Louise is his acute sense of guilt. She knows that this is her one source of power over him and does her best to appeal to his notion of right and wrong. She tries to make him go to Mass, although she knows that he has no faith. He jokes that her faith is great enough for both of them, and she says that he became a Catholic only because he wanted to marry her. To give himself and his wife a little relief from such tiresome disputes, he sends her on a long holiday to South Africa. While Louise is away, he falls in love with a young woman who is vulnerable and alone. The affair dooms not only his marriage but also his life. After Louise returns he finds himself trapped between the emotional demands of both women, and his sense of guilt soars out of control, driving him toward death.

Helen Rolt does not fit the stereotype of the other woman. She is neither sexy nor charming, and she is certainly not beautiful; in fact, at one point Scobie admits to himself that she is "ugly." In part, he seems to want an affair simply to make himself more miserable. There is no question that a love of pain attracts him to Helen. He tells himself that her ugliness is more exciting because no one else will give her a second look. If he cannot have beauty and love, he will make a pleasure of ugliness and pain. In no time his "love" for Helen gives rise to a nasty fight. She

is deeply jealous of Louise and complains that Scobie will never leave his wife. He falls back on the empty excuse that he is Catholic, and she explodes in anger, pointing out that his scruples keep him from marrying her but not from having sex with her. In time, Scobie thinks, Helen and Louise will be "indistinguishable" in his mind. He will have two women to dread, two women to keep him trapped. The situation is never as bad as Scobie seems to think. As we later discover, both women *can* live without him. But his passion for overdramatizing his troubles causes him to contemplate suicide, and the more he thinks about it, the more it appeals to him as the perfect escape from a seemingly impossible problem.

There is also the added appeal of defying God, who has failed to rescue him from his plight. As Scobie gets closer to committing suicide, he thinks less about the women in his life and more about his confrontation with God. He tells God that he will be doing him a favor by taking his own life. But the pleasure is all Scobie's. At Mass he has a vision of devilish priests celebrating a Black Mass and tells himself that their hatred of God is a kind of "perverse devotion" to him. He regards himself as too weak to reach the level of their power and glory, but his aspirations lie in that direction. Having found so much unhappiness in his life, he wants to wallow in it, making every good thing bad. It is a path of destruction that must lead to the sin of suicide. It is the only way that he can carry pain to the ultimate extreme, and the only way that he can imitate those devilish priests in their proud orgy of hatred.

The Heart of the Matter is the story of a man who seems determined to break the rules. He is a policeman who cannot maintain law and order in his own life, violating the moral prohibitions against adultery and suicide. And, as does *The Ministry of Fear*, the novel makes the emotional turmoil in one man's life the center of attention in a world at war. In Sierra Leone the war is barely felt. There are blackouts but no raids. Wounded people are brought ashore from torpedoed ships, but the actual attacks take place hundreds of miles away. Stuck in an alien land at the margin of an enormous battleground, Scobie is free to pursue his lonely duel with God. The rest of the world can take care of itself....

Source: Michael Shelden, "The Undiscovered Country: *The Heart of the Matter*," in *Graham Greene: The Enemy Within*, Random House, 1994, pp. 291–93.

Martin Turnell

In the following essay, Turnell discusses some of the religious themes in Greene's novel.

The Heart of the Matter might fairly be described as a companion piece to *The Power and the Glory*, but we shall see that in one respect at least it is notably inferior to the earlier novel. It deals like *The Power and the Glory* with an immature world, a world whose inhabitants are morally, mentally, and emotionally undeveloped. They are arranged broadly in three tiers: police, administrators, and natives who correspond to the police, expatriates, and natives in *The Power and the Glory*. Children play an important part, but in this novel they underline and prolong the immaturity of the adult world instead of providing a criticism of it as to some extent they do in *The Power and the Glory*. What is more obvious in *The Heart of the Matter* than in almost any of the other novels is that Greene's world is a world of mediocrities. His protagonists are examples of what has been called, in another context, "the unheroic hero." They are never distinguished by their moral or intellectual qualities: the hallmark of the Greene hero is grievous moral weakness. The only two saints in his work appear to achieve sanctity by accident. The clergy are remarkable mainly for their inadequacy, which seems a reflection of the moral weakness of the laity. Their futility or their silence hastens the disaster; they arrive on the scene with empty words of comfort when it is too late and the protagonist is dead.

There is, as I have already suggested, the same sharp contrast in *The Heart of the Matter* and *The Power and the Glory* between the "inner" and the "outer" man, between the public and the private image, the office and its holder. The policeman's uniform confers an outward authority which is markedly at variance with the lack of inner authority of the individual. It also has the effect of concealing personal weakness from public view. The same is true of the civilian administrators whose position as state employees sometimes hides criminal tendencies. One is given premature retirement, another is transferred, for putting his hand into the till. A third commits suicide as the only escape from an intolerable situation created by his dishonesty.

Scobie, working as a police officer in an appalling backwater, has earned a reputation for integrity. He is known as "the Just": a local Aristides in the British bureaucracy who is

> **THE RESULT IS THAT WE HAVE AN INCREDIBLE CHARACTER USED AS AN INADEQUATE ILLUSTRATION OF AN IMPOSSIBLE THESIS."**

respected alike by colleagues, friends, and the native population. The novel is largely devoted to an exposure of the man, to showing how undeserved the flattering title is. It is true that he is not scruffy or disreputable or given to the bottle or other men's beds. The source of his downfall is precisely what is esteemed a virtue by the secular world: his humanity, his feeling for his fellow human beings; in a word—a very terrible word in this novel—his "pity." It is a terrible word because virtue is turned inside out, because what is ordinarily a virtue becomes a fatal weakness. We are reminded here of the essential mediocrity of Greene's characters and of the "uncomfortable questioning critic" of his first novel. It is a sign of Scobie's immaturity and of his singular lack of insight into his own motives that he is taken in by his private cant about "pity":

> He had no sense of responsibility toward the beautiful and the graceful and the intelligent. They could find their own way. It was the face for which nobody would go out of his way, the face that would soon be used to rebuffs and indifference that demanded his allegiance. The word "pity" is used as loosely as the word "love," the terrible promiscuous passion which so few experienced.

The word occurs again in an account of Scobie watching his poor, silly, snobbish wife sleeping:

> He watched her through the muslin net. Her face had the yellow ivory tinge of atrabine: her hair which had once been the colour of bottled honey was dark and stringy with sweat. These were the times of ugliness when he loved her, when pity reached the intensity of a passion. It was pity that told him to go, he wouldn't have woken his worst enemy from sleep—leave alone Louise.

One would hardly feel inclined to describe either of these passages as distinguished prose, but their purpose is clear. Scobie's special pleading is really aimed at the reader. The comparison between the fortunate and the unfortunate, the use of a phrase like "terrible promiscuous passion," the pathetic account of Louise's ugliness, are intended to make us swallow the author's thesis about "pity." The faults in the writing are more pronounced in another passage in which Scobie reflects on his responsibilities towards his wife:

> He had always been prepared to accept the responsibility for his actions, and he had always been half aware too, from the time he made his terrible private vow, how far *this* action might carry him. Despair is the price one pays for setting oneself an impossible aim. It is, one is told, the unforgiveable sin, but it is the sin the corrupt or evil man never practices. He always has hope. He never reaches the freezing point of knowing absolute failure. Only the man of good will always carries in his heart the capacity for damnation.

There is a similarity between the tone and content of this passage and the passages I quoted from *The Power and the Glory*. It, too, is filled with special pleading and unconvincing arguments. The wicked man has a better chance of salvation than the man of good will who, we are told in a characteristically emotive phrase, has taken a "terrible private vow," which after all is nothing more than to make an unprepossessing wife happy.

In *The Power and the Glory* we watch a movement which looks like a descent leading to martyrdom: in *The Heart of the Matter* we watch the descent of a man who seems, but only seems, to be betrayed by his good qualities and are left in doubt about his salvation. For if *The Power and the Glory* is one of the most popular of Greene's novels it is because there are genuine motives for the whisky priest's actions when he finds himself on the run in a hostile country. Scobie's "pity" is far less convincing. He is a very ordinary individual with the traditional public school virtues—decency, uprightness, kindness, integrity—who finds himself married to the wrong woman. He also has the characteristic public school vice: the sentimentality which underlies the heartiness and supposed manliness that are sedulously inculcated by the schools. In the supercharged atmosphere of a Greene novel the sentimentality produces disproportionate results because Scobie's sentimental pity for the underdog completely undermines his character, revealing the extreme brittleness of his virtues. He is guilty of one betrayal after another: his duty as a police officer, his loyalty to a faithful

servant, his marriage vows, and finally his vows to the Church. A blubbering Portuguese captain is more than enough to make him betray his trust to his country and to do so without any serious struggle or apparently without any realization of the enormity of the offence. He is a believing Catholic, but simply in order to avoid paining his wife or arousing suspicion about his liaison with another woman, he makes a sacrilegious communion which could have been avoided without the slightest difficulty. Finally, he commits suicide on the pretext that it is the only way to avoid making two women unhappy, but in reality because he is too cowardly to face the situation created by his weakness—it would be too much for his "pity."

I have suggested that in one particular *The Heart of the Matter* compares unfavorably with *The Power and the Glory*. The superiority of *The Power and the Glory* lies primarily in the fact that the priest's simple faith does provide a point of reference, a positive standard which enables us to see the actions of the other characters in perspective. It is precisely this that is lacking in *The Heart of the Matter*. I have tried to show that Scobie's "pity" is a sentimental illusion. What is more serious is that the illusion is bolstered up by an element of casuistry. It is suggested in one place that the Crucifixion was a form of suicide. This unorthodox suggestion becomes the excuse for Scobie's suicide which by implication is compared favorably with the suicide of the civil servant who could not face material difficulties which were more real than Scobie's sentimental difficulties. We hear much in the novel of corruption and decay, but the casuistry seems to me to point to something corrupt in the novel itself. For what we find in it is not so much an absence of moral perspective as a deliberate destruction of perspective in the interests of melodrama.

The truth is that sensational events like the sacrilegious communion and the suicide have no real motivation. The author set out to write a "theological thriller" about a Catholic gambling with his soul, which leaves us in doubt (as it was bound to) about the result of Scobie's "last throw." The protagonist is "rigged." What seems to have happened is that situation preceded character as it would in an adventure story. The result is that we have an incredible character used as an inadequate illustration of an impossible thesis.

Source: Martin Turnell, "*The Heart of the Matter*," in *Graham Greene: A Critical Essay*, edited by Roderick Jellema, William B. Eerdmans, 1967, pp. 27–31.

SOURCES

Allitt, Patrick, "Introduction: Intellectuals Becoming Catholics," in *Catholic Converts: British and American Intellectuals Turn to Rome*, Cornell University Press, 1997, http://www.nytimes.com/books/first/a/allitt-converts.html (accessed March 5, 2013).

"Blue Plaque for Graham Greene," English Heritage website, April 1, 2011, http://www.english-heritage.org.uk/about/news/blue-plaque-for-graham-greene/ (accessed March 4, 2013).

Coles, Robert, Review of *The Heart of the Matter*, in *New Oxford Review*, April 1996, http://www.newoxfordreview.org/article.jsp?did=0496-coles (accessed March 6, 2013).

Davies, Roy, "Dangerous Diamonds: Scandals behind the Sparkle of the World's Most Desirable Gems," 2007, http://projects.exeter.ac.uk/RDavies/arian/scandals/diamonds.html (accessed March 5, 2013).

Donaghy, Henry J., *Graham Greene: An Introduction to His Writings*, Rodopi B.V., 1986, p. 58.

Du Bois, William, "A Searching Novel of Man's Unpaid Debt to Man," in *New York Times*, July 11, 1948, http://www.nytimes.com/books/00/02/20/specials/greene-matter.html (accessed March 6, 2013).

Evans, Rob, and David Hencke, "In Life as in Fiction, Greene's Taunts Left Americans in a Quiet Fury," in *Guardian* (London, England), December 1, 2002, http://www.guardian.co.uk/uk/2002/dec/02/film.books (accessed March 3, 2013).

Flamini, Roland, "Still Here: The Case of British Catholics," in *World Affairs*, March–April 2011, http://www.worldaffairsjournal.org/article/still-here-case-british-catholics (accessed March 5, 2013).

Ford, Tamasin, "Sierra Leone's Diamonds Still a Source of Contention," NPR website, November 23, 2012, http://www.npr.org/2012/11/23/165271466/sierra-leone-holds-a-vote-not-a-war-on-diamonds (accessed March 5, 2013).

"Graham Greene, 86, Dies; Novelist of the Soul," in *New York Times*, April 4, 1991, http://www.nytimes.com/books/00/02/20/specials/greene-obit.html (accessed March 1, 2013).

Greene, Graham, *The Heart of the Matter*, Penguin Books, 2004.

Hargreaves, J. D., "The Establishment of the Sierra Leone Protectorate and the Insurrection of 1898," in *Cambridge Historical Journal*, Vol. 12, No. 1, 1956, pp. 56–80.

Howard, Allen M., Abstract of "Freetown, Sierra Leone and World War II: Assessing the Impact of the War and the Contributions Made," March 17, 2011, http://www.ascleiden.nl/?q=news/events/seminars/freetown-sierra-leone-and-world-war-ii-assessing-impact-war-and-contributions (accessed March 6, 2013).

Ibhawoh, Bonny, "Second World War Propaganda, Imperial Idealism and Anti-colonial Nationalism in British West Africa," in *Nordic Journal of African Studies*, Vol. 16, No. 2, 2007, pp. 221–43.

"James Tait Black Prizes: Fiction Winners," University of Edinburgh website, http://www.ed.ac.uk/news/events/tait-black/winners/fiction (accessed March 1, 2013).

Joannon, Pierre, "Graham Greene's Other Island," in *Conversations with Graham Greene*, edited by Henry J. Donaghy, University Press of Mississippi, 1992, p. 163.

Lacayo, Richard, "*The Heart of the Matter*," in *Time*, January 27, 2010, http://entertainment.time.com/2005/10/16/all-time-100-novels/slide/the-heart-of-the-matter-1948-by-graham-greene/ (accessed March 6, 2013).

Liu, Aimee, "Reaching for *The Heart of the Matter*," in *Los Angeles Review of Books*, August 5, 2012, http://lareviewofbooks.org/article.php?id=807&fulltext=1 (accessed March 6, 2013).

Orange, Michelle, "Not Easy Being Greene: Graham Greene's Letters," in *Nation*, May 4, 2009, http://www.thenation.com/article/not-easy-being-greene-graham-greenes-letters (accessed March 3, 2013).

Orwell, George, "The Sanctified Sinner," in *New Yorker*, July 17, 1948, pp. 61–62.

Pearce, Joseph, "Why Tolkien Says *The Lord of the Rings* Is Catholic," Catholic Education Resource Center website, http://www.catholiceducation.org/articles/arts/al0161.html (accessed March 4, 2013).

Quartey, Kwei, "How West Africa Helped Win World War II," in *Foreign Policy in Focus*, June 6, 2012, http://www.fpif.org/articles/how_west_africa_helped_win_world_war_ii (accessed March 5, 2013).

Review of *The Heart of the Matter*, in *Kirkus Reviews*, July 1, 1948, https://www.kirkusreviews.com/book-reviews/graham-greene/heart-of-matter/ (accessed March 6, 2013).

Sherwood, Marika, "Colonies, Colonials and World War Two," BBC News website, http://www.bbc.co.uk/history/worldwars/wwtwo/colonies_colonials_01.shtml (accessed March 5, 2013).

"Sierra Leone Profile: A Chronology of Key Events," BBC News website, November 28, 2012, http://www.bbc.co.uk/news/world-africa-14094419 (accessed March 5, 2012).

Sinclair, Peter M., "Graham Greene and Christian Despair: Tragic Aesthetics in *Brighton Rock* and *The Heart of the Matter*," in *Renascence: Essays on Values in Literature*, January 1, 2011, http://www.thefreelibrary.com/Graham+Greene+and+Christian+despair%3A+tragic+aesthetics+in+Brighton...-a0250032597 (accessed March 6, 2013).

Watts, Cedric, "*The Heart of the Matter* and the Later Novels of Graham Greene," in *A Companion to the*

British and Irish Novel, 1945–2000, edited by Brian W. Shaffer, John Wiley & Sons, 2008, pp. 278–88.

Woods, Katherine, "Graham Greene's Stirring Tale of Beleaguered Souls," in *New York Times*, October 1, 1939, http://www.nytimes.com/books/00/02/20/specials/greene-agent.html (accessed March 4, 2013).

FURTHER READING

Greene, Graham, *Graham Greene: Collected Essays*, Penguin, 1995.

> This volume, first published in 1969, contains a generous sampling of the author's nonfiction prose. The essays span the author's life, from describing how a novel called *The Viper of Milan* (1906) by Marjorie Bowen inspired him to become at writer at age fourteen, to a description of his last trip to Sierra Leone in 1968.

Greene, Richard, ed., *Graham Greene: A Life in Letters*, W. W. Norton, 2008.

> Greene (who is no relation to the author) creates a biography of the author out of his own words in the thousands of letters he left behind. Many of these letters were not even made available to authorized biographer Norman Sherry. Among his correspondents were Evelyn Waugh, Muriel Spark, Kurt Vonnegut, Ralph Richardson, Michael Korda, Anthony Burgess, the future Pope Paul VI, and Swiss theologian Hans Küng.

Hynes, Samuel, *Graham Greene: A Collection of Critical Essays*, Prentice-Hall, 1973.

> This volume is a collection of critical essays about Greene and his fiction. Included are seminal essays by such scholars as Morton Dauwen Zabel, R. W. B. Lewis, Richard Hoggart, Ian Gregor, and Frank Kermode.

Parkinson, David, ed., *The Graham Greene Film Reader: Reviews, Essays, Interviews, and Film Stories*, Applause Theatre and Cinema Books, 2000.

> This volume assembles Greene's film reviews, along with his essays, lectures, and letters on film. The reviews provide valuable insights into Greene's aesthetic views. Many of Greene's novels were filmed, so the book includes several of his film treatments and lists all of the films made from Greene's fiction.

Sherry, Norman, *The Life of Graham Greene*, 3 vols., Penguin, 2004–2005.

> This three-volume biography of Greene, regarded as the definitive biography, was written by the biographer Greene himself chose. Volume 1 covers the author's early life up to 1939; volume 2 covers the years 1939 to 1955; and the third volume covers the years 1955 until the author's death in 1991.

SUGGESTED SEARCH TERMS

African diamond smuggling AND World War II

British Catholic novelists

British colonialism

British West African colonies AND World War II

French West Africa AND World War II

Graham Greene

Graham Greene AND Catholicism

Graham Greene AND Heart of the Matter

scramble for Africa

Sierra Leone AND World War II

Vichy government AND Africa

World War II AND black market colonies

The House behind the Cedars

CHARLES W. CHESNUTT

1900

Charles W. Chesnutt is the author of *The House behind the Cedars*, published in 1900. The novel, regarded as among the author's major works, is about "passing," that is, the ability of people with black ancestry but fair skin to assume a white identity in white society. Set in the years following the Civil War, the novel features Rena Walden, a woman of mixed-race ancestry who leaves her home to join her brother, John Warwick, in a new town, where she, like her brother, passes as white. She falls in love with a white aristocrat, but he rejects her when he learns the truth about her ancestry. *The House behind the Cedars* was well received by critics, but because it dealt with racial themes that were controversial at the time, including interracial relations and racial identity, it was not highly successful in the marketplace.

Chesnutt began writing the novel in 1889, although he originally conceived it as a short story titled "Rena Walden." However, the publisher, Houghton Mifflin, urged Chesnutt to revise and rewrite the story, and in the process it evolved into a novel, though a relatively short one (some 73,000 words). Chesnutt was personally qualified to write such a novel. He, like his protagonist, came from a mixed-race background, and although his heritage was predominantly European, he celebrated his African American roots. He remarked later in life that the issue of the position of mixed-race people became an overriding one for him.

The House behind the Cedars is available online at the Documenting the American South website at http://docsouth.unc.edu/southlit/chesnutthouse/menu.html.

AUTHOR BIOGRAPHY

Charles Waddell Chesnutt was born on June 20, 1858, in Cleveland, Ohio, the first of six surviving children of Andrew Jackson Chesnutt and Ann Maria Sampson Chesnutt. His parents, who came from Fayetteville, North Carolina, were among the 465 free blacks living there in 1850, according to the US census. Ann was the daughter of a mixed-race mother and a white slave owner, although there remains some doubt about the identity of her father. Andrew was the son of a mixed-race mother and a white landowner in Fayetteville. These details are relevant to an understanding of Chesnutt's exploration of racial issues and racial identity in his writings.

Chesnutt's parents left Fayetteville in 1856 and traveled north with a small band of free blacks to settle in Cleveland in 1857. Shortly after Charles was born, the family moved to Oberlin, Ohio, where the father worked as a horse-car driver. During the Civil War he worked as a teamster for the Union army. After the war, the family returned to Fayetteville, where Andrew opened a grocery store and was later elected county commissioner and justice of the peace. In 1867 Chesnutt began attending the Howard School, a public school for black children built with Freedmen's Bureau funds. He began a career as an educator in 1872, when he became a pupil-teacher at the school. In 1873 he was appointed assistant to the principal of the Peabody School in Charlotte, North Carolina, and in 1877 he was appointed to a similar post at the State Colored Normal School in Fayetteville, where he rose to principal in 1880. In 1878 he married Susan Perry, a teacher at the Howard School, and the two had four children.

Chesnutt's career as an educator ended in 1883 when he moved to New York City to work as a reporter for the Dow Jones news agency. That same year he returned to Cleveland to take a job in the accounting department of the Nickel Plate Railroad Company, where he later worked as a stenographer. He published his first short story, "Uncle Peter's House," in 1885. Later sketches, anecdotes, and stories appeared in such periodicals as *Tid-Bits*, *Puck*, the *New York Independent*, *Century*, and *Atlantic*. Meanwhile, he passed the Ohio bar examination and began working for a law firm in 1887, although he left the law firm in 1889 and established his own stenographic service. In the 1890s, publishers were rejecting much of his work, but his fortunes changed in 1899 when *The Conjure Woman* (a short-story collection including "Po' Sandy," "The Goophered Grapevine," "The Gray Wolf's Ha'nt," and others), *Frederick Douglass* (a biography of the social reformer), and *The Wife of His Youth and Other Stories of the Color Line* were published.

After *The House behind the Cedars* was published in 1900, Chesnutt closed up the stenography business and tried to succeed as a full-time writer, although he would reenter the business with a partner in 1918. In 1900 he began working on *The Marrow of Tradition*, a novel inspired by an 1898 race riot in Wilmington, North Carolina; the novel was published the following year. In subsequent years, he published numerous nonfiction articles addressing racial issues, and in 1905 he accepted membership on Booker T. Washington's Committee of Twelve for the Advancement of the Interests of the Negro Race. He was also a public speaker and became what today would be called a political activist on racial issues. He succeeded, for example, in persuading the authorities in Cleveland to ban showings of the racially incendiary film *The Birth of a Nation*. He continued to publish the occasional short story, and his novel *The Colonel's Dream* was published in 1905.

Although Chesnutt's work was only modestly successful during his lifetime (and only one of his books was in print at his death), he was awarded the Spingarn Medal by the National Association for the Advancement of Colored People in 1928. That year, too, he completed a novel, *The Quarry*, that was not published until 1999. Chesnutt died at his home in Cleveland on November 15, 1932, of arteriosclerosis and hypertension.

PLOT SUMMARY

Chapters I–III

The novel begins in the years just after the end of the Civil War. John Warwick, a lawyer from Clarence, South Carolina, is seen leaving his

MEDIA ADAPTATIONS

- *The House behind the Cedars* was adapted as a 1927 silent film produced by noted African American director Oscar Micheaux. However, no print of the film is known to exist, and it is regarded as a lost film.

- Micheaux remade the film under the title *Veiled Aristocrats* in 1932. This version, too, is largely lost, although portions have been preserved by the Library of Congress, and 48 minutes of the film are available on a DVD released by Grapevine Video in 2012. The film stars Lucille Lewis, Walter Fleming, Laura Bowman, Lawrence Chenault, and Lorenzo Tucker.

hotel in Patesville, North Carolina. He strolls about the town he used to live in and tries to pay a visit to Judge Archibald Straight, but the judge is not in his office. He notices an attractive-looking young woman and concludes that she has to be Rowena (or Rena) Walden. He follows her home to "the house behind the cedars." He cautiously approaches the house and tries to avoid being seen. After the home's owner, Molly Walden, invites him in, he says that he has a message for her from her son. Molly, however, realizes that John is in fact her son, whom she has not seen in a number of years, for Warwick left the state before the Civil War began.

Molly, John, and his sister Rena have a joyful reunion, and John tells them about his life. Passing as white, he has become a successful lawyer. He also was married and has a son, although his wife has died. He would like Rena to come live with him and help care for the son. Rena does not want to leave her mother, and Molly is reluctant to part with her daughter, but John ultimately convinces them that Rena, who will also be able to pass as white, can have a better life in South Carolina with him. The following morning, John visits Judge Straight, who years earlier had employed John as an office boy.

The judge counsels John not to remain in town for too long, for people might recognize him and his identity would be exposed. He believes that John should have moved farther away than South Carolina.

Chapters IV–VI

Rena bids good-bye to her mother and to Frank Fowler, a workman who is devoted to the Walden family and has long been in love with her. She and John then make the journey back to South Carolina, much of it by steamboat. John tells Rena that she will take the name Warwick. They arrive at Clarence, South Carolina, where they attend a mock tournament in which men dressed as medieval knights take part in a jousting competition. Rena and John sit among prominent white attendees. After Rena drops her handkerchief into the ring, one of the "knights," George Tryon, seizes it and regards it as a good-luck charm. He wins the tournament and names Rena as his Queen of Love and Beauty. Since he is the winner, he has earned the right to invite his "queen" to the annual tournament ball. A young widow, Mrs. Newberry, visits to instruct Rena on the proper etiquette for the ball.

Chapters VII–IX

Rena grows accustomed to a more lavish style of living. As she does so, John begins to think about their family secret and the precautions he has taken to make sure that his position in Clarence's white society is not threatened. George begins to court Rena and professes his love for her, even though his mother is trying to arrange a marriage with another woman in North Carolina, Blanche Leary. Rena consents to marry him, but she is troubled by her family secret and wonders whether she should tell George about her background. She discusses her fears of being discovered as part black with John, who maintains that George will love her despite her ancestry. He has a conversation with George in which he emphasizes that his and Rena's family is not in any way distinguished or anything other than humble. George responds by saying that he does not care about family background; his only care is for Rena. Rena concludes that she should leave her secret in the past.

Chapters X–XII

John and George leave Clarence to tend to George's legal case. During their absence, Rena is haunted by dreams that her mother is sick and dying. She receives a letter from her mother informing her that she is in fact very ill, so she boards a train for Patesville. George receives a letter from his mother asking him to contact her cousin, Ed Green, a doctor in Patesville, whom she has not seen for many years; Green can recommend a lawyer who will help with a legal matter in the area. After he leaves, he discovers a letter to him from Rena saying that she is on her way to Patesville as well. George visits the doctor in Patesville, and while he is waiting, he hears the voice of a woman who wants Green to attend to her sick mother (but he does not see her). As Green takes George to the office of Judge Straight, they discuss the woman's beauty and Green remarks that it is a shame that she has to live the life of a black person when she could pass as white.

Chapter XIII–XV

George leaves the judge's office. He inadvertently leaves behind the note he received from Rena, which the judge finds among George's other papers and reads. He begins to make the connections between Rena, John, their mother, Dr. Green, and George. He concludes that he is being punished for having helped John, the son of an old friend, years earlier. He knows that he has to prevent a meeting between George and Rena in Patesville, for such a meeting would surely lead to exposure of Rena's racial heritage, and George would break off his engagement with her in disgust. He writes a note to Molly Walden urging her to keep Rena at home. Molly, however, cannot read, so the note from the judge goes unread.

Frank Fowler found work with the railroad near Clarence, so he was able to follow Rena there and learn about her relationship with George. When he sees George in town, he knows that he has to prevent him from running into Rena, so he rushes off to the Walden home, where he reads the judge's note to Molly. George is having lunch with Dr. Green and his family when the doctor is summoned to the drugstore. George accompanies him, and he sees the black woman who had come to Green's office earlier. George recognizes her as Rena; when Rena sees George, she faints.

Chapter XVI–XVIII

George is devastated by what he has learned about Rena's antecedents. John receives two

letters. One is from his mother, informing him that Rena is not well and will not be returning to Clarence. The other is from George, stating coldly that he will not marry Rena but promising to keep the family secret.

Chapter XVIII is a lengthy flashback. It returns to the period before the Civil War. John as a child (John Walden) visits Judge Straight and says that he wants to become a lawyer. John is the son of one of the judge's old friends. The judge had promised the friend, now deceased, that he would help his children, so he takes John on as an office boy and allows him to read his law books. They decide that John's chances of becoming a lawyer will be greater if he leaves home and passes for white in another state, so John moves to South Carolina in the mid-1850s.

Chapters XIX–XXI

The narration returns to the present. Rena is lamenting the loss of George. Her brother tries to persuade her to move away with him to start a new life, but she is reluctant to once again leave Molly. George returns home, where his mother, Elizabeth Tryon, senses that something is troubling him, but he does not tell her the source of his disquiet. Although Blanche Leary would marry him, he cannot get Rena out of his mind. Mary B. Pettifoot, Molly's second cousin, visits the Walden home. She has information about a teaching opportunity for Rena at a school for black children run by a cousin, Jeff Wain. Molly and Mary would like to see Rena marry Jeff. When Rena agrees to take a position at the school, the women throw a party for Rena and Jeff.

Chapters XXII–XXIV

George has been called back to Patesville on business, but he wants to see Rena again, for he still loves her and wants to believe that what he has learned about her ancestry is false. At the celebratory party, Rena refuses to dance, but Molly persuades her to dance with Jeff Wain. George arrives at the party just in time to see her dancing; he is upset to think that Rena appears to be happy rather than grieving for the end of their engagement.

Chapters XXV–XXVIII

Rena travels with Wain to Sampson County, where Rena takes a teacher's examination, but the person administering the exam hints that

Wain is not a man to be trusted. George seems to be recovering from his grief over the loss of Rena and appears to be growing more interested in Blanche. The two take a buggy drive and happen to stop before the schoolhouse where Rena teaches. He talks to a young boy, Plato, who informs him that the teacher is a black woman who appears to be white. Elizabeth, George's mother, later enters the schoolhouse and indicates to Rena that she would like to help support the school; Rena does not know who she is. Elizabeth tells Rena that Jeff Wain is not a widower but that he beat his wife, who left him. Rena learns the woman's identity from Plato, who used to work for the Tryon family. Rena is now afraid to be alone with Jeff, so she has a student accompany her home every day after school. Jeff, however, sends the student away and tries to kiss Rena, who runs away and stays with the family of one of her students.

Chapters XXIX–XXXIII

George discovers that Rena is teaching at the school. He sends her a letter asking her to meet with him, but she replies that such a meeting would serve no purpose. George bribes Plato to inform him when he is walking Rena home so that he can intercept her. As Rena sees him approaching her one day, she flees into the woods. There she loses consciousness, and later she becomes ill. She begins to grow delirious, and a few days later she disappears from her bed. George searches for her, but it is Frank Fowler, at a roadside camp, who hears a noise and finds Rena on the ground. He picks her up and takes her home, but he is stopped by others who grow suspicious at the sight of a black man carrying a sick "white" woman. George learns what people have seen and pursues Rena to the house behind the cedars. Rena, who now understands that Frank has always loved her, dies just as George arrives.

CHARACTERS

Frank Fowler

Frank Fowler is a black workman for the Waldens and is intensely devoted to the family. He grew up with Rena and is in love with her, so he would do anything for her. After Molly Walden is left alone, he takes care of her and reads and writes letters for her. When Rena falls ill and disappears from her sickbed, Frank is the one who finds her and carries her home, although he encounters suspicion from others witnessing a black man carrying a woman who appears to be white.

Peter Fowler

Peter is Frank Fowler's father. He is a cooper by trade, but new industrial processes are driving him out of business. He empathizes with his son about his love for Rena.

Ed Green

Green is Elizabeth Tryon's cousin and a doctor. Elizabeth urges her son, George, to contact Green in Patesville and ask him to recommend a lawyer who can help deal with a legal matter. Green becomes a plot device that brings George and Rena together in Patesville, leading to the revelation of her racial heritage.

Blanche Leary

Blanche is the young woman George's mother would like to see him marry. She is described as a "demure, pretty little blonde, with an amiable disposition, a talent for society, and a pronounced fondness for George Tryon."

Mrs. Newberry

Mrs. Newberry is a young widow who instructs Rena in the etiquette of the tournament ball.

Mary B. Pettifoot

Mary is Molly's second cousin. She visits the Walden home with information about a teaching opportunity for Rena at a school for black children run by Jeff Wain.

Plato

Plato is a young African American boy who used to be a slave on the Tryon estate. He is now a student at the school where Rena teaches.

Judge Archibald Straight

Judge Straight was John Warwick's mentor when John was an office boy for the judge. Straight promised John's father, now deceased, that he would help provide for his children. It was he who counseled John to move away so that he could pass as white and become a lawyer. Later, he tries to prevent Rena and George Tryon from meeting in Patesville, for he knows that such a meeting will lead to the revelation of Rena's racial heritage.

Elizabeth Tryon

Elizabeth is George Tryon's mother. She is eager to see her son marry Blanche Leary. She later visits Rena's school and offers to help support it. She informs Rena that Jeff Wain is not a widower and that his wife left him because he beat her.

George Tryon

George Tryon, twenty-three years old, is a close friend of John Warwick's. He comes to Patesville often to deal with the settlement of his grandfather's estate, and John is his attorney. He is described as "a tall, fair young man, with gray eyes, and a frank, open face." He falls in love with Rena when he meets her at the jousting tournament in Clarence. While his mother would prefer that he marry Blanche Leary, he sets his heart on marrying Rena. When he discovers as a result of a chance meeting in Patesville that she is part black, he leaves her, although he continues to love her. After she takes a teaching job, he pursues her and tries to arrange a meeting with her. When she becomes ill and delirious, he follows her to her family home, arriving just as she dies.

Jeff Wain

Jeff Wain is a mixed-race man who owns the school where Rena comes to teach. Although he initially seems polite and good natured, his appearance seems to hide a darker reality: "Upon a close or hostile inspection there would have been some features of his ostensibly good-natured face—the shifty eye, the full and slightly drooping lower lip—which might have given a student of physiognomy food for reflection." After she joins him at the school, Rena grows afraid to be left alone with him, particularly after he tries to kiss her. He says that he is a widower, but according to Elizabeth Tryon, his wife is not dead but left him because he beat her.

Molly Walden

John and Rena's mother, Molly Walden, is of mixed race and comes from a family of relatively well-off free African Americans. Unlike her children, she is not fair skinned. After her son leaves home, she is left with Rena in "the house behind the cedars." She is illiterate, so she is unable to read the letter from Judge Straight warning her to keep Rena at home—an inability that contributes to the novel's plot.

Rowena "Rena" Walden

The novel's protagonist is Rena Walden, a young woman who is "strikingly handsome, with a stately beauty seldom encountered." Further, "she walked with an elastic step that revealed a light heart and the vigor of perfect health." Rena, the daughter of Molly Walden, is the younger sister of John Warwick. She is of mixed race, so she would legally be considered black or mulatto, but she is fair skinned, so she can pass as a white woman, which she does when she joins her brother in South Carolina. Rena becomes engaged to George Tryon, but after he discovers her racial heritage, he rejects her, their relationship ends, and she joins Jeff Wain to become a schoolteacher for black children. She rejects George's efforts to meet with her, but when she encounters him on the way home from the school one day, she flees into the woods, loses consciousness, and becomes delirious. Later, she leaves her sickbed and is discovered by Frank Fowler, who carries her back home, where she dies.

Albert Warwick

John's son is named Albert Warwick.

John Warwick

John Warwick, born John Walden, is Rena's twenty-eight-year-old brother. He moved away from his home in North Carolina when he was younger to become a successful lawyer in South Carolina; he owed his success in part to the fact that he was seen as a native southerner and not a carpetbagger from the North. He is protective of Rena and wants her to forge a new life that will provide her with the opportunities she deserves. Like Rena, he is fair skinned, allowing him to pass as white, but to hide his identity, he has to stay away from Patesville, his hometown. He was married, but his wife died and left him with a young son.

THEMES

Race Relations

The central theme of *The House behind the Cedars* is race relations, particularly race relations in the years after the Civil War. As a result of the war and the ratification of the Thirteenth Amendment to the Constitution, former slaves were now free and no longer regarded as the property of white families. These events,

TOPICS FOR FURTHER STUDY

- The first school Chesnutt attended, the Howard School in Fayetteville, North Carolina (which would in time evolve into Fayetteville State University), was built with support from the Freedman's Bureau. Investigate the history of the bureau and the role it played in Reconstruction following the Civil War. Prepare a time line and post it on a blog; invite your classmates to comment.

- Conduct online and print investigation of the meaning of the word *hypodescent*. What role did the concept of hypodescent play during the post–Civil War period up to the end of Chesnutt's life? Prepare an oral report for your classmates in which you explain hypodescent as it pertains to *The House behind the Cedars*.

- In 2000, Paramount released *A House Divided*, starring Sam Waterston and Jennifer Beals. The movie is based on the true story of a mixed-race woman who returns to post–Civil War Georgia and has to fight in court to claim her inheritance from her slave-owner father. The movie's plot closely parallels a subplot in Chesnutt's novel *The Marrow of Tradition*. Watch the movie, then write a report that explains how it shares themes with *The House behind the Cedars*.

- Mark Twain's 1894 novel *Pudd'nhead Wilson* is a satiric examination of passing in the pre–Civil War South. It tells the story of Roxy, a slave who is one-sixteenth black and who exchanges her daughter (who is one-thirty-second black) with a white baby she is caring for. Her own child is spoiled by his aristocratic family. Read Twain's novel, then write a dialogue in which you imagine Roxy and Rena Walden having a conversation about the racial and gender issues that affect them. With a partner, perform your dialogue for your classmates.

- Walter Dean Myers's young-adult novel *Riot* (2009) is set during the Civil War. Using cinematic techniques, it examines the tension in New York City between the Irish and African American communities after President Abraham Lincoln called for a draft to replenish the Union army. At the center of the conflict is Claire, the daughter of a black father and an Irish mother. Read the novel and, comparing it to *The House behind the Cedars*, prepare a report on the similarities and differences you see in the authors' treatment of nineteenth-century race relations.

- Joseph Bruchac's middle-grade novel *Hidden Roots* (2004) provides commentary on passing from a different cultural perspective. Eleven-year-old Harold is an Abenaki Indian whose family for decades has passed as French to escape the Vermont Eugenics Program, a forced sterilization scheme in the 1930s. Over time, Harold discovers his "hidden roots." Read the novel, then write a report in which you discuss how the experiences of African Americans and Native Americans differed (or were similar) as they may have tried to pass in white society.

- Marion Kilson's *Claiming Place: Biracial Young Adults of the Post–Civil Rights Era* (2001) examines how young-adult biracial Americans who have grown up in the post–civil rights era see racial identity issues in their lives. After reading portions of Kilson's book, prepare a chart comparing the experiences of her subjects and those of the characters in *The House behind the Cedars*.

---

however, by no means created a climate of racial harmony, and racial relations continued to be strained at best. George, for example, is scornful and dismissive of "colored people," and when he discovers that Rena is the daughter of a mixed-race woman, he is taken aback:

> At first he could see nothing but the fraud of which he had been made the victim. A negro girl

The house, tucked behind cedar trees, is a symbol for the family's hidden past. (© YuryZap | Shutterstock.com)

had been foisted upon him for a white woman, and he had almost committed the unpardonable sin against his race of marrying her.

He goes on to think:

Such a step, he felt, would have been criminal at any time; it would have been the most odious treachery at this epoch, when his people had been subjugated and humiliated by the Northern invaders, who had preached negro equality and abolished the wholesome laws decreeing the separation of the races.

For Blanche Leary, Plato, a student at Rena's school, is "a funny little darkey."

These and similar passages indicate the extent to which race relations remained problematic during the Reconstruction period.

Some white characters, however, display more enlightened attitudes. In particular, Judge Straight was a mentor and friend to John Walden, even though he was aware of the boy's racial heritage. John's ambition to be a lawyer meets with the judge's support rather than derision. Further, Elizabeth Tryon pays a visit to the school for black children where Rena teaches and offers her support, recognizing the nobility of Rena's efforts.

Identity

A related theme is racial identity. The novel raises the question of what it means to be black and to what extent blackness and whiteness are matters both of self-identification and of the perceptions of others. In the novel, the Waldens are all to be regarded as black, even though they are of mixed-race ancestry. In this regard, Chesnutt is not entirely accurate, for in the antebellum South, a person who was as much as one-quarter black (that is, had one black grandparent) could be considered legally white, and such persons, on the basis of appearance, were routinely accepted in the white community. But the author was not writing from the perspective of the 1850s; he was writing from that of the late nineteenth century, when racial tensions ran high and even one drop of "Negro blood" could define a person as black and therefore subject to punitive Jim Crow laws. Thus, a person with black ancestry often could succeed only through the ability to pass as white. John can use his light skin to pass as white and become a successful lawyer; Rena can follow him and achieve a position in white society. Racial identity thus becomes a matter of perception rather than reality. People are white or black in large part on the basis of how others see them. A good example occurs when Elizabeth Tryon visits the school where Rena teaches and is surprised by Rena's refined manner; her perception of Rena conflicts with her expectations.

Economic Change

As part of Chesnutt's portrait of post–Civil War American society, he touches on the nation's growing industrialization. In Chapter XIV, the reader learns about Frank Fowler and his father, Peter. The narrative notes that "business in the cooper shop was dull. A barrel factory had been opened in the town, and had well-nigh paralyzed the cooper's trade. The best mechanic could hardly compete with a machine. One man could now easily do the work of Peter's shop." The narration continues: "An agent appeared in town seeking laborers for one of the railroads which the newly organized carpet-bag governments were promoting." Frank takes a job, which allows him to relocate to the vicinity of Clarence, South Carolina. This passage underscores the nature of the changes taking place in the United States after the Civil War. The era was one of growth and industrialization, which was putting small artisans out of business. Also, in the South, so-called carpetbaggers were arriving from the North. These were northerners who were out for political or financial gain in exploiting the defeated Confederacy, though in time they would contribute to the modernization of the South's economy. The term *carpetbagger* comes from the tendency of these northern "invaders" to carry luggage made of sturdy used-carpeting material.

STYLE

Third-Person Point of View

The point of view adopted in *The House behind the Cedars* is third-person omniscient. The story is narrated in the third person, with the characters referred to as "he," "she," and "they." In contrast would be first person, with the story narrated by a character who refers to him- or herself as "I" and "me." Further, the narration adopts an omniscient point a view; *omniscient* is derived from the Latin and literally means "all knowing." Thus, the narrative voice is able to move about freely in time and space (such as with the flashback in Chapter XVIII) and, more importantly, enter into the minds of the characters to comment on their thoughts, perceptions, emotions, and reactions to events. Additionally, Chesnutt uses a convention that is sometimes referred to as the intrusive narrator, although "intrusive" is not intended to be pejorative. This is a narrator that does not just report but also comments on the action. Thus, the very first words of the novel, "Time touches all things with destroying hand...," are commentary by an intrusive narrator.

Dialect

In his short stories, Chesnutt adopted some of the conventions of the local-color school of writing. This term refers to writing that re-creates the characters, dialects, customs, folkways, history, and landscape of a region, in this case, of the South. Local colorists often recreated in particular the dialects of the people of the region. In *The House behind the Cedars*, Chesnutt often makes use of the conventions of black dialect to distinguish black characters who are former slaves from more educated and refined characters with black ancestry, such as John and Rena. Thus, for example, when Plato, a young black boy, encounters George Tryon, he greets him with "Hoddy, Mars Geo'ge" ("Howdy, Master George"). When George asks him what he is doing at the school, Plato replies, "Gwine ter school, Mars Geo'ge, larnin' ter read an' write, suh, lack de w'ite folks" ("Going to school, Master George, learning to read and write, sir, like the white folks"). Notice that Plato, although free, shows the deference that would be associated with the slave plantation.

Coincidence

The plot of *The House behind the Cedars* is fairly conventional. After some exposition that makes clear who John, Rena, and Molly are, the plot is complicated when Rena follows her brother to South Carolina, falls in love with a white aristocrat, and worries that her secret will be revealed. The plot reaches a climax as Rena's racial heritage is revealed and George rejects her. The chapters dealing with her teaching career, her illness, and her death become a kind of extended coda that wraps up the story of her life.

One feature of the plot, however, merits comment, and that is the author's reliance on coincidence. A reader could argue that some of the coincidences of the novel are not entirely credible. For example, it seems somewhat unlikely that John would not immediately recognize his own sister when he spots her on the street in Patesville. Later, Rena dreams that her mother is ill, then learns that she is in fact ill, prompting her to return to Patesville. George then also winds up in Patesville to make contact with Dr. Ed Green, which sets in motion the events that lead to the revelation of Rena's racial heritage. It might seem coincidental to some readers that George just happens to be waiting in Green's office when Rena comes in to seek help for her mother, then that he just happens to spot her outside the pharmacy later on, where the two see each other. Additionally, the reader learns that Frank Fowler, who has long been in love with Rena, happens to find work with the railroad near Clarence, South Carolina, so he is aware of her relationship with George. It seems particularly coincidental that Rena would take a teaching position near the home of George and that George and Blanche would appear at the school; similarly, the appearance of George's mother at the school seems coincidental. Another major coincidence is that Frank Fowler is the one who finds the delirious Rena and returns her to her home. A final coincidence is that Rena dies just as George appears at her home. These and other coincidences suggest that Chesnutt intended to manipulate the events of the novel in a way that would help him develop his thesis about the post–Civil War racial climate in the South.

HISTORICAL CONTEXT

African Americans in the Postbellum Era

The House behind the Cedars takes place during the Reconstruction era following the Civil War, and race relations during this period dominated Chesnutt's interests until his death in 1932. *Reconstruction* refers to the process of reintegrating the rebellious Confederate states into the Union following the war. An important event had been the passage of the Thirteenth Amendment to the Constitution (1865), which ended slavery and other forms of "involuntary servitude." Other legislation and constitutional amendments further reconfigured the racial landscape of the United States: the Civil Rights Act of 1866; the Reconstruction Acts of 1867; the Fourteenth Amendment (1868), adopted to guarantee "due process" and "equal protection"; the Fifteenth Amendment (1870), which protected voting rights; the Ku Klux Klan Act of 1871, which gave the president powers to combat Klan violence; and the Civil Rights Act of 1875, which made it unlawful for public facilities to deny access to any individual based on race or

color. The Freedmen's Bureau was created in 1865 to aid newly freed African Americans and ensure that their rights were protected. Despite these initiatives, people like Rena Walden and her brother concluded that they had to pass as white to claim their share of American opportunity.

The racial climate in the South improved marginally during the period in which *The House behind the Cedars* is set, when African Americans were elected to the US Senate and the US House of Representatives, as well as to state and local offices; at one point, blacks outnumbered whites in the South Carolina legislature. The climate began to deteriorate, however, in the 1870s. In 1876, Wade Hampton, a former Confederate general dedicated to white supremacy, was elected to the governorship of South Carolina. The Compromise of 1877, which arose from the disputed presidential election between Democrat Samuel Tilden and Republican Rutherford B. Hayes, formally ended Reconstruction and launched a new era that enabled some southern whites to reassert dominance using fraud, intimidation, and violence. A series of US Supreme Court decisions undermined the Fourteenth and Fifteenth Amendments, culminating in the Court's decision in *Plessy v. Ferguson* (1896), which created the separate-but-equal doctrine. The result of these and other setbacks was the passage of Jim Crow laws, which denied blacks access to white-designated transportation, housing, employment, recreation, and education and created a racially segregated society.

A resolution of the unsettled question of the status of the black population was found in the unlikely person of a former slave, Booker T. Washington, who established a school in rural Alabama. At what became the Tuskegee Institute, Washington developed an educational program that emphasized industrial education, providing training for brick masons, carpenters, and other artisans. Women were trained in the domestic arts. Tuskegee's program was based on Washington's belief that black students would be served best by training for practical vocations rather than for professions—in contrast to John Warwick, who was able to become a lawyer because he was able to pass as white (and because he was not seen as a carpetbagger—that is, as one from the North trying to exploit the South's defeat for his own gain). In 1895 Washington delivered his historic "Atlanta Compromise" speech in Atlanta,

COMPARE & CONTRAST

- **Post–Civil War:** A young man can become a lawyer by working in a law office and learning the law on the job as an office boy and apprentice (as John Warwick did with Judge Straight), a process referred to as "reading law."

  1900: The Association of American Law Schools is formed this year. Over a hundred law schools, many of them private, for-profit enterprises, provide legal education for prospective lawyers.

  Today: In most (but not all) US states, prospective lawyers are required to attend law school to be admitted to the bar.

- **Post–Civil War:** African Americans have achieved full emancipation as a result of the Thirteenth Amendment, ratified in 1865, which ended slavery and all forms of involuntary servitude.

  1900: African Americans suffer the ill effects of Jim Crow laws, passed by states and municipalities to segregate public schools, transportation facilities, restrooms, and public accommodation.

  Today: While African Americans continue to endure some forms of prejudice, all forms of legal segregation are strictly outlawed.

- **Post–Civil War:** The term *mulatto* is widely used to refer to people of mixed race, usually black and white but sometimes Caribbean or Native American and white.

  1900: Some fair-skinned mulattos, often those whose fathers or grandfathers were white slave owners who fathered children by their slaves, choose to pass as white and thus evade Jim Crow laws and societal prejudice.

  Today: Few people identify themselves as mulattos because of the word's archaic associations with slavery and colonialism; the preferred terms are *biracial*, *mixed-race*, or *multiracial*. As stereotypes fall, being of mixed race generally carries less of a stigma than it once did.

- **Post–Civil War:** In the aftermath of the Civil War, a person such as John Warwick from a Confederate state, in this case South Carolina, is required to sign an oath of allegiance to the US government in order to be licensed to practice a profession.

  1900: Typically, oaths of allegiance are required only from those wishing to become naturalized American citizens; such oaths emphasize renunciation of loyalty to a king or queen, and specifically to the emperor of Germany.

  Today: Some states retain laws requiring the administration of a loyalty oath to state employees to ensure that they are not subversives or Communists, despite rulings by the US Supreme Court questioning their constitutionality.

Georgia, before a large and mainly white audience. He invoked a metaphor that would be seen as the solution for race relations. He held out one hand and said, "In all things that are purely social we can be as separate as the fingers, yet as one hand in all things essential to mutual progress." He then closed his fingers into a fist to emphasize his point. The implication was clear: African Americans would be trained to be reliable workers who would not challenge white supremacy.

Washington would go on to form the Committee of Twelve for the Advancement of the Interests of the Negro Race, of which Chesnutt was a member.

Much about Washington's philosophy irritated many African Americans, among them such figures as W. E. B. Du Bois, a prominent black intellectual who published essays that took a very different, more militant position—often in the same *Atlantic* magazine that published

Rena is a beautiful young African American woman, but her skin is fair enough for her to "pass" as white. (© White Room / Shutterstock.com)

Chesnutt's short stories. In one of his articles, "Strivings of the Negro People" (1897), he made a statement that sheds light on the issues raised by Chesnutt's fiction:

> Between me and the other world there is ever an unasked question.... How does it feel to be a problem?... One feels his two-ness,—an American, a Negro; two souls, two thoughts, two unreconciled strivings; two warring ideals in one dark body.... The history of the American Negro is the history of this strife,—this longing to attain self-conscious manhood, to merge his double self into a better and truer self.... He does not wish to bleach his Negro blood in a flood of white Americanism, for he believes— foolishly, perhaps, but fervently—that Negro blood has yet a message for the world.

Du Bois then remarked that the African American "simply wishes to make it possible for a man to be both a Negro and an American without being cursed and spit upon by his fellows." It was in the context of this racial divide that *The House behind the Cedars* was published at the turn of the twentieth century.

CRITICAL OVERVIEW

The House behind the Cedars was well received by critics and reviewers after it was published in 1900. A reviewer for the *Chicago Daily Tribune*

remarks that the narrative is "well constructed," but the same reviewer concludes that "neither in style nor in characterization is there any freshness or originality." This view, however, was not shared by most other reviewers. The reviewer for the *Toronto Globe* writes that "Chesnutt never forces his reader's feeling" and that he "does not lack the two things that keep so many [authors] back: he cares and he knows." More enthusiastic was the *Philadelphia Record*, whose reviewer calls the novel "deftly written" and one that "gives a clear insight into the race difference of that day resulting from the freeing of the slaves." The *Denver Times* also emphasizes the historical and thematic elements of the book, concluding that Chesnutt's novel "is the more artistic for his not attempting to carry the problem further. He reaches a dramatic climax in his sorrowful tragedy and then merely drops the curtain." In a similar vein, the *Detroit Free Press* reviewer comments on Chesnutt's "able presentation" of the book's issues and calls it "a story of sustained strength and interest, wrought out to an artistic finale."

Some reviewers were still more highly enthusiastic. The reviewer for the *Boston Courier*, for example, writes, "It is necessary... to peruse the book carefully to appreciate its merit." Chesnutt is "exceptionally able in describing circumstances which are decidedly important in this story." The reviewer goes on to praise the author's "laudable perspicuity" in his depiction of Rena and concludes, "Such presentation of the finer emotions is far from usual in fiction, and marks the author as being of subtle artistic qualities." For the *Nation*, Chesnutt has a "fine literary temperament" and an "easy, educated way of telling a tale; and a special interest in the 'negro question' is not at all necessary for enjoying this work," which is marked by "sincerity, simplicity, and restrained expression of deep feeling." The *Boston Evening Transcript* finds the novel "rich in incident and suggestion" and admires the characters, "all close studies from real life." The reviewer finally states,

> This novel of his, with its strong conclusion— the race prejudice conquered late by love—may be taken as symbolical of what the author regards as the eventual solution of the race question. His book is admirably worth reading.

A more modern critic, Donald B. Gibson, in his introduction to *The House behind the Cedars*, notes that the novel also raises issues of class and gender: "In the end, Chesnutt draws us... into the labyrinthine intricacies of color and race as they are and have been historically inflected by gender and class in the United States."

CRITICISM

Michael J. O'Neal

O'Neal holds a PhD in English. In the following essay, he examines The House behind the Cedars *as an example of the social-problem novel of the nineteenth century.*

The House behind the Cedars, published at the precise turn of the twentieth century, is representative of a literary trend that emerged in the United States earlier in the century and culminated during the years that encompassed Charles W. Chesnutt's writing career. American novelists (along with their British counterparts) were abandoning the romanticized and stylized presentation of narrative that characterized earlier fiction in favor of what is now termed literary realism. This movement emphasized depictions of contemporary society as it was, as well as those of everyday life and experiences. An extension of literary realism was a movement called naturalism. Naturalist writers, among them Hamlin Garland, Frank Norris, Jack London, and Stephen Crane, strove for a faithful representation of reality without passing moral judgments on their characters. The naturalists took a deterministic view of life, presenting characters as victims of their heredity and/or their environment. Naturalism can be thought of as realism pushed to a logical extreme.

While no writer conforms entirely to the conventions of any particular literary movement, writers exhibit tendencies. Chesnutt in this novel shows many of the characteristics of the naturalist movement in creating a social-problem novel about race and racial identity in the post–Civil War era. During this period, writers were highly aware of social change. They paid deference to such emerging disciplines as sociology, psychology, and anthropology. In creating fiction, they drew individual characters while simultaneously showing how those characters emerged from the milieux in which they lived. Put differently, their characters were representative of a way of life, one that reflected social developments. These writers, too, understood that human affairs change and develop over time, and the novel became a major means

> CHESNUTT DOES NOT QUESTION THE WISDOM OR MORALITY OF PASSING. RACE PREJUDICE EXISTS; PEOPLE OF MIXED RACE FACE OBSTACLES; PASSING IS A WAY OF OVERCOMING, OR AT LEAST SIDESTEPPING, THOSE OBSTACLES."

by which writers imagined their immediate past—in this case the post–Civil War years—and a possible future that could emerge from that past—in this case, an America that offered opportunity to all of its citizens, not just those with fair skin. In this intellectual climate, writers wrote about crises having to do with class, gender, religious doubt, and other social problems that came about because of societal evolution.

Clearly, Chesnutt defined a problem he wanted to explore: the belief that a person of mixed-race ancestry who could pass as white should do so as a path to success and achievement. Even Molly, who is a dark-skinned black, recognizes the merit in this. As her daughter is about to depart with John, she reflects: "Her daughter was going to live in a fine house, and marry a rich man, and ride in her carriage." She goes on to think, "Of course a negro would drive the carriage, but that was different from riding with one in a cart." When Rena arrives in Clarence, one of the first things she does is attend a mock jousting tournament, where she passes as white and sits with the town's leading white citizens. She drops her handkerchief, which is captured by George Tryon, one of the community's most prominent citizens and eligible bachelors. George wins the tournament and proclaims Rena the Queen of Love and Beauty, entitling him to take her to the tournament ball. Clearly, these and other events detail Chesnutt's belief that being white conferred social advantages and, more importantly, that being able to pass as white enabled persons of mixed-race backgrounds to attain status, comfort, and perhaps even wealth that would otherwise have eluded them.

What is noteworthy about *The House behind the Cedars*, however, is that Chesnutt never judges his characters. They judge themselves, to

WHAT DO I READ NEXT?

- *The Marrow of Tradition* is Chesnutt's 1901 novel inspired by an 1898 race riot in Wilmington, North Carolina.

- *The Conjure Woman* is Chesnutt's 1899 collection of seven short stories that reflect the "local color" school of American writing, that is, fiction (or poetry) that focuses on the characters, dialects, customs, history, and landscape of a region.

- One of the most famous local colorists of the nineteenth century was Joel Chandler Harris, author of the famous Uncle Remus stories. The full title of his 1881 collection of tales is *Uncle Remus, His Songs and His Sayings: The Folk-Lore of the Old Plantation*.

- *Reconstruction* (2008), by Michael V. Uschan, is a nonfiction book for young adults that examines the post–Civil War era in the United States.

- Nella Larsen is the author of a 1929 novella titled *Passing*. The novella depicts the social experiences of two biracial women. One passes for white and is married to a white man. The other is married to a black man and lives in the black community of Harlem, New York.

- *Black Like Me* (1961), by journalist John Howard Griffin, is a nonfiction account of his experiences as a white man passing as black in the South in the late 1950s. The book continues to be a popular selection in high-school and middle-school curricula.

- Werner Sollors is the author of *Neither Black nor White yet Both: Thematic Explorations of Interracial Literature* (1997). The book, drawing from literary works, asks such questions as why, in the United States, it is believed that a white woman can give birth to a black baby, while a black woman is never thought of as giving birth to a white baby; what makes racial passing different from social mobility; and why interracial and incestuous relations are often confused in literature.

- Some readers may recognize a variant of the author's name in Mary Boykin Chesnut, a South Carolinian who kept a voluminous, witty diary written from the standpoint of the Confederate plantation class during the Civil War, although she rewrote much of it during Reconstruction. A Pulitzer Prize–winning version of the diary edited by C. Vann Woodward was published in 1981 under the title *Mary Chesnut's Civil War*.

be sure. When Molly faces the prospect of losing her daughter, she reflects:

> She must lose her daughter as well as her son, and this should be the penance for her sin. That her children must expiate as well the sins of their fathers, who had sinned so lightly, after the manner of men, neither she nor they could foresee.

Similarly, Judge Straight passes judgment on himself for urging John to leave Patesville and secure his future by passing as white. When John returns, the judge feels haunted by his decision. But what is important here is that while the characters pass judgment on themselves, the narration does not. Chesnutt does not question the

wisdom or morality of passing. Race prejudice exists; people of mixed race face obstacles; passing is a way of overcoming, or at least sidestepping, those obstacles. It poses the risk of exposure, but exposure in the novel comes about through convoluted circumstances, not through anyone's dogged search for truth. Passing is seen as a form of social adaptation that just *is*, without comment or condemnation. In this regard, it might be hard for a modern reader to swallow Chesnutt's thesis, for in the twenty-first century, the hiding of one's racial heritage seems antiquated, racist, and counterproductive.

What is equally important, however, is that Chesnutt, through the narration, does not judge his white characters either, for he is able to see them as the product of their times. Take, for instance, the scene in which John and Rena are traveling to John's home in South Carolina. The narration describes John's encounters with others on the steamboat:

> It was learned that he was a South Carolina lawyer, and not a carpet-bagger. Such credentials were unimpeachable, and the passengers found him a very agreeable traveling companion. Apparently sound on the subject of negroes, Yankees, and the righteousness of the lost cause, he yet discussed these themes in a lofty and impersonal manner that gave his words greater weight than if he had seemed warped by a personal grievance.

The narration goes on to recreate an exchange with one of the passengers:

> His attitude, in fact, piqued the curiosity of one or two of the passengers.
>
> "Did your people lose any niggers?" asked one of them.
>
> "My father owned a hundred," he replied grandly.
>
> Their respect for his views doubled.

The reader must remember that John, as well as John's creator, is part black. In the twenty-first century, readers might expect, with good reason, that an author would somehow convey indignation or contempt for the attitudes reflected here. Chesnutt, however, presents the matter with virtually no commentary. It is the other passengers who find his view "unimpeachable" and find John "agreeable." It is they who find his views "sound." John does not express his views as if "warped by a personal grievance." The use of the offensive word *nigger* passes without comment. The narration here and throughout is a curious mixture of authorial commentary and journalistic reporting. Chesnutt philosophizes when he wants to, but when he presents his characters, he allows them to take center stage without remark. His characters, whether they are black, white, or mixed race, whether they are former slaves or were formerly free, whether they are aristocratic, middle class, or lower class, are products of their environment and presented for the reader's inspection without judgment or, in the case of those with objectionable attitudes, condemnation. In this regard, Chesnutt conforms to many of the conventions and narrative approaches of the nineteenth-century problem novel.

This narrative approach might help explain Chesnutt's apparent reliance on coincidence— coincidences that some readers might find strain credibility. Near the end of the novel, for instance, Rena sees George, flees into the woods, falls ill, and becomes delirious. Clearly this is authorial manipulation; Chesnutt is trying to bring his novel to a tragic conclusion. She leaves her sick bed and disappears, only to be found by, of all people, Frank Fowler, the man who has long loved her and just happens to be at a roadside camp when Rena falls unconscious nearby. Frank hears a noise, discovers Rena, and carries her back to her home. This sequence of events, so clearly staged by the author, allows him to depict the suspicion with which Frank is met. Frank is clearly black. Rena is fair skinned and can pass as white, so what people *see* as he carries her is a black man touching a white woman, raising the possibility (in their minds) that he is up to no good. The matter is so remarkable that it reaches the ears of George, who follows to the house behind the cedars just in time to witness Rena's death. This authorial manipulation of events, however, serves a larger purpose. The characters are victims of circumstance and of the social and historical environment that shapes their lives. The novel's multiple coincidences make clear that its tragic occurrences as they affect Rena are not a function of character flaws but of circumstances over which she has little or no control.

John is another matter. John is representative of a class of men who strive to become self-reliant individualists and successful professionals in the expansive era following the Civil War. He takes in Rena at least in part because she is attractive and not stupid or ugly. He regards her ability to keep the family secret as a matter of self-interested pragmatism on her part rather than sisterly affection. He knows that Frank Fowler has to be kept quiet, so he buys Frank's silence with a new mule and cart. He is shrewd and successful, but he is also self-centered. The way he is characterized constitutes an implicit judgment on him, but that judgment is passed on his individual psychology as a function of his efforts to achieve success, and perhaps of his views regarding women. It is not a judgment on his racial attitudes. Again, those are a given, and Chesnutt, whose overriding issue was racial identity, asserts his thesis without mounting a soapbox.

When Rena and John arrive in Clarence, they attend a jousting tournament and Rena meets George Tyron. (© Raulin | Shutterstock.com)

Source: Michael J. O'Neal, Critical Essay on *The House behind the Cedars*, in *Novels for Students*, Gale, Cengage Learning, 2014.

Coleman C. Myron

In the following excerpt, Myron explains how Chesnutt, as an African American, had to be careful about what he wrote because of racial prejudice.

Post-slavery African American writer Charles Waddell Chesnutt, who like many other African American authors, often had to lessen the blow of his message or employ masks to hide unpleasant truths incurred by African Americans that otherwise might not get voiced in leading American literary magazines and publishing houses, refrains from this technique that he used so marvelously in *The Conjure Woman* (1899) to craft his novel *The House Behind the Cedars* (1900). In *The House Behind the Cedars*, Chesnutt deals directly with the social, cultural, and racial upheavals that the freed African American faced in the post-Reconstruction South.

If I do write, I shall write for a purpose, a high, holy purpose, and this will inspire me to greater effort. The object of my writings would not be so much the elevation of the colored people as the elevation of the whites—for I consider the unjust spirit of caste . . . a barrier to the moral progress of the American people; and I would be one of the first to head a determined organized crusade against it. Not a fierce indiscriminate onslaught; not an appeal to force, for this is something that force can but slightly affect; but a moral revolution which must be brought about in a different manner. . . . The subtle almost indefinable feeling of repulsion toward the negro, which is common to most Americans—and easily enough accounted for—, cannot be stormed and taken by assault; the garrison will not capitulate: so their position must be mined, and we will find ourselves in their midst before they think of it. . . . It is the

AS CHESNUTT MOVES HIS READERS FORWARD IN HISTORICAL TIME WITH THE PRESENTATION OF MOLLY, HE ALSO MOVES THEM BACKWARD IN TIME, SHOWING THAT EVEN THOUGH SLAVERY HAD ENDED, THE MINDSET OF THOSE WHO HAD INFLICTED THIS SOCIAL INSTITUTION ON HUMAN BEINGS AND THOSE WHO HAD SUFFERED IT ENDURED."

province of literature . . . to accustom the public mind to the idea; and . . . while amusing them to . . . lead them on imperceptibly, unconsciously step by step to the desired state of feeling [Chesnutt, May 29, 1880, *Journals* 139–40].

By crafting a complex, multi-layered novel that makes use of several characters whose identities as mulattoes allow them to cross racial boundaries, Chesnutt exposes the racism of white America while shaping a character in young Miss Rena Walden, whose heroism places her in line with other great American literary figures, both historical and fictional, such as Thomas Jefferson, Henry David Thoreau, and Huck Finn. They rebel against society, either real or imagined, to show people that other truths do exist.

Although African Americans had been granted their freedom, their release from the chains of slavery provided for them only a physical removal from their situations. As newly freed people, African Americans remained more enslaved than if they had been slaves, since their new-found condition involved a constant struggle to define their role alongside their former oppressors, who did not accept them as equals but adopted them into the framework of their lives on an as-need basis. What increased the difficulty of assimilation for these former slaves was the frequent unwillingness of their fellow Southern brethren to view their past lives as slaves as egregious. Rather than interpret the facts in clear terms, those in power romanticized the situation of slavery by publishing works along the lines of Joel Chandler Harris's Uncle Remus tales, which idealized the view of race relations. The publication of these works

and others similar to it served to disguise the deplorable reality of the past and to help explain the reasons for the present situation. By choosing this path, Southerners and Northerners tainted history by painting a picture of themselves as liberators of a pagan people from their roots in a savage and uncivilized world. This story of deceit ameliorated the conscience of white society and allowed it to move forward, not swayed by the needs of those whom it had liberated.

Through the tale of mulatto siblings John and Rena Walden, who could pass for being white, Chesnutt (who could also pass for white but chose not to) provides in microcosm the theme of the growing race consciousness between African Americans and whites, which had escalated and even turned into a conflict between African Americans and African Americans. Former slaves and even previously freed African Americans now faced life under much different circumstances than the "system that made it possible to convert human beings into disposable property with supposedly no more feeling or consciousness than a tree" (Andrews, 43). As property, African American slaves owed to their masters and mistresses complete allegiance. If they failed to provide complete allegiance, they could end up being sold or even killed. Often for female slaves—more so than males—this allegiance included fulfilling the base sexual needs of their masters. Sexual intercourse with a young girl or woman was often enticed with gifts and other favors, but more often than not, the woman, as the property of her master, was forcibly raped. In either scenario, women gave birth to illegitimate offspring with their fathers' features but not their name, which would have provided them some measure of legitimacy. Once freed from slavery, however, the situation for African Americans of mixed race changed little, as they often found it necessary to prostitute themselves to survive in society. When Molly's father "died prematurely, a disappointed and disheartened man, leaving his family in dire poverty," Molly's own fortunes as a free woman of color changed, and followed a similar path to the ones her ancestors had traveled:

The slim, barefoot girl, with sparkling eyes and voluminous hair, who played about the yard and sometimes handed water in a gourd to travelers, did not long escape critical observation. A gentleman drove by one day, stopped at the well, smiled upon the girl, and said kind words. He came again, more than once, and soon, while scarcely more than a child in years, Molly was living in her own house, hers by deed of gift, for her protector was rich and liberal [*Cedars*].

As Chesnutt moves his readers forward in historical time with the presentation of Molly, he also moves them backward in time, showing that even though slavery had ended, the mindset of those who had inflicted this social institution on human beings and those who had suffered it endured. In this view, history repeats itself, and Molly follows the precedence of her parents and ancestors, "old issue free negroes," who had "mingled their blood with great freedom and small formality" among the "many Indians, runaway negroes, and indentured white servants from the seaboard plantations" (*Cedars*). However, Molly's decision to become the mistress of this Southern gentleman is blinded by the innocence of youth. As a young girl, she willingly sacrificed herself morally and damned her offspring to a life of hardship so that her "mother [would] nevermore [know] want. Her poor relations could always find a meal in [her] kitchen" (*Cedars*). Molly herself "did not flaunt her prosperity in the world's face, but as her lord had done with her, she hid it discreetly behind the cedar screen" (*Cedars*).

After presenting the relationship between Molly and the white "gentleman," Chesnutt briefly demonstrates to his readers that racial inequality does not discriminate between Southern or Northern whites or even between the races but is a contagion found in all peoples. In *The House Behind the Cedars*, Chesnutt showcases it in the free colored people who had "exercised the right of suffrage as late as 1835," had worked hard, "and dreamed of a still brighter future when the growing tyranny of the slave power crushed their hopes and crowded the free people back upon the black mass just beneath them." As Chesnutt states: Molly "did not sympathize greatly with the new era opened up for the emancipated slaves; she had no ideal love of liberty; she was no broader and no more altruistic than the white people around her, to whom she had always looked up; and she sighed for the old days, because to her they had been the good days," in large measure because "her king" lived (*Cedars*), but also because "Molly's free birth carried with it certain advantages, even in the South before the war.... They were not

citizens, yet they were not slave," and this knowledge allowed "Mis Molly [to feel] herself infinitely superior to Peter and his wife,—scarcely less superior than her poor white neighbors felt themselves to Mis' Molly." In Molly, Chesnutt shows us the wide-ranging conflicts in race consciousness felt toward other African Americans, considered of a lower caste....

Source: Coleman C. Myron, "Charles W. Chesnutt's *The House behind the Cedars*: An Outlaw(ed) Reading," in *Charles Chesnutt Reappraised: Essays on the First Major African American Fiction Writer*, edited by David Garrett Izzo and Maria Orban, McFarland, 2009, pp. 91–94.

Matthew Wilson

In the following excerpt, Wilson discusses issues of race in The House behind the Cedars.

...Chesnutt's mixed-race character, John Warwick (Walden) seems absolutely free from this fear of reversion to type. He is a racial conundrum, a "white negro" who has grown up with a knowledge of his own liminality and his paternal heritage: a bookcase that is, Richard Brodhead writes, "the primal scene for the Walden children ... the bookcase ... stands for their absent white father, the place where they read his literary classics" (*Cultures* 207) and where access to literature fuels his desire to escape the limitations of the racialized world in which he finds himself. By sheer force of will, John convinces a local magistrate, Judge Straight, who in a "moment of sentimental weakness" allows John to read law. In the face of John's insistence that he is white in spite of his mixed-race ancestry, the judge looks up a statute that gives John the warrant he needs to pass as a white man, the 1831 South Carolina law discussed in "What Is a White Man?" As the judge says, since John has "all the features of a white man, you would, at least in South Carolina, have simply to assume the place and exercise the privileges of a white man." Taking advantage of this law, John moves to South Carolina and during the Civil War marries the daughter of a "good family," who dies after giving birth to their son.

As John tells this story to his sister and mother during a clandestine visit to them, they find that it has "the charm of an escape from captivity," and that comparison is more telling than they realize. His story, in their view, could be a high romantic tale of capture and providential escape, or it could be like an escape from the

> TRYON WAS A REPRESENTATIVE OF CHESNUTT'S WHITE AUDIENCE, WHICH SAW THE POSITION OF WHITE SUPREMACY AS RATIONAL."

captivity of slavery. Although he has escaped the disadvantages of his ancestry, his decision to pass is made at a high cost to him and to his mother and sister, the same cost that escaped slaves paid and one to which the narrator points in this exchange between John and his mother. She says, "I thought I'd lost you forever," and he responds, "'I couldn't live without seeing you, mother,' . . . He meant it, too, or thought he did, although he had not seen her for ten years." From the beginning of the novel, Chesnutt pointed to the anguish of the mother, abandoned and unacknowledged because she was unable to pass, and the necessary withering of the affections of the separated son. Warwick (Walden) does feel, however, a momentary "blind anger" that he must sever all family ties to become white, but he also quickly banishes that thought as "pure sentiment." He has lived his life by "principles of right and reason" even though his individual principles were "at variance with what society considers equally right and reasonable." His decision, then, involved a devaluation of sentiment, of feeling in favor of "argument, of self-conviction. Once persuaded that he had certain rights, or ought to have them, by virtue of the laws of nature, in defiance of the customs of mankind, he had promptly sought to enjoy them," even though the cost of that enjoyment was nearly permanent separation from his family.

Sedlack has shown that the character of John Warwick (Walden), like George Tryon, came rather late in Chesnutt's revision of "Rena Walden," and Sedlack sees John as providing, in structural terms, the "necessary bridge between the world of Rena Walden and that of George Tryon." (In other words, John is needed to introduce Rena to George.) If John bridges the white and black worlds of the novel, he also provides an instructive contrast to George, who finds it more difficult than John to live his by "principles of right and reason." Unlike John, Tryon reasons from a position of racist rationality, while John's rationality is antiracialist;

both, as characters, have the same effect on the women around them. John separates himself from his mother, annealing his sense of affection, and George attempts to do much the same thing when he discovers that Rena is passing as white. Thematically, then, Chesnutt equated these two characters, who struggle to differing degrees with what they consider rationality and sentiment. In staging this struggle, Chesnutt extended the effect of the tragic mulatta genre to the privileged white male character, and he hoped that his audience would feel sympathy for Tryon. Part of the strategy of that genre (in its antiracist versions) was to demonstrate to the white audience that given the proper education and upbringing, the mulatta—the white negro—was no different from the white reader, and what she felt (whether the loss of a child, as in Stowe, or the stifling of ambition) was no different from what putative white readers would experience in similar circumstances. However, with these two male characters, Chesnutt was showing that they were internally almost identical in terms of a masculinist view of the world in which masculine rationality overruled female sentiment. Of course, Chesnutt was critical of both of these men for sealing themselves off from sentiment, and despite the similarities between Chesnutt and John Warwick (Walden), Chesnutt established a certain ironical distance between himself and John. In representing John's decision to pass, Chesnutt explored the consequences of the denial of family history and connection, a choice Chesnutt refused to make in his life. He was aware that mixed-race families were most often constructed on white denial: the white fathers refused to acknowledge their mixed-race children. Passing was also predicted on a similar denial—the denial of the African American family left behind and its heritage, which must be shunned to prevent any accidental racial revelations.

Warwick (Walden), who says that he has been almost completely successful in banishing sentimental considerations except in this single visit to his hometown, claims that in coming home he has yielded to a "sentimental weakness," but he also has an instrumental reason for seeing his sister and mother after such a long separation. He wants to ask his sister to live with him and care for his motherless child. Chesnutt wanted his readers to be aware of the human cost of annulling sentiment, not only in John's separation from his family but also in his separation from almost all human feeling, except for that regarding his son. In contrast to John's utilitarian view of passing, his sister, Rena, is filled with doubts, which only grow when she decides to marry George Tryon. He, on the other hand, has no doubts, either about her as a white woman or about his love for her, but Tryon instinctively draws the color line when he reads an article in a contemporary "medical journal" that argues, from a position of scientific racism, for the impossibility of race mixing. This "scientist" argues that "negro blood," no matter how "diluted," will always "revert to the African type, [and] any future amalgamation of the white and black races . . . would therefore be an ethnological impossibility; for the smallest trace of negro blood would inevitably drag down the superior race to the level of the inferior." Lest we think Chesnutt was exaggerating for effect here, it is important to remember that ideas such as these were accepted orthodoxy in the late nineteenth and early twentieth centuries. As Nancy Leys Stepan and Sander L. Gilman have observed, "In studying the history of scientific racism, we have been struck by the relative absence of critical challenges to its claims from within mainstream society." In its heyday, the "concepts within racial science were so congruent with social and political life . . . as to be virtually uncontested from inside the mainstream of science." The article that Tryon reads, though, moves beyond science and concludes with a peroration in which the southern man is enjoined to "maintain the supremacy and purity of his all-pervading, all-conquering race, and to resist by every available means the threatened domination of an inferior and degraded people." Tryon concludes that this seems to be "a well-considered argument, albeit a trifle bombastic." Tryon's judiciousness here is a sign that he is not a racist ideologue, a notion that Chesnutt reinforced in a subsequent chapter by introducing another white character, Dr. Green, who obsesses about the "negro problem" as in this sample of dinner conversation: "The negro is an inferior creature; God has marked him with the badge of servitude, and has adjusted his intellect to a servile condition. We will not submit to his domination." This statement has the tone of George in the earlier "Rena Walden," where he was characterized, Sedlack has observed, as a "loud, blustering bigot"; however, in *The House Behind the Cedars*, Tryon is more moderate, and Dr. Green is the hyperventilating racist. Chesnutt was trying to make Tryon more

sympathetic to a northern white audience that would have found Green's level of unabashed bigotry to be slightly embarrassing and would have been more comfortable with George's understated, more gentlemanly, less overly ideological racial prejudice.

Tryon was a representative of Chesnutt's white audience, which saw the position of white supremacy as rational. Such racist rationality, though, concealed a deep-seated irrationality that can be uncovered in Chesnutt's reference to the reversion to "the African type" in the article that Tryon reads. This phrase conjured up for Chesnutt's white readership a nightmarish vision articulated by a character in Dixon's *The Clansman* who says that the African lived in an undifferentiated time out of history. He "stole his food, worked his wife, sold his children, ate his brother, content to drink, sing, dance, and sport as the ape!" The African is further characterized as a "creature, half-child, half-animal, the sport of impulse, whim and conceit . . . whose speech knows no word of love, whose passions once aroused, are as the fury of the tiger—they have set this thing to rule over the Southern people." Attitudes such as these were exactly the kinds of naturalized, essentialized prejudices that Chesnutt, as a writer attempting to affect a white audience, needed to take into consideration—the nightmare vision of the inevitability of racial hierarchy and the sense of violation involved in any action that breached that "natural" hierarchy. The anxiety of that breach was acute during Reconstruction, the era in which both *The House Behind the Cedars* and *The Clansman* are set, and in both the cause of anxiety was the rule of blacks over whites—political rule in one case and racial, almost genetic rule in the other. Chesnutt also found Tryon's use of the term *argument* to describe the racist "scientific" article to be quite ironic because the word concealed something more uncontrollable than rational conviction, something that was revealed when Tryon discovered the truth about Rena.

Through a series of coincidences, Tryon and Rena end up in the town where Rena was raised and where she cannot pass, and she is revealed to him as a colored woman. When she confronts Tryon, she sees "a face as pale as death, with staring eyes, in which love, which once had reigned there, had now given place to astonishment and horror." As Rena subsequently says to her brother, Tryon "looked at me as though I were not even a human being." In seeing her instantaneously slide from one order of being to another, Tryon faces the fundamental instability of appearances within the racist imaginary. Although racists insisted that they could infallibly tell when anyone had any admixture of black "blood" (as the Supreme Court implied in its 1922–23 decisions defining whiteness), their anxiety of course resulted from the fact that they were unable to do so, either by external signs or by behavior, because in this period the one-drop rule had rendered race as potentially invisible. The sexual transgressions of the fathers, then, haunted their sons in the nightmare of the simulacrum, the white negro . . . .

Source: Matthew Wilson, "*The House Behind the Cedars*: Race Melodrama and the White Audience," in *Whiteness in the Novels of Charles W. Chesnutt*, University Press of Mississippi, 2004, pp. 73–77.

Dean McWilliams

In the following excerpt, McWilliams examines Chesnutt's treatment of perception and identity.

. . . The discrepancy between things as they are and things as they are perceived—dramatized in Warwick's encounter with the town—takes us to this novel's thematic heart. The woman Warwick seeks is Rena Walden. Rena is, in literary terms, Mandy Oxendine's sister—or at least her near cousin. Both are fictional protagonists conceived by Chesnutt during the 1890s, and both are light-colored black women who cross the color line and live as whites. In *The House behind the Cedars*, Chesnutt explores once again the consequences of his heroine's decision to change her racial identity. But these consequences are imagined differently in the two novels. The consequences that flow from Mandy's choice are felt most powerfully in the lives around her, in the convulsive sexual passions her presence arouses in two white males and in the vindictive jealousy it elicits from a black girl. Tragedy in *Mandy Oxendine* occurs around the central couple, in the deaths of Bob Utley and Rose Amelia, but Mandy Oxendine and Tom Lowrey themselves escape and begin a new life elsewhere. We do not know where or how Mandy and Tom will live their lives, but we are told that they will freely elect their social affiliation in terms of their own interests. The narrative thus defends the mulatto couple's right to choose their own racial identity.

> CHESNUTT'S NOVEL CALLS INTO QUESTION THE VIABILITY OF FABRICATIONS THAT BLATANTLY IGNORE THE PAST."

Rena Walden's story casts doubt on this assertion of the mulatto's sovereign independence. In *The House behind the Cedars*, emotional confusion occurs not only around Rena, but within her. She cannot escape this confusion because not only does she live in a racist society, but that society also lives within her. She is not exempt from the contradictory pressures of her culture: they blind her, they frustrate her hopes, and finally they destroy her life. John Warwick's entry into Patesville at the beginning of the novel initiates the chain of events that leads to Rena's death at its end. Warwick comes, he believes, to rescue his sister from life as a Negro, but he brings instead another form of imprisonment—entrapment within white Southern ideology. John and Rena are the illegitimate children of a white man and his mulatto mistress, and thus they are, under North Carolina law, black, and they bear their mother's family name, Walden. Ten years earlier, John left home and became a white man in South Carolina. He married into the white social elite, and he acquired property. More important, he embraced the privileges and the values of his new class. He was, his white peers judged, "sound on the subject of negroes, Yankees, and the righteousness of the lost cause." It is this ideological "soundness" that locks Warwick in the distorting historical nostalgia noted in the opening paragraph. He has affirmed his new identity by changing his family name from Walden to Warwick. He has read avidly in the library left by his white father, and he has chosen his new name from Bulwer-Lytton's historical novel *The Last of the Barons* (1843). Unfortunately, Warwick reads literature as poorly as he did the townscape he surveyed in the novel's opening paragraph. The mulatto parvenu is obviously infatuated with Bulwer-Lytton's protagonist, Warwick, the king-maker who deposed Edward IV and placed Henry VI on the throne. Warwick does not care to notice, however, that his namesake's career ended, in history as in fiction, with defeat, disgrace, and death. Similarly, Warwick renames his sister Rowena, after the blond princess in Scott's *Ivanhoe*. A friend suggests, however, that Warwick's dusky sister might better bear the name of Rebecca, Rowena's tragic, Jewish rival.

Warwick is not alone in venerating Walter Scott; the Scottish novelist was a revered figure in the South before and after the Civil War. In the Clarence Social Club's tournament, Southern planters and businessmen solemnly imitate Scott's medieval warriors by donning cardboard armor, poking poles through iron rings, and swinging swords at wooden balls. The South's Scott cult, which Mark Twain also mocked, reflected a central tenet of Southern myth: the specious claim that the South's governing elite descended from England's cavaliers and embodied its aristocratic ethos. Warwick's commitment to his new white identity is the primary force driving his behavior. For it he abandoned his mother and sister, and for it he embraced the culture that placed an uncrossable gulf between him and his former life. John Walden was denied his father's name and forced to bear the name of his Negro mother. He attempts to name himself and to author his own identity. J. Lee Greene's description of Warwick—"a New World Ishmael who metamorphoses into a New World Adam"—suggests the conflicting narratives implicit in his project. John would trump the racist biblical account of black servitude with the American myth of self-invention. In pursuing this project, he makes several fundamental miscalculations.

The first has to do with time. Warwick assumes a naive, overly simple opposition of past and future. At different moments, he will value one or the other of these seemingly opposed terms, without properly appreciating the way they interpenetrate one another. In the reflections that begin the novel, John overvalues the past, but it is a specious view of the antebellum South, the pastoral of plantation legend. At the same time, rather contradictorily, he undervalues the connection between past and future. He believes that, in crossing the state line, he leaves his past behind. This leads us to his second miscalculation, a reliance on another reductive binary: the opposition between subjective, psychological identity versus public, social identity. Warwick leaves home believing that *what* he is depends on *where* he is. Legally, he is correct on

this point: in North Carolina he was a Negro, and in South Carolina he is a white man. But law is the least of it. He is still—regardless of space, time, and legislative fiat—Rena's brother and Molly's son. These powerful personal bonds pull him back in space and time, convulsing his life and the life of his family. John, anticipating none of this, moves ahead in his project of self-authoring. What he accomplishes, however, is not invention, but replication. He inscribes himself within the dominant cultural narrative, the racist ideology that consigns his mother to inferior status. His fabrication is a lie within a lie, for the myth of a white Southern chivalry was itself a fiction, a cover for a brutal social order based on slavery and exploitation. Chesnutt's novel calls into question the viability of fabrications that blatantly ignore the past.

The House behind the Cedars also reminds us of the consequences of fictions that ignore our ties to others. The novel's first chapter introduces connections that seriously threaten the identity Walden/Warwick has constructed. Warwick left home ten years earlier at the age of eighteen, and he has not seen his family during the war or after. Now he returns to the house behind the cedars where he was raised and where his blood kin still live. Warwick knows that this journey into the past can put his new identity at risk, but he feels compelled to make it. His wife has died, and his son is without a mother; the child "needs some woman of its own blood to love it and look after it intelligently." The natural solution, reinforced by Molly's "tearful yearning," would be to place the child in his grandmother's care, but Molly bears the "mark of the Ethiopian," and her presence would threaten John's white identity. He will instead take his sister with him, leaving his mother alone. Warwick speaks of his son's need, not of his own, and in fact, he seems to have no strong feelings for his blood relations, although there is a disturbing hint of a sexual attraction for Rena. For the most part, Warwick is less concerned for the family he left than for the one he will found. His son, Albert, first of the Warwick line, needs care; so the boy's aunt will become his surrogate mother, his "mammy." Here again Warwick fatally miscalculates, ignoring the connection of future and past. Rena cannot so easily cut her ties to her mother; they draw her fatally back to her past life and explode her and her brother's new identities.

The pull between natural feelings and social identity provides the emotional armature for the novel's three tragedies: the death of Rena Walden and the ruined hopes of George Tryon and Frank Fowler. In all three lives flow the forces of affection, love, and desire; in all three this natural flow is frustrated by the ideologies of race and class. Judge Straight, a jurist who spent his life in the South and who has tried to mitigate some of its worst features, comments on the general problem that Chesnutt's narratives illustrate. Humans band together, tell stories, and create systems of belief, which help them to organize reality. But at some point these systems become more powerful than the people who created them, and they crash the lives they were meant to enrich: "We make our customs lightly; once made, like our sins, they grip us in bands of steel; we become the creatures of our creation." One of its victims, George Tryon recognizes the destructive power of ideology and the greater value of human feeling: "Custom was tyranny," he concludes, too late. "Love was the only law." George Tryon meets Rena as "Rowena Warwick," sister of the prominent South Carolina attorney and planter John Warwick. He falls in love immediately and as "Sir George," victor of the Clarence tournament, crowns Rena "Queen of Love and Beauty." However, when he learns of her African ancestry, he sees her through an ideological lens: the same woman becomes, in his fevered dream, "a hideous black hag." Tryon's natural feelings for Rena gradually reassert themselves, and he sets out in search of her, determined, against all social odds, to "make her white." . . .

Source: Dean McWilliams, "*The House behind the Cedars*: 'Creatures of Our Creation,'" in *Charles W. Chesnutt and the Fictions of Race*, University of Georgia Press, 2002, pp. 134–38.

SOURCES

"Anti-Communist Loyalty Oaths Persist Despite Court Rulings," Associated Press, February 23, 2013, http://www.pennlive.com/midstate/index.ssf/2013/02/anti-communist_oaths_persist_d.html (accessed March 17, 2013).

Benedict, Michael Les, "History of American Law: Gilded Age to the Great Depression (1877–1929)," in *Oxford Companion to American Law*, edited by Kermit L. Hall and David S. Clark, Oxford University Press, 2002, p. 383.

"The Booker T. Washington Era," *African American Odyssey*, Library of Congress website, http://memory.loc.gov/ammem/aaohtml/exhibit/aopart6.html (accessed March 17, 2013).

Chesnutt, Charles W., *The House behind the Cedars*, Penguin, 1993.

Du Bois, W. E. Burghardt, "Strivings of the Negro People," in *Atlantic*, August 1897, http://www.theatlantic.com/magazine/archive/1897/08/strivings-of-the-negro-people/305446/ (accessed March 15, 2013).

Gevison, Alan, "Veiled Aristocrats," in *Within Our Gates: Ethnicity in American Feature Films, 1911–1960*, University of California Press, 1997, p. 1096.

Gibson, Donald B., Introduction to *The House behind the Cedars*, Penguin, 1993, p. xxiii.

"An Issue in the Race Problem," in *Detroit Free Press*, November 11, 1900, p. 11.

"The Mixture of Blood: New Novel Dealing with the Old Race Problem," in *Denver Times*, November 11, 1900, p. 13.

Moore, Jacqueline M., *Booker T. Washington, W. E. B. Du Bois, and the Struggle for Racial Uplift*, Rowman & Littlefield, 2003, p. 76.

"Race Problem in a Novel," in *Chicago Daily Tribune*, November 10, 1900, p. 10.

"Reconstruction and Its Aftermath," *African American Odyssey*, Library of Congress website, http://memory.loc.gov/ammem/aaohtml/exhibit/aopart5.html (accessed March 17, 2013).

Review of *The House behind the Cedars*, in *Boston Courier*, December 29, 1900, p. 2.

Review of *The House behind the Cedars*, in *Boston Evening Transcript*, October 31, 1900, p. 12.

Review of *The House behind the Cedars*, in *Nation*, February 28, 1901, p. 182.

Review of *The House behind the Cedars*, in *Toronto Globe*, January 5, 1901, p. 6.

Sedlack, Robert P., "The Evolution of Charles Chesnutt's *The House behind the Cedars*," in *CLA Journal*, Vol. 29, No. 2, 1975, p. 126.

Sollors, Werner, ed., *Charles W. Chesnutt: Stories, Novels, and Essays*, Library of America, 2002, pp. 915–23.

"A Story of Love and Race Prejudice," in *Philadelphia Record*, November 16, 1900, p. 10.

Washington, Booker T., "An Address Delivered at the Opening of the Cotton States and International Exposition," September 18, 1895, *African American Odyssey*, Library of Congress website, http://memory.loc.gov/ammem/aap/aapaddr.html (accessed March 15, 2013).

Watson, Bruce, "*Black Like Me*, 50 Years Later," in *Smithsonian*, October 2011, http://www.smithsonianmag.com/arts-culture/Black-Like-Me-50-Years-Later.html (accessed March 19, 2013).

FURTHER READING

Andrews, William L., *The Literary Career of Charles W. Chesnutt*, Louisiana State University Press, 1980.
This volume is a literary biography, meaning that it examines the author's writings in the context of his life. It provides insight not only into his literary corpus but also into his role in the evolution of social-problem literature in the late nineteenth and early twentieth centuries.

Barney, William L., *The Civil War and Reconstruction: A Student Companion*, Oxford University Press, 2001.
Part of the Student Companions to American History series, this volume is written for audiences ranging from junior-high-school students to adults. It is an alphabetized reference work that examines a wide range of topics pertaining to the Civil War and the postwar Reconstruction era about which Chesnutt wrote.

Chesnutt, Helen M., *Charles Waddell Chesnutt: Pioneer of the Color Line*, University of North Carolina Press, 1989.
This volume, by Chesnutt's oldest daughter, was first published in 1952. Helen Chesnutt, born in 1881, followed her father into a teaching career, first in Baltimore, then in Cleveland. She was able to tour Europe with her father as well. This volume is a standard biography written from a familial perspective.

Nelson, Emmanuel S., ed., *African American Authors: 1745–1945*, Greenwood Press, 2000.
Readers interested in the larger topic of black American literature will find this volume a useful reference source. It includes profiles, written by different authors, of seventy-eight African American writers. It includes a profile of Chesnutt by Tracie Church Guzzio.

Render, Sylvia Lyons, *Charles W. Chesnutt*, Twayne, 1980.
This volume is part of Twayne's United States Authors Series. It provides a succinct overview of Chesnutt's life and a critical examination of his work.

SUGGESTED SEARCH TERMS

African American authors

Booker T. Washington

Charles W. Chesnutt

Charles W. Chesnutt AND House behind the Cedars

Committee of Twelve for the Advancement of the Interests of the Negro Race

Freedman's Bureau

Jim Crow laws

mixed race

passing AND race

post–Civil War AND American history

Reconstruction AND Civil War

W. E. B. Du Bois

A Map of the World

JANE HAMILTON

1994

Jane Hamilton is a popular and award-winning novelist, and *A Map of the World*, published in 1994, is her most important and widely read work. *A Map of the World* is written in the idiom of the American gothic, a literary tradition stretching back to nineteenth-century writers like Nathaniel Hawthorne and Edgar Allan Poe. American gothic reshapes the stylistic vocabulary of gothic literature, with its haunted castles, damsels in distress, and love of the grotesque, into an exposition of the dark underside of American culture, seeing America not as a land of limitless opportunity but as a wild land filled with threatening danger lurking in the shadows. *A Map of the World* recalls the real-world phenomenon, all too common in the 1980s and 1990s, of what has been called the satanic panic, a wave of hysterical accusations against day-care providers and others working with children that they not only molested their charges but were also part of a vast conspiracy bent on sacrificing children to Satan. These utterly false charges, which saw many innocent Americans wrongly imprisoned, were soon likened to the witch hunts that marred early American history at Salem, Massachusetts, and which were equally fantastic. The Salem experience was also an integral feature of older American gothic literature. Readers of *A Map of the World* should be aware that while there is no actual child abuse in the novel, there are discussions of such abuse and sexuality in general.

Jane Hamilton *(© Dave Schlabowske / Time & Life Pictures /*
Getty Images)

AUTHOR BIOGRAPHY

Hamilton was born in Oak Park, Illinois, a suburb of Chicago famous for its many early examples of Frank Lloyd Wright's architecture, on July 13, 1957. She took an undergraduate degree in English at Carleton College, in Minnesota. She was encouraged by her professors there to become a professional writer. In 2006, Hamilton told interviewer Mark Hertzberg for the *Journal Times* of Racine, Wisconsin, that she was deeply affected by overhearing her creative writing professor say that he thought Hamilton would someday write a novel. Hamilton told Hertzberg,

> It had a lot more potency, the fact that I overheard it, rather than his telling me directly.... I was just stunned.... I didn't tell anyone. I suppose, in a way, it was like getting an unexpected letter from someone you love dearly, as a teenager, saying "I love you." You have to walk outside and walk around and absorb this marvel. It had great impact.

By 1982 Hamilton was already publishing short stories in *Harper's*, beginning with "My Own Earth." In 1988 she published her first novel, *The Book of Ruth*, an examination of small-town poverty and spousal abuse. The following year, the book won the Hemingway Foundation/PEN Award and several regional awards in the upper Midwest, the setting of all of Hamilton's fiction. She published *A Map of*

the World in 1994. She followed this in 1998 with *The Short History of a Prince*, a novel about the failure of artistic aspiration. In 2000 she published *Disobedience*, which concerns the senior year of high school of a young man who discovers his mother's infidelity to his father through prying into her e-mail account.

Hamilton's 2007 novel *When Madeline Was Young* deals with the impact on a young family of the mother's traumatic brain injury. Hamilton was inspired in this work by Elizabeth Spencer's 1960 novella *The Light in the Piazza*, whose main character is also reduced to a childlike mental state by a brain injury. Her most recent novel, published in 2009, is *Laura Rider's Masterpiece*, a domestic satire also based on unrealized artistic desires. Her novels have enjoyed tremendous popular success, and *The Book of Ruth* and *A Map of the World* were both adapted by Hollywood. Highly reclusive, Hamilton has settled in Rochester, Wisconsin, a small town outside Racine, where she devotes a good deal of time to charity work to benefit the local library.

PLOT SUMMARY

A Map of the World is divided into three sections, each named after its narrator.

Alice

CHAPTERS 1–8

Alice and Howard Goodwin live on a farm in the (fictitious) town of Prairie Center, Wisconsin. They have adopted this way of life because of Howard's romanticized view of farming. Alice works as the nurse in the local grade school. They have the last working farm in the county, which has rapidly turned into a suburb.

Alice is close friends with Theresa Collins, a psychologist who lives nearby. They both have two daughters—Claire and Emma Goodwin, and Lizzy and Audrey Collins—and during the summer break, each of them takes one day a week to watch all four girls, so as to give the other a rest from child-care duties. The novel begins on a day that Alice has the four girls and has decided to take them swimming in a pond on the farm. While she is getting ready to go out, Alice is momentarily distracted upstairs by finding some old maps that had been part of her inner fantasy life as a child. She recalls how

MEDIA ADAPTATIONS

- *A Map of the World* was filmed in 1999 by director Scott Eliott, off a screenplay adapted by Peter Hedges and Polly Platt. The movie stars Sigourney Weaver as Alice Goodwin and also features Julianne Moore, David Strathairn, and Chloë Sevigny.

the unreal world they depict represented the one moment of closeness and joy she had shared with her father. While she is distracted, Lizzy, who is two years old, wanders down to the pond on her own. Alice eventually surmises what has happened and rushes to follow her, only to find the girl floating apparently lifeless in the water. Alice's inner monologue now takes over the narrative, and she consonantly denies that anything serious has happened, expecting that at any moment paramedics, doctors, or someone will make everything all right. Alice, herself a school nurse, cannot even rouse herself to properly perform CPR on the girl. Eventually, Howard sees what is happening and calls an ambulance, and Lizzy is taken to the hospital.

The Collins family keeps a vigil in Lizzy's hospital room with constant prayer, while the Goodwins, exiled from the room, keep watch in the waiting room. Alice continues her denial. She prays herself, though she recognizes how out of place this is for her. Alice encounters the Presbyterian minister, Reverend Nabor, Lizzy's father's pastor, and appeals to him too for salvation, though she mistrusts his spirituality.

Alice happens to see Carol Mackessy in the hospital. She is the mother of Robbie, a child Alice often sees at school and whom she suspects is being criminally neglected. The two women argue, and Carol curses Alice. Alice broods over all the money and good advice that Howard's mother, Nellie, gives them; she feels it is always offered in view of controlling them.

Nellie visits the family to help manage the children and try to console Alice. Alice assures

her daughters that nothing can happen to them because Lizzy has already been sacrificed. She does not seem to believe this, but she is struggling to understand the Christian doctrine of salvation. At the funeral at the Presbyterian Church, Alice feels a crushing burden building up on her and is horrified upon seeing Carol Mackessy and a hideous and offensive woman named Glevitch leering at her like figures out of a painting by Hieronymus Bosch. Alice finally makes a scene by running out of the church.

As the daily routine of life settles back in, Alice builds up her guilt by insisting to herself that she is the greatest villain in history. She visits the pond where Lizzy drowned and then walks in the woods that separate the farm from the subdivision where the Collinses live. She comes upon Theresa wandering alone also, weeping and screaming. There is neither hostility nor forgiveness between the two women, but Theresa tells Alice that she visited Albert Santinga. He had been her parish priest and the English teacher at the Catholic school Theresa attended. But he left the church for a short-lived marriage. After his wife left him, Theresa worked with him in her role as a psychologist. Now he has acted as her confessor and helped Theresa deal with her grief, bringing down what Theresa interpreted as a visitation of the Holy Spirit.

Alice contemplates the absurdity of reconciling Christian mythology with physical science—for example, where in outer space is heaven located? She recalls her resentment of God over the death of her own mother. It was in the aftermath of that tragedy that she retreated into the fantasy world of her maps. Alice has to attend a school-board meeting about her employment status, a sign of the community turning against her. But she retreats to the hallway under the excuse of feeling unwell. Two police officers corner her in the hallway and start questioning her, not about Lizzy but about Robbie Mackessy. Alice blurts out, "I hurt everybody!" blowing up her negligence in the case of Lizzy to a cosmic scale. But the police interpret it as a confession of the charges Carol Mackessy has made against Alice, that she has molested Robbie. The police do not tell her their suspicion at the time, but Alice recalls confronting Carol Mackessy over the poor health of her child, implying that she is negligent and ought to be reported to child services. Mackessy lashed out at her: "'I'll report *you*,' she snarled, coming past me with Robbie slung over her shoulder. She turned, almost cracking her son's head in the molding of the door. 'I'll get you put away if anything is the matter with him.'" Shortly thereafter, Alice is arrested.

Howard

CHAPTERS 9–16

Howard takes up the narration at the moment Alice is led off in handcuffs. As more accusations emerge from the community, Alice's bail is set at $100,000. Alice wants Paul Rafferty, whom they know slightly, as her lawyer, although Howard does not see how his fee can be paid. Howard tries to secure a babysitter for their daughters. He asks several neighbors, such as Miss Bowman and Suzannah Brooks, but their religious concerns and prejudices make the situation impossible.

On top of Alice's misfortunes, Howard is put under pressure by a drought that endangers the farm. Theresa starts to visit the Goodwin farm to watch the children as Howard attends court. During a preliminary hearing, Rafferty establishes that no molestation such as Robbie Mackessy testifies to could have taken place because the nurse's office is in full public view, but Alice is bound over for trial anyway. The trial is set for October, several months away. Theresa gradually becomes a regular visitor at the Goodwins as her husband Dan withdraws into his work. One night Emma and Claire insist that Theresa sleep over, and Howard nearly makes love with her. They agree they must stop seeing each other after that.

Howard decides that he has no choice but to sell the farm. The community's turning against them makes it impossible for the Goodwins to stay even aside from their need for cash.

Alice

CHAPTERS 17–22

Alice takes over the narration again, and the novel focuses on her life in jail. Her cell mate is Debbie Clark, a young woman charged with killing her twin sons when they were born. Alice's cell block is dominated by a violent woman named Dyshett, who particularly torments Alice and Debbie because they are charged with harming children. Dyshett is looking for any excuse for hostility toward Alice and eventually attacks her while they are watching Oprah Winfrey's television show, sending her to the hospital. Alice

thinks this attack a just punishment for her neglect of Lizzy.

When Alice returns, she finds that Dyshett has been dethroned by an inmate called Sherry. Dyshett seems to have collapsed emotionally after the attack. Sherry decides to protect Alice but spreads the rumor that Alice injured herself by bashing her own head against a table, so she is feared by the other inmates as a madwoman. Alice spends most of her time reading, especially studying Buddhism. Lynelle Duchamps, a mentally unbalanced inmate, gives Alice a bookmark with the text of the twenty-third psalm, which makes a deep impression on her.

Rafferty, meanwhile, is intent on winning the case because he hates the hysteria that is being whipped up contrary to justice. He has discovered that the other boys who are charging Alice with abuse are all friends of Mackessy and were probably bullied by him into perjury.

Alice is soon released on bond, and the family now lives in an apartment in Racine. Howard, unable to remain idle, takes a job with the Motor Vehicle Registration Office. The boys besides Robbie withdraw their accusations.

Free now, at least until the trial is over, Alice feels reborn and looks back on a swim she took with Howard in the pond the first night they moved to the farm as a baptism.

As the trial begins, Rafferty works to discredit Robbie as a witness, particularly by attacking Myra Flint, the social worker in charge of questioning Robbie for the prosecution, as using coercive and leading techniques that have already been discredited by the psychological profession.

As the trial progresses, Rafferty is able to call witnesses, including Nancy Sheridan, Robbie's sometime babysitter, who establish that Robbie has often seen his mother having sex with various men, suggesting a source for the details of his false accusations. Rafferty also calls Theresa, a trained psychologist, as an expert to refute Flint's evaluation of Robbie. Alice imagines that Mackessy's hatred of her stems from her own guilt at failing as a mother.

Alice is acquitted, and the Goodwins move to Chicago, again helped by Nellie. Alice sees Theresa one last time and is forgiven by her, but she knows their friendship is over.

CHARACTERS

Miss Bowman

The Goodwins buy their eggs from Miss Bowman, who keeps chickens. Howard considers that her oddity would have singled her out for charges of practicing witchcraft in an earlier time.

Suzannah Brooks

Brooks is the Goodwins' neighbor. When Howard approaches her about babysitting, she calls on him to surrender his life to Jesus, oblivious that he is already a Lutheran. Despite her show of Christian virtue, she is a notorious gossip and snubs the Mackessys out of class antagonism.

Debbie Clark

Clark is Alice's cell mate in jail. The charges against her stem from the deaths of her twin children. She had denied to herself the fact that she was pregnant. Her babies died at birth, and her degree of guilt in the matter is unclear.

Audrey Collins

Audrey is the five-year-old daughter of Dan and Theresa Collins and the sister of Lizzy.

Dan Collins

Dan is the husband of Theresa Collins and the father of Lizzy and Audrey. He deals with the depression that follows Lizzy's death by immersing himself in his work and withdrawing from his family. He is also the organist at the Presbyterian Church and runs a museum devoted to dairy farming. This resonates with Howard's idealization of America's rural past.

Elizabeth "Lizzy" Collins

Elizabeth, or Lizzy, is the two-year-old daughter of Dan and Theresa Collins. Her accidental death by drowning is the event that sets the plot of the novel in motion.

Theresa Collins

Theresa is Alice's best friend and the mother of Lizzy, the girl who drowns under Alice's care. Unlike Howard and Alice, she comes from a small town, went to university to become a psychological counselor, and moved to Prairie Center to take up a suburban, rather than a rural, life. She is Catholic, and her reaction to her daughter's drowning and death is conditioned by her faith. However, she seeks out

Albert Santinga, her old family priest, as a counselor even though he had left the church; the personal connection is more important to her than the office. In the aftermath of Lizzy's death, Alice is soon isolated in jail, and Dan's depression makes him turn inward and become emotionally unavailable to Theresa, so she tries to start a relationship with Howard. They can express their grief to each other. But Howard refuses her after sore temptation. She makes a formal reconciliation with Alice, but it seems doubtful their friendship will revive.

Susan Dirks

Dirks is the assistant district attorney who prosecutes Alice. She is generally outmaneuvered by Rafferty.

Lynelle Duchamps

Duchamps is a prisoner in jail with Alice. Dying of AIDS, she hovers between insanity and prophecy and influences Alice's spiritual journey more than any of the regular clergy in the novel.

Dyshett

Dyshett is a fellow prisoner of Alice's in jail. She is the dominant figure in inmate culture because she is readier than most to commit violence. She is serving time for assaulting a police officer. But she is also more intelligent and sophisticated than most of the others. She was abused herself growing up in foster homes and is hostile to Alice. At one point she assaults Alice, and loses the respect of the other inmates.

Myra Flint

Flint is the child protection worker in charge of the Mackessy case. She imagines that she understands the psychology of children and how to interrogate them, but she is exposed as a fraud by Rafferty's cross-examination.

Mrs. M. L. Glevitch

Glevtich is a loud, tasteless, and unpleasant woman who attends Lizzy's funeral. For Alice she comes to signify the condemnatory face of the Prairie Center community.

Alice Goodwin

Alice is the main character of *A Map of the World* and the narrator of most of the text. Her life is overshadowed by a feeling that falls somewhere between doubt and denial. She is not able to embrace the commonplace religiosity that surrounds her, not because she analyzes and rejects religion rationally, but because she cannot summon up enough faith to embrace it. Paradoxically, she seems unable to accept adverse realities because of the same flaw. It is a desire to be detached, living in an internal exile of isolation, while still in the world. Her first response to the disaster of Lizzy's drawn-out death is to simply deny what is happening: "No. It could not be true that there was nothing behind her eyelids. . . . It could not be true that she was like an egg that has been blown out." Alice constantly imagines that nothing bad can really happen and insists to herself that this fantasy must be true.

Tall and blond, Alice is withdrawn and socially inept. The pressures that she experiences at Lizzy's funeral cause her to flee, and this rupture of conventions, almost as much as the accident itself, turns the community against her. She also provokes retaliation from Robbie Mackessy's mother and from the other inmates in prison. At her trial, her testimony does little to help her because she is pursuing some inner code of honesty rather than speaking in her own interest to the jurors. Her husband, Howard, a reserved Lutheran, was initially drawn to her because of what he viewed as her self-containment, but it is more nearly an inability to make connections with others.

Claire Goodwin
Claire is the three-year-old daughter of Alice and Howard. Alice suspects that Claire is the reincarnation of her grandmother.

Emma Goodwin
Emma is the six-year-old daughter of Alice and Howard. Even before the tragedy that befell her young friend Lizzy, Emma was trying and given to tantrums; it was partly distraction from Emma that made Alice inattentive to Lizzy before the accident.

Howard Goodwin
Howard, Alice's husband, idealizes an earlier way of living, signified for him by farming and small-town life. To pursue his own version of the American dream, he moves his family to the farm in Prairie Center, setting up the circumstances of the novel. A Lutheran, he is naturally reserved and stoic. He believes that he has a duty to God to succeed on the path of life set for him by divine providence. He is overwhelmed by the

enormity of the accusations against Alice and cannot conceive that they were fabricated out of mere spite. He is ostracized by the community because of Alice's supposed crimes, the flip side of the traditional village life he had idealized. On a symbolic level, nature turns against him too, wracking his farm with drought. During Alice's imprisonment, he grows close to Theresa Collins but eventually recoils from her in horror as a temptation to his concept of virtue. In pursuing his duty to Alice, he feels he must sacrifice his whole carefully chosen way of life, selling the farm to pay her legal fees. His loyalty to her keeps them together through the end of the novel.

Nellie Goodwin
Nellie is Howard's mother. She exists in the novel principally as the focus of Alice's resentment. She helps the couple financially and with good advice. But her help is offered in exchange for the control it gives her. Howard comes to realize this, but he is nevertheless dependent on her, as, at the end of the novel, she pays for her granddaughters' education in private schools. She has little understanding of her son's and daughter-in-law's character beyond what she needs to know to dominate them.

Carol Mackessy
Carol is Robbie's mother. She is resentful of the responsibility of having a child and dangerously neglects her son, to the point where he becomes dehydrated and ill. She reacts with hostility to Alice's criticism of her and vows revenge, which comes in the form of her own child-abuse accusation against Alice.

Robbie Mackessy
Neglected and abused by his own mother, Robbie is both frequently ill, coming to Alice's professional attention, and bullying to other students. He is easily manipulated by his mother to testify falsely against Alice. The social workers and others who deal with Robbie on behalf of the state are eager to assign diagnoses such as PTSS (post-traumatic stress syndrome) or APD (antisocial personality disorder) but do little to help him.

Reverend Joseph Nabor
Nabor is the young minister of Prairie Center's Presbyterian Church. He visits the Collins family in the hospital and conducts Lizzy's funeral. Alice sees him as a fraud, as if he is playing the

part of a preacher rather than being truly spiritual. He seems to work from a small repertoire of memorized Bible verses and to put on a facade he learned at seminary. He spends most of his time speculating in real estate. Alice nevertheless hopes to find some sort of spiritual authority in him.

Horace Peterson
Peterson is the judge presiding over Alice's trial. He generally favors Rafferty but is nevertheless harsh to and suspicious of Alice.

Paul Rafferty
Rafferty is Alice's defense attorney. The Goodwins know him socially through the Collins family. They do not know what to make of his aggressiveness and competence, sometimes admiring him, sometimes thinking he must be essentially fraudulent. He wins Alice's case because he is able to persuade the jury to view the facts involved through a different interpretive lens from that which the authorities use. He sees that the heart of the matter is Carol Mackessy's character, not Alice's.

Albert Santinga
Santinga is the old family priest of the Collins family, and he also taught Theresa Collins at her Catholic school. He fell in love and left the church to marry but was quickly rejected by his wife. Nevertheless, he acts as Theresa's spiritual guide after the death of her daughter.

Nancy Sheridan
A neighbor of the Mackessys', Mrs. Sheridan dislikes Carol and testifies to impugn Robbie's testimony at Alice's trial.

Sherry
Sherry is one of the inmates in Alice's ward in prison. She takes over leadership of the community after Dyshett's spiritual collapse.

THEMES

Grief
Alice's principal experience in *A Map of the World* is the emotion of grief. The dominant factor in her life before the novel begins was grief over her mother's death, but this is far exceeded by what she feels after her negligence

causes Lizzy's death. Yet her feelings are complicated. At the time of the drowning she is paralyzed by denial, in the absence of which she might have been able to save the girl. Thereafter she feels guilt more than any other emotion. She also fears losing Theresa's friendship. Are these emotions expressions of grief, or do they arise in place of grief? They are conditioned by what may be described as Alice's self-centeredness. Her grief impels her on a path of spiritual growth, but it is the catharsis, or washing away by expression, of Theresa's grief that allows the two women to reconcile to the degree they do. Within the plot of the novel, guilt is certainly Alice's most powerful and significant reaction. In that respect, Alice's later experiences of accusations and prosecution for child abuse can be seen as byproducts of her feelings of guilt over Lizzy's death.

Religion
One way of looking at the plot of *A Map of the World* is as a spiritual journey Alice is impelled upon by Lizzy's death. She begins in a state of questioning skepticism (rather than atheism) and proceeds, in accord with the narrative structure of the novel, to move through several spiritual possibilities before settling on a new spiritual life for herself. Alice's first thought upon finding Lizzy in the water is "She's fine! She's fine!" and her mind keeps on fighting against reality up until the girl's death in the hospital three days later. Is this denial or prayer? She focuses all of her attention on building up a mental picture of the way things ought to have been if the disaster had never happened. Hamilton seems to be exploring the mental process of prayer detached from its ritual context. Alice's desperate clinging to a manufactured reality seem irrational, but if she were trying to invoke a deity to miraculously reorder reality, then that would find a social context as prayer, which is what the Collins family spends the same time doing. Alice begins with a doubt of basic religious tenets: "I wasn't always sure that there was any such thing as a soul to begin with, if there was an essence that was independent of our bodies, and that doubt made it all the more difficult to think of a little soul." But she quickly moves through a series of experiences that enable her to come to terms with faith, although none is fully formative with regard to her transformation.

TOPICS FOR FURTHER STUDY

- In *A Map of the World*, a central part is played by a map Alice made that is the summation of her childhood hopes. Reading J. R. R. Tolkien's *The Hobbit*, you will see that a central role is played by another map, the map of the Lonely Mountain that is the bearer of Thorin Oakenshield's heritage. In both cases the map is an expression of the innermost desire of the character. Interestingly too, where Tolkien was the creator of a fantasy mythos based in part on his boyhood love of mapmaking, Hamilton presents a character more analogous to Tolkien himself than to the personae of Tolkien's fiction. Make your own map of a fantastic world expressing your innermost hopes and frustrations.

- Khaled Hosseini's 2003 novel *The Kite Runner* begins in Afghanistan on the eve of the Soviet invasion in 1979 and follows its characters as they become refugees in Pakistan and immigrants in the United States. It shares some themes with *A Map of the World*, including an act of child abuse that destroys lives and the interaction of such charges with traditional culture. Write a paper comparing the cultural responses that led to hysterical accusations of child abuse in American culture to the widespread

ignoring or toleration of such abuse in Afghanistan.

- Give a presentation to your class on the history of false accusations of child abuse in American culture. This is a lively topic of interest on the Internet, and much information can be found there as the basis for your report, from blogs and discussion-board posts by therapists who continue to insist that organized ritual abuse is widespread and by individuals who fear that they have lost memories of traumatic abuse, to systematic debunking of such claims. The website of the False Memory Syndrome Foundation (http://www.fmsfonline.org/) is a useful place to start your research.

- *A Map of the World* uses many themes of the American gothic movement: the distrust between city and countryside and the irruption of unexpected horror in an idyllic landscape, among others. Write a paper comparing Hamilton's novel with another modern expression of American gothic literature, such as Flannery O'Connor's *Wise Blood* (1952) or Joyce Carol Oates's *Bellefleur* (1980).

Alice's husband, Howard, offers a workman like view of religion. A Lutheran, he believes that God set him a certain job to accomplish in life and gave him what he needed to succeed, and that the purpose of his life is working to carry out the task he has been set. Alice is deeply impressed by Theresa Collins's encounter with her old family priest, Albert Santinga, who left the church to marry but was quickly divorced. Because of the authority he has with her, Theresa feels that simply going over with him what happened secures the blessing of the Holy Spirit on her. In prison Alice encounters Lynelle

Duchamps, a prostitute who is dying of AIDS and whose delusions—for example, that Oprah Winfrey is her fairy godmother—seem almost schizophrenic. But somehow her use of familiar Bible passages impresses Alice with a spiritual conviction in contrast to the falseness she perceived in the same usage by Reverend Nabor at Lizzy's funeral.

Alice finally feels that she has become a spiritual person and can resolve her grief and guilt. She puts this down to a private experience that she had when she was first married and moved to the farm. She and Howard had gone

Alice and her husband moved recently to their dairy farm. *(© auremar | Shutterstock.com)*

swimming in the fatal pond. She now interprets this as

> something on the order of a baptism, a kind of blessing. It had been impossible to see at the time, to understand what was taking place right under our noses. Without minister and feast and candlelight and absolution, our swim had marked a beginning.

But she had not felt so at the time. Is this different from the constructed memories of the children that resulted in the false accusations against her? The novel concludes with Alice's disappointment that Howard has not made a similar spiritual journey but remains unchanged by everything they have experienced.

STYLE

Fantasy World Creation

The title of *A Map of the World* refers to a map, really a series of maps, that the main character Alice created as a little girl. They were the kinds of maps that grade-school children often make

as a project when studying the geography of various states or countries:

> I had designed a whole world when I was a child, in secret. I had made a series of maps, one topographical, another of imports and exports, another highlighting mineral deposits, animal and plant species, another with descriptions of governments, transportation networks, and culture centers.

This world was not one that existed at the time the maps were made or at any time in the past; rather, it is an entirely different world which Alice called Tangalooponda. It was not an alien planet or a magical realm, but it was the secret place where Alice could experience happiness. She considered that as a child she had only felt happiness once, on one of the rare occasions when her father physically touched her as a sign of affection, when he took her to see a giant coal-mining machine he had helped to build, the Gem of Egypt. Ironically, it is while Alice is distracted by coming across these maps that Lizzy wanders out of the house and drowns. Although it is not possible to conclusively draw on Hamilton's own background in this respect, this kind of essentially childish play in creating maps, histories, and other pseudo-facts about an imagined world is often the foundation of literature. Charlotte's Brontë's *Jane Eyre* and her sister Emily Brontë's *Wuthering Heights* grew out of their childhood creation of the worlds of Angria and Gondal, while J. R. R. Tolkien's Middle Earth has helped to turn the concept of world creation into a well-known and widespread style of literature.

Intertextuality

Intertextuality is a way for a writer to address other works of literature without quoting from them or explicitly referring to them. The author simply engages the ideas or content of another work directly. This subtly involves the reader in a three-way conversation, since the reader must use her own knowledge of the other work to fully understand the work at hand. Some of these kinds of intertextual references are of central importance to *A Map of the World*. For example, when Elizabeth drowns, she spends three days in the hospital alive, but in any meaningful sense already dead, and finally dies; moreover, the reader might reasonably expect that Alice, as a nurse, might have saved the girl's life by performing CPR when she first found her, but she did not. Hamilton does not explicitly put these elements of the story into any symbolic framework. But they take on their full meaning only in light of the reader's knowledge that according to the Gospels, Jesus spent three days in the tomb supposedly dead, while really alive, and was resurrected at the end in a way no one could have reasonably expected. The death, burial, and resurrection of Jesus is the foundation for Christian faith. In the same way, Elizabeth's death becomes the foundation for Alice's spiritual transformation from an essentially irreligious person to one with faith at the end of the novel, albeit a very individualistic and personal faith. This is signaled by her rite of baptism having been carried out in the form of her midnight swim in the same pond where Elizabeth died.

HISTORICAL CONTEXT

Child-Abuse Hysteria in the Late Twentieth Century

The plot of *A Map of the World* concerns accusations of child abuse brought against Alice, a school nurse, by several of her clients. This reflects a disturbing phenomenon that was all too common in the 1980s and 1990s, when many day-care works and others in charge of children were accused of child abuse, with many serving terms in prison and others killing themselves under the weight of the social condemnation the charges brought about. Hamilton actually presents a case in which the false charges are relatively mild compared to many fantastic accusations made at the time. The actual facts would have worked against the illusion of realism she strives for.

The usual pattern was that one child would say something to make his parents suspicious, and soon gossip and other social pressures would bring about accusations from dozens of children against all the workers at a day-care center or school. The most famous of many incidents occurred at the McMartins' preschool in Manhattan Beach, California, beginning in 1983 and entailing one of the longest and costliest trials in US history. In fact, none of these incidents involved actual molestation. Interrogators who had no scientific methodology for understanding children's psychologies (despite frequent claims that they did) paradoxically helped the children to fabricate false stories and then memorize them for testimony. Parents in the affected communities were understandably outraged by the cases and often unknowingly coerced their own children into making false accusations.

In a number of incidents, these accusations stirred up a frenzy or panic in the community that has been likened to a witch hunt, and innocent people were convicted despite the bizarre nature of the children's charges. At the McMartin preschool, for instance, the day-care workers were said by the children to be able to fly around the room and to molest the children either in public places, such as a car wash near the school or a local airport, or in tunnels under the school that did not in fact exist. Many episodes became actual witch hunts when the accused were said to be part of a nationwide network of Satan worshippers who carried out the abuse for their rituals. Hamilton alludes to this facet of what is now known as satanic ritual abuse hysteria when the lawyer Rafferty refers to the charges against Alice as a witch hunt, as well as in her description of Miss Bowman, from whom the Goodwins bought their eggs:

COMPARE
&
CONTRAST

- **1990s:** The late 1980s and early 1990s see a wave of accusations and charges of sexual abuse against day-care workers and a widespread belief that an international satanic conspiracy is behind it.

  Today: It is now recognized that such accusations were false and the result of mass hysteria.

- **1990s:** The United States is in the grip of a housing boom that sees rapidly rising prices and the construction of a large number of suburban housing units.

  Today: The housing bubble, fueled by speculation and illegal banking practices, burst, resulting in the worst economic recession since the Great Depression of the 1930s.

- **1990s:** AIDS is a new and terrifying disease with little to no means of medical treatment.

  Today: Although AIDS remains a dreaded disease, its spread in the United States has slowed, and treatments offering prospects of long-term survival have been developed.

> If it had been Salem in witch-hunting times she would have been the first to go. She would have been suspect because she talked to her animals, because she was a single-woman property owner, and because she was disfigured.

These are, indeed, all qualities that might have attracted a charge of witchcraft. The unifying principle is that they are all things that are out of place, that put her out of the mainstream of the community. But there was another quality that even more clearly defined a witch, which Miss Bowman does not possess but which Alice does. She herself is an outsider.

Hamilton moves closer to her historical context when she reveals that the charges against Alice were fostered by the investigators' amateurish questioning of the children. Myra Flint is the child protection worker responsible for questioning Robbie and the other children who accuse Alice of molesting them. Testifying at the trial, she describes her working methods:

> Children's memories...can become locked inside their minds. One possible key to unlocking those memories is to ask very specific questions, or even leading questions. In the legal context, of course, we are not allowed to do so.

Rafferty sees through this and accuses her of trying to "enhance their memories," in other words, to manufacture false memories. It is now clear that this is what the social workers and psychologists who investigated such accusations of child abuse did. They would ask a very specific set of questions over and over until the children realized that they were expected to answer yes, and their "memories" came to consist of being able to tell the story that was outlined in the questions. Memory, after all, is not an exact record of the personal past but a constantly changing mental flux that reacts to new experiences. It is easy to believe that children would not lie about being molested—even Sigmund Freud, the founder of modern psychology, was deceived in the same way at the beginning of his career—but the children were rather coached to recite a script, or become ventriloquist's dummies, as Hamilton puts it.

CRITICAL OVERVIEW

Hamilton was already a popular novelist when she published *A Map of the World* in 1994, so the book was widely reviewed in the popular press, but it has attracted as yet little scholarly attention. The novel also became a selection for Oprah's Book Club, derived from Oprah Winfrey's television show, perhaps not least because Oprah figures in the book in a small

Alice is consumed by guilt after a young girl in her care drowns in the farm pond. (© Leene | Shutterstock.com)

way as Lynelle Duchamps's supposed fairy godmother. Reviewing the novel in the *New York Times*, Bill Kent picks up on its mythic themes, describing the plot as a witch hunt and noting that Howard's character is "strengthened by hard labor and an almost mystical love of the land." But Kent views Hamilton's engagement with religious ideas as ultimately a failure of oversimplification:

> Unfortunately, the narrative grows muddled when Ms. Hamilton returns to Alice to describe her ennobling but unconvincing jailhouse epiphany. Ms. Hamilton apparently wants us to believe that Alice's time in prison, during which she does little more than eat bad food and read great books, is a cleansing period that allows her to experience her cell mates' suffering. With an almost Buddhist quiescence, Alice comes to think that her depression is the result of her attachment to an imagined world, a world in which she tries to atone for all of life's victims.

In fact, Kent sees the novel as ultimately failing by simplifying away the complexity of character of its rural denizens:

> Ms. Hamilton . . . labors mightily to have Alice understand the citizens of Prairie Center who

have ranged themselves against her. Despite their vile behavior, she looks on them as plain people caught up in their own imaginary worlds, much as she was in hers. But . . . these other figures seem merely rapidly sketched heartland types. In fact, they come across in a way Ms. Hamilton may not have intended: as stupid, venal, cravenly cruel practitioners of small-town xenophobia.

John Skow, in the *Time* review, perceives the same lack of development in character and place as representations of Alice's disorientation amidst her calamities. Carol Anshaw, reviewing the novel in the *Women's Review of Books*, sees the main theme as Alice's surrender to fate. Despite its veering into melodrama, Anshaw thinks that the novel succeeds in evoking the universal fears of parents. Laura Shapiro, the reviewer in *Newsweek*, agrees that Hamilton's treatment of her material is a triumph over its melodramatic subject matter. Laura E. Tanner, writing in *American Literary History* in 2002, examines the disorientation the Goodwins suffer in the environment of the hospital waiting room, a common locale for modern Americans' experience of tragedy.

CRITICISM

Rita M. Brown

Brown is an English professor. In the following essay, she situates Hamilton's A Map of the World *in the American gothic tradition.*

The American gothic tradition in literature was established primarily by nineteenth-century authors; Nathaniel Hawthorne was one of the most important. Through many of his works, particular issues are brought into relief in order to examine the American experience and what it means. Some of these issues include tension between the city or town and the woods, forest, or rural country; unknown forces controlling lives and events; the experience of madness; taboo themes such as sexual impropriety; the place of the individual as opposed to the community; and the very common examination of the good and evil in human nature. These ideas have been developed by other authors in the American gothic tradition ranging from Edgar Allan Poe to Flannery O'Connor. Jane Hamilton's novel *A Map of the World* can be classed as part of the American gothic tradition because it examines many of these themes in an effort to illustrate that the simple farm life, where one makes his or her way through honest hard work, is just as subject to corruption and evil as any other way of life or kind of existence.

One of the most common themes in all of Hamilton's works is the conflict between civilization and the natural world. In *A Map of the World*, this relates especially to the setting of the novel. The rural countryside is in any case a stage of development between the forest and the city. The town of Prairie Center is a rural landscape that is in the process of becoming suburban, in flux between nature and culture. One way of looking at the city in American literature is as a place of decadence and corruption. The virtuous farm boy who goes to the city and has his character destroyed through exposure to strong drink, gambling, and loose women is a cliché. This is how the relationship between town and country is viewed by the Lutheran tradition of Hamilton's character Howard. This is why he idealizes farm life and wants to get his family away from the city. But the American gothic tradition sees things the other way around. The city is after all the home of civilization and its many virtues, while the forest is savage and

> HOWARD THINKS HE IS TAKING HIS FAMILY TO A PLACE OF SAFETY ON THE FARM, BUT REALLY HE IS BRINGING THEM TO A NEST OF VIPERS."

threatening. Originally, this perspective was often expressed as a racist slur against Native Americans as savages: the inhabitants of the forest were portrayed as brutal murderers, given to practicing black magic and pagan idolatry. In *A Map of the World*, Howard's idealized view of the country as the seat of virtue comes squarely up against the gothic view of small-town, rural-minded Americans as vicious and vile. They are the ones who bring false charges against Alice. They are the ones who ostracize and drive out an innocent family. They are the ones who attack the law and truth as elements of civilized virtue. The plot of the novel is driven by Howard's mistake. Howard thinks he is taking his family to a place of safety on the farm, but really he is bringing them to a nest of vipers. Carol Mackessy is the one who abuses and corrupts her son. When she accuses Alice of the same crimes, she is projecting her own guilt onto innocence.

Howard's view of the world comes up against the American gothic reality of the world he inhabits in many instances. He is shown to be mistaken not only in his understanding of the countryside but also in his view of order. According to his Lutheran theology, God ordained the course of his life even before the foundations of the world were laid. The only choices he has are to work to go along with God's plan or to rebel and fight against it. He has decided to follow God, so he expects God to help him along and smooth his way. This view is perhaps symbolized in the family name *Goodwin*. If one reads it as ordinary words, it means that the good win—in Lutheran terms, that the sheep are separated from the goats and are saved by God's grace. But this is not at all what happens as the novel develops. Instead, Howard and his family find themselves living though an American gothic nightmare where chaotic and destructive events occur unpredictably and for no rational reason.

WHAT DO I READ NEXT?

- Garrison Keillor has created his own fictional small town and farming community in Lake Wobegon, Minnesota. It is the setting for short stories he reads on his weekly radio show on NPR, *A Prairie Home Companion*, as well as for several novels. He has rewritten many of his short stories for publication in a series of books, of which the first was *Lake Wobegon Days* (1985). Keillor lovingly treats the American idyll of small-town life, but not through idealizing it, and not without sometimes mordant satire.

- *The Abuse of Innocence: The McMartin Preschool Trial* (1993), by Paul Eberle and Shirley Eberle, gives an account of the initial climate of fear and hysteria that led to the accusations of child abuse against the staff of the McMartin preschool and traces the eventual triumph of rationalism. The then most expensive trial in US history ended in the acquittal of the defendants of the false charges against them, but only after driving one of them to suicide.

- Pearl S. Buck's *The Good Earth* (1931), a novel today commonly assigned in high-school English classes, is set in the rural China of the 1920s, a land racked by famine and civil war. It concerns the Wu family,

onetime prosperous farmers who fall on hard times. Their crisis is so great that the mother kills one of her own daughters so that she will not use up the scarce resources the family needs to survive.

- Nathaniel Hawthorne's *The Scarlet Letter* (1850) is a classic work of the American gothic tradition. Set in Salem on the eve of the witch trials, it tells the story of a young woman who is ostracized from her community because she has an illegitimate child. The conflict between the undeveloped wild countryside and the ordered civilization of the city, as well as that between religious community and the autonomy of the individual, largely originate as themes in American literature with this novel.

- Kathe Koja's 2003 novel *Buddha Boy* is a young-adult work that deals with the social isolation of a young man who seriously practices Buddhism in a typical American high school.

- Hamilton's first novel is *The Book of Ruth* (1988). It deals with the destruction of a poor family in rural Wisconsin through the forces of mental illness, drug and alcohol abuse, and spousal and child abuse.

This is most true with respect to the death of Lizzy. Her drowning strikes the Goodwins like a thunderbolt falling unexpectedly from a blue sky. So far from divine intervention protecting them, the nature of events seems to be working against them in a random and inexplicable way. Again, Alice tries to be virtuous, and to follow the rules that have been set up for her, by moving to report Carol Mackessy for child neglect. But this too has chaotic and destructive results. The very people whose supposed goodness ought to help protect the Goodwins turn against them, as Alice's principal attacks and denounces her,

even testifying to her bad character in court, and as the people of Prairie Center, who claim to be agents of God's righteousness, shun Alice and her family, driving her out into prison and finally back to what turns out to be the safety of the city. In the American gothic reality of the novel, the countryside turns out to be evil and destructive, a place where evil events befall for no intelligible reason.

As is common in the American gothic, many of the characters in *A Map of the World* are touched to one degree or another by madness. Alice is plagued with what might be diagnosed as

Alice is arrested because of the unfair accusations made against her. (© albund / Shutterstock.com)

depression throughout much of the novel. Her reaction to Lizzy's death after the initial shock is to withdraw into herself. She feels physically ill for no somatic reason and sleeps for as much as twenty hours a day. She just wants to go on sleeping because that is the only way she can avoid thinking about what has happened. But her initial reaction is more interesting. She invests all of her psychic energy in denying that the calamity that is ongoing around her, in the form of the nearly lifeless body she drags from the lake and in the crisis in the hospital emergency room and intensive care wards, is actually happening. She tells herself that nothing bad is happening or even can happen despite all evidence to the contrary, up until the moment Lizzy is pronounced dead. Alice acts, or at least seems to think, as though constantly repeating that it is not happening will make it not happen. Whether this can be likened to prayer or even to casting a spell, this level of denial is certainly delusional. While Alice does eventually come to some kind of terms with reality, what is less obvious is that Howard is equally delusional and that he never reestablishes contact with reality. In his basic worldview, shared with the founding community of Pilgrims in New England and with deep roots in American culture, his hard work and virtue ought to be rewarded by providence. But the events of the novel amply

demonstrate that the world he lives in simply does not work that way. Yet his view remains unchanged.

Lynelle Duchamps is a typical character of the American gothic. She is obviously insane but at the same time acts as a sort of spiritual guide to Alice, making a deep impression on her and giving her advice that she finds spiritually uplifting. While the twenty-third psalm is one of the best-known religious texts in American culture, to the point of being hackneyed, it takes on a special significance for Alice because Lynelle seems so inspired. The character of Lynelle draws on a deep tradition that is nearly shamanic. She is a true channel for the divine to irrupt into the world, but taking on that role has both driven her to the margins of human culture and driven her mad.

The expression of sexuality has been taboo throughout much of American history. A great deal of American literature ignores sexuality, particularly any sexuality that exists outside a fairly narrow spectrum that is called normal, as if ignoring it could make it go away. But the American gothic concentrates on themes of forbidden sexuality like adultery or incest, recognizing that they are significant exactly because they are condemned and marginalized. The act of child abuse that Alice is accused of, which is central to *A Map of the World*, stands squarely in this tradition. The accusation exposes what Prairie Center pretends it wants to keep hidden, even as it takes a prurient interest in denouncing Alice. And the charge can only be defended against by exposing the sexual impropriety of Carol Mackessy. Interestingly also, what Howard and his Lutheran tradition views as normal sexuality, marital relations, has to give way before the irruption of the abnormal.

The American gothic offers a competing view of the ideals of progress and the self-made man. It recognizes that events proceed with no direction or guidance but are random and chaotic. Any attempt to build a life in defiance of these facts is doomed. Alice and Howard choose to raise their family on a farm in deliberate isolation from what they perceived as the corrupting influence of the city, only to find that the countryside they romanticized harbors worse evil than they had imagined.

Source: Rita M. Brown, Critical Essay on *A Map of the World*, in *Novels for Students*, Gale, Cengage Learning, 2014.

Amy Levin

In the following excerpt, Levin compares A Map of the World *to Jane Smiley's* A Thousand Acres, *showing how in both novels, the security of family is tied to the health of the farm and the community at large.*

. . . Jane Hamilton, too, focuses on issues of ideology, power, and memory in her construction of a region. Her second novel, *A Map of the World* (1994), exposes the harmful effects of governmental involvement in social and farm policy, yet it diverges from *A Thousand Acres* in several significant ways. First, *A Map of the World* is set about ten years later. Sex crimes have come into public discourse instead of remaining hidden. The community is more suburban than agrarian; one of the characters is creating a "Dairy Shrine," to "commemorate" a passing way of life (Hamilton 1994). Second, the heroine and her husband have *chosen* to farm. They resemble the Ericsons, a family whose farm fails early in Smiley's novel. Third, Alice has never acquired household management skills. It is all she can do to contain the household chaos, be patient with her daughters, and seem caring in her part-time job as a nurse.

Despite these dissimilarities, Hamilton's work resonates with many of the themes found in Smiley's fiction. Initially, the farm of Alice

> SHE WILL BE SILENCED BY THE WEIGHT OF OTHERS' VERSIONS OF EVENTS, WHICH REFLECT LARGER SOCIAL BELIEFS."

and Howard Goodwin (an ironic choice of surname), is described as "a self-made paradise," studded with a pond and an orchard. The rich, almost sensual, details build a careful picture of the locale, where Alice does her "best to be a good farm wife" (Hamilton 1994), and her husband throws himself into local history. As in *A Thousand Acres* and the works studied by Kolodny, some of the details instruct, such as when Alice notes that she "made butter in the food processor" or when Howard states, "It is a rule of nature that taking a day off on a farm sets a person back at least a week." Other details document information for historical reasons, as when Alice explains the workings of their hay baler.

These facts must be recorded because a "dream of a Midwest Arcadia is destroyed" (Kent 1994, 26) by the novel's central events. Yet, from the beginning, the "dream" is as deceptive as the Cook family enterprise in *A Thousand Acres*. The presence of an old orchard suggests that this Eden contains evil as well as good, that it exists after the creation of labor: "the tedium of work and love—all of it was my savior," says Alice (Hamilton 1994). Even as they face the "usual problems that came with farming in what was becoming suburbia," Alice notes that the Goodwins are "labeled from the first as that hippie couple," existing "[o]utside the bounds of the collective imagination."

The Goodwins' neighbors, "very few [of whom] seemed to make the connection between the sustaining white liquid they poured on their breakfast cereal and Howard's clattering, stinking enterprise across the way," cannot face what they have left. They are so distant from nature that their streets bear the names of other states and connect through fake covered bridges. Instead of owning livestock, they possess refrigerators "with juice spigots hanging down like goat tits." Given the way the townspeople have abandoned farming, they offer a vision of what might have occurred to the inhabitants of Zebulon County in Smiley's novel within ten years of the book's events.

Political and economic policy are visible in the townsfolk's decision to leave farming, as well as in the transformation of the landscape into neatly separated subdivisions. Moreover, the Goodwins are heavily in debt, and the young couple must constantly borrow from Howard's mother. Families have been disrupted as well. Alice lost her mother while she was young, as did Ginny in *A Thousand Acres*, and the absence of mothers seems correlated to a growing alienation from "Mother Nature." Significantly, Alice's friend Teresa, who is in many ways the moral center of the novel, works as a therapist, helping to keep or bring other families together.

The Goodwins' fall is precipitated by two crises: first, one of Teresa's daughters drowns while Alice is supposed to be watching her, and second, Alice is accused of molesting boys at the elementary school where she works as a nurse. Alice's guilt over the drowning incapacitates her. While public opinion supported Larry Cook against allegations that he committed sexual abuse, it is not so kind to Alice Goodwin. Indeed, the accusations confirm her scapegoating and throw the family into emotional and financial crisis. As in the household in *A Thousand Acres*, family roles have been rigidly distinguished. Howard does not know how to manage the farm while tending the children. Further economic hardship is created by Alice's legal expenses. As in *A Thousand Acres*, the heroine's family finds itself feverishly trying to create an impression of "normalcy" for a community that is reinforced by predatory governmental agencies: "If we let ourselves fall apart, the neighbors, or the police, might descend upon us and pick our bones clean."

If the Cook farm floats on pesticide-laced water as well as on its hidden past, Prairie Center in *A Map of the World* is contaminated solely by spiritual pollutants. While Smiley seems to cast blame primarily on the men in the community, Hamilton distributes blame equally, noting the importance of another mother in accusing Alice. At the elementary school, values are so skewed that instead of being seen as a healer, the nurse is perceived as a criminal who gives children shots and molests them. A single mother whose sexual acts are witnessed by her son paints herself as a

martyr to virtue. Instead of being innocents, boys spread vile rumors of a sexual nature.

In contrast to Smiley's novel, where the family colludes to keep secrets from the community (and the community chooses not to see these secrets), the town in *Map of the World* is the source of malicious gossip. Innuendo becomes a means of asserting power, ideology a crushing machine. Howard argues, "Lawyers, people in the system, politicians, were so crippled by bureaucracy and jargon they no longer had common sense." A domestic policy that finally begins to attend to sex crimes becomes an agency of power against the very people it was designed to help when social service employees attempt to deprive Howard and Alice of their children.

Ironically, Alice finds a kind of peace and redemption in prison, a community of women created and regulated by the state, so marginalized that it bears no regional markers. Bill Kent is critical of Alice's "ennobling but unconvincing jailhouse epiphany" (1994, 26), yet it seems necessary because Alice believes her incarceration compensates for the girl's drowning. When she is attacked by another inmate, Alice "took it, like a sponge" (Hamilton 1994).

More importantly, Alice finds herself in a community that is not built on illusions of righteousness or truth. Even though prison life is highly regimented, the prisoners find ways to subvert the system. Cruelty and violence are out in the open, and the inmates acknowledge that truths may be varied, multiple, and anarchic:

> Jail is one of the last holdouts on earth, a place where there is still an oral tradition. Sometimes I think the inmates made trouble not only so there'd be a story to tell, but so there'd be five stories to tell, each rendition becoming funnier or more grotesque or outlandish. There were stories to tell certainly, but there were also stories to tell about the telling of the stories. Although I long ago lost faith in the idea of Truth, I knew that once I spoke, the stories would take on their own shape, their own truth.

Alice's neighbors gain tremendous satisfaction in telling stories, too. The difference is that the women in jail do not—and cannot—exert power over others by insisting their accounts are the "legal" versions. Their marginality resembles the isolation of Ginny and Rose's daughters at the end of *A Thousand Acres*.

The scars left by the community's stories are indelible. The accusations that cause Alice's incarceration are designed to protect the children of the community, but disrupt her family irremediably. Howard and Teresa seek solace together temporarily, creating guilt and discomfort. Later, Howard must sell the farm in exchange for a sterile, minuscule townhouse: "The whole place was deceptive. Here, it seemed to squeak and stink, is the American dream. Except that everything we were supposed to want, everything that looked so good, was too small or too flimsy for use." When Alice is freed, the family is reunited, but, as in *A Thousand Acres*, the victory, if one could call it that, is small. The farm is lost and becomes a retreat for urban Boy Scouts. The Goodwins have become separated from the land, from the myth of regionalism that sustained them.

The tone of the ending is muted. If Smiley's novel is a manual on family relations, Hamilton's book tells us that even Arcadia contains ponds that may be dangerous. Alice observes: "the terrible thing is that there is so much good, and gradually it slips away from you. I had not believed until last summer that loss is determined, charted." The map Alice made as a child was of a dream world, where she sat, "imagining myself in an ideal country, alone and at peace." Now her family remains alone, even though they are "outcasts making a perfect circle" of forgiveness.

Like Smiley's heroine, Alice must carry the scars of the past in her mind and on her body. The conclusion of this novel provides more resolution, though it, too, connects the downfall of the family farm with corruption in the country's moral fiber. In locating the corruption primarily outside the family, Hamilton does not ultimately condemn farmers or families themselves. Perhaps this is because she depicts a universe after the farm crisis of 1985. The Goodwins, who were not born farmers, have tried to insert themselves in a story about the Midwest that is already over. Their farm has always been a zoo (literally and figuratively), so it is appropriate that Howard ends up working in one.

Moreover, like Ginny, Alice invokes the various and deceptive faces "truth" can wear. While Ginny challenges public perceptions of *wife* and *daughter*, Alice throws into question the ideological agendas implicit in definitions of such terms as *mother* and *nurse*. Alice is perceived as a failure in the community, even as a force of evil, because she embodies alternate visions of these common occupations. Even

though her idealized existence is shattered by her experiences, her story exists, a small nub embedded in the fabric of society. Howard is pessimistic, however, about its permanence: "She would be the great-great-grandmother who spent several months in jail. The ancestor who abused the boy.... It seemed cruel that her afterlife was already determined." She will be silenced by the weight of others' versions of events, which reflect larger social beliefs.

... Ultimately, the ambiguous endings of all three novels, including the heroines' mixed success at finding a more liberated existence, have significant implications for our readings of contemporary women's regionalist fiction. While this fiction succeeds in giving voice to the unheard and offering a critique of agrarian idealism, the authors are unable to conceive of a world where women can extricate themselves from powerful discourses pertaining to gender, social policy, and politics. The protagonists offer readers advice, but the advice is not what it seems, outdated, or useless. The strength of regionalist fiction—that it comments from inside the region rather than from outside—is also its weakness, for it cannot rise above community structures and social ideology. For women heroines, this means that their narratives must express nostalgia for a past that never was and dream of future unity that may never be.

Source: Amy Levin, "Familiar Terrain: Domestic Ideology and Farm Policy in Three Women's Novels about the 1980s," in *NWSA Journal*, Vol. 11, No. 1, Spring 1999, pp. 30–34, 40.

Moureen Coulter

In the following review, Coulter praises Hamilton's portrayal of Alice's emotional turmoil in A Map of the World.

What does it mean to fall from grace, and where do the fallen go? Are they forever banished from their former blessedness, or can they hope to regain its heights? These theological questions have structured many a catechism over the years, but even children who learn the answers "by heart" can later have trouble applying them to the unforeseen messiness of their adult lives. Alice Goodwin, the protagonist of Jane Hamilton's remarkable new novel, *A Map of the World*, confesses to just such bewilderment at the beginning of her narrative:

I used to think if you fell from grace it was more likely than not the result of one stupendous error, or else an unfortunate accident. I hadn't learned that it can happen so gradually you don't lose your stomach or hurt yourself in the landing. You don't necessarily sense the motion. I've found it takes at least two and generally three things to alter the course of a life: You slip around the truth once, and then again, and one more time, and there you are, feeling, for a moment, that it was sudden, your arrival at the bottom of the heap.

Alice's fall does seem to be literally the result of "an unfortunate accident": the death of her neighbor and best friend's two-year-old daughter Lizzy one summer morning when the child and her older sister have been left in Alice's charge. Her "stupendous error" is allowing herself to be distracted, while changing for a swim, by the rediscovery in a dresser drawer of the maps of a fictional world she had invented during her childhood. "My maps had taken over my life for months at a time," Alice recalls wonderingly. But by the time she finishes dressing, Lizzy has left the house and made her way unaccompanied to a nearby pond, where she drowns.

"When I am forced to see those ten minutes as they actually were, when I look clearly, without the scrim of half-uttered prayers and fanciful endings, I am there, tall and gangly and clumsy and slow, crying out unintelligibly, splashing through the water to Lizzy," Alice reports, but no amount of retrospection, however clear-sighted, can alter the outcome. The lives of Alice and her husband, Howard; of Lizzy's parents, Theresa and Dan; of both couples' other children and relatives are irrevocably and decisively altered by both the fact and the circumstances of the child's death. No one, least of all Alice, can escape the conclusion that she is to blame.

If there can be any greater torment for a woman than the loss of her own child, it may be the knowledge that she is responsible for, or at least implicated in, the loss of another. It is to Hamilton's credit that she is able to convey the paralyzing confusion of Alice's thoughts and feelings in the months that follow Lizzy's death in language that is so clear and credible. Alice's guilt isolates her by erasing the familiar patterns of communication with Howard and Theresa that had helped to demarcate her adult "map of the world." It also renders her vulnerable to attack by people outside the boundaries drawn by marriage and close friendship, so that

before the fateful summer is over Alice finds herself jailed on unrelated charges of child abuse and threatened with the loss of her own daughters. Falling from grace does indeed turn out to be a more protracted experience than she had imagined, with more hands ready to push her off of the precipice than to pull her back.

The novel ends with Alice's legal exoneration and her reconstituted family's move to a new house in a new city. The grace that she seems to have regained might best be described as a restored sense of herself and of her place in the world, her bearings according to the compass of the heart. Its source is not judgment but forgiveness: Alice's forgiveness of others, especially Howard, as much as theirs of her. This, too, is a theological truth, but one usually taught by parable rather than catechism, and that is how Alice and Howard learn it and how they teach it to us. "I had that marvelous clarity for an instant," says Alice, "and so I understood that the forgiveness itself was strong, durable, like strands of a web, weaving around us, holding us." Thus are the fallen raised.

Source: Moureen Coulter, Review of *A Map of the World*, in *Belles Lettres: A Review of Books by Women*, Vol. 10, No. 1, Fall 1994, p. 25.

SOURCES

Anshaw, Carol, "Culture Clash," in *Women's Review of Books*, Vol. 12, No. 1, October 1994, pp. 7–8.

Ceci, Stephen J., and Maggie Bruck, *Jeopardy in the Courtroom: A Scientific Analysis of Children's Testimony*, American Psychological Association, 1999, pp. 7–46, 87–126.

Hamilton, Jane, *A Map of the World*, Doubleday, 1994.

Hertzberg, Mark, "First, She Threw One Away—Jame Hamilton Discarded a Book before Completing her Latest Novel," in *Journal Times*, November 4, 2006, http://journaltimes.com/news/local/first-she-threw-one-away-jane-hamilton-discarded-a-book/article_5d0b217a-b557-52bd-80db-8921c96ca3f5.html (accessed May 10, 2013).

Jones, Maggie, "Who Was Abused?," in *New York Times*, September 19, 2004, http://www.nytimes.com/2004/09/19/magazine/19KIDSL.html?pagewanted = print&position = &_r = 0 (accessed May 10, 2013).

Kent, Bill, "Witch Hunt in Prairie Center," in *New York Times*, July 17, 1994, http://www.nytimes.com/1994/07/17/books/witch-hunt-in-prairie-center.html (accessed May 10, 2013).

Shapiro, Laura, "Lost World," in *Newsweek*, Vol. 123, No. 34, June 13, 1994, p. 55.

Skow, John, "Mom's Horror," in *Time*, Vol. 143, No. 26, June 27, 1994, p. 75.

Talbot, Margaret, "The Devil in the Nursery," in *New York Times*, January 7, 2001, http://newamerica.net/node/6298 (accessed May 10, 2013).

Tanner, Laura E., "Bodies in Waiting: Representations of Medical Waiting Rooms in Contemporary American Fiction," in *American Literary History*, Vol. 14, No. 1, 2002, pp. 115–30.

FURTHER READING

Hamilton, Jane, *Disobedience*, Doubleday, 2000.
> In this novel, Hamilton explores the difficulties faced by a high-school senior who accesses his mother's e-mail account only to discover that she is carrying on an adulterous affair.

Hill, Sally, and Jean Goodwin, "Satanism: Similarities between Patient Accounts and Pre-Inquisition Historical Accounts," in *Dissociation*, Vol. 2, No. 1, March 1989, pp. 39–44.
> This article attempts to link the reports of recovered memories of modern psychiatric patients to medieval accounts of devil worship, in an attempt to give credence to the myth that Western civilization has housed a shadow religion in which torture and sacrifice of children to Satan were treated as a sacrament. This ridiculous thesis represents the nadir of the so-called satanic panic of the 1980s which inspired Hamilton's *A Map of the World*. *Dissociation* was the house organ of the International Society for the Study of Multiple Personality and Dissociation (which still exists under the name International Society for the Study of Trauma and Dissociation), published between 1988 and 1997. It was the professional home of mental-health workers who wished to believe such outlandish fantasies, such as Myra Flint in the novel.

Mackay, Charles, *Memoirs of Extraordinary Popular Delusions and the Madness of Crowds*, 2 vols., Office of the National Illustrated Library, 1852.
> Kept continuously in print since its publication, Mackay's book is an early and classic study of the power of irrational ideas to become crazes of mass hysteria.

Victor, Jeffrey S., *Satanic Panic: The Creation of a Contemporary Legend*, Open Court, 1993.
> This is one of the most outstanding books of several written in the early 1990s to debunk the outlandish idea that the United States was host to a secret organization of child-murdering satanists.

SUGGESTED SEARCH TERMS

Jane Hamilton

A Map of the World AND Hamilton

American gothic

satanic child abuse hysteria

Oprah Winfrey

American Lutheranism

Buddhism

small town America

Never Let Me Go

Director Mark Romanek's 2010 film *Never Let Me Go* tells the unsettling story of a world that is very much like the present day, except that, as explained when the story starts, the average human can live over a hundred years. The film quickly explains that this is possible through organ transplants. The characters whom viewers get to know as children—Kathy (played as a young adult by Carey Mulligan), Tommy (Andrew Garfield), and Ruth (Keira Knightley)—form friendships, then love relationships, before viewers find out why they and others at their exclusive boarding school are considered special: they are clones, raised from infancy to have their organs harvested until they die young. When they hear a rumor that couples in love can stall off their deaths for a few years, the pressure is on to find a way to make their love "verifiable." Though it deals with issues of relative quality of life, the rights of society versus the rights of individuals, and what it means to be human, most viewers will agree that the film centers around the question of love.

The film's quiet tone and universally acclaimed acting earned it multiple award nominations when it was released, scoring a Best Actress award at the British Independent Film Awards for Mulligan. The same body nominated it for Best Film, Best Director, Best Screenplay (by Alex Garland), and Best Supporting Actor and Actress for the other two leads.

Never Let Me Go is based on a 2005 novel of the same name by Kazuo Ishiguro, best known as the author of *The Remains of the Day*. Viewers should be advised that the film, rated R, includes scenes of a sexual nature. The film was first released in England in 2010 and was released on DVD by DNA Films and Fox Searchlight.

PLOT SUMMARY

The title of *Never Let Me Go* is followed by none of the usual information about actors, writers, producers or directors. Instead, the film starts with text explaining how the world presented here is different from the common world. It says that there was a breakthrough in medical science in 1952, leading to an average life expectancy of over one hundred years by 1967. These facts, and what they have to do with the lives of the characters in the story, are never stated directly in the book.

The story begins with voice-over by Kathy H., the novel's narrator. She says that she is twenty-eight years old and has been a "carer" for nine years. She is watching through a pane of glass as doctors prepare an operation on a man named Tommy, one of the story's other main characters. He has a long scar down his side from previous operations. This is a scene that will be repeated later in the film.

The end of Kathy's narration mentions "the Cottages" and "Hailsham." As she mentions herself, Tommy, and Ruth, the camera shows each of them as children in a group setting at school. A title establishes the next setting as Hailsham in 1978, showing a huge mansion with nothing but trees nearby. On a raised dais, Miss Emily and the other instructors talk to the assembled children, warning them that smoking cigarettes is especially dangerous for Hailsham students because they are special and maintaining good health is imperative.

Watching the boys play, Kathy and Ruth talk. Ruth fantasizes about the horses she imagines having as she holds a little toy horse. She admires a string of flowers Kathy has woven, and Kathy gives it to her. They notice Miss Lucy, the new guardian. Later, when the children play cricket, the ball goes over the fence. Miss Lucy wonders why Tommy will not go to get it, and they tell about the horrible things that have happened to children who have gone outside of the fence, showing how fear and superstition keep children in line at Hailsham.

In art class, all of the children join Ruth in mocking Tommy's painting. He has to explain that it depicts an elephant. Kathy looks on uncomfortably.

As the children run outside, they each scan a bracelet on a sensor by the door (a device not mentioned in the novel). The boys are chosen for teams: when Tommy is left unchosen, he flails his arms and screams. Across the field, Ruth and the other girls laugh, but Kathy goes to comfort him. When she touches his shoulder, though, he spins quickly, hitting her in the face. Miss Lucy walks Tommy away to comfort him. Later, Tommy sits alone and ostracized at lunch, and Kathy joins him. He apologizes for hitting her. Miss Lucy sees them sitting together and smiles.

When the children are all gathered together enjoying an old film, George Formby's 1940 musical *Let George Do It*, Kathy looks back at Tommy and is pleased to see him having fun. Later, the class does a role-playing exercise about how to behave in a tea shop, but Tommy is unable to imagine what his character would order. The other children laugh at him.

Madame Marie-Claude arrives at the school to select the best art and poetry for inclusion in her gallery. There is also going to be a sale, at which students who have earned tokens at the school can buy items. The items left out for them to pick from are old, used, and sometimes broken. At the sale, Miss Lucy picks up an old baby doll and looks sadly at Kathy. Tommy buys Kathy a cassette tape of Judy Bridgewater, a singer from the 1950s. This is a combination of scenes from the novel. In the novel, Kathy buys Judy Bridgewater's tape *Songs after Dark* for herself but eventually loses it, and Tommy, years later, insists that they look for it at resale shops while they are in the town of Norfolk, eventually finding a tape that is probably different, though Tommy believes it might be the one Kathy once owned. When Tommy gives her the tape in the movie, Kathy kisses his cheek.

Alone in her room, Kathy dances to the slow, dreamy song "Never Let Me Go" on the tape, clutching a pillow to her chest. She turns to see Ruth watching her from the open doorway. (In the novel, it is Miss Emily who watches Kathy dance.)

FILM TECHNIQUE

- In discussing film technique, critics often refer to the film's *mise-en-scène*, a catchall phrase to describe a film's one unified mood. The early scenes at Hailsham have a mood of docile complacency, which is conveyed by the way the children are often filmed in groups, either outside or in wide-open interiors. As their situation becomes more hopeless, they are viewed in darker, limited spaces: the scene of Ruth watching from a window as Tommy and Kathy walk off into the meadow captures the juncture of these moods. Hope for a deferral coincides with wide-open vistas of the ocean: first at the seaside town where Ruth's "possible" works, then at the site of the beached ship (moved for the film from the novel's swampy inlet), then along the sea walk across from Madame's house. These settings, along with the film's visual design focusing on muted earth tones (browns and greens), its mournful soundtrack music, and the quiet, reserved acting, create its unique tone, its mise-en-scène.

- Kathy H. narrates this film, usually between scenes. A narrator is necessary because the film is not able to present as many details of the story as the novel can. It is also desirable because Ishiguro gives Kathy such a unique voice in the novel that hearing her words, and the way she looks at the world, helps viewers understand the clones' passivity about their fate and their confusion in separating what is real from what is just rumor.

- *Title cards* are written pieces of information that are interwoven with the visual story. The term was first used in silent movies, when they were necessary for clarifying plot and conveying dialogue. Director Mark Romanek establishes key facts about the world the story takes place in early in the film with title cards that tell viewers about a medical breakthrough that allowed people to live much longer than they really do. Doing this reveals more about the fictional setting before the story begins than Ishiguro's entire novel ever reveals. After the beginning of the film, title cards are also used to announce the three basic sections of the story: "Hailsham, 1978"; "the Cottages, 1985"; and "Completion, 1994." Title cards are also referred to as *intertitles*.

- An *establishing* shot prepares viewers for the scene to come. Usually, its function is to establish the location of the scene, but it can also be integral for setting the mood. An example of this is the scene in which Miss Lucy tells the children the dismal truth about their existence, that they are being raised to donate their vital organs and die young: the scene opens with a shot of a dead flower on an open windowsill in the rain, followed by a map being blown by the wind, before any characters appear. Another use of establishing shots occurs when Kathy and Tommy enter Madame's house. With quick shots of a travel alarm clock, medicine bottles, a magnifying glass, and mahjong tiles, the film immediately tells what kind of life Madame and Miss Emily have been leading in retirement.

- A *composite* shot mixes multiple images on-screen. Modern technology gives films the ability to seamlessly merge shots filmed at different times at different places, but this film uses a realistic style, filming through reflective glass. The first shot of Kathy watching Tommy being prepared for surgery introduces this technique, and it returns at the end, when the story comes back to this scene. Using a composite shot, the film can simultaneously show the action and a character's reaction to that action.

Miss Lucy interrupts a lesson to tell the students the truth about what their futures will hold: as donors, they will not grow up to be actors or teachers, nor will they marry. Their futures are settled. Before they can reach middle age, they will donate their vital organs, and by their third or fourth donation they will die.

A shot shows the cricket ball that went outside of the fence lying in the rain, a symbol of the confined, shielded lives the Hailsham students lead.

Miss Emily explains to the assembled children that Miss Lucy has been removed from her job. When she talks about the problem of fighting deliberate subversion, the children applaud. Kathy watches Tommy and Ruth locking hands together. Later, she walks down a garden path herself and sees Tommy and Ruth kissing in the garden. Packing her belongings to leave Hailsham, Kathy muses, in voice-over, about why Tommy would choose Ruth. She thinks that maybe she should have teased him, as Ruth did.

A title card announces that the scene is "The Cottages, 1985." Kathy's voice-over explains that she and Tommy and Ruth were moved there from Hailsham at age eighteen. She introduces readers to Rodney and Chrissie, who have been at the Cottages for a year. As the assembled students watch a comedy on TV, Kathy observes how Rodney and Chrissie pick up mannerisms from the television, and then she looks at how Ruth and Tommy mimic them.

Kathy and Tommy take a walk, and Ruth spies on them through a curtained window. Later, at breakfast, Kathy watches Ruth and Chrissie joke together, and she sees Ruth squeeze Tommy's shoulders in the same way Chrissie squeezed Rodney's. She asks later why Ruth has picked up Chrissie's behavior, and Ruth concludes that Kathy is just jealous.

Kathy finds a stack of pornographic magazines in the garbage. She takes them to the barn to study them, sitting at a desk, thumbing through quickly. Tommy comes in and she denies that she is looking for anything specific in them. She tells him she is just viewing them for fun, but he explains that if she wants to look at them for fun, she would have to look at each picture more slowly.

Ruth comes to Kathy. Last weekend, she explains, Rodney and Chrissie were in "a town up the coast" (identified as Norfolk in the novel) where they saw, working in an office, a "possible" of Ruth's, an adult who could be the person she was cloned from. The novel explains that Ruth had previously dreamed of growing up to work in just this sort of office.

Driving up to the coast, Rodney and Chrissie find out that the Hailsham students have very little experience with the outside world. They eat at a diner, and the three of them sit stiff and awkward, intimidated by the waitress, and then, mumbling, they order exactly what Rodney just ordered. They eventually loosen up. Chrissie says that she and Rodney have heard a rumor: donors could delay their first donations for a few years if they could prove that they were truly in love with each other, to give them some time together. Kathy and Ruth tactfully look confused, but Tommy states outright that he does not know what they are talking about. Rodney accuses them of being secretive. Kathy says that she has heard this among many other false rumors. Rodney and Chrissy are crestfallen.

They go to the office, a travel agency, to see Ruth's possible. All five press against the window, admiring how happy people are with ordinary jobs. The woman Rodney identified looks up and locks eyes with Ruth, who walks away angry. Her friends try to console her, but Ruth shouts that they all know that if they were modeled on anyone, it would not be middle-class office workers, but prostitutes and drug addicts. "Look in the gutter," she exclaims; "that's where we came from."

Days later, Tommy and Kathy take a walk, and he explains his theory about the deferment. If it were true, he says, it would explain why Madame collected the students' pictures, poetry, and sculptures at Hailsham: when students came and claimed they had true love, looking at their artworks would help verify it by revealing what they really feel in their souls. The gallery would tell them the truth. Kathy asks if Tommy and Ruth are thinking of applying for a deferment, but he says that it would not work. For a moment it seems an admission that he does not love Ruth, but he explains the problem: none of his childhood works were collected for the gallery.

One night, to block out the sound of Ruth and Tommy having sex, Kathy puts on her earphones and listens to "Never Let Me Go." Ruth comes in and climbs on top of her in bed. Kathy is wrong to believe herself to be a more natural couple with Tommy, Ruth tells her. She kisses Kathy's tear-stained face before leaving.

The next day, Kathy finds the old porter of the Cottages, Keffers, and asks for an application to leave and become a carer. In a voice-over, she explains that by the time she left the Cottages, Ruth and Tommy had separated.

A title card announces "Completion, 1994." "Completion" is the euphemism used in Ishiguro's novel to describe the death of a donor after they have given their organs.

Kathy, an adult, goes about her lonely business as a carer: waking in a cramped apartment, driving long distances to sit by the bedside of a woman who is preparing for surgery. When the woman she is caring for dies, Kathy goes to the nurse's desk to fill out forms. On the computer screen, she sees Ruth's picture. The nurse explains that Ruth has done two donations and might not survive the third. In the nurse's opinion, Ruth wants to "complete."

Kathy goes to Ruth's room. They walk together down a dark, empty hospital corridor. Ruth is bitter, but she also states that she knew she would see Kathy one last time before she completes.

Later, Kathy is Ruth's carer. Ruth expresses interest in taking a trip, and their discussion leads to a boat left on a beach that people have been talking about. It is near Tommy's recovery center. At Kingsfield Recovery Center, Tommy meets their car. Kathy hugs him, and he awkwardly kisses Ruth's cheek.

When they reach the beach, there is a gate. Ruth begins to panic, but Tommy unlocks it and lets them through. This reflects the novel's explanation that Ruth is too weak to climb through a barbed-wire fence. The movie shows her frailty by having Tommy and Kathy hold her up from both sides as they walk. At the beach, they see an abandoned boat not far from the water's edge. Tommy runs to the boat and explores it, though the exertion leaves him short of breath, for he has already donated two organs.

On the beach, Ruth asks them to forgive her for having kept them apart: she acknowledges that Kathy and Tommy are the ones who should have been a couple. To make amends, she will help them get a deferral: over the course of years,

she has worked to obtain the home address of Madame, who they assume must be the person who gives out the deferrals. Ruth gives them the address on a slip of paper.

Tommy and Kathy's relationship grows. He shows her the hundreds of complex, intricate drawings he has done over the years, feeling that he would have to show them to someone to apply for a deferral.

Kathy sees that the address Ruth gave her is indeed Madame's house. She goes and tells Ruth that she and Tommy do intend to apply for a deferral, and soon after, during a donation, Ruth dies on an operating table.

Kathy and Tommy find Madame in her front yard, gardening, and explain who they are. Inside, they tell her that they are in true, "verifiable" love, which she will understand if she looks at Tommy's pictures, to make up for the art that he did not do when in school. They are joined by Miss Emily, the former director of Hailsham, now confined to a wheelchair. She remembers them both. Miss Emily explains to them that Hailsham was an experiment in showing respect to the clones raised to be donors. The point of the gallery, she says, was not to look into the souls of the students, as Tommy thinks, but simply to prove that the students there, clones, actually had souls. In the end, however, society did not want to be confronted with the idea that the people who had been created and raised for organ donations were actually human. Miss Emily says she used to get two or three couples a year asking for this deferral because they were in love. However, there was never any deferral program for lovers.

On the drive back to Kingsfield in the dark, Tommy asks Kathy to stop the car on an abandoned road. He walks forward into the headlights a few feet and then falls into the kind of shouting, flailing fit that he had regularly in childhood. Kathy comes to him and hugs him.

The film returns to its first scene: Kathy is watching through glass as Tommy is brought into surgery. He smiles at her before the anesthetic knocks him out, and he dies before her eyes.

Later Kathy goes to a fenced field in an unnamed place. In the novel, Ishiguro explains that this fence was in Norfolk, rumored among the students of Hailsham to be the place where lost things end up: it is the town where Kathy found a copy of her Judy Bridgewater tape years after she lost the first copy. In the novel she imagines scraps of paper caught in the fence to be things that she has lost over the course of her life. In the film's voice-over, she explains that she will begin donating in a month. She looks at scraps of cloth that have been caught on the barbed wire fence and thinks about Tommy, wondering whether anyone, donors or the people who benefit from those donations, has a full enough life before they complete.

CHARACTERS

Chrissie

Chrissie is an older girl who is already living at the Cottages when Kathy, Tommy, and Ruth arrive there. She is in love with Rodney, another student, and together they hope to get a deferral so that they can explore their love for a few extra years before starting the painful and ultimately lethal process of organ donations.

When the Hailsham students arrive at the Cottages, Ruth looks up to Chrissie as a role model. She models her relationship with Tommy on the relationship between Chrissie and Rodney, adopting particular mannerisms and behaviors from Chrissie.

Miss Emily

Miss Emily is the headmistress at Hailsham. She is played by veteran film actress Charlotte Rampling and is an intimidating figure, the one who lectures the whole school when they are assembled. Because of her power over them, and her bearing, the children are frightened of her. The film even indicates some degree of evil in Miss Emily when she explains to the assembled students why Miss Lucy, a kind, sympathetic teacher, had to be dismissed, referring to Miss Lucy as a "radical." As the main characters are growing up, Miss Emily seems to be the authoritarian figure working hardest to keep control of their lives.

When Kathy and Tommy meet her at Madame's home much later, however, the story shows her sympathetic side. She is old and feeble and defeated by society, She explains that her experiment at Hailsham was a social failure. It turns out that she was actually the students' greatest advocate in the world outside. The entire premise of Hailsham was to fight society's prejudices against cloned children and give them

some degree of dignity. Her reason for objecting to Miss Lucy's openness about their situation was based on her humanitarian theory that the children would be better off if their fate were not made clear to them. Miss Emily presents a cold attitude, but she is actually sympathetic toward the children raised at Hailsham.

Hannah

Hannah is the woman Kathy is shown caring for when she first becomes a carer. Hannah has a patch over one eye socket, indicating that she has already donated one of her eyes for a transplant. She is only in the film briefly, soon dying during surgery.

Kathy

Kathy H., played by Carey Mulligan, is the narrator of Ishiguro's novel and of the film. In the novel, her narrative voice has a calming effect, assuring readers that the way the children are raised at Hailsham is, at least from her perspective, normal. In the film, though, Kathy seems more disturbed by the events that unravel.

In both the film and the book, Kathy is introduced as a detached professional, a "carer" who is able to empathize with those who are dying without becoming too crushingly close to their plight. The novel explains that she has been doing it for longer than most carers are allowed to, twelve years, because she is so good at it. The film shows her loneliness as she wakes in a small, featureless apartment in an anonymous high-rise and drives by herself from town to town.

The film makes a point of showing Kathy's affection for Tommy from the earliest scenes. They exchange glances in public places, and she is shown looking at him from afar with sadness. She is the only one who will approach him when he has a fit, and when he accidentally hits her as she is trying to calm him, she quickly forgives him. The novel leaves the question of love open until later in the story, but Alex Garland's screenplay is quite clear about their love for each other, which drives Kathy to scenes that show her loneliness in the middle of the film, when Tommy is dating Ruth. Ruth accuses Kathy of resenting her relationship with Tommy out of jealousy because Kathy has no one to connect with: though she denies it, the film implies that Kathy is in fact jealous.

In the end, Ruth is the one to tell Kathy that her love for Tommy is obvious to everyone. This gesture makes Kathy and Ruth close friends, as they were when they were young, and throws Kathy and Tommy together as a couple. Kathy watches both of the people closest to her die doing their duty as donors, and she does her duty as a carer, remaining relatively emotionless.

Keffers

Keffers is the old man who takes care of the Cottages. In Ishiguro's novel, more is explained about his aloofness: he is the students' one connection to the outside world, but he is gruff and unsocial toward them. His few spoken lines in the film come when Kathy tells him that she does not want to stay at the Cottages anymore and would like to begin her practice as a carer: Keffers tells her that he will bring the paperwork for her to fill out.

Miss Lucy

Miss Lucy is a new young teacher at Hailsham. She is idealistic and honest, but she is quickly dismayed by the life led by the students there. When Tommy refuses to go beyond the fence to get a cricket ball hit beyond the yard, she asks the students why he would hesitate, and the answers they give her, involving legends that are obviously false, make her uncomfortable. She still keeps her thoughts to herself. After Tommy has a fit and inadvertently hits Kathy, Miss Lucy takes him aside and talks to him, assuring him that it is not important that he excel at art or sports.

Eventually, Miss Lucy talks to her fourth-year students about the truth of their situations. They are not going to grow up to be athletes or artists, or parents, she tells them, because they were bred to have their vital organs taken from them, a process that will kill each of them early. Soon after this frank talk, Miss Lucy disappears from Hailsham, and the headmistress, Miss Emily, explains her dismissal to the children as necessary because Miss Lucy was a radical element. The children, though most of them liked Miss Lucy, cheer her firing.

Madame Marie-Claude

The woman known to the children of Hailsham as Madame is referred to in one scene late in the book as Marie-Claude, and in the film she is introduced in her first scene as "Madame Marie-Claude." In both the novel and the film, the children view Madame as a shadowy, controlling presence. She comes to Hailsham intermittently to pick through their artworks and take the best ones away with her to put in her mysterious "collection." When they grow up and pin their hopes upon the rumors of a possible deferral from donating their organs, the former Hailsham students naturally assume that Madame would be the one to see, the one who has power over the system.

The woman that Kathy and Tommy meet when they go to her house later in life is quite different. She is gardening and taking care of a wheelchair-bound Miss Emily and is not the imposing, powerful figure she once was. In Ishiguro's novel, Miss Emily calls her "darling" several times, suggesting a romantic relationship between them.

One reason the children assume that she is the one in control of the entire situation is her coldness, which they read as power but which is actually fear of the unnatural clones. In an earlier scene, she looks at them warily as she goes from her car into Hailsham. When they come to her house, she is quick to get away from them, leaving Miss Emily to talk to them. In the novel, her fear of them is an early indicator of a central point of the story, that many people, even those who want to help them, feel uncomfortable around the clones.

Rodney

Rodney is a student who has been at the Cottages for about a year when the Hailsham students arrive there. He is romantically involved with Chrissie, another student.

Rodney is the person who says that he thinks he has seen a "possible" of Ruth's, an older person she may have been cloned from. It is not clear if he really believed the woman he saw was related to Ruth, however, because he has an ulterior motive for driving Ruth, Kathy, and Tommy to the town of the sighting. He and Chrissie want to ask about a rumor they have heard about possible deferrals, assuming that the privileged Hailsham students would know the truth. When they know nothing about it, Rodney and Chrissie are crestfallen, having hoped that their love for each other could gain them a few more years of life.

Ruth

Keira Knightley and Ella Purnell play Ruth, as an adult and as a child, respectively, as someone who is scheming and manipulative. Director

Mark Romanek often goes to reaction shots of Ruth frowning at things that she witnesses. For example, she belittles Tommy and calls him stupid when they are children. Later, when they are a couple, she is superficial, copying the actions of the older student, Carrie, who is in turn basing her actions on characters on television.

The most obvious example of Ruth's pettiness is her jealousy. It is immediately after she sees Kathy and Tommy walking together that Ruth takes Tommy's hand during a class assembly. The implication is not that Ruth is reacting out of sympathy with Tommy's sorrow at the dismissal of Miss Lucy, but out of jealousy at Kathy's relationship with him.

Near the end of the film, at the beach, Ruth admits to jealousy, telling Tommy and Kathy that her long relationship with Tommy was her way of keeping them apart, knowing that they had real love and that she did not. She redeems herself with the confession during the beach scene and the gift she gives them of Madame's home address, leaving audiences with a sense that Ruth was, in the end, a good person after all.

In Ishiguro's novel, Ruth does the same petty things, but Kathy as narrator makes a point of showing the true friendship at the core of their relationship. For example, the novel elicits both sympathy for and suspicion about Ruth when she first befriends Kathy and invites her to play with her imaginary horses: young Kathy enjoys the make-believe game, but Ruth is careful to control the limits of their play. The novel also has a thread that the film leaves out about Ruth being at the center of a group of girls who imagine themselves to be "guardians" of a favored teacher, as well as a sequence about a pencil case that Ruth, probably lying, says the teacher gave her. In each case, different levels of sympathy are raised in both Kathy and the reader toward Ruth's need to be important. These nuances are missing from the Ruth character in the film, who is almost always jealous and manipulative.

Tommy

Ishiguro's novel makes clear that Tommy has frequent fits of rage when he is a boy, which accounts for the other children's ostracizing him. In the book he is shown having one fit, when he mistakenly strikes Kathy. Even his friends, including Kathy in the novel, make fun of Tommy because they think he is not able to follow complex ideas.

Although people think of him as being slow in his thoughts, Tommy is actually a complex thinker. His theory about the administration's use of artwork to verify whether or not people are truly in love is not very wrong, it just gives those in power more credit than they actually deserve: as Miss Emily explains to them, the art collection is not to read the students' souls, but to determine whether they even have souls. Another example of Tommy's clear thinking is when, questioned about the existence of "deferrals," he tells Rodney and Chrissie that he has no idea what they are talking about: the way Andrew Garfield, who plays Tommy, delivers the line might make it sound as if he is confused, but he is actually being direct in explaining what Ruth and Kathy are clearly feeling.

The depth of Tommy's emotions and intellect can be seen in his artwork. Ishiguro describes his drawings as being a complex, intricate merging of animals and machines. The film shows an early scene of his peers, including Ruth, mocking Tommy, which causes him to withdraw into himself and produce no art for the gallery. But the artworks Tommy produces later in the film, though mostly seen from angles, are clearly works of intelligence.

Tommy's biggest problems are that he is socially awkward and eager to please. He has no defenses to stand up to bullies, which causes him to be labeled as "odd" by his classmates. When Ruth decides that they should be a couple, he goes along with her, even though, as she herself admits later in the film, he is a more natural match for Kathy.

THEMES

Love
The relationships between Kathy, Tommy, and Ruth become more complicated as they grow up and Tommy and Ruth become a romantic couple, which isolates Kathy. She continues to associate with them in the closed social world of Hailsham and, later, the Cottages, but she finds herself disapproving of the way that Ruth behaves toward Tommy. Ruth dismisses her concern as jealousy since Kathy does not have her own love interest. The scene when Ruth comes to Kathy's room after having sex with

READ, WATCH, WRITE.

- After watching *Never Let Me Go*, write a brief essay explaining your feelings about organ transplantation. Then watch the 2002 Nick Cassavetes film *John Q.*, starring Denzel Washington as a father who finds his son blocked by his insurance plan from being put on the list for heart transplants, driving him to desperation and violence. In a paper, explain whether your feelings about the possibility of creating people as organ donors have been changed by *John Q.* and how you think the problem of obtaining organs for donation should be handled.

- Watch *The Remains of the Day*, the acclaimed 1993 film based on Ishiguro's most famous novel. Note the ways that film, by the acclaimed producing/directing/writing team of Ishmael Merchant, James Ivory, and Ruth Prawer Jhavbala, captures the tone of Ishiguru's prose. Write an explanation of three or four stylistic techniques used in that film that you think could have helped *Never Let Me Go* stay closer to its source material.

- Read Ishiguro's novel *The Unconsoled* (1995), a fantasy about an acclaimed piano player's bizarre adventures in a nameless European city. Prepare an argument, supported with examples of how it would be done, explaining why you think that book would be easier or more difficult than *Never Let Me Go* to adapt to film. Present your argument to your class in an oral report.

- Read Neal Shusterman's young-adult novel *Unwind* (2007), which presents a futuristic society that uses organ donations from unwanted children as a replacement for abortion. Shusterman wrote his novel as a thriller, while the quiet tone of *Never Let Me Go* keeps viewers wondering what the actual situation is. Write a comparison that explains which work is more convincing for showing people how you personally feel about the controversial issues it covers, and which work you think makes the other side's point better.

- One of the central questions raised in this film is whether Kathy, Tommy, and Ruth, who seem like normal children, should actually be considered human. Before explaining your opinion about this difficult topic, read Jesse Bering's article in the *Scientific American* edition of February 13, 2009, called "Would Your Clone Have Its Own Soul, or Be a Soulless Version of You?" Write an essay about whether human clones would have souls, using Bering's article, the film, and one other source that agrees with your religious or spiritual beliefs as your sources.

- Watch Kenneth Branagh's 1994 film *Mary Shelley's Frankenstein*, which is much more true to Shelley's 1818 novel than the more famous 1931 monster movie starring Boris Karloff. Robert DeNiro's sympathetic portrayal of the monster that Dr. Frankenstein creates raises questions about whether people should create life, if the science to do so existed. Write dialogue for the Frankenstein creation, explaining in his own way how he thinks the children of Hailsham should be treated. Post your dialogue on a blog and allow your classmates to comment.

Tommy and sits atop Kathy on her bed, insulting her but then kissing her, implies that she might be suppressing romantic feelings for Kathy. Later in the film, long after they have all gone their separate ways, Ruth confesses that she was wrong to stand between Kathy and Tommy, who she feels are obviously in love.

The students who grew up at Hailsham have an almost superstitious belief in love. They think that true love can extend their lives through the legendary deferral program. They know that they are destined to have their organs removed until they die, but they think that their fates might be changed if the depth of their love could only be conveyed to the right people. Tommy's theory is that their artworks from childhood can be used as proof that, as adults, they have the ability to love.

Dystopias

A *utopia* is an imagined ideal of social order, deriving its name from the title of a book written in the 1500s by Sir Thomas More about a place where all is right. The reverse—a society based on negative principles—is called a *dystopia*.

The world imagined in this film is presented in the first few minutes after the title as a utopia, where disease has been conquered and the human life span is extended to a hundred. It is not until later in the film, when viewers can see the cost of these medical advances, that the question arises about whether it might actually be a dystopia. In the world of the film, society grows clones of human beings specifically to harvest their organs, and when these clones show that they have human feelings and emotions, society turns its back on them.

Miss Emily explains to Kathy and Tommy why Hailsham was considered a failed experiment: trying to show the humanity of clones only made people uncomfortable about bringing them to life in order to kill them. The film, unlike Ishiguro's novel, is explicit early on about the ways these characters are destined to be maimed for society's benefit. The cruelty of the way the clones are treated becomes most obvious in the scene of Ruth's death, when the doctors coldly shut down the entire operating room and turn off the lights after Ruth dies during an organ removal, leaving her body on the table as if she were just a machine or surgical device they have finished using.

Humanity

A central question that is never explicitly addressed in either the book or the film of *Never Let Me Go* is whether the clones who are raised for organ donations are humans. Because audiences of both versions get to know the children of Hailsham from childhood, with their worries and loves, their jealousy and artistic expression, the answer seems obvious. To people who live in the world they live in, though, the opposite answer would seem just as obvious: being brought to life by cloning, they are not humans but, as Miss Emily calls Kathy, "creatures."

To Tommy, the point of collecting their artwork as children must have been to look into their souls, so that the caretakers of Hailsham could judge whether they were actually as in love as they claimed to be. To Miss Emily, the point of the artwork was to prove that they possessed souls. Her desire to prove this backfired, however, when she found out that the world did not want evidence that the cloned donors had souls because that raised ethical concerns that most people could not square with their own conscience.

Self-Image

Like young people in the real world, the three main characters here grow up wondering about who they are and what their roles are to be in this world. This is most clearly depicted in the behavior of Ruth. When they are young adults and move from Hailsham to the Cottages, Kathy observes Ruth trying on personal traits that she copies from others. She laughs the way Chrissie laughs and touches Tommy the way Chrissie touches Rodney, a behavior that was in turn learned from watching a comedy on television. When there is a possibility that Ruth might be able to see a woman who was her "model," the person she was cloned from, Ruth tries to hide her excitement at first and her disappointment later, after she realizes that she probably has no relationship to the woman.

Later, Tommy explains to Kathy his belief that her own interest in the pornographic magazines she found stems from the same curiosity: as Kathy's sexual instincts kicked in, she was drawn to looking at the women who posed for such a magazine, seeking some sort of relationship to them. Being born without parents—created in laboratories—has left these people with no sense of where they belong. That is why any connection to their childhood at Hailsham is so important to them and why Tommy is so fascinated with the picture of the old mansion that he finds in Miss Emily's study.

The three main characters are trapped in a love triangle: Kathy (Carey Mulligan), Ruth (Keira Knightley), and Tommy (Andrew Garfield). (© DNA Films | The Kobal Collection)

STYLE

Chronology

The narrative voice of Kathy H. is a controlling force in Ishiguro's novel. In adapting the story for film, screenwriter Alex Garland included limited sections of narration. Without the voice of the narrator constantly involving audiences in the story, he runs the risk of losing attention, so the decision was made to tell the story chronologically.

Instead of the viewer slowly discovering who the children at Hailsham are, why they are there, and the fact that it takes place in a parallel universe where things have happened that did not happen in the normal universe, the script tells the story from the very beginning. The first title cards on-screen, after the credits, reveal the idea of a medical breakthrough in 1952 and indicate that this film's action begins in 1978. The first scene with the children depicts Miss Emily telling the Hailsham children that they must maintain their health because they are "special." Viewers of the film understand what is meant by "carer" and "donation" within the very first minutes of the film, and it is explicitly related to them in Miss Lucy's speech to the children, about twenty-two minutes in. These are ideas that only slowly become known to readers over the course of the novel.

Flashback

Most of the story told in the film of *Never Let Me Go* is framed between scenes of Kathy looking on as Tommy undergoes his final surgery. In the beginning of the film, she is looking through a divider as a young man is brought into the operating room, though viewers have no idea who this young man is or what his relationship is to her. In voice-over, she identifies herself as a "carer" and refers to her "patients," so viewers might reasonably assume that her relationship to the young man is a professional one.

When the film returns to the same scene at the end, viewers know of her history with Tommy, and how the last weeks of their life together were spent trying to defer the very moment being depicted—his final donation—so that they could explore the love for each other that they only recently discovered. This puts the repeated scene in a new light, raising questions and emotions that could not have been understood when the film began.

Ishiguro's novel uses the same framing device. Starting with the declaration as told by twenty-eight-year-old Kathy sets a tone for the novel that tells readers what they can expect. It prepares readers for the cases where the narrator refers to things that have not yet been explained in the book, letting them know that this story is being told out of chronological order, as a person remembers things.

In both the film and the book, Kathy's narration in the first scene sets up the contrast between the moral uncertainty of organ harvesting and the calm, professional tone of someone who has spent her life in the middle of the situation.

Soundtrack

Throughout the film, the drama of the plot is augmented by Rachel Portman's soundtrack, which uses slow, dreamy piano solos and strings to heighten the sense of loneliness and despair. Portman, an Academy Award–winning veteran film composer, has composed the scores for dozens of films. In this film, her music is gentle, but it is almost always present, telling viewers the mood that goes with the images on-screen—David Denby of the *New Yorker* refers to Portman's soundtrack as "overly insistent."

An important part of this film is the song "Never Let Me Go," which gives the film and its source book its title. Ishiguro made up the singer Judy Bridgewater, basing her on similar torch singers of the 1940s and 1950s. The filmmakers created a design for the imaginary Bridgewater's audio cassette *Songs after Dark*, giving it graphics that would be appropriate for its time, and had a song written by the late Luther Dixon and performed by jazz singer Jane Monheit to approximate the kind of music that would have been on the sort of cassette that Ishiguro describes in his novel.

CULTURAL CONTEXT

Transplantation

Human organ transplants were long considered possible. The basic idea is the same one that drove human blood transfusions, first successfully accomplished in 1818, and bone transplants, which were accomplished in 1878. Mary Shelley's classic novel *Frankenstein*, published in 1831, shows the early hope that science could one day put together organs from different bodies, while also raising suspicions about what would happen if the scientists involved were to compromise their ethics.

Organ transplants became a reality in the twentieth century. In 1905 Austrian surgeon Eduard Zirm was successful in putting the cornea of an eleven-year-old donor into the eye of a patient with chemical burns on his eyes, restoring his sight. The first attempt at kidney transplant to have moderate success occurred in 1908, when the slices of the kidney of a rabbit were put into a young patient who survived for two weeks. The first human-to-human kidney transplant, performed in Soviet Russia in 1936, was sustained only two days before the patient died, but the process was successful in 1954 with the transfer of a kidney from one identical twin to the other. This transplant, and the lives of both the donor and the recipient twin after it, gave the medical community hope that human organ transplants could indeed save lives. The film *Never Lets Me Go* identifies a "medical breakthrough" in 1954 that it implies would be the advent of human organ transplantation.

The process of transplantation accelerated in the 1960s, with the first successful lung transplant in 1963 followed by a pancreas transplant in 1966 and a liver transplant in 1967, which was also the year of the first heart transplant. Soon after that, organ donor programs were established so that people could make legal arrangements for donation before something happened to them. The American Association of Tissue Banks was established in 1976, and the National Transplant Network was established in 1984.

The success of organ transplantation, along with the limited supply of available organs through legitimate, carefully screened programs, has driven some people with means to obtain organs through illegal channels. According to the *American Journal of Transplantation*, the

World Health Organization estimated in 2007 that as many as 5 to 10 percent of kidney transplants worldwide were the result of organ sales, generally from people in poor countries. Organ trafficking has gone from being the stuff of urban legends to a serious ethical concern in the global medical community

Cloning

The theory of cloning has been practiced on plant life for hundreds of years in the form of plant propagation, or using a cutting from a mature plant to grow a new plant with the same characteristics as the donor. In animals, however, the possibility of successful cloning has only been taken seriously by scientists since later in the twentieth century.

In 1901, researcher Hans Spemann, a German embryologist, was successful in separating the cells of a two-cell salamander embryo and growing two identical organisms from them. Having established that the necessary DNA for a mature organism was carried in each cell, the prospect for successful cloning seemed clear. Nearly four decades later, in 1938, Spemann published his theory that the nucleus of a cell could be transferred into a cell without a nucleus, a theory that, once proven, would provide the basis for the cloning experiments that were to follow. The isolation of genes in 1969 gave science the tools it needed to achieve the cloning of mammals. In the world of the film, the children at Hailsham, who moved to the Cottages in 1985 at age eighteen, would have already been successfully cloned by 1967.

In 1969 there was a claim of three mice being cloned. The first verified case of successful mammalian cloning on record came in 1984, when a sheep was cloned in Denmark. A groundbreaking event occurred in 1996 with the cloning of Dolly, another sheep. It was the first time an adult organism had been cloned from the cell of another adult. In 1998 Dolly gave birth to three sheep conceived through natural reproduction.

Since Dolly, the prospect of cloning human beings has been considered controversial. In 2002 President George W. Bush pushed for a ban on human cloning, saying, "Cloning would contradict the most fundamental principle of medical ethics, that no human life should be exploited or extinguished for the benefit of another. Life is a creation, not a commodity."

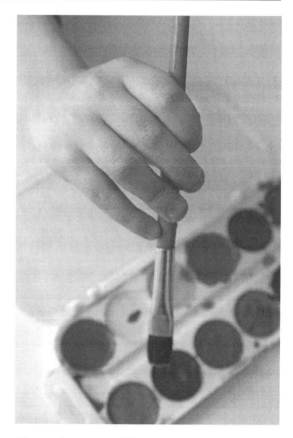

The students at Hailsham House are encouraged to create artwork, which is displayed in the Gallery. *(© nulinukas / Shutterstock.com)*

The law that he was supporting, along with several other national bans on cloning, have failed to gather enough support in the Senate and House of Representatives to be passed into law; however, several states have bans on cloning.

CRITICAL OVERVIEW

The film version of *Never Let Me Go* received mixed reviews, with some reviewers finding it too dull and, predictably, unable to rise up to the standards set by the novel it is based on, while the majority feel that it is a sensitive and intelligent film. An example of the negative reviews comes from Tom Long of the *Detroit News*, who feels that the film's whole premise is "oddly cold and detached, as if director Mark Romanek and screenwriter Alex Garland couldn't decide precisely how to interpret Kazuo Ishiguro's popular novel and so they just laid it out flat. And flat it feels." David Denby echoes that sentiment when he writes in the *New Yorker* that the film is "a stiff." Despite impressive technical achievements, Denby feels that "nothing in it takes hold of us emotionally" and that the film "is in such good taste that we never feel any horror over the idea at the center of it." Tom Huddleston, writing for *Time Out London*, also feels that the film lacks emotion, even as he acknowledges the good work of the director and the actors: his two-out-of-five-star review ends with the dismissive observation, "The result is pretty, empty, and immediately forgettable."

Supporters of the film, however, tend to be more passionate than the detractors. For example, Australian critic Paul Byrnes starts his review in the *Sydney Morning Herald* by saying, "Don't walk, run. This is one of the best films of the year, but don't expect it to be in cinemas for long." He attributes its box-office failure in the United States to the misconception that its dark, depressing subject does not appeal to men, dismissing that theory with, "Real men will see this and weep, as I did. It is one of the most moving and profound films in a long time." Peter Travers of *Rolling Stone* calls it "a movie you can't get out of your head, a sci-fi horror story with the seductive allure of a classic romance," and takes care to "praise the visual skill with which Romanek creates this world, the delicate power of Alex Garland's screenplay, and the stellar performances." Richard Corliss of *Time* magazine is one of the most enthusiastic fans, comparing "the poignant, troubling and altogether splendid new film version" favorably with Ishiguro's novel and, in the end, putting it third on his year-end top-ten list.

CRITICISM

David Kelly

Kelly is an instructor of creative writing and literature. In the following essay, he talks about why Never Let Me Go *is not really a love story, even though presenting it as one is good commercial marketing.*

Anyone who has seen a few movies can probably think of one or two that pretend to be more deep than they really are. Maybe the film has people in silly body armor hauling colossal weapons, pretending to be about the potential destruction of the universe. Maybe the film is

> " AND IT IS HERE THAT THE LOVE STORY FALLS AWAY, REVEALING ITSELF TO BE JUST A HANDY PROP TO SELL MOVIE TICKETS."

shot darkly, in different languages, trying to rip the pretense off an international scandal, but is easily recognizable as the basic "one just person fights an unjust system" fare that Hollywood has been churning out forever. Film is about overstatement, and it is geared toward the lowest expectations for the intelligence of audiences.

Rare, though, is the film that hides its intellectual depth from its audience. This appears to be the case with the 2010 film adaptation of Kazuo Ishiguro's novel *Never Let Me Go*. It has been sold to audiences as a love story, and indeed, love is an issue discussed in it, but love is not the main point of the novel or the film. Audiences who watch the film thinking of it as a meditation on love will finish it thinking about much more significant issues. The potential for love that lingers around this film is the sheep's clothing, but inside it, the case for human relevance is a lurking wolf.

Viewers are certainly steered toward the love aspect by the story. At its center is a romantic triangle that would have been hackneyed in silent films a century before this one was made. A sweet-natured but awkward boy, Tommy, is loved by drab, dutiful Kathy, but before she can let him know of her love, the fiery, scheming dark-haired Ruth, a duplicitous friend, lures Tommy into her clutches. Before dying, Ruth repents, confessing that she did not love Tommy, practically willing him to her former friend, the good girl, on her deathbed.

On film, this basic love story is conveyed tastefully: young Kathy looks on as Tommy is humiliated (by Ruth); he does her a good turn and she kisses him on the cheek; he hits her mistakenly during a temper tantrum, but she forgives him; she watches Ruth and Tommy holding hands and kissing, while, for her part, she is left dancing with a pillow to a dreamy, romantic song that was popular a generation or

WHAT DO I SEE NEXT?

- The film's sense that Hailsham children are special reflects the social dynamics of many movies about boarding schools. It is clearly evident in *A Little Princess*, based on Frances Hodgson Burnett's classic 1905 novel. This heartwarming fantasy concerns a British girl, Sara, sent to school in New York when her father goes off to war. While Sara maintains that she is "a princess," the school's headmistress struggles to keep her ego in check. The latest, acclaimed film version, rated G, was released by Warner Brothers in 1995, starring Liesel Matthews, Eleanor Bron, and Liam Cunningham.

- The sense of secrets and rumors at Hailsham is echoed in one of the great movies about boarding schools, 1961's *The Children's Hour*, based on Lillian Hellman's 1934 stage play. The unrated film stars Audrey Hepburn and Shirley MacLaine as teachers whose careers are jeopardized when a malicious student starts rumors that they are lesbians. James Garner and Miriam Hopkins also star. It was released on DVD in 2002 by Warner Brothers.

- *Logan's Run* (rated PG) is a 1976 science fiction classic that raised questions about government controls on the lives of individuals that *Never Let Me Go* only hints at. Set in the year 2444, it presents a world where the population is controlled by a law that requires everyone to report for extermination at age thirty. Michael York plays one of the men responsible for capturing people who try running from their appointment with death but starts questioning the system. Starring Roscoe Lee Browne and Jenny Agutter and directed by Michael Anderson, it is available on DVD from Warner Brothers.

- Mark Romanek, the director of *Never Let Me Go*, has only produced a few feature films, having worked in music videos for artists such as Nine Inch Nails and Jay-Z for most of his career. Viewers can get a good sense of his earlier career by watching *The Work of Director Mark Romanek* (unrated), which is number 4 in Palm Pictures' Director's Label DVD series. Directed by Lance Bangs, it was released in 2005, before *Never Let Me Go* was produced.

- Another classic science-fiction film that raises questions about what it is to be human is *Blade Runner*, based on Philip K. Dick's novel *Do Androids Dream of Electric Sheep?* Harrison Ford plays a detective who is charged with capturing escaped "replicants" (androids) and "retiring" them, only to find that, like the clones in *Never Let Me Go*, they are more human than society feels comfortable believing. Frequently cited as one of the best of its genre, Ridley Scott's film also stars Sean Young, Rutger Hauer, and Daryl Hannah. This 1982 film is available from Warner Brothers and is rated R for violence.

- Alex Garland, the screenwriter for *Never Let Me Go*, wrote the novel *The Beach* and worked on the screenplay for its adaptation, released in 2000. The movie stars Leonardo DiCaprio, Virginie Ledoyen, Guillaume Canet, and Tilda Swinton. Danny Boyle directed this mysterious tale of a young man backpacking through Thailand who comes into possession of a map that is supposed to take him to a beach that might or might not be paradise. It is available on DVD from 20th Century Fox and is rated R for violence, sexuality, language, and drug content.

---

two earlier. The images on screen all suggest heartache, and if they do not suggest it powerfully enough, the soundtrack is always pouring out sad violins and piano solos that are so slow and meditative that the pianist always seems on the verge of collapsing of world-weariness.

If this were just a case of mistaken identity—of guileless Tommy coupling up with the bad girl instead of his true love—the film could be a comedy and maybe even have a happy ending. But this is a story of doomed love. The theatrical trailer for the film alternates creepy scenes of the three friends at their boarding school, Hailsham—scenes reminiscent of the ghost film *The Awakening*—with title cards that read "Welcome to Hailsham . . . the students have everything they need . . . except time."

The first scene of the film has grown-up Kathy, not yet thirty but looking pale and drawn, as the sole observer while Tommy, already sporting a huge jagged scar down his side, is wheeled into a surgical room. Ishiguro lets this sense of impending doom grow slowly on the novel's readers through the first two-thirds of his book, dropping hints about "donors" and "carers" and "completion." But the film dispenses with the mystery, announcing a medical breakthrough as soon as the film's title has run, which gives a context to the first plot development, in which the children are told that Hailsham students need to take particular care of their health. Before the first half hour is up, the entire mystery is cast aside, as idealistic and beloved young teacher Miss Lucy tells the children, and audiences, that these students are raised to be organ donors and are destined to die young.

For the middle of the film, the lingering aura of death mixes into the love triangle. The temporality of the situation heightens its romance in the way that only tragedy can. Viewers know that Tommy and Ruth start dating at Hailsham, and they hope that something will intercede to provide Tommy with the right love interest. They know from a scene at the beginning that Tommy will be wheeled in to have one of his organs taken, and somewhere in the backs of their minds there must be the belief that such foreshadowing is destined to be interrupted when real time catches up: a reprieve by sympathetic powers in the National Donor Programme, perhaps, or maybe Kathy will pull a gun and tell the doctors to back away.

The story's mechanism for hope is a deferral program, which would allow donors to put off relinquishing their organs for a few years if they are really "verifiably" in love. In both the novel and the film, it is introduced as just a subject of wishful gossip, like the spook stories that the

Hailsham children scare one another with: not at all unexpected in a world where the adults keep the children in the dark about rules and regulations (in other words, the actual world). What starts as gossip is latched onto desperately, especially when Ruth, with the shadow of death over her head, takes a hand. She knows that she is dying, so she tells Kathy and Tommy that it is they who are truly in love, and she gives them a big clue to how they can get a deferral for themselves.

At this point, love and death are merged. Death is threatening the love that Kathy and Tommy put off too long, but love might be able to literally conquer their scheduled deaths, if they can prove the sincerity of that love. This is the apex of the love story driving the film. Kathy and Tommy finally spend time together as a couple. They go to see Miss Emily, the former headmistress of Hailsham, played by one of the iciest British actresses alive, Charlotte Rampling. And it is here that the love story falls away, revealing itself to be just a handy prop to sell movie tickets.

This meeting readjusts the film's focus. The pipe dream of being able to out-love death is quickly dispensed with as a common rumor, and the talk turns to what made society even think they could cut short the lives of Kathy, Ruth, Tommy, and the dozens of beautiful little Hailsham students like them: they are clones and as such are not considered actual human beings. The most memorable line from the scene, even from the movie itself or from the book, is when Miss Emily tells them, "We didn't have the gallery [of students' art] to look into your souls; we had the gallery to see if you had souls at all." The right response, which is never spoken, would be that yes, of course Kathy and Tommy and maybe even Ruth have souls, even though the merciless wheels of society simply cannot let them live because society needs a source for transplantable organs.

As much as audiences who see this as a story about love might hate to admit it, though, the question of the souls of clones is never actually settled. Once they are pushed together, Kathy and Tommy seem awkward with one another. The film shows them exchanging glances since childhood, and, after Ruth pushes them together, they spend more time together and eventually enter into a physical relationship one rainy afternoon. But there is never any sign that they are fighting to be next to one another. One way to look at this is that they have such a deeply felt love for each other that any physical display would just be counterfeit, just as Ruth based her actions when she was with Tommy on what she saw the older, established couple, Chrissie and Rodney, doing.

But what if they really do not feel love? If their lives are spent artificially trying to respond to situations the way humans would? It would explain a whole lot, from the film's slow, deliberately paced acting, to the shudder that comes over Madame and other humans in their presence, to the way that Ruth picks up Tommy with nothing but sad muted stares from Kathy, to the way she then gives Tommy to Kathy and tells them, "You are in love," to the way the soundtrack seems so intent on explaining what the appropriate human response would be at any given time.

Tommy and Kathy seem to want to love each other, but there is no real evidence that they have that ability. Alex Garland's screenplay for the film conflates love with survival: proving that one has the capacity for true love just might earn one a few more years of life. It does not show love for its own sake. Tommy and Kathy are not fighting for their love (remember, Kathy watches her friend Ruth carry Tommy off and then accepts him when Ruth brings him back), they are fighting for a deferral.

And that is the film's ultimate triumph. It is easy to make film audiences root for characters whose love is being denied, either by a cruel society or by death. It is awfully difficult to make audiences wonder if sad people like Kathy, Tommy, or Ruth even have the ability to love, and, if they do not, then whether they are human. If these clones, who have been brought to life on-screen by some of the most talented actors of their generation, can act as human as they do and still not have souls, then where do we draw the line about what a human is? Introverts? Autistics? The ramifications of accepting a society where one's humanity is measured and judged are just too appalling to contemplate.

But questions like these do not get audiences into a mass-market film. Love stories do. *Never Let Me Go* has love in it, but it would not be right to say that this is a film about love.

Source: David Kelly, Critical Essay on *Never Let Me Go*, in *Novels for Students*, Gale, Cengage Learning, 2014.

Mark Fisher

In the following excerpt, Fisher explains how Never Let Me Go *does not allow its characters any avenue for escape.*

. . . There is no such conversion of fatalism into resistance in Mark Romanek's *Never Let Me Go*. The peculiar horror of the film, in fact, resides in the unrelieved quality of its fatalism. *Never Let Me Go* focuses on an "ideological state apparatus," an English boarding school, Hailsham, in an alternative twentieth century. The film is about the success of such ideological apparatuses in destroying even the thought of rebellion. The truth of the school is known to all, but, in the typical English way, it cannot be said out loud (one teacher is sacked for explicitly stating what the pupils already know): Hailsham is a training academy for clones, whose role will be to be provide organs for the wider human population. Unlike in *The Hunger Games*, the lead characters in *Never Let Me Go* are not kept in line by a police force or an army. Here, heartbreakingly, and surprisingly, there are no dreams of escape into the woods (as the threshold to an outside world coded as threatening, the woods at the perimeter of Hailsham are precisely not understood as a place of freedom, but mythologized as a site of terror); there is only a terrible compliance, and a slave's desperate capacity for self-delusion. By contrast with *The Hunger Games*, in which brute force is always visible through the veneer of ideology, *Never Let Me Go* is about a form of power that does not need to exhibit force. It is instructive to compare *Never Let Me Go* with Michael Bay's *The Island*; indeed, such a comparison is inevitable. Bay's film works from a premise that is practically identical—clones whose body parts will be harvested—but its treatment of the concept could not be more different. *The Island* is a story of escape, full of spectacular Hollywood action sequences. In *Never Let Me Go*, however, there is nowhere to escape to. Once they leave the school, the clones are not confined in some carceral space; they share the same world as those to whom, in a chilling yet appallingly convincing-sounding euphemism, they must "donate" their organs. Nothing could be further from *The Island*'s adrenal bustle than *Never Let Me Go*'s atmosphere of lassitude, languor, and longing. The fact that the clones' time is short lends their thwarted love affairs, their lazy afternoons spent reading in meadows, and their day trips to the coast a nearly unbearable intensity.

If there is nowhere to escape to—the clones are already in the world; the world is their prison—then nor is there any attempt to escape. The hopes and fantasies of the three lead clone characters, Kathy (Carey Mulligan), Ruth (Keira Knightley), and Tommy (Andrew Garfield), are entirely shaped by the bureaucratic organization of the donation program. For reasons that are never fully clear but which we can surmise are down to the success of the Hailsham ideology, fleeing the program is unthinkable for them. Their hopes rest instead on the kind of collective fantasy that seems to spontaneously grow in institutions like Hailsham, and without which, in a cruel twist, the institution could not do its work. The fantasy is the unofficial supplement which the official ideological program relies upon—and may even cultivate—without explicitly sanctioning. The fantasy is of a reprieve in the form of a "deferral" (Ishiguro's language here echoes the "indefinite postponement" in Kafka's *The Trial*), which is supposedly available to couples that can prove they are really in love. Without this fantasy, the clones would have no hope, and thus no reason not to rebel, or to destroy themselves. But, as Tommy and Kathy discover—and we sense that Kathy never really believed it anyway, except as a kind of superstition for the condemned to console themselves with—there is no deferral. Their love, like their bodies, will not survive much longer. Kathy's concluding voiceover notes that this is the same for everyone, whether clone or not—except that there is nothing natural about the clones' fate. They die—or, in another wonderfully chilling euphemism, they "complete"—because they belong to an exploited class, and what a harrowingly incisive image of exploitation "organ donation" is . . . .

Source: Mark Fisher, "Precarious Dystopias: *The Hunger Games*, *In Time*, and *Never Let Me Go*," in *Film Quarterly*, Vol. 65, No. 4, Summer 2012, pp. 31–33.

J. H. de Villiers and M. Slabbert

In the following excerpt, de Villiers and Slabbert discuss some of the ethical and legal issues raised by Never Let Me Go.

. . . Like so many other novels that inspire a law and literature interpretation, Ishiguro's novel prompts us to examine, question and rethink a specific area of legal theory. Our reading of this novel therefore reiterates the notion

IT IS NOT ISHIGURO'S INTENTION TO CONSIDER A SPECIFIC LEGAL FRAMEWORK IN *NEVER LET ME GO*, YET HE INDIRECTLY RAISES AND HIGHLIGHTS THE PROBLEMATIC NATURE OF CURRENT MEDICO-LEGAL ISSUES SUCH AS CLONING, ORGAN DONATIONS, THE SHORTAGE OF TRANSPLANTABLE ORGANS, AND MEANS OF MEETING THE SHORTFALL."

that literature can play an important role as a critical tool through which to examine various aspects of the law. Many works of science fiction thus have practical significance. Hans Vaihinger (1935:viii) states that

> . . . an idea whose theoretical untruth or incorrectness, and therewith its falsity, is admitted, is not for that reason practically valueless and useless; for such an idea, in spite of its theoretical nullity may have great practical importance.

Ishiguro's novel, albeit a work of fiction, may thus have great practical importance in that it also alludes to the reality that someone's healthy organ can save another's life. The overwhelming demand for healthy organs and events like the recent Netcare scandal in KwaZulu-Natal where kidneys were bought from the poor to be transplanted into Israeli patients (*The State v Netcare Kwa-Zulu Natal* 2010), suggest that the events depicted in the novel might indeed be closer to possible realisation than we would like to believe. With this in mind, we look at systems of procuring donor organs and propose an alternative approach in the second part of this article. We side with a legal framework that respects autonomy and balances the various factors that intersect to configure the subject.

2. NEVER LET ME GO—LAW(LESSNESS) IN LITERATURE

Ishiguro's novel does not take law as a theme in the same way as is the case in Franz Kafka's *The trial* (Kafka, 1968), or William Gaddis's *A frolic of his own* (Gaddis, 1994). The storyline does not evolve around any legal proceedings, nor is there any direct reference to the law. Instead, Ishiguro actually confronts the reader with a state of lawlessness; he depicts a world characterised by an uncertain distance separating the characters and (the existence of) the law. The expression "lawless" has more than one meaning—inter alia referring to instances of disregard for the law. For the purpose of this article, "lawlessness," however, designates a status of a-legality, the non-application (or non-existence) of an ethically-sound regulatory legal framework. By reading Ishiguro from a law and literature perspective, we can generate a new understanding of the various nuances that intersect to form the complex socio-legal configuration that comprises the status quo pertaining to organ donations.

Set during the late 1990s in England, *Never Let Me Go* is an unsettling story about three young people, Kathy H, Tommy D and Ruth, as it unfolds through their eyes. The reader first encounters them as students at a seemingly idyllic private school called Hailsham. The story is written in the first person with Kathy H, now 31 years old, narrating the story with hindsight. From the onset the author creates an unusual yet credible milieu and rhythm that form the backdrop to the lives of the students at Hailsham. We are introduced to a world of "guardians," "carers," "donors," "completions," "possibles" and "the Gallery." This unfamiliar vocabulary draws the reader into the leitmotif of uncertainty that haunts the lives of the characters. Having "been told and not told," the students of Hailsham are left to speculate on the significance of these constants that form part of their everyday existence.

Their (often misguided) search for truth propels the storyline and also presents a source of conflict within the complex triadic relationship between Kathy, Ruth and Tommy, as it gradually changes from innocent childhood friendship to a love triangle. Because of her dominant personality, Ruth dictates the relationship and she initially fosters a somewhat artificial romantic connection with Tommy, thereby suppressing the love between Kathy and Tommy. It is only towards the end of her (short) life that Ruth reflects on her destructive role in the relationship.

> It should have been you two. I'm not pretending I didn't always see that. Of course I did, as far back as I can remember. But I kept you apart. I'm not asking you to forgive me for that.

The reader, being dependent on Kathy's narration, which draws on her imperfect and, therefore, inevitably flawed reflections, has to read between the lines to make sense of the situation. The same applies to Kathy and the other students who are left to interpret their lives, relying only on their limited, censored and superimposed frames of reference. The students are constantly told that they are "special" and they progressively realise exactly what this means. Miss Lucy, a "guardian" at Hailsham, is one of the very few characters in the novel who engages in candid discussions with the students. After overhearing a conversation between two students contemplating the pursuit of careers in the American film industry, she is profoundly affected by the innocent unawareness typifying the students' lives and thinking. She then acts on her unwillingness to be a complacent bystander:

> [. . .] none of you really understand, and I dare say, some people are quite happy to leave it that way. But I'm not. If you're going to have decent lives, then you've got to know and know properly. None of you will go to America, none of you will be film stars . . . Your lives are set out for you. You'll become adults, then before you're old, before you're even middle-aged, you'll start to donate your vital organs. That's what each of you was created to do. You're not like the actors you watch on your videos, you're not even like me. You were brought into this world for a purpose, and your futures, all of them, have been decided.

The students' reactions of dismissal to Miss Lucy's frank words are symptomatic of their obscured views of their reality, and their inability (and unwillingness) to reflect on the significance of their inescapable fates: "Well so what? We already knew all that." This illustrates Miss Lucy's concern that they have "been told and not told," and one is reminded of the proverb that half a truth is ever the blackest of lies. In portraying the students' initial inability and unwillingness to interpret and conceptualise the significance of their predetermined essence, Ishiguro introduces the abstraction that the students are en route to "becoming"—to realising a project. This usage links him with existentialist themes like being-in-the-world, becoming, angst, and ultimately death . . . .

It is not Ishiguro's intention to consider a specific legal framework in *Never Let Me Go*, yet he indirectly raises and highlights the problematic nature of current medico-legal issues such as cloning, organ donations, the shortage of transplantable organs, and means of meeting the shortfall. The main characters in the novel, the students, are actually cloned so that their organs can be harvested. Their predetermined essence (of providing transplantable organs) precedes their existence. They are believed by some to be subhuman, without a free will or soul, but the events depicted in the novel suggest otherwise. We "see" their souls through their artwork and, later in life, how their relationships and accompanying emotions explicitly illuminate their humanness. Yet, they are stripped of choice; they are not the conductors of their own lives and occupy a space as objects to be used for someone else's purpose. They furthermore embrace the roles carved out for them, in essence fitting the description of an article of manufacture—like Sartre's paper-knife. One can only imagine what Sartre would have said about this scenario. He explicitly distinguished a (human) being from a thing, but could he have foreseen the practice of cloning and the resulting questions? What are clones? Are they fully human or not? What exactly constitutes a human and what does it mean to be human?

The primary aim of this article was to utilise Ishiguro's popular and since filmed novel as a platform from which to consider, interpret and propose an alternative approach to the more specialised issue of organ donation. Ishiguro destabilises and disrupts the law through narrative, portraying a fictional but possible scenario of procuring organs and, thereby, illustrating the need for a comprehensive legal framework regulating the supply of organs for transplantation. Whilst cloning, as depicted in the novel, does not offer a satisfactory option, the current systems of organ procurement also clearly fall short in various regards. An alternative that is not science fiction and which recognises and balances personal autonomy, free choice and the right to self-determination is imperative (but keeping in mind that a donor should be allowed to choose between donating and selling a kidney) (Lawlor, 2011:250–259; Kishore, 2005:362–365). The approach of financially rewarding a donor seems to present such an alternative.

Source: J. H. de Villiers and M. Slabbert, "*Never Let Me Go*: Science Fiction and Legal Reality," in *Literator: Journal of Literary Criticism, Comparative Linguistics, and Literary Studies,* Vol. 32, No. 3, December 2011, p. 85.

> DESPITE THE STORY'S SCI-FI ELEMENT, THE ENGLAND THESE MARGINALIZED CHARACTERS INHABIT IS QUIET, RURAL, BLEAK."

Kristin M. Jones

In the following essay, Jones praises the film's casting and its gradual revelation of what will happen to the characters.

What does it mean to live a good life? That's a question raised by Kazuo Ishiguro's piercingly sad 2005 novel *Never Let Me Go*. The book derives some of its power from its simplicity and symmetry: in three acts, it follows a trio of friends whose lives have been preordained to be shortened by three unspeakably dire events. In their film adaptation, director Mark Romanek and screenwriter Alex Garland pare Ishiguro's story down even further, eerily evoking the late-life impulse to winnow down memories in search of the essential.

Although a thread of biotechnological horror runs through the story, it is set in the recent past rather than a dystopian future, generating an uneasy sense of familiarity. Ishiguro initially aimed to write a novel about a group of young people facing a strange fate, then imagined an alternate postwar history in which an infatuation with scientific progress led to a sinister kind of baby boom. Early in the film a title tells us: "By 1967, life expectancy passed 100 years." But whose life expectancy? Not, it becomes clear, the story's central characters, Kathy (Carey Mulligan), Tommy (Andrew Garfield), and Ruth (Keira Knightley). Their journey—and haunting love triangle—is shown through the eyes of Kathy, a wonderfully ordinary but mournful narrator who as the movie begins is sifting through her all-consuming memories of the years they spent together.

As a child growing up during the Seventies, Kathy (at this point played by Isobel Meikle-Small) first becomes friends with magnetic but manipulative Ruth (Ella Purnell) and volatile, sensitive Tommy (Charlie Rowe). She meets both of them at Hailsham, an isolated rural boarding school housed in a handsome brick mansion set amid lush gardens and playing fields—a place of quiet gray days and golden evenings. There, the pupils are instructed and cared for by a team of tweedy "guardians," led by the dedicated Miss Emily (Charlotte Rampling), who addresses assemblies with bracing zeal, her inscrutable, hooded gaze sweeping across their fresh, upturned faces. The guardians strictly monitor the students' physical well-being but also emphasize the importance of creativity and select student artwork for a mysterious, never-seen Gallery.

In the magical yet sometimes ominous world of Hailsham, students are repeatedly reminded that they are "special," their talents seemingly nurtured as if at any cheerfully progressive school. Rumors abound of Hailsham runaways who have had their hands and feet cut off as punishment or have been left to starve outside the gates, but these seem mostly to heighten the children's sense that they are safe within the grounds. Nor do they seem bothered by their worn, mismatched uniforms, and they eagerly anticipate the periodic "Sales," where they can purchase armless dolls and stubby crayons with tiddlywinks-like tokens they earn when their artwork is selected for the Gallery by an intriguing Frenchwoman the children call "Madame" (Nathalie Richard).

But Madame recoils disconcertingly when they playfully crowd around her on one of her occasional visits, and her behavior isn't the only glimmer that their "specialness" may not be such a good thing. When a new guardian, Miss Lucy (Sally Hawkins), arrives, she seems troubled by certain aspects of the school, and she later offers odd advice to Tommy after he draws a primitive elephant in art class. Weather has a potent presence in the film—filtered as the story is through Kathy's memory—and it's on a day of torrential rain that Miss Lucy finally breaks with protocol to address her class frankly, eschewing the usual euphemisms. "The problem is that you've been told and not told," she says. None of them will travel to America, become movie stars, or work in supermarkets. Their adult lives will be brief. The children listen in silence to her revelations. A breeze blows some papers from her desk and Tommy picks them up; shots follow of a rain-soaked statue and a child's ball left in the grass.

Hailsham's seclusion, its sense of enchantment, and the elusive Gallery recall another flawed childhood utopia: the luminously cloistered realm in *Innocence*, Lucile Hadzihalilovic's 2004 film based on Frank Wedekind's Symbolist novella *Mine-Haha*, or *On the Bodily Education of Young Girls*, in which preadolescent dancers are periodically plucked from ballet classes at a strange, remotely located girls' school for a mysterious purpose. But whereas the future of Hadzihalilovic's beribboned sylphs remains tantalizingly uncertain—despite hints that they are being prepared for sexual maturity and reproduction—the fate of Hailsham's boys and girls will, eventually, be all-too-painfully revealed.

Knowledge is meted out in small doses, like a series of inoculations. In the story's second act Kathy, Ruth, and Tommy—now teenagers on the verge of adulthood—are transported to the Cottages, a lonely cluster of ivy-covered farm buildings where they will live with other young people and occasionally venture into the outside world, before going on to fulfill their chilling predetermined roles. There they read poetry, giggle at Eighties sitcoms, and experience romantic entanglements, misunderstandings, and petty betrayals. Their interactions take on unusual weight, however, when they grapple with troubling anxieties about the nature of their existence and about their seemingly hopeless prospects, as if in a warped version of the typical college experience.

The country setting feels like a temporary balm: the teenagers can take walks in the woods and a stray songbird perches in the kitchen. Belying their origins, they seem to have a special affinity for nature. In fact, as their story unfolds it brings out in them a natural grace, as with Thomas Hardy's tragic "daughter of the soil" Tess of the d'Urbervilles—another social castaway during an era of technological transformation—although they don't seem to wonder, as she did, "why the sun do shine on the just and unjust alike." They only wonder where they come from, whom to love, how best to live their lives, and whether they might secure a temporary reprieve from what awaits them.

Despite the story's sci-fi element, the England these marginalized characters inhabit is quiet, rural, bleak. In keeping with the melancholy sense of living on the fringes, the visuals in Romanek's adaptation eschew primary colors. The palette varies slightly for each of its three sections: earth tones and greens for the

Hailsham years; more saturated colors found in nature for the purgatory-like interlude at the Cottages; and cooler, paler tones for the harrowing final act. In addition to a whiteout at a crucial moment, the film is periodically punctuated by muted gray-green or mauve fade-outs, evoking a foggy netherworld. (In creating the look of the film, Romanek drew on the restrained style of Mikio Naruse's films, which Ishiguro admires.)

The film's sensitive casting is a big part of its success in bringing Ishiguro's story, with its delicately elegiac tone, to the screen. Mulligan and Garfield inhabit their roles with aching naturalism, while Knightley, flashing hurt from beneath mop-like bangs that movingly diminish her beauty, delivers her best performance to date as the brittle, sometimes cruel, but ultimately heartbreaking Ruth. Rampling, Richard, and Hawkins sketch out their briefly seen but complicated characters with a subtlety that becomes more evident at the conclusion, when two of them turn out to have cultivated spectacularly muddled attitudes toward their pupils.

"I feel a great sense of pride in what we do," the adult Kathy points out in her voiceover. At the same time, she says, "In the end, it wears you down." *Never Let Me Go* is filled with sadness and muffled brutality, but it also offers a compelling affirmation. At Hailsham Miss Lucy speaks to her charges of the need for them to know the truth in order to "live decent lives," and in the end, what is important is not the appalling fate that looms over these three characters, but the clear-eyed choice they make to sacrifice themselves for one another. Ultimately, the challenges they face in their artificially compressed lives are revealed to be not so dissimilar from our own.

In a lecture on Kafka's *The Metamorphosis*, Vladimir Nabokov observed: "*Beauty plus pity*—that is the closest we can get to a definition of art. Where there is beauty there is pity for the simple reason that beauty must die: beauty always dies, the manner dies with the matter, the world dies with the individual." *Never Let Me Go* fits that definition.

Source: Kristin M. Jones, "Childhood's End: The Mortal Concerns of Mark Romanek's *Never Let Me Go*," in *Film Comment*, Vol. 74, No. 10, September–October 2010, pp. 32–33.

SOURCES

Budiani-Saberi, D. A., and F. L. Delmonico, "Organ Trafficking and Transplant Tourism: A Commentary on the Global Realities," in *American Journal of Transplantation*, April 14, 2008, http://onlinelibrary.wiley.com/doi/10.1111/j.1600-6143.2008.02200.x/full (accessed April 24, 2013).

Byrnes, Paul, Review of *Never Let Me Go*, in *Sydney Morning Herald*, March 31, 2011, http://www.smh.com.au/entertainment/movies/never-let-me-go-20110330-1cg3b.html (accessed April 15, 2013).

Corliss, Richard, "Everlasting Love," in *Time*, September 13, 2010, http://www.time.com/time/magazine/article/0,9171,2015774,00.html (accessed April 15, 2013).

Denby, David, "English Tests," in *New Yorker*, September 27, 2010, http://www.newyorker.com/arts/reviews/film/never_let_me_go_romanek (accessed April 15, 2013).

"History of Cloning," Harvard Medical School website, https://bsp.med.harvard.edu/?q=node/18 (accessed April 24, 2013).

"History of Transplantation—Timeline," The Gift of a Lifetime, http://www.organtransplants.org/understanding/history/ (accessed April 24, 2013).

Huddleston, Tom, Review of *Never Let Me Go*, in *Time Out London*, February 8, 2011, http://www.timeout.com/london/film/never-let-me-go?cpage=3&ccat=11 (accessed April 15, 2013).

"Human Cloning Controversy," NewsHour Extra, PBS website, April 17, 2002, http://www.pbs.org/newshour/extra/features/jan-june02/cloning.html (accessed April 24, 2013).

Long, Tom, "Parts Lacking in 'Never Let Me Go,'" in *Detroit News*, October 8, 2010, http://www.detroitnews.com/article/20101008/OPINION03/10080333 (accessed April 15, 2013).

Never Let Me Go, directed by Mark Romanek, Fox Searchlight Pictures, 2010, DVD.

Travers, Peter, Review of *Never Let Me Go*, in *Rolling Stone*, September 15, 2010, http://www.rollingstone.com/movies/reviews/never-let-me-go-20100915 (accessed April 15, 2013).

FURTHER READING

Kato, Norihiro, "Send in the Clones," in *American Interest*, Vol. 6, No. 4, Spring 2011, pp. 90–97.
    This study gives a comprehensive look at the film, discussing its relationship to Ishiguro's novel and the ethical and political issues raised in both.

Levy, Titus, "Human Rights Storytelling and Trauma Narrative in Kazuo Ishiguro's *Never Let Me Go*," in *Journal of Human Rights*, Vol. 10, No. 1, 2011, pp. 1–16.

Levy writes a complex, graduate-level examination of the ways that Ishiguro's novel fits into the study of human rights, looking at Kathy H. as an example of someone who has survived horrible abuse and lived to tell about it.

Lochner, Liani, "'This Is What We're Supposed to Be Doing, Isn't It?': Scientific Discourse in Kazuo Ishiguro's *Never Let Me Go*," in *Kazuo Ishiguro: New Critical Visions of the Novels*, edited by Sebastian Groes and Barry Lewis, Palgrave Macmillan, 2011, pp. 225–35.

Lochner examines the ethical ramifications raised in the novel and the film, looking at the controversies that Ishiguro leaves unstated.

Maio, Kathi, "Spare Parts with a Soul," in *Fantasy & Science Fiction*, January/February 2011, pp. 172–77.

This is ostensibly a review of the film, but from the perspective of a science fiction–oriented publication. It is very thorough, with ample comparisons to other films with similar themes woven into the discussion.

O'Kane, Paul, "Life and Death," in *Art Monthly*, Vol. 365, 2013, pp. 5–8.

This article, primarily about British artist Paul O'Kane and his 2010 film *Robinson in Ruins*, turns into a discussion of cloning as depicted in art, including an extended examination of the film *Never Let Me Go*.

SUGGESTED SEARCH TERMS

Kazuo Ishiguro AND Mark Romanek

Mark Romanek AND Alex Garland

Kazuo Ishiguro AND Alex Garland

Ishiguro AND clone

Ishiguro AND transplant

cloning AND organ transplant

Carey Mulligan AND British Independent Film Award

cloning AND life expectancy

Ishiguro AND boarding school

Romanek AND movie

Alex Garland AND screenplay

Sons and Lovers

D. H. LAWRENCE

1913

When British novelist D. H. Lawrence first published *Sons and Lovers* in 1913, the novel was praised by many reviewers, though some criticized its frank depiction of the maturation of its protagonist, Paul Morel. Described by some as semiautobiographical, the novel stands among Lawrence's best works, alongside such works as the more risqué *Lady Chatterly's Lover*. In *Sons and Lovers*, Lawrence narrates the childhood and young adulthood of Paul Morel. Paul's intensely close relationship with his mother, Gertrude Morel, and her deep-rooted instinct to protect him and keep him close to her are at the heart of the novel. Their relationship generates the tension Paul experiences with women as he grows older and develops romantic relationships. Paul's bond with his mother and his desire to break free from this bond are what informs the novel's exploration of love, family, and identity. The work also realistically depicts daily life in an English working-class coal-mining community and explores the gender and class issues of this society.

AUTHOR BIOGRAPHY

David Herbert Richards Lawrence was born on September 11, 1885, in Eastwood, Nottinghamshire, England. He was the fourth child of Arthur John and Lydia Lawrence. Lawrence's father worked as a collier (a coal-mining worker). From 1891 through 1898, Lawrence attended Beauvale

D. H. Lawrence *(© Pictorial Press Ltd / Alamy)*

Board School. He won a scholarship to attend Nottingham High School, where he graduated in 1901. He soon secured a position as a clerk at a surgical appliance factory.

In 1902, Lawrence was introduced to the Chambers family and spent time at their farm. During this period he formed a friendship with Jessie Chambers. He worked as an uncertified teacher at the British School in Eastwood from 1905 through 1906. At that time Lawrence began writing poetry and his first novel, which would be published in 1911 as *The White Peacock*. Lawrence studied at University College Nottingham from 1906 through 1908. There he earned a teaching certificate. After graduating, he began teaching elementary-school children at Davidson Road School in Croyden.

In 1910, Lawrence had a brief affair with Jessie Chambers. His mother died in December that year. At that time he also began to write *Paul Morel* the novel that would later become *Sons and Lovers*, which was published in 1913. Not long after, Lawrence became engaged to Louie Burrows, but in 1912 he broke off the engagement. He continued to work on *Paul Morel*. Frieda Weekley and Lawrence met that same year. She soon left her husband and children to be with Lawrence. The two traveled to Italy together, where he wrote the final version of *Sons and Lovers*.

Lawrence, after settling in England with Frieda for a time, continued to write. He published *The Rainbow* in 1915 and *Women in Love* in 1920. In 1919, Lawrence contracted influenza and convalesced in Italy. In the 1920s, the couple traveled to Australia, the United States, and Mexico. In New Mexico, where Lawrence settled for some time, he nearly died of typhoid and pneumonia. In 1928, he finished *Lady Chatterly's Lover*. The controversial novel was published in Italy later that year. In February 1930 Lawrence entered a sanatorium in Vence, France, but he discharged himself on March 1. He died at a rented villa in Vence of tuberculosis and pleurisy on March 2, 1930.

PLOT SUMMARY

Part One

CHAPTER I: THE EARLY MARRIED LIFE OF THE MORELS

The opening chapter of *Sons and Lovers* introduces the Morel family. The narrator describes the way the mining communities of Nottinghamshire and Derbyshire evolved and within this context discusses Mrs. Gertrude Morel and her husband, Walter Morel. Walter works in the coal mines. The Morels have two young children, William and Annie, and Mrs. Morel is pregnant with a third child. Walter and Gertrude struggle as a poor working-class family. Gertrude has a youthful attraction to Walter, an attraction that is in part to blame for her social decline from the daughter of a reasonably well-off family to the wife of an impoverished coal miner. Gertrude's duties as a wife and mother have left her feeling disconnected from the man she once adored. She transfers the affection she once had for her husband to her children. Walter Morel's heavy drinking contributes to his wife's disaffection. When Walter comes home drunk, the two argue bitterly. Walter roughly pushes his wife out of the house and locks the door behind her. After she spends hours out in the cold, Gertrude knocks at the window, attempting to wake Walter from his stupor so that he will let her in. Eventually he lets her back into the house.

CHAPTER II: THE BIRTH OF PAUL AND ANOTHER BATTLE

Gertrude gives birth to the baby, Paul, without incident. Not long after, Gertrude once

MEDIA ADAPTATIONS

- A British production of *Sons and Lovers* was released on film in 1960, featuring Trevor Howard, Dean Stockwell, and Wendy Hiller. The film was directed by Jack Cardiff and was released on DVD by Twentieth Century Fox in 2013. (A previous DVD version of the film was released in a format nonstandard in the United States.)

- A 2003 adaptation of *Sons and Lovers* was directed by Stephen Wittaker and stars Sarah Lancashire, James Murray, and Hugo Speer. It was released on DVD by Koch Vision in 2007.

- An unabridged audio recording of *Sons and Lovers*, read by Paul Slack, was published by Naxos AudioBooks in 2008. It is available as an audio CD and as an MP3 file.

- An unabridged audio edition of *Sons and Lovers*, read by Simon Vance, was published by Tantor Media in 2010. It is available as an audio CD and as an MP3 file.

- An abridged audio recording of *Sons and Lovers*, read by Ramsey Hill, was published by Saland Publishing in 2010. It is available as an MP3 file.

- A full-cast, unabridged audio dramatization of *Sons and Lovers*, featuring Michael Butt and Fiona Clarke, was published by BBC Radio 4 in 2012. It is available as an MP3 file.

- A 2013 audio recording of *Sons and Lovers*, read by Robert Powell, was published by Fantom Films in 2013. It is available as an audio CD.

again finds herself arguing with her drunken husband, who has demanded to be fed. Walter drops a drawer as he clumsily attempts to find a bread knife. When Gertrude chastises him, he flings the drawer in her direction, and it strikes the side of her head. She binds the head wound while the stunned Walter looks on. The next day, as Walter is getting ready to depart to drink with his friends, Gertrude accuses him of stealing money from her purse, which he denies. Walter threatens to leave her but nevertheless returns at the end of the day.

CHAPTER III: THE CASTING OFF OF MOREL—THE TAKING ON OF WILLIAM

Walter Morel becomes ill after an all-night excursion with his friend Jerry Purdy, and though Gertrude nurses him devotedly, her love for him diminishes. Yet the house is more peaceful. Gertrude is more patient with Walter now that her feelings have cooled and become increasingly mild. When Paul is seventeen months old, Arthur, a fourth child, is born. Time passes. William trains to be a clerk and bookkeeper when he reaches the age of sixteen. At nineteen, he finds employment in Nottingham and must take the train to work every morning. As William becomes more independent and with Annie studying to be a teacher, Gertrude becomes increasingly close to Paul. When William turns twenty he is offered a job in London.

CHAPTER IV: THE YOUNG LIFE OF PAUL

The Morels move out of the crowded row house where they spent their early years and into a new place. The children have grown to hate their father. Walter bullies Gertrude as the fourth chapter opens. He continues to drink heavily and rage at the family, inspiring hate and fear in his children. Increasingly, the children and Gertrude leave him out of their discussions and experiences. He becomes a presence that is endured. The Morels periodically manage, however, to share a few meaningful moments together as a family. Arthur is closer to Walter than the other children are. When Paul becomes ill with bronchitis, he spends long hours with his mother, and his love for her deepens. They share a common love of nature, flowers in particular, and discuss at length the flowers Gertrude purchases at the market, or those growing in their garden. William's return visit from London at Christmastime causes great excitement in the household.

CHAPTER V: PAUL LAUNCHES INTO LIFE

Walter is severely injured in a mining accident and is hospitalized. Although Gertrude dutifully tends to him, she finds within herself a "failure to love him." During Walter's stay in the hospital, Gertrude and the children enjoy a reprieve from his unpredictability. The household is peaceful. Paul realizes he must contribute to the family's income now that William is sending less money home and his father is injured. In his letters home William describes his interest in a particular young woman; his courting of her takes much of his income. Paul interviews at a local surgical appliances manufacturer. Meanwhile, William's relationship grows serious, and he announces his plan to bring Louisa Lily Denys Western, or Lily, home to meet his family. Paul begins work, eagerly taking the train on his first morning. While his first day is filled with some awkward moments, overall it is a success. He especially enjoys spending time with the girls who make stockings in the factory. Upon returning home, Paul details the events of the day to his mother, as will become his fashion.

CHAPTER VI: DEATH IN THE FAMILY

As time passes, Walter Morel becomes increasingly detestable. He and Arthur are often in conflict. William and Lily are engaged. They journey home at Christmas. His pet name for her is Gypsy, or just Gyp. Gertrude dislikes her. She acts as if William's family is beneath her. One May day Gertrude and Paul pay a visit to the family of Gertrude's friend Mr. Leivers. Paul meets the children of Mr. and Mrs. Leivers, Miriam and her brothers, Edgar, Geoffrey, Maurice, and the youngest, Hubert; Miriam also has a sister, Agatha. Paul and Miriam share an immediate and mutual interest in one another, but also a spark of tension. William returns home with Lily for another visit. William begins to express his displeasure with Lily to his mother. He is frequently annoyed with her, regarding her as petty and silly. Although Gertrude does not disagree with him, she does scold him for his frequent rudeness toward Lily. After William returns to London, he writes to his mother often. He returns home for a visit by himself and seems to Gertrude to be overworked and unwell. Shortly after William is back in London, Gertrude receives a telegram reporting that he is ill. She rushes to London as quickly as she can. The doctor diagnoses William with pneumonia. He soon dies. Gertrude arranges for his body to be returned home. The family is devastated. Gertrude's intense grief worries Paul, who is now sixteen years old. Soon Paul is diagnosed with pneumonia. Gertrude nurses him devotedly for seven weeks until he begins to improve.

Part Two

CHAPTER VII: LAD-AND-GIRL LOVE

Paul begins to spend a great deal of time at Willey Farm, where Miriam and her family live.

Paul is friends with Miriam's brothers but increasingly drawn to Miriam and her thoughtful, spiritual, and introspective nature. Paul also enjoys being doted upon by Miriam's mother, who treats him as one of her own children. Paul helps out on their farm and is refreshed by the isolation of the location. Miriam and Paul increasingly seek one another's company, yet Paul finds Miriam to be intense and emotional. He sometimes hates her, yet he cannot leave her alone. Mrs. Morel's dislike of Miriam is intense. She feels that Miriam is the type "who will want to suck a man's soul out till he has none of his own left." Paul is aware of his mother's disapproval of Miriam. Despite their emotional connection, Paul and Miriam seem put off by the idea of exploring a physical relationship. Paul is now nineteen. He organizes outings with the two families. Miriam begins to sense Paul's family's disliking of her and avoids seeing him for a time. Yet their relationship continues to grow, and Paul starts to desire Miriam. He resists acting on this impulse, fearing Miriam's response.

CHAPTER VIII: STRIFE IN LOVE

Arthur gets a new job at an electrical plant. Paul and his mother regard him as reckless and irresponsible. After Arthur fails to come home one night, Gertrude receives a letter from him stating that he has enlisted in the army and that it has been a mistake. He asks his mother to try and figure out a way to extricate him from the situation. Gertrude is furious and disappointed that he will be nothing more than "a common soldier." Paul attempts to comfort her. He and his father disagree with her decision to try and bail him out. Gertrude does visit Arthur but is unable to secure his release. Meanwhile, Paul enjoys painting and drawing as he has since his youth. He wins two first-prize awards for his work in a local exhibition. Not long after, Paul meets Miriam in town. Mrs. Clara Dawes, a married woman who has been separated from her husband for some time, accompanies Miriam. Clara's interest in women's rights and her separation from her husband fascinate Paul. Clara was formerly employed at Jordan's, the business that employs Paul. Her husband, Baxter Dawes, still works as a smith in the factory there. While visiting Miriam, Paul questions her intently about Clara. Miriam and Paul are increasingly drawn to each other physically, but both resist. Paul finds her intense spirituality to be off-putting. To Paul it is as if Miriam's perceived need to elevate their relationship to an abstract and cerebral level makes him feel ashamed to desire her physically. While Miriam, now twenty years old, becomes increasingly devoted to her religious beliefs, Paul, now twenty-one, begins to reject them. Paul and his mother discuss her intense dislike of Miriam. Paul tries to avoid Miriam. He receives a promotion and a raise at work. Annie is now working as a teacher and engaged to be married. Gertrude begins to develop health problems, growing tired at tasks she used to perform with ease. Paul grows concerned for her. In an intimate discussion, Gertrude again expresses her dislike of Miriam, as well as what appears to be jealousy. She describes the way her own marriage has been a disappointment to her. As Gertrude despairs that Miriam is taking Paul away from her, Paul insists he does not love Miriam. The discord between Gertrude and Walter intensifies when Walter comes home drunk again.

CHAPTER IX: DEFEAT OF MIRIAM

Paul behaves cruelly toward Miriam, accusing her of having an "abnormal raving" to be loved. He attempts to break things off with her. Still friends with the family though, Paul continues his visits to the farm. Clara is sometimes there. Clara, Miriam, and Paul go on an outing and Paul's attraction to Clara intensifies. Later, when spending time with his mother, Paul observes how weak she is getting and expresses his sadness that she is aging so rapidly. He tells her about Clara. Gertrude points out the difference in their ages. Clara is thirty; Paul is now almost twenty-three. Annie marries Leonard, a friend of the family. Paul sends Miriam a letter attempting to explain why they cannot marry. He asserts that while they have a spiritual connection, they do not have the type of relationship that could lead to a fulfilling marriage.

CHAPTER X: CLARA

Paul continues to submit artwork for exhibition. He also designs prints for fabrics. He sells one of his paintings that had been on display. Once Arthur leaves the army, he marries Beatrice Wyld, a longtime family friend. She gives birth six months after their wedding. Paul meets Mrs. Radford, Clara's mother. He helps Clara secure a position at Jordan's in the department that manufactures hosiery. It is the department Paul oversees. The other girls who work in the department find Clara's superior attitude to be off-putting. As Paul and Clara grow closer, he questions her about her husband and expresses

some sympathy for him. At the same time, Clara rightly guesses that things are not truly over with Paul and Miriam. When she questions him about Miriam, he tells her that Miriam is not interested in anything beyond a spiritual connection. Clara tells him that he is wrong, that Miriam in fact wants Paul in a more physical way.

CHAPTER XI: THE TEST ON MIRIAM

Acting on what Clara has told him, Paul approaches Miriam and broaches the subject of a physical relationship. Feeling as though she must submit if she is to keep him, she promises Paul that she will be with him. They consummate their relationship and lose their virginity to one another in the process. Their relationship progresses and Paul suggests they marry, but Miriam insists that at twenty-four and twenty-three, they are too young. He feels his love for her dwindling and recognizes Miriam's distaste for their physical relationship. He vows to break things off with her. Miriam is angry when he tells her he no longer wishes to marry. Paul becomes bitter when Miriam characterizes their eight-year relationship as a series of battles.

CHAPTER XII: PASSION

Free of Miriam, Paul begins to pursue Clara in earnest. They escape together for an interlude in the woods and begin their affair. Their desire for one another is a relief to Paul, for he knows his feelings are reciprocated. He invites her to meet his mother over tea. The two get along much better than Miriam and Gertrude. Paul takes Clara to see a play and later spends the night at the home Clara shares with her mother.

CHAPTER XIII: BAXTER DAWES

At a bar, Paul is accosted by Clara's husband, who saw them leaving the theater together. Clara warns Paul that Baxter might still come after him for revenge. When Baxter confronts Paul at work, Mr. Jordan, the owner of the business, steps in and asks Baxter to leave the premises. Baxter pushes Mr. Jordan down a flight of steps. Baxter is fired from the factory and brought up on assault charges. Paul testifies to the origin of the conflict between Baxter and himself. As the relationship between Paul and Clara progresses, Paul begins to question his feelings for her. He detects a lack of connection, which she too feels. She begins to see that despite her conflict with Baxter when they were together, she did in fact establish a connection with him, in that he was willing to give her all of himself. By comparison, she feels that Paul holds something back. Not long after, Paul, walking alone on a deserted stretch of road, is accosted and beaten severely by Baxter. Paul is bruised and beaten, has a dislocated shoulder, and later develops bronchitis. Paul is determined to be through with Clara. After he has recovered from the bronchitis, he goes on a four-day holiday. He sends his mother to the nearby town of Sheffield to stay with Annie and Leonard. After his holiday, Paul arrives in Sheffield to find that Gertrude has become very ill. She has a tumor on her side that she has not told anyone about and suffers moments of severe pain. Doctor visits are arranged. Walter comes to visit Gertrude at Annie's house in Sheffield. She remains there for two months without improving. Eventually her children make arrangements to take her home, knowing she likely does not have much time left.

CHAPTER XIV: THE RELEASE

One of Gertrude's doctors, Dr. Ansell, informs Paul that he has a man in his hospital who, like Paul, comes from Nottingham. It is Baxter Dawes. At the doctor's request, Paul visits Baxter, who is ill with typhoid fever. Paul reveals to Baxter that his mother has cancer. Despite their antagonism, the two men begin an awkward conversation. Paul informs Clara of Baxter's whereabouts and his condition. Clara reflects on her treatment of Baxter. Back at home, Paul tends to his dying mother. Months pass, and her condition deteriorates slowly. Paul and Clara continue their affair, but the warmth of their initial love is absent. Clara takes Paul to the seaside for his birthday, where he mostly laments his mother's suffering and how she will not let go of this life. At this point, he wishes she would die. After returning from the trip, Paul visits Baxter in the hospital again. For the first time, the two men directly discuss Clara. Paul explains that she has grown tired of him. Annie has come home to help Paul care for their mother. Gertrude dies. Not long after, Walter goes to Sheffield to stay with Annie. Baxter is now well, and Paul encourages his reconciliation with Clara by explaining that his own affair with Clara is over and that Clara had always "belonged" to Baxter. Baxter has secured lodgings in Sheffield with Paul's help, and Leonard has helped Baxter find a job.

CHAPTER XV: DERELICT

Clara decides to return to Baxter and once again takes up residence with him. Walter moves in with a family friend in the town of Bestwood

while Paul takes lodgings in Nottingham, close to his job. Paul is alone, unsure of what to do next. He considers the possibility of marrying Miriam and seeks her out He invites her to his home. Miriam, who has become a teacher, questions him about his life now, and about the end of his relationship with Clara. With her once again, though, he realizes he would feel "smothered" in a marriage to her. Still he asks if she would marry him. He waits for her to assert herself with him, to claim him rather than to view marriage to him as a sacrifice or a surrender. At the same time, Miriam wishes the same thing, that he would assertively claim her. They part, and Paul considers the way he still feels bound to his mother, even after her death. He vows to turn from his memory of her and toward the future.

CHARACTERS

Dr. Ansell

Dr. Ansell treats Gertrude Morel when she becomes seriously ill. He also informs Paul that Baxter Dawes is in the hospital and encourages Paul to visit him.

Baxter Dawes

Baxter Dawes is Clara Dawes's husband. He is employed at Jordan's Surgical Appliances. After five years of marriage to Baxter, Clara has left him. She tells Paul that Baxter treated her brutally and that he never fully knew or understood her. Baxter learns of Clara and Paul's affair and attacks Paul. Over time, Clara begins to recognize that she treated Baxter unfairly. Once her passion for Paul cools, she returns to Baxter, who accepts her back.

Clara Dawes

Clara Dawes is married to Baxter Dawes, but they are separated. A friend of the Leivers family, Clara meets Paul through Miriam Leivers. She has been separated from her husband for three years when she and Paul begin their affair. She is interested in women's rights. Clara lives with her mother and makes lace for a living. Paul helps her secure a position at Jordan's Surgical Appliances, where she was formerly employed. Although her relationship with Paul is initially passionate, their lust for one another tempers, and she eventually returns to her husband.

Mr. Heaton

Mr. Heaton is a friend to Gertrude Morel. He is a minister. When the children are young he visits her frequently, and she finds some solace in their friendship.

Mr. Jordan

Mr. Jordan owns Jordan's Surgical Appliances. He hires Paul to work as a bookkeeper and eventually promotes him to a managerial position. When Baxter Dawes confronts Paul at work, Mr. Jordan attempts to intervene. Baxter pushes him down a flight of stairs. Mr. Jordan fires Baxter and then presses charges against him for assault.

Agatha Leivers

Agatha Leivers is Miriam's older sister. She is a schoolteacher and has only one significant scene in the novel, when she and Miriam are excitedly anticipating Paul's arrival at their home. Miriam is angered by her sister's eagerness.

Edgar Leivers

Edgar Leivers is Miriam's brother and the eldest of the Leivers children. He is eighteen when Paul first meets him. He becomes a close friend of Paul's. Even when there is tension between Miriam and Paul, Edgar and his friendship repeatedly draw Paul back to Willey Farm.

Geoffrey Leivers

Geoffrey Leivers is Miriam's brother. He is twelve when Paul first meets him. Along with Maurice and Edgar, he becomes good friends with Paul.

Hubert Leivers

Hubert Leivers is Miriam's brother. He is five when Paul first meets him.

Maurice Leivers

Maurice Leivers is one of Miriam's brothers. He is thirteen when Paul first meets him. Along with his brothers Edgar and Geoffrey, he becomes one of Paul's close companions.

Miriam Leivers

Miriam Leivers is one of Mr. and Mrs. Leivers's daughters. She is fourteen when Paul first meets her. Miriam is intensely spiritual, emotional, and intellectual. She is also shy and introverted. Paul is drawn in by these qualities initially, but Miriam perpetually seeks to communicate with him on this higher spiritual and intellectual level, and Paul finds it fatiguing. Miriam seems to desire Paul in her own way, but she also appears to be ashamed of having a physical relationship. She feels betrayed by Paul's ultimate rejection of her. Her negative feelings toward Paul are heightened by the sacrifice of her self that she felt she would be making to be with him.

Mr. Leivers

Mr. Leivers is the gentleman farmer who asks Gertrude Morel to come to his new farm and visit his wife. Paul regards Mr. Leivers as lively and robust and is pleased that Mr. Leivers allows him to help his sons do some of the chores on the farm.

Mrs. Leivers

Mrs. Leivers is the object of Paul and his mother's first visit to Willey Farm. As the two women converse, Paul becomes acquainted with Mrs. Leivers's sons and with her daughter Miriam. As the novel progresses, Paul increasingly appreciates Mrs. Leivers's personal warmth toward him. She is welcoming and doting. However, at times Paul finds Mrs. Leivers and her children to be overly emotional. He notes how rational his own mother seems in contrast.

Leonard

Leonard is a family friend of the Morels. He eventually marries Annie and moves with her to Sheffield. He is instrumental in helping Baxter Dawes secure a job in Sheffield.

Annie Morel

Annie Morel is the only daughter of Gertrude and Walter. She is older than Paul and is a close companion to him when they are young. Annie becomes a teacher and marries Leonard, a longtime family friend.

Arthur Morel

Arthur Morel is the youngest child of Gertrude and Walter. He is reckless, much like his father. On a whim, he enlists in the army with his friend but almost instantly regrets his decision. When he is released from the army, he marries Beatrice Wyld, a friend of the family. Beatrice gives birth to their child not long after the wedding.

Gertrude Morel

Gertrude Morel is the wife of Walter and the mother of William, Annie, Paul, and Arthur. She is a devoted and protective mother. Although she initially loves her husband passionately, her affection dwindles as their children grow and begin to enter the world and Walter turns increasingly to alcohol. Her criticism of him and his drinking sends him into violent rages. He injures her gravely when he throws a drawer at her. Gertrude pours all of her ambitions into her children, feeling as though she can be satisfied with herself if her children succeed in life. Her son William dies of pneumonia. It is a severe blow. Gertrude relies heavily on Paul as a friend and confidante after William's death. She finds the greatest peace when Walter is away and she is home with her children. As they grow older and more independent, she grows bitter and frail. Yet Paul alone remains devoted to her. Gertrude's harsh judgment of Miriam, and later Clara, shapes the course of Paul's relationships. Her resistance in particular to Miriam is fueled by her sense that Miriam will possess all of him and leave nothing to her. Gertrude's characterization of Miriam informs Paul's opinion of Miriam and in some ways prevents him from furthering his relationship with her in a fruitful fashion. Gertrude develops cancer and dies a long, slow death. Paul suspects that she clings to life because she does not wish to leave him. After her death, Gertrude remains an overwhelming presence in Paul's consciousness.

Paul Morel

Paul is the second son of Walter and Gertrude Morel. As a boy he is quiet, sensitive, and easily upset. He clings to his mother and is prone to bouts of inexplicable sadness. His close relationship with his mother persists into young adulthood. He stands with her in opposition to his father on many occasions. As he begins to develop a relationship with Miriam, Paul repeatedly rejects his feelings for her, knowing that his mother intensely dislikes her. He alternates between an almost resentful attraction to Miriam and a hatred of his mother for her disapproval. Every time Gertrude expresses her dissatisfaction with Miriam, Paul draws away from Miriam and feels as though he hates her. They have a deeply spiritual connection, and Paul enjoys their philosophical discussions, until it seems as though that is the only pursuit Miriam wishes to engage in. Eventually, they explore a physical relationship, but Miriam's distaste for it is disappointing to Paul. He makes a break with her and pursues Clara, whom his mother seems to like personally. Yet Clara is older and married. She is therefore unavailable to

Paul as a mate. When Gertrude becomes ill, Paul nurses her in the same way that she took care of him when he was a young boy. Her death causes him great grief. At one time he imagined he would be free to love someone only when his mother died, but her passing does not entirely break the bond she forged during her lifetime. He remains haunted by her presence. As the novel ends, though, Paul vows to walk away from this bond from her. He heads instead "towards the faintly humming, glowing town, quickly." He heads toward the future.

Walter Morel

Walter Morel is the husband of Gertrude. As a young man, he is handsome and carefree and attracts Gertrude with his gregarious nature. He works in the coal mines and earns a meager living for his family. Walter frequently comes home drunk and gradually becomes so unreliable that Gertrude feels her love for him ebbing. When he is ill and injured, she cares for him but grows to resent his neediness and his often-violent nature. A thundering presence in the household when the children are young, and a source of great angst for Gertrude, Walter in many ways fades into the background as the novel progress. He muddles along in the same fashion throughout his life, working and drinking.

William Morel

William Morel is the oldest child of Gertrude and Walter. He is doted on by his mother and shows every sign of being a success. A smart youth, he is hired as a bookkeeper. As a young man, he secures a position in London. There he meets Lily. During their engagement, he becomes ill with pneumonia. His mother is summoned to London. She is present when William dies. Upon William's death, Gertrude transfers all of the hopes she had for her eldest son onto Paul.

Jerry Purdy

Jerry Purdy is a close friend of Walter Morel's. When the two are out all night together, Walter sleeps on the ground in the cold and becomes gravely ill.

Mrs. Radford

Mrs. Radford is Clara Dawes's mother. She is protective of her daughter and of Clara's reputation, but recognizes as well that she is a grown woman who will do as she pleases with Paul.

Louisa Lily Denys Western

Lily is William's girlfriend and later becomes his fiancée. She is shallow and superior. Gertrude does not think very highly of her. Lily moves on to another man not long after William's death.

Beatrice Wyld

Beatrice is a family friend of the Morels'. She eventually marries Arthur and has a child six months after the two are wed.

THEMES

Parent-Child Relationships

Sons and Lovers focuses heavily on the relationship between Paul Morel and his mother, Gertrude. The mutual love most children share with their mothers is the root of the bond that exists between Paul and Gertrude. Yet Lawrence characterizes Gertrude's relationship with Paul as different from the relationships she has with her other children. Unlike his brothers William and Arthur and his sister, Annie, Paul is quiet, sensitive, and introverted. In his childhood, he clings to his mother for comfort and companionship. Gertrude readily provides this throughout Paul's youth, even though his moods sometimes frustrate her. After William's death, Gertrude, who has high hopes for all of her children, turns to Paul seeking not only to help make him as successful as she knew William would have been, but also to attempt to protect him from the potential dangers posed by the other women in his life. Having seen William fall prey to Lily, whom Gertrude believed would spend all of William's money the second he earned it, Gertrude is alert to the ways the women in Paul's life might hurt him.

Gertrude finds in Miriam a particular threat. She repeatedly expresses to Paul her feeling that Miriam will take all of him and leave nothing for her. Throughout Paul's youth, Gertrude responds to his need for her, a need her other children express less intently. Grateful for this response, Paul does not seem to outgrow his need for his mother's love and approval. Having established this relationship dynamic early on, Paul and Gertrude continue to perpetuate a cycle of dependence. Paul needs his mother; Gertrude increasingly needs to be needed. Gertrude's affection for her husband rapidly dwindles over time, largely due to his drunkenness.

Her other children look elsewhere for companionship and grow independent, yet Paul continues to seek out her opinion and approval. When he rejects her advice regarding Miriam, he is tormented knowing how unhappy he has made her. He responds by shunning Miriam and consoles himself with the knowledge that he has pleased his mother. Despite his misery in rejecting Miriam "he was at peace because he still loved his mother best. It was the bitter peace of resignation." Paul's struggle to simultaneously maintain and break the bond with his mother continues throughout the novel and lasts even beyond Gertrude's death.

Love

As Paul Morel comes of age in *Sons and Lovers*, he explores different notions of love. Although his relationships are informed by his mother's opinions and withholding of approval, Paul nevertheless forms two distinct ideas about how a person gives and receives love. At different times, he expresses love for both Miriam and Clara, but the former love causes him torment and the latter leaves him feeling empty. With Miriam, Paul experiences an intense emotional connection. This intrigues him, but he also finds Miriam's apparent desire to elevate all of their interactions to a spiritual level to be exhausting, off-putting, and eventually unfulfilling. As they grow older, he wants more from her and thus seeks a whole relationship, in which the physical and spiritual aspects of love are balanced. She gives this to him but clearly regards the giving of herself to Paul physically as a sacrifice. For Paul this is insufficient and hurtful. When he imagines what marriage should be like, he feels as though he needs someone who can be a companion, a lover, and a friend. With Miriam he achieves only that spiritual connection. He claims that she refuses to just be with him as a companion and that she does not find satisfaction in their physical relationship. Paul observes that Miriam "was prepared for the big things and the deep things, like tragedy. It was the insufficiency of the small day-life she could not trust."

After Paul moves on to Clara, he discovers the physical satisfaction of being with a partner who feels as overcome with desire as he does. Yet this passion cools, and Paul finds that Clara keeps part of herself from him. She accuses him of doing the same thing. Clara tells Paul that she feels "as if I hadn't got you," as in when they are making love. She feels it is not *her* that Paul

TOPICS FOR FURTHER STUDY

- *Sons and Lovers* is similar in some ways to modern "coming-of-age" novels in which an adolescent journeys toward emotional and sexual maturity. One popular contemporary coming-of-age novel, *The Perks of Being a Wallflower*, by Stephen Chbosky, deals with themes similar to those found in *Sons and Lovers*. In each work a sensitive protagonist attempts to develop relationships and find his place in the society outside of his home. Though originally published in 1999, Chbosky's novel was adapted for film in 2012, and the novel was then re-released. Read or watch *The Perks of Being a Wallflower* with a small group. Consider the ways Chbosky's protagonist, Charlie, is similar to the young Paul. In what ways are they different? What types of struggles do the characters face? How effectively are they able to deal with the conflicts in their lives? Are there parallels between other characters in Chbosky's and Lawrence's works? Create a forum that you can use as a means of discussing these issues and others that are of interest to your group.

- Lawrence incorporated some of his own life experiences into his novel *Sons and Lovers*. Like Paul, he was the son of a coal miner. His friend Jessie Chambers is regarded as the inspiration for Miriam Leivers. Research Lawrence's life and write a biographical essay in which you discuss his youth, his major works, and his personal relationships. Be sure to cite your sources. If you like,

present your work in an electronic format, such as a web page.

- The coal mine where Walter Morel works is essentially the center of his life and a prominent feature of the otherwise rural landscape in which Paul and his siblings are reared. Using print and online sources, research the history of the coal industry in England and discuss the way it transformed the countryside in the late nineteenth and early twentieth centuries. Present your findings as a research paper, PowerPoint presentation, or other visual display, such as a time line. Consider the effects of the industry on politics, class issues, and the environment.

- *Sons and Lovers* has been studied as an example of the bildungsroman genre. A sub-genre of the bildungsroman, a *kunstlerroman* traces the maturation of the protagonist but focuses in particular on the character's formation or maturation as an artist. In *Sons and Lovers*, Paul's art plays an important role in his life. Consider the novel as a kunstlerroman and explore the way Lawrence depicts Paul's transformation from a child who likes to sketch to a more mature artist. Reflect on the ways other characters react to his art and how these reactions influence Paul. Write an essay arguing for or against the idea that *Sons and Lovers* may be read as a kunstlerroman. Provide specific details and descriptions of scenes that support your argument.

---

wants, but the act itself. She notes that when she was with her husband, Baxter, she felt "as if I had all of him," and this gave her a feeling of wholeness. She goes on to accuse Paul, "you've never given me yourself." Clara finds that the withholding of their true selves characterizes their relationship, while Miriam had the opposite experience. She felt that she had access to the

true Paul, his spirit or essence, but that was all she wanted. Near the novel's conclusion, Paul considers the matter, observing that Clara "felt that she wanted the man on top, not the real him that was in trouble." In meeting one final time, both Miriam and Paul seem to challenge each other to assert themselves and claim one another, but Miriam recoils from their physical

Mr. and Mrs. Morel's marriage disintegrates: he heads to the pub every day after work, and she gives her attention and affection to her sons. *(© Victor Torres / Shutterstock.com)*

relationship and continues to regard it as an act of sacrifice rather than mutual desire. In the end, Paul can only regard his relationship with her as "another failure."

STYLE

Bildungsroman

The German term *bildungsroman* means "formation novel." It is a novel that explores the psychological and moral journey of a character from youth to adulthood. The term has been used to describe this type of fiction since the late eighteenth century. *Bildungsroman* was applied to numerous novels of the early twentieth century, including Lawrence's *Sons and Lovers* as well as James Joyce's *A Portrait of the Artist as a Young Man* (1916) and Thomas Mann's *The Magic Mountain* (1924).

In *Sons and Lovers*, Lawrence begins Paul Morel's story before he is even born by describing the familial context into which he enters upon his birth. He then demonstrates how the family's experiences, such as his brother William's death, contribute to the development of his identity. For example, after William dies, Gertrude Morel transfers many of the ambitions and desires she had for her eldest son onto Paul. She seeks to protect him in a way that she was unable to protect William. In turn, this creates within Paul an intense focus on his mother's love and approval and establishes a unique bond between the two of them that is both comforting and restrictive for Paul. His efforts to establish romantic relationships with women are negatively affected by his close relationship with his mother. He fights against his devotion to her even after her death. By detailing these struggles, Lawrence narrates Paul's maturation and his eventual embracing of his own life and dreams.

Realism and Modernism

In *Sons and Lovers*, Lawrence wrote using a realist mode, taking care to depict with detailed accuracy the physical and social environment of the novel. In literature, realism may be contrasted with romanticism, a style that in general is characterized by an idealized or sentimentalized view of the world. Realism gained prominence at the close of the nineteenth century and beginning of the twentieth century. Lawrence's work is also at times regarded as modernist. Modernism is seen as a rejection of realist aims, or as the evolution of realism. Rather than focusing on the stark objectivity with which realism is associated, modernist writers experimented with narrative formats and explored the subjective responses of their characters to their world. Modernism is similarly contrasted with realism in its rejection of the realist tendency to write as a means of advancing a social agenda or exploring societal ills.

Sons and Lovers captures the nuances of various types of realism, and also explores the personal and individual emotions and psychological motivations of its characters. Lawrence uses an omniscient third-person narrator to achieve this end. An omniscient third-person narrator relates the events of the story from an all-knowing perspective and exists outside of the narrative construct. This narrator refers to the characters by their names or by such personal pronouns as "he" or "she" (in contrast to a first-person narrator, who typically is part of the story and refers to himself or herself as "I"). The omniscient third-person narrator additionally describes the events of the story from various points of view, allowing the reader into the thoughts of multiple characters. Providing an array of sensory details, Lawrence invites the reader into the home of the Morels and offers an intimate and realistic view of their daily life.

The novel has also been discussed in terms of its social realism. Lawrence's characters are members of the working class who live in a rural area that is becoming increasingly industrialized and in close proximity to a bustling manufacturing town. Lawrence does not simply focus on the daily lives of the individual characters who populate his novel, but offers the reader a view of a particular social class and their collective struggle toward the comforts of middle-class life. Lawrence also writes in a psychologically realistic mode, depicting the interior life and internal struggles Paul undergoes. Paul's desire for and resisting of Miriam become as much of a focus in the novel as his intense love for his mother and his struggle against her emotionally charged power over him. Lawrence details Paul's torment in particular, but his omniscient third-person narration allows the reader access to the minds of Gertrude and Miriam as well, providing glimpses into their own emotional battles.

HISTORICAL CONTEXT

Social Class in Prewar England

Lawrence uses *Sons and Lovers* to some extent as a means of exploring his society, with its class struggles and with the pervasive tension generated in rural communities by the expansion of industries such as coal mining. In *The Social Impact of the Novel: A Reference Guide*, Claudia D. Johnson observes that *Sons and Lovers* is "one of the most realistic pictures of working-class life in England before World War I." Johnson goes on to note that in depicting the mining community Lawrence "provided one of the most vivid pictures of the disruption of rural society by the continuing growth of industry." In Lawrence's novel, Paul and his mother disagree about class issues. Mrs. Morel accuses Paul of being "snobbish about class." He seems to reject the middle class and their focus on "ideas" in contrast to his ideas about the "common people," who are interested in "life itself, warmth." Yet Mrs. Morel wants Paul "to climb into the middle classes, a thing not very difficult, she knew."

In *The Remaking of the British Working Class, 1840–1940*, Mike Savage and Andrew Miles discuss the relationships between the working and middle classes in England. Despite Mrs. Morel's belief that climbing the social ranks would be an easy thing for Paul, Savage and Miles observe that members of the middle class seemed to strive to distance themselves from the working class, moving out of areas densely populated by the working class. The authors note further that the middle class itself had its own divisions, the lower and the elite middle class. Savage and Miles specify that "the elite middle classes moved out of the city," leaving the urban areas to the working-class people. Likewise, the lower middle class, those whom Savage and Miles identify as "clerks and small business people," also moved out of the city and into the suburbs. As a coal miner, Walter Morel is quite clearly a member of the working class, yet by the definition Savage and Miles posit, Paul seems to have pushed his way at least into the lower middle class. In that the working classes

COMPARE & CONTRAST

- **1913:** British society in rural and urban areas is marked by divisions between social classes. Working-class individuals seek to improve their status by expanding their role in their communities and bettering their working conditions and wages, while middle-class individuals often attempt to distance themselves from their working-class counterparts by moving away from urban areas and by decreasing their participation in the social institutions in which they used to play a more prominent role.

  Today: Although some British politicians have declared that class issues are no longer prevalent in British society, others argue that British society remains divided along class lines and that the possibility for upward mobility has diminished following an increase in class mobility after World War II. Income inequality is cited as a major contributing factor in the current lack of upward social mobility.

- **1913:** Members of the women's movement in Britain struggle to improve their standing in society. They stage demonstrations and protests in order to gain support for the suffragist cause and to draw attention to the need for reform in divorce legislation.

  Today: Women's rights advocates in Britain are focused on such issues as reproductive rights, marriage equality, and employment equality.

- **1913:** Trends in British fiction include the still-pervasive realism that has characterized the literature of recent decades, a resurgence of bildungsroman novels, and an evolution toward more experimental modernist fiction.

  Today: Realist fiction and experimental fiction are both popular literary modes in Britain. Dystopian literature has been particularly prevalent in recent years. Many critically acclaimed new British writers come from diverse backgrounds and are foreign-born British citizens or the children of immigrants, and so bring to modern British literature a broad worldview.

expanded, evolved, and took over some of the roles of the middle class with their communities, it could be said that the boundaries between classes were in some ways blurred. In religious institutions, the working class became increasingly active as "middle-class involvement in urban religious provision declined." Savage and Miles further describe the broadening of the working class and its institutions, tracing the way "many towns and cities" transitioned "from middle-class to working-class environments" in the years leading up to World War I.

The Women's Movement in Prewar England

In *Sons and Lovers*, Clara Dawes has left her husband, and she is involved in the women's movement. During the first decade of the twentieth century, the women's movement in England was concerned with issues such as women's suffrage (the right to vote) and divorce reform. In 1909, the British government appointed a Royal Commission on Divorce due to pressure from Great Britain's High Court and its Probate, Admiralty, and Divorce Division, the president of which insisted on reform due to the inconsistencies and inequalities prevalent in divorce law at the time.

As Lawrence Stone explains in *Road to Divorce: England 1530–1987*, the Royal Commission on Divorce implemented an exhaustive investigation of divorce law and in 1912 offered two reports on the subject, a Majority Report and a dissenting Minority Report. The three Minority Report commissioners objected to "any extension of the causes for divorce beyond female adultery" and cited a religious justification for this contention. The Minority Report commissioners also opposed proposals designed to make

Paul takes long walks with Miriam, a farm girl he meets at church. (© Kevin Eaves | Shutterstock.com)

divorce easier. The Majority Report commissioners, on the other hand, advocated equality of access to divorce for all citizens—rich, poor, men, and women. Yet with the onset of World War I in 1914, the government did not make any changes to divorce law until after the conclusion of the war in 1918. Similarly, the women's suffrage movement refrained from intensive activity until the end of the war. In 1918 women over the age of thirty were granted the right to vote with the passage of the Representation of the People Act. It was not until 1928 that all women aged twenty-one and over were given the right to vote. Prior to World War I, women's rights organizations sought to draw attention to the suffragist cause through demonstrations, protests, and marches. Robert Colls describes the way women were viewed in society prior to the success of the suffragist movement, stating, "Before suffrage, the identity of women rested on institutions entirely defined by masculine authority—the household, the business, the church, and especially the state."

CRITICAL OVERVIEW

When *Sons and Lovers* was published in 1913, it received many favorable reviews. In *D. H. Lawrence: "Sons and Lovers,"* Andrew Harrison states that "contemporary reviews of the novel were rather celebratory." R. P. Draper, in *D. H. Lawrence: The Critical Heritage*, similarly observes that the tone of these reviews was "laudatory" but comments further that the details of the reviews were "unfavorable." Draper states that many critics objected to the book's erotic nature, while Harrison delineates other objections, including the book's lack of a "coherent plot." Harrison also states that some contemporary critics objected to Lawrence's "putting lyrical words and sentiments into the mouths of working people."

In summarizing later critical responses to the novel, Harrison comments on attempts to categorize the work, noting that it was considered by some as exemplifying the realism associated with fiction of the Edwardian or even Victorian age. At the same time, Harrison notes, it was regarded as a "modernist Bildungsroman."

Other scholars have examined the issues of psychology, class, and gender in *Sons and Lovers*. In *Writing against the Family: Gender in Lawrence and Joyce*, Cynthia Lewiecki-Wilson maintains that according to his correspondence about the novel, Lawrence regarded *Sons and Lovers* "both as a cultural critique of the social relations that shape mental and sexual life and as an uncovering of the hidden, mythic relations that construct the gendered subject." Lewiecki-Wilson argues that Lawrence uses "omniscient point of view and subjectivity" in order to create a "textual voice that authorizes each character's experiences as equally legitimate." The critic further explores the relationship between gender and class issues, claiming that for Gertrude, as a "female subject under patriarchy, the sexual struggle and the sexual relation to power are primary and displace class struggle and class relations."

CRITICISM

Catherine Dominic

Dominic is a novelist and a freelance writer and editor. In the following essay, she examines the intensely close relationship between Paul Morel and his mother and its effects on his relationships

WHAT DO I READ NEXT?

- Lawrence's 1928 novel *Lady Chatterly's Lover*, once considered shockingly explicit, is regarded as rather tame by today's standards. The work is highly acclaimed for its lyrical tone and masterfully developed characters.

- Lawrence was a prolific writer of short fiction, but these short stories have received less attention than his novels. A two-volume collection, *The Complete Short Stories of D. H. Lawrence*, was published in 1961.

- An accomplished poet as well as fictionist, Lawrence wrote poetry concerned with depictions of daily life as well as with romantic themes. A modern edition of his poetry was published as *The Complete Poems of D. H. Lawrence* in 1994.

- W. Somerset Maugham was a contemporary of Lawrence's. His 1915 novel *Of Human Bondage* has been regarded as bildungsroman or kunstlerroman and is considered Maugham's masterpiece. The work, considered to be semiautobiographical, traces the maturation of a young artist, Philip Carey.

- *Waiting for Appa*, a 2009 young-adult novel by Korean-born author Jennifer Kim, explores the adolescence of a young Korean girl whose father emigrates to the United States. Her father's subsequent death shapes the protagonist's life and relationships for years to come.

- Martin J. Wiener's 1981 volume *English Culture and the Decline of the Industrial Spirit, 1850–1980* examines the industrialization of England and its impact on class consciousness, class conflict, and other social issues.

---

with women, arguing that Gertrude was not solely to blame for Paul's failed relationships in Sons and Lovers.

The relationship between Paul Morel and his mother Gertrude is at the heart of D. H. Lawrence's

Sons and Lovers and the subject of much critical debate. Not long after the publication of the novel, critics began to regard the relationship in Freudian psychoanalytic terms, seeing in Paul's attachment to his mother evidence of what Freud termed an Oedipal complex. Freud believed that in general, a young boy regards his mother as an object of desire and subconsciously wishes to supplant his father as his mother's lover. The son suppresses his desire, and it becomes a source of anxiety. (The origin of the term Freud assigned to this phenomenon comes from a story written by Sophocles where the protagonist, Oedipus, unknowingly murders his father and marries his mother.) As R. P. Draper explains in *D. H. Lawrence: The Critical Heritage*, Lawrence's novel was reviewed by psychologist Alfred Kuttner in 1915. Kuttner's review appeared in an expanded form in 1916. Lawrence responded to this version of Kuttner's psychoanalytic reading and largely rejected Kuttner's views. Yet Draper comments on the similarities between Kuttner's analysis and Lawrence's own interpretation of the novel's theme. Draper states, "Lawrence's account stresses the mother's devotion to her sons, William and Paul, as compensation for the lack of satisfaction in her marriage." Freudian readings of the work gradually gave way to fresh evaluations of the novel. Yet there remains within the text an undeniably tense aspect to Paul's relationship with his mother. Lawrence implies—in both the title of the novel and in his response to Freudian readings—that the sons in the novel are chosen by their mother as lovers. It is important to note the subtleties of these relationships. William and Paul both are primary objects of their mother's love, attention, and hopes for the future. They are confused in their romantic relationships with women and seek out their mother's advice. Paul, especially after William's death, becomes his mother's friend. She is his confidante. He relies on her to nurture him, and in turn she thrives on Paul's dependency on her. The relationship between Paul and his mother is characterized by intensity, mutual dependency, and a type of passion not imbued with the sexual desire that the term "lover" suggests. However, the bond Paul feels for his mother does sculpt the contours of his desire for other women.

The relationship between Paul and his mother is unique. It is different from the relationships she shares with her other children. It is intense and flawed. They seek in each other the companionship they should be able to find with a romantic partner, yet their relationship is not shaded with romantic or sexual overtones. Their

> GERTRUDE'S NEED TO CONTINUE TO PROTECT HER SON INTENSIFIES AS HE FACES THE DANGERS OF ADULT RELATIONSHIPS. SHE HAS MOMENTS WHEN SHE REALIZES SHE MUST ALLOW PAUL HIS FREEDOM, BUT SHE CANNOT BEAR TO SEVER THE RELATIONSHIP INTO WHICH SHE HAS PUT THE MOST EFFORT."

relationship is characterized by loss and by love. The failure of Paul's romantic relationships results from the fact that the women in his life cannot, or will not, fully devote themselves to the relationship, and from Paul's response to this withholding. Paul is no more or less culpable than any of the women in his life. Vesting the blame for Paul's romantic failures in Gertrude, as many critics have done, is an unfair analysis of their relationship.

In Part One of the novel, Lawrence outlines the ways in which Paul is different from his siblings. He delineates the way Paul's mother's treatment of him shifts to accommodate his singular nature. Paul's sensitivity inspires in Gertrude an intense protectiveness. Paul, feeling cared for and understood, is grateful, loving, and loyal in return. In the second part of the novel, this bond blossoms into a friendship. When Paul begins to mature sexually, their companionship is tested. He battles with the desire to remain devoted to his mother and the need to be free of her to pursue his own romantic interests. Gertrude's need to continue to protect her son intensifies as he faces the dangers of adult relationships. She has moments when she realizes she must allow Paul his freedom, but she cannot bear to sever the relationship into which she has put the most effort.

From early childhood, Paul is singled out by his mother as different from her other children. He clings to her more. He is intensely sensitive. As a child, Paul "trotted after his mother like her shadow." When he was as young as three or four, he would cry for no reason and could not be consoled: "These fits were not often, but they caused a shadow in Mrs. Morel's heart, and her treatment of Paul was different from that of the other children." Mrs. Morel's feeling of helplessness as she watches her child struggle bonds her to him in a special way. As Paul grows older, and has witnessed his father bullying his mother, he, like his siblings, feels opposed to his father. Yet Paul is "particularly" against Walter. Sometimes he prays that he will stop drinking. Other times he wishes him dead.

Paul's health, too, separates him from his siblings. William, Annie, and Arthur are all strong, while Paul frequently suffers from bronchitis. Gertrude's anxiety regarding Paul's ability to survive fuels her love for him. Paul is guiltily aware of this. He watches his mother and despairs that "she had never had her life's fulfillment: and his own incapability to make up to her hurt him with a sense of impotence, yet made him patiently dogged inside."

As Paul grows older and begins to earn his own wages at Jordan's Surgical Appliances, he proudly gives his mother all he earns, unlike William, who spends his wages on his girlfriend, and unlike Walter, who spends his wages on alcohol. After Paul and his mother make their first visit to the Leivers family on Willey Farm, Paul is instinctively drawn to Miriam Leivers. Even at the onset of Paul's friendship with Miriam, though, he finds Miriam's nature to be irritating. He contrasts her character with that of his mother. Miriam's "intensity, which would leave no emotion on a normal plane, irritated the youth into a frenzy." He is startled by how exposed Miriam seems. Paul "was thankful in his heart and soul that he had his mother, so sane and wholesome." Yet he continues to spend time with Miriam. Gertrude intensely dislikes Miriam. She has the sense that Miriam "is one of those who will want to suck a man's soul out till he has none of his own left." She worries that Paul will "let himself be absorbed" and that Miriam "will never let him become a man." After Paul returns home late one night after visiting Miriam, Gertrude chastises him. Mrs. Morel insists that Paul and Miriam are too young to be courting one another. Paul retorts that they are not courting. The attraction between Paul and Miriam deepens. Paul tells himself that he does not act on his desire to kiss Miriam because she is too spiritual. He supposes that "she could scarcely stand the shock of physical love," and so he suppresses his desires.

As Paul navigates his complex relationship with Miriam, he endures the angst any young man might. However, his mother sees him "growing irritable, priggish, and melancholic. For this she put the blame on Miriam." Gertrude's feelings toward Miriam are harsh, but they are motivated by the same love that has defined her relationship with Paul his entire life. She seeks to protect him from someone with the power to hurt him, as Miriam, or any woman, might. Paul, aware of his mother's disapproval, is keenly attuned to the fact that Miriam makes him uncomfortable: "Paul hated her because, somehow, she spoilt his ease and naturalness." What Paul and his mother overlook is the commonplace nature of these feelings. Paul senses the way his friendship with Miriam is altered by a budding sexual desire for her. Miriam, fearful of this change in Paul and unready to explore these feelings herself, creates tension through her guarded reaction to Paul. Gertrude, like any mother of a young man, seeks to protect her son from a broken heart, or from a young woman who seems to be transforming her son from the child she once knew into a vague somebody. So much weight is placed upon these very human feelings by all three characters that their intersecting relationships become overly fraught with negativity.

Paul draws inspiration from Miriam's intensity, despite the fact that he is often put off by it. He transfers the passion she sparks in him to his artwork: "She brought forth to him his imaginations." While neither one of them understands this, "this was life for her and for him." Yet Paul finds Miriam's love "too good for him." He feels "inadequate." He continues to be drawn to her and to simultaneously pull away. Sensing the intensity of Paul's feelings for Miriam, Gertrude expresses defeat, telling Paul, "You only want me to wait on you—the rest is for Miriam." Given the distance Annie and Arthur have put between themselves and her by this point in their young-adult lives, and given that Gertrude long ago ceased loving her husband, she fears the impending loss of Paul. As Paul draws closer to Miriam, Gertrude begins to lose her friend, not just the little boy who needed her and whom she protected. Now that Paul has grown into a young man who takes care of her, he fills the roles of both companion and provider that Walter should have been fulfilling. Gertrude's fear of losing Paul is real and deep. Paul is stung by her words: "Instinctively he realized that he was life to her. And, after all, she was the chief thing to him, the only supreme thing."

A scene between Paul and his mother occurs that embodies the intensity of their bond for one another. Paul denies that he is in love with Miriam. His mother clings to him and weeps, lamenting that Miriam will leave nothing left for her. Haltingly, she states, "I've never had a husband—not really." She kisses her son. It is "a long, fervent kiss." Just before Gertrude kisses Paul, he asserts that he does not love Miriam and bows his head, "hiding his eyes on her shoulder in misery." Yet the most Gertrude could do with Paul's head on her shoulder is fervently kiss the top of her son's head. Despite the intensity of the underlying passion, Gertrude's actions remain maternal. Gertrude goes on to speak to Paul "in a voice trembling with passionate love." Paul strokes her face without being fully aware that he is doing so. Then Gertrude composes herself and states, "Perhaps I'm selfish. If you want her, take her, my boy." Paul, confused, kisses her. He trembles.

Taken out of context, the passionate action between Paul and his mother plays out like a scene between romantic lovers. Their passion seems charged with sexual desire. When regarded within the context of an intense parent-child relationship, the scene, while tense, is perhaps less disturbing. Gertrude confronts the prospect of Paul's continued pursuit of Miriam with a deep sense of loss. She lost a companion in her husband long ago when he chose alcohol over her love. She then lost her beloved eldest son, William. Sensing Paul is to be consumed by his relationship with Miriam, Gertrude is pushed beyond reason and acts out of pure emotion. Compelled by grief and the prospect of old age and loneliness, Gertrude fails to restrain herself and throws herself at her son: "As he stooped to kiss his mother, she threw her arms around his neck, hid her face on his shoulder." The fervency, trembling, and emotion seem inspired by the passion and wildness of panic rather than by any sort of deviant romantic tendencies. Gertrude clutches at her son, at the only close relationship left in her life. The potential loss of Paul fills her with terror. Compelled by the depth of his love for his mother, Paul responds to his mother's pleas. He, too, fears the loss of their bond, and is likely frightened by the intensity of her emotions. His trembling suggests his own anxiety over the pain he fears he is causing her.

Despite this exchange, Paul still pursues Miriam, eventually consummating his relationship

Paul returns to his mother, but after her death realizes that he is all alone. *(© clearimages | Shutterstock.com)*

with her. He then discovers in Clara a new partner, and a new type of love, one less fraught with the spirituality that characterizes his ultimately doomed relationship with Miriam. Gertrude seems to prefer Clara to Miriam, but senses that Clara will not be able to hold Paul. When Gertrude and Paul discuss his prospects for the future, he asserts that being happy is not important to him. This shatters Gertrude, who insists that he should *try* to find happiness. Lawrence states, "her passion of grief over him broke out." Here Lawrence offers the reader an indication of what motivates Gertrude's "passion." It is grief, it is fear for Paul that compels her to act as she does.

Although Gertrude is typically blamed for Paul's inability to cultivate a fruitful romantic relationship, the trouble in his relationship with Clara stems from the fact that Clara is married. Through Paul's own efforts to comprehend Clara and her relationship with her husband, Baxter, Clara begins to sense she has treated Baxter unfairly. This plays as big a role in the ultimate demise of the relationship as Paul's apparent inability to give his whole self to another woman. Paul reflects that "he could not be free to go forward with his own life, really

love another woman," because of his love for his mother.

Trapped by the bond between himself and his mother, Paul eventually concedes to her, "I shall never meet the right woman while you live." Paul is right. He does not meet the right woman, but all of the blame cannot be placed upon Gertrude. When Paul was small and needy, when he clung to her, she provided him with comfort and security. He repaid her with grateful devotion, which she grew to need, particularly so in the absence, or failure, of other relationships. Paul's attempt to love Miriam and then Clara tests their mutual dependence, but the failure of his relationships with these women to some extent rests with the women themselves. Miriam's elevated, spiritual nature keeps her from enjoying a physical relationship. She repeatedly suppresses her physical desire for him and consequently inspires in Paul a sense of shame for his desire. For her part, Clara cannot entirely give herself to Paul either. Their withholding is mutual.

After Gertrude's death, Paul's interactions with Miriam and Clara confirm that his efforts to love have been in vain. He considers that he is still yoked to his mother, but vows to symbolically and literally move forward, away from his rural home and toward the glittering city. His grief over the loss of those relationships, and of his mother, is proportionate to the depth of feeling Paul has always possessed. Similarly, Gertrude's love for her son rises up in response to the depth of the losses she suffers in her life. The loving relationship between Gertrude and Paul skews the losses of Miriam and Clara. Likewise, the ways Miriam and Clara relate to Paul are shaped by their own personalities, families, and experiences. Gertrude's sense of loss does not make her a failed mother. Paul's sensitive, thoughtful, deep nature does not make him a failed son or lover.

Source: Catherine Dominic, Critical Essay on *Sons and Lovers*, in *Novels for Students*, Gale, Cengage Learning, 2014.

MacDonald Daly

In the following excerpt, Daly examines issues of class among the characters in Sons and Lovers.

... It is virtually impossible for a reader (although not for the characters) to consider sexuality separately from class in the novel. Not surprisingly, however, the unity of the two is most evidently stressed at the beginning, where it provides an origin for everything that follows. The key circumstances here are those surrounding the marriage of Gertrude Coppard and Walter Morel in Chapter I. She is twenty-three and he is twenty-seven. Walter is a miner, 'full of colour and animation,' his grandparents a French refugee and an English barmaid; Gertrude hails from a 'good old burgher family' that has gone bankrupt. Each sees the other, across this class division, as an embodiment of the exotic, as the possessor of desired qualities which he or she does not have: 'He came and bowed above her. A warmth radiated through her as if she had drunk wine'; 'she was to the miner that thing of mystery and fascination, a lady.' Their initial meeting is a seeming testament to the ability of erotic power to overthrow class barriers: Gertrude and Walter liaising on the classless ground of their mutual sexual attraction. But Lawrence's account of the meeting is consistent with the way he deals with the marriage throughout the novel. It is essentially told from Gertrude's, not Walter's, point of view, and it is in Gertrude's perceptions of

Walter that the notion of a 'classless' sexuality is exploded. Watching him, Gertrude registers Walter as 'well-set-up, erect and very smart,' a description which is primarily a sexualised reference to his physical bearing. But 'well-set-up' carries other colloquial insinuations: Walter gives the impression of being a man who has good material prospects. If he affects her like intoxicating liquor, this does not prevent her noticing (nor he from showily displaying) that he 'wore the blue ribbon of the teetotaller': an outward sign of a sober mind and, in all likelihood, equally sober finances. A year later, on Gertrude's mistaken assumptions about Walter's misleading public image, they openly pronounce their sexual and economic compatibility in a sexual and economic contract: marriage.

It is from the failure of this marriage that the enormous conflict and heartache at the centre of *Sons and Lovers* unspool. The failure is not, primarily, sexual: by all accounts there is a great deal of passion early in the marriage. 'There were many, many stages in the ebbing of her love for him,' we are told, 'but it was always ebbing.' What ruins it decisively is Walter Morel's inability to deliver to Gertrude the bourgeois material standards she has been led to expect their marriage to secure. A fundamental feature of this lifestyle is the ownership of property. Gertrude's first disappointment is the discovery that Morel, far from owning two houses as he claimed, in fact pays rent to his mother for the one in which they are living. A generous disposable income is another mark of bourgeois living, but the Morels are, in their early married life, far from having one. They are in arrears with their furniture and Morel's habitual drinking drains whatever small sums are left over. His anti-authoritarian attitude at work irritates Mrs Morel because, in her view, it ensures that he is allotted difficult and unprofitable seams of coal to mine. It should be said that this does not seem always to remain the case, and there is some evidence that telling the story largely from Mrs Morel's point of view leads to an exaggeration of Morel's irresponsibility: for all his drinking Morel is a steady worker, and in the course of the novel the family becomes gradually more prosperous. But Mrs Morel's bitterness starts to entrench itself in the initial stages of her coming to understand what her husband is really like: 'At last Mrs Morel despised her husband. She turned to the child, she turned

> THIS SHUTTLING TO AND FRO IN THE
> NARRATIVE POINT OF VIEW GOES ON THROUGHOUT
> *SONS AND LOVERS*, AND SUCH A CONSTANT SHIFTING
> ARGUES AGAINST THE IMPRESSION THAT LAWRENCE
> IS CRUDELY TAKING SIDES."

from the father . . . There began a battle between the husband and wife, a fearful, bloody battle that ended only with the death of one. She fought to make him undertake his own responsibilities, to make him fulfil his obligations.'

This is the first of many instances in which it is made clear that one of Mrs Morel's most frequently chosen weapons is a certain language. The bourgeois vocabulary of contract ('responsibilities,' 'obligations') is prevalent in the discourse which attaches to her to the extent that it seems so natural that we are often in danger of failing to notice it. The effect of this language is to make her unhappiness seem a result exclusively of Walter Morel's financial libertinism rather than the wasting and dehumanising long-term pressure of poverty in the working-class community into which she is seen as having 'descended,' and of which Walter Morel is himself a victim. Morel's personal behaviour—mainly his frequent withholding of money for household necessities so that he can buy drink—is depicted as the sole source of economic deprivation within the family. This deprivation causes severe disaffection, including sexual disaffection, between husband and wife. Exchange of intimacy and exchange of cash become fairly closely related in the Morel household. It is no surprise that the young Paul hands over his entire wage packet to his mother once he starts working.

One of the shortcomings of the novel is its failure to deal adequately with the consequences of the discovery that Walter Morel is much poorer than he originally makes out, and to place readers in a position where they might understand both his motivation for deceit and the damaging result of exploding his personal mythology. Mrs Morel simply sees her husband as selfish, perhaps malicious: it is certainly with this view that she indoctrinates her children. More importantly, there is no point in the novel where we are invited to see things in a larger perspective than the rather confined view of Mrs Morel and the children. In particular, Morel's sub-literacy and inarticulacy conveniently prevent his own voice from being heard. In this respect, the novel puts readers in the curious position of being asked to ignore the tragedy of Walter Morel as a disadvantaged and impoverished worker (if one is to adopt the terms of Lawrence's précis, this was the tragedy of millions, rather than thousands, of people in the England of his time) in favour of the tragedy of Paul's and other young men's Oedipus complexes.

However, for all its ambiguous and evasive dealings with the emotional and material realities of working-class life, *Sons and Lovers* offers a fascinatingly 'social' reading of sexuality. Nowhere is this more profound than in the microcosmic class struggle between man and wife, which leads to an even greater polarisation than that which engendered it. We learn that it 'drove [Morel] out of his mind' and 'caused him, knowingly or unknowingly, grossly to offend her where he would not have done':

> The pity was, she was too much his opposite. She could not be content with the little he might be, she would have him the much that he ought to be. So, in seeking to make him nobler than he could be, she destroyed him. She injured and hurt and scarred herself, but she lost none of her worth. She also had the children.

For all that later commentators have found the narrator's loyalties unduly skewed in Mrs Morel's favour, there is extraordinary narrational insight into the nature of class deadlock in these early pages. Linguistically, the paragraph quoted above reveals a complex manoeuvring of perspective. For instance, 'the little he might be' can hardly be the phrase Walter Morel would use to describe his own potential: it is the narrator's, and it tells us a great deal about the narrator's own far from charitable view of the miner. With 'the much that he ought to be' and 'nobler' we pass to the vocabulary of Mrs Morel's own moral judgements. But then the narrator resumes control to describe the effects of her psychologically terroristic onslaught on Morel.

This shuttling to and fro in the narrative point of view goes on throughout *Sons and Lovers*, and such a constant shifting argues against the impression that Lawrence is crudely taking sides. From the paragraph quoted we learn that the narrator is caught between Walter and Gertrude Morel, is able to differentiate his own perceptions of conflict from theirs, but regularly *tends* towards sympathy with the woman. In other words, the narrator is very much in the position of one of the Morels' children, and indeed the case has often been made that, with the exception of the earliest scenes, *Sons and Lovers* reads like a first-person narrative of Paul Morel rewritten in the third person. But one of the main points of the novel is to demonstrate the great dangers of the kind of relationship which Paul and his mother have, and this in part explains the curious narrative vacillation. To live independently, in sexual and emotional and even economic terms, Paul must progressively grow apart from his mother in a way that Mrs Morel, because of her own described transference of affections, constantly inhibits. It is thus hardly surprising that the narrator of the novel is self-divided between obvious loyalty to Mrs Morel and a critical attitude towards her. In that sense the narrative formally takes us through the very process it is describing. In its final form it does not achieve anything like omniscience or objectivity; but the narrator does attain a sufficient degree of separation and detachment from the relationships he describes to distinguish him from the hero.

Mrs Morel takes possession of her sons by directing the course of their futures: "'He is *not* going in the pit,'" she says authoritatively of William, her first son. William's rise to the lower middle class, aged twenty, is marred by the equation of financial reward with emotional attachment ("'And I can give you twenty pounds a year, Mater—we s'll all be rolling in money'"), a confusion which Mrs Morel, too late, recognises keenly ('It never occurred to him that she might be more hurt at his going away, than glad of his success'). This should be a moment of great triumph for Mrs Morel, since William is crossing a class boundary; but the price of doing so, she realises, is painful separation from her. The beginning of his 'upward' journey into the bourgeoisie is also the beginning of a 'downward' spiral, a moral and physical decline. In London, he squanders his extra money on the consumerist luxuries of the bourgeois world (for his girlfriend, 'Gyp,' more than himself) instead of sending it home as promised. It is implied that, in his final illness, geographical distance is the fatal factor: in the time taken for Mrs Morel

> THUS, ALTHOUGH LAWRENCE AT TIMES CRITICIZES GERTRUDE'S TEMPERAMENT AND INNER NATURE—ALTHOUGH HE SHOWS US THAT HER PRIDE AND INTEGRITY CAUSE A GREAT DEAL OF SUFFERING—HE ALSO UNDERSTANDS THAT THIS YOUNG WOMAN HAS NOT CHOSEN HER NATURE."

to reach him, 'No one had been with him.' William's death is a clear sign of the contradictory consequences of the class mobility Mrs Morel continues to advocate. It brings greater material security, but with it come the new dangers of isolation and distance: individualised self-sufficiency can easily become a form of exposure....

Source: MacDonald Daly, "Relationship and Class in *Sons and Lovers*," in *D. H. Lawrence's "Sons and Lovers": A Casebook*, edited by John Worthen and Andrew Harrison, Oxford University Press, 2005, pp. 81–86.

Ross C. Murfin

In the following excerpt, Murfin examines Mrs. Morel's strengths and weaknesses.

The last two critics discussed in the previous chapter differ somewhat in ideology and emphasis. The views of Peter Scheckner, unlike those of Judith Ruderman, are neither feminist nor psychological in their orientation, and whereas Ruderman focuses on women in Lawrence's fiction, Scheckner is interested in the communal life of the men. Both critics, though, see *Sons and Lovers* in terms of conflict—specifically, male-female conflict—and both are interested in the social bases of conflict. Scheckner sees women pitted, like the male managers they can never be, against their own working-class husbands, while Ruderman analyzes the "deadly smothering of women" by a male-dominated society.

My contention is that *Sons and Lovers* is characterized by a conflict between male and female that goes on within several of the novel's characters as well as among almost all of them. External conflicts between individuals often involve, in a triangle, a pair of opposed characters plus a third, radically self-divided one. These tense, triangular relationships not only give impetus to the plot but also provide a formal pattern or structure that supports everything from the novel's symbolic colors and images to its most profound ideas.

The seminal opposition in the novel is, of course, the one that pits Gertrude Morel against her husband, for it is that opposition that is responsible for Paul Morel's deep and destructive self-division. Consideration of the parental opposition and conflict begins, moreover, with the study of Gertrude Morel, for if she is the novel's primary example of what Ruderman calls "the deadly smothering of women," she is also, in many ways, the most important character in the book. (This is true even though her son Paul is not only the protagonist of the novel but also a fictional version of the young D. H. Lawrence.) No sooner has Lawrence described the setting of the novel—the coal-mining fields of Nottinghamshire that lie "on the edge of Sherwood Forest"—than he begins to characterize the mother of the "sons" referred to in his novel's title.

We can see from Lawrence's first description of Gertrude that she is a proud and independent-minded woman, one who is, not surprisingly, lonely and dissatisfied with her life in the dirty, male-dominated world of a coal-mining village. When we meet her for the first time, she is at her new home in "the Bottoms," which she enjoys only because it is the "end house" on a long row of identical miners' dwellings. "[H]aving an end house," Lawrence tells us, "she enjoyed a kind of aristocracy among the other women of the 'between' houses.... But this superiority in station was not much consolation to Mrs. Morel." Her "new" house, after all, is only new to her; although it is only twelve years old, it is already on "the downward path." Worse yet, Gertrude feels imprisoned in the house, for she is thirty-one, the mother of two small children, pregnant with a third, and married to a man with no ambition to better himself.

Only a few pages further into the novel, we see Gertrude home "alone" with her children, William and Annie, waiting for her husband, Walter. He is still at the "wakes," a fair at which miners get drunk while their wives take their children from one tawdry sideshow to another. From the garden just outside her door, she watches women and children "coming home from the wakes.... Occasionally a man lurched past," and "sometimes a good husband came along with his family, peacefully. But usually the women and children were

alone." Other women we are to meet in the novel seem relatively insensitive to the injustice of being abandoned by hard-drinking men, but Mrs. Morel—who expects people and places to be "good"—feels deeply oppressed by her situation and environment. "The world seemed a dreary place" to her, a place in which "nothing else" could possibly "happen for her—...nothing but this dreary endurance—till the children grew up. And the children! She could not afford to have this third. She did not want it. The father was...in a public house, swilling himself drunk. She despised him, and was tied to him. This coming child was too much for her.... [S]he was sick of it, the struggle with poverty and ugliness and meanness." The last five words of this passage are telling. Gertrude Morel is a woman with economic, aesthetic, and moral standards and aspirations. She despises lowness in all forms; she would like to have a higher income and live in a beautiful world with a "good" husband, next to refined neighbors. Since she does not, she longs for change—change that her husband is unlikely to bring about and that she is impotent to bring about for herself.

Mrs. Morel comes to realize her powerlessness as she watches a drunk young man crash into a stile at the edge of the road. Lawrence subtly allows the reader to watch this scene through Mrs. Morel's discriminating, even judgmental, eyes as he describes the fellow "pick[ing] himself up" and "swearing viciously, rather pathetically, as if he thought the stile had wanted to hurt him." We know that Mrs. Morel finds the scene pathetic, the sound of swearing vicious, because the combination sends her immediately "indoors, wondering if things were never going to alter. She was beginning to realize that they would not." She wonders what she has "to do with all this"; "it doesn't seem as if *I* were taken into account," she thinks to herself. "I wait," she says to herself, "and what I wait for can never come."

Lawrence begins his novel, then, by picturing a lonely woman who has not only high, unreachable goals but also a degree of understanding and self-knowledge that make her condition extremely painful. That is to say, Gertrude knows that what she waits for can never come. The fact that she continues wanting what she knows she can never have may make her seem somewhat pretentious, smug, and unrealistic. She is a dreamer whose dreams make her despise the shortcomings of others, whether they be young men tripping over stiles or mothers who, unlike herself, are content to "gossip...at the corners of the alley...folding their arms" stoically "under their white aprons." Next to such women, Gertrude seems "frail"—physically and psychologically. "The heat suffocated her. And looking ahead, the prospect of her life made her feel as if she were buried alive." And she may even seem somewhat self-indulgent as she stands alone in her garden feeling sorry for herself, "trying to soothe herself with the scent of flowers and the fading, beautiful evening." Even nature seems somehow not good enough for her, not quite beautiful enough to offer adequate solace or consolation.

Lawrence, who provides us with pairs of characters who possess opposite strengths and opposite weaknesses, is both critical of and sympathetic with Mrs. Morel, who is, as we have seen, a literary character modeled after his own mother. He is sympathetic, in part, because he knows that all human character is to some extent a given, something present from birth and unalterable. It is difficult enough for human beings to be other than what they have been raised to be, but it is virtually impossible to suspend aspects of identity that have been genetically inherited.

Mrs. Morel is the beneficiary—and victim—of both her social and her biological inheritance. She "came of a good old burgher [middle class] family, famous independents who had fought with Colonel Hutchinson, and who remained stout Congregationalists," the narrator tells us. Such families teach certain values, but they also seem to pass along such characteristics as ambition, willfulness, and rigidity. Certainly, Gertrude's father was born with just such characteristics, which Gertrude seems to have inherited as surely as she inherited her mother's physical traits. George Coppard "was an engineer," the novel tells us: "a large, handsome, haughty man, proud of his fair skin and blue eyes, but more proud still of his integrity. Gertrude resembled her mother in her small build. But her temper, proud and unyielding, she had from the Coppards." Lawrence thus uses the word *proud* three times (and its synonym *haughty* once) in describing the character of George and Gertrude Coppard. When he says that the daughter "had" her pride from her father, he clearly suggests that she inherited as well as learned her father's temper.

Thus, although Lawrence at times criticizes Gertrude's temperament and inner nature—

although he shows us that her pride and integrity cause a great deal of suffering—he also understands that this young woman has not chosen her nature. She is not just indulging a passing whim to dream impossible dreams; the dissatisfaction that Gertrude Morel feels with life in the Bottoms has been virtually fated by her background and makeup. After all, her father, too, had felt "bitterly galled by his own poverty." Gertrude may have "favoured her mother" physically, and even "loved her...best of all; but she had the Coppard's clear, defiant blue eyes and their broad brow." And that brow, the narrator makes us realize, is more than just a physical characteristic. It is an outward sign of that which lies unalterable at her inner core: a proud, willful, unyielding inner spirit.

The fact that Gertrude Morel is like her father in all but outward appearance is extremely important to *Sons and Lovers*, for perhaps the most important idea set forth by the novel is this: the traits that a given society defines as "male" and "female" are not always to be found in biologically male and female bodies. The world is dreary, suffocating, and unfulfilling indeed for a woman like Gertrude, who has inherited traits that can most usefully be used in playing a man's social part. If Gertrude's father, George, was "bitterly galled at his poverty," how much more galled must his daughter be? George was prevented neither by lack of educational opportunity nor by society's expectations of parents and spouses from becoming an engineer, from trying to better his standard of living. His "gentle, humorous, kindly-souled" wife may have been perfectly content to let her proud and independent husband struggle for her family's betterment. But Gertrude cannot be so content, for she is her father's spirit in her mother's body. And her husband, who has a male body like her father's, has nothing like her father's spirit. He would not, could not, struggle for his family's betterment, even if Gertrude were willing to sit back and let him.

Gertrude is, in addition to being proud, unyielding, and independent, "intellectual" and "spiritual" (as opposed to physical and sensual). Because she is intellectual by nature, she is not only "curious" but also argumentative, especially when the subjects of God and religion come up. Thus, although her curiosity causes her to find "much pleasure and amusement in listening to other folk," she is also "clever in leading folk to talk. She loved ideas," and "what she liked most of all was an argument on religion or philosophy or politics with some educated man." Such talks, unfortunately, "she did not often enjoy," for educated men did not regularly meet to discuss ideas with women in Lawrence's day. "So she always had people tell her about themselves, finding her pleasure so."

The one man she can, occasionally, discuss ideas with is Mr. Heaton, the "young, and very poor" Congregational clergyman who has come to the Bottoms to minister to the miners and their families after receiving his "Bachelor of Arts at Cambridge." Occasionally he called, stayed to tea with Mrs. Morel, and "for hours he talked to her."

> Then she laid the cloth early, got out her best cups...and hoped [her husband] would not come too soon; indeed, if he stayed for a pint, she would not mind this day....Mr. Heaton would hold the baby, whilst Mrs. Morel beat up a batter-pudding or peeled the potatoes, and he, watching her all the time, would discuss his next sermon. His ideas were quaint and fantastic.

Even with Mr. Heaton, however, Gertrude has to do more listening than talking; "For hours he talked *to* her," Lawrence makes pointedly clear. He comes to "discuss his next sermon"; her role is to bring him "judiciously to earth" (italics mine). Thus, the "curious" side of her intellectual nature is satisfied far more often than the "clever" one. Gertrude is forced to be a listener. When Mr. Heaton comes, she gets to listen and respond to quaint and fantastic ideas. The rest of the time she must listen to what every other woman must content herself with: the details of personal, familial, domestic lives.

Although Lawrence says that Gertrude finds "her pleasure so," he means that she finds what pleasure she finds in listening. That is not to say that she finds a great deal of pleasure, this "lady" who is "considered very intellectual" and who speaks with "a purity of English" that is seldom heard in the Bottoms or in the thatched houses of neighboring "Hell Row." For she is not, by nature, a listener; she is not, by genes and by background, what she must, as a woman, be: receptive and sympathetic. She is, after all, "puritan, like her father." He was a "rather bitter" man "who preferred theology in reading, and who drew near in sympathy only to one man, the Apostle Paul." To Gertrude "her father was...the type of all men," and so was Paul, the apostle who was "harsh in government, and in familiarity ironic."

Like her father and like Saint Paul (who in addition to being harsh and ironic "ignored all sensuous pleasure"), Gertrude by nature is "high-minded, and really stern." In characterizing Gertrude, Lawrence repeatedly uses adjectives that describe socially acceptable male—but unacceptable female—characteristics. Gertrude is not only "stern," but she is also "cold," "hard," and "rigid." She sits "rigid with bitterness," for instance, when her husband reveals that he has not yet paid off his wedding bills. She "[is] her father," suddenly, when her mother-in-law reveals that Walter has lied about owning a house. "Then we ought to be paying you rent," she pronounces "coldly," and shortly thereafter "something in her proud, honourable soul...crystallise[s] out hard as rock." Not long after that, "a battle" begins "between husband and wife," one in which Gertrude struggles "to make him undertake...responsibilities, to make him fulfil his obligations. But he was too different from her. His nature was purely sensuous, and she strove to make him moral, religious. She tried to force him to face things." Gertrude is inevitably disappointed with her husband's lack of "grit." She has grit, and a sense of obligation or responsibility to go with it, but a woman's grit goes unused and unappreciated outside the household. Men "force" women—not vice versa—in the world into which Gertrude has been born, the world she can no more revolutionize in a short lifetime than she can entirely change her own proud, willful nature....

Source: Ross C. Murfin, "Opposition and Conflict: Gertrude and Walter Morel," in *"Sons and Lovers": A Novel of Division and Desire*, Twayne Publishers, 1987, pp. 29–35.

SOURCES

Colls, Robert, "Extending the State," in *Identity in England*, Oxford University Press, 2004, pp. 69–142.

Draper, R. P., Introduction to *D. H. Lawrence: The Critical Heritage*, Routledge, 1997, pp. 1–30.

Harrison, Andrew, "Reception and Subsequent Critical Approaches," in *D. H. Lawrence: "Sons and Lovers,"* Humanities-Ebooks, 2007, pp. 46–53.

Johnson, Claudia, *"Sons and Lovers,"* in *The Social Impact of the Novel: A Reference Guide*, Greenwood, 2002, pp. 110–11.

Law, Cheryl, "Setting the Scene: The Movement's Response to the First World War," in *Suffrage and*

Power: The Women's Movement, 1918–1928, I. B. Tauris, 1997, pp. 13–41.

Lawrence, D. H., *Sons and Lovers*, Barnes and Noble, 1996.

Lewiecki-Wilson, Cynthia, "D. H. Lawrence: The Sexual Struggle Displaces the Class Struggle," in *Writing against the Family: Gender in Lawrence and Joyce*, Southern Illinois University Press, 1994, pp. 67–116.

Norfolk, Lawrence, "Lawrence Norfolk on Dystopian Fiction," in *Telegraph* (London, England), March 28, 2013, http://www.telegraph.co.uk/culture/books/author interviews/9946330/Lawrence-Norfolk-on-dystopian-fiction.html (accessed May 8, 2013).

Rohter, Larry, "British Writers, World Citizens: *Granta*'s List of Young Literary Stars," in *New York Times*, April 15, 2013, http://www.nytimes.com/2013/04/16/books/granta-best-of-young-british-novelists-ranges-wide.html?pagewanted = all (accessed May 8, 2013).

Savage, Mike, and Andrew Mills, "Working Class Formation and the City," in *The Remaking of the British Working Class, 1840–1940*, Routledge, 1994, pp. 57–72.

Stone, Lawrence, "Epilogue: The Century of Divorce Law Reform, 1857–1987," in *Road to Divorce: England, 1530–1987*, Oxford University Press, 1990, pp. 383–422.

Toynbee, Polly, "Why the Class Struggle Is Not Dead," BBC News website, September 1, 2011, http://www.bbc.co.uk/news/uk-politics-14721315 (accessed May 8, 2013).

Wilson, Sarah, "Sigmund Freud and the Oedipal Complex," in *Observer* (London, England), March 7, 2009, http://www.guardian.co.uk/lifeandstyle/2009/mar/08/sigmund-freud-oedipal-complex (accessed May 8, 2013).

"Women's Timeline," in *Gender Resources*, Manchester Metropolitan University website, http://www.mmu.ac.uk/humanresources/equalities/doc/gender-equality-timeline.pdf (accessed May 8, 2013).

Worthen, John, "A Biography," in *D. H. Lawrence: A Reference Companion*, edited by Paul Poplawski, Greenwood Press, 1996, pp. 3–7.

FURTHER READING

Jones, Gareth Stedman, *Languages of Class: Studies in English Working Class History, 1832–1982*, Cambridge University Press, 1984.

Jones details the history of class conflict in England and distinguishes between the everyday understanding of class consciousness and class differences, and Marxist theories about class.

Sagar, Keith, *D. H. Lawrence's Paintings*, Chaucer Press, 2004.

Sagar presents high-quality color reproductions of Lawrence's paintings, which were only on display for a limited time during Lawrence's lifetime. The volume also contains Lawrence's essays and letters in which he discusses his art and his views on art.

Seelow, David, *Radical Modernism and Sexuality: Freud/Reich/D. H. Lawrence and Beyond*, Palgrave Macmillan, 2004.

Seelow studies the way sexuality informs much of the modernist movement, as displayed in the works of writers such as Lawrence and Freud.

Worthen, John, *D. H. Lawrence: The Life of an Outsider*, Greenwood, 1996.

Worthen, a highly regarded Lawrence scholar, offers a biographical portrait of Lawrence drawn from extensive research and the novelist's letters. Worthen's study explores Lawrence's life and work and reflects on his sense of alienation.

SUGGESTED SEARCH TERMS

D. H. Lawrence AND Sons and Lovers

early twentieth-century social realism

early twentieth-century psychological realism

early twentieth-century modernism

D. H. Lawrence as modernist

D. H. Lawrence as realist

D. H. Lawrence AND Freud

Sons and Lovers AND autobiography

Gertrude Morel AND Hamlet's mother

early twentieth-century British women's movement

early twentieth-century British class conflict

British working class AND coal industry

Stargirl

JERRY SPINELLI

2000

Written for adolescent readers, *Stargirl* (2000) is an allegorical tale of the conflict between conformity and individuality. An unconventional new student who calls herself Stargirl captures the heart of the shy Leo Borlock and the imagination of her classmates at Mica Area High School. All too soon, however, Stargirl's enthusiasm crosses unseen lines, bringing on the scorn of her peers. Although she remains blissfully unaware of the collective cold shoulder they give her, Leo finds himself caught in the middle, unsure of where his loyalties lie.

Named a 2001 Book of the Year by *Book Sense*, a New Atlantic Independent Booksellers Association Book of the Year, and an American Library Association (ALA) Best Book, *Stargirl* is one of Jerry Spinelli's best-loved novels.

AUTHOR BIOGRAPHY

Jerry Spinelli was born February 1, 1941, in Norristown, Pennsylvania. His first career aspiration was to be a cowboy. He states on his website:

> One day in second grade I dressed up in my cowboy outfit, complete with golden cap pistols and spurs on my boots. I went to school that way. It was not Halloween. When the teacher asked if I "would like to do something for the class," I got up and sang "I Have Spurs That Jingle Jangle Jingle."

He later set his sights on baseball, which he features in a number of his books. During a high-school football game, he wrote a poem that was subsequently published in his hometown newspaper. Spinelli identifies the day of its publication as the day he decided to become a writer.

He wrote his first short stories and edited the literary magazine at Gettysburg College, in Gettysburg, Pennsylvania. After attending writing seminars at Johns Hopkins University, he took a job as a men's wear editor for a department store, writing during his free time. He published his first novel, *Space Station Seventh Grade*, fifteen years later. The novel, like the four unpublished manuscripts he had written previously, was initially aimed at an adult audience but features an adolescent. When a children's publisher signed on for the book, Spinelli found his calling. He has since published thirty books for children and young adults. Spinelli is most famous for his fifth book, *Maniac Magee* (1990), which won the prestigious Newbery Award in 1991. His 1997 novel *Wringer* was a Newbery Honor Book. He published *Stargirl* in 2000 and a sequel, *Love, Stargirl*, in 2007.

Spinelli is married and has six children and twenty-one grandchildren. He has noted that, in addition to his own childhood, his children have provided great source material for his fiction. Like Stargirl, he has also owned pet rats. "They're smart and friendly and make terrific pets," he declares on his website.

PLOT SUMMARY

Porcupine Necktie
In this prologue, the book's narrator, eleventh grader Leo Borlock, relates that when he was a child, his uncle wore a necktie that had a porcupine on it. Leo adored the tie, and when his family moved from Pennsylvania to Arizona, his uncle gave it to him. Leo decided to collect porcupine ties but up until his fourteenth birthday had only one. One day Leo returned home one day to find a necktie with porcupines on it on his front porch with an unsigned note wishing him a happy birthday. No one seemed to know anything about it.

Chapters 1–3
On the first day of school in eleventh grade, all the students are buzzing about a new girl, said to have been previously homeschooled, who says

MEDIA ADAPTATIONS

- Listening Library released an unabridged audiobook of *Stargirl* in 2007. It is read by John H. Ritter and the running time is 4 hours and 25 minutes.

her name is Stargirl Caraway. She is dressed in a long, white, ruffled dress and carries a ukulele on her back. She plays it and sings during lunch. Leo and his best friend, Kevin, see her as a potentially exciting subject for their in-school TV talk show, *Hot Seat*.

The next day, a student named Hillari Kimble declares that Stargirl must be a fake, that the school has planted her there to improve school spirit. The rumor circulates, and Leo debates it. During lunch, Stargirl walks among the students and stares at them. Leo worries irrationally that she might be looking for him. She stops in front of a student named Alan Ferko and sings happy birthday to him.

Kevin and Leo surmise that Stargirl will not last long at Mica Area High School, where all of the students dress, act, and talk the same way and have the same taste. Stargirl continues wearing outrageous clothes to school and singing happy birthday to students in the lunchroom. She decorates her desk with flowers and carries a bag with a gaudy sunflower on it. She has a pet rat that she brings to school. Leo thinks that Hillari must be right—that Stargirl cannot be real—but he lies awake at night thinking about her, while the moonlight streams in his window. One night he realizes that she is real.

Kevin and Leo argue over whether or not to invite Stargirl onto *Hot Seat*. Leo refuses; he has a vague premonition that she should be left alone. Hillari develops outlandish theories about Stargirl's origins, and the students of Mica continue to be astonished by her dreamy, uninhibited, and friendly ways. Leo observes her "as if she were a bird in an aviary." One day he follows her after school. She delivers an unsigned card to someone's mailbox and then wanders to the edge of town and into the desert and the setting sun. At that point, Leo leaves her.

Chapters 4–6

Leo describes Hillari Kimble and her boyfriend, Wayne Parr. Hillari is known for her mouth, for turning down the cheerleading squad, and for her affiliation with Wayne. Wayne has few distinctive characteristics except for good looks, and Leo realizes that it is precisely his blandness and disinterest that the entire school, Leo included, unconsciously imitates.

Stargirl makes a splash at one of the football games, which are generally sparsely attended, by joining the marching band, and then the players, on the field. She marches, plays imaginary instruments, twirls, cheers, and does acrobatics. Attendance swells at the next game, but all are disappointed when they realize Stargirl is not coming. The following Monday cheer captain Mallory Stillwell recruits her to the cheerleading squad.

Hillari's birthday approaches, and she commands Stargirl not to sing to her. During lunch on the day of Hillari's birthday, all the students wait nervously to see what Stargirl will do. She walks over to Leo, and the words of her song say happy birthday to Hillari but her singing is aimed at him. He is embarrassed. The students go wild with applause. Kevin asks why she chose Leo, and Stargirl says it is because he is cute.

Chapters 7–9

Kevin and Leo visit their friend Archie, a paleontologist who, on Saturdays, turns his house into a progressive school called the Loyal Order of the Stone Bone. He collects bones and has a thirty-foot cactus he named Señor Saguaro. Kevin and Leo discuss Stargirl with Archie and find out that he taught her one day a week for the past four to five years. He tells them that her demeanor is definitely not an act and that her parents are normal people. He reinforces the sense of mystery surrounding her.

Soon Stargirl is the most popular girl in school. Leo guesses that this may be due to her unconventional and highly entertaining cheerleading practices, the distasteful cruelty of Hillari Kimble, the emergence of a sidekick-like companion, Dori Dilson, or perhaps a change in the student body itself. Students begin to imitate her, carrying their own ukuleles and buying pet rats. Stargirl

competes in and handily wins a local speech competition. While conferring, the judges show a film of a previous state champion who receives a hero's welcome upon returning to his school.

Leo observes a blossoming of individuality and empathy in the school. Students begin to celebrate each other's joys and mourn each other's sorrows. They begin to do things and dress in ways that express their individuality. Leo feels a sense of freedom, but no direction to it. He tells Archie that it is a miracle, but Archie warns that miracles do not last long.

Chapters 10–12

At the height of Stargirl's popularity, Leo changes his mind about having her on *Hot Seat*, and he and Kevin schedule an interview. Things begin to take a turn for Stargirl, who offends some people with her unconventional ways. She recites her own ludicrous version of the Pledge of Allegiance. She shows up at the funeral of a classmate's grandfather, whom she presumably did not know, and is castigated by the classmate's mother for intruding on a very personal moment. The local paper publishes a photo of a sick child's homecoming, and Stargirl is seen in the photo. She is also suspected of giving the boy a bike.

At the basketball games, Stargirl cheers for both teams. At school, she cheers for even the most minor actions, like someone picking a candy wrapper off the floor, calling attention to and embarrassing that person.

The basketball team, finally feeling support from the student body, goes on a winning streak. After ten games, they are undefeated. Feeling a new pride and ownership, the students become intolerant of the idea of losing. They begin to hate opposing teams and boo them. Then they begin to boo Stargirl, who cheers indiscriminately. At one game, the students trick the bus driver so that she is left behind.

The day comes for Stargirl to appear on *Hot Seat*. As usual, Leo has chosen a "jury" of twelve students who are directed to fire tough, embarrassing, or nosy—but not mean—questions at the subject. Kevin will act as host. Although he anticipates record viewership, Leo feels dread. The interview begins with a bang, as Stargirl convincingly pantomimes that she is literally in the hot seat—that it is burning her. Then her pet rat escapes.

Chapters 13–15

In the interview, she shares that her given name is Susan, and that before taking on the name Stargirl, she called herself Pocket Mouse. The jurors then go on the attack, calling her a traitor to her country and her school. She explains that she is on everyone's side, but they ridicule her for meddling in people's business and for being intentionally different. Hillari calls her crazy and tells her to leave their school. The advisor, Mr. Robineau, ends the show. The interview never airs.

In the first basketball play-off game, a player from the opposing team gets hurt, and Stargirl comforts him. The Mica team wins, but they are outmatched in the next game. Although it is clear to the Mica fans that they are doomed in the second half, Stargirl cheers relentlessly to the Mica fans, only to be hit in the face by a tomato. Leo discovers a Valentine's card Stargirl created for him. It says "I LOVE YOU."

At school, Stargirl walks up to Leo and says hello. Leo is embarrassed and runs away. Her greeting replays in his head all evening. The next day, Kevin and Leo visit Archie and discuss their disappointment about the game. Archie answers mysteriously, as he usually does.

Chapters 16–18

Stargirl approaches Leo at lunch. Once again he is embarrassed, but he thanks her for the card. He looks for her after school and overhears some girls saying Stargirl was kicked off the cheerleading squad. When they see him, they call him Starboy. He is secretly thrilled.

Feeling nervous anticipation, Leo walks slowly to Stargirl's house, arriving in the dark. She soon emerges and mentions the time he followed her. She introduces him to her rat, Cinnamon. Cinnamon licks his ear, and he admits to enjoying it. Leo and Stargirl banter playfully, and Leo is sad to say goodnight.

Within two weeks, Leo is "loopy with love," though he still feels uncomfortable in the lunch room, believing everyone is staring at him. Stargirl takes him to her "enchanted place," a spot in the desert which Leo finds ordinary looking. She explains the beauty of meditation, of shutting down one's senses to become nothingness and let the universe speak. Leo attempts it and struggles but ultimately steps into "a territory of peace, of silence."

Leo feels as if he and Stargirl are the only people in school, but soon he notices that they are being shunned. At lunch, Kevin confirms that the student body is giving Stargirl the silent treatment and that Leo has been deemed guilty by association. They blame her for the basketball team's loss. Leo begins to feel a deep sense of isolation, whereas Stargirl does not seem to notice.

Chapters 19–21

Leo seeks advice from Archie, who speaks mystically about Leo's predicament. Archie asks Señor Saguaro for questions, not answers, and says that the cactus has boiled Leo's dilemma down to one question: "Whose affection do you value more, hers or the others'?"

Stargirl wins the district speech championship and practices in the desert for the state finals, with Leo as her audience. She speaks entirely extemporaneously. In her presence, Leo becomes lighter. She points out, and Leo notices for the first time, the many small wonders that make up daily existence. He joins her as she does good deeds for strangers and realizes she gave him the tie.

Stargirl explains how she gets her information about people in need from newspapers and bulletin boards and how she surmises what kind of encouragement might help them. She demonstrates this skill by taking Leo to the mall, where together they observe people and imagine what their lives might be like and what they might need.

Chapters 22–24

Leo meets Stargirl's family and sees her bedroom, both of which are more unremarkable than he anticipated. The most notable object in her room is a small trinket shaped as a wagon. She calls it her happy wagon; when something makes her happy, she adds a pebble to it, and when something makes her unhappy, she removes one. There are twenty pebbles in all, and usually it stands around ten in and ten out. She states that it once got down to three pebbles. Leo is surprised, not seeing her as a person who might ever be unhappy. Now it is piled high.

Later Stargirl takes pictures of the little boy across the street and explains that she is writing a biography of sorts for him. Leo asks if she is trying to be a saint, and the words hurt her. He apologizes, and she decides he must be jealous. The two kiss.

Leo relishes time outside school with Stargirl but begins to feel more deeply the pain of being shunned by his peers at school. He resents feeling that he has to choose between them.

One day Stargirl paints a giant sign declaring her love for Leo on a bedsheet and posts it on the Roadrunner, the large bulletin board that all students consult for the latest news. Leo first feels a pang of pride, but an impulse to destroy the sign swiftly follows. Humiliated, he blows her off after school.

Chapters 25–27

Leo continues to avoid Stargirl until one day she corners him, and he tells her that things have to change. He asks why she does not care what people think of her. She says she cares what Leo and her close friends, like Cinnamon and Señor Saguaro think, but he says that it should matter to her what everybody thinks. He challenges her about caring for Kovac, the injured basketball player from the other team, whom he classifies as being the enemy. He tells her that she cannot continue ignoring other people's opinions, which she would be able to intuit if she were connected. She is shocked and wounded to discover that she is not connected. Leo feels sad for her.

In the following days, Leo attempts to explain the ways of society to Stargirl and ends up telling her that nobody likes her. She looks at him with hurt eyes, and he tries to put it on "*them*," stating, "We live in a world of them, whether we like it or not." Secretly, he hopes she will change for his sake. Two days later, Stargirl vanishes.

She reappears as Susan, dressed like a typical teenager, without Cinnamon or a ukulele. Leo is overjoyed by the transformation, noting that "Stargirl had vanished into a sea of *them*." He suddenly walks with pride and is thrilled to identify himself as Susan Caraway's boyfriend. Susan attempts to learn everything she can about "them," buys things for their designer labels, and adjusts mannerisms such as her laugh to conform with others' expectations. However, she continues to be shunned. She is disheartened, but her hope is revived when she has a vision: she will be popular when she wins the state speech competition and receives a hero's welcome, just like the boy in the video.

A week later a teacher named Mr. McShane drives Susan and Leo to Phoenix for the competition. Susan says that Dori Dilson, her best friend, refused her invitation to join them, as she thinks Stargirl betrayed herself by becoming Susan. Unaffected, Susan giddily envisions what it will be like when she wins, how the crowd will swarm her. Mr. McShane encourages her, but

Leo tries to adjust her expectations. She remains confident. She asks Mr. McShane to pull over, and she spends a few minutes dancing playfully about before looking off in the distance, deep in concentration. When she returns to the car, she asks Mr. McShane about extinct birds, and he talks about the moa. She says Archie told her that mockingbirds may be singing songs of ancient birds, "pitching fossils into the air."

Chapters 28–30

At the contest, Susan delivers a brand-new speech called "I Might Have Heard a Moa," and it is mesmerizing. Leo is shocked to discover that she made it up on the spot. In the final round that evening, she enchants the entire audience, which bursts into thunderous applause after her speech.

Susan wins and is the star of the competition, receiving congratulations and praise from all who encounter her. Leo is amazed by her. As they journey home, Susan eventually grows quiet. She nervously instructs Leo as to how to handle the silver plate she won when the crowd waiting for her back at school hoists her onto their shoulders. She makes him promise to stick close to her. Leo's sense of foreboding is confirmed when they arrive to the school to a welcoming committee of three people—two teachers and Dori Dilson.

Susan is stunned. At school on Monday, she has become happy-go-lucky Stargirl again. She hands out cookies to everyone at lunch, including Hillari, and plays her ukulele with Cinnamon on her shoulder. Leo confronts her, and she says with a smile that she has given up on being normal or popular. She says goodbye and that she knows he will not be asking her to the upcoming Ocotillo Ball. He recognizes her smile as one she had given to other needy souls, and he feels hatred for her. That night as he lies in bed, he closes his shade on the moonlight.

Stargirl invites students to join her new ukulele band, the Ukee Dooks. Dori is the only one to join. Kevin, and soon the rest of the students, decide it is acceptable to say nasty things about Stargirl to Leo, which Leo resents. She and Dori perform a duet in the courtyard, and despite feeling that he should go out and applaud them, Leo leaves by another door.

Chapters 31–33

Leo does not attend the Ocotillo Ball, but Stargirl does. She arrives in a bicycle sidecar festooned with flowers, the bicycle pedaled by a tuxedo-clad Dori. Leo relates varying secondhand accounts of her stunning appearance. The parents, there to make a fuss over their own children, are moved by her. She dances ethereally by herself, and the students begin to feel more alone than she is. Then an ordinary boy named Raymond Studemacher begins to dance with her. Other boys leave their dates and head toward her, but before they can reach her, she goes to the band and asks them to play the bunny hop. Almost everyone joins in, and Stargirl leads them in a line. Following her, they wander off the dance floor and slowly make their way into the desert. Hillari and Wayne do not join them, and Hillari grows agitated about their disappearance and the band's refusal to play a new song. Eventually Stargirl and her followers, even more energetic than before, reappear. Hillari slaps her. In return, Stargirl kisses her on the cheek and then departs with Dori, her bicycle chauffeur. No one sees Stargirl again.

The summer after Stargirl's disappearance, Leo discusses her with Archie. Leo wonders if she was a dream, but Archie says she was real, made of stardust, a person more primitive than others and thus even closer to what is real. He says that she loved Leo enough to give herself up for awhile. Leo feels ashamed.

Later, just before Leo leaves for college, Archie shows him Stargirl's office in his toolshed. She kept decorative materials, a map of Mica, and files for the residents. Leo sees a file for him. It says that he likes porcupine neckties.

Leo becomes a set designer, a career he realizes he chose when he visited the enchanted place with Stargirl. On his last visit to see Archie, the two drive into the foothills, and Archie digs into a stone with his pick. There he buries Barney, a Paleocene rodent skull that had long been a favorite companion. He fills in the hole with cement, in essence returning Barney to being fossil. Inside Barney's cement tomb, he also places a piece of paper with a word on it. The next time Leo visits, someone else is living in Archie's house, and an elementary school occupies the enchanted place.

More Than Stars

Leo does not attend his class reunions, but he gets reports from Kevin, who says there is still much discussion of Stargirl. She has left her imprint on the school. There is a group called the Sunflowers whose members do kind deeds for others. The basketball team has never done as well as they did

that season, but there is always a small contingent of students who cheer the first time the opponent makes a basket. Leo sees traces of Stargirl in everyday experiences. He wonders about her, about whether he will ever get another chance. He does not feel alone—he feels she is watching him. The day before his birthday, he receives a porcupine necktie in the mail.

CHARACTERS

Barney

Barney is the skull of a Paleocene rodent that Archie keeps in his house. Archie and Leo often look at, refer to, and sometimes speak directly to Barney. The effect is usually to illustrate the commonalities between ancient and modern life. Just before Archie dies, he restores Barney to being a fossil, carefully cementing him into a rock. In giving Barney back to the earth, Archie seems to be preparing to return to it himself.

Leo Borlock

Leo is the protagonist, or main character, and narrator of *Stargirl*. Because he falls in love with Stargirl, he is drawn into the conflict between her extreme individuality and the expectations of his peers, and he must determine where his loyalties lie through trial and error. Leo is shy and embarrasses easily, a sign of a heightened social awareness. This sensitivity can also be seen in his early intuition that Stargirl should be left alone and in his bad feeling before her interview on *Hot Seat*. At the same time, he is intrigued by, if also skeptical of, the enchanted world that Stargirl inhabits. His earlier fondness for something so unusual as porcupine neckties betrays a similar nonconformist streak. Time spent in the moonlight in his bed takes him to a more fanciful place, a world of "otherness."

However, perhaps because he has been part of the collective at Mica Area High School, his personality seems something of a blank slate. When, inspired by Stargirl, the school experiences a brief flowering of individuality, Leo says:

> I felt lighter, unshackled, as if something I had been carrying had fallen away. But I didn't know what to do about it. There was no direction to my liberation. I had no urge to color my hair or trash my sneakers. So I just enjoyed the feeling and watched the once amorphous student body separate itself into hundreds of individuals.

There is one realm in which Leo seems most self-assured: when he is discussing or running his television program. However, the advisor, not Leo, calls off Stargirl's interview when things turn ugly. For most of the novel, Leo seems to vacillate between wondering about and discovering Stargirl's point of view or considering that of his fellow students. When he is happy with Stargirl, he shows a funny, sarcastic side; when the shunning becomes too much for him and he tries to change Stargirl, he identifies strongly with "them" and becomes more aggressive. By making Leo so malleable, Spinelli enables him to serve as an everyman, demonstrating the universality of the book's themes. Leo becomes a stage upon which the conflict between individual and society is dramatized.

Leo is also a great observer. He spends almost the entire first half of the book observing Stargirl from afar. Later, he says that Stargirl teaches him how to observe other people, but it is clear that Leo already makes it a habit. After Leo decides not to continue his relationship with Stargirl, he rides his bike to the Ocotillo Ball and observes her most spectacular moment from a distance.

Archie Brubaker

Archibald Hapwood Brubaker, known as Archie, is a paleontologist who invites students to his house on Saturdays for a progressive school that he calls the Loyal Order of the Stone Bone, so named because of his affinity for bones and fossils. With no kids of his own, he serves as a mentor to Leo and Kevin, who visit him when they are troubled by something. He knows more about Stargirl than anyone else, having known and taught her for four or five years. Leo later discovers that she keeps her "office," where she works on her good deeds, in his toolshed. Stargirl tells Leo that Archie is like a grandfather to her.

Archie tells the boys that Stargirl is very real, but he discusses her mysteriously, thereby honoring her elusive nature. He uses various metaphors to describe her, especially the stars, and suggests multiple times that she reflects something more primitive about humanity.

Leo often does not understand Archie's talk but has a premonition that he will one day. Archie also shows signs of having been in Leo's position. He says that Leo cannot know how lucky he was to be so loved by Stargirl, that he might understand someday. Leo maintains a

relationship with Archie until his death. Archie is mysterious to the end, crumpling up and fossilizing a piece of paper with a word on it during his last encounter with Leo. Archie's character would seem to suggest that there is wisdom in mystery.

Mr. and Mrs. Caraway

Leo imagines Stargirl's parents to belong in "a leftover hippie scene from the 1960s," but they surprise him by being fairly unremarkable. He finds her mother running a sewing machine barefoot and her balding father painting shutters. After Susan's (Stargirl's) first performance at the state speech competition, Leo and Mr. McShane are ecstatic, but her parents are "more reserved... full of smiles and 'well dones,' but... no more surprised at her success than Susan" is. When she is crushed by her poor reception back at school, "as in all things, they did not appear especially surprised or emotional." Their levelness provides yet another contrast to Stargirl's exuberance and serves to further emphasize her individuality.

Stargirl Caraway

Born Susan Caraway, the appropriately self-named Stargirl is the heroine and star of the novel. Her behavior, dress, demeanor, and outlook are highly unconventional and cause a sensation in the homogeneous (unvaried) environment at Mica Area High School. She is said to have been homeschooled, one possible explanation for her unusual ways, which include wearing pioneer dresses, playing the ukulele and singing happy birthday to people at lunch, and bringing her pet rat to school. However, her behavior is so far out of the norm—for instance, she runs out onto the field during a football game and joins the players—that the students swiftly suggest she cannot be real.

Leo wrestles with this question, and it is clear that Spinelli intends Stargirl to be something of a mythic or legendary figure. Her background is mysterious and, just as suddenly as she arrives, she leaves Mica like a shooting star in a blaze of glory, leading the students in an epic bunny hop through the desert that seems to last forever. Archie speaks of her as if she is a spirit or an idea rather than a person. She spends much of her time performing anonymous good deeds, and Leo wonders if she is running for sainthood. However, Spinelli reveals her means and methods for doing so, suggesting that there is no magic behind uncommon kindness, just attention and thoughtfulness.

Stargirl serves as a foil, or contrast, to the conformity of Mica students, who are alternately enthralled and revolted by her. She goes from being the most popular girl in school to the biggest outcast. For the most part she brings out the worst in her peers. They call her "'weird' and 'strange' and 'goofy'" and then "a traitor...a nut roll...crazy." For a time, however, she brings out a new spirit of liveliness and considerateness, and she ultimately leaves a positive legacy. Most of all, she causes Leo to consider his own values and loyalties.

For much of the first half of the novel, she seems to be a flat character, lacking much depth. She is always outrageously enthusiastic and apparently immune to cruelty or hurt. However, when Leo becomes involved with her, she shows both a sarcastic, teasing side and the ability to feel pain or sadness.

Her rapid and wholesale conversion into the generic Susan, who looks and behaves just like everyone else, seems as unlikely as her behavior as Stargirl and reinforces the notion that Stargirl is more of a symbol (an object representing an idea) or device than a realistic character. However, she shows herself to still be Stargirl under the new facade, enchanting everyone at the state speech competition with her meandering yet mesmerizing improvised speech. Notably, while Leo (and likely the reader) find her expectations of a hero's welcome back to school to be unrealistic, in the end her magical performance makes reality—the rather pitiful welcome she does receive—seem unjust.

Susan Caraway
See Stargirl Caraway

Cinnamon
Cinnamon is Stargirl's beloved pet rat. He is another accessory that makes Stargirl seem strange, and Hillari Kimble threatens to drop him down the stairwell. Leo too is initially repulsed by Cinnamon but upon further acquaintance comes to bond with him. Cinnamon is like Stargirl in that, while some people find him off-putting, he offers warmth of spirit.

Dori Dilson
Dori is Stargirl's most loyal friend at school. She joins Stargirl at lunch every day and is devoted to her even when she is unpopular. However, Dori stops speaking to Stargirl when she becomes Susan, feeling that her friend has betrayed her true self. She still welcomes Susan home after the speech competition, the only student to do so. When Stargirl becomes herself again, Dori joins her ukulele band, the Ukee Dooks, and, dressed in a white tuxedo with tails, accompanies her to the Ocotillo Ball. Unlike Leo, Dori loves and accepts Stargirl as she is.

Alan Ferko
Alan is the first student to whom Stargirl sings happy birthday.

Anna Grisdale
Anna Grisdale is a Mica student whose grandfather dies. Stargirl shows up at the funeral and wake, and Anna's mother yells at her and kicks her out, finding her presence there intrusive. This is one incident of several that turn the tide against Stargirl.

Kevin
Kevin is Leo's best friend and his partner in producing the show *Hot Seat*. Kevin is more outgoing, outspoken, and playful than Leo. He sees Stargirl mainly as an entertaining curiosity, but he also demonstrates character when he tries to keep her *Hot Seat* interview from derailing, as it ultimately does. Kevin is loyal to Leo regardless of how the rest of the students feel about his relationship with Stargirl, but he also suggests that he agrees with them to some extent, which is one of the last straws for Leo. Kevin and Leo keep in touch after high school.

Hillari Kimble
Often depicted sneering, scowling, and spreading rumors, Hillari is the school snob. She is dating the most popular boy in school, Wayne Parr, which Leo says is one of the most significant things she is known for. The other two are her mouth and "The Hoax," which is how the school refers to the time when she tried out for the cheerleading squad and turned down the spot she was offered.

Hillari hates Stargirl and would be her nemesis (archenemy) if Stargirl could comprehend such a thing. Hillari spreads rumors about Stargirl, commands her not to sing happy birthday to her, and threatens to drop Cinnamon down the stairwell. During the fateful *Hot Seat* interview, Hillari calls Stargirl crazy and tells her to get out of their school. She is outraged when Stargirl enchants everyone at the Ocotillo Ball and slaps her. In response, Stargirl kisses her. As critics have compared Stargirl to a savior, one could see this moment as a reversal of the Biblical story of Judas, who kisses Jesus of Nazareth to identify him to his tormentors. By kissing Hillari, Stargirl exemplifies the unconditional love that Jesus preached.

Kovac

Kovac is the basketball player from another school whom Stargirl comforts when he is injured during the first play-off game. This moment seals Stargirl's fate in terms of her social standing at Mica.

Mr. McShane

Mr. McShane drives Susan (Stargirl) and Leo to the state speech competition in Phoenix. He banters playfully with Susan and Leo and encourages Susan's confidence—overconfidence in Leo's mind. He also supplies her with the name of the extinct bird—the moa—that becomes the touchstone of her winning speech.

Wayne Parr

The most popular boy in school, Wayne is remarkable only for being gorgeous. He rarely speaks, does not participate in anything, and earns average grades. Leo refers to him as "grand marshal of our daily parade," a parade of conformity and apathy. He does not care about much of anything. The rest of the students, including Leo, follow suit. Leo wonders, "Did Parr create us or was he simply a reflection of us?" Regardless, Leo feels that at the core of the school is not spirit, but Wayne. Leo has him on *Hot Seat* precisely "*because* he was so monumentally good at doing nothing," and on the show, Wayne says his role model is the magazine *GQ*. Wayne personifies, or represents, the sea of bland conformity that Stargirl disrupts.

Danny Pike

Danny Pike is a nine-year-old boy whose bike injury leads to serious complications. The *Mica Times* prints a photo of his family and neighbors welcoming him home after treatment, and Stargirl can be seen among them. She is also rumored to have given him a new bike that appeared with no explanation. This is another incident that Mica students find inappropriate.

Mr. Robineau

Mr. Robineau is the advisor to Kevin and Leo's in-school television show, *Hot Seat*. He says that Stargirl's pantomime of the hot seat burning her was the greatest moment in the show's history, but he also ends the interview when the jury turns on Stargirl. He destroys the tape so that it can never air.

Señor Saguaro

Senor Saguaro is a thirty-foot-tall aging cactus that lives at Archie's house. Leo describes him as somewhat ratty and mostly dead, but to Archie he is a sage, or advisor. Archie says he bought the house because of Señor Saguaro, and he often consults the cactus for guidance. According to Archie, Señor Saguaro provides answers by asking questions. He boils down Leo's dilemma to one question: "Whose affection do you value more, hers or the others'?"

Peter Sinkowitz

Peter is Stargirl's five-year-old neighbor. She says she is writing his biography. She takes pictures of him, writes notes of what she sees him doing, and collects discarded artifacts like used candy wrappers so that one day she can present him with a realistic scrapbook of his life. Leo finds this project astonishing and asks if she is running for saint. He immediately regrets the question, realizing she is hurt by it.

Mallory Stillwell

Mallory is the captain of the cheerleading squad. After Stargirl impresses the entire school with her cheering and acrobatics at a football game, Mallory recruits her to the squad.

Raymond Studemacher

Raymond Studemacher is an unremarkable, largely unknown student who dances with Stargirl at the Ocotillo Ball. This act of connection and defiance breaks the spell of isolation the students have imposed upon her. Soon most of the school is dancing with Stargirl.

THEMES

Individualism

Stargirl represents extreme individuality. She violates nearly every established social guideline at Mica Area High School and, more than that, in

TOPICS FOR FURTHER STUDY

- Read Chris Crutcher's novel *Whale Talk* (2001), and compare its multiracial protagonist, T. J. Jones, to Spinelli's whimsical Stargirl. Write an essay in which you analyze their similarities and differences and what they say about the authors' views of the individual, society, and conformity.

- In contemporary film, heroes are often nonconformists or social misfits, as in the beloved Star Wars and Harry Potter series. Create a web-based catalogue of films that feature nonconformity. Include your own comments on how nonconformity is treated in each.

- Archie, a paleontologist, states that Stargirl is something "a little more primitive... a little closer to our beginnings, a little more in touch with the stuff we're made of." Evaluate Archie's claim by researching early humankind, such as represented by indigenous peoples; an early civilization, such as the Phoenicians or Sumerians; or a spiritual tradition aimed at establishing a connection with divine or worldly energy. Do you find evidence of some of the qualities that characterize Stargirl, such as empathy, selflessness, or unique behavior? What does your research say about individuality, society, and conformity? Give a multimedia presentation of your findings to your class.

- Do you find Stargirl to be a sympathetic character, one to whom readers can relate? Why or why not? Lead a discussion on your class discussion board, outlining your reasoning and responding thoughtfully to comments from your classmates.

- Write an alternative ending for the novel in which Leo chooses Stargirl instead of his peers. How is Leo changed? Does he still lose something valuable?

American culture. Indeed, she appears completely oblivious to such guidelines. This frequently puts

her at odds with her fellow students, but when she is being true to herself (that is, when she is Stargirl and not Susan), she does not notice their scorn. To Leo, she is puzzling yet compelling, an unexplainable exception to the group mind-set that dominates Mica, which he admits to having adopted. However, falling in love with her eventually pits Leo against society, and he struggles in this position. He resents having to choose between Stargirl and everyone else:

> I imagined my life without her and without them, and I didn't like it either way. I pretended it would not always be like this. In the magical moonlight of my bed at night, I pretended she would become more like them and they would become more like her, and in the end I would have it all.

Through Archie, Spinelli suggests multiple times that Stargirl represents something in Leo and something primitive and rare in humanity in general. One apparent interpretation is that she represents the truly individual spirit. Thus, Leo's attempt to resolve the conflict by changing Stargirl, by teaching her the rules of society, is doomed to fail. In the process, the power of the collective is demonstrated in Leo's sweeping declarations, such as "I'm in touch with everybody," "I'm one of them," and "Nobody likes you." He tells Stargirl, "We're talking about them. *Them.* We live in a world of them, like it or not." While she restores her individuality, Leo chooses to rejoin society.

Through this outlandish character and her equally unrealistic actions, Spinelli exaggerates the conflict between the individual and society. Interestingly, while he paints these forces in a polarized fashion—there is no compromise between the two—he does not suggest that one or the other is the right path. (Leo does have some regret about losing Stargirl, but he is also content in his life.) By avoiding a tidy solution, Spinelli emphasizes the difficulty of the conflict. Students are likely to identify with this difficulty, as they may find themselves shunned by peers for even the most minor social violation. Spinelli also concludes the book on a hopeful note: before she departs, Stargirl's unique spirit triumphs and leaves a positive mark on the town and Leo.

Notably, and somewhat ironically, Spinelli's representation of the individual spirit is also entirely unselfish. Stargirl is wholly empathetic and demonstrates little self-awareness. When meditating, she erases herself and finds a connection to the entire universe. In this sense, she may represent

Stargirl wears unusual outfits, like kimonos and pioneer clothes, not seeming to care what anyone at school thinks of her. (© takayuki / Shutterstock.com)

an alternative path for society, one built on more generous, unselfish, and empathetic impulses.

Conformity

A theme closely related to individualism is that of conformity, which is a powerful force in *Stargirl*. Leo states:

> Within pretty narrow limits we all wore the same clothes, talked the same way, ate the same food, listened to the same music.... If we happened to somehow distinguish ourselves, we quickly snapped back into place, like rubber bands.

Wayne Parr, the "grand marshal of our daily parade," represents this value of conformity. Unconsciously, the student body mimics Wayne's style of dress, preferences, and generally apathetic outlook.

The students respond dramatically to Stargirl, who challenges their conformity in every way. They alternate between finding her threatening, because she violates the patterns of social conduct that they have all unconsciously agreed to, and enchanting, given the novelty and outlandishness of her behavior. After she joins the cheerleading squad, Leo notes:

> She was entertaining. At the same time, we held back. Because she was different. Different. We had no one to compare her to, no one to measure her against. She was unknown territory. Unsafe. We were afraid to get too close.

For a time, Stargirl ignites both a flowering of individuality and a new school spirit. However, this spirit soon gives way to tribalism, a dangerous version of conformity characterized by intense loyalty to a group or clan. The Mica students view opposing basketball teams as the enemy and boo them. Stargirl breaks the rules of tribalism by cheering for the opponents, and her peers punish her cruelly, throwing a tomato at her, leaving her behind at a game, ignoring her and Leo at school, and demeaning her during the *Hot Seat* interview.

STYLE

Allegory

Stargirl is an allegory, a story in which characters represent ideas and are used to present a message or moral. Characters are not necessarily meant to be believable or realistic; often they are larger than life, as Stargirl unquestionably is. However, because the book's setting is relatively realistic, and its core conflicts so familiar, readers may struggle, as Leo does, with how to understand Stargirl. The characters in the book consistently pose the question of whether or not she is real, and Spinelli repeatedly answers in the affirmative. He also suggests, however, that she may be real on a symbolic, universal level—that is, she is not real in the concrete sense, but rather in the human quality she represents. Archie says that she is "as real as *we* get" (emphasis added).

Allegories are often used in religious teachings, and Stargirl shares some qualities with religious figures like Jesus of Nazareth, who taught unbound compassion, violated social norms, and was ostracized by society. An ancient genre, the allegory has become an established format for children's books, such as C. S. Lewis's Chronicles of Narnia, Antoine de Saint-Exupéry's *The Little Prince*, and William Golding's *Lord of the Flies*, books that have also been popular among adults.

COMPARE & CONTRAST

- **2000:** Schools, civic institutions, and businesses increasingly tout the importance of diversity. Multiculturalism becomes an important educational value.

  Today: The term *diversity* now generally encompasses differences in sexual orientation, although not in all contexts. Bullying of students with differences in sexual orientation has become a hot-button issue in education.

- **2000:** The shooting at Columbine High School in Littleton, Colorado, in 1999, believed to be a result of bullying, sparks a national debate over the issue.

- **Today:** The shooting at Sandy Hook Elementary School in Newtown, Connecticut, sparks a national debate over gun control.

- **2000:** As it has long been, pressure to conform at school is a powerful force in the lives of teens.

  Today: Social media create new avenues for peer pressure, as social interactions extend into most every facet of life. At the same time, social media offer a platform for individuality and expressing a unique voice.

Other popular allegories include J. R. R. Tolkein's *Lord of the Rings* trilogy and Paulo Coelho's novel *The Alchemist*.

Bildungsroman

Bildungsroman is the formal name for a coming-of-age novel, one that focuses on the psychological and/or moral growth of the protagonist, or main character. The bildungsroman portrays the protagonist's transition from youth to adulthood with an emphasis on achieving maturity, often slowly and arduously. In *Stargirl*, this occurs when Leo realizes that social norms matter but that by subscribing to them, something valuable may be lost. A traditional and beloved genre, the bildungsroman is especially well suited to a young-adult audience, because readers may find parallels to their present lives.

HISTORICAL CONTEXT

Conformity in Late Twentieth-Century Young-Adult and Juvenile Literature

Conformity is a common theme in twentieth-century literature, particularly after World War II and throughout the Cold War, a period of intense confrontation in which the United States

(and its allies) faced off against the Soviet Union (now Russia and smaller republics). During this conflict, which lasted roughly from 1945 to the early 1990s, the United States and its allies considered Communism to be the ultimate system of conformity and the highest threat to the individualism and democracy so cherished in American culture. A prime example of literature dealing with these concepts is George Orwell's novel *Nineteen Eighty-Four* (1949), in which individualism, including independent thought, is illegal.

The topic of conformity also frequently appears in the young-adult and juvenile literature of the period, and appropriately so, because pressure to conform in behavior and dress is often keenly felt in the teenage years. The issue is usually closely related to questions about human nature and the struggle between the individual and society, topics of great concern to authors in the latter half of the twentieth century.

Perhaps the most classic work of young-adult fiction dealing with these issues is British author William Golding's *Lord of the Flies* (1954). In the novel, a group of boys are stranded on an island and form their own new society, rules, and leaders. Civilization does not last long, however, as the group breaks down into two tribes, one of which turns violent. The work is

The other kids do not understand Stargirl, so rumors about her spread. (© *Valua Vitaly | Shutterstock.com*)

considered an allegory that demonstrates humans' need for society; the book suggests that without order, humans become savages. This moral would seem to cast a shadow on the notion of our ancient selves that *Stargirl*'s Archie so admires. At the same time, the novel shows that a democratic society is an antidote to the most dangerous kind of conformity, tribalism, because it must make room for multiple points of view.

Tribalism also plays a crucial role in S. E. Hinton's *The Outsiders* (1967). This novel follows the rivalry between a group of social misfits, poor and struggling teenage boys known as the Greasers, and a more privileged group of students known as the Socs. As it does in *Lord of the Flies*, tribalism results in the death of one of the youths.

Robert Cormier's *The Chocolate War* (1975) also pits the individual against society. The novel tells of a high school dominated by a secret society called the Vigils. When Jerry refuses to sell chocolates for the school, a cause that the Vigils have agreed to enforce, he becomes subject

to their wrath, facing harassment, isolation, and ultimately violence.

Lois Lowry's 1993 young-adult novel *The Giver* offers an extreme and provocative portrayal of conformity. Jonas lives in a strictly run, utopian (ideal) society known as the Community. Here citizens have converted to "Sameness" and use conformity to avoid the pain of life, such as wars and violence arising from tribalism. They take pills to suppress their emotions and senses, and their lives are happy and free of strife. However, they cannot see color, hear music, or experience true joy, love, sensuality, or sorrow. Because he is selected for a special role in the society, the Receiver of all its past memories, Jonas soon discovers what they have been missing. Worse, he discovers that their seemingly perfect society is upheld by murder: individuals who break important rules multiple times, as well as children deemed less than ideal, are "released"—injected with fatal poison.

Ji-li Jiang's 1998 juvenile book *Red Scarf Girl: A Memoir of the Cultural Revolution* relates the heroine's adolescent experience of the

Cultural Revolution in China in the 1960s, during which the Communist Party chairman Mao Zedong attempted to rid the nation of threats to Communist rule and instill his own values in the nation. His attempt to achieve conformity of thought and values was carried out with harassment, imprisonment, and brutality.

Although conformity does not lead to dangerous violence in *Stargirl*—rather, it leads to shunning—one can sense its lurking possibility when Hillari threatens Cinnamon and slaps Stargirl, when students throw a tomato at her, and when they harass her on *Hot Seat*. Spinelli addresses hostile conformity in the form of racism in his Newbery Award–winning novel *Maniac Magee*. Its nonconformist hero, Jeffrey Lionel Magee, is blind to the racism that divides the fictional town of Two Mills.

CRITICAL OVERVIEW

Aside from *Maniac Magee*, *Stargirl* is one of Spinelli's most popular books. Critics have drawn comparisons between the two works, positing that Stargirl may offer a female counterpart to the mystical hero of the earlier book. However, critics differ over whether or not *Stargirl* is successful. A *Kirkus Reviews* critic asserts that "Spinelli spins a magical and heartbreaking tale," and a contributor to *Journal of Adolescent & Adult Literacy* deems *Stargirl* "an elegant and lifelike microcosm of high school life." Betsy Groban, writing in the *New York Times Book Review*, characterizes Stargirl as "a poetic allegorical tale about the magnificence and rarity of true nonconformity."

Other reviewers found Stargirl too outrageous to be effective in conveying the author's message. Ilene Cooper writes in *Booklist* that "Spinelli's point about the lure and trap of normalcy is a good one. But to make it real, Stargirl needed to have at least one foot on the ground." Similarly, a reviewer for *Horn Book* states that "while it is true that we are meant to see Stargirl as larger-than-life... there are no shadows to contour her character, and thus her gestures seem empty." *Stargirl* "prominently features issues of difference and conformity in stereotypical ways that seem not only contrived but also unbelievable," writes Kelly Emminger in another review published in the *Journal of Adolescent & Adult Literacy*. She continues: "As with

most saviors, Stargirl is constructed as a martyr.... Unlike most saviors or martyrs however, Stargirl seems oblivious to reality." Emminger further points out that Stargirl, Spinelli's poster child for individuality, consists of qualities "specific to white popular culture... reminiscent of 'hippie-chicks' in the 1960s and 1970s."

Emminger nonetheless finds that Stargirl offers opportunities for engaging students in valuable considerations of identity and diversity. A number of reviewers also commended the author for portraying the difficulty in the struggle between conformity and individuality and for not offering pat answers. A *Publishers Weekly* critic writes, "As always respectful of his audience, Spinelli poses searching questions about loyalty to one's friends and oneself and leaves readers to form their own answers."

CRITICISM

Andrea Betts

Betts is a freelance writer specializing in literature. In the following essay, she analyzes Stargirl *as an allegory for Sigmund Freud's theory of the psyche.*

In *Stargirl*, Jerry Spinelli suggests a number of times that his whimsical title character reflects some deep and ancient impulse in humanity, some essence that has been lost over thousands of years of civilization. Indeed, Stargirl is often held up as a sort of mirror to the ancient self. When Leo is first puzzling over her, his sage advisor Archie says, "You'll know her more by your questions than by her answers. Keep looking at her long enough. One day you might see someone you know." After she vanishes, Archie says of her, "I think that every once in a while someone comes along who is a little more primitive than the rest of us,... a little more in touch with the stuff we're made of." She is like the mockingbird reviving the ancient song of the moa, "pitching fossils into the air."

Leo and the rest of the Mica High students frequently question whether Stargirl is real. She often seems to be a dream, and it is in dreamlike moments that she appears most real. Lying awake in bed, bathed in the moonlight, Leo acquires "a sense of the otherness of things." He says,

WHAT DO I READ NEXT?

- Laurie Halse Anderson's young-adult novel *Speak* (1999) tells the story of an ostracized high-school student whose isolation hides a dark secret.

- *Love, Stargirl* (2007), Spinelli's sequel to *Stargirl*, consists of a series of letters that Stargirl writes to Leo after moving away from Mica, offering insight into her character and revealing how much her relationship with him affected her.

- Arthur Miller's famous play *The Crucible* (1953) is another allegory about the dangers of nonconformity. It was written in response to the persecution of alleged Communists in the United States in the 1950s, a movement known as McCarthyism. The protagonist, John Proctor, faces a dilemma similar to Leo Borlock's but with more severe consequences.

- *Prehistoric Life: The Definitive Visual History of Life on Earth*, released in 2009, offers a detailed look at the history of hundreds of species through artwork and images of fossil and skeletal evidence.

- Roy Cormier's famous novel *The Chocolate War* (1974) tells of a student who refuses to conform and faces dire consequences.

- Georges Bizet's 1875 opera *Carmen*, with libretto by Henri Meilhac and Ludovic Halévy, tells of a man who falls in love with a free-spirited, sensual gypsy named Carmen. She is ultimately punished with death. Author J. D. McClatchy published an English-language translation in 2001.

I liked the feeling the moonlight gave me, as if it wasn't the opposite of day, but its underside, its private side, when the fabulous purred on my snow-white sheet like some dark cat come in from the desert. It was during one of these nightmoon times that it came to me.... Stargirl *was* real.

Archie, who says that Stargirl is "as real as we get," talks about her by describing a similar

> PERHAPS THAT PRIMITIVE, UNRULY SPIRIT WE KEEP BURIED IS NOT ENDLESSLY SELFISH, BUT BOUNDLESSLY GENEROUS."

---

sensation in early-morning moments between sleep and waking:

> For those few seconds, we are something more primitive than we are about to become. We have just slept the sleep of our most distant ancestors, and something of them and their world still clings to us. For those few moments we are unformed, uncivilized.... We are untitled, unnamed, natural, suspended between was and will be.... We are, for a few brief moments, anything and everything we could be. And then ... we open our eyes and the day is before us and ... we become ourselves.

What is this ancient quality, this "private side" that is "uncivilized" and accessible only in such dreamy moments?

Readers familiar with the work of Sigmund Freud, often called the father of psychology, may begin to see hints of his theory of the mind in Spinelli's allegory. Freud theorized that dreams offer humans rare access to a more primitive part of the psyche, which he called the unconscious. Freud refined his concept of the unconscious in his books *Beyond the Pleasure Principle* (1920) and *The Ego and the Id* (1923). He argues that the human mind or psyche is composed of three structures: the id, the ego, and the superego. The id is drawn from his concept of the unconscious, "the most obscure and inaccessible region of the mind," as he puts it in *Beyond the Pleasure Principle*. Driven by primitive urges, instincts, and passions, the id is unorganized and unrestrained, and it lacks social awareness. According to Freud, the id is most driven by the desire for pleasure. The id as he describes it is totally selfish and seeks only to meet its own needs; the metaphor of a newborn baby is often used to describe the id.

At the other end of the psychological spectrum is the superego. This part of the psyche seeks most of all to conform to cultural rules and expectations for appropriate behavior, rules that the mind has internalized. In Freud's model, the superego enforces society's rules by punishing one with feelings of guilt and self-criticism when one breaks such rules. Freud further developed the idea of the superego in his book *Civilization and Its Discontents* (1930), introducing the concept of the "cultural super-ego" to describe the societal values, ideals, and behavioral expectations that drive the individual superego.

According to Freud, the superego and the id are often working against each other. Standing between these forces is a third component of the psyche, the ego. "The ego is that part of the id which has been modified by the direct influence of the external world," he writes in *The Ego and the Id*. "The ego represents what may be called reason and common sense, in contrast to the id, which contains the passions." A key task of the ego is to assess the world around us and deter-mine what is real. The ego then works to find balance between the primitive drives of the id, the rules of the superego, and reality, operating on what Freud calls the reality principle. This is often a frustrating task for the ego and one that frequently leads to the development of anxieties. Freud notes that there is not a sharp divide between the ego and the id, but they merge into one another.

It is not difficult to see elements of Freud's theory at work in *Stargirl*. Caught between his affection for and kinship with Stargirl, the expectations of his peers, and his understanding of reality, Leo can be seen as representing the ego. He struggles to make sense of Stargirl, to determine whether or not she is real. He is drawn to her passion, and for a time he shares in her unusual world. All too soon, however, he is faced with a conflict: how to live with both her and "them." Notably, the tipping point for Leo is when she announces her love for him to the school. As with most of Stargirl's actions, and in character with the id, this display of passion violates the social rules for acceptable behavior. However, this time Leo is the target, and he is humiliated. The conflict begins to paralyze him: "I wanted her. I wanted them. It seemed I could not have both so I did nothing. I ran and hid."

Although he avoids her, Stargirl is persis-tent. (Notably, Freud's id is also a persistent force.) When Leo finally acknowledges her, he emerges as the superego. Lecturing Stargirl, he tries to explain all of society's rules and why they matter. He is harsh with her, telling her that

nobody likes her and that she is not connected, much as the superego might deliver emotional punishment in the form of criticism for social failures. For a time the superego triumphs and the id, in this case Stargirl, falls in line: she becomes the highly conventional Susan. But the id is untamed by nature; the charade cannot last, and Leo once again faces his old dilemma.

Interestingly, once Leo chooses "them" and decides not to continue his relationship with Stargirl, she vanishes after one last dazzling dis-play. This is in keeping with one of Freud's key theories: that of repression. The drives of the superego and the anxiety of the ego become so powerful that they force the desires of the id out of the conscious mind—these desires become hidden, or repressed, and it is as if they never existed. However, the id continues to try and make itself known, sending signs and messages from that underside of the psyche, particularly in dreams. Similarly, as an adult Leo sees signs of Stargirl in the world around him and even feels she is watching him.

If Leo clearly enacts the dilemma of the ego and the superego, Stargirl does not so easily fit Freud's model. According to Freud, the unruly, chaotic, passionate, primitive, and socially unaware id is entirely selfish and often aggres-sive. While she fits many of the id's character-istics, Stargirl is almost entirely self*less* rather than selfish. Above all, she is driven by compas-sion and empathy for others. She celebrates their births, cheers their successes, mourns their losses, and aids them in need, all in ways that ignore social boundaries. Her empathy is so strong that she becomes offensive to a society that is accustomed to less.

Thus Spinelli seems to offer a revision of Freud's model of the psyche. Perhaps that prim-itive, unruly spirit we keep buried is not endlessly selfish, but boundlessly generous. Might the more aggressive element come from culture? At our most primitive, do we give off light, like stars?

Because of the extremeness with which Spinelli paints Stargirl's character, some readers may not buy his message. Indeed, as critics have noted, readers will at times find her repulsive and sympathize with the Mica students. This may be part of Spinelli's point: he asks us to consider where this impulse originates. Our sense of loy-alty to reality (ego)? Our sense of appropriate behavior (superego)? Spinelli suggests that,

The novel's climactic scene occurs at the school dance: popular Hillari slaps Stargirl, who responds by sweetly kissing Hillari's cheek. *(© Monkey Business Images | Shutterstock.com)*

however distasteful it may be to our cultural values, what opposes these forces might be wildly beautiful.

Still, Spinelli does not moralize about how to incorporate this primitive element into our modern lives. Instead he illustrates the struggle. Even readers who find Stargirl mostly distasteful are likely to feel conflicted over Leo's decision to break up with her, as Leo himself does. And yet, one senses that in the end, his life is in balance—real, practical, but sprinkled at the edges with stardust.

Source: Andrea Betts, Critical Essay on *Stargirl*, in *Novels for Students*, Gale, Cengage Learning, 2014.

Steve Redford

In the following excerpt, Redford discusses the Japanese concept of amaeru *in* Stargirl.

...As a long-term resident of Japan, I am struck by these two fictional characters as near perfect exemplifications of Takeo Doi's theoretical model of the Western psyche. In *The Anatomy of Dependence*, Doi's discussion of

Japanese and Western psyches focuses on the Japanese verb *amaeru*: to forge relationships with others in a way that allows one to indulge, like an infant, in passive dependence. Doi argues that Japanese culture encourages individuals to *amaeru* throughout their lives, whereas Western culture encourages them to outgrow the desire to *amaeru* as quickly as possible—the end result being an emphasis on the group in Japanese society and on the individual in the West. Public spirit can flourish in the Western world, Doi concludes, because the individual is not stifled by restrictive group loyalties.

To what extent Doi's theory applies to the American mindset is certainly open to debate, but the pattern of individual psychological growth in Western culture that he outlines—freedom from a suffocating conformity, discovery of self, the subsequent development of a larger sense of connectedness with humanity as a whole—was the prime focus of the nineteenth century American Transcendentalists, and that the pattern still looms large in the American imagination is clearly demonstrated by the two novels with which this paper is primarily concerned: Paul Fleischman's *Whirligig* and Jerry Spinelli's *Stargirl*.

...As the narrator of *Stargirl*, junior Leo Borlock tells us, Mica Area High School (MAHS) is "not exactly a hot bed of nonconformity." Students are so scared of being anything but mediocre—or different—that if they "happened to distinguish [them]selves, [they] quickly snapped back into place, like rubber bands." They "all wore the same clothes, talked the same way, ate the same food, listened to the same music" (*Stargirl*). The role model for most boys is Wayne Parr, an attractive but extraordinarily ordinary and boring boy who is admired "*because* he [is] so monumentally good at doing nothing."

Into this environment walks Susan "Stargirl" Caraway. Homeschooled up until then, she is unconcerned with fashion trends and wears whatever she likes: a 1920 flapper dress one day, a kimono another. Unlike the other girls, she wears no make-up. She recites her own personal version of the Pledge of Allegiance. She brings a pet rat to school. She joins the cross country team, but when the course bends right, she goes left. When the P.E. teacher calls everyone in from the rain, she stays outside and dances. Most perturbing to her new classmates, she is not fazed at all that they think she is crazy.

A consummate individual not beholden to any small group, Stargirl has been free to develop an enormous sense of public spirit. Her days are consumed with doing good for others, without the slightest concern for receiving credit or payback. She scours the newspaper and bulletin boards for information about people's wants and needs and sends them cards and presents. She somehow discovers the birthday

of all her schoolmates and sings "Happy Birthday" to them in the cafeteria. She takes pictures of the little boy down the street, believing a scrapbook of candid shots will bring him and his family great joy a few years down the road. Knowing what a thrill finding a penny can be for a small child, she leaves small change everywhere she goes.

At first, the MAHS students consider Stargirl a quirky freak. However, when she becomes a cheerleader, her enthusiasm is so inspiring that it dawns on everyone that individualism might just be interesting, and Leo is amazed to watch "the once amorphous student body separate itself into hundreds of individuals." He also notes how their new individualism leads to public spirit.

> It was wonderful to see, wonderful to be in the middle of: we mud frogs awakening all around. We were awash in tiny attentions. Small gestures, words, empathies thought to be extinct came to life. For years, the strangers among us had passed sullenly in the hallways; now we looked, we nodded, we smiled.

> Ironically, as we discovered and distinguished ourselves, a new collective came into being—a vitality, a presence, a spirit that had not been there before.

The novel's focus, though, is on Leo and his feelings toward Stargirl. Her arrival affects him more than any of his schoolmates, for he falls head over heels in love with her. At first, Leo is confused by his feelings, and he pays a visit to the neighborhood guru, Archie Brubaker, a retired archaeologist whose opinion is highly respected by Leo and his friends. When Leo's buddy Kevin suggests that Stargirl is of a different species, Archie quickly disagrees: "On the contrary, she is one of us. Most decidedly. She is more us than we are. She is, I think, who we really are. Or were." Immune to peer pressure, Archie means, Stargirl has been able to create and maintain her original relation to the universe. She is just like Emerson's "great man," who "in the midst of the crowd keeps with perfect sweetness the independence of solitude" ("Self-Reliance"). All this really hits home with Leo. He has felt himself drifting in a malaise and senses the opportunity for an awakening.

Soon Stargirl is leading Leo into her "enchanted places," especially the desert at the edge of their town. She knows in her heart what Archie later explains to Leo: the stars "supplied the ingredients that became us, the primordial elements." For a while Leo has sensed that her voice came "from the stars," and now she tells him: "The earth is speaking to us, but we can't hear because of all the racket our senses are making. [. . .] The universe will speak. The stars will whisper." She advises Leo to tune out the trivial chatter in his life and tune in the universe. When *she* tunes in, she explains, "[T]here is no difference anymore between me and the universe. The boundary is gone. I am it and it is me." Here, she is the quintessential Transcendentalist.

Under Stargirl's Transcendentalist tutelage, Leo's vision clears. "She was bendable light: she shone around every corner of my day," he tells us. "She saw things. I had not known there was so much to see. [. . .] After a while I began to see better." As she points out things she sees, things he had never noticed before, he understands from where her public spirit has sprung. For a brief while, they are "two people in a universe of space and stars."

Unfortunately for Leo, he is an apprentice Transcendentalist at best, and when the student body turns against Stargirl again (because she insists on helping and cheering for *everybody*, including players on the opponents' teams), he is left in a terrible bind. He does not want to lose her, but "the silent treatment" that descends upon the two of them, "the chilling isolation," causes him great emotional pain. Doi suggests that, in Japanese society, the indulged desire to *amaeru* leads to such a strong dependence on a particular group that "to be ostracized by the group is the greatest shame and dishonor." This is exactly what Leo experiences. He is terribly ashamed of being shunned by his schoolmates—those who have liked him and comforted him even though he has done nothing of any particular merit—and his loss of their indulgent acceptance proves more than he can bear.

The only solution that comes to him is ill-conceived: he will change Stargirl. He will make her understand that she must bend her will to that of the group's. Their discussions on the matter, though, reveal how different their deep-rooted ways of thinking are.

> This group thing, I said, it's very strong. It's probably an instinct. You find it everywhere, from little groups like families to big ones like a town or school, to really big ones like a whole country. How about really, really big ones, she said, like a planet? Whatever, I said. The point is, in a group everybody acts pretty much the same, that's kind of how the group holds itself together. Everybody? she said. Well, mostly, I said. That's what jails and mental hospitals are for, to keep it that way. You think I should be in jail? she said. I think you should try to be more like the rest of us, I said.

Leo, though more understanding of Stargirl's individuality and altruistic sense of public spirit than any of his schoolmates, ultimately finds himself valuing the comfort of the group over the self-actualizing energy and love that she can give him. Finally, he chooses the group over her.

Whirligig and *Stargirl* are novels, not empirical sociological studies, so we must be careful in suggesting how much they represent an American mindset. Still, it is interesting to compare how Brent and Stargirl fit into their local societies with how Emerson and Thoreau fit into the nineteenth century. In his introduction to the nineteenth century in *The Heath Anthology of American Literature*, Paul Lauter describes, basically, the irrelevance of the Transcendentalists to their contemporaries. Their ideas may have held sway in certain literary circles, Lauter writes, but their "immediate effect on their time was not extensive." Their journal, the *Dial*, only had a circulation of about three hundred, and Thoreau's publisher had to return him most of the copies of his first book. Emerson was considered a heretic by the church, Thoreau a crank by his neighbors. According to Michael Meyers, one reason Thoreau liked speaking of himself as a Transcendentalist was it greatly dismayed the people around him.

Stargirl also dismays those around her. Her classmates at MAHS can revel in a spontaneous moment with her, as when they join her in the Bunny Hop at the school dance, but most of them are likely to remember her as they first saw her: "weird," "strange," and "goofy." While Leo's memory of their relationship will color his outlook for the rest of his life, most of the others seem unlikely to absorb and retain significant amounts of her Transcendental vibrations. . . .

In the world of these two novels, then, the western psyche that Doi describes seems alive and well in Brent and Stargirl, but it is hardly observable—or *fleetingly* observable—in other characters. Both Fleischman and Spinelli seem eager to encourage their readers to think and act transcendentally, while seeming to recognize that most of their readers' peers will only occasionally, and many of their readers' peers hardly ever or not at all. Thus, while *Whirligig* and

Stargirl demonstrate that Transcendentalist ideas still thrive in the American imagination— they also seem to express Fleischman's and Spinelli's belief that the spiritual void felt by Emerson and Thoreau is still in need of filling.

Source: Steve Redford, "Transcending the Group, Discovering Both Self and Public Spirit: Paul Fleischman's *Whirligig* and Jerry Spinelli's *Stargirl*," in *ALAN Review*, Vol. 33, No. 2, Winter 2006, pp. 83, 85–87.

Kelly Emminger and Brooks Palermo

In the following review, Emminger and Palermo discuss the issue of conformity in the novel and point out that many of the characters in the book, other than Stargirl herself, are indistinguishable from one another.

Stargirl is a nonconformist, home-schooled teen with the lead role in Spinelli's book of the same name. The story takes place during her first year in a U.S. high school. It is told by Leo, an unremarkable youth who becomes her boyfriend. The novel follows Stargirl from her rocky school debut in September when no one knows what to think of her, through her rise to popularity in December when other students in the school emulate her, and finally to her dramatic plunge to the bottom of the social ladder as her classmates tire of her and her different way of being.

Stargirl prominently features issues of difference and conformity in stereotypical ways that seem not only contrived but also unbelievable. The story unfolds in a suburban Arizona high school that is predominantly white and middle upper class (the school has a TV studio) with a culture that replicates itself through the students' allegiance to conformity. As Leo explains it, "We all wore the same clothes, talked the same way, ate the same food, listened to the same music." This description seems odd in a modern U.S. high school, especially one in the heavily Latino southwest. All students would have to come from the same socioeconomic background and from the same cultural milieu to look the same, talk the same, and have the same musical interests. Stargirl seems to be the antithesis of teen conformity and apathy in the school. She is portrayed as the savior of Mica Area High School who suddenly appeared at school from out of town bringing laughter, kindheartedness, and sunshine (or should I say "starshine") to the apathetic students of Mica High.

As with most saviors. Stargirl is constructed as a martyr who, after her brief, inexplicable period of popularity, falls out of favor with her classmates and is banished with Leo to the fringes of the dominant high school inner circle. Unlike most saviors or martyrs however, Stargirl seems oblivious to reality. It is Leo who tells her that she is a social outcast, at which point she takes one last stab at saving the soul of Mica High by leading a conga line during a school dance before suddenly moving away, never to be heard from again.

The students in the novel are portrayed as indistinguishable from one another. This could be Spinelli's attempt to make Stargirl as distinct and different as possible. However, he gives her characteristics that are not only unoriginal (Stargirl seems to be a throwback to the "flower power" era in vogue 35 years ago) but also specific to white popular culture. Her flowing dresses and sunflower bag along with her ukulele playing, her love of meditation, and her barefoot dancing in the grass is reminiscent of "hippie-chicks" in the 1960s and 1970s.

In spite of its shortcomings, *Stargirl* can be used to begin a discussion about conformity in high school culture. The following are some questions that could push such discussions.

> What effects do multiculturalism and diversity have on conformist trends in high schools?
>
> What different ways of being would cause one to stand out in a school setting? Who decides what is different?
>
> If the "hippie" stereotype is most relevant to white American culture, what are some examples of stereotyped personas in other cultures?
>
> How is the need for self-validation constructed in the story?

Jerry Spinelli's *Stargirl* deals with the individuality of a young high school girl living in a world of conformity. The story is narrated by Stargirl's first love Leo, as he looks back on their days together 15 years earlier. Leo, like the rest of the students at Mica High, is intrigued with Stargirl's unique way of viewing the world. At first she is feared because she is so different, then she is loved and mimicked because she is so different, and finally she is hated because she is so different. Stargirl's love for Leo is portrayed in her ultimate act of conformity. She transforms herself into a normal alter ego, Susan.

Stargirl touches upon many issues that teens can relate to such as individuality, conformity, first love, school, the power of love and hate, the power of an individual over a group and the power of a group over an individual, loneliness, and cliques. Stargirl had the power to ignite and captivate the attention of an entire high school. She captivated the other students simply because she was not like "them." What could possibly be so scary about a genuinely nice person like Stargirl? She is not a part of any existing groups or cliques such as the jocks, the nerds, or the pretty cheerleaders. She is an outsider. The cliques are "them" and Stargirl is simply Stargirl. Soon, as a result of his affection for Stargirl, the students also shun Leo. In the end he chooses "them" over her.

Spinelli's novel raises issues about individuals who live on the fringe. Stargirl is an example, because other students see who she is as unacceptably different. She can never be one of them.

Source: Kelly Emminger and Brooks Palermo, Review of *Stargirl*, in *Journal of Adolescent & Adult Literacy*, Vol. 45, No. 2, October 2001, p. 170.

Horn Book

In the following review, a critic warns that more cynical readers might not appreciate Spinelli's benevolent heroine.

Cynics might want to steer clear of this novel of a contemporary Pollyanna, whose glad-game benevolences include singing Happy Birthday to her classmates, dropping change in the street for children to find, and—to her downfall—joining the cheerleading squad and rooting for both teams. High school junior Leo is at first nonplussed by Stargirl's not-so-random acts of kindness, but he really loves her from the start. After Stargirl is shunned for her disloyal cheerleading, Leo persuades her to go along with the crowd, and she even reclaims her birth name, Susan. Predictably, this doesn't work for Stargirl; on the author's part, it occasions much heavy-handed moralizing about conformity. While it is true that we are meant to see Stargirl as larger-than-life ("She seems to be in touch with something that the rest of us are missing"), there are no shadows to contour her character, and thus her gestures seem empty. While Spinelli's *Maniac Magee* was on the run for a reason and Pollyanna needed something to be glad for, *Stargirl* has nothing to lose. But as a story of high school outsiders and light romance, this will find an audience, and the book does bear many strong similarities to *Maniac Magee*, offering a charismatic female counterpart.

Source: Review of *Stargirl*, in *Horn Book*, Vol. 76, No. 4, July 2000, p. 465.

SOURCES

"Biography: Jerry Spinelli," Scholastic website, http://www.scholastic.com/teachers/contributor/jerry-spinelli (accessed April 18, 2013).

Cooper, Ilene, Review of *Stargirl*, in *Booklist*, Vol. 96, June 1, 2000, p. 1883.

Emminger, Kelly, Review of *Stargirl*, in *Journal of Adolescent & Adult Literacy*, Vol. 45, No. 2, October 2001, p. 170.

Flowers, Ann A., Review of *The Giver*, in *Horn Book*, Vol. 69, No. 4, July–August 1993, p. 458.

Freud, Sigmund, *Beyond the Pleasure Principle*, Pacific Publishing Studio, 2010, pp. 1–2.

———, *Civilization and Its Discontents*, Martino Publishing, 2010, pp. 136–39.

———, *The Ego and the Id*, Stellar Books, 2013, pp. 1–16.

Groban, Betsy, Review of *Stargirl*, in *New York Times Book Review*, September 17, 2000, p. 33.

Kramer, Mark, "Cold War," in *Encyclopedia of Russian History*, edited by James R. Millar, Vol. 1, Macmillan Reference USA, 2004, pp. 274–81.

Parsons, Christi, Kathleen Hennessey, and Michael A. Memoli, "Sandy Hook and Grief: Gun Control Advocates Plead Their Case," in *Los Angeles Times*, April 13, 2013, http://www.latimes.com/news/politics/la-pn-sandy-hook-gun-control-20130413,0,3866737.story (accessed April 28, 2013).

Review of *Stargirl*, in *Horn Book*, Vol. 76, No. 4, July 2000, p. 465.

Review of *Stargirl*, in *Journal of Adolescent & Adult Literacy*, Vol. 46, No. 3, November 2002, p. 218.

Review of *Stargirl*, in *Kirkus Reviews*, June 15, 2000, https://www.kirkusreviews.com/book-reviews/jerry-spinelli/stargirl/ (accessed April 18, 2013).

Review of *Stargirl*, in *Publishers Weekly*, Vol. 247, No. 26, June 26, 2000, p. 76.

Slayton, Paul, "Teaching Rationale for William Golding's *Lord of the Flies*," in *Censored Books: Critical Viewpoints*, edited by Nicholas J. Karolides, Lee Burress, and John M. Kean, Scarecrow Press, 1993, pp. 351–57.

Spinelli, Jerry, Jerry Spinelli website, http://www.jerryspinelli.com/newbery_002.htm (accessed April 18, 2013).

———, *Stargirl*, Dell Laurel-Leaf, 2000.

"Spinelli, Jerry," Library of Congress Authorities web site, http://authorities.loc.gov/ (accessed April 18, 2013).

Stines, Joe, "Robert Cormier," in *Dictionary of Literary Biography*, Vol. 52, *American Writers for Children since 1960: Fiction*, edited by Glenn E. Estes, Gale Research, 1986, pp. 107–14.

Sutherland, Zena, "The Teen-Ager Speaks," in *Saturday Review*, January 27, 1968, p. 34.

Sutton, Roger, Review of *Red Scarf Girl: A Memoir of the Cultural Revolution*, in *Horn Book*, Vol. 74, No. 1, January–February 1998, p. 76.

Toppo, Greg, "10 Years Later: The Real Story behind Columbine," in *USA Today*, April 14, 2009, http://usato day30.usatoday.com/news/nation/2009-04-13-columbine-myths_N.htm (accessed February 15, 2013).

FURTHER READING

Frosch, Mary, ed., *Coming of Age in America: A Multicultural Anthology*, New Press, 1994.

> Appropriate for ages nine and older, this anthology includes writings from such notable writers as Tobias Wolff, Paule Marshall, Dorothy Allison, and Eugenia Collier.

Plato, *The Allegory of the Cave*, translated by Benjamin Jowett, edited by Brian Burns, P&L Publications, 2010.

> In this well-known allegory, taken from Plato's classic work of philosophy *The Republic*, humans who first encounter the sun find it overwhelming and seek to return to the cave from which they emerged. The allegory provides an interesting complement to *Stargirl*, whose mystical female subject is often compared to light, the stars, and the moon.

Spinelli, Jerry, *Maniac Magee*, Little, Brown Books for Young Readers, 1990.

> Winner of the 1991 Newbery Award, *Maniac Magee* is one of Spinelli's most celebrated novels. Many critics have drawn comparisons between its protagonist and Stargirl, though several find the former more compelling.

Spradley, James, and David W. McCurdy, *Conformity and Conflict: Readings in Cultural Anthropology*, 13th ed., Pearson Prentice Hall, 2008.

> This book collects nearly forty articles on the stated topic, providing readers a multifaceted approach to understanding this aspect of human behavior.

SUGGESTED SEARCH TERMS

Jerry Spinelli

Stargirl AND Spinelli

Stargirl AND conformity

Stargirl AND individuality

allegory

young-adult literature AND conformity

Spinelli AND interview

Spinelli AND coming of age

Sunrise over Fallujah

WALTER DEAN MYERS

2008

Acclaimed young-adult author Walter Dean Myers's *Sunrise over Fallujah* introduces readers to Robin Perry, an eighteen-year-old African American soldier from Harlem. The story, told from Robin's point of view, follows the young man and his squad as they navigate the first months of the Iraq War in 2003, from February to June. A heartfelt war novel that also constitutes a coming-of-age tale, *Sunrise over Fallujah* touches on the trauma, violence, and confusion of Operation Iraqi Freedom, the bonds between Robin and his fellow soldiers, and the challenges of trying to effect positive change in the midst of chaos.

First published in 2008, *Sunrise over Fallujah* serves as a companion to Myers's 1988 novel *Fallen Angels*, which features Robin's uncle, Richie, and his experiences as a seventeen-year-old soldier in the Vietnam War. Both books are personal for the author, a veteran whose brother died in the Vietnam War and whose son and grandson served in the Iraq War.

AUTHOR BIOGRAPHY

Myers was born Walter Milton Myers on August 12, 1937, in Martinsburg, West Virginia, and later changed his name to honor his adoptive parents. Myers's biological mother, Mary Myers, died while giving birth to his younger sister. Afterward,

Walter Dean Myers (© *Howard Earl Simmons / NY Daily News Archive / Getty Images*)

his biological father, George Ambrose Myers, sent him to live with Herbert and Florence Dean in New York City's Harlem neighborhood. Herbert worked as a shipping clerk, and Florence, George's first wife, was a factory worker and English teacher.

As a boy, Walter struggled in school and suffered from a speech impediment. A teacher told him he might communicate better by writing, and Myers was soon filling his notebooks with poetry and short stories. But he dropped out of high school when he learned that his family could not afford to send him to college. Myers joined the army when he turned seventeen, serving from 1954 to 1957. The experience would serve as the inspiration for the 1988 novel *Fallen Angels* and its 2008 follow-up, *Sunrise over Fallujah*.

Myers held a variety of odd jobs after he left the army, mostly as a factory or clerical worker. He married and fathered two children, Karen and Michael Dean, and he continued to write through it all, publishing articles in the *National Enquirer* and *Alfred Hitchcock's Mystery Magazine*. Myers's first story, the picture book

Where Does the Day Go? (1969), won a Council on Interracial Books for Children contest. Additional picture books followed, but in 1975 Myers released his first young-adult novel, *Fast Sam, Cool Clyde, and Stuff*. Most of his work since then has been categorized as young-adult fiction, coming-of-age tales that feature African American teens as they navigate social issues from drug use and racism to gang violence and war.

As his early writing career took hold, Myers joined the Bobbs-Merrill publishing company, working in the editorial department from 1970 to 1977. He attended college in his forties, earning a bachelor's degree at Empire State College. Myers married his second wife, Constance Brendel, on June 19, 1973, and the couple had one son, Christopher. Father and son often work together, and several of Myers's novels and children's books feature Christopher's illustrations. Myers has also published nonfiction and several collections of poetry. He touches on much of his life and work in the 2001 young-adult memoir *Bad Boy*.

Myers has received several awards for his work, including Newbery Honor Book designations for the 1988 young-adult novel *Scorpions* and the 1992 young-adult novel *Somewhere in the Darkness*. His 1997 epic poem *Harlem* was a Caldecott Honor Book. Myers won the first Michael A. Printz Award for his 1997 young-adult novel *Monster*, and *Sunrise over Fallujah* earned a Christopher Award in 2009. He was honored with the Coretta Scott King–Virginia Hamilton Award for Lifetime Achievement in 2010. Two years later, Myers was named the Library of Congress National Ambassador for Young People's Literature. As of 2013, he was living in Jersey City, New Jersey, with his wife, Constance, and continuing to write.

MEDIA ADAPTATIONS

- *Sunrise over Fallujah* was adapted as an audiobook with a running time of 7 hours and 27 minutes, narrated by J. D. Jackson and released by RecordedBooks in 2008.

PLOT SUMMARY

Prologue

Sunrise over Fallujah begins with a letter from eighteen-year-old Robin Perry to his uncle, Richie Perry (the protagonist in *Fallen Angels*). The letter is dated February 27, 2003, and Robin tells his uncle that he is on the way to Iraq. He joined the army after the terrorist attacks of September 11, 2001, and he mentions that his father is angry because he skipped college to enlist. Robin is curious about his uncle's experiences in Vietnam.

Chapter 1

In Kuwait, which borders Iraq, Major Spring Sessions briefs the soldiers, including Robin and his friend, Jonesy. She turns the meeting over to Captain Coles. Robin is part of the Civil Affairs unit under the Third Infantry. The war may or may not happen. If it does begin, Robin's unit will aid civilians and help them rebuild their country.

Robin meets a soldier named Marla Kennedy, who teases him and calls him Birdy. The name sticks, and the rest of the soldiers adopt the nickname. Robin does not like it at first.

Chapter 2

Robin is assigned to a Humvee with Jonesy, Marla, and Captain Coles. Two other Humvees are part of Robin's unit. They are occupied by Darcy, Evans, and Sergeant Harris and by Danforth, Pendleton, and Corbin. The unit wonders whether or not the war will happen. They watch a film about Iraq's dictator, Saddam Hussein, and the mass murders he has caused. Robin silently admits that he is scared, but the other soldiers appear angry and ready to enter battle.

A colonel and Captain Coles stress that the team's mission is to help civilians. The squad spends the next few days waiting and training. Robin sends an e-mail to his uncle, dated March 17. He mentions the reporters on the base and the security rules regarding what he is and is not allowed to write about. Robin also says that he wrote a letter to his father but his father has not replied.

Chapter 3

Robin knows that he and his fellow soldiers are being primed for battle with films about the Persian Gulf War and rousing speeches from their commanders. Later, Darcy complains about the confusing Rules of Engagement (ROE), which outline when they can and cannot use their weapons. The soldiers struggle to understand the cultural differences between Iraqi tribes, unable to tell who is an enemy and who is an ally.

Fighting starts with bombing in Baghdad, which Robin and his friends watch from a television on base. They get their orders to cross over into Iraq and discuss the complicated ROE with soldiers from the 507th as they wait in line to fuel the Humvees. Then they drive in a long convoy across the Kuwaiti desert all day and night. Robin can hear heavy artillery fire in the distance, and the next morning they enter Iraq. Green body bags, filled with the war's first victims, are lined along the border.

Chapter 4

Robin and his unit continue into Iraq for the rest of the day before stopping. They set up a television and watch CNN together. The next morning, they prepare to move out but are delayed by a sandstorm that lasts for two days. Afterward, they clean their gear and watch the news, which is filled with images of bombed-out buildings and cheering Iraqis.

The squad is driving through Iraq when they hear that members of the 507th have suffered heavy casualties in An Nasiriyah, and some have been captured. They are told to pull over and await further orders. Robin and his friends pass the time by watching the news, which shows images of the captured men and women, some of whom Robin recognizes. He silently prays for their safety.

Robin's squad is redirected to An Nasiriyah to befriend the civilians and try to gather intelligence regarding the whereabouts of the captured soldiers. They are joined by an interpreter named Ahmed. Sounds of a battle rage in the distance, and civilians wave white flags as Robin's squad searches houses and provides medical care. In one house, a soldier from the Third Infantry has found a rocket-propelled grenade (RPG) launcher that has been recently fired. The inhabitants—an old man, old woman, teenage boy, and little girl—are gathered in the living room. The soldiers suspect the boy, and his grandmother cries and begs them not to arrest him.

When Robin's squad brings the boy outside to explain the situation to an officer, a sniper opens fire. A gunner in a Humvee kills him. The boy starts to run, and the gunner shoots and kills him as well. His grandmother runs into the street, sees her grandson, falls to the ground, and begins to wail. Robin walks away from her, unable to see through his own tears.

Chapter 5

Robin spends the rest of the day in shock. The squad is followed by curious children, and the soldiers give them candy. In a March 25 letter to his uncle, Robin mentions the boy and his attempts to deal with what happened. He writes that none of the other soldiers have talked about it, and he probably will not send the letter.

The medics do their best to help the civilians, many of whom have never had access to basic health care. Then Robin's squad heads to An Najaf to provide medical care to civilians injured in the fighting there. Heavy artillery fire rages through the city, and Robin's convoy stops to wait it out. Robin is terrified, and Marla cracks jokes. They take turns sleeping and keeping watch throughout the night.

They proceed into the city the next morning. A green car speeds toward Robin's Humvee, and Marla opens fire. Civilians exit the car with their hands up, and people are running everywhere. A rocket lands in the street and explodes, followed by grenades. Coles orders the squad to check the nearby buildings. A wounded man waves a pistol in the air, and Harris shoots him.

Robin's squad heads to a café that is being used as a field hospital, where they search wounded civilians for weapons. Robin is sickened by the carnage and lives in a constant state of terror. Robin and Jonesy watch as soldiers load body bags, filled with other soldiers, onto a truck.

The squad transports an Iraqi prisoner, a scared old man who speaks English and tells them that he worked as a cab driver in London. He was arrested because he had an old AK-47 in his house, a gun he used to ward off robbers. Afterward, Robin's squad picks up three intelligence officers to take them to Shuyukh. Robin and his team start to realize that Iraq is not as easy to invade and control as they anticipated.

On the way, Robin's Humvee gets stuck in a marsh. At first the soldiers are terrified that they will be attacked. But Iraqi civilians tie a rope to the car and use their mules to tow it out. The squad finally arrives in Shuyukh, and the intelligence officers search for weapons of mass destruction. They do not find any.

Robin writes an April 14 letter to his parents. He says that things are going well and the war should be over soon. In another letter, dated eight days later, Robin tells his uncle that the war is officially over. They have arrived in Baghdad to cheering citizens and may be coming home soon.

Chapter 6

The sewers in Baghdad have been shut down so the military can search them for weapons, and Robin's squad paints outhouses to set up around the city. They hire Iraqis to do odd jobs on the base. One is an old man named Jamil Sidqi al-Tikrit.

Robin's unit heads to a school near Tallil Air Base with Captain Miller. The school was accidentally bombed, and they want to provide medical care and financial reparations to the victims. Ahmed and Robin speak to the town chief. Coles joins them, along with two mothers whose children were killed. They scream in a dialect Ahmed does not understand. Then the chief takes the offered money and signs a receipt.

As they drive away, an ambulance approaches, and two men fire an RPG from the back of it. The squad returns fire, and the Iraqis are killed. It is over in minutes, but Robin, Jonesy, and Marla struggle to cope once they are back at the base. Robin tells his uncle things are going well in a May 3 e-mail. He says his dad sent him a picture of Morehouse College.

The squad spends the next two weeks on base, until they are sent to Ba'qubah to help a village with a herd of sick goats. Lieutenant Maire and his command serve as security detail. When they arrive, they learn that the chief lied about the goats in order to trick them into providing medical care for Iraqis who have been wounded while fighting against the Americans. Maire wants to leave, but Miller insists on helping. They learn that the injured are children who were forced to fight by the fedayeen, a commando group that supports Saddam Hussein. Ahmed helps an Iraqi dig a child-sized grave.

Chapter 7

Back at the base, Robin feels homesick. He watches the news with his squad, but now they know a lot of it is not true. Robin gets a May 11 letter from his mother, Jackie. She asks him to stay safe, mentions the church and community gossip back home, and tells Robin his father sends his love.

Chapter 8

Even though the war is officially over, there is still fighting. Robin's squad listens to two different versions of the war: one on the news on Jonesy's radio and one on the Third Infantry's transmissions on the Humvee's radio. They spend most of their time on the base, bored. The squad offers to drive a few chaplains to visit a nearby mosque. Robin, Jonesy, and Marla leave their weapons in the Humvee in order to enter the mosque. Infantrymen from the Third Infantry stay outside and stand guard. As they leave, a Humvee across the street explodes, and the marines open fire. Some try to save the soldiers in the burning vehicle. The incident is over in seconds.

In a May 9 letter to his father, Robin says that things are going well and his base is in the Safe Zone. He tells his father he loves and respects him, even if they do not always have the same opinions.

Chapter 9

Second Squad soldier Victor Ríos receives a large package in the mail. He ordered a small monkey figurine as a good-luck charm, but the owner has decided to send him a taxidermic monkey instead, as thanks for his service in the military. Victor does not like it, so Marla names it Sergeant Yossarian and decides that it should ride in her squad car.

Robin's squad and Victor's squad are sent to Al-Uhaimir, another bombing site with civilian casualties. Captain Miller befriends some of the women, who invite the soldiers to have tea. One of them speaks English, and she tells them the Ba'athists (Arab nationalists) forced the men in town into a truck and were taking them to fight the Americans. One of the Ba'athists shot at a military plane as they were driving away, and the plane bombed the truck. All of the children were waving goodbye and witnessed the carnage. After tea, Robin's squad befriends the youths, showing them the monkey and playing soccer with them. The soldiers lose the game. When they get back, Coles reports that the bombing was justified because the men were enemy combatants. Robin knows that it is not that simple.

Chapter 10

Sergeant Harris makes a sexist comment, and he and Jonesy nearly come to blows over it. The next day Robin's squad is sent to search a mansion that is believed to be a hub for insurgent activity. They burst into the home in the middle of the night, with Robin and Jonesy assisting the more battle-experienced infantrymen. The family inside appears to be innocent, and the soldiers do not find anything. The infantry commanders are embarrassed and are about to leave when Marla discovers detonators hidden in a tub of flour.

Chapter 11

Tribal tensions between the Sunnis, Shiites, and Kurds continue to mount, and Robin compares them to inner-city gangs. His squad searches for a missing Iraqi teen, beginning with the hospitals and morgues, but both are so overrun the search is useless. They try the prison instead and learn that the boy was arrested for breaking curfew.

They bring him to Major Sessions, who ordered the mission, and she holds a press conference celebrating its success. The reporters choose to interview Marla because she is blonde and pretty. They take the boy back to his village the next day, and Robin observes, "It felt good to see people happy with something we had done for a change."

The chapter ends with a May 13 e-mail to Uncle Richie, in which Robin says some of the soldiers are so scared they are committing suicide. The ROE changes every day.

Chapter 12
A soldier named Jerry Egri temporarily joins Robin's squad. He is a great soccer player, so they practice and schedule a rematch with the youths from Al-Uhaimir. A camera crew records the game, and Marla says that they are going to be on CNN. The soldiers lose, twenty to zero. Omar, one of the Iraqi boys, speaks English. Although he is friendly, he says the Americans lost the game because they are infidels (non-Muslims).

Back at the base, the soldiers play poker and discuss the war. Next, after a boring afternoon of cartoons and trashy TV, Robin's squad is sent north. The Iraqi police will be taking over a water project in Ba'qubah, and Robin's team will help with the transition. They escort a bus full of reporters and a bus full of Iraqis to the event. Everything goes well, and they return with the buses back toward the base.

An abandoned bus blocks the road, and the convoy spreads out to clear it. The bus explodes, and another explosion follows, along with gunfire. Two men on a nearby ridge are firing at them. The soldiers fire back, and everything is quiet. The driver in the first truck is injured, one cameraman has a mild head injury, Jonesy has a small cut, and Major Sessions is badly bruised. Second Squad's Humvee is in a ditch. Pendleton and Victor are seriously hurt.

Medevacs clear the injured, and Robin's squad returns to the base. They learn that Victor will lose his fingers and has been transferred to Germany. They also learn that Pendleton has died. They hold a memorial two days later. The tearful ceremony is followed by a cheery May 29 letter from Robin to his mother.

Chapter 13
The base is on lockdown after five Sunni civilians are found murdered, victims of tribal fighting, which continues to worsen. Robin thinks about how the war has changed him.

Chapter 14
Robin's squad, Major Scott, and several infantrymen meet in Fallujah with tribal leader Hamid Faisal Al-Sadah. The sheik speaks English, and he wants the military to provide his people with security. Scott says they will grant his request if he helps them find weapons of mass destruction. Hamid says he will see what he can do, and the soldiers head to the local hospital to learn how they can be of assistance.

The only supplies the hospital has are dirty bandages that must be washed and reused. Miller insists on trying to help the patients, and the rest of the soldiers wait for the marine escort that will take them from Fallujah to Baghdad. Robin goes inside to use the restroom before they leave. When he opens the door, he sees two men dragging Miller out of the bathroom. One reaches for his gun, and Robin shoots both of them. It is the first time he is sure he has killed someone. Every time he has used his weapon before, he has been firing into the distance with the rest of the squad.

Darcy has a birthday party at the base the next day. Then First, Second, and Third Squads are sent to As Sayliyah. The base there is meant to provide rest and relaxation, although Captain Coles is nervous, and the squads are told to leave their gear and dress in civilian clothes. They are flown to the base, which has a pool, volleyball courts, and a rec room, and given the day off. Robin tries to relax, but he has nightmares. He tries to flirt with Marla, but she wonders how Victor will get by with only two fingers on his hand.

Robin's squad is sent on a secret mission and told they will be reassigned afterward. In a June 8 letter to his uncle, Robin says things are good and he might be reassigned. Tribal fighting is getting worse, and he misses Harlem. Robin wants his uncle to tell his mother not to worry; the army does not send Civil Affairs soldiers into battle.

The soldiers are given new gear and sent to Al Amarah, a rural region near the Iran border. A politically friendly tribe is trading with the Badr fighters (an Islamist Iraqi political party). The Badrs are using the tribe to smuggle detonators into Iran. Fifth Group is stationed in the area, and they want the detonators so they can trace their origins. The army has kidnapped some of the tribe's children and blamed the crime on an enemy clan. Robin's squad will be sent in as negotiators to persuade the tribe to exchange the detonators for their children.

The squad heads to the local camp where Fifth Group is stationed. They meet with Colonel Roberts and are given a translator. They head to the tribe's village with one of the children as proof that they can retrieve them, then set a second rendezvous point. An hour later, Robin's squad brings the rest of the children to the hand-off. Roberts's men act as security. The exchange seems to go well, but as Robin carries the detonators back to the truck, the Iraqis open fire. Roberts covers them as they run to safety. The children are caught in the crossfire and Jonesy covers one of them, a blind boy crying for help. Robin's leg is wounded, and Jonesy is shot. Robin prays for his friend.

Chapter 15

Back at the camp, Roberts's men prepare for a possible attack. Morning arrives, and Jonesy is dead. The attack never comes, and Robin's squad is flown back to Baghdad, where they hold a memorial for Jonesy. The unit is reassigned, and they do their best to say goodbye, promising to stay in touch. Robin confesses his love to Marla, and she says she will be thinking about him. He is sent to Germany so that his leg can heal before he resumes duty.

In a June 17 letter to his uncle, which Robin says he will not send, Robin is finally honest about his experiences and the pain and sadness he feels. He signs the letter as both Robin and Birdy.

CHARACTERS

Birdy
See Robin Perry

Captain Coles
Captain Coles is Robin's squad leader. He is a fair commander, and his troops like and respect him. He is also honest about the chaos and confusion they face. Coles often successfully leads negotiations between the military and Iraqi tribal leaders. He is a career military man and a natural diplomat.

Toby Corbin
Corbin is a soldier in Robin's unit. He rides in the unit's third Humvee with Danforth and Pendleton.

Dad
Although Robin's father never appears as a character, Robin often refers to him in his letters. He is angry that Robin chose the army over college, and his only communication with Robin during the war is a picture of Morehouse College. Despite their differences and his silence, Robin writes to his father and says he loves and appreciates him.

PFC Shelly Danforth
Danforth is a soldier in Robin's unit. He rides in the unit's third Humvee with Corbin and Pendleton. When a colonel and Captain Coles stress that the team's mission is to help civilians, Danforth points out the irony of blowing people up and healing them afterward.

Jean Darcy
Darcy is a soldier in Robin's unit. She rides in the unit's second Humvee with Evans and Sergeant Harris. Like Danforth, she is aware of their confusing duties. She celebrates her twenty-first birthday on the base in Baghdad.

Jerry Egri
Jerry Egri is a soldier temporarily assigned to Robin's squad. He is a good soccer player, and he helps the soldiers hold a soccer match with Iraqi civilians. The game is filmed as good publicity for the war effort.

Corporal Eddie Evans
Evans is a soldier in Robin's unit. He rides in the unit's second Humvee with Darcy and Sergeant Harris.

Sergeant Robert Harris
Harris is a soldier in Robin's unit. He rides in the unit's second Humvee with Evans and Darcy. Harris is a showoff with a big ego, and most of the soldiers in the unit do not like him. He makes a sexist comment about the female soldiers and then tries to pick a fight with Jonesy. When the other soldiers stop the altercation, he throws a tantrum.

Jackie
See Mom

Corporal Charlie Jones
See Jonesy

Jonesy
Jonesy, a soldier in Robin's squad and Robin's closest friend, is a blues musician who sings and

plays guitar whenever he has a chance. He plans to open a blues club when he leaves the army, but he is killed while trying to save an Iraqi child. Jonesy has a bad feeling before the war starts, and he wakes Robin in the middle of the night and asks him to pray with him, reciting the Lord's Prayer. The next day, when they are invited to join a prayer group, Jonesy declines.

When Harris makes a sexist comment about the female soldiers, Jonesy point out that the women fight alongside the men. He is brave, and he stands up for what he believes in. He also provides much of the novel's humor, cracking jokes at every opportunity.

Marla Kennedy

Marla is a soldier in Robin's squad as well as Robin's love interest. His decision to call Marla by her first name is likely a sign of his interest in her, but she teases him relentlessly and comes up with his nickname, Birdy. Marla is a sharp-tongued observer who calls it as it is. She is brave and unflinching and insists on operating the gun on the squad's Humvee.

When the squad searches a mansion rumored to harbor insurgent activity, Marla alone finds the detonators. They are hidden in a tub of flour, and she explains that she knew to look there because the flour had been smoothed out. As a foster child, she helped with the cooking, and the flour was never smooth.

When Robin finally confesses his love for her, she says that he is confusing the bonds of battle for romance, but then she admits that that is "all I have the courage to deal with right now.... But I'm thinking heavy on you, Birdy Boy."

Lieutenant Maire

Lieutenant Maire and his command serve as security detail when Robin's squad is sent to Ba'qubah to help a village with a herd of sick goats. When they arrive, they learn the chief lied about the goats in order to trick them into providing medical care for conscripted Iraqis. Maire wants to leave, and he threatens to do so even though Miller insists on staying. Although he is brash and loud and Robin's squad does not like him that much, Maire does not carry out his threat.

Captain Miller

Captain Miller is a medic attached to Robin's squad. She helps everyone regardless of the reason they were wounded. She is sensitive and kindhearted and frustrated by how little she can do to help. With limited medical supplies, Miller does her best to heal the sick and wounded, but there is only so much she can do. When two men in a Fallujah hospital attempt to attack her and Robin saves her, she tells him he stopped them from hurting her, "but you didn't stop them from ripping up what was left of my soul."

Miller takes her job very seriously and serves as the group's conscience, even pointing out that the army is untrustworthy when they learn about their secret mission. She tries to save Jonesy, and when she fails, she apologizes, as if his death is her fault.

Mom

Robin's mother, Jackie, writes to him, and Robin writes back. She fills him in on the gossip from home and sends him dolls to give to the Iraqi children. She worries about her son's safety and tells Robin that his father loves him.

Omar

Omar is one of the Iraqi boys with whom Robin's squad plays soccer. He speaks English and talks about going to America to attend college. Although he is friendly, he believes that the Americans lose their soccer games because they are infidels.

Corporal Phil Pendleton

Pendleton is a soldier in Robin's unit. He rides in the unit's third Humvee with Danforth and Corbin. He is a big and jolly guy who makes a bad first impression when he inadvertently makes a racist comment. He tries to recover from the blunder by showing the soldiers a picture of his two young daughters. Robin does not look at the photo, and later, after Pendleton is killed, Robin feels guilty about this.

Richie Perry

See Uncle Richie

Robin Perry

Robin Perry is the protagonist and first-person narrator of *Sunrise over Fallujah*. He is honest and well meaning. He joined the army after September 11, 2001, and believes in fighting for freedom, but he is also scared of the war and what might happen to him and the people he cares about. He is deeply upset by the death and carnage he witnesses; when he prays, he asks for his safety and the safety of others.

He writes mostly cheerful letters to his uncle, mother, and father, and tells them not to worry about him. Some of Robin's letters to his uncle are more honest about the hardships of war, but those are the messages he says he probably will not send.

As the war progresses, Robin becomes aware that things are far more complicated than he expected and that it is hard to know how much good he is actually achieving. He is also aware of how the war has changed him. He lives with low-level fear at all times, effectively describing post-traumatic stress disorder (PTSD), an anxiety disorder caused by exposure to violence and common among soldiers. He mourns for himself after he is forced to kill the men who are attacking Captain Miller. He mourns for Pendelton and Jonesy when they die, and he has lost almost all of his faith in the war by the time Jonesy is killed. When Robin tries to find what little faith he has left, he thinks of Jonesy's giving his life to save an Iraqi child.

The novel begins with Robin's letter to his uncle as he flies to Kuwait, in which he asks Uncle Richie what it was like to be a soldier. The story ends with another letter to his uncle, but now he understands what being a soldier means and why everything they have both witnessed is so hard to talk about. Robin's character arc traces his loss of innocence, and he is slowly transformed from Robin the boy to Birdy the soldier.

Uncle Richie

Uncle Richie is Robin's uncle and the protagonist of *Fallen Angels*. Although he never appears in *Sunrise over Fallujah*, Robin writes letters and e-mails to him. Uncle Richie served in Vietnam as a soldier when he was seventeen, and Robin reaches out to him for guidance. It is clear that Robin feels his uncle is the only person who can understand what he is going through. While it is implied that Uncle Richie responds to Robin's letters, those responses are never shown.

Victor Ríos

Victor Ríos is a soldier in the second squad. His *abuela* (grandmother) once gave him a monkey charm, and he is inspired to order a similar one for good luck. The owner sends him a large taxidermic monkey instead, as thanks for his service in the military. Victor does not like it, so Marla names it and decides that it should ride in her squad. When Victor loses most of his

fingers, Robin wonders if he should have kept the monkey as a good-luck charm.

Colonel Roberts

Colonel Roberts is the commander of Fifth Group, which has been stationed near Al Amarah, a rural region near the Iran border, since the beginning of the war. He and his men provide security for Robin's squad and help them with their mission to exchange kidnapped children for detonators. When Miller points out that what they are doing is unethical, Roberts replies, "After the war . . . we'll talk about the philosophy. . . . Until then we'll do what we have to do to keep our people alive."

Ahmed Sabbat

Ahmed Sabbat is the translator who works with Robin's squad in and around Baghdad. He is a mostly quiet, solid, and trustworthy man. He cries with the Iraqis who have lost loved ones and helps them dig a grave. He calmly straddles the divide between the Americans and Iraqis.

Hamid Faisal Al-Sadah

Hamid Faisal Al-Sadah is a sheikh Robin's squad meets with in Fallujah. He wants the military to provide protection to his people. In exchange, he will try to help them find weapons of mass destruction. Al-Sadah tells Robin's squad that the Americans won Operation Iraqi Freedom but now are in the middle of a second war, one between Iraqi factions struggling for control of the country.

Major Scott

Major Scott travels to Fallujah with Robin's squad to meet with Hamid Faisal Al-Sadah.

Major Spring Sessions

Major Sessions is an attractive commander who is one of Robin's original unit leaders. She greets the troops in Kuwait and gives them their orders. She is mostly concerned with public relations, arranging press conferences whenever possible. Robin and his squad lose respect for her because she contributes to the media's overly positive portrayal of the war.

Jamil Sidqi al-Tikrit

Jamil Sidqi al-Tikrit is one of the Iraqis hired to work on the base in Baghdad. He is an old man who is rumored to be a distant cousin of Saddam Hussein's. He speaks some English, and whenever the soldiers ask him about the war, he speaks in cryptic parables: "When you kill a camel, it is better to cut off the body than the head.... If you cut off the head then the camel doesn't know what he is."

THEMES

Wars

While Robin's experiences reflect the chaos and confusion of the Iraq War, the theme in *Sunrise over Fallujah* extends to all wars, a device that is underscored by the novel's allusions to *Fallen Angels* and the Vietnam War. Robin and his squad want to depose a dictator and help the Iraqi people, but their good intentions are waylaid by tribal infighting. They live in constant fear. They struggle to help the people the army has harmed, and they often lose hope. War, as Robin experiences it, is the terrible result of noble intentions. Regardless of politics and press coverage, it oscillates between two realities. "I've always thought of life as being precious," Robin says; "I don't want the image of body parts ... in my head. I don't want to think about shooting somebody." Later, in his final letter to his uncle, Robin attempts to find meaning in the fighting, death, and sacrifice: "Once you have seen a Jonesy or a Pendleton ... offering themselves up, you don't think about losing or winning so much. You think there is more to life."

War, as Myers portrays it, is a complicated and terrible undertaking, a theme he addressed in an interview appended to the 2009 paperback edition of *Sunrise over Fallujah*. In that interview, the author stated:

> Today's teenagers ... will be the ones asked to fight this nation's wars.... They need to do a lot of thinking before either picking up a weapon or casting a vote to go to war. It's my hope that *Sunrise over Fallujah* will be the start of that thinking process.

Trauma

Trauma, particularly PTSD, is evident throughout *Sunrise over Fallujah*. Although PTSD is never directly referenced, Robin's constant fear and its integration into his very personality are highly indicative of the disorder. PTSD occurs after acute or repeated exposure to violence, such as, most notably, when Robin watches the

TOPICS FOR FURTHER STUDY

- Read Julia Alvarez's 2002 young-adult novel *Before We Were Free*, which features a Dominican girl named Anna. Her father is part of a conspiracy to overthrow the government. In a book report, compare and contrast Robin's experiences as a soldier with Anna's experiences as a citizen, focusing on their attempts to navigate civil and political unrest.

- Robin's squad moves through several parts of Iraq as they fulfill their duties. Use the Internet to access maps of the area and trace their journey. Then create a multimedia presentation that includes commentary on the different locations.

- Once Saddam Hussein is deposed, the main source of conflict in Iraq stems from long-standing tensions between the Sunnis, Shiites, and Kurds. Research these tensions and, forming three groups to represent each faction, stage a class debate. How should Iraq be governed? Can you find a way to agree?

- Is Robin's experience of war (particularly his feelings of fear and stress, his concern about ethics, and his distaste for violence) typical of real soldiers? Conduct an interview with a veteran or find first-person reports via the Internet. Edit the results into a short documentary.

- In retrospect more than at the time, the Iraq War has been considered highly controversial. Write a research paper on the controversy surrounding the war, addressing such key topics as the Iraqi informant known as Curveball, Secretary of State Colin Powell's address to the United Nations, Secretary of Defense Donald Rumsfeld's role in planning for the war, President George W. Bush's "Mission Accomplished" speech, the search for weapons of mass destruction, and the prolonged fighting in and American occupation of Iraq.

Much of the protagonist's time in Iraq is spent in Baghdad, where he is part of a unit negotiating matters between the troops and the citizens of Iraq. (© Frontpage / Shutterstock.com)

Iraqi boy die and when he sees his friends Pendleton and Jonesy sustain fatal injuries. But trauma also occurs when Robin is forced to kill the men who attack Miller. It occurs every time Robin and his fellow soldiers fear for their lives.

Robin drives by a café and imagines the people inside of it tracking his movements. He sees a truck and thinks of a recent car bombing. He says that the "vibrations" of explosions and gunfire become constant even when they are not there, "as if, little by little, I was bringing the crash of war inside me." It is "as if . . . the war was becoming part of me."

The Iraqi people are traumatized as well. Women cry in the street, and innocent men and children are forced to fight.

Moral Ambiguity

Moral ambiguity is consistently present as the Civil Affairs unit attempts to help civilians while gathering information, looking for bombs and weapons, and preventing further violence—all

while defending themselves against imminent attack. This ambiguity is first pointed out by Danforth's comment about blowing up Iraqis in order to help them afterward. It is also apparent in the constantly changing ROE; the soldiers are confused about when they can use their weapons and whom they can use them against. They have trouble separating civilians from insurgents, especially when civilians are being forced into battle against their will. Robin's squad is aware of the questionable and complicated morality of their situation.

Civilians in Al-Uhaimir are bombed after being forced to fight by the Ba'athists, but Coles reports that the bombing was justified because the men were enemy combatants. Miller attempts to combat such ambiguity by helping the injured without question and by confronting Colonel Roberts about their unethical mission. Robin addresses these concerns best in his final letter to his uncle, stating, "There's a distance between what my brain says I'm doing . . . and what I'm feeling inside."

STYLE

Humor

Throughout the novel, Robin's fellow soldiers rely on jokes and humor to break the tension. Readers experience this humor the same way, as the novel's stressful moments are relieved by the soldiers' banter. Danforth points out the irony (the contrast between how things are expressed and how they really are) of blowing people up only to patch them back together again. Jonesy makes up silly blues songs about their experiences. Marla picks on Robin and relies on sarcasm. She names the taxidermic monkey and carries it around with the squad, an absurd act. Although Robin is not without a sense of humor, he tends to play the straight man in the group. In one such earnest moment, he comments, "I hoped God wouldn't think it was funny to let me die sitting next to a monkey."

Epistolary Novel

While most epistolary novels are told entirely, or mostly, through letters, *Sunrise over Fallujah* contains only a handful. Nonetheless, Robin's e-mails and letters to his uncle, mother, and father provide a valuable counterpart to the action. They reveal the difference between the horrors Robin experiences and his mostly cheerful messages. Almost all of Robin's letters mention that things are going well, and in those that do not, Robin writes that he probably will not send them.

Robin's letters also allow him to discuss his problems with his father and his desire to help the people of Iraq. They relate his experiences to those of his Vietnam veteran uncle. Most importantly, the epistolary aspects of *Sunrise over Fallujah* allow Robin to connect to the world outside Iraq and to a life that exists outside the war.

Juxtaposition

Juxtaposition places two or more items beside one another for an inevitable comparison. This device can occur in both literary and visual mediums, and it is most effective when the juxtaposed items serve as contrasting elements. Several notable juxtapositions are found in *Sunrise over Fallujah*. The soldiers are cracking jokes one moment and taking gunfire the next, and they often career between feelings of boredom and fear. There is little to do on base but watch TV, but boredom is immediately replaced by terror as soon as Robin and his squad leave the safety of the base. After

Pendleton's heartbreaking memorial, Robin writes a happy letter to his mother. After Robin kills Miller's captors, the soldiers celebrate Darcy's twenty-first birthday. These latter examples seem to indicate that life goes on, that happiness, celebration, and love persist, even as they are surrounded by fighting, sadness, and death.

HISTORICAL CONTEXT

Vietnam War

The Vietnam War, which stretched from 1954 to 1975, was primarily fought between North Vietnam and South Vietnam. The Communist-led North and its allies in the South, the Viet Cong, sought to unify the North and South under one Communist government. The United States, allied with the South, provided military assistance throughout the first decade of the war, finally entering active combat in 1965. US involvement in the war was increasingly unpopular among American voters, especially in the face of heavy casualties, and US troops withdrew in 1973. The South subsequently fell to the North in 1975.

More than two million Vietnamese citizens were killed during the war, while roughly 1.3 million Vietnamese soldiers died on both sides, More than fifty-eight thousand American soldiers were killed as well. Like the Iraq War, the Vietnam War was typified by insurgent and guerrilla warfare. Both wars featured political infighting among the populace, and both US war efforts were motivated by an American foreign policy that focused on removing or preventing nondemocratic forms of government. Neither war had a clear winner or loser.

Saddam Hussein

Saddam Hussein joined the revolutionary Ba'ath Party in 1957 and took part in a failed attempt to assassinate Iraqi prime minister Abd al-Karim Qasim in 1959. He fled the country and remained in Egypt until the Ba'athists came to power in 1963. The party's power was short-lived, and Hussein was arrested and jailed later that year. He escaped and became Ba'ath Party leader, executing a coup against the Iraqi government and installing himself as vice president under Ahmad Hasan al-Bakr.

Hussein succeeded al-Bakr in 1979 and ordered troops to invade Iran in 1980. The invasion was an attempt to take over the country's oil

There is a seemingly endless stream of military vehicles traveling to Baghdad. *(© Anton Hlushchenko |*
Shutterstock.com)

production and bolster Iraq's economy, but it resulted in an eight-year military standoff instead. Hussein's army invaded Kuwait with the same goal in 1990. After economic sanctions and diplomatic negotiations between Iraq and the United Nations failed to put an end to the occupation, the Persian Gulf War began on January 17, 1991. The war, led by the US military, lasted for six weeks and ended when Iraqi troops withdrew from Kuwait.

This defeat led to political unrest and tribal tensions in Iraq, but Hussein relied on violence, intimidation, and secret police to retain political control. The United Nations levied further sanctions against Iraq, prohibiting the country from owning nuclear, chemical, or biological weapons. Hussein refused to cooperate with UN inspectors, which caused a brief air strike against the country in 1998. Even so, Hussein continued to bar weapons inspectors from entering Iraq. Pressure increased after the terrorist attacks of

September 11, 2001; while Hussein complied briefly in 2002, his cooperation was limited and short-lived.

The United States and United Kingdom at length severed diplomatic relations with Iraq and began transporting troops into the area. On March 17, 2003, President George W. Bush told Hussein to abdicate power and leave Iraq or prepare to be invaded. Allied troops entered the country on March 20, marking the first day of the Iraq War.

CRITICAL OVERVIEW

Critical response to *Sunrise over Fallujah* has been largely positive, as reviewers have commended Myers for offering young readers an engaging examination of modern warfare. Discussing the novel's link to *Fallen Angels* in her

Booklist review, Jennifer Mattson finds that both "deliver a searing statement about how the lessons of history go unheeded as the fog of war envelops generation after generation." Betty Carter in *Horn Book* focuses on *Sunrise over Fallujah*'s emotional powers, writing that the novel "takes readers behind the headlines to . . . an existence full of fear, bravery, boredom, confusion, compassion, and violence." As a *Kirkus Reviews* contributor points out, "This is an important volume, covering much ground and offering much insight."

Some critics, however, warn that Robin, in focusing on the events and people around him, fails to become a well-defined character. *Kliatt* correspondent Paula Rohrlick writes, "Myers succeeds in making the reader feel what it's like to be in Iraq, though Robin remains something of a blank slate." A *Publishers Weekly* contributor seconds this opinion, asserting, "Robin serves more as a lens on the war than as a narrator whose voice surprises or compels the reader." The contributor nevertheless concludes that *Sunrise over Fallujah* "will allow American teens to grapple intelligently and thoughtfully with the war in Iraq."

The Iraq War was declared over on May 1, 2003, by President George W. Bush, but Myers's 2008 novel suggests how fighting continued well past that date. "This is an astonishing book," Leonard S. Marcus remarks in the *New York Times Book Review*, and he stresses that Robin and his friends are reassigned—not relieved from duty—as the novel ends. They are still soldiers serving in the midst of war. US troops were not fully withdrawn from Iraq until 2011, and Marcus notes in his 2008 review that "like the war it chronicles, its main characters' stories have not yet come to a close. . . . We leave them not knowing who will make it home."

CRITICISM

Leah Tieger

Tieger is a freelance writer and editor. In the following essay, she examines the soldiers' changing attitude toward media and the news as the war progresses in Sunrise over Fallujah.

Walter Dean Myers's *Sunrise over Fallujah* follows a small group of soldiers who sincerely hope to help the Iraqi people. Robin and his squad are frustrated by the increasing hopelessness

WHAT DO I READ NEXT?

- Myers's *Fallen Angels* is the ideal complement to *Sunriseover Fallujah*, featuring crossover characters and similar themes. In his *Sunrise over Fallujah* interview, Myers shared that *Fallen Angels* (1988) was easier to write because "as a younger man I thought there might eventually be a time when there would be no more wars. I no longer feel that way."

- For a different approach to Myers's work, try his young-adult memoir *Bad Boy* (2001), which outlines the author's rebellious adolescence. Myers recounts his decision to drop out of school, his refuge in books, and how he came to terms with race and class divides.

- The taxidermic monkey that Marla names Sergeant Yossarian in *Sunrise over Fallujah* references the main character of Joseph Heller's 1961 novel *Catch-22*. Set during World War II, *Catch-22* is considered the definitive war novel and satire, combining sarcasm, irony, and ridicule to lambast the experience of war and military policies.

- Ji-li Jiang's young-adult memoir *Red Scarf Girl: A Memoir of the Cultural Revolution* shares the author's experiences as a twelve-year-old in China during the Cultural Revolution. Published in 1997 and set in the 1960s, *Red Scarf Girl* offers further insight into the impact of war.

- Another personal take on war can be found in *Stolen Voices: Young People's War Diaries, from World War I to Iraq*. Edited by Zlata Filipovic and Melanie Challenger, the 2006 collection includes fifteen diaries kept by young adults during the wars of the twentieth and twenty-first centuries.

- *A Historical Atlas of Iraq*, by Larissa Phillips, was released in 2003. The book offers students a valuable resource for tracing Iraq's changing geography.

of their goals, and their feelings are reflected in their attitude toward the news and other media. As they begin their tour of duty, Robin and his squad watch war movies, films about Saddam Hussein, and the news. They turn to these sources for comfort, guidance, and information. After the war begins and they gain experience, the unit realizes that the news does not reflect reality. Robin's squad begins to appear in press conferences and human-interest stories, and they resent the way the media has turned them into performers who contribute to this inaccurate portrayal.

In the first chapter of the novel, Captain Coles takes roll call, asks the soldiers to introduce themselves, and tells them they are not on *American Idol* (a popular reality-TV program). In the second chapter, the soldiers watch a film about Hussein, one that features images of the genocide he led against the Kurds. The soldiers watch training films and *Top Gun*, a blockbuster movie about fighter pilots. As they wait for the war to begin, Robin notes, "Most of what we learned was from the television news." Yet, while the squad relies on the news for information, part of them already acknowledges that the truth feels like fiction. The soldiers get to know each other, and Marla comments that she feels as if they are actors in a war movie. A few sentences later, Robin says that a televised speech by the president sounds like something from a cowboy film.

When the third chapter begins, Robin and his fellow soldiers watch films about the Persian Gulf War. The Iraq War starts with bombing in Baghdad, and Robin and his squad watch the action from a television on base. In the fourth chapter, Robin's unit travels into Iraq and stops along the way to watch CNN. A soldier tells an interviewer about sacrifice and duty. Marla states that they would not put him on television if he admitted he was scared, and Jonesy says he would do the same thing to get on TV. This conversation indicates that the soldiers are beginning to understand that the war, as seen on the news, contains an element of performance. This point is underscored when the soldiers watch the news a second time and are shown images of cheering Iraqis. Coles asks, "If they weren't cheering, would they be on television?"

The fourth chapter also ends with a reference to films and the divide between fact and fiction. After he watches a teenager die in front of him, Robin thinks of it as a horror movie that is "out of focus." But in his mind, "the images . . . [are] crystal clear." Robin's views continue to change as he experiences more and more violence. In the fifth chapter, he realizes that the war looked "better" in the training movies, "when it was all just a video game." Now the war is "connected with real people." Robin repeats this realization in the next chapter, as he says that the war on TV "seemed so simple" but the "clarity disappeared" after he got close to the fighting.

The soldiers' loss of faith in the media is complete in the seventh chapter. Robin admits that he and his squad look away from the television when it makes reports "we knew weren't true." The soldiers' awareness of the gap between the news and their experience increases in the following chapter. They listen to two different wars: the media version broadcast on Jonesy's radio and the Third Infantry's transmissions sent to them through the radio in their Humvee. Goofing around on base, Jonesy uses his flashlight as a microphone to "interview" his friends, and Robin acknowledges that the fighting is worse than the news will report.

By the ninth chapter, Robin and his squad have given up on the news altogether, and they watch reruns of baseball games from the 1980s instead. In the tenth chapter, they watch a trashy reality show about the police. After Robin's squad finds a missing Iraqi teenager in the eleventh chapter, they return to the base and learn that Major Sessions has arranged a press conference. "That pissed us off," Robin remarks. The reporters decide to feature Marla in the interview because she is a pretty blonde, and Jonesy sarcastically recreates the event, using his spoon as a microphone.

Robin's squad appears on the news a second time in the next chapter. They play soccer against a team of Iraqi teens, and Marla makes a joke about it, suggesting that she and Captain Miller should "strip down to our shorts and shake our booties for the camera." The soldiers continue to choose bad TV over the unreliable news, spending three hours watching cartoons. Afterward, they escort a bus full of reporters and a bus full of Iraqis to Ba'qubah to, as Coles describes it, "show our pretty faces for a camera op." The American soldiers transfer control of a water project to Iraqi police, and Robin thinks the Special Ops officers at the hand-off look as if they came from "central casting." No longer naive, Robin's squad knows they are performing for the news, creating a veritable fiction that passes for reality.

In the thirteenth chapter, Robin tries to read a newspaper, but he is not sure why he bothers.

Although Myers's characters are not on the front lines, they see the effects of war on civilians and other soldiers. *(© Pavel Bernshtam | Shutterstock.com)*

His experiences are only a small part of the war, and he wants to see the bigger picture, only he cannot find it on the television, on the radio, or in the paper. When the squad regroups on the base in As Sayliyah in the next chapter, they watch the news for the last time. Robin says that the war is a game with no rules, and the television is a scoreboard that tells them how the game is going. The observation makes it seem as if Robin is trying to believe in the news again, but his squad takes part in an unethical secret mission immediately after, and the media is not mentioned once during the entire episode. Robin's mission reveals the complicated truth about the war and the tactics being used to fight it. The closer the soldiers are to the truth, the farther they are from the news; the deeper they enter into the game, the farther they are from the scoreboard.

In his final letter to his uncle in the fifteenth chapter, Robin makes one last comment about the news, writing that a recent copy of the *New York Times* makes no mention of the war on the front page, and only a small section buried within lists the names of the dead. The optimistic news coverage comforted Robin as he entered the war, but now it saddens him because it cannot honor the sacrifices his fellow soldiers have made. As Myers explained in his interview about the book, the Iraq War was "hailed as an easy victory." He knew, however, "that there were men and women being killed, that behind the easy headlines there were tragedies." By the end of *Sunrise over Fallujah*, Robin and the surviving members of his squad know this as well.

Source: Leah Tieger, Critical Essay on *Sunrise over Fallujah*, in *Novels for Students*, Gale, Cengage Learning, 2014.

Diane P. Tuccillo

In the following review, Tuccillo appreciates Myers's memorable characters and vivid setting.

Instead of heading to college as his father wishes, Robin leaves Harlem and joins the army to stand up for his country after 9/11. While stationed in Iraq with a war looming that he hopes will be averted, he begins writing letters home to his parents and to his Uncle Richie, the main character from Myers's acclaimed Vietnam War novel, *Fallen Angels* (Scholastic, 1988). Robin finds himself in a diverse Civil Affairs unit of both men and women, with a mission to serve as a buffer between winning over the Iraqi people and concurrent military operations. As the war unfolds, the military angle of Robin's job escalates, and he experiences increasing horrors of violence, death, destruction, insecurity, sorrow, and extreme fear. Ultimately, he comprehends the reasons Uncle Richie never wanted to talk to their family about what happened in Vietnam, saying, "...are there really enough words to make them understand?" Myers brilliantly freeze-frames the opening months of the current Iraq War by realistically capturing its pivotal moments in 2003 and creating a vivid setting. Memorable characters share instances of wry levity that balance the story without deflecting its serious tone. Through precise, believable dialogue as the catalyst, tame compared to that warranted in *Fallen Angels*, Myers's expert portrayal of a soldier's feelings and perspectives at the onset of this controversial war allows the circumstances to speak for themselves.

Source: Diane P. Tuccillo, Review of *Sunrise over Fallujah*, in *School Library Journal*, Vol. 54, No. 4, April 2008, p. 146.

Publishers Weekly

In the following review, a reviewer praises the effective, if predictable, climax in Sunrise over Fallujah.

Here it is at last—the novel that will allow American teens to grapple intelligently and thoughtfully with the war in Iraq. Robin Perry, nephew of the soldier central to Myers's Vietnam novel *Fallen Angels*, has joined up because, as he fumblingly writes to his uncle on the eve of the invasion in 2003, "I felt like crap after 9-11 and I wanted to do something, to stand up for my country." Massing in Kuwait, assigned to a Civil Affairs unit, he finds that his motives continue to elude him as he assesses his fellow soldiers, all of whom seem tougher, braver, better directed. Even as the author exposes Robin's ambivalent feelings and doubts, he re-creates the climate of the earliest days of the war, when victory seems definable and soldiers credibly talk in March or April of being home by Christmas.

Robin serves more as a lens on the war than as a narrator whose voice surprises or compels the reader. His comrades, too, conform to type; rather than individuals, they are representatives of characters familiar to war movies and genre fiction: the soulful musician whose awareness of irony does not stop him from heroism; the medic who defies military protocol in her humanitarianism; the tough-talking gunner female—who quips her way through danger. In this novel, the conventions are helpful: they ground the reader. For as the Civil Affairs unit moves from a mission of winning "hearts and minds" to having to apologize for the "collateral damage" of having bombed a school and killed children in the "fog of war," the characters realize they are in the middle of many wars, none of which they understand. Readers will get a sense of the complexities of the war, and of the ways the rank-and-file, as represented by Robin, are slowly drawn into covert or morally dubious engagement. The action builds toward a climax that is affecting despite being easily foreseen. At the end, when Robin writes his uncle one last letter, asking, "[A]re there really enough words to make [kids] understand [about war]," the book itself dares readers to lift that question off the page; it is a forceful bid for their hearts and minds.

Source: Review of *Sunrise over Fallujah*, in *Publishers Weekly*, Vol. 255, No. 16, April 21, 2008, p. 59.

Rudine Sims Bishop

In the following excerpt, Bishop discusses Myers as one of the few African Americans writing specifically for young adults.

MYERS THE AFRO-AMERICAN NOVELIST

One of Myers's major contributions has been his authentic and generally positive portrayal of Black life in urban United States. The significance of this contribution becomes clear when it is placed in its historical context. Myers's first book was published in 1969. Just four years earlier, Nancy Larrick had lamented in the pages of the *Saturday Review* the near-total absence of Blacks in books published by juvenile publishers between 1962 and 1964. Historically, when Blacks had been portrayed in books for young people, the images presented had been laughable and insulting stereotypes, such as the servants in

> AT THE SAME TIME THAT HIS BOOKS OFFER INSIGHTS ABOUT BLACK LIFE, THEY ALSO DEAL WITH THEMES THAT CAN BE FOUND IN OTHER YOUNG ADULT LITERATURE AND IN LITERATURE IN GENERAL: FRIENDSHIPS AND PEER RELATIONSHIPS, FAMILY, INDIVIDUAL AND SOCIAL RESPONSIBILITY, LOVE, GROWING UP, FINDING ONESELF."

series like Tom Swift and the Bobbsey Twins. The advent of the civil rights movement of the sixties and the war on poverty of the Johnson administration, along with the generally liberal attitude in the country, stimulated a major increase in the numbers of books by and about Blacks and other so-called minorities.

During the early part of this period, books about Blacks were frequently written by white authors, and many suffered from a lack of authenticity. However, by 1975, when *Fast Sam* was published, Myers saw himself as a part of a new beginning. A number of young adult novels by Black authors had already been published. Kristin Hunter's *The Soul Brothers and Sister Lou* had won, in a different category, the same Council on Interracial Books for Children Minority Writers Contest that had given Myers his start. Other novels with urban settings were Sharon Bell Mathis's *Teacup Full of Roses* and *Listen for the Fig Tree*; June Jordan's *His Own Where*; Rosa Guy's *The Friends*; Eloise Greenfield's *Sister*; Alice Childress's *A Hero Ain't Nothin' but a Sandwich*. The year of *Fast Sam* was also the year that Virginia Hamilton became the first Black author to win the Newbery Medal, although it should be pointed out that *M. C. Higgins, the Great* was not an urban novel.

The urban novels of the late sixties and early seventies were part of the new realism in adolescent literature. They not only presented Black characters, but they included previously avoided topics such as drugs, sex, and street violence. The characters often lived in harsh circumstances, and the authors portrayed them realistically. Parents were not always positive role models, and endings were not always happy. Growing up Black in the city was shown to be a very difficult task.

Myers's contribution in his early books was to add a much needed touch of humor to the developing portrait of Black life in the city. Other Black authors were offering hope for overcoming adversity and focusing on the tradition of survival that is strong in the culture and an important theme in Afro-American novels. But Myers called attention to the laughter that is also a strong tradition and one of the tools for survival.

Although he is not unique in presenting authentic representations of Blacks and Black life, his is a unique voice. At this writing he is the only Black male currently and consistently publishing young adult novels. Although he shares certain aspects of his world view with Black women authors, his voice has been tuned by barbershops and street corners, bongo drums and fatherhood, basketball and military service. His brand of humor, his facile rendering of the rhetoric of Black teenage boys, his strong focus on fathers and sons, are all shaded by his experiences as a Black male. A look at Myers's urban novels reveals not only two sides of Black urban life, but also two important threads woven through the books. One thread is an authentic picture of life within a cultural group. The other is a set of themes, an offering of wisdom and insights into what it means to grow up a member of the Black community. In one set of his books, the harshness of the urban setting is backdrop; the focus is young people and their escapades. In the other, the urban setting is an integral part of the story itself. The portrayal of the Black experience and the insights he offers can be found in both.

The authenticity of Myers's portrayals of Black life is heightened by his weaving of important elements of Black culture into his stories. He is best known for his realistic representation of the rhetorical, grammatical, and semantic characteristics of Black English. Whenever his Black characters speak, they sound like real Black people. It should be noted that although his informal vernacular is most noticeable to critics, his characters reflect the full range of Black urban speech, both female and male, from street corner rapping to formal standard English.

Another cultural thread that Myers weaves through the urban novels is religion. Particularly in the novels that include older female characters (such as Grandma Carrie in *It Ain't All for Nothin'* and Sister Gibbs in *Crystal*) the language and the music of the Black church are used to build character and setting. On the other hand, particularly in *Mojo and the Russians*, Myers recognizes that non-Christian belief systems can still exist in the Black community side by side with Christianity.

Other aspects of Black culture are woven into the stories as a part of the setting, a reflection of the details of daily living of people who belong to a distinct cultural group. References to sacred and secular music and to musicians are sprinkled throughout the books. Aphorisms turn up frequently, often in the mouths of older women. Occasionally the names of a few Black heroes can be found. In one book, *The Legend of Tarik*, Myers offers to young Black readers an epic Black hero whose qualities—strength, determination, endurance, intelligence, compassion—represent a cultural ideal.

Myers himself identifies what he and the other Black novelists were doing: "I had learned from [Langston] Hughes that being a Black writer meant more than simply having one's characters brown-skinned, or having them live in what publishers insist on describing on book jackets as a 'ghetto.' It meant understanding the nuances of value, of religion, of dreams. It meant capturing the subtle rhythms of language and movement and weaving it all, the sound and the gesture, the sweat and the prayers, into the recognizable fabric of black life."

Also woven into the tapestry of Black life that Myers offers his readers are insights that might help them understand what it means to grow up Black in the urban centers of this nation. Myers is clear about the obstacles and hardships that often must be faced in such a setting, especially by people who are poor. Drugs, gangs, and violence are a fact of life in many large cities. Social agencies cannot always be depended on to provide support, or if they do help, their support sometimes comes at the expense of a loss of pride, dignity, or control over one's own life. Racism is a given. Myers is also clear about the potential for overcoming the hardships. He writes of love and laughter and offers compassion and hope. He writes of the need to find strength within oneself and of the possibility of finding strength within the group, whether the group is the family, the peer group, or the community.

This notion of community support, of Blacks helping Blacks, is important to Myers. He notes that television programs and books by white authors often portray whites helping Blacks (as in "Different Strokes" or "Webster," in which white families adopt Black children), or they portray Blacks helping whites, whites helping whites, but not usually Blacks helping Blacks. Myers says, "I find that a very precious relationship, and it's being omitted, so when I write I thought I should write about that."

At the same time that his books offer insights about Black life, they also deal with themes that can be found in other young adult literature and in literature in general: friendships and peer relationships, family, individual and social responsibility, love, growing up, finding oneself. Myers succeeds, therefore, in embedding the universal inside the particulars of the reflected lives of people whose image, in the field of children's and young adult literature, had for too many years suffered neglect and abuse. Again, Myers speaks for himself: "What I wanted to do was to portray this vital community as one that is very special to a lot of people. I wanted to show the people I knew as being as richly endowed with those universal traits of love, humor, ambition as any in the world. This, I ·hope, is what my books do. That space of earth was no ghetto, it was home. Those were not exotic stereotypes, those were my people. And I love them."

MYERS THE GENERALIST

Myers is proud to be an Afro-American young adult novelist, but he is first of all a writer and can and does write about other people, in other genres, and about other topics. He has written short stories, nonfiction magazine pieces, nonfiction children's books, books for older elementary-age readers, mysteries, adventure stories, easy-to-read science fiction, picture books, and a new novel offering some blank space and invitations for the reader to add his or her own writing to the book.

The adult stories, published in the seventies, reveal some of Myers's versatility. The stories offer a different world view from that in his work for young people. There is some bitterness ("How Long Is Forever?"), tragedy ("The Vision of Felipe"), loneliness ("The Going On"), insanity ("The Dark Side of the Moon"). One or two may be precursors of the work to come. "The Vision of Felipe," set in Peru, features a gentle, sensitive, and compassionate young boy, who when orphaned by his grandmother's death goes off to the city to seek his fortune. Felipe is in many ways similar to Tito, the Puerto Rican boy in *Scorpions.* Like Tito, Felipe has been greatly influenced by his beloved grandmother's teachings, and his relationship with his friend Daniel is in some ways similar to that between Jamal and Tito. Other stories are related to Myers's young adult work only in that they explore similar topics. "Juby" includes a white person studying voodoo, though the story is in a much darker vein than *Mojo and the Russians.* The dialect used in the narrative has a Caribbean flavor similar to the one in *Mr. Monkey and the Gotcha Bird.* Both "Juby" and "Gums," in which a grandfather and his young grandson are overcome by their fear of a personified Death, may have their roots in the scary stories Myers remembers his father telling. "Bubba" features a white soldier who is part of the military escort for the funeral of a Black soldier killed in Vietnam. He spends the night in the home of the deceased soldier's mother and has to confront the issue of racism as it sometimes operates in the military. The issue is one of those touched on in *Fallen Angels.*

Myers has also produced two nonfiction books for young people, *The World of Work* and *Social Welfare. The World of Work* draws on the knowledge Myers acquired when he was a vocational placement supervisor for the New York State Employment Service. It is a guide to selecting a career, including descriptions of numerous jobs, their requirements, the method of entry, possibilities for advancement. True to his storytelling self, Myers introduces *The World of Work* with an imaginative speculation about how a hungry cave man might have created for himself the first job.

Social Welfare is a brief history and explanation of the welfare system, how it operates, who it serves, its problems, and some possible solutions. Both are well written—clear and straightforward. Both are over ten years old and somewhat dated, although *Social Welfare* is not nearly as dated as its author might wish it to be, given his expressed desire for change in the system. The books are nonfiction that is accurate, clear, and interestingly written.

Myers is willing to take risks with format, genre, and style, and he does so with varying degrees of success. *Brainstorm* is a science fiction story written with a limited vocabulary and designed for reluctant or remedial readers in fifth through eighth grades. Although Myers says that he would like to "bring some good literature" to the easy reader form, the restrictions on length and vocabulary make that a difficult task. It *is* possible to do what he did with *Brainstorm*—present interesting but undeveloped characters in a fast-moving plot. *Brainstorm* appeals also because it uses black-and-white photographs of a diverse group of teenagers who are the crew of a space ship sent to an alien planet to investigate the cause of a spate of "brainstorms" that have been destroying humans on earth.

Brainstorm received reasonably good notices, but the reviews of *The Black Pearl and the Ghost* range from scathingly negative to a cheerful acceptance of the book as spoof and a recognition of its good points. *Kirkus* called it "clunkingly obvious . . . hollow, creaky." The *Children's Book Services* reviewer found it "static . . . neither well-written nor interesting . . . trivia." On the other hand, *Booklist* saw "funny characters . . . sprightly pace," and *Horn Book* accepted it as "exaggerated in style and designed to meet the tastes of children."

A good reviewer must consider what the author was trying to do. *The Black Pearl and the Ghost; or One Mystery after Another* is a spoof meant for children somewhere between ages seven and ten. The humor starts with the subtitle (the book consists of two mysteries, one after another) and continues through the joke shared with the reader but not the ghost-busting detective. It is a profusely illustrated book, although not quite a picture book, and an important part of the story is told in Robert Quackenbush's amusing pictures.

Myers's books for elementary school readers, including his picture books, show a vivid imagination at work. His realistic stories, *Where Does the Day Go?* and *The Dancers*, are built on premises that were unusual at the time of their publication: a group of Black and Hispanic children speculating about a natural phenomenon and receiving answers from a Black father, and a Black boy from Harlem intrigued by ballet. *Fly, Jimmy, Fly* shows a young boy using his imagination to soar above the city. *The Golden Serpent*, set in India and illustrated by the Provensens, sets up a mystery that it leaves unresolved. *The Dragon Takes a Wife* takes the traditional knight-fights-a-dragon tale and twists it to make the dragon the protagonist, as Kenneth Grahame did in *The Reluctant Dragon.* Then Myers adds a touch of Blackness in the form of Mabel Mae Jones and her hip, rhyming spells. Although Kirkus called it "intercultural hocus pocus," other reviewers found it amusing, even delightful. The imaginative humor works. *Mr. Monkey and the Gotcha Bird* dips into African and Caribbean folk traditions for its narrative voice and its trickster monkey who outsmarts the gotcha bird who would have him for supper.

Myers's novel for readers under twelve, *Me, Mop, and the Moondance Kid*, echoes some of the concerns and qualities of his young adult novels. The story is told by T.J., who, along with his younger brother, Moondance, has been recently adopted. Their task is to help their friend Mop (Miss Olivia Parrish), who is still at the orphanage, to be adopted too, preferably by the coach of their Little League team, which they are trying to turn into a winner. The style is typical Myers: T.J.'s narration is easygoing and humorous, characters are credible and likable, the plot moves along briskly, and the human relationships are warm.

Sweet Illusions is a young adult novel, published by the Teachers and Writers Collaborative, that experiments with format. It is an episodic novel focusing on teenage pregnancy. Not only is each chapter narrated by a different character, but at the end of each chapter the reader is invited to help create the story by writing a letter, a song, a list, a daydream. Lined pages are available for writing directly in the book (with a caution about not writing in library books). The characters are Black, white, and Hispanic, and all of them are learning of the difficulties and responsibilities involved in becoming parents. Both the young women and the fathers of their children tell their stories, which raise hard issues involved in teenage pregnancy: decisions about abortion and adoption, parental and community attitudes toward the mothers, irresponsibility on the part of the fathers, continuing their education, providing for the child. The book works. Myers has, in a brief space, managed to create believable characters with individual voices. Their stories are unique and at the same time recognizable to anyone who has thought about or grappled with the problems of teenage pregnancy. The purpose is to provoke thought, which happens as readers get caught up in the characters and their stories.

In spite of its workbook format, *Sweet Illusions* received some serious critical attention. *Booklist*, for example, gave it high praise, calling it "an astute, realistic consideration of some of the problems associated with teenage pregnancy, valuable for personal reading as well as classroom discussion." Further, the reviewer found that "Myers' profiles are quick and clever; his characters, stubborn, confused, and vulnerable, draw substance and individuality from tough, savvy dialogue and credible backdrops." It is an unusual book that succeeds because it draws on Myers's highly developed craftsmanship....

Source: Rudine Sims Bishop, "The Present and the Future: Myers the Artist," in *Presenting Walter Dean Myers*, Twayne Publishers, 1991, pp. 93–101.

SOURCES

Anderson, Dale, *Saddam Hussein*, Lerner, 2004, pp. 57–104.

Arnold, James R., *Saddam Hussein's Iraq*, Twenty-First Century, 2008, pp. 30–64, 124–36.

Austin, Lloyd James, III, *The Iraq War, 2003–2011*, US Department of the Army, 2012, pp. 21–45, 143–57.

Bosman, Julie, "Children's Book Envoy Defines His Mission," in *New York Times*, January 3, 2012, p. C1.

Carter, Betty, "Walter Dean Myers: *Sunrise over Fallujah*," in *Horn Book*, Vol. 84, No. 3, May–June 2008, p. 324.

"Christopher Winners," in *Publishers Weekly*, Vol. 256, No. 16, April 20, 2009, p. 8.

Marcus, Leonard S., "Boys to Men," in *New York Times Book Review*, May 11, 2008, p. 26.

Mattson, Jennifer, Review of *Sunrise over Fallujah*, in *Booklist*, Vol. 104, No. 12, February 15, 2008, p. 76.

McElmeel, Sharron L., "A Profile: Walter Dean Myers," in *Book Report*, Vol. 20, No. 2, September–October 2001, p. 42.

Miller, Mara, *The Iraq War: A Controversial War in Perspective*, Enslow Publishers, 2011, pp. 7–36, 71–83.

Myers, Walter Dean, *Sunrise over Fallujah*, Scholastic Press, 2009.

Review of *Sunrise over Fallujah*, in *Kirkus Reviews*, April 1, 2008, https://www.kirkusreviews.com/book-reviews/walter-dean-myers/sunrise-over-fallujah (accessed April 10, 2013).

Review of *Sunrise over Fallujah*, in *Publishers Weekly*, Vol. 255, No. 16, April 21, 2008, p. 59.

Rohrlick, Paula, Review of *Sunrise over Fallujah*, in *Kliatt*, Vol. 42, No. 3, May 2008, p. 15.

Schiraldi, Glenn, *The Post-traumatic Stress Disorder Sourcebook: A Guide to Healing, Recovery, and Growth*, 2nd ed., McGraw-Hill, 2009, pp. 3–13.

Subryan, Carmen, "Walter Dean Myers," in *Dictionary of Literary Biography*, Vol. 33, *Afro-American Fiction*

Writers after 1955, edited by Thadious M. Davis, Gale Research, 1984, pp. 199–202.

Willoughby, Douglas, *The Vietnam War*, Reed Educational/Heinemann Library, 2001, pp. 4–8.

FURTHER READING

Hughes, Langston, *Montage of a Dream Deferred*, Holt, 1951.
> Myers noted in his *Sunrise over Fallujah* interview that Hughes read at his church when he was a boy. This volume is one of the Harlem poet's most famous works.

Myers, Walter Dean, *Scorpions*, HarperCollins, 1988.
> Published the same year as *Fallen Angels*, *Scorpions* portrays a Harlem seventh grader and gang member who comes face to face with gun violence. The story was named a Newbery Honor Book in 1989.

Polk, William R., *Understanding Iraq: The Whole Sweep of Iraqi History, from Genghis Khan's Mongols to the Ottoman Turks to the British Mandate to the American Occupation*, HarperCollins, 2005.
> Iraq has a long and complicated history, one that continues to influence the region and its likely future. In *Understanding Iraq*, Polk attempts to condense this history into a concise and readable volume.

Smith, Huston, *The Illustrated World's Religions: A Guide to Our Wisdom Traditions*, HarperOne, 2009.
> Most of the American soldiers in Myers's novel are Christian, while most of the Iraqi citizens are Muslim. This book offers brief but comprehensive overviews of both religions, as well as Hinduism, Judaism, Buddhism, and others.

SUGGESTED SEARCH TERMS

Walter Dean Myers

Sunrise over Fallujah AND Myers

Fallen Angels AND Myers

Harlem

Iraq War

Vietnam War

Saddam Hussein

history of Iraq

Persian Gulf War

Swallowing Stones

JOYCE MCDONALD

1997

Joyce McDonald's 1997 novel *Swallowing Stones* is her second foray into the world of young-adult literature. In the work, seventeen-year-old Michael MacKenzie aimlessly shoots a rifle into the air, only to find out the next day that the bullet killed a man who was working on his roof a mile away. The story is told in sections that alternately focus on Michael and Jenna Ward, the fifteen-year-old daughter of the man who was killed. The work thus has two protagonists, both Michael and Jenna, making it somewhat unconventional. Jenna struggles with anxiety attacks after the death of her father, while Michael is consumed by intense feelings of guilt that he compares to the feeling of swallowing a stone. As Michael and Jenna suffer in their own ways, the themes of guilt, chance, and intuition are explored throughout the work, as are the social issues of gun control and teenage mental health. *Swallowing Stones* has been lauded by critics for the emotional depth with which McDonald has portrayed her characters.

AUTHOR BIOGRAPHY

McDonald was born on August 4, 1946, in San Francisco, California, but was raised in Chatham, New Jersey. Books were important to her from a young age. She has stated that in her childhood, her mother would read to her every night before bed, a tradition that she has kept up

Michael receives a rifle for his seventeenth birthday. (© Sari Oneal / Shutterstock.com)

on her own ever since. McDonald studied English in college, receiving both her bachelor's and master's degrees in English from the University of Iowa, in 1972 and 1974 respectively.

After university McDonald embarked on a career in the publishing industry. She was a production assistant at Charles Scribner's Sons from 1976 to 1978, a production editor at Springer-Verlag from 1978 to 1980, and a freelance editor from 1980 to 1984. In 1984 McDonald started her own small publishing press in New Jersey, McDonald Publishing Company/ Shoe Tree Press, which she ran from 1984 to 1989. She then went on to work as an editor for Betterway Publications from 1989 to 1990.

In the late 1980s McDonald began shifting her career from publishing and editing to writing and teaching. Her first book, a children's work titled *Mail-Order Kid*, was published in 1988. In 1989 she became an adjunct lecturer at Drew University, in Madison, New Jersey, a position she would hold until 2000. She also worked as an assistant professor of English at East Strouds-burg University, in Pennsylvania, from 1990 to

1996. She went back to school during this time and completed her doctorate in English at Drew University in 1994. While at Drew, McDonald was awarded the Helen LePage and William Hale Chamberlain Prize for her PhD dissertation, "The Incommunicable Past: Willa Cather's Pastoral Modes and the Southern Literary Imagination." The prize acknowledges a dissertation that is "singularly distinguished by creative thought and excellent prose style." During that period she also wrote and published another children's book, *Homebody* (1991), and her first young-adult novel, *Comfort Creek* (1996).

In 1997 McDonald's second young-adult work, *Swallowing Stones*, was published. It was named one of the American Library Association's Top Ten Best Books for Young Adults and one of *Booklist*'s 100 Best of the Best 1966–2003. In 2001 she published what is perhaps her best-known work to date, a young-adult novel called *Shades of Simon Gray*. That work was nominated for an Edgar Allan Poe Award. Her young-adult novels *Shadow People* and *Devil on My Heels* were published in 2000 and 2004.

For eight years beginning in 2002, McDonald taught at Spalding University's brief-residency MFA in Writing Program, in Louisville, Kentucky. She also served for twelve years on the Rutgers University Council on Children's Literature. She lives in Forks Township, Pennsylvania, with her husband, Hubert McDonald, where she continues to write and teach.

PLOT SUMMARY

Prologue
Swallowing Stones begins with a description of a bullet flying through the air on a hot summer day in the fictional town of Briarwood, New Jersey. A fifteen-year-old girl named Jenna Ward looks up at her father, Charlie Ward, as he is making repairs on the roof of their house. Just as he looks up from his work to wave at Jenna, he suddenly collapses, his body goes entirely limp, and he rolls off of the roof to land at Jenna's feet. It is implied here that the cause of his collapse was his being hit by the previously mentioned bullet.

Meanwhile, on the other side of town a high-school senior named Michael MacKenzie and his best friend, Joe Sadowski, admire the .45-70 Winchester rifle that Michael has just received that day in honor of his seventeenth birthday, which also happens to be the Fourth of July. Because Michael could not wait to fire the gun, he has just shot one single bullet aimlessly into the air. It is implied that that bullet is the same one that hit Charlie Ward. This has taken place during a large pool and barbecue party that Michael's parents have thrown for his birthday, though Joe and Michael snuck off into the woods to fire the gun where no one would see.

The chapter ends with the omniscient narrator informing the reader that at the end of the day, Michael will reflect on it as the best day of his life because he will not yet know that he has accidentally committed murder.

Chapter 1: Michael
Beginning with the first chapter, the story is told in segments that alternate in focus between Michael and Jenna, the two protagonists of the work. The first chapter follows Michael. The chapter begins early on the day after Michael's party. He has awoken early in anticipation of taking the test to receive his driver's license. As

MEDIA ADAPTATIONS

• *Swallowing Stones* was recorded as an audiobook, narrated by Ed Sala, and released by Recorded Books in 1998. The running time is 6 hours and 30 minutes.

he gets dressed for the day, he reflects on a makeout session he had the previous day during his party in his garage with Amy Ruggerio, a girl from his high school known for being promiscuous, despite the fact that his unsuspecting girlfriend, Darcy Kelly, was also at the party, helping his mother in the kitchen. Michael experiences conflicting feelings about his interaction with Amy. He enjoyed it, but it has made him feel remorseful. Michael eventually puts thoughts of Amy aside to finish getting ready, then heads over to his friend Joe's house. After he wakes up Joe and coaxes him out of bed, the two boys head to the DMV in Joe's Mustang, with Michael driving. In the midst of practice parallel parking the car, the two boys are distracted by a story on the radio about a man in their town being killed by a rogue bullet the previous day. They both immediately realize that the bullet probably came from Michael's gun, though they entertain the possibility that it may have come from elsewhere.

After discussing the ways that an involuntary manslaughter charge would affect Michael's future, the two decide to make a pact to get rid of the gun and pretend they had never shot it, though Michael feels uneasy about this plan. Nevertheless, he goes home and hides the gun, burying it in his backyard.

Chapter 2: Jenna
The morning after her father's death, Jenna wakes feeling emotionally numb. She goes about her morning routine indifferently, noticing little reminders of her father all around the house. She goes down to her father's workshop in the basement and reflects upon the events of the previous day in disbelief. She is called back

upstairs by her mother, who asks her to help clean the house in preparation for guests.

Soon police chief Dave Zelenski arrives to interview Jenna and her mother about the events of the day before. When Chief Zelenski informs Jenna and her mother that the ballistics team that will try to determine where the bullet came from will not be available until they finish their current case, Jenna erupts in a fit of anger, screaming at Zelenski. She tries to leave the house to go for a walk and calm down but is shocked to find a flurry of reporters and photographers blocking the front of her house.

Chapters 3–5: Michael
The next day, Michael makes breakfast by himself in the kitchen. While eating, he notices a story about the Wards in the local paper and is deeply affected by a picture of Jenna, knowing she is the daughter of the man he killed. His younger brother, Josh, comes downstairs and, to Michael's horror, explains that the entire town has heard about the shooting.

After breakfast, Michael heads to the local pool for his shift as a lifeguard. There he is confronted by his girlfriend, Darcy, who wants to know why he never showed up for their date the previous day. In truth he was so distracted about the shooting that he forgot. While on the lifeguard stand, he reflects on a story he heard about a local girl who died from inhaling a stone in a nearby lake. He thinks that if she had just swallowed the stone, it may have torn apart her insides but she would have survived. To him, keeping what he did a secret is akin to swallowing a stone.

Back at home after work, Michael eats dinner with his family while they discuss the Ward funeral. He leaves to pick up Darcy for a party in the midst of his father's rant about how stupid and senseless the death was. On the way to the party he thinks about how he should break up with Darcy. After overhearing some girls discuss Charlie Ward's murder, Michael makes an attempt to ditch the party but is distracted by Amy Ruggerio on the way out. When the party is broken up by the cops, Michael, his drunk friend Joe, and Darcy all flee.

The next day after finishing his work shift, Michael cannot stand the thought of going home. Instead, he walks around town mindlessly, ending up at Jenna's house. He sits in front of it for several hours. On his way home

he comes upon Amy's house by chance. She invites him in. The two accidentally end up spending the night together after falling asleep while playing board games.

Chapters 6–8: Jenna
A few days after her father's death, Jenna wakes up from a nightmare. She had been dreaming that a local sycamore tree known as the Ghost Tree was attacking her with its limbs. She has had this same dream three nights in a row, which perplexes her because she has never thought of the tree as scary at all.

In the wake of her father's death, Jenna finds comfort in obsessively rearranging and tidying her room and working complex math problems, which distract her and help clear her mind. At her father's funeral, she simply feels numb and does not even cry. Since his death she has only been able to cry in her sleep.

One night a few weeks after the accident Jenna and her mother finally discuss it. They wonder why they have been stricken with this tragedy instead of someone else. Afterward, Jenna goes up to her room and notices that the same boy who has been sitting on the church steps across from her house almost every night since her father's death is there. She does not yet know that that boy is Michael MacKenzie.

The next morning Jenna heads to the pool after being coaxed to go by Andrea. She looks for her boyfriend, Jason Freidman, who has just gotten back from camping with his family. When she finally meets up with him, she notices something very odd—he is making her feel nervous in a way that he never has before. Before leaving she notices one of the lifeguards, who Andrea informs her is Michael MacKenzie, staring at her.

Later that night at dinner, Jenna's mother informs her that the ballistics team has traced the origin of the bullet that killed her father to a four-block area. Desperate to know more Jenna heads to the police station, but she is not able to get any more information there. Not willing to give up, Jenna asks the town gossip, Annie Rico, and quickly learns where the four-block location is.

Later, on a movie date with Jason, Jenna has a panic attack when he slips his arm around her shoulders. In the bathroom at the theater, Amy Ruggerio helps her recover and confides that she has had panic attacks before herself.

Chapters 9–12: Michael

Chapter 9 begins with Michael having a vivid dream that he is a bullet headed toward a man's head. Upon waking, he believes that the dream was caused by his seeing Jenna Ward at the pool earlier that day. He goes into the kitchen and runs into his brother Josh, who informs him that the police are questioning everyone in their neighborhood and who makes a snide joke suggesting that Michael could be the killer. Michael begins to panic internally.

As time goes on, Michael spends more and more time hanging out with Amy at her house. He becomes increasingly attracted to her but tries to resist pursuing anything because he does not want to feel as if he is using her to escape his problems. One night, however, after she asks him why he never tries to kiss her, he finally does. At this point he fully realizes how much he actually likes her and knows that he has to break up with Darcy.

After avoiding Darcy for as long as possible, he is finally confronted by her about why they have not been hanging out and why he has been spending time with Amy. Darcy is furious that their relationship is dissolving and blames Amy for coming between them.

On a stormy night in early August, police officers Doug Boyle and Ralph Healey show up at the MacKenzie house to do some routine questioning concerning the Ward case. They are visiting everyone in a four-block area that encompasses both Michael's and Joe's houses. When asked to produce all of the guns in the house for inspection, Michael explains that he cannot give them his Winchester rifle because he lent it to Joe. When forced to call Joe in front of the police, Michael makes up a story about the gun being stolen out of Joe's car. After the police leave, Michael meets up with Joe, and the boys decide to stick to the story about the gun being stolen.

The next morning, Joe goes to the police station to file a police report about the missing gun. Later that day, when the police come to Joe's house for routine questioning, he tells them the same story.

A few days later Michael goes by Amy's house, only to find her on the front porch, her face blotchy from crying. Later at school he learns that Darcy and her friends told Amy that Michael had only been hanging out with her as part of a

bet to see how much he would be able to manipulate her.

Chapters 13–15: Jenna

One day in mid-August while hanging out with Andrea, Jenna tells her that she has been having a fantasy about shooting her father's killer. At home later that day Jenna receives a letter from Amy Ruggerio. In the letter, Amy explains that she understands what Jenna is going through because she lost both of her parents when she was seven. She says that she wrote the letter so that Jenna would know she is not alone. After reading it, Jenna begins to cry the first tears she has shed since her father died.

That night Jenna has the same dream about vines attacking her, but this time Amy appears in it, leading her to the Ghost Tree. In the morning Jenna's mother tells her that someone has been mysteriously completing chores around their house, such as cleaning the gutters and weeding the garden. This makes both of the women feel uneasy.

Later that day at the mall, Andrea talks Jenna into going to a party. At the party Jenna almost immediately runs into Jason. While the two of them talk outside, Jenna begins to feel anxious. She is thankful when Andrea interrupts them to excitedly inform Jenna that Michael has arrived. Jenna walks right up to his car and tells him that her friend, Andrea, wants to meet him. Jenna's presence seems to make Michael nervous, and he leaves immediately. When Jenna turns around, she notices Amy on the porch watching her.

Chapters 16–18: Michael

At the beginning of chapter 16 it is revealed that Michael is the one who has been tending to the Ward house, cleaning the gutters, taking care of the flower beds, and doing other tasks he believes Charlie Ward would have done if he were alive. One of his other routines has been going by Amy's house to try to talk to her, but so far he has had no luck. On one of his daily runs he spots Amy at the 7-Eleven. He tries to explain that he never meant to hurt her. Though things are still not back to normal between them, Michael feels elated about having reestablished contact.

This feeling quickly dissipates when he arrives home to find a flurry of policemen searching his backyard with metal detectors. To Michael's horror, they find the casing of the bullet that Michael fired in the woods, but are not able to find the gun itself. When questioned about the found casing, Michael claims that he had taken the gun out but had not fired it. He also says that he could not remember whether or not he locked it back up after taking it out. Michael's father says that anyone could have taken it and fired it, and Josh throws out the idea that it was probably Joe. Michael feels guilty for letting suspicion turn toward his friend. He realizes that the police probably never believed the gun was stolen.

The next day the boys meet up and go to the Ghost Tree, in the swamp, so that Michael can fill Joe in in private. Joe is not happy to learn that he is becoming the lead suspect in the case. Because Joe had been drinking, Michael insists on driving them home. On the way, they get into a minor car accident with Amy. Joe flies into a rage, jumping on her car and smashing the windshield, though Michael knows the person he is really angry at is him.

Chapters 19–20: Jenna
After having another dream about the Ghost Tree, as well as Michael, Amy, and this time her father, Jenna reflects on what her father had told her about the tree. Local Native American legend, that of the Lenape, designated it as a place where one could communicate with ancestors. According to her father, it was also a place of healing.

In the morning Jenna and her mother pack up some of Mr. Ward's things to give to charity. On their way out of the house, Annie Rico shows up claiming that she came by to check on them after hearing about new developments in the case. They immediately run inside to call the police department, only to be disappointed by the news that they had not caught the killer but had merely taken a suspect in for questioning. Without telling her mother, Jenna calls Annie Rico to learn that the suspect is Joe Sadowski. Desperate for more information, she goes by Joe's house just in time to see Michael show up at his front door.

Chapters 21–22: Michael
After working a shift at the pool, Michael comes home to the news that Joe has been taken in for questioning. He immediately runs over to Joe's house to hear what happened. He thinks for a moment that he sees Jenna across the street but convinces himself that he is being paranoid, not knowing that it really was her watching him. Joe seems agitated as Michael questions him about

what happened. He tells Michael that he stuck to the story but seems less confident that they will get away with everything. In the midst of this, the police arrive to search Joe's house. Michael tells him that if they charge Joe with anything, he will come forward and tell the truth. On the way home he wonders whether or not he would let Joe take the fall for him.

He stops by Amy's house and is surprised to actually find her there, and willing to talk to him. Amy reveals that Joe once told her he had brought her to Michael's party as a gift to Michael, with the expectation that she would have sex with him. She also tells him that the police were at her house that afternoon. Michael comes close to telling Amy the truth about shooting the bullet, but she interrupts him, explaining that she already knows what he is about to tell her. She witnessed him coming out of the woods at his party with Joe and the gun. As they embrace, Michael bursts into tears.

Chapters 23–24: Jenna
At the pool Jenna watches Amy, trying to work up the nerve to speak to her. She senses that Amy knows something about the case but is afraid of what her friends will think if they see her talking to Amy. She finally walks over to where Amy is sitting and thanks her for her letter. The two girls discuss the experience of losing a parent. Jenna is surprised when Amy tells her that the hardest part for her has been living with the guilt that she survived and her parents did not. When Jenna finally works up the nerve to ask Amy about Joe, Amy tells her that she does not believe that Joe is the one who killed her father. Jenna then notices that Michael is watching her and Amy talk, and he looks worried.

Later that night, Jason shows up at Jenna's house and asks to go for a walk. On the walk she finally tells him that she has been having anxiety attacks around him. As they are talking about this, Jason brings up how they had been talking on the phone right before her father's death, a fact that Jenna had completely forgotten. As soon as he says this, the memories of the moments immediately preceding the accident come flooding back to Jenna. She realizes that her mom had been nagging her to get off the phone and call her father in to lunch, but she had not listened. She is suddenly overwhelmed with guilt. If she had just gone to get her father when her mother told her to, he would still be alive.

Back at home Jenna confesses all of this to her mother, who assures her that the death was not her fault. As they discuss the fate of the person whose fault it actually is, Jenna realizes that she knows it was Michael who pulled the trigger.

Chapter 25: The Healing

The final chapter of the book is written in a different style than the rest of the work: it is written in the present tense and follows both Jenna and Michael. The night before Labor Day, Jenna has a dream about the Ghost Tree and her father, except this time she is not being attacked. Her father takes her by the hand, and everything around them disappears except the stars. When she wakes up a few hours before dawn, without thinking about it she instinctively heads to the Ghost Tree.

At the same time Michael is also awake. He knows that he has to confess what he has done and is afraid. He goes outside and digs up the gun. He takes it into his dad's car and drives off.

When Jenna arrives at the Ghost Tree, she senses that her father is there with her. She has come here to say goodbye to him and finally find some peace of mind. She realizes that the dreams she has been having were her mind's way of telling her to come to this place and heal herself.

Meanwhile Michael drives up to Jenna's house. He wants to speak with her personally and tell her what he has done before he turns himself in, as he knows he probably will not have a chance to afterward. When he arrives, he realizes that there is still at least an hour before dawn. Because he cannot think of anywhere else to wait, he heads to the Ghost Tree. When he arrives there he is surprised to find Jenna sleeping at the base of the tree. He decides to wait until she wakes up to talk to her.

CHARACTERS

Doug Boyle

Doug Boyle is a police officer also known as the Hangman. He helps Chief Zelenski investigate the Ward case by going door to door to question people.

Jason Friedman

Jason is a boy whom Jenna has been going out with for a few months. She has had a crush on him since the seventh grade. Besides her mother, Jason was the last person Jenna talked to before the accident. Because he left to go camping with his family the day that it happened, he did not find out about it until he returned a few weeks later. Every time Jenna sees Jason after her father's death, his presence inexplicably causes her to have an anxiety attack. Toward the end of the novel, Jenna and Jason realize that her anxiety attacks may have been triggered by the fact that she was subconsciously associating him with her father's death.

Ralph Healey

Ralph Healey is a sergeant on the local police force. Along with Doug Boyle, he is one of the policemen who visits the MacKenzie house for the first time.

Darcy Kelly

Darcy Kelly is Michael's girlfriend. She is known for being one of the most attractive and popular girls at school. After the accident, Michael begins to feel increasingly distant from her and eventually breaks things off. She blames Amy for the demise of their relationship, believing that Michael has feelings for her, and along with her friends begins to bully Amy relentlessly.

Josh MacKenzie

Josh is Michael's younger brother. He is highly interested in the Ward murder case, to the point of fascination. Much to Michael's annoyance, he is eager to keep up with any developments in the case and to aid with the investigation when police visit the MacKenzie residence. He sometimes teases Michael by implying that he is the murderer, not knowing that this is the truth. He is the one who first suggests to the police that Joe may be the culprit.

Karen MacKenzie

Karen MacKenzie, Michael's mother, works at the local florist. Michael worries that she suspects he may be the murderer.

Michael MacKenzie

Along with Jenna Ward, Michael MacKenzie is a protagonist of the story, and he is the one who has fired the shot that kills Charlie Ward. Michael is a well-liked, athletic, and popular soon-to-be high-school senior whose life was fairly normal prior to the accident. He is known for being a big track star at school and a lifeguard at the local pool. He was planning on going to a good college the next year.

Though he does not always do the right thing, he is a thoughtful and caring individual. He has always stuck by his best friend Joe, despite the fact that he is much less popular and has some bad habits. He takes care of Joe when Joe drinks too much and helps him stay out of trouble. He is also kind to Amy, whom he has feelings for, even though she is a social outcast.

After he has fired the shot that kills Charlie Ward, Michael's world is turned completely upside down. He is racked with guilt almost every waking moment and has trouble sleeping as well. Even when he can sleep, he has haunting dreams about the accident. He tries to make amends in every way he can think of, keeping vigil outside of the Wards' home and secretly completing chores for them in the dead of night. He constantly feels the urge to admit what he has done but is too afraid of the consequences he will suffer for it. Toward the end of the investigation he has a moment of moral weakness when he considers letting Joe take the fall for him; however, he soon realizes that he could never live with himself if he were to do that. At the end of the novel, he finally decides that he must do the right thing and turn himself in at the police station. But he wants to personally admit the truth to Jenna first.

Tom MacKenzie
Tom MacKenzie is Michael's father. He is outraged by the carelessness of the shooter. Michael worries that, like his mother, his father may also suspect him to be the person who fired the gunshot that killed Charlie Ward.

Pappy
Pappy is Amy's grandfather. He has been her primary caretaker ever since the deaths of both her parents. He is a kind and gentle old man who loves Amy deeply. He sometimes plays cards with Michael and Amy. He is fond of Michael but seemingly oblivious to the fact that Michael has spent the night in his house several times. He protects Amy by keeping Michael away from her when she decides that she does not want to see him anymore.

Annie Rico
Annie Rico works behind the cosmetics counter at the local pharmacy and is notorious for being the town gossip. Early on in the investigation, Jenna goes to her to find out which streets the police have homed in on in the search for suspects. Later, Jenna asks Annie for information

about whom the police have taken into custody as a suspect.

Amy Ruggerio
Amy Ruggerio is a high-school senior who wears a lot of makeup and has a reputation for being promiscuous, even though she is not particularly so. She is a warm and compassionate person but does not have many friends because of her reputation, and thus is somewhat of a loner. Still, she shows up at the pool and parties despite often being by herself.

Like Jenna, Amy has experienced great loss in her life. When she was younger, she was in a car accident that killed both of her parents. Because of this she feels a connection with Jenna and wants to help her in any way that she can. When she sees Jenna having an anxiety attack in the movie theater, she rushes to her aid. She also reaches out to Jenna by writing her a letter describing her own experience of losing her parents.

Amy has had a crush on Michael ever since he and her made out at his birthday party. She enjoys spending time with him, but his ex-girlfriend Darcy attacks her, telling her that Michael only ever paid any attention to her because he thought she would easily have sex with him. After this, Amy distrusts Michael and avoids him, though she eventually comes around to beginning to trust him again when he has a chance to explain that Darcy was lying. Yet around this same time she figures out that Michael is the person who shot Charlie Ward and implies as much to him. She indirectly tells him that he should come clean and that she does not want to see him until he does.

Joe Sadowski
Joe is Michael's longtime best friend. They grew up together. As they have gotten older, Michael has become significantly more popular than Joe, whose behavior and appearance are frowned upon by some of his classmates. He often wears a bandanna around his head and a dangling skull earring. He drives a Mustang, from which he blares loud rock and metal music. He has difficulty expressing his emotions in a healthy way and is a heavy drinker despite the fact that he is several years too young to drink legally.

Joe was the only person who was with Michael when Michael fired the bullet that killed Charlie Ward. He and Michael were also together when they learned that Charlie Ward had been killed by a stray bullet. Joe convinces Michael that they should keep the fact that Michael shot the gun a secret, thereby voluntarily incriminating himself as an accessory to the crime. Joe adamantly believes that if the police cannot locate the murder weapon, they cannot charge Michael with murder. Yet when questioned about the whereabouts of his rifle by the police, Michael reports that he let Joe borrow it, casting direct suspicion on him. As the investigation progresses, Joe is taken down to the police station for questioning and becomes the primary suspect in the case. Even still, he sticks to the story the two boys have fabricated about the gun being stolen and does not rat out his friend.

Andrea Sloan

Andrea has been Jenna's best friend since they were little. They grew up as neighbors. She is described as being attractive and fairly popular at school. She is a good friend to Jenna and tries to lift Jenna's spirits after the death of her father by coaxing her to go out to the pool and to parties. She has a crush on Michael MacKenzie and often persuades Jenna to accompany her to events on the grounds that he might be there.

Charlie Ward

Charlie Ward, the father of Jenna Ward, is killed by a stray bullet at the beginning of the novel. He was enthusiastic about his tools and worked in upper management at AT&T.

Jenna Ward

Jenna Ward is the other protagonist of the story, besides Michael. She is the fifteen-year-old daughter of Charlie Ward, the man whose murder is the catalyst for the entire story. She was present at the time of her father's death and actually witnessed the bullet hitting his head and his falling off of the roof. She had always been closer with her father than her mother, as she and her mother sometimes do not see eye to eye. She is a good student and well liked at school. Like Michael, she led a fairly normal life prior to the death of her father.

After the accident, she has a difficult time accepting what has happened. It is almost as if her brain cannot process the fact that her father has died. She cannot remember anything that happened directly before his death. She also cannot cry about the incident and has trouble feeling much of anything at all, aside from sporadic bouts of anger. She also has dreams about the Ghost Tree and Michael which she believes are related to her father's death. She is obsessed with the idea of finding her father's killer and does some detective work of her own when she cannot get the information she wants from the police. She wants revenge on her father's murderer.

Jenna obsessively organizes and rearranges her bedroom and works complex math problems as a way of calming herself down when she begins to feel overwhelmed. A few days after the accident, she begins to suffer from anxiety, particularly around her boyfriend, Jason, who was the last person she spoke to before her father's death. It is not until Jason reminds her that he was talking to her on the phone right before the accident happened that her memories begin to return and her anxiety begins to dissipate.

Thanks to her own detective work and the intuitive connection she feels with Michael, toward the end of the story she realizes that he is the one who killed her father before he has a chance to tell her. Once she knows this, she can truly accept that her father is dead and begins to feel a sense of peace. She no longer wants revenge.

Meredith Ward

Meredith Ward is Jenna's mother and Charlie Ward's widow. She is an account executive at a large New York advertising agency. She and Jenna have a somewhat strained relationship due in part to her type A, hyper-organized personality. However, over the course of the novel they bond over the loss of their family member.

Dave Zelenski

Dave Zelenski is the local police chief. He keeps Jenna and her mother apprised of any developments in Charlie Ward's murder investigation. He is middle-aged and rather large.

THEMES

Guilt

Guilt, particularly the guilt associated with the loss of a loved one, is a major theme in *Swallowing Stones*. It affects the majority of the main characters. When Jenna and her mother have their first heart-to-heart talk after Charlie Ward's death, Meredith Ward expresses the deep remorse she has over having been unable

TOPICS FOR FURTHER STUDY

- Read the young-adult novel *Lovely, Dark and Deep* (2012), by Amy McNamara. Like several of the characters in *Swallowing Stones*, the protagonist of this novel, Wren Wells, is dealing with the trauma of losing a loved one. Think about how Jenna and Wren are similar or different in the ways that they deal with trauma and loss. Then write an essay comparing and contrasting the two characters.

- When Jenna is feeling upset and overwhelmed, she retreats to her bedroom to work complex math problems. For Jenna, math has a therapeutic effect. This is only one of many surprising applications for mathematics. In fact, there are many connections between math and the world of the arts. For example, some artists use mathematic formulas to generate patterns or determine the size scale of a work. Using the Internet, research an artist of any kind (visual, musical, dance, etc.) who has implemented mathematics in his or her work. Using a camera and video-editing software, create a short film explaining to your fellow classmates how the artist you have

chosen uses math. Be sure to insert visual aids such as pictures or graphs into your video.

- The death that serves as the focal point of *Swallowing Stones* was caused by an accidental gunshot wound. Every culture has a different way of approaching the subject of gun control, and every country has formed different laws to regulate guns. Research the history of gun-control legislation in the United States as well as in another country of your choosing. Create a PowerPoint presentation with information demonstrating what you have leaned. Be sure to include slides explaining how gun laws in the two countries are similar and different.

- One of the themes of *Swallowing Stones* is chance. Sometimes there is no discernible reason for an event like Charlie Ward's death, it is just a matter of coincidence. Choose one detail of the story, large or small, to change. Then write your own alternate ending based on how you imagine the story would be different as a result of the detail you chose to change.

---

to prevent the accident. As she explains, she is overwhelmed with the feeling that if she had done something differently, her husband would still be alive.

Amy, who was in the car with both of her parents with they died from a crash, confides in her letter to Jenna that for her, the hardest thing about losing her parents was the overwhelming feelings of guilt. This was initially surprising to Jenna, but Amy explained she somehow felt guilty that she was the one who survived. Amy suffered from a phenomenon called survivor's guilt, which occurs when a person feels that one has done something wrong or unfair by surviving when others did not.

Because Jenna initially suffers from the post-traumatic stress of having watched her

father be hit in the head with a bullet and fall to his death, she initially does not feel guilty or even very sad. She mostly feels numb but goes through bouts of feeling shocked, angry, and anxious. Toward the end of the novel, when she begins to uncover the cause of her anxiety, feelings of guilt come forward to replace those feelings. She suddenly feels as if she was the cause of her father's death because she did not go out to beckon him inside as soon as her mother told her to. Just like her mother, she begins to experience the guilt of having been unable to save her father.

Michael, on the other hand, experiences a totally different type of guilt—the guilt of taking another man's life. While Jenna and her mother only feel as if they were the cause of his death,

Michael's thoughtless shot into the sky has disastrous consequences. (© *Olga Miltsova | Shutterstock.com*)

Michael actually was. Moreover, he also feels guilt over constantly lying to everyone around him about what he has done. These feelings of guilt eat away at him, until eventually he cannot stand it any longer and knows that he has no choice but to come clean.

Chance

The concept of chance is another theme that is explored in the work. Charlie Ward's death is characterized as a freak accident because the circumstances were so unusual, and because there was no possible way that it could have been predicted. Oftentimes human beings like to feel as if there has to be some order to life, as if there is a reason behind everything that happens. Sometimes when bad things happen to good people, they begin to search for a potential reason. They believe they are being punished in some way. Yet Charlie Ward did nothing to deserve to die, his family did nothing to deserve to lose him, and Michael did not intently do anything to deserve the punishment of becoming a murderer. Charlie Ward's accidental death was merely a matter of chance. Michael's circumstances cause

him to fully realize that his fate is entirely out of his control and that, to a certain degree, control is always an illusion.

Intuition

Amy and Jenna, the two characters in the novel who have lost parents, are also the characters in the novel who are highly intuitive. They are able to sense other people's feelings, particularly feelings of pain, nonverbally. Their intuition plays a major role in the novel, as it draws them each toward one another, and toward Michael. Even before Jenna knows Michael by name, she feels connected to him. For example, when she sees him sitting on the church steps across from her house, she senses that they share a similar type of pain. He also turns up in her dreams quite often, indicating a subconscious connection. And toward the end of the novel Jenna realizes without being told that Michael is the killer. At this point she and Michael are drawn to the Ghost Tree at the exact same time. Amy also feels drawn toward Michael, and he toward her. Their unlikely friendship prevails despite the fact that they are both teased for it.

Additionally, Amy senses Michael's secret and the pain he is carrying far before she lets on. Finally, Amy and Jenna connect on a deep intuitive level as soon as Amy reaches out and writes her letter to Jenna. They are the only two characters in the book who fully understand the type of pain each other is feeling. Furthermore, Jenna senses that Amy knows something about her father's death that she is not saying.

STYLE

Symbolism

The most evident example of symbolism in *Swallowing Stones* is the Ghost Tree. The Ghost Tree is surrounded by local folklore and legend and is said to have healing properties. While it does serve as a symbol for healing throughout the novel, it also encompasses all of the pain that goes along with the healing process. Throughout the novel Jenna has a recurring dream that the tree's branches are coiling around her, restraining her body. The pent-up emotions associated with her father's death that she is not able to express while conscious are manifest in these dreams. Michael also feels drawn to the tree throughout the book. He ends up going there several times without ever realizing that he is heading there until he has nearly arrived. It is almost as if the tree is seeking out both Michael and Jenna in their states of emotional trauma. In the final chapter of the book, the two instinctively go there at the same time to confront their demons. Both are finally ready to begin the healing process.

The other major symbol in the book is the figurative stone that Michael has swallowed. After the accident, he remembers an incident a few years before when a young girl suffocated to death while playing a game in the lake with a friend. The two girls were diving down to the bottom of the lake and picking up stones with their teeth, when the young girl tragically inhaled one. Michael remembers thinking that if she had just swallowed it, it would have damaged her internally but she would have most likely survived. To him, the secret of his killing Charlie Ward is like a stone he has to swallow and carry around with him as it tears him up on the inside. However, at the end of the book he realizes that actually he has been carrying the stone around in his throat the entire time, and the work of swallowing it will be to admit to everyone what he has done.

Multiple Protagonists

Swallowing Stones has two protagonists, Michael and Jenna, who are both equally important to the story. A *protagonist* is the main character of a story and is typically the character that readers most closely identify with. While it is not unheard of for a novel to have more than one protagonist, in literature it is more common for a novel to have a single protagonist. Because the portrayals of Michael and Jenna are equally vivid and both emotionally salient, the reader can empathize with both and will not necessarily favor one over the other, or identify with one more than the other. Though Michael may initially seem like an antagonist because he committed an accidental murder, it is obvious from the beginning that he had no intention to kill anyone and is absolutely horrified that he did. From the way McDonald chronicles his internal struggle, it is clear that readers are meant to sympathize with him, not despise him for what he has done.

There are pros and cons to creating a story with multiple protagonists. While having more than one main character can aid in the development of a complex plot, some readers do not appreciate works that have multiple protagonists because they tend to make the meaning of a story less straightforward and to pull the reader's sympathies in two, sometimes opposing directions. However, this is a matter of personal taste.

HISTORICAL CONTEXT

Gun Culture in the United States

Swallowing Stones is centered around an accidental death by gunshot. Unfortunately, in the United States death by gunshot, accidental or otherwise, is far from unheard of. As Michael A. Bellesîles notes in his 1996 article "The Origins of Gun Culture in the United States, 1760–1865,"

> An astoundingly high level of personal violence separates the United States from every other industrial nation. . . . The weapon of choice in 69.6 percent of those murders [in the United States in 1993] was a gun, and thousands more are killed by firearms every year in accidents and suicides.

In fact, the United States has the highest rate of gun ownership in the entire world and also has

COMPARE
&
CONTRAST

- **1990s:** Between 1990 and 1999, there are twenty-three mass shootings in the United States. One of the most widely covered shootings, the 1999 Columbine High School massacre, prompts a national debate about gun-control laws.

  Today: In the wake of seven mass shootings in 2012 alone, including the Aurora theater shooting and the Sandy Hook Elementary School shooting, the gun-control debate is just as widespread today as it was in the 1990s, if not more so.

- **1990s:** According to the US Centers for Disease Control and Prevention (CDC), from 1990 to 2003 the rates of suicide among young people ages ten to twenty-four steadily decrease.

  Today: A 2007 CDC report reveals that in 2004, 4,599 children and young adults committed suicide, an 8 percent increase from 2003 and the largest increase in suicides among young people in fifteen years.

- **1990s:** In 1999, Georgia becomes the first state to pass anti-bullying legislation to help protect students such as Amy who suffer emotional distress at the hands of their peers.

  Today: As of 2012, forty-eight states have passed anti-bullying laws.

---

some of the most lenient gun-control laws. In some places in the world it would be unthinkable to give a seventeen-year-old a firearm for his birthday, but in suburban New Jersey, where the novel is set, it does not seem unusual at all. Michael is eager to show off his new rifle to his friend Joe.

Mental Health Issues among Teenagers

Swallowing Stones depicts a group of teenagers who are dealing with different types of mental health issues and emotional distress. Jenna experiences intense grief and anxiety attacks after the death of her father. Michael struggles with the overwhelming guilt of having accidentally killed a man. Joe deals with the stress in his life by turning to alcohol. Amy, who has experienced the deaths of both of her parents, describes struggling with survivor's guilt. She is also mercilessly bullied by her classmates, who falsely accuse her of being promiscuous. Although these instances are of course fictional, they are representative of a very real and long-standing problem in the United States: the high rate of emotional distress among teenagers. The teen years are a highly formative time not only

physically but also mentally. The majority of mental health issues diagnosed in adults have their roots in adolescence, and over half of all diagnosed cases of mental disorders begin by age fourteen. According to the National Adolescent Health Information Center, as of 1995 (two years prior to the publication of *Swallowing Stones*), a survey indicated that among young people ages twelve to seventeen in the United States, 16 percent of males and 19 percent of females "met most of the diagnostic criteria in the DSM-III for one of three psychiatric diagnoses—major depression, post-traumatic stress disorder, or substance abuse/dependence disorder." Additionally, as of 1999, nearly 25 percent of young people ages seven to sixteen had one or more emotional or behavioral problems.

Depression has been the most widely reported disorder among teens in the United States and is almost twice as common among females. The cause of depression in teens varies from case to case and can sometimes be difficult to determine, but the effects are often tangible and evident. Depression has a negative impact not only on the individual suffering from it but

Michael feels guilty for what he did, especially when his friend Joe takes the blame. (© Ilike | Shutterstock.com)

also on that individual's friends and family. It is particularly dangerous in that it can lead to other concerns, such as substance abuse, self-harm, and suicide. Anxiety disorders are also prevalent among teens and often occur in conjunction with depression. Conduct disorders, learning disabilities and attention deficit/hyperactivity disorder (ADHD), and eating disorders are also significant problems among teens.

CRITICAL OVERVIEW

Swallowing Stones, McDonald's second young-adult novel, received a flurry of critical attention upon its publication in 1997, though it has not been heavily addressed by scholars since. By and large critics lauded McDonald's ability to make the emotional states of her characters resonate with readers.

For example, in a review of the work a contributor to *Publishers Weekly* claims that the portrayal of the characters' emotions is true to life and one of the strongest parts of the novel.

The contributor comments, "While the novel's sequence of events is rather farfetched, the characters' reactions are real. Readers will quickly become absorbed." Other critics likewise claimed that McDonald's vivid characterization is a feat unto itself. Joel Shoemaker, who reviewed the work in *School Library Journal*, observes, "This mesmerizing story largely derives its power from the respect McDonald demonstrates for these teens and their emotions."

In another contemporary review, a *Kirkus Reviews* contributor also notes the characters' emotional journey as one of the most significant aspects of the book. Although the contributor describes the ending as somewhat "awkward," overall the reviewer calls the work a "deliberately paced but deeply felt drama." This reviewer was not the only one to take issue with the ending, which varies in style and tone from the rest of the work. *Booklist* contributor Frances Bradburn writes in her review, "McDonald masterfully moves both teens to an inevitable, if somewhat nebulous, final confrontation." Indeed, Bradburn cites the ending of the work as its only weak spot.

Nevertheless, reviews were generally positive. *Book Report* contributor Brooke Selby Dillon cites "believable and empathetic characters; fascinating minor characters, who defy stereotypes;" and "poetic, haunting, yet easily accessible language" as some of the main draws of the work. Dillon concludes, "McDonald has crafted a gem."

CRITICISM

Rachel Porter

Porter is a freelance writer and editor who holds a bachelor of arts in English literature. In the following essay, she argues that McDonald's portrayal of Michael as a second protagonist in Swallowing Stones, *rather than an antagonist, forces the reader to investigate the moral and philosophical consequences of his actions.*

Among literary critics there has historically been some debate about whether or not a work can truly have multiple protagonists. In critic Henry Fowler's seminal 1926 work *A Dictionary of Modern English Usage*, he argues that the term protagonist can only ever be used in the singular form. To Fowler, the term *protagonist* means the character in a work of literature who is the most important. Logically speaking, designating two or more characters as each being the *most* important is impossible. If one character is the most important, then it follows that the other is not, and vice versa. Since Fowler's time, many authors and critics have subscribed to his way of thinking, but many have also swayed. *Swallowing Stones* firmly places Joyce McDonald in the latter camp, as one of the individuals who believes not only that having a work with multiple protagonists is possible, but further that in some cases having two different perspectives that seem equally valid can enrich the work with deeper layers of meaning. McDonald's decision to structure the work in sections that alternate between Michael's and Jenna's perspectives, as well as her portrayal of their parallel experiences of emotional trauma, indicate that their experiences are to be read as equally valid, and in turn prompt the reader to think deeply about the concepts of chance, blame, and becoming a victim of circumstance.

The way that McDonald has chosen to structure the story is perhaps the biggest indicator that Michael is meant to be read as a protagonist

WHAT DO I READ NEXT?

- *Izzy, Willy-Nilly*, published in 1986, is a young-adult novel by Cynthia Voigt. Like *Swallowing Stones* it addresses how one accident can change a person's life instantly and permanently. After fifteen-year-old Izzy loses her leg in a car accident, her entire world changes.

- *Devil on My Heels* is McDonald's 2004 young-adult novel. Protagonist fifteen-year-old Dove Alderman has a relatively easy and happy life in 1959 Benevolence, Florida. Yet when fires begin breaking out around town and rumors of Ku Klux Klan activity spread, Dove's sense of security and safety in her town begins to waver.

- The 1997 book *Guns, Violence, and Teens*, by Vic Cox, is an overview of the place of guns in American society with particular attention to how guns affect young people. The author covers both sides of the gun-control debate equally.

- Sherman Alexie's 2007 young-adult novel *The Absolutely True Diary of a Part-Time Indian* is about Arnold, a Native American teenager who leaves life on the reservation to attend an all-white high school. Though at first Arnold finds life at his new school difficult, he eventually finds ways to fit in. Outside of school, Arnold struggles through many hardships over the course of the novel.

- *Speak* is a 1999 young-adult novel by Laurie Halse Anderson about a high-school freshman who is ostracized by her peers after calling the police at a party. What she does not tell anyone is that she called the police because she was raped.

- In McDonald's 1996 young-adult novel *Comfort Creek*, eleven-year-old Quinn and her family endure a string of bad luck. Her mother has left the family to play in a band, and her father has lost his job.

MCDONALD'S DECISION TO STRUCTURE THE
WORK IN SECTIONS THAT ALTERNATE BETWEEN
MICHAEL'S AND JENNA'S PERSPECTIVES, AS WELL AS
HER PORTRAYAL OF THEIR PARALLEL EXPERIENCES
OF EMOTIONAL TRAUMA, INDICATE THAT THEIR
EXPERIENCES ARE TO BE READ AS EQUALLY VALID."

rather than as an antagonist. She has broken the work into sections, half of which focus on the story from Michael's perspective, and half of which focus on the story from Jenna's. The story begins with a chapter devoted to Michael, another indicator that he must be an important character in the work. The second chapter follows Jenna. Thereafter, every few chapters McDonald shifts perspective from one to the other. Her decision to dedicate equal amounts of the work to each of their stories indicates that their stories are equally important. The reader spends the same amount of time getting to know the personalities, characteristics, and inner thoughts and feelings of both Michael and Jenna, which has the effect of leaving the reader feeling equally well acquainted with both characters. Their stories run parallel, meaning that oftentimes readers are exposed to a single event from both Michael's and Jenna's perspective. In this way, readers do not get a one-sided version of an occurrence but are rather able to see the event from dual angles. If the story were told purely from Jenna's perspective, it would be easy to vilify Michael. The reader would constantly be exposed to the rage and anguish of Jenna and her mother without understanding that Michael is suffering a great deal as well. McDonald's use of a dual narrative enables readers to empathize with both Michael's and Jenna's sides of the story, and at times to feel equally sorry for them both.

It is McDonald's vivid portrayal of Jenna's and Michael's emotional anguish that allows readers to empathize with the both of them. Jenna's turmoil is possibly more easily relatable for readers, as many people are familiar with what it feels like to lose someone they love.

Moreover, Jenna is merely a victim of circumstance. Her tragedy comes about completely unexpected, and she had no role in creating it. Because of this, it makes perfect sense that her initial reaction is shock. In the wake of the accident, she feels almost nothing besides anger. She is numb, unable to cry about her father's death except in her sleep. This is only one of the many symptoms she exhibits of anxiety disorder. She feels particularly anxious around her boyfriend Jason and eventually has a full-fledged panic attack when she is with him at the movies. At times she is also filled with overwhelming aggression. As she tells her best friend Andrea, she frequently fantasizes about telling her father's killer that he has destroyed her life before shooting him in the face. The only thing that seems to calm her down and take her mind off of things is working long and complicated math problems.

Although Michael was the one who pulled the trigger and ultimately caused a tragic death, his despair is nearly as deeply felt as Jenna's. Though he was careless in his handling of his new rifle, he certainly does not take the consequences of his actions lightly. He is entirely consumed by guilt, to the point that Mr. Ward's death is nearly all that he thinks about. He can no longer enjoy spending time with his friends, or at the pool, or going to parties. He experiences a great deal of anxiety as well, especially around Jenna and the police. He becomes obsessed with Jenna and her mother, wanting to help make their lives a little easier in every way that he can. He sneaks out of his house at night to do things for them that he thinks Mr. Ward would have done if he were still alive, like cleaning out the gutters, replacing the porch light, and weeding the garden. By including chapters from Michael's perspective, McDonald makes it clear that in a way, he has been a victim of the accident as well. It has had a profound and lasting impact on his life, just as it has had on Jenna's.

Even though Michael and Jenna do not know each other very well, their mutual grief bonds them. Despite the fact that Michael actively tries to avoid Jenna, she is drawn to him. She senses his pain and inexplicably feels like she understands it. Several times throughout the work McDonald writes of an intuitive connection between Michael and Jenna. Describing Jenna as she watches Michael on the steps of the church across from her house, McDonald writes, "she could not have said why, but something deep inside her seemed to sense his pain." Later, after Michael hits Amy's car with Joe's car, the narrator explains,

> For a split second he thought he saw Jenna Ward's face in Amy's stunned expression. Not in her features, but in her eyes. Something in Amy's eyes made him think of that first newspaper photograph of Jenna.

As with Jenna, Michael cannot articulate exactly what it is, but there is something he understands about Jenna instinctively. Somehow, being on either side of the same terrible accident has forged a deep and unspoken bond between the two. They each understand, at least in part, what the other is going through.

Their dreams are another important way in which Michael and Jenna are connected. Since the accident they have both been haunted by somewhat similar recurring nightmares. Jenna has a recurring dream about the vines of a tree enwrapping her and dragging her into a forest. She eventually recognizes the tree as the Ghost Tree, a large old sycamore known around town as a place that can connect one to one's ancestors. She believes that these dreams have something to do with her father's death. Eventually Michael appears in one of these dreams, indicating that in her subconscious at least, Jenna knows he has something to do with the death of her father. Michael's nightmares are always somehow related to Charlie Ward. At times he is a bullet flying toward his head, and at times he just sees Mr. Ward's face. While their dreams are different, the fact that they both have symbolic dreams is another way in which McDonald draws a parallel between Jenna and Michael.

Though Jenna's and Michael's emotional pain manifests itself in very different ways, by presenting their experiences as parallel and demonstrating how the incident has brought them together rather than repel them from one another, McDonald presents them as fellow victims of a tragic accident, rather than as victim and perpetrator. Their parallel journey ends with them both at the Ghost Tree at the same time, ready to start the process of healing together. Their trauma has entirely consumed both of their lives, to the point where they are finally ready to face it. By depicting Michael as a victim of circumstance alongside Jenna, McDonald inadvertently asks her readers to consider the important question as to just how much he can

Jenna and Michael meet under a huge sycamore tree, a place of healing, according to local Lenape legend. (© Lusoimages | Shutterstock.com)

truly be blamed for his crime. Were he not portrayed as a second protagonist alongside Jenna, the reader would never be forced by the work to consider, what exactly constitutes a murder? How much should someone be punished for a brief moment of carelessness? How much does chance play a role in our lives? By ending the story moments before Michael begins to come clean, McDonald insists that readers find their own answers to these questions.

Source: Rachel Porter, Critical Essay on *Swallowing Stones*, in *Novels for Students*, Gale, Cengage Learning, 2014.

CRITICISM

Kristen Sarlin Greenberg

Greenberg is a freelance writer and editor with a background in literature and philosophy. In the following essay, she examines the transformation Michael goes through in Swallowing Stones.

> SOMEHOW, KNOWING THAT SHE KNOWS THE TRUTH ABOUT THE TERRIBLE THING HE HAS DONE AND SEEING PROOF THAT SHE STILL CARES FOR HIM MAKE MICHAEL ABLE TO FULLY ADMIT THE TRUTH TO HIMSELF AND DO THE RIGHT THING."

Joyce McDonald's novel *Swallowing Stones* begins with a boy doing a foolish thing, leading to disastrous consequences. By the story's end, that boy and the girl whom he has hurt by his thoughtless actions will both be drawn to a legendary tree believed to be "a place of healing." The boy, Michael MacKenzie, believes that he has changed after learning that he has unintentionally killed a man. When his girlfriend wants to discuss everyday matters, like making plans to go to a party, he stares at her in disbelief, thinking, "Couldn't she see he wasn't the same person she'd been going out with for the past six months?" Certainly Michael feels guilty about what he did. But does he really heal? Does he really change? Throughout the book, there is evidence for both sides of the argument.

One of the first things we learn about Michael is that he cheats on his girlfriend. At his birthday party, he sneaks off to the garage to be with Amy without the knowledge of his girlfriend, Darcy. Not only does he not seem to care that Darcy will be hurt if she finds out, he does not think at all about what Amy might feel once she realizes that he is using her. He is careless with her emotions and careless with her physically: he tears one of the straps of her bikini and "couldn't even remember how it happened." He thinks only about himself and what he wants.

Michael's treatment of Darcy is not much better. He feels uncomfortable being with her after the accident, and he begins to pull away from her. Driving to Stephen Chang's party, Michael thinks about breaking up with Darcy but worries that his reasons for doing so will sound "so phony." For a moment, when she touches his hand, "the gentle pressure of her soft skin hurt him in a way he had never known." This seems to indicate that he has at least a vague idea of how he might hurt her, but in the end, he gives in to his selfishness. He avoids her

at the party and for days afterward. He believes that he "just couldn't be with her right now. He couldn't be with anyone." When Michael finally breaks up with Darcy, his reasons all center on his own feelings: "this breakup wasn't about Amy or Darcy; it was about carrying a secret so terrible that it shut him off from the rest of the world." Michael cannot see past his own pain and confusion to imagine how Darcy might feel.

Michael's self-centeredness is also evident in his relationship with Joe. When Joe has been drinking and the police come to break up the party, Michael asks for Darcy's help getting Joe away from the scene. "We can't leave him here for the cops to find," Michael says, like a true best friend. However, it is impossible to tell whether Michael is more concerned about Joe getting into trouble for underage drinking or about protecting himself against Joe possibly letting something slip to the police while his judgment is impaired.

It is clear that Michael feels bad about what he has done, but it does not seem completely real to him. He knows that he did something wrong when he fired that rifle into the air, but the fact that he caused Charlie Ward's death, even if only by accident, is too big, too abstract, and too scary for Michael to face. He cannot truly believe that he did it.

Initially, Michael tries to distance himself from what happened. When the boys first hear a radio report of the shooting, Joe says, "It could have been anyone," and Michael "wanted to believe his friend." Throughout the entire novel, there are moments when Michael allows himself to hope that maybe his shot was not the one that killed Charlie. Near the end of the story, when it comes out that Joe had touched the rifle while Michael was kissing Amy during the party, he begins "to entertain the possibility that he wasn't a murderer after all."

Perhaps the most shocking example of Michael's selfishness and inability to come to terms with what he has done relates to Joe. Because Michael cannot accept what he has done, he considers letting Joe take the blame. For a short while, when the police begin to focus their investigation on Joe, Michael contemplates the possibility of letting Joe take the blame and saving himself:

> He couldn't let Joe take the rap for Charlie Ward's death. Or could he? He knew that even though Joe hadn't done it, and even if it

never came to trial for lack of evidence, most folks would think Joe was guilty anyway.... It was the perfect setup, really. And he knew it.

However, even while McDonald provides these many instances where Michael acts selfishly or thoughtlessly, she also leaves small hints in the text to show that he is changing. From the first time he sees Jenna's picture in the newspaper, he feels terrible that she lost her father. He has many nights when he cannot sleep because he cannot stop thinking about what he did.

Part of Michael's change is due to the guilt he feels. It is significant that Michael starts to take on small tasks that he would never have done before, perhaps as a way to atone for his mistake: he cleans up some dishes in the kitchen and secretly weeds the Wards' garden and cleans out their gutters. Although he must realize that doing a few chores cannot truly make up for the tragedy, it shows that Michael is starting to feel remorse and the desire to help repair the damage however he can. What begins as simple guilt, perhaps combined with anxiety about how he will be punished, transforms into something else. Michael becomes more aware of the feelings of others.

One important clue to Michael's growing awareness is his relationship with his parents. When Mr. MacKenzie first appears in the book, he is watching a game show with Michael's little brother, being his "personal trainer" in his plan to be on *Jeopardy!* As Michael watches this "nightly ritual," he thinks, "That was his dad for you. Whatever his sons aspired to, he was right behind them every step of the way." It is clear that Mr. MacKenzie is a supportive father. The assurance Michael has of his parents' love and support makes it all the more painful for him when the police come to the house asking questions about the rifle. Michael begins to realize "with horror that his father had at least considered the possibility that the shot had come from his own house." He cannot stand the idea of his father knowing what he has done, and he has to force "himself to look at his mother. The fear in her face was terrible to see."

Through his parents' reactions, Michael begins to understand the seriousness and the enormity of what he has done with his careless, thoughtless act. He starts to realize that his actions affect other people and that he should be considering their feelings, not only his own. Joe's reactions to Michael's behavior also drive home the truth; when Michael realizes how much danger he has put Joe in, "the look on his friend's face was more than Michael could bear."

Perhaps it is Michael's relationship with Amy that best shows his transformation. Even at the start of the story, Amy brings out something in Michael that he has never experienced. After he tore her bikini, she looked "so vulnerable. He had said he was sorry. And he was. She had smiled and said it was okay, she'd fix it later. But somehow it didn't seem okay." After Michael hears the radio report of Charlie Ward's death, he tries to pretend that nothing is wrong and get his driver's license as planned, but he fails the driving test because he "thought, for some crazy reason, about Amy Ruggerio and her torn bikini top, and suddenly he wanted to cry." Whenever Michael hears Amy say something that makes it clear she has heard the rumors other kids spread about her, "something inside him cringed." It makes him uncomfortable to know that she is hurting.

It is Amy who is able to help Michael finally accept what has happened. When he realizes that Amy may very well have suspected his crime for a long time, Michael is horrified: "He could face Joe's anger and resentment. And he would face the police when the time came. But Amy, who trusted and believed in him—that was something else. He wanted to die." He cannot bear that Amy knows his terrible secret, but she surprises Michael by hugging him. Somehow, knowing that she knows the truth about the terrible thing he has done and seeing proof that she still cares for him make Michael able to fully admit the truth to himself and do the right thing. Perhaps because Amy seems to forgive him, he can forgive himself.

It is only after this scene with Amy that Michael decides to confess to the police, to find Jenna and tell her face to face what he has done. He has clearly changed. The transformation occurs not because he breaks the law and worries about getting caught, but because he starts to truly think about his actions and the consequences of those actions. It is not the law—some external force—making him confront Jenna and decide to tell the truth to the police. Rather, he develops an inner sense of what is right and wrong by seeing how he affects the people around him.

Source: Kristen Sarlin Greenberg, Critical Essay on *Swallowing Stones*, in *Novels for Students*, Gale, Cengage Learning, 2014.

Publishers Weekly

In the following review, a reviewer praises the realism of characters' reactions in Swallowing Stones.

A bizarre Fourth of July accident, which leaves an innocent man dead, sets McDonald's (*Comfort Creek*) spiraling drama in motion, drawing together four teenagers whose lives are drastically changed by the incident. Caught in the eye of the storm are 15-year-old Jenna Ward, whose father is struck by a stray bullet, and Michael MacKenzie, the 17-year-old who unknowingly fires the fatal shot. More distanced from the action are witnesses Joe Sadowski, Michael's loyal buddy and Amy Ruggerio, a misunderstood teen with a "loose" reputation. The alternating points of view of Jenna and Michael reflect their psychological turmoil. Jenna's grief surfaces in anxiety attacks, usually occurring when she is around her boyfriend, the last person she spoke to before her father's death. Michael is racked with guilt, but admitting his involvement in the accident is as difficult as "swallowing stones." The intensity of the teens' emotions increases to a feverish pitch as the police edge closer to the truth. At a crucial moment, Amy forces Michael and Jenna to face the facts that they have tried to avoid. While the novel's sequence of events is rather farfetched, the characters' reactions are real. Readers will quickly become absorbed in this electrifying portrayal of fear and deception.

Source: Review of *Swallowing Stones*, in *Publishers Weekly*, Vol. 244, No. 39, September 22, 1997, p. 82.

Frances Bradburn

In the following review, Bradburn criticizes the ending of Swallowing Stones *as somewhat unclear.*

When Michael MacKenzie fires his grandfather's Winchester rifle into the air to celebrate his Fourth of July birthday, he has no idea that he will kill Jenna Ward's father as he patches the roof of his home a mile across town. Handsome, popular Michael knows immediately that it is his gun that killed Charlie Ward when he hears the radio news story the next day, but he and his friend Joe decide it will be smarter to bury the gun and feign ignorance rather than own up to the crime. Alternating chapters focus on Michael and then Jenna, examining the effect that an unpredictable tragedy can have on seemingly totally unrelated lives. McDonald masterfully

moves both teens to an inevitable, if somewhat nebulous, final confrontation, as Michael appears to accept the consequences of his actions. Indeed, only the ending mars an otherwise classic example of Burns' oft-quoted lines, "Oh, what a tangled web we weave when first we practice to deceive."

Source: Frances Bradburn, Review of *Swallowing Stones*, in *Booklist*, Vol. 94, No. 4, October 15, 1997, pp. 397–98.

SOURCES

Bellesîles, Michael A., "The Origins of Gun Culture in the United States, 1760–1865," in *Journal of American History*, Vol. 83, No. 2, September 1996, pp. 425–55.

"Bio," Joyce McDonald website, http://www.joycemcdonald.net/bio.html (accessed April 15, 2013).

Bradburn, Frances, Review of *Swallowing Stones*, in *Booklist*, Vol. 94, No. 4, October 15, 1997, pp. 397–98.

Cox, Ruth, "Unspoken Words—Words Left Unspoken," in *Emergency Librarian*, Vol. 25, No. 5, May–June 1998, pp. 46–48.

Dillon, Brooke Selby, Review of *Swallowing Stones*, in *Book Report*, Vol. 16, No. 3, November–December 1997, pp. 37–38.

Follman, Mark, Gavin Aronsen, and Deanna Pan, "A Guide to Mass Shootings in America," in *Mother Jones*, February 27, 2013, http://www.motherjones.com/politics/2012/07/mass-shootings-map?page=2 (accessed May 1, 2013).

Heise, Jennifer, "Helen LePage and William Hale Chamberlain Prize," Drew University website, https://uknow.drew.edu/confluence/display/DrewHistory/Helen + LePage + and + William + Hale + Chamberlain + Prize (accessed May 1, 2013).

"Joyce McDonald," Random House website, http://www.randomhouse.com/author/19835/joyce-mcdonald?sort = best_13wk_3month (accessed April 15, 2013).

"Joyce McDonald (1946–) Biography," Brief Biographies website, http://biography.jrank.org/pages/1877/McDonald-Joyce-1946.html (accessed April 15, 2013).

Khazan, Olga, "Here's How U.S. Gun Violence Compares with the Rest of the World," in *Washington Post*, December 14, 2012, http://www.washingtonpost.com/blogs/worldviews/wp/2012/12/14/schoo-shooting-how-do-u-s-gun-homicides-compare-with-the-rest-of-the-world/ (accessed May 1, 2013).

Knopf, David, M. Jane Park, and Tina Paul Mulye, "The Mental Health of Adolescents: A National Profile, 2008," National Adolescent Health Information Center, 2008, http://nahic.ucsf.edu/downloads/MentalHealthBrief.pdf (accessed May 1, 2013).

Lange, Sydney, "Birthday Bios: Joyce McDonald," Children's Literature Network website, http://www.childrensliteraturenetwork.org/birthbios/brthpage/08aug/8-4jmcdnld.html (accessed April 15, 2013).

McDonald, Joyce, *Swallowing Stones*, Ember, 2012.

Review of *Swallowing Stones*, in *Kirkus Reviews*, July 1, 1997, https://www.kirkusreviews.com/book-reviews/joyce-mcdonald/swallowing-stones/ (accessed May 1, 2013).

Review of *Swallowing Stones*, in *Publishers Weekly*, September 1, 1997, http://www.publishersweekly.com/978-0-385-32309-3 (accessed May 1, 2013).

Ruff, Morgan, "*Shades of Simon Gray*," Prezi, February 12, 2013, http://prezi.com/syiedmoulzuz/shades-of-simon-gray/ (accessed April 15, 2013).

Sacco, Dena T., Katharine Silbaugh, Felipe Corredor, June Casey, and Davis Doherty, "An Overview of State Anti-bullying Legislation and Other Related Laws," Harvard Law School website, February 23, 2012, http://cyber.law.harvard.edu/sites/cyber.law.harvard.edu/files/State_Anti_bullying_Legislation_Overview_0.pdf (accessed May 1, 2013).

Shoemaker, Joel, Review of *Swallowing Stones*, in *School Library Journal*, Vol. 43, No. 9, September 1997, p. 219.

Webber, Carlie, "Joyce McDonald: Interview," Teenreads.com, July 2004, http://www.teenreads.com.asp1-14.dfw1-2.websitetestlink.com/authors/au-mcdonald-joyce.asp (accessed April 15, 2013).

FURTHER READING

Feinman, Jay M., *Law 101: Everything You Need to Know about American Law*, 3rd ed., Oxford University Press, 2010.
> *Law 101* is a comprehensive and engaging introduction that will familiarize readers with the American legal system. This work will help readers understand the charges Michael would be up against if he were to be tried for involuntary manslaughter.

Krementz, Jill, *How It Feels When a Parent Dies*, Knopf, 1981.
> In Krementz's book, eighteen children and teens share their experience of losing a parent. This book is designed to comfort youths who have experienced the loss of a parent and also to illuminate the experience for others.

Salmore, Barbara G., and Stephen A. Salmore, *New Jersey Politics and Government: The Suburbs Come of Age*, 4th ed., Rivergate Books, 2013.
> Barbara and Stephen Salmore's book educates readers about the culture of New Jersey, where *Swallowing Stones* is set, and the politics that made it the way it is today.

Souter, Gerry, *American Shooter: A Personal History of Gun Culture in the United States*, Potomac Books, 2012.
> In this work Souter provides a history of gun culture in the United States through the lens of his own personal experience. Souter was raised with guns and is himself a gun-sport enthusiast, but he is highly critical of some current aspects of gun control.

SUGGESTED SEARCH TERMS

Joyce McDonald

Joyce McDonald AND Swallowing Stones

Joyce McDonald AND YA fiction

Swallowing Stones AND YA fiction

YA fiction AND gun violence

Swallowing Stones AND gun control

Swallowing Stones AND teens AND guns

loss of a parent AND survivor's guilt

involuntary manslaughter AND gun-control laws

involuntary manslaughter AND guilt

The Way to Rainy Mountain

N. SCOTT MOMADAY

1969

The Way to Rainy Mountain (1969) is a ground-breaking work of Native American literature that posits several narrative voices and gradually blends and unifies them to create a moving exploration of Kiowa legend and history through the prism of one individual's life in the modern era. N. Scott Momaday is of Kiowa as well as Cherokee heritage, but under his schoolteacher parents, much of his early life was spent among the Navajo and Jemez Pueblo Indians in Arizona and New Mexico. The parents' intimate understanding of education was passed on to their son, who excelled in high school as well as college; at the age of twenty-nine he received a doctorate from Stanford University.

Given a great deal of encouragement by mentors to polish his superlative literary skills, Momaday soon became both a professor and an acclaimed writer. A significant source of inspiration as well as material would be his Indian heritage and perspective. By his thirties, having thoroughly adapted to the Anglo-dominated academic world, Momaday realized that a part of him—the Kiowa part of him—would remain incomplete until he could take the time to delve into the lore and history of his people. Being unable to speak Kiowa, he drew on his father to gather oral legends, and he also embarked on a journey tracing the route followed by the Kiowas during the migration that brought about their golden age, from Montana down through the Great Plains to Oklahoma. Momaday merged

N. Scott Momaday (© Giulio Marcocchi / Getty Images)

the legends, the history, and his own experiences to form what he would call his favorite among his books, *The Way to Rainy Mountain*, which features a unique textual design and signifying illustrations by his father, Al Momaday.

AUTHOR BIOGRAPHY

Momaday was born on February 27, 1934, in the Kiowa and Comanche Indian Hospital in Lawton, Oklahoma. On his birth certificate his name is Navarro Scotte Mammedaty, but his father had recently changed his last name to Momaday, and the son would follow suit. Al Momaday was Kiowa, while Natachee Scott, his wife, was part Cherokee, with their son officially documented as being of seven-eighths Indian blood. His mother was raised in middle-class circumstances and only later in life reconnected with her Indian heritage, which would prove an inspiration to Momaday. She was also a writer, publishing books and short stories. In the first year of his

life Momaday was brought north to Devils Tower, in Wyoming, where an elder gave him the Kiowa name Tsoai-talee, meaning "Rock Tree Boy"—he was named after the boy in the Kiowa legend about the monumental volcanic structure's origins.

Through Momaday's youth, his parents taught and administrated at several schools through the Southwest, ranging from Tuba City, Chinle, and the San Carlos Reservation, Arizona, to Shiprock, Hobbs, and Jemez Pueblo, New Mexico. The last destination especially, reached in 1946, allowed the family a strong connection with the land and the people, though as Kiowas they remained just outside the Jemez community. Momaday grew able to comfortably navigate both Indian and Anglo worlds, and he flourished in academics. For his final year of high school he attended Augustus Military Academy, in Virginia, where the English master was flabbergasted to find that among all his students an Indian should have the best command of the language.

Momaday enrolled at the University of New Mexico in 1952, earning—after a couple of intervening years studying law at the University of Virginia—a bachelor of arts degree in 1958. He then went to teach on the Jicarilla Reservation, in New Mexico, but he soon applied for a creative-writing scholarship at Stanford, where Yvor Winters, the poetry judge, immediately perceived his potential and extended him a fellowship. Winters would play an outsized role in ushering Momaday toward literary success.

Momaday's first publication, in 1965, was his doctoral dissertation, an edition of the verse of the largely forgotten nineteenth-century poet Frederick Goddard Tuckerman. Momaday's own writings would begin with Kiowa lore collected as *The Journey of Tai-me* and privately printed in 1967. Momaday then wrote the novel that earned him the Pulitzer Prize, *House Made of Dawn* (1968). Meanwhile, he would adapt the Tai-me lore for inclusion in *The Way to Rainy Mountain*, published in 1969, a banner year for Momaday: he was awarded the Pulitzer, recognized as Outstanding Indian of the Year by the American Indian community, and formally initiated into the Kiowas' Gourd Dance Society. Momaday's career evolved further from there: he has taught at such universities as California at Berkeley, New Mexico State, Princeton, and Columbia, and he has published books including novels, essays, poetry, and autobiography. Later in his career he shifted focus to visual arts, with his drawings, paintings, and etchings critically appreciated enough to allow him to stage independent exhibitions. Having taught at the University of Arizona since 1982, Momaday recently became a professor emeritus.

PLOT SUMMARY

Prologue

The Way to Rainy Mountain opens with a poem, "Headwaters," followed by a prologue recalling the migration undertaken by the Kiowas from the northern mountains down through the Great Plains. The journey and the era would end around Rainy Mountain, in Oklahoma, with the demise of the tribe's culture. The journey was the Kiowas', but it was also universal, and those who listen to the story can take part in it.

Introduction

Next the narrator speaks more personally, relating the harsh weather and magnificence of the land around Rainy Mountain. His grandmother Aho died in July, and he returned to visit her grave. She grew up when the Kiowas' still-young culture was coming to an end. The narrator, deciding to retrace the Kiowas' journey, headed north to the shadowed wilderness of Yellowstone. Down the foothills to the east, the land turns golden, the sky opens up, and Devils Tower—object of a Kiowa myth about seven sisters and a brother-turned-bear who chases them into the sky—thrusts up from the land. The sun became holy to the Kiowas, as signified by the sacred doll Tai-me. Aho was seven when the last Sun Dance was held on the Washita River in 1887. The narrator remembers her as an ancient woman whose house was once filled with community and culture; now it is empty.

In the text that follows, there are three titled chapters, each with a number of sections. Each section consists of three passages differentiated by font, each suggesting a different voice. For clarity, they are identified here with lowercase Roman numerals.

The Setting Out

SECTIONS I–III

(i) The Kiowas emerged into the world through a hollow log. They are few because a pregnant woman got stuck and blocked the way.

MEDIA ADAPTATIONS

- A reading of *The Way to Rainy Mountain* by Momaday himself was released on audiocassette in 1969, with a running time of 42 minutes, and is available in a number of college libraries.

(ii) The Kiowas' original name, *Kwuda*, means "coming out." Their custom of cutting their hair unevenly brought about the name *Gaigwu*, describing something with differing halves. Their allies the Comanche softened this to *Kiowa*. (iii) The sight of the great distances of the open plains revolutionized the narrator's view of the earth.

(i) When two chiefs argued over an antelope's udders, one chief led his followers away forever. (ii) A people in the Northwest speak a language similar to Kiowa. In the winter of early 1849, scarcity of buffalo forced a return to an ancient hunting method, the encircling of an antelope herd. (iii) The narrator once saw two pronghorns far off, living in a timeless "wilderness dimension."

(i) A Kiowa with no arrows left, surrounded by enemies, was led to safety by a dog. (ii) The Kiowas had a long-standing closeness with dogs. Their elite warrior society, the Ka-itsenko— "Real Dogs"—was founded by a man who dreamed of a dog leading warriors. (iii) Dogs were always around at the narrator's grandmother's house.

SECTIONS IV–VI

(i) Before the time of Tai-me, a girl was placed in a cradle in a tree to stay safe. But a redbird led her up into the sky, became a man, and claimed her as his wife. He was the sun. (ii) The mountains of the North mark the top of the continent. (iii) The narrator has seen the wildflowers, high pines, and rose-colored birds of the mountain meadows.

(i) Having borne a son, the woman tried to climb down the sky, but the sun killed her, leaving the child below. (ii) Up in the sky, the plant that grew where the woman descended was the *pomme blanche*, with nutritious roots. The Kiowa were always hunters, never farmers. (iii) The Kiowa have remained meat eaters. The raw liver and tongue of buffalo were delicacies.

(i) A grandmother spider managed, with some trouble, to capture the sun's child. (ii) In 1874, when the Kiowas were surrounded by troops in the rain near the Staked Plains, swarms of tarantulas emerged. (iii) The narrator has seen great ornery tarantulas on the deserted dirt roads.

SECTIONS VII–IX

(i) The boy had kept the gaming ring with which the sun killed his mother. He tossed it in the air and split himself in half, becoming twins. (ii) Mammedaty, the narrator's grandfather, prized horses—a defining Kiowa trait. (iii) In summers the narrator would swim in the Washita, secluded from the endless plains. He once saw his image in the muddy water.

(i) The twins chased their rings into a giant's cave. They avoided suffocation by smoke by repeating a mantra, *thain-mom*, "above my eyes," and were set free. (ii) Words are powerful and even sacred. The Kiowa would no longer speak the names of the deceased. (iii) Aho would utter *zei-dl-bei*, "frightful," to ward off evil and the unknown.

(i) The twins killed a snake, but it was their grandfather. The grandmother spider then died, too, but the twins lived long and were honored. (ii) In another version of that story, the sun appears as a porcupine, not a redbird, and one twin dies, while the other is transformed into ten portions of sacred, eucharistic medicine. (iii) The narrator's father, as a boy, saw one sacred medicine bundle with Keahdinekeah, his grandmother.

SECTIONS X–XI

(i) During a famine, a Kiowa man wandered for four days and found Tai-me, a hooved, feathered idol that promised anything. (ii) The ceremonial "taime" figure is a two-foot bust of dark green stone exposed only during the Sun Dance—not since 1888. (Mooney, an anthropologist quoted earlier, is cited as the source for this passage.) (iii) The narrator saw the Tai-me bundle just once, hanging from a small ceremonial tree, its holiness filling the room.

(i) Once when food was scarce, two brothers found plentiful food outside their home. One partook and became a water beast. (ii) The peyote ritual involves sacred song and steady rhythms from rattle and drum. (iii) A "peyote man," Mammedaty once fled the overflowing, strangely turbulent Washita River and later saw the tracks of a water beast there.

The Going On

SECTIONS XII–XIV

(i) Once when enemies surrounded an old man, wife, and boy and demanded food, the wife cast burning fat on them, and the three escaped. (ii) In the winter of 1872–1873, a tipi emblazoned with battle scenes, the *Do-giagya guat*, was destroyed by fire. (iii) At day's end at Rainy Mountain Cemetery, there is a period of profound silence.

(i) Once a man was making arrows in his tent and sensed an enemy without. Speaking as if to his wife and discerning that the enemy knew no Kiowa, he slew him. (ii) The old men made the best arrows, prized by the young hunters and warriors. (iii) Cheney, an old arrow maker, used to pray in the silence of the dawn.

(i) The Kiowas can entreat the storm spirit to pass over them because it knows their language. (ii) The plains can be quiet or violent with weather but are always windy. (iii) The narrator once climbed down to his grandmother's storm cellar and saw the world aglow in a flash of lightning.

SECTIONS XV–XVIII

(i) The warrior Quoetotai had an affair with a wife of Many Bears and ran off with her. Fifteen years later, Many Bears welcomed Quoetotai and the wife back with friendship and horses. (ii) George Catlin, an artist, found the Kiowa nobler than the Comanche and Wichita in appearance. (iii) Catlin drew a portrait of Kotsatoah, a seven-foot warrior of legendary bearing.

(i) A man tried to escape a buffalo with steel horns by jumping between the tops of four trees, but the buffalo felled them—until the man shot his one weak spot, the cleft of the hoof. (ii) Forty years earlier (circa 1929), two old Kiowa men staged a hunt of a tame, bewildered buffalo. (iii) The narrator and his father were once briefly charged by a mother buffalo and felt truly alive.

(i) A blinded Kiowa was left behind with his wife and child, and though he slew two buffalo, his wife deceived him, took the meat, and left. When she was found out, she was thrown away. (ii) Kiowa women good or bad have known subjugation. One was stabbed for accepting a ceremonial ride with a chief; another was left ignored in the cold, and her feet froze. (iii) The narrator's great-great-grandmother, Kau-au-ointy, was a Mexican captive of the Kiowas' who rose to become a proud, powerful woman of elite status.

(i) Several young Kiowa men once followed the summer south until they discovered the strangest beings—monkeys. Then they turned back. (ii) The advent of the horse transformed the Kiowa and other tribes from pitiable, creeping subsistence hunters into daring buffalo chasers and warriors. (Mooney is again cited.) (iii) The narrator was fond of living in his grandmother's arbor—an outdoor shelter—in summers and feeling the vastness of open nature.

The Closing In

SECTIONS XIX–XXI

(i) In a raid by Utes, a Kiowa man was captured, as was his brother in a rescue attempt. But after a feat of balance and strength—the second brother carried the first over greased buffalo skulls—the Utes released them. (ii) When the Kiowas surrendered at Fort Sill (in 1874), some eight hundred horses were killed and another two thousand lost. The buffalo disappeared by 1879. (iii) Riding horseback, the narrator came to know the New Mexican terrain near Jemez Pueblo intimately.

(i) One proud hunting horse died of shame after his owner turned him away from a charge. (ii) In 1861, one horse was sacrificed as an offering to Tai-me; another, by Gaapiatan, to ward off smallpox. (iii) The narrator understands how Gaapiatan must have felt in sacrificing one of his finest steeds.

(i) Once Mammedaty caught sight of a boy in the tall grass, but then he could not be found. (ii) There is one photograph of Mammedaty in traditional garb and accoutrements, with a noble aspect. (iii) Mammedaty saw four fantastic things in his life: the ghostly boy, the water beast tracks, three small alligators (never seen again), and a mole blowing out the fine dirt left around his hole.

SECTIONS XXII–XXIV

(i) In frustration at a defiant horse leading others in circles, Mammedaty shot and killed the wrong one. (ii) In the winter of 1852–1853, a young Pawnee captive ran away with the Kiowas' greatest hunting horse, Little Red. (iii) Mammedaty had the bones of a horse called Little Red, and the narrator understands why such bones would be cherished.

(i) Once when Aho visited the Tai-me keeper's wife, the Tai-me bundle fell, seemingly of its own accord. (ii) For a time Mammedaty wore one of the medicine bundles on behalf of his mother. (iii) At the narrator's grandmother's house, there was a huge kettle—used to catch rainwater.

(i) Somewhere southeast of the narrator's grandmother's house, a woman is buried in a beautiful dress. (ii) Aho had richly ornamented high moccasins. (iii) The narrator believes that a man should give himself up to the landscape once in his life, feeling it from all angles, at all times.

Epilogue

On November 13, 1833, a great meteor shower lit up the sky and seemed to foretell the fall of the Kiowa culture. The year before, Tai-me had been tragically stolen; in 1837, the Kiowas made their first treaty with the United States. The golden age had come to an end, with Kiowa culture persisting in decline until about 1875, when materially it disappeared. What remains are the memories and the oral tradition. The centenarian Ko-sahn, who was a grown woman when the narrator's grandparents were born and yet outlived them, once recalled before the narrator the singing and rites of the Sun Dance: "...There were many people, and oh, it was beautiful!" The narrator imagines that Ko-sahn came to embody that history—in her telling, an old woman bore the first bag of sandy earth for dancing on and proclaimed a time of play. The narrator wonders if Ko-sahn would dream herself into that old woman; if she would see the falling stars in her mind. The book closes with a poem, "Rainy Mountain Cemetery."

CHARACTERS

Aho

The person who serves as the narrator's gateway to the past is Aho, his grandmother, who recently died. He can distinctly recall her physical presence—especially how she prayed when he last saw her—and his visit to her grave leads into his journey along the Kiowas' path of migration from Yellowstone to Rainy Mountain. The narrator admires Aho's sense of sacredness, her reverence for those things, like the sun and the medicine bundles, deemed sacred. Her home as filled with passing old and young Kiowas signified the narrator's sense of being a part of the community; the present-day silence of the house reflects the demise of the living Kiowa culture. Once the narrative begins, Aho appears now and again but mostly gives way to the narrator's Kiowa grandfather, Mammedaty.

Cheney

The narrator's father has spoken of an arrow maker named Cheney, a wrinkled old man who would paint his face to go out and pray to the rising sun. The narrator feels that he could watch Cheney pray as if the old man were still there.

Guipahgo

Briefly mentioned is Guipahgo, grandfather of Mammedaty and thus great-great-grandfather of the narrator. Guipahgo's renown extended to his grandson.

Kau-au-ointy

Mammedaty's grandmother—the narrator's great-great-grandmother—was a blue-eyed Mexican taken captive (and effectively adopted) by the Kiowa at eight or ten years of age. From slave status, she rose to become a powerful woman with many cattle and exceptional horse-back-riding skills.

Keahdinekeah

Keahdinekeah is Mammedaty's mother, thus the narrator's great-grandmother. The narrator says that he could see the holiness of the eucharistic medicine bundle, which Keahdinekeah once prayed to, shine out of her sightless old eyes. Her touch felt like water.

Ko-sahn

A hundred-year-old woman by the time the narrator knew her, Ko-sahn was a grown woman even when his grandparents were born. She was one of very few remaining Kiowas who could recall the Sun Dance for him. Her description renders a ceremony remembered both fondly and precisely; it was truly memorable.

Mammedaty

The kin of the narrator's mentioned most often in the course of the book is Mammedaty. He was a "peyote man," a medicine man with exceptional powers of vision and sensation, and some extra-ordinary things happened to him. His witnessing a mole puffing out the dirt encircling its hole—Mammedaty was perhaps sitting exceptionally still for a very long time—is considered evidence of his power. He is also mentioned with reference to ordinary aspects of the era, like how he owned and cherished horses and how he unsuccessfully tried his hand at wheat and cotton farming.

Narrator

In this work of postmodern literature that defies classification as fiction or nonfiction, whether the narrator should or should not be seen as the author himself is an open question. But Momaday's name is known to be a shortened version of his real-life grandfather's name, Mammedaty, and in all other respects the representations of his family members ring true. Thus, it is reasonable to conceive of the narrator not generically but indeed as N. Scott Momaday. Nonetheless, the narrator is not named within the course of the book.

The book is, in part, the story of the narrator's journey toward a greater understanding of the Kiowa culture of his forebears. The golden-age culture had passed away well before his birth, but this text so immerses the narrator in Kiowa history that it seems that he, like the pronghorns he saw, is living in a timeless dimension. Alongside his relatives, nature is what most offers the narrator a link to the past. For example, his looking up into the branches of the mountain-meadow pines is associated with the story of the girl led up the sky by the redbird; his own experiences riding horseback and getting to know the land are associated with stories of cherished horses. It is as if the narrator succeeds in envisioning himself right into the past, transporting the reader along with him. Beyond the personages of the legends and tales, nearly all the named characters are relatives of the narrator, reflecting his central role.

Narrator's Father

Like the narrator he is not named, but N. Scott Momaday's father, Al Momaday, is understood to be the father of whom the narrator speaks several times. The father was with the narrator when they were briefly chased by a buffalo cow, and the father once saw one of the medicine bundles with his own grandmother, Keahdinekeah.

THEMES

Memory

Through its intricate structure and patterns *The Way to Rainy Mountain* encompasses a swirl of significant themes, all of which are put eloquently forth in the prologue. What stands out through the introduction is the primacy of memory, specifically the memories that the narrator is delving into, his people's as well as his own. With the Kiowa golden age long over, since the youth of his now-deceased grandmother, and with the oral tradition being the only record of that age, it is through memory alone—whether silent, spoken, or written—that the height of Kiowa culture can be preserved. The narrator seeks to augment the communal memories of the golden age through a personal reenactment, a physical journey following the migration undertaken by the Kiowa over many years. In this way the narrator can embed the memories of his people more firmly in his consciousness, by virtue of direct witness of the locales that engendered them. The memories are not merely imagined but are actualized as their settings are experienced firsthand. Interestingly, the narrator characterizes the enhanced memories that his journey will establish as inferior to the pure memories once held by his grandmother, who could recall the northerly Crows and Black Hills despite having never encountered either. These "she had seen more perfectly in the mind's eye." A question, then, is why the narrator would wish to forsake such pure memory in absentia by undertaking his journey.

Identity

Suggested in the introduction but left unaddressed through most of the remaining text is the author's desire to solidify his Kiowa identity. His own distance from the Kiowa golden age is made clear by his framing its end as occurring in his grandmother's youth, but he does not explicitly state feeling an absence of Kiowa-ness within himself. Yet there must be a reason why the narrator wishes to undertake a journey that will intrude upon what he characterizes as the pure collective memories of the imagination, like those his grandmother is said to have had, and perhaps the closest he comes to voicing his motivation is a comment made on the eve of his journey: "A warm wind rose up and purled like the longing within me." The suggestion, then, is that the narrator's identity is in a sense incomplete, and he longs to complete it. The living Kiowa culture has

disappeared—there are no more buffalo, no more war parties, no more Sun Dances. Aho at least had her own youthful memories of that culture, but the narrator has only the stories. Thus, while Aho could be sustained by her memories of the culture, he cannot be—not without forging some deeper connection with that culture, such as by tracing it back to its origins. Through this journey, this search for a deeper connection, the narrator is establishing less an individual identity than a cultural identity, a Kiowa identity. Instead of discovering how the community's past reflects on his particular present, he discovers how his experiences in the present reflect on the community's past.

Legends

That the legendary past, not the personal present, is of central importance is suggested by the structure of the sections. In each section, the legendary passage comes first, occupies its own page, and is presented in the normative text, that is, in the font and style used also in the prologue, introduction, and epilogue. In turn, the second passages, the history, are modified by italics—which is perhaps an inversion of the ordinary Western orientation regarding history and myth: most people regard history as normative, as the truthful standard, while legends are a modification of history, oft-fantastic fictionalizations of what perhaps really happened.

That Momaday would invert this orientation speaks to his narrator's circumstances: he is trying not to reach back and inhabit merely the historical truth of the Kiowa people—whose history as a culture ended in tragedy—but to inhabit the very mind-set of the Kiowas of the golden age, for whom myth indeed played an integral role in shaping reality. An example of this is to be found in the myth of the seven sisters turned into the stars of the Big Dipper, a myth that deposited the Kiowas' kin in the heavens, extending the existential sphere of the people and figuring their societal evolution: "Whatever they were in the mountains, they could be no more." Myth was what helped the Kiowa reimagine themselves as a warfaring people of the Great Plains, and myth allows the narrator to reach back through history and touch the Kiowa consciousness of the golden age.

Native American History

Though history may be assigned a secondary role in the arrangement of the text, its significance is not obscured. History is what brought

TOPICS FOR FURTHER STUDY

- Using *The Way to Rainy Mountain* as a model, draw on significant moments in your life to write three sections of a work of literature, each with three passages—one written from a legendary perspective, one from a historical perspective, and one from a personal perspective. For each section, you may choose to treat the same moment in these three different styles—as a legendary occurrence, as a historical event, and as a personal experience—or you may choose to narrate moments from real legends and history that relate to each personal experience.

- Like Momaday's text, *Night Flying Woman: An Ojibway Narrative* (1983), a work of young-adult literature by Ignatia Broker, draws on the author's kin to explore family as well as tribal history. Read Broker's book and write a paper comparing the woman of Broker's title with either of the narrator's grandparents, Aho or Mammedaty, in Momaday's book. Discuss the ancestor's importance to the narrative structure, the plot, and the narrator's consciousness, among other topics of note.

- Interview your own relations, especially the eldest ones, to learn of significant events in your family's history and what previous eras were like in your family's experience. Then create a website archive of what you learn, including photos of your relatives, biographical capsules, and excerpts and/or audio clips from your interviews. Also include faithful re-creations of their stories in your own narration, an approach that allows you to unite multiple relatives' perceptions of an episode in a single narrative.

- Write a research paper that provides an in-depth look at traditional Kiowa life, as during the tribe's golden age, expanding on the capsules of ethnographic information available in Momaday's book.

- Write a research paper on military engagements between the United States and any of the Kiowa, Comanche, and Apache tribes. Discuss the different sides' advantages and disadvantages and address the role that warlike activity played in the progress of US-Indian relations.

---

the Kiowa to their culture's endpoint at Rainy Mountain, and as filled with misfortune as it became vis-à-vis US imperialism, that history cannot be denied. As much as the golden age must be remembered, so must the tragedies of the slaughter of the buffalo and the horses and the suppression of Kiowa religion, perhaps less for the sake of the Kiowa than for the sake of an American culture that must be regularly confronted with those injustices, lest they be ignored and intentionally forgotten.

More positively, the narrator wishes to memorialize the Kiowa traditions that shaped the golden-age culture, like the reverence for Tai-me and for the medicine bundles, which amounted to a historical extension of the legend of the sun's twins (just as the Christian sacrament of Holy Communion is an extension of the legend of the resurrection of Jesus Christ). The Kiowas' history was their own until it was usurped by the US government, which annihilated their communal culture by slaughtering the buffalo and horses and outlawing the Sun Dance. The narrator addresses these atrocities, which must be mentioned for Kiowa history to be fully understood, but he does not wish to dwell on them. The last section, "The Closing In," is noted for its reference to how US culture closed in on the Kiowas, whose culture was then in essence closed up. But after the Kiowas' surrender at Fort Sill (in 1874) is recalled in section XIX, section XX rewinds the time frame to the preceding decade, and the last four sections make no mention of US encroachment. As the sun sets, so to speak, Mammedaty,

A period photograph of a Kiowa man wearing a war costume (© *HP Robinson | Interim Archives | Getty Images*)

Aho, and the Kiowa culture are allowed to live proud again, on the page and in the narrator's and reader's minds.

Vision

In the end, the narrator does not simply recall the migratory journey undertaken by his people, nor does he simply retell the old stories or the post–golden age history. Whether or not he had particular powers of vision prior to the period of the tale, the narrator, in embarking on his reenactment of the Kiowas' journey, demonstrates that the act of envisioning is what will provide him with the deepest connection to both past and present. Regarding the vastness of the land in Oklahoma, he remarks, "To look upon that landscape . . . is to lose the sense of proportion. Your imagination comes to life." That is, real vision activates creative vision. He goes on to note that "the Kiowas reckoned their stature by the distance they could see," positioning vision as central to Kiowa identity.

And in the personal passages throughout the text, what is essential is what the narrator has seen. Emerging onto the Great Plains after the relative confinement of Yellowstone, he could "see the earth as it really is," and henceforth his sense of perception would be forever changed. Seeing antelope in the distance enables him to sense the perfect immersion in the present that animals, and even people, can experience. Phrasings like "I saw," "I have seen," "You see them," and so forth are iterated over and again, and in time the narrator can say even of someone like Cheney—an old man when the narrator's father was a boy, a man the narrator has presumably never seen—"In my mind I can see that man as if he were there now. I like to watch him . . . ." Cultivated in such a way as the narrator has cultivated his, vision can be an extraordinarily powerful, veritably magical tool for understanding the world, not only the visible present but the now-only-imaginable past, the memories, as well.

STYLE

Postmodernism

The Way to Rainy Mountain is a classic of post-modernism. There are various definitions of what constitutes a postmodern literary work, but the most frequently cited approaches include deconstruction, fragmentation, and open-endedness, with regard to characters, plot, and the text as a whole. The ways in which Momaday's text—a fragmentary one that draws on disparate narrative voices, lacks a conventional plot, and defies classification in a particular genre—exemplifies these traits is largely self-evident. The events related throughout the novel are presented in an associational order, not a chronological one, disrupting the reader's sense of the passage of time. Also, certain events—like the Kiowas' setting off on their migratory journey and their surrender to US troops at Fort Sill—are presented multiple times in versions that give different pieces of information about those events, such that the reader absorbs the significance of the event in a circular, rather than linear, way.

In terms of character, the work deconstructs personhood in that the narrator goes unnamed and is not given any sort of individual identity. The narrator is widely recognized as Momaday himself, who has classified the book as a memoir, but the narrator's namelessness forces the reader to accept him perhaps as autobiographical but ultimately as a not-quite-nonfictional (that is, fictional) construct of the author's. The narrator's reenactment of the journey of the Kiowas is established as a framework in the introductory sections, yet this journey is only implicitly alluded to for the remainder of the text, and Momaday never gives closure to that journey by relating how it came to an end. In effect, the book sets off on that journey and then loses itself in Kiowa legend and history, reflecting how the narrator's identity is subsumed within the collective Kiowa identity.

Perhaps the most intriguing postmodern aspect of Momaday's work is the variance in the three narrative voices in each section. From the beginning the differences between these voices are clear, presenting legendary (or mythical), historical, and personal narratives, respectively. These voices at times play off of each other in self-referential ways (textual reflexiveness being another postmodern trait). Toward the end of the book the differences between these voices are blurred. In section XXI, Mammedaty, established as a figure in the narrator's personal life—his grandfather—appears in the legendary passage. The narrative phrasing and the curiosity of the tale (of the ephemeral boy) are such that the story is readily appropriated as legend, and indeed, as the reader realizes, this is what Momaday is doing: extending the legends of his people by including the life of his own grandfather, who lives in the narrator's mind with a mythic stature. Mammedaty also appears in the historical and personal passages in that section, and thus are the three voices unified into one, just as the legendary, historical, and personal are all facets of a single realm of existence. In many ways, *The Way to Rainy Mountain* presents deconstructed and fragmented views of reality as a means of unifying that reality, of merging before the reader's eyes the legends, history, and living experiences of a people.

Native American Literature

Published just a year after Momaday's Pulitzer Prize–winning novel *House Made of Dawn*, *The Way to Rainy Mountain* was like the second half of a one-two punch that recalibrated the consciousness of the mainstream literary world. Many consider Momaday's two major works to mark the beginning of a Native American renaissance—representing the rebirth of Native oral literature as written literature—and Momaday himself to be the patriarch of Native letters. In part thanks to his wide exposure, writers such as Joseph Bruchac, Leslie Marmon Silko, and Gerald Vizenor gained recognition and appreciation from all literary audiences through the 1970s. Like Momaday, many Native authors have drawn on both their own and their tribe's histories in their writings. By the mid-1980s, William M. Clements could say of Native authors as a group, "It would indeed be difficult to identify a group of writers who have developed historical sense more effectively than the Native American poets, essayists, and novelists" of the era.

The Way to Rainy Mountain is distinctly Native American in that Kiowa myths and legends, as well as Kiowa history, play essential roles in the narrative. But beyond its accepted status as a landmark Native work, Momaday's text is recognized as one with universal appeal. The author enables such appreciation in his prologue, which depicts the Kiowas' migration as representative not just of Indians but of humanity and of the American past:

> The way to Rainy Mountain is preeminently the history of an idea, man's idea of himself.... And the journey is an evocation of three things in particular: a landscape that is incomparable, a time that is gone forever, and the human spirit, which endures.

Thus, the communal self that Momaday creates is specifically Kiowa but can encompass people of all ethnicities. This is reflected especially in the personal passages that conclude each section, which allow the reader to inhabit the narrator's perspective from the inside without regard for his externalities. While many of these passages revolve around specific Native memories or events, like the amazing things Mammedaty has witnessed, many others are straightforward descriptions of what the narrator has seen or done that do not restrict his identity in any way. The passages beginning "One morning on the high plains," in section II, and "I have walked in a mountain meadow," in section IV, exemplify this universality. In such passages, the narrator could be anybody, and so anybody could be the narrator—anybody can readily inhabit the perspective that Momaday presents.

HISTORICAL CONTEXT

The Kiowa Tribe and the United States of America

The Way to Rainy Mountain loosely covers more than two centuries of Kiowa history, from the beginning of the tribe's migration away from the northern mountains around 1700 through the 1960s, with a focus on the mid- to late nineteenth century. Yet Momaday avoids any cut-and-dried discussion of that history, giving dates as reference points but no easily digested chronology. The Kiowas are said to have specifically originated at the three forks of the Missouri River in western Montana. Moving eastward, they were befriended by the Crow and remained around the Black Hills in Wyoming and South Dakota, where they conflicted with the Lakota, until 1760. After occupying the Cheyenne and Platte river regions through 1790, they ended up in a stretch of the southern plains—around the headwaters of the Cimarron River in the borderlands of Kansas, Colorado, New Mexico, Texas, and Indian Territory (Oklahoma)—considered by Anglo-American observers so dry and windy

as to be inhospitable. But the Kiowa found adequate game, shelter, water, and botanical riches for subsistence, with the grasslands especially valuable as a food source for their plentiful horses, the linchpin of their intertribal economy. Their yearly settlement patterns largely followed the vast herds of buffalo.

With Momaday providing an assortment of legends and details reflecting Kiowa life during their golden age, which he frames as the century or so from 1740 to the 1830s, the modern reader may be left most curious about how the tribe was subordinated by US interests. Politically, as the author notes, the first Kiowa treaty with the United States (also involving the Kataka and Tawakaro nations) was signed in 1837, establishing peace among the different tribes and US citizens while granting the Indians hunting and trapping rights. In most respects, as with many early treaties between Native tribes and the US government, this one allowed the tribes their own sovereign governments and internal authority. Later treaties, however, would gradually diminish this sovereignty, especially after the US territorial position was strengthened by the acquisition of the bulk of the modern American Southwest after the Mexican-American War in 1848. Outnumbered and outprovisioned by the US military, tribes were left with few options. With the 1853 Treaty of Fort Atkinson, the Kiowas, Comanches, and Apaches were no longer permitted to govern their own external relations with other tribes or republics—including the United States itself. Also, for violations like raids the tribes were threatened with the loss of previously promised capital sums, and they conceded to the United States rights to build roads and military posts through their territory. By this time, tribes like the Kiowa were primarily perceived by Anglo society as an obstacle to the gross fulfillment of Manifest Destiny—US occupation of the span of the North American continent.

US privileges increased further with the 1865 Treaty with the Comanches and Kiowas. Tribal law was to be replaced by US law, even with regard to crimes involving Indians only, while regular censuses would now enable the US government to limit the financial sums allotted tribes based on proportions of Indian blood and populations restricted to reservations. The 1867 Treaty of Medicine Lodge Creek, in turn, would restrict the Kiowas, Comanches, and Apaches alike to a minimal reservation in the

COMPARE
&
CONTRAST

- **Mid-eighteenth century:** The Kiowas migrate east and south from Montana to inhabit the Great Plains.

  Mid-nineteenth century: Having ranged the borderlands of Kansas, Colorado, New Mexico, and Texas, the Kiowas are gradually confined by US-dictated treaties and congressional legislation to a corner of Indian Territory called the Kiowa-Comanche-Apache Reservation.

  1960s: Since the Kiowa-Comanche-Apache Reservation was opened up to white settlement at the beginning of the century, the Kiowa persist as a people with individually held lands but only the nominal homeland of Kiowa County, Oklahoma.

  Today: While they remain independent of any reservation, Kiowas are able to solidify community identification and interests through the website of the Kiowa Tribe, which lists over two dozen organizations bringing together members of the Kiowa community.

- **Mid-eighteenth century:** Kiowa storytellers propagate stories and legends that reflect the history and pride of a migrating, flourishing people.

  Mid-nineteenth century: In addition to the persisting legends, Kiowa storytellers may also relate the sorrow of defeat and subjugation at the hands of US military forces and the US government.

  1960s: Following up on myth collections and ethnographic studies published by Anglo authors, Momaday's *The Way to Rainy Mountain* provides one of the earliest creative literary explorations of Kiowa culture and identity by a Kiowa writer.

  Today: Momaday's works, including *The Names: A Memoir* (1976), remain among the most valuable literary resources regarding Kiowa history and life, while the Kiowa language is preserved through local classes as well as the website Kiowa Kids, which provides resources such as dictionaries and recordings.

- **Mid-eighteenth century:** The thirteen colonies of eastern North America gradually unite to stage a revolution against an empire perceived as oppressive, the British Empire. Meanwhile, conflicts such as the French and Indian War (1754–1763) reflect growing antagonisms among colonial powers and Native Americans.

  Mid-nineteenth century: With the United States determined to fulfill what is perceived as the nation's Manifest Destiny, US political leaders are content to trample Native Americans' rights and subjugate tribes by any means necessary, including dishonesty, deceit, bureaucratic maneuvering, unilateral legislation, and military assaults and massacres.

  1960s: At the end of a decade marked by the successes of the civil rights movement and advancing feminism, Native American activists—with over 5,600 participating for at least a day—advance their cause by staging an eighteen-month occupation of the abandoned Alcatraz Island, from 1969 to 1971, making it a symbol of Indian reclamation. The effects prove profound, with some ten legislative acts passed or emended to restore and recognize Native rights.

  Today: Institutions like the American Indian Movement and the Native American Church continue to sustain and advance the rights and interests of US Indian nations, which number over 550. In an era marked by the environmental degradations of modern civilization and the potentially catastrophic effects of global warming, there is a resurgence of interest in the sacred view of nature inherent in Native cultures and traditions.

Momaday's ancestors surrendered to the U.S. Cavalry at Fort Sill in 1889. (© MPI / Getty Images)

midst of a broad expanse of previously recognized Indian territory. These treaties reflected a shift in the perceptions of the American bureaucracy: tribes were already constrained enough to no longer be feared, and US legislators saw no need to be generous, or even fair, with regard to tribal interests. Many figures of authority argued that the Indians never rightfully owned the land to begin with. Thus were appropriations bills swamped by indifference, and in the words of Jacki Thompson Rand in *Kiowa Humanity and the Invasion of the State*, "The hubris of empire...consigned Indian people to suffer indignities, starvation, and illness."

The Kiowas in particular were branded by US leaders as outlaws; as Momaday notes in *The Way to Rainy Mountain*, "War was their sacred business," as seen in their reliance on raiding parties for the procurement of goods. The US military presence in the region was strengthened in the mid-nineteenth century, with offensives against Kiowas and Comanches carried out before and after the Civil War. As Anglo settlers increased population pressures and made buffalo increasingly scarce, while Kiowa hunting grounds were increasingly limited in expanse by the US-dictated treaties, the Kiowas depended ever more on US rations promised in those

treaties—which nonetheless depleted as the United States reduced those rations and often simply failed to provide them. Corrupt Bureau of Indian Affairs agents played a substantial role in diverting resources to enrich themselves and in forcing tribes to barter for goods they had been promised gratis.

By the 1870s the downward spiral was painfully evident: under US constrictions the Kiowas could not procure enough food to feed their people, and their necessarily aggressive responses only further minimized their allotments. In 1874, reservation-based Kiowas, who were being officially enrolled, were left with little option but to declare the abandonment of those young Kiowas who continued to raid in order to support their families. That particularly cold fall, the US Army kept the Kiowa raiding parties on the run through freezing rain until, having left their stores behind in Palo Duro Canyon, as Momaday records, they surrendered in defeat at Fort Sill. Following such a protracted history of oppression, the reader of *The Way to Rainy Mountain* cannot be surprised to find Kiowa culture and history rendered with admiration and pride and US relations treated marginally—countering the course of history by inverting it, subordinating US concerns to the "wonder and delight" of the Kiowa golden age.

CRITICAL OVERVIEW

In the wake of Momaday's Pulitzer Prize for Fiction in 1969, the public was primed to offer his ensuing major publication, *The Way to Rainy Mountain*, a broad and admiring reception. As Mick McAllister notes in his 1980 essay "The Topology of Remembrance in *The Way to Rainy Mountain*," initial reviewers "praised Momaday's eloquence and conciseness, the gentle dignity of his prose, and the book's 'simplicity that approaches purest poetry.'"

In the extended critical reception, few have had anything but positive comments for Momaday's title. In *Twentieth-Century Young Adult Writers*, Charmaine Allmon Mosby calls *The Way to Rainy Mountain* "arguably his most important work," and likewise Suzanne Evertsen Lundquist, in the *Dictionary of Literary Biography*, calls the book "undoubtedly Momaday's greatest contribution to world literature."

An especially insightful and commendatory study was offered by McAllister. He likens the structure of the book to a musical concerto or string quartet, and he offers an extended analysis of the subtle significances of the artwork by Al Momaday, such as with how the imagery of the falling-stars scene at the book's end connects to that of the seven stars of the Big Dipper at the beginning. McAllister declares that *The Way to Rainy Mountain*

> is a loving book, not an anatomy of human suffering nor, primarily, an indictment of white culture, but a celebration of 'nobility and fulfillment,' a celebration of a great people who became, for a time, whole and complete, and a celebration of the imagination.

McAllister concludes that, like the cultural material it draws upon, *The Way to Rainy Mountain* "is simple, organic, primitive, and at the same time a thing of order and measured form. Structures interplay and weave a fabric of beauty, wonder, and meaning."

In an *American Indian Culture and Research Journal* essay, Kenneth Lincoln calls *The Way to Rainy Mountain* a "book of magical passages, a miracle document of tribal journey toward the dawn. Momaday has charted an ongoing cultural treasure of tale-telling and dance-singing and deep-rooting in the storied places of time and human imagining." Calling Momaday's works "mysterious, chiseled, and crafted," Lincoln goes on to conclude that the author's

"words will be pondered and remembered for a long time," and he "will long be regarded as the Grandfather Bear of a Native American Renaissance in Western letters."

CRITICISM

Michael Allen Holmes

Holmes is a writer with existential interests. In the following essay, he traces how Momaday uses the personal passages in The Way to Rainy Mountain *to guide the reader toward a goal of his own—the dissolution of individual identity.*

Many of the world's traditions deemed mystical entail the dissolving of one's individual identity to some extent. As exemplified in the Upanishads, those Hindus who reach the highest spiritual consciousness do so by merging theirs with that of Brahman, the universal essence also called the Atman or Self. Brahman is said to be everywhere and to inhabit everything. This is broadly similar to the Christian conception of God. Less known is the Taoist tradition, whereby one seeks unity with a very similar—but unpersonified—fundamental essence called the Tao. One may do so in part by shedding the egotistic aspects of one's existence, including emotions, desires, attachments to others, and pride in accomplishments. Such traditions were given a nineteenth-century spin in the guise of transcendentalism by Ralph Waldo Emerson, who spoke of a Universal Soul and of union with Nature. N. Scott Momaday's project in *The Way to Rainy Mountain* is not so far removed from these mystic traditions. He does not explicitly express a goal of identity dissolution, and in fact much of what he addresses is linked to his specific self: he closely identifies with his family, discussing his ancestors in such a way that the reader senses his pride of kinship, and of course, he remains an individual with some degree of worldly ambition, as suggested by the impressive output of the early phase of his literary career. Nonetheless, a process of identity dissolution becomes evident in *The Way to Rainy Mountain*, a work of literature that tends to accomplish the same dissolution in the reader.

Notable from the book's outset—though perhaps not quite noticeable until further in—is the fact that the narrator's background is ignored almost entirely. He does not discuss his birthplace, his early life, or any other biographical

WHAT DO I READ NEXT?

- Momaday's Pulitzer Prize winner, *House Made of Dawn* (1968), is about a Pueblo Indian who seeks to center himself after returning from military service during World War II.

- The work in which Momaday delves furthest into his family's history is *The Names: A Memoir* (1976). He provides a genealogical chart, photographs of his ancestors, detailed family history, and a narrative of his explorations of the lands of his people and his past.

- *The Names* has been considered analogous to Alex Haley's volume *Roots: The Saga of an American Family* (1976), which traces the author's African heritage back through American slavery to Gambia in the eighteenth century.

- Nonfiction writings by Momaday are collected in *The Man Made of Words: Essays, Stories, Passages* (1997). In the title story, the author discusses the genesis of *The Way to Rainy Mountain*.

- Among Chippewa author Gerald Vizenor's many works is the comic novel *The Heirs of Columbus* (1991), which draws on the significance and value of Indian oral literature to posit a genetic research center dedicated to extracting the stories and survivance written in the blood of Native Americans.

- Paula Gunn Allen, of mixed Laguna Pueblo and European heritage, wrote the novel *The Woman Who Owned the Shadows* (1983), about a mixed-blood woman named Ephanie who confronts a racist world by turning back to her Indian heritage.

- The theme of the destruction of Native culture is prominent in the collection *The Man to Send Rain Clouds: Contemporary Stories by American Indians* (1974), edited by Kenneth Rosen, which among fourteen tales features six by Leslie Marmon Silko.

- A notable influence on Momaday was William Faulkner, whom Momaday met at the University of Virginia. *The Way to Rainy Mountain* has been compared with Faulkner's *Absalom! Absalom!* (1936), which uses a fragmented, nonchronological structure while following three southern families to explore the life of protagonist Thomas Sutpen in the Civil War era.

- *They Dance in the Sky: Native American Star Myths* (1987), edited by Jean Guard Monroe and Ray A. Williamson with black-and-white drawings by Edgar Sturat, provides a collection of star myths—including about the Big Dipper and the Pleiades—from different Indian cultures, including Plains Indians. Appropriate for young adults, the book includes a glossary with pronunciation guide.

---

details. He does name family members, effectively fixing his identity as the descendant of Keahdinekeah, Mammedaty, Aho, and the others. Yet his own name goes unspoken, as do the names of his parents, despite the fact that Momaday's father was the one who illustrated the book. There is no explanation for why his mother goes unmentioned entirely. (Momaday's mother was of Cherokee descent.) Indeed, these seem to have been deliberate choices. It would have been a most simple matter for the narrator

to provide his own father's name when mentioning him, and in the context of a historically oriented work in which virtually all other family members are named, the father's going unnamed can only be explained by intention. In effect, the namelessness of both the narrator and his father—and his unmentioned mother—creates a cocoon of anonymity that shields the narrator from any fixed conception of his existence. The reader can never really formulate an image of who the narrator is as a person, not even in

MOMADAY BEGINS TO FILL IN THE NARRATOR'S BLANKS—WITH THE READER'S OWN SELF-IMAGE."

name, other than through the tribal and family history that he relates. In other words, the reader's sense of the narrator's identity depends strictly on his family and community; it is not an egotistic, internally determined identity but a communal, externally determined one.

A few of the grammatical strategies used by Momaday serve to further suppress the reader's sense of the author's identity. In the introduction, the author begins relating his own journey down the plains from the North by remarking, with reference to himself as perceiver, "Yellowstone, it seemed to me, was the top of the world." His individual existence is established. But he proceeds in the ensuing sentence to hide his narratorial presence by making the subject third-person generic: "One might have the sense of confinement there." He then assigns an active role to what he is witnessing, making an aspect of nature—the skyline—the subject of the following sentence; and the sentence after that further diminishes the author's existence by using the passive voice: "There is a perfect freedom in the mountains." In effect, this sequence of sentences gradually removes the author as subject, leaving the author as a vaguely outlined medium between the reader and the experience embodied in the text. The narrator does return as a subjective presence, as he proceeds to discuss, with many uses of first-person pronouns, his approach to Devils Tower, the character of his grandmother, and his visit to her grave. But the pattern of the removal of the author as subject has been established, and after the book's introduction, there is no specific account of the proceedings of the journey the narrator has undertaken. Rather, there are capsules of experiences that are not strictly chronologic and thus are, in a sense, timeless—many could be occurring almost anytime, especially where the capsules involve only the anonymous narrator interacting with elements of nature.

An example of such a nature-narrator–centered recollection occurs as soon as the first chapter, "The Setting Out," begins, in section I. In the personal passage here, the narrator frames the Great Plains in the spring as a setting so grand that they fill one's consciousness: "At first there is . . . nothing but the land itself, whole and impenetrable." The land is ubiquitous, and it is only impenetrable at first, as the narrator soon finds his eye absorbed in the various distant sights of herds, rivers, and groves. There is a suggestion of enlightenment in this viewing of the land: all that the narrator sees is perceived to have "perfect being," and the narrator can declare, "Now I see the earth as it really is." The tone of the personal passage in section II echoes that of the first section, as the narrator discusses a particular natural sight experience and the impression it made upon him. Here the pronghorn antelopes are recognized as existing in a "wilderness dimension of time"—that is, a timeless one, unburdened by history or concern for the distant future; as animals, the antelopes simply *are*. Once again, then, the narrator is absorbed in what he sees to such an extent that his identity tends to dissolve: not his own self but what he sees becomes all that concerns him. That he is viewing nature is essential, as there is a suggestion of infinity, of universality, in the expanses of the plains and the consciousnesses of the animals that cannot be found in human civilization.

Section III continues the narrative trend. In the personal passage here, the author breaches the notion that dogs might reside in and around a household and belong there "in a sense that the word 'ownership' does not include." Thus the narrator is now subtracting the notion of possession—a hallmark of the modern capitalist Anglo world—from his consciousness. People often define themselves by what they possess, what their accomplishments and wealth have enabled them to possess; in throwing the very notion of possession out the window, this passage advances the dissolution of individual identity.

After section IV presents, like the first two sections, a passage in which the author loses himself in a vision of nature, section V marks the return of the narrator's subjective presence. He speaks of his grandfather, Mammedaty, and an experience of his own, where he witnessed a boy relishing a raw calf's liver. But rather than dwelling on his own role in this experience, the narrator uses it to transition into a recollection of the Kiowa past: "I have heard that the old hunters of the Plains prized the raw liver and tongue of the buffalo above all other delicacies." Such transitions are consistently suggested by the juxtaposition of legendary, historical, and personal passages. In being presented side by side in alternation, the personae of the various sections begin to overlap in the reader's mind (a process that will culminate in the merging of the various narrative voices in the last chapter).

The personal passage in section VI is, once again, focused on a vision of nature—spiders on old dirt roads—but an interesting difference is that the author here introduces the use of the second person:

> There are dirt roads in the Plains. You see them, and you wonder where and how far they go.... Now and then there comes a tarantula, at evening, always larger than you imagine.

The use of the second person is common in letters, when a specific individual is indeed being addressed, but not so common in literature. Some consider it risky because it forces a readerly identification with the text that may not ring true for everyone. In this case, Momaday has expertly set the scene for the use of the second person: In the introduction he spoke of the Kiowas' journey as being "an expression of the human spirit," such that no ethnicity is excluded from the implications of that journey. In turn he has preserved the anonymity of his narrator for long enough that the reader is likely feeling an urge to formulate a more concrete image of him; the reader is by now thirsting for details about who the narrator is. And with the narrator being primarily an observer, not an actor, he is not someone whom the reader him- or herself cannot imagine being. In section VI, then, Momaday begins to fill in the narrator's blanks—with the reader's own self-image.

The use of the second person proves momentary, but the effect is lasting. In section VII the narrator plants himself back swimming in the Washita River, but now the reader is likely subconsciously associating the narrator with oneself. What is related is a specific but not exclusive experience; anyone who has swum in a pond or lake can imagine oneself there where the narrator is. Momaday proceeds to highlight his concealment of the narrator's identity by ending the section in the moment when the narrator's image in the water breaks apart. That broken, rippling image, as extended indefinitely,

signifies precisely the process of the dissolution of the narrator's identity.

From this point onward the personal passages increasingly reference the narrator's family members, most often Aho and Mammedaty. In a sense this tends to prevent the reader from projecting oneself onto the narrator's identity, because of course each reader has had one's own grandparents and so forth. Yet typically the passage closes with a generalization of the circumstances related. In section VIII the narrator tells of how Aho would mutter a particular word to ward off "ignorance and disorder," and one can readily substitute one's own elderly kinfolk muttering phrases that over time have become mantras—sayings with soothing, veritably mystical effects. Similarly, section IX regards Keahdinekeah, but anyone who has interacted with a very old relative can relate to the notion of this woman's "glad weeping and the water-like touch of her hand." The scene is particular, but the sense is universal. Section X, too, is a specific scene, the narrator's viewing of the Tai-me bundle, that ends with a generalized characterization: "There was a great holiness all about in the room, as if an old person had died there or a child had been born." Nothing is more universal to humanity than death and birth.

Section XI, the last of the first chapter, is perhaps the most specific personal passage in the book, but opening the second chapter, section XII returns to a vision of nature, set in a cemetery. In light of its connection with the title and the narrator's journey, the cemetery is named, but the description is, once again, universal—it could be any silent cemetery at sunset. Section XIII specifies an old man, Cheney, but here again Momaday introduces the second person: "There, at dawn, you can feel the silence. It is cold and clear and deep like water. It takes hold of you and will not let you go." This phrasing not only reintegrates the reader into the narrator's persona but also formulates precisely what the book is accomplishing with respect to the reader: taking hold of one and not letting one go. Even if the reader does not make this association, the wording is strong and clear enough to make an impact on the reader's subconscious.

The same patterns are found in the personal passages throughout the remainder of the book. There are homages to specific individuals that fade to generalized images—like the great Kotsatoah silhouetted "alone and against the sky" in section XV; the proto-feminist Kau-au-ointy, who "could ride as well as any man," in section XVII; and Mammedaty, who like any sage or shaman is seen in section XXI to possess "a powerful medicine." Furthermore, beyond merely paying homage to past individuals, the narrator explicitly speaks of feeling able to inhabit the perspectives of Gaapiatan the horse sacrificer, in section XX, and of any who might preserve or steal a horse's bones, in section XXII.

There are accounts of personal and familial experiences that speak to the universal human condition—like the brief charge of the mother buffalo in section XVI, when the narrator and his father "knew just then what it was to be alive"; the view in section XVIII of "the long sweep of the earth itself" at Aho's arbor; the account in section XIX of how the narrator "came to know that country" of his youth "truly and intimately, in every season, from a thousand points of view"; and the image in section XXIII of the great, seemingly unmovable kettle—the narrator does not "know where it came from; it was always there." The second person is invoked to enhance the reader-narrator connection in two of these sections: At Aho's arbor "you could see far and wide . . . ; there was nothing to stand in your way." And regarding the kettle, "It rang like a bell when you struck it, and with the tips of your fingers you could feel the black metal sing."

And there are visions of nature, namely, the lightning-lit landscape in section XIV and "the remembered earth" of section XXIV, which, in closing the last section and the entire inner portion of the book, presents one of its most quoted passages. Here Momaday perhaps astutely avoids the second person, which might have been construed as either overly sentimental or didactic. The narrator is declaring what he believes "a man ought to" do, and the power of this declaration would have likely been compromised by a direct address to the reader, which might have seemed like a presumptuous command. Thus, the final section's association between reader and narrator is not forced but entirely voluntary. The reader is given the freedom to decide whether one would conform to the narrator's conception of what a man (or woman) ought to do—"to concentrate his mind upon the remembered earth, . . . to give himself up to a particular landscape in his experience." The reader has been subtly coaxed into identifying with the narrator's perspective, and by this point this identification

may be effortless. The reader who has been enlightened by Momaday's text need not think twice about the propriety of conforming to the narrator's vision; the fulfillment of this vision is instinctively recognized as a genuine ideal.

Throughout the text, the narrator has been losing himself in the legends and history of his people. He is not dwelling on Kiowa stories in order to gain perspective on his own life, but rather is dwelling on his own experiences in order to gain perspective on the last several centuries of life for the Kiowa people—on the collective life and collective identity of the community. Through the various stylistic approaches employed in the text, the reader is carried along on the narrator's journey and encouraged to participate in the dissolution of individual identity in favor of a communal identity. Appropriately, this process itself is at last imaged in the epilogue. There, after relaying the centenarian Ko-sahn's girlhood recollections of the Sun Dance, the narrator closes with questions about whether Ko-sahn came to envision herself as that old woman she witnessed initiating the Sun Dance: "Was she become in her sleep that old purveyor of the sacred earth, perhaps, that ancient one who, old as she was, still had the feeling of play?" In other words, had Ko-sahn, by the time of her old age, experienced such a successful dissolution of her individual identity that in her mind she literally conceived herself as a Kiowa woman she once witnessed? The question that implicitly follows is, did the narrator, through his journey, accomplish such a dissolution for himself—has he, or will he, come to envision himself as Mammedaty or, perhaps more likely, the old man praying aloud to the rising sun? And finally, has the reader been enabled to experience such a mystical dissolution of identity for oneself, if only momentarily, through the book's most powerful passages, like the declaration of how "a man ought to concentrate his mind upon the remembered earth"? If all has gone well in the reading, the answer to this last question would be yes.

Source: Michael Allen Holmes, Critical Essay on *The Way to Rainy Mountain*, in *Novels for Students*, Gale, Cengage Learning, 2014.

Jim Charles

In the following excerpt, Charles addresses the intricate and unusual structure of The Way to Rainy Mountain.

> "HIS JOURNEY COMPLETE, MOMADAY HAS CONNECTED HIMSELF TO HIS FAMILY AND TO THE STORIES OF HIS TRIBE. HE KNOWS WHO HE IS. IF HE HAS SUCCEEDED IN THIS WORK, READERS KNOW SOMETHING MORE OF THEMSELVES AS WELL."

... Momaday's *The Way to Rainy Mountain* retraces the migration of the Kiowa people, his people, from western Montana, through the Black Hills, Wyoming, and Colorado into their present homeland—southwestern Oklahoma. He leads readers on a journey, weaving together the threads of tribal oral tradition, of anthropological and historical research, and of personal narrative. The work challenges teachers and students on structural and thematic grounds and because it speaks directly and in fresh ways to students about crucial elements of their being—identity and self-understanding.

In many ways, *The Way to Rainy Mountain* is a difficult book, defying categorization into a particular genre. Like Jean Toomer's *Cane* (1923), *The Way to Rainy Mountain* contains prose passages and poems as well as vivid illustrations that are fully integrated into the text. It is a book that students say "looks different." For our purposes, *The Way to Rainy Mountain* fits categorization as a short novel because it tells a story and does so in an imaginative way. It is primarily written in prose (albeit, in the third section of each triad, some of the most lyrical prose). There is clear plot movement within a beginning-middle-end structure. There is a frame story and others within it. There are memorable characters and events. Much of the book, however, is historical. One of the three "strands" into which the book is divided derives from historical or anthropological texts. Therefore, roughly one-third of the book is overtly non-fiction. Traditional Kiowa stories comprise another third. Some may consider the stories themselves fiction, but their accurate transcription and careful retelling is non-fiction. Of course, there is no contradiction necessarily between the novel form and non-fiction as illustrated in the "non-fiction novels" of Norman Mailer (*The Executioner's Song*, 1979) and Truman Capote (*In Cold Blood*, 1965) or in the universal truths one derives from reading a well-written novel. So, then, the categorization of *The Way to Rainy Mountain* as a novel proves to be yet another of its interesting aspects, more food for discussion and debate between teacher and students!

Framed by two poems, *The Way to Rainy Mountain* contains a prologue, introduction, three main sections—"The Setting Out," "The Going On," and "The Closing In"—and an epilogue. Figure 4 conveys something of the structural intricacy of the work.

The poem "Headwaters" begins the book, referring to "a log, hollow and weather-stained," an allusion to the origin story of the Kiowa people. According to their oral tradition, the Kiowas, who refer to themselves as "coming out people," emerged into this world one by one through a hollow log. The poem speaks of sources—of the Kiowa people, of their oral traditions, and of Momaday's family. In so doing, the poem presages the triadic structure of other stories in the book. In the Prologue, Momaday retells the Kiowa story of *Tai-me*, the sacred bundle used in the Sun Dance, the most sacred ceremony of the Kiowas. The story clearly conveys that while the tribal oral tradition may change, it nonetheless persists. Today, for example, crucial elements of the Kiowa Sun Dance persist in the Gourd Dance (Ellis, 1990, 21, 23), a dance in which Momaday participates. Momaday asserts a major theme of this and many of his other works: the power of the oral tradition rests in its ability to preserve in language the essence of a people, their concept of themselves.

The Introduction continues these ideas, tying them to the landscape of the central plains of the United States. Momaday establishes his personal connection to the Kiowa stories by way of his personal journey to and connection with the story of "rock tree," Devils Tower located in Wyoming. Momaday's Kiowa name, *Tsoai-talee*, translates "Rock-tree Boy." The defining nature of names among his people connects Momaday in a very *real* way to the story. In the story a boy, while chasing his sisters, turns into a bear. Fearing for their lives the seven sisters climb upon a tree stump that begins to grow skyward. The boy-bear reaches up for them as they rise and his claws dig deep grooves into the bark of the tree. Eventually, the sisters are borne into the heavens and become the stars of the Big Dipper; the scoriated tree, Devils

Tower. Momaday stated in an interview with Charles Woodard (1989), "...[A]fter the end of the story, the bear remains and the boy remains and they come together now and then. The boy becomes a boy again and becomes a bear again, and this goes on and has gone on through the centuries, and probably in every generation there is a reincarnation of the bear—the boy bear. And I feel that I am such a reincarnation...." Here, Momaday establishes direct linkages between tribal, familial, and personal experiences. Here, too, he treats the theme of identity simultaneously on several levels—tribal, familial, and spiritual.

The first major section of *The Way to Rainy Mountain* entitled "The Setting Out" contains Kiowa oral narratives and traditions as told by Momaday's relatives and "validated" by the anthropological/historical record. The journey motif is established in this opening section. The movement of the Kiowa people southward and out onto the Great Plains is reflected in Momaday's personal recollection of gazing upon the Plains landscape: "... At first there is no discrimination in the eye, nothing but the land itself, whole and impenetrable. But then the smallest things begin to stand out of the depths—herds and rivers and groves—and each of these has perfect being in terms of distance and of silence and of age. Yes, I thought, now I see the earth as it really is...." Throughout the section Momaday binds other Kiowa oral traditions to his personal experience. He connects his childhood memory of the many dogs at his grandmother's house to the tribe's use of dogs as beasts of burden and to the time, documented in Kiowa oral tradition, when dogs could talk. Thus, the reality of his childhood, through family, story, and imagination extends into and becomes part of the tribal past. What to some seems unreal, even impossible, is imagined into existence, into plausibility, by Momaday.

In the major section entitled "The Going On," Momaday conveys the persistence of the Kiowas and the strength of their traditions. Both people and traditions possess the power to continue. He weaves together tellings of the craft of arrowmaking and a family story about Cheney, an old arrowmaker. Momaday writes, "In my mind I can see that man as if he were here now. I like to watch him as he makes his prayer. I know where he stands and where his voice goes on the rolling grasses and where the sun comes up on the land. There, at dawn, you can feel the

silence. It is cold and clear and deep like water. It takes hold of you and will not let you go." As with braiding, the strength of interconnecting strands of experience—here tribal past, family tradition, and personal experience—is what Momaday captures and clarifies.

The book's third major section, "The Closing In," speaks of the Kiowas settling in the southern plains in Oklahoma. This is the landscape of Momaday's youth, and it is within this geographic context that he establishes a connection to his father's family, particularly to his father's mother. He writes:

> East of my grandmother's house the sun rises out of the plain. Once in his life a man ought to concentrate his mind upon the remembered earth, I believe. He ought to give himself up to a particular landscape in his experience, to look at it from as many angles as he can, to wonder about it, to dwell upon it. He ought to imagine that he touches it with his hands at every season and listens to the sounds that are made upon it. He ought to imagine the creatures there and all the faintest motions of the wind. He ought to recollect the glare of noon and all the colors of the dawn and dusk.

In the Epilogue Momaday underscores his belief in the power of the oral tradition to preserve any culture. He details two instances in tribal history which, to him, are interconnected and which, through the old woman *Ko-sahn*, are linked to him personally. In short space, the triadic weaving of ancient, tribal, and personal experiences is again accomplished. The Kiowas recorded the Leonid meteor shower of 1833 on their calendars and the importance of the Sun Dance in their songs. Momaday recalls *Ko-sahn* telling of an old woman who carried sacred soil on her back, soil necessary for the Sun Dance ceremony. The old woman sang,

> We have brought the earth.
> Now it is time to play
> As old as I am, I still have the feeling of play.

Through *Ko-sahn* and her retelling, such events "... [are] in the reach of memory still...." To Momaday,

> It was—all this and more—a quest, a going forth upon the way to Rainy Mountain. Probably *Ko-sahn* too is dead now. At times, in the quiet of evening, I think she must have wondered, dreaming, who she was. Was she become in her sleep that old purveyor of the sacred earth, perhaps that ancient one who, old as she was, still had the feeling of play? And in her mind, at times, did she see the falling stars?

Structurally, *The Way to Rainy Mountain* concludes as it begins—with a poem. Entitled "Rainy Mountain Cemetery," the poem commemorates Momaday's visit to his grandmother's grave, the culmination of his personal, historical, and tribal journey. In this contemplation upon his grandmother's grave, Momaday hears in the silence of the graveyard his grandmother's voice and feels her presence in heat, sunlight, and shadow. His journey complete, Momaday has connected himself to his family and to the stories of his tribe. He knows who he is. If he has succeeded in this work, readers know something more of themselves as well.

Similar to its structural uniqueness, *The Way to Rainy Mountain* possesses a different thematic "sound and feel," evoking multiple responses from readers. Through a multivoiced telling, Momaday weaves together different versions of several aspects of *his* journey, his family's journey, his tribe's journey. These braided triadic tellings are connected linearly, chronologically, and therefore historically. But more importantly, I think, the parts of each triad are linked through image and metaphor. As in the above examples of the dogs, the arrowmaker, and the Plains landscape, Momaday conveys a more complete version of these essential experiences when he describes them from three perspectives, rather than one. A more complete telling results; a more truthful telling results. A new history, with emphasis on *story*, results. As Momaday puts it, "There are on the way to Rainy Mountain many landmarks, many journeys in the one."

The book invites readers to join Momaday on his quest for self-knowledge. Readers wrestle with issues of personal, familial, and national identity; the role of spirituality in peoples' lives, and an orientation toward landscape, one that shapes identity of those who, as Momaday would put it, "live in it." The process of reading the book is, in itself, an act of self-discovery. Bataille, elaborating this idea (in Roemer, 1988), argues that "[w]hat [Momaday] shows students is that finding one's identity is a personal quest, a going forth to discover 'who and what and that we are.'"

From the outset, readers know they are reading an "American Indian book," a book about Indian identity, but this is a subtle treatment of "Indianness," underscoring the work's thematic universality. It speaks to the power of a

people to carry on, to survive, by means they themselves devise and hold meaningful. Specifically, Momaday links the survival of his people to their ability to remember, preserve, and pass on stories. Taking the idea one step further, Momaday models necessary personal involvement in the stories through use of the imagination. That is, to make sense of and find a place in the *contemporary* world, one must connect on a personal level with the stories of one's past. Limiting categories do not apply to *The Way to Rainy Mountain*. It is not a protest book, nor is it an overtly political book. Rather, it describes a process: a people, one person and one family at a time, preserves essential aspects of its heritage, connects through imagination to that heritage, and in so doing, assures its survival. The book, then, speaks to Indians today. Mistakenly, it has been read as a nostalgic backward glance at the "rise and fall" of Kiowa culture. To not make connections to the *contemporary* Kiowa experience is to misread the book; to not connect it to *universal* contemporary experience is to miss an opportunity for student and teacher self-discovery.

The work's universality is evident. Readers participate with Momaday in a parallel personal journey of introspection and analysis. According to many psychologists, there is no more important task during adolescence than the development of a healthy, well-integrated sense of identity; the resolution of the identity crisis within each individual is a crucial step toward healthy development. Reading and responding to Momaday's *The Way to Rainy Mountain* are means through which students can further develop an identity rooted in history, family, and heritage....

Source: Jim Charles, "*The Ancient Child, House Made of Dawn*, and *The Way to Rainy Mountain*," in *Reading, Learning, Teaching N. Scott Momaday*, edited by P. L. Thomas, Peter Lang, 2007, pp. 53–60.

Charles L. Woodard

In the following excerpt, Woodard points out the importance of place in Momaday's work.

There are many journeys in the writings of N. Scott Momaday. In *House Made of Dawn* there are restless displacements from villages to cities, and questing movements across the surfaces of the earth, and long, ritualistic runs, and migration memories. In *The Names* there are frequent references to nomadic experiences and impulses, and the book concludes dramatically with factual and imaginative descriptions of journeys. In *The Way to Rainy Mountain* the central focus is, of course, on movement across time and space; and that movement is again a strong element in *Set*, the novel in progress. Additionally, many of Momaday's essays discuss migration experience and explore the implications of movement.

There have also been many journeys in Momaday's life. He moved frequently with his parents during his childhood, and they centered themselves on several southwestern landscapes across which he could move in imaginative play. In adulthood, he has chosen to live in a variety of places and has traveled often and widely, most recently to his wife's native Germany, where he occasionally lectures and exhibits his paintings, and from where he travels to other places. He travels often in this country as well, lecturing and exhibiting.

All of this would seem to be consistent with modern restlessness and the frequent displacements of modern life. Americans, especially, are on the move, sociologists tell us, and for them there is usually no turning back. The typical response to the idea of return is often some paraphrase of Thomas Wolfe's melancholy assertion that one cannot "go home again." That sense of loss, of irreversible movement forward, of the price of movement, of the price of linear "progress," is dramatized by Robert Frost in "The Road Not Taken." The speaker is stopped at a crossroads and must choose one "way." Although he forlornly hopes to return eventually to that physical and emotional place, it is quite clear that he will not. "Yet knowing how way leads on to way," Frost's speaker tells us, "I doubted if I should ever come back." One sacrifices where one has been for where one is going. Severing one's "roots" is simply the price one must pay.

Yet N. Scott Momaday pays no such price, nor have his people, traditionally. That is because Momaday also has a strong sense of place and an intense belief in the sustaining permanence of origins. Throughout his life and art, he has emphasized the importance of having an intimate knowledge of one's own landscape. He has dramatized that importance in many ways, but nowhere is the idea more eloquently presented than it is in *The Way to Rainy Mountain*, where he declares that a person "ought to give himself up

to a particular landscape in his experience, to look at it from as many angles as he can, to wonder about it, to dwell upon it."

This idea of the importance of place is therefore not contradicted by Momaday's nomadism. In his world, as was the case in the traditional world of the nomadic tribes, one departs and returns. The journey is not linear and permanent, as is so often true of modern displacements, but circular and, in interesting ways, continuous. And no version of the essential journey is complete until the return is made. Often the return is physical, as it was with the tribes that moved with the seasons, spiritually and in pursuit of game, returning always to their origin places, to their native grounds. One returns to one's native landscape whenever possible, to renew oneself. But the return is as importantly spiritual, and can be accomplished through the oral tradition. One can circle back imaginatively to one's origins. One can actualize those origins through storytelling. That is the "way" of Momaday's *The Way to Rainy Mountain*. In that book, his grandmother's grave is "where it ought to be." It is "at the end of a long and legendary way," a phrase that is, in several ways, a summary statement of the book. In an important sense, Momaday and his people have never left the seventeenth-century Yellowstone area from which they began their long migration. In a very real sense, through tribal memory, they have not left the mouth of that hollow log out of which they emerged to begin their journey.

But how does one actualize the past fully enough to retain one's origin places? Momaday's response to that question is delivered near the end of *The Names*. "The events of one's life," he declares, "take place, *take place*." That is, human experience has definition and permanence only within the larger context of the physical world. One understands one's past, retains one's past, through recollections of symbolic physical events. One imagistically recalls the world, with all of its implications and attendant meanings. One is connected through those recollections. That idea is beautifully summarized in *The Way to Rainy Mountain* when Momaday concludes the story of Devils Tower by speaking of the seven sisters who became the stars of the Big Dipper. "From that moment, and so long as the legend lives," he says, "the Kiowas have kinsmen in the night sky."

So N. Scott Momaday is a physical and philosophical traveler, a nomad whose life is movement and whose art is a steady progression through time and place to the origins that define him and his people. Beginning with the roughly contemporary *House Made of Dawn*, he has journeyed steadily back through his writings in a creative and definitive celebration of origins. In doing so, he has demonstrated the power of those origins, and he has also demonstrated the power of place....

Source: Charles L. Woodard, "Into the Sun," in *Conversations with N. Scott Momaday*, University of Nebraska Press, 1989, pp. 47–49.

SOURCES

Allen, Chadwick, "Blood (and) Memory," in *American Literature*, Vol. 71, No. 1, March 1999, pp. 92–116.

Blaeser, Kimberly, "*The Way to Rainy Mountain*: Momaday's Work in Motion," in *Narrative Chance: Postmodern Discourse on Native American Indian Literatures*, edited by Gerald Vizenor, University of New Mexico Press, 1989.

Cederstrom, Lorelei, "Myth and Ceremony in Contemporary North American Native Fiction," in *Canadian Journal of Native Studies*, Vol. 2, No. 2, 1982, pp. 285–301.

Clements, William M., "Folk Historical Sense in Two Native American Authors," in *MELUS*, Vol. 12, No. 1, Spring 1985, pp. 65–79.

Cole, Burna, "Kiowa County," in *Encyclopedia of Oklahoma History & Culture*, http://digital.library.okstate.edu/encyclopedia/entries/K/KI019.html (accessed May 6, 2013).

Dickinson-Brown, Roger, "The Art and Importance of N. Scott Momaday," in *Southern Review*, Vol. 14, No. 1, January 1978, pp. 30–45.

Elder, Arlene, "'Dancing the Page': Orature in N. Scott Momaday's *The Way to Rainy Mountain*," in *Narrative*, Vol. 7, No. 3, October 1999, pp. 272–88.

Garrait-Bourrier, Anne, "N. Scott Momaday: A Postmodern Rebel *with* a Cause?," in *Journal of the Short Story in English*, Vol. 54, Spring 2010, pp. 71–80.

Kracht, Benjamin R., "Kiowa-Comanche-Apache Opening," in *Encyclopedia of Oklahoma History & Culture*, http://digital.library.okstate.edu/encyclopedia/entries/K/KI020.html (accessed May 6, 2013).

Lincoln, Kenneth, "N. Scott Momaday: Word Bearer," in *American Indian Culture and Research Journal*, Vol. 33, No. 2, January 2009, pp. 89–102.

———, "Tai-me to Rainy Mountain: The Makings of American Indian Literature," in *American Indian Quarterly*, Vol. 10, No. 2, Spring 1986, pp. 101–17.

Lundquist, Suzanne Evertsen, "N. Scott Momaday," in *Dictionary of Literary Biography*, Vol. 256, *Twentieth-Century American Western Writers, Third Series*, edited by Richard H. Cracroft, The Gale Group, 2002, pp. 203–18.

McAllister, Mick, "The Topology of Remembrance in *The Way to Rainy Mountain*," in *Denver Quarterly*, Vol. 12, No. 4, 1980, pp. 19–31.

Molesky-Poz, Jean, "Reconstructing Personal and Cultural Identities," in *American Quarterly*, Vol. 45, No. 4, December 1993, pp. 611–20.

Momaday, N. Scott, *The Way to Rainy Mountain*, illustrated by Al Momaday, University of New Mexico Press, 1998.

Mosby, Charmaine Allmon, "N. Scott Momaday: Overview," in *Twentieth-Century Young Adult Writers*, edited by Laura Standley Berger, St. James Press, 1994.

"N. Scott Momaday," University of Arizona website, http://www.ais.arizona.edu/people/n-scott-momaday (accessed May 4, 2013).

Nicholas, Charles A., "N. Scott Momaday's Hard Journey Back," in *South Dakota Review*, Vol. 13, No. 4, Winter 1975–1976, pp. 149–58.

Rand, Jacki Thompson, *Kiowa Humanity and the Invasion of the State*, University of Nebraska Press, 2008, pp. 33–57, 76–92.

Schubnell, Matthias, *N. Scott Momaday: The Cultural and Literary Background*, University of Oklahoma Press, 1985, pp. 13–39, 140–66.

Teuton, Christopher B., "N. Scott Momaday's *The Way to Rainy Mountain*," in *Deep Waters: The Textual Continuum in American Indian Literature*, University of Nebraska Press, 2010, pp. 53–94.

———, "Theorizing American Indian Literature: Applying Oral Concepts to Written Traditions," in *Reasoning Together: The Native Critics Collective*, edited by Craig S. Womack, Daniel Heath Justice, and Christopher B. Teuton, University of Oklahoma Press, 2008, pp. 193–216.

Winton, Ben, "Alcatraz, Indian Land," Redhawk's Lodge, http://siouxme.com/lodge/alcatraz_np.html (accessed September 1, 2013); originally published in *Native Peoples Magazine*, Fall 1999, p. 2.

Zachrau, Thekla, "N. Scott Momaday: Towards an Indian Identity," in *American Indian Culture and Research Journal*, Vol. 3, No. 1, 1979, pp. 39–56.

FURTHER READING

Deloria, Ella Cara, *Waterlily*, 1988, University of Nebraska Press.

> An earlier Native American work than Momaday's, Deloria's text—written in the 1940s but not published until forty years later—is a fictionalized version of a nineteenth-century Sioux woman's life in South Dakota. Deloria

expressed the intent to reflect the cultural life of the Sioux for white people convinced that Indians had no culture as such.

Marriott, Alice, *The Ten Grandmothers*, University of Oklahoma Press, 1983.
This book's title is derived from the ten medicine bundles of Kiowa myth created by the transformation of one of the twins born to the sun and the woman who climbed up the sky. Marriott combines legend and history in a novelistic way.

Mayhall, Mildred P., *The Kiowas*, University of Oklahoma Press, 1962.
A source that Momaday drew upon in his research of Kiowa history was Mayhall's comprehensive ethnography, part of the Civilization of the American Indian Series. Like Momaday, Mayhall draws on James Mooney's "Calendar History of the Kiowa Indians" (1898), which directly conveys the Kiowas' recorded history.

Welsch, Roger, *Touching the Fire: Buffalo Dancers, the Sky Bundle and Other Tales*, Villard Books, 1992.

This work by Welsch, a noted observer of humanity, presents stories that explore the roles played by sacred artifacts and rituals in the daily life of a fictional Plains tribe. The introduction discusses the modern-day peyote-centered Native American Church.

SUGGESTED SEARCH TERMS

N. Scott Momaday AND The Way to Rainy Mountain

N. Scott Momaday AND biography

N. Scott Momaday AND interview

Kiowa history

Kiowa AND legend OR myth

Native American literature

Manifest Destiny AND Native Americans

Plains Indians AND buffalo

Plains Indians AND peyote

Wuthering Heights

Emily Brontë's *Wuthering Heights*, published in 1847, is an acknowledged masterpiece of English literature. It is regarded as the greatest gothic novel and one of the first modern psychological novels. Considered marginal when it was published, *Wuthering Heights* gained in reputation throughout the twentieth century. In particular, it became a favorite of the surrealists because of its exploration of unmediated, uncontrolled raw emotion. William Wyler's 1939 film of *Wuthering Heights*, however, takes an entirely different approach to the novel. The producer, Samuel Goldwyn, wanted to make a prestige film that would increase the aesthetic reputation of the MGM studio as well as be a popular success. He decided therefore that the film should be worked over as a classic love story. The resulting film is regarded as one of the great triumphs of the golden age of the Hollywood studio system. The film was also intended by its creators as a tribute to British culture and the shared Anglo-American bond to Western civilization that would help prepare the American public for the war with Germany that already seemed inevitable.

PLOT SUMMARY

As *Wuthering Heights* begins, Lockwood, the narrator of the novel, explains the meaning of the title: "Wuthering Heights is the name of

FILM TECHNIQUE

- Although there is no reason to assume that Heathcliff is not English, the other characters in the film, as in the novel, belittle him by calling him a "dark-skinned gypsy." Wyler treated this in the film by applying dark makeup to Lawrence Olivier's face in the scenes from his days as a stable boy. This was so exaggerated that producer Samuel Goldwyn, on seeing the dailies (the segments of film shot each day during production) of such a scene, complained that Olivier looked like he was in blackface (a technique begun in minstrel shows whereby white and black actors alike applied makeup to suggest stereotypes of black features and skin color). Wyler assured Goldwyn that in later scenes, when Heathcliff returns as a wealthy American, Olivier's makeup would show his natural skin tone.

- Wyler and Goldwyn never considered filming *Wuthering Heights* in England but created their impression of a Yorkshire moor in Chatsworth, California, importing thousands of heather plants for the purpose; heather has since become an invasive species in the area. The landscape was so carefully worked over that the exterior shots often appear to have been filmed on a studio soundstage. Because the film is set in agricultural countryside, many scenes are full of domestic animals. The geese in particular posed problems, as their honking often drowned out the actors during recording. Wyler had their vocal chords cut out to silence them, which would scarcely be allowed in a film today because of considerations of animal cruelty.

- Film is distinguished from literature by the visual language that it uses and from photography by its control of the viewer's vision through editing (*montage*). The director and editor of a film can use framing and scene cutting to communicate profound emotions and mood, whether comic, horrific, elegant, or sublime, in a way that no other medium can achieve. In *Wuthering Heights*, Wyler aimed to create a sense of spectacle through the slow cadence of his editing and the lingering of the camera over scenes of aesthetic beauty, whether in the sets and landscape or the bodies of the actors. The viewer is invited to feast on visual excess.

- The soundtrack for 1939's *Wuthering Heights* is notably uninspired compared with other period films of that era. During Edgar and Cathy's wedding, it plays the traditional wedding march, the Bridal Chorus from Wagner's *Lohengrin*, which, in the historical context of the film, would not yet be composed for several decades. At one of the Lintons' glamorous parties, a guest is prevailed upon to demonstrate her particular talents as a harpsichordist and play Schubert's *Marche militaire*. The harpsichord would have been in keeping with the original setting of the novel around 1780, but the instrument would have been out of fashion by the 1850s, and Schubert composed the march with the piano in mind. The piece is also played at an incredibly fast tempo, as classical music often was in early Hollywood films, as if it was suspected the audience could not wait to get it over with. However, the inclusion of this miniature concert was part of Goldwyn's strategy to provide the audience with what they would consider a culturally uplifting experience.

Mr. Heathcliff's dwelling. 'Wuthering' being a significant provincial adjective, descriptive of the atmospheric tumult to which its station is exposed in stormy weather." The film begins with Lockwood fighting his way through a snowstorm to get to Wuthering Heights (rather than to get away as in the novel), to introduce himself as Heathcliff's new tenant at Thrushcross Grange. He is received brusquely by Heathcliff, the owner of both Wuthering Heights

© United Artists / The Kobal Collection

and Thrushcross Grange, who must nevertheless give him shelter for the night. As he falls asleep, Lockwood, but not the eye of the camera, sees a woman outside the window. As Lockwood explains to Heathcliff, the woman was running through the snow and called herself Cathy. Heathcliff rushes out into the storm to find her. Ellen, the maid, begins to explain who Cathy is and begins the narration of the main story of the film, beginning forty years earlier. The film dissolves to show the events she is describing after a brief spoken narrative.

In the story, Ellen is the teenage nursemaid of the young Catherine (often called Cathy) and Hindley, who is her brother, rather than a playmate of the same age as in the novel. The children's father, Mr. Earnshaw, returns from a trip to Liverpool with a dirty young boy riding with him on his horse. The boy is Heathcliff. Earnshaw explains that he found Heathcliff homeless and starving in the streets of Liverpool. Moved by pity, he decided to bring the boy back home and raise him. He describes Heathcliff as "dark as if it came from the Devil." He took the boy only after "trying to find out who its owner was." This phrasing suggests that Heathcliff is less than human, an *it* with an *owner*, and it closely echoes the language of the novel. Heathcliff is soon shown becoming fast friends with Cathy, but Hindley brutally bullies the boy behind his father's back. Mr. Earnshaw soon dies, leaving Hindley in control of Wuthering Heights. Hindley sends Heathcliff out of the house to work in the stables.

After a brief intrusion of Ellen's narration, the scene shifts to a dinner some years later when the Earnshaw children and Heathcliff have grown into adults. Hindley is shown to be far gone in alcoholism. He continues to act sadistically toward Heathcliff, who bears the bad treatment because of the intense joy he finds in private moments stolen with Cathy. They meet at Penistone Crag, their old playground on the moors around Wuthering Heights. There, Cathy suggests that Heathcliff ought to leave, make his fortune, and then come back and rescue her, a romantic scene that never occurs in the novel.

From the crag, Heathcliff and Cathy hear the music from a party being given by the Lintons at Thrushcross Grange, the nearest country estate to Wuthering Heights. They spy through the window and see a different world than the grim, dark bleakness of Wuthering Heights. The scene is full of light and gaiety and exquisite details of art, architecture, and the clothes of the partygoers. The camera moves languidly over the scene, stimulating the viewer to desire what is seen in the same way Cathy does. Cathy makes clear to Heathcliff that he must gain the ability to provide her with the same expensive clothes and extravagant style of living that they see at the Lintons' party.

Cathy and Heathcliff are attacked by guard dogs. When the Lintons realize that Cathy is a member of their own class, they send for the doctor and treat her with due respect. They treat Heathcliff as no better than a common criminal. When they are on the verge of throwing him out, Catherine tells him to go and make his fortune. Heathcliff accedes and curses the Lintons, boasting that he will eventually destroy them for the way they have treated him.

Ellen's narration again briefly intrudes to indicate the passing time, and the film shifts to Cathy's return to Wuthering Heights after a few weeks' recuperation from her dog bite at the Lintons' home. When Edgar Linton brings her back, she is disappointed to find that Heathcliff had gone away on the night of the party but had lately returned. Edgar begins to insult Heathcliff and dismisses him as belonging to the servant class, but Cathy defends him. She confesses to Edgar that she loves Heathcliff, in such a way that it is hard to imagine she does not mean a romantic attachment. Feeling himself insulted, Edgar leaves. Cathy destroys the fine dress that Edgar's sister had given her. Dressed again as a peasant, she runs off to Penistone Crag, where she reconvenes with Heathcliff in the famous scene of them sitting atop a rock there in rapturous union. Heathcliff tells her that he set out on a ship for America, but he swam back because he could not bear to be separated from Cathy for years.

Ellen's narration again moves the story through an ellipsis of time, speaking of Cathy's "wild uncontrollable passion for Heathcliff." A romance with Edgar nevertheless advances, and Cathy adopts the stylish and elegant fashions of the Linton household. Catherine seemingly spurns Heathcliff, dismissing him as a "dirty stable boy." Heathcliff leaves when he hears of Edgar's proposal to Cathy, yet she chases after Heathcliff through a terrible rainstorm, professing her love for him. She collapses on the moor from a fever and is once again rescued and nursed back to health by the Lintons. Hindley is indifferent to his sister's plight and goes on drinking. Edgar presses his proposal, and Cathy, dismissing her identification with Heathcliff as a sort of demonic possession, accepts. During their wedding, Cathy feels a premonition of doom.

Ellen's narration advances the story several years, covering Cathy's elegant new life at Thrushcross Grange, filled with art and beauty. Heathcliff returns and comes to call, filling Cathy with revulsion. He went to America and made a fortune, causing Edgar to accept him as a gentleman. Heathcliff announces that he has bought up Hindley's gambling debts, making him effective owner of Wuthering Heights. Isabella, Edgar's sister, falls in love with Heathcliff partly because of his mysterious and swaggering allure but mostly, it seems, to spite her brother, who forbids her to feel any such thing.

Heathcliff becomes the master of Wuthering Heights. He allows Hindley to stay on, taking pleasure in seeing him drink himself to death. Heathcliff humiliates Hindley, who cannot gather the courage to shoot him. When Heathcliff's servant announces a lady visitor from Thrushcross Grange, he hopes it is Cathy, but it turns out to be Isabella, who pretends that her horse has gone lame. Heathcliff begins to seduce her.

The next scene is another elegant party at Thrushcross Grange, which Heathcliff attends at the invitation of Isabella. Cathy suggests that Heathcliff must be happy with his new circumstances. He replies that his life is ended. Heathcliff makes clear that he returned to reclaim Cathy as his beloved, despite her marriage. Cathy insists that this is impossible. Heathcliff realizes that marrying Isabella will accomplish his oath of revenge against Edgar and also now against Cathy. Isabella announces that she has already secretly accepted Heathcliff's marriage proposal.

Catherine visits Heathcliff at Wuthering Heights to insist he give up Isabella, but he refuses. Once Heathcliff and Isabella elope, Cathy encourages Edgar to murder Heathcliff in a duel, but he realizes that her real objection is that despite everything she is still in love with Heathcliff.

Sometime later, Hindley is finally dying from drink, and Isabella, reduced to a shell of her former self, is still living with Heathcliff. She is tortured by her discovery that Heathcliff loves Cathy and not her. Cathy, meanwhile, is dying of pneumonia. Heathcliff learns of Cathy's illness when Ellen is sent to bring Isabella back to console her brother, but Heathcliff instead gallops across the moor to be at her side. While Edgar goes to fetch the doctor, Heathcliff attends Cathy at her deathbed. They finally share a romantic embrace just as she dies. She confesses that she prefers to die than to live without him. Heathcliff condemns her for abandoning him for Hindley; his final speech to her removes any possibility of doubt that their relationship had been a romantic one, and Cathy confesses that she had only truly loved Heathcliff, never her husband. After she dies in his arms, Heathcliff prays that Cathy's ghost will return to haunt him.

The film returns to Ellen telling the story to Lockwood, as Heathcliff is outside chasing what can now be understood as Cathy's ghost, or rather, as Ellen says, the ghost of Cathy's love. Heathcliff dies in the snow searching for the apparition on Penistone Crag. The film ends with the ghosts of Heathcliff and Cathy walking off to infinity together, arm in arm. William Wyler, the director, refused to film this scene, invented by the producer, Samuel Goldwyn, because he felt the happy ending too directly betrayed the original story.

The film compresses the second half of the novel. In the book, Isabella bears Heathcliff a son named Linton, and Catherine bears Edgar a daughter also named Cathy, while Hindley's brief marriage also produces a son, Hareton, whom Heathcliff devotes many years to corrupting and degrading. After Cathy's and Edgar's deaths, Linton inherits Thrushcross Grange, but he soon dies himself, passing it to his father, Heathcliff. Heathcliff enters a long decline and finally dies grieving in Catherine's former bedroom. At the end of the novel, Lockwood pays a last visit to Wuthering Heights and learns that Hareton and Cathy will soon be married. He visits the graves of the elder Catherine and

Heathcliff, which lie next to each other in the parish churchyard.

CHARACTERS

Ellen Dean

Ellen Dean, frequently called Nell or Nelly, is played by Flora Robson. It is commonly observed that the Earnshaw family is destroyed by the passion between Catherine and Heathcliff, even if it never takes on an adult, romantic character. Their connection is often viewed as tantamount to incest, since Cathy and Heathcliff were raised together as children. They had another virtual sibling in Ellen Dean, who spent her childhood in a manner little different than if she had been Cathy's and Hindley's sister. However, when it suits Hindley, Ellen is, as it were, thrown out of the family and cast into the role of servant. Moreover, the same pattern recurs when, as nursemaid to Hindley's son, she virtually becomes the boy's mother as he is neglected by his father, only to have the boy ripped away from her when Hindley finds it convenient. In the film, the character of Ellen has a smaller part, because the role of the ensuing generation at Wuthering Heights is stripped out of the plot. Also, whereas in the novel Ellen is a major narratorial voice, in the film the camera takes on that role.

Catherine Earnshaw
See Catherine Linton

Hindley Earnshaw
Hindley is played by Hugh Williams. His role is diminished in the film as compared to the book, and the story of his marriage and the birth of his son is omitted. For psychological reasons that are only hinted at, Hindley squanders his life on alcoholism and gambling. Certainly in the book this was partly due to depression following the death of his wife from tuberculosis. Because Heathcliff is almost an adopted son to Mr. Earnshaw, Hindley comes to view him as a hated rival and treats him with a bullying brutality when they are children and young men. When Heathcliff returns, he gains control of Hindley by playing on his weaknesses and addictions and exposes him as a weak and pathetic coward. Heathcliff takes out his revenge on him with daily humiliations. In the film, Heathcliff buys up the massive gambling debts Hindley had contracted with

others. The treatment in the book is more subtle, as Heathcliff seduces Hindley into serious gambling, directly winning the Heights from him piece by piece.

Mr. Earnshaw

Earnshaw appears only briefly in the film and is notable for his act of kindness in adopting Heathcliff. He is visibly disappointed by Hindley's selfish attitude toward the orphan. He had certainly intended to bring Heathcliff into his family, since he gave him the name Heathcliff after the elder brother of Catherine and Hindley, who had died in infancy.

Heathcliff

Heathcliff is played by Lawrence Olivier, in his first major screen role in Hollywood. The young Heathcliff is played by Rex Downing. Olivier was nominated for the Academy Award for Best Actor for this part.

Heathcliff is the main character of *Wuthering Heights*, an antihero rather than a hero. When Lockwood, the narrator, first encounters Heathcliff in the novel, he describes him as

> a dark-skinned gypsy in aspect, in dress and manners a gentleman, that is, as much a gentleman as many a country squire.... His reserve springs from an aversion to showy displays of feeling—to manifestations of mutual kindliness. He'll love and hate, equally under cover, and esteem it a species of impertinence to be loved or hated again.

Cathy knows Heathcliff far better than Lockwood can and, because of this knowledge and despite her own love for him, is profoundly shocked when Isabella Linton confesses her love for Heathcliff. "I wouldn't be you for a kingdom, then!" Cathy tells her. She goes on to denounce Heathcliff's character in great detail, saying that he is "an unreclaimed creature, without refinement, without cultivation, an arid wilderness of furze and whinstone" (i.e., thorns and stones).

In particular, Cathy derides Lockwood's idea that there is an essential innocence hidden within Heathcliff, telling Isabella, "Pray don't imagine that he conceals depths of benevolence and affection beneath a stern exterior! He's not a rough diamond—a pearl-containing oyster of a rustic; he's a fierce, pitiless, wolfish man." The agreements and contradictions of these characterizations add great depth to the reader's understanding of Heathcliff. He acts just as he is inclined to, without any kind of screen of reason

or sociability deflecting his desires. If he is cruel, it is to those who were cruel to him. The film suggests this temperament, but Olivier's performance lays a facade of stoic self-control over Heathcliff's passions.

The character of Heathcliff in *Wuthering Heights* is the focus of a sophisticated and critical exploration of race and class in Victorian England by Brontë. When he is first introduced, he is called "a dark-skinned gypsy," a charge—and in the mouths of Brontë's character it is clearly meant as a charge—that is often repeated throughout the book. During their make-believe play as children, even Cathy suggests to Heathcliff that he is an Indian or Chinese prince who was kidnapped by pirates and taken to Liverpool. She is attempting to make the best of what everyone in the novel believes is a very bad situation. Heathcliff is not merely portrayed as a foreigner and a member of what readers at the time would have thought of as an inferior race, but is repeatedly referred to not as *him* but as *it*, something that is clearly less than human. This kind of objectification of non-Europeans is today generally known as orientalism thanks to the pioneering scholarship of Edward Said. Europeans conceived of non-Europeans as "others," less human than themselves, whose political and economic exploitation through imperialism and colonialism could be justified.

Heathcliff is clearly presented in these terms in *Wuthering Heights*. In fact, it does not seem as if Heathcliff is anything but English. Ellen affirms that he is not "a regular black" (which in Victorian England meant more nearly non-European than African). Heathcliff's blackness is metaphorical. Brontë's point is that Heathcliff is objectified as an other, *as if* he had been black, because he is a member of the lower class. It is his poverty that makes him seem inhuman. Brontë is writing about the class oppression in her own time. Heathcliff represents the oppressed poor striking back at the aristocracy. Emily and her sisters were acutely aware of the economic injustice of their society, which prevented them as women from pursing any profitable career. Their father had risen by tremendous effort from the working class to become an Anglican priest, and they felt themselves in danger of slipping back into poverty. Wyler brings much of the discourse about Heathcliff's race and identity as an other into the film, somewhat incongruously in view of his reshaping of Heathcliff as a romantic lead. Perhaps, in the generally progressive environment of Hollywood, he hoped to make a subtle criticism of the racial oppression that troubled 1930s America.

Joseph

Joseph is played by Leo G. Carroll. Joseph is the head servant at Wuthering Heights, although he is more like a farm overseer than a butler. In the novel, Joseph makes a show of being very religious and is continually quoting Bible verses to chastise the other servants. It is clear, however, that this is only a means for him to try to control and dominate whomever he views as his social inferiors. Joseph is a Yorkshire man who speaks the local dialect, which is hard to understand for standard speakers and is often explained in editions of *Wuthering Heights*. Dialect became of serious interest to the romantic movement because it represented for them a link to authentic tradition. The Brontë children, raised in close contact with servants, may have grown up speaking Yorkshire dialect also; they certainly understood it. Regional dialects of English are not incorrect forms. English developed in the Middle Ages in villages all over the country where speakers of Old English, Old Norse, and Old Danish lived together, often in mixed families. These languages shared the same word roots but had different grammatical endings, so a pidgin developed between them using only the roots. This process developed differently in each region, resulting in dialects. The Cambridgeshire accent only became standard as it was adopted by the government and the education system throughout the eighteenth and nineteenth centuries. In the film, Joseph's language is slightly archaic standard English.

Catherine Linton

Catherine, née Earnshaw, is played by Merle Oberon. The young Cathy is played by Sarita Wooten. Cathy's character is mostly defined by her relationship with Heathcliff. In the novel, she and Heathcliff appear nearly as the male and female halves of the same person, connected on a level far removed from ordinary human experience. She is as wild and elemental in character as Heathcliff. In the film, her character is diminished and moves much closer to that of a standard romantic heroine. (Wyler felt that Oberon's acting ability was not up to a more serious interpretation.) She tells Heathcliff quite directly that he needs to leave Wuthering Heights and make

the kind of fortune that could support the aristocratic lifestyle she wants, and if he does not, he will lose her to someone who can. In the novel, Catherine's decidedly nonromantic relationship with Heathcliff posed no difficulties in reconciling her marriage with Edgar Linton, but in the film her alternation between what are effectively two suitors makes her appear fickle and immature.

Edgar Linton

Edgar Linton is played by David Niven. Edgar is elegant and sophisticated, offering Catherine a path to a grander and more elegant way of life that she finds seductive. However, Edgar is also weak compared to Heathcliff and is ultimately destroyed by him in retaliation for his ill treatment of a person he thinks of as a mere stable boy. When Catherine suggests to him that the only way they have out of the web of Heathcliff's revenge is for Edgar to kill him (probably meaning in a duel), Edgar has no stomach for the task. He seems completely overwhelmed by the chaos that Catherine and Heathcliff introduce into his life.

Isabella Linton

Isabella is played by Geraldine Fitzgerald, who was nominated for the Academy Award for Best Supporting Actress. In the novel, Isabella is presented as silly and childish, expressed largely through her obsession with fashionable clothes (which were an object of horror to the Brontë sisters, perhaps not only because of their sense of the frivolity of fashion but also because they could never have afforded them in real life). Isabella provides an interesting comparison to Cathy, who is tempted away from Heathcliff by pretty clothes, the adoration of which were not part of her intrinsic nature. Isabella is tormented by her love for Heathcliff, which does not diminish even when she learns her husband's true intentions toward her.

Judge Linton

Judge Linton is the father of Edgar and Isabella. He plays only a very minor role in the film before his death allows Edgar to come into his own as the squire of Thrushcross Grange.

Lockwood

Lockwood, though he tells the entire story, is a relatively minor character in the book and still more so in the film. He fails to take the measure of the depths of Heathcliff's character and imagines that in Thrushcross Grange and Wuthering Heights he has found "a perfect misanthropist's Heaven: and Mr. Heathcliff and I are such a suitable pair to divide the desolation between us." However, Lockwood clearly understands what Heathcliff's revenge has created.

Nell
See Ellen Dean

THEMES

Gothicism

Gothic literature is a popular form of romanticism. It derives its name from a common nineteenth-century term for the Middle Ages. If the Renaissance held up antiquity as a shining example distinct from the dark and irrational Middle Ages, the gothic sensibility takes that very darkness and irrationality as its ideal. The gothic novel began with Horace Walpole's *The Castle of Otranto* (1764) and Anne Radcliffe's *The Mysteries of Udolfo* (1794), tales of supernatural horror set in the Middle Ages. What Brontë found in the gothic, largely mediated through the historical romances of Sir Walter Scott, was the past as the receptacle of a sense of alienation from the present and a language of the unconscious, which allows characters to act, think, and feel irrationally, but nevertheless coherently, on a different level.

The gothic's interest in fantasies and morbid states of mind gave rise in Brontë's work to an interest in her characters' interior life, letting her reach for a character's psychological depths. *Wuthering Heights*, alongside Charlotte Brontë's *Jane Eyre*, transformed the gothic into the modern psychological novel. The result is a work in which characters act on the basis of emotion unfiltered by reason. Charlotte Brontë, in her preface to the 1850 edition of *Wuthering Heights*, excuses the raw emotion of the novel:

> Men and women who, perhaps, naturally very calm, and with feelings moderate in degree, and little marked in kind, have been trained from their cradle to observe the utmost evenness of manner and guardedness of language, will hardly know what to make of the rough, strong utterance, the harshly manifested passion, the unbridled aversions, and headlong partialities of unlettered moorland hinds and rugged moorland squires, who have grown up untaught and unchecked....

Charlotte wants to rescue her sister from the charge of writing a mere gothic novel, which in her view was something less than serious literature. It is precisely the free and unrestrained exercise of emotion that contributes most to the novel's reputation today. The fact that the characters act on their primitive desires without the restraint of social convention attracted the attention of the surrealists, which has led to new understandings of *Wuthering Heights* as a precursor to the modern psychological novel.

Magic

The scholarly study of folklore was just beginning in the mid-nineteenth century, but Brontë's knowledge of the subject probably stems rather from her own firsthand exposure to folk culture among the population of the English countryside rather than from secondhand reading. Brontë, for instance, vividly refers to folk beliefs about magic and witchcraft. Early in the novel, the younger Catherine taunts the religiously hypocritical servant Joseph by pretending to be a witch. She is certainly not serious in her claims but is intent on causing him outrage by appealing to the folklore that underpins his cultural beliefs. She shows him a book which she pretends is a grimoire, or book of spells, and taunts him:

> I'll show you how far I've progressed in the Black Art—I shall soon be competent to make a clear house of it. The red cow didn't die by chance; and your rheumatism can hardly be reckoned among providential visitations!

In folk belief, nothing happens without a reason or a conscious agent causing it, so any misfortunes such as the death of valuable livestock or personal illness that might otherwise seem to occur by chance are attributed to some supernatural agency such as witchcraft. Catherine is putting on a mock-threatening front by pretending to have such powers. Of course, many people did make such claims and made a living from those who believed them, although a greater part of their practice consisted of claims to be able to heal, remove curses, and the like. The spell book was part of the stock in trade of such people and village priests, and so-called cunning folk kept books like the Renaissance grimoire *The Key of Solomon*, circulating in manuscript copies through the early nineteenth century.

Later in the narrative, the elder Catherine playfully mocks Ellen by accusing her of witchcraft. Cathy tells her servant, "I see in you,

READ, WATCH, WRITE.

- *Wuthering Heights* has been filmed numerous times, with eighteenth-century settings, modern settings, and settings in Mexico, India, France, and feudal Japan. View several versions, and then write up comparisons of them with Wyler's film. Post your comparisons on a blog, and allow your classmates to comment.

- In Wyler's *Wuthering Heights*, the tortured conflict that is seething beneath the surface in Heathcliff's mind is suggested by his contorted postures and motions, which derive from the tortured characters of German expressionist cinema of the 1920s, such as Robert Wiener's *The Cabinet of Dr. Caligari* (1920), and ultimately from the depictions of wounded and dying soldiers of the Great War in the art of painters like Otto Dix. Viewers may find themselves reminded of Boris Karloff's portrayal of the monster in *Frankenstein*. Make a presentation to your class discussing the interconnections and influences of these various moving and still images. It may prove useful to concentrate on a particular aspect, such as the characters' and figures' hands.

- Robert Stevenson's 1943 film *Jane Eyre* was made to capitalize on and compete with the success of Wyler's *Wuthering Heights*, as what Goldwyn called a prestige film. Watch *Jane Eyre*, and then write a paper comparing the artistic, commercial, and cultural success of the two films.

- The concept of the meme was created by the biologist Richard Dawkins. Just as a gene carries the basic information necessary for an organism to reproduce, a meme is a discrete carrier of the base information that lets an idea spread and reproduce through a

culture. Patsy Stoneman in her *Brontë Transformations* has argued that Wyler created a new meme in *Wuthering Heights*, symbolizing profound romantic love in its spiritual dimension through the meeting of two lovers on a mountaintop in communion with each other and the universe. If Stoneman's hypothesis is correct, it should be easy to find examples of this meme broadly distributed throughout culture, especially in advertising. Reuse in other films should also be considered. A meme's presence in satire, where the audience must be relied upon to "get it" in order to understand the joke, might provide a good index of its cultural diffusion. Internet search engines, especially image searches, are ideally suited to help find such images. Make an illustrated report to your class showing the cultural diffusion of this meme, what contexts it is displayed in, and what meanings and variations it has taken on.

- David Lean's 1946 film *Great Expectations* was another prestige Hollywood project based on British literature. It shares many plot elements with *Wuthering Heights*—a young boy plucked out of poverty and placed in the middle class, along with the return of a scoundrel as a wealthy man. With *Great Expectations*, however, the newfound wealth is used to promote a happy ending. Make a presentation to your class analyzing how the film caters to young-adult taste through the ages of its main characters, with their concerns and actions shaped by their youth. Show clips that contrast with the more cursory treatment of the younger lives of the child characters in Wyler's *Wuthering Heights*.

Nelly...an aged woman—you have grey hair, and bent shoulders. This bed is the fairy cave under Penistone Crag, and you are gathering elf-

bolts to hurt our heifers; pretending, while I am near, that they are only locks of wool." Whatever folk memory Catherine and Brontë are

The story is set in the wild countryside of Yorkshire. *(© Capture Light | Shutterstock.com)*

relying on accurately records the fact that victims of witchcraft accusation were precisely a community's most defenseless members, old women living on the economic margins of society (although to stretch this to Ellen's case is an exaggeration). The mention of elf-bolts shows the degree to which charges of witchcraft, supposedly couched in Christian theological terms, mixed with folk belief. Elf-bolts, or elf-shot, were the purported means by which fairies caused sickness in human beings. Logically, this is an alternative explanation to witchcraft for random sickness and is couched within the non-Christian framework of fairy belief, which is probably a descendant of pre-Christian Celtic religion.

STYLE

Fantasy World Building

Emily Brontë and her siblings, Anne, Charlotte, and Branwell, engaged in a highly unusual form of collective play throughout their childhoods and early adulthoods. They were fanatically devoted to making handwritten imitations of *Blackwood's Edinburgh Magazine*, a popular literary and news review of the time. They copied the style and format, while the text material was entirely their own invention. They began writing about their toys, but they soon began writing about a fantasy analog of England, the Empire of Angria, with its capital Glasstown (later Verdopolis after Branwell started the study of Greek and Latin), in the unexplored interior of Africa.

As they grew older, they became more specialized, with Emily and Anne working on their own separate project, a history of the Empire of Gondal, set on an imaginary island in the North Pacific. Gondal in particular allowed Emily to express powerful chaotic emotions that she could never have indulged in during her daily life because of her role as a schoolteacher and her social position on the margin of the middle class, which essentially made her accept the role of servant within her family and ruled out any chance of marriage (because her father could never have provided a dowry).

The creation of such detailed and fully realized fantasy worlds, revolutionary at the time, is now common in popular literature, thanks to the similar project carried out by J. R. R. Tolkien in the creation of Middle Earth. The writing practice provided by these fantasy worlds allowed the Brontës to burst onto the literary scene as practiced writers, already with a sophisticated literary sensibility. At the time, without public knowledge of Gondal and the Brontës' lifetime of fantasy writing, *Wuthering Heights* and the novels of Emily's sisters seemed to spring fully formed out of nowhere. They were admired, but as the wild and crude products of a genius arising from nature rather than culture.

As the Brontë childhood writings came to light in the 1920s, it became clear that *Wuthering Heights* was the fruit of a long apprenticeship in writing. Emily had slowly learned her art by long practice. The Brontës kept the existence of Gondal and their other fantasy worlds secret, as their literary instincts rightly judged that any revelation would have had them dismissed as eccentrics. Nevertheless, Emily published some poetry set in Gondal, with only minor changes to generalize them. Although the prose works associated with Gondal were destroyed by Emily, a reconstruction of the plot shows clearly that the story of unrestrained emotion leading to passionate affairs, murder, cruelty, and civil war within families was the proving ground for *Wuthering Heights*. Her plots and characters came ever closer and closer to that work until the novel emerged from Gondal.

Metaphor

A *metaphor* is a figure of speech in which the author presents two unlike things and explains one by invoking the other. A particularly striking metaphor used in *Wuthering Heights* is the description of Heathcliff as a cuckoo. At the beginning of Ellen's narration in the novel, Mr. Earnshaw returns from Liverpool with Heathcliff rather than the whip that Cathy asked for as a present and the violin that Hindley wanted (in the film he brings back the gifts along with Heathcliff). It is often suggested that Heathcliff's substitution is a kind of curse that destroys Catherine's autonomy and Hindley's creativity, symbolized by the gifts, dooming them to the tragic circumstances of the novel. This in itself is an extended metaphor, but Heathcliff's role as a substitute or interloper in the family is frequently emphasized by his likeness to a cuckoo.

Mother cuckoos do not build a nest, but rather spread their eggs around the nests of other birds. When the cuckoo chick hatches, the nesting birds assume that it is one of their own offspring and consequently feed and care for it. However, a cuckoo matures more quickly than other birds and soon outgrows its nest mates and kills them, so that all of the care given by the adoptive parents will be lavished on the cuckoo. This is a metaphor for Heathcliff's destruction of the Earnshaw and Linton families. Even Catherine warns Isabella that Heathcliff will "crush you, like a sparrow's egg," when she reveals her romantic attachment to him.

Narration

The novel *Wuthering Heights* has an unusually densely nested hierarchy of narrators. Lockwood is responsible for telling the reader the entire text of the novel, the greater part of which is reported to him by Ellen, who is relating both things she had witnessed and others that had been told to her, often repeating conversations that themselves have several levels of narration. This too has its origin in the juvenilia; the Brontë children acted as reporters and writers in their *Blackwood's* pastiches, with each child having her or his own character and characteristic narrative voice. They also acted as editors, who shape news of the same event submitted by different writers and select and refashion an official version. The narrative structure of the book would have lent itself well to the cinematic technique of the flashback, but in the actual film matters are greatly simplified, and the viewer is essentially listening directly to Ellen's single level of narration.

CULTURAL CONTEXT

Propaganda

Samuel Goldwyn, the producer of *Wuthering Heights*, and William Wyler, its director, were both politically progressive and of Jewish cultural background, as were many Hollywood executives and artists. They had little reason to care for the anti-Semitic fascist regime in Nazi Germany. Hollywood was therefore quite ready to use its tremendous popular and artistic power to prepare America for war with Germany. This feeling was shared by the considerable colony of

Much of the action in Wuthering Heights *takes place on the moors.* *(© petejeff / Shutterstock.com)*

British writers and actors in Hollywood, including Olivier and Niven.

The threatening sense of impending war in Europe hung over the production of *Wuthering Heights*. The principal filming took place in the spring of 1939, during the illegal German occupation of Czechoslovakia. One of the stage crewmen who spoke German was more or less excused from his duties to listen to the German shortwave radio service to keep the crew appraised of developments as they were reported. There was a general expectation that Britain and France would declare war on Germany at any moment, although this declaration was delayed until the German invasion of Poland in September.

Films like *Wuthering Heights* were considered to create a shared sense of Anglo-American culture that would educate the audience in viewing Britain's impending conflict as America's also. The characterization of Heathcliff in the film, so different from the book, owed much to the Anglo-American experience of the First World War. Heathcliff is presented as constantly

suppressing his emotions under a stoic facade of self-control, as soldiers are required to do. The American audience was still filled with veterans who would pick up on Olivier's subtle cues of physical and emotional restraint in his expressions and gestures.

Period

Wuthering Heights has a historical setting in the Regency period at the turn of the nineteenth century, roughly fifty years before the book was published in the Victorian period. The historical setting serves to distance the novel from the everyday reality of the reader, as does its geographical setting in the remote moorlands of Yorkshire. The film, however, is set at approximately the time the book was published. Because this is still a time remote from the 1939 release date of the film, the setting retains its basic feature as a romanticized historical era. The reasons for the change are less than clear. It does not make any difference in the gentry society of the English countryside that the film is at pains to celebrate but that the novel deprecates as a system of rustic decadence oppressive of women's rights and the poor.

It is clear, however, that the difference has something to do with the costuming and the changes in fashion between the two eras. It has been suggested that producer Goldwyn simply preferred the Victorian-era clothing (although it is not imitated with much fidelity even to the high fashion of the era and still less to the dress of ordinary country gentry) or else sought to increase the commercial appeal of the film by exposing the shoulders of the leading actresses. Similarly, it might be that director Wyler found the aesthetic qualities of the Victorian clothes more useful for the sumptuous display of luxury he wished to make in the film. It may also have been an economic decision, reusing costumes from films set during the American Civil War (roughly the mid-Victorian period in Britain) that the studio had on hand.

CRITICAL OVERVIEW

Critical reception of Wyler's *Wuthering Heights* in 1939 was highly subdued. Film reviewers, especially in Britain, wished to support the translation of classic literature onto the screen but may have been shocked by the massive transformation Wyler and Goldwyn effected in making *Wuthering Heights* over as a conventional love story. Reviews mostly consisted of praise for the effort rather than the film itself.

Modern scholars have mostly been interested in how interaction with the contemporary culture of the 1930s determined the character of Wyler's translation, acknowledging a network of economic, artistic, and political concerns. The scene of Heathcliff's and Catherine's ecstatic union atop Penistone Crag, invented by Wyler, has been taken as an important emblem of the director's effort. Patsy Stoneman, in *Brontë Transformations* (1996), focuses on the mountaintop scene on Penistone Crag as the central image of the film: "The picture of Catherine and Heathcliff together, as adults, on the hilltop, silhouetted against the sky which represents their mutual aspiration, has become a visual emblem of what the novel 'means.'" Stoneman continues by asserting that the image became so fixed in the popular imagination that "Monty Python's Flying Circus could assume that two

lovers on a hilltop constituted a cultural icon to which a mass audience would respond."

She somewhat inaccurately describes the satirical scene from a Monty Python episode in which Heathcliff and Catherine stand on distant hilltops and signal to each other with semaphore flags. Stoneman sees the whole idea of the film reduced to that single scene as a meme, a self-replicating element of cultural language that in turn has become embedded in popular culture, like the line "Play it again, Sam" from *Casablanca* (a line never actually uttered in the film). Hila Shachar, in her 2012 *Cultural Afterlives* volume, expands on this idea, addressing the same scene in its political ramifications as a symbol of Anglo-American cultural unity.

CRITICISM

Bradley Skeen
Skeen is a classicist. In the following essay, he analyzes the ideological and aesthetic repurposing of the story of Wuthering Heights *in the 1939 William Wyler film.*

Wuthering Heights may fairly be called one of the first psychological novels, because its purpose is an introspective exploration of its characters' minds, especially that of its antihero, Heathcliff. However, it is also a gothic novel that repurposes the gothic themes of supernatural horror and psychological morbidity into a tool to expose the inner workings of character. No single description or analysis of the novel can exhaust its meaning and complexity, but the 1939 film adaptation of the novel is something else entirely. The director, William Wyler, and the producer, Samuel Goldwyn, did not adapt the novel per se but received its contents into their own frame of reference and created a new work of art that functioned within their own quite different understanding of art. This ability of later readers to transform a work through reception is an important concept in postmodern criticism, revealing a new form of creativity. Reception creates a new meaning that was not present in the original but functions in the cultural terms of the reader (in this case the artists who adapt the novel to film) rather than the author.

Wyler's film adaptation of *Wuthering Heights* was made at the height of the studio system in the late 1930s. Film requires a tremendous economic

WHAT DO I SEE NEXT?

- One of the most notable film adaptations of *Wuthering Heights* was made in 1954 by the surrealist director Luis Buñuel. It was filmed on location in Mexico during his political exile there and is performed in Spanish. Often called *Wuthering Heights* in English-speaking countries, it also has the Spanish title *Abismos de pasión* (Depths of passion). Buñuel focuses on the intense, irrational emotions of the characters to the same degree Wyler suppresses them in this unrated film.

- While Wyler was searching for a new film project in the late 1930s, he had wanted to make a documentary about the Spanish Civil War, but his producer Samuel Goldwyn overruled him and persuaded him to film *Wuthering Heights* instead. Wyler succeeded in exercising his social consciousness after World War II, when he made *The Best Years of Our Lives* (1946, not rated), a documentary-style film about the difficulties that veterans faced in fitting in again with civilian American society. The film won the Academy Award for Best Picture.

- *Jane Eyre* was directed in 1943 by Robert Stevenson. It stars Orson Welles as Rochester and was based in part on his Mercury Theater radio adaption of the novel. The unrated *Jane Eyre* is the natural companion to *Wuthering Heights* among the Brontës' works and was produced by Twentieth Century Fox in direct competition with MGM's film. Bernard Hermann composed the soundtrack and worked in tandem on his own operatic adaptation of *Wuthering Heights* (which was not performed fully until 2011).

- A version of *Wuthering Heights* was directed in 2011 by Andrea Arnold and filmed on location in Yorkshire. The unrated film is notable for casting black actors—Solomon Glave as a youth and James Howson as an adult, both of whom were actually born in Yorkshire—in the role of Heathcliff.

- *The Tenant of Wildfell Hall* (unrated), based on the novel by Anne Brontë, was filmed as a BBC miniseries in 1996. In contrast to *Wuthering Heights* and *Jane Eyre*, which have both been filmed at least a dozen times, this is the only screen adaption of this Brontë work.

- In 1959, Wyler filmed *Ben Hur* (rated G), widely considered his masterpiece. Starring Charlton Heston, the film treats a Jewish nobleman's conversion to Christianity.

---

investment that literature does not, so all filmmakers, even the lone amateurs like Ingmar Bergman and modern independent filmmakers, have to consider the economic viability of their projects. Moreover, the Hollywood studios were businesses and had profit as their primary motivation. Accordingly, their highest priority for *Wuthering Heights* as a film was to appeal to a mass audience that would generate the highest ticket sales and the maximum revenue. To accomplish this, the complexities of the novel had to be reduced to a simple visual story that the largest possible audience could easily understand and identify with.

The emotional bond between the two lead characters, Heathcliff and Catherine, is absolute, as Cathy expresses when she says, "I *am* Heathcliff." The relationship is one of the most effective character studies in literature. Its fascination derives from its primitive and elemental nature. It seems to exist at a level prior to mere romance in some evolutionary or ontological sense. It is too profound to support an ordinary human custom like courting or marriage. Nor is there the slightest hint of any physical relationship between them in the novel (which is hardly to be accounted for by Victorian prudery). The world of the novel that this relationship creates is

> IN THE CLIMACTIC MOMENT OF
> HEATHCLIFF'S AND CATHERINE'S ECSTATIC UNION
> ON THE MOUNTAINTOP, *WUTHERING HEIGHTS*
> BECOMES A METAPHOR FOR ANGLO-AMERICAN
> CULTURAL UNITY."

equally primitive in the sense of being unformed and uncontrolled, but Wyler's film, to the contrary, is an appealing love story told through beautiful images. It could not be more conventional, and given the economic and artistic pressures on the film, it could not have been made in any other way. Goldwyn (as quoted in Hila Sachar's *Cultural Afterlives*), as producer, could not see "why an audience would pull for a capricious, irresponsible girl or a hate-filled man bent on revenging his miserable childhood." He reduced the novel to simple terms that function on the level of the mass audience he desired, cutting away the novel's psychological and dramatic complexity. He gave orders that instead a different story had to be told, transforming *Wuthering Heights* into "a story of undying love . . . that transcends the gloomy nature of its backgrounds."

Many Hollywood films of the golden age were adaptations of classics of English (as opposed to American) literature. Such sources were chosen because they had a certain prestige. This meant that they could generate revenue from exhibition in Great Britain and the British colonial empire as well as in Europe. American audiences would also flock to them because of a certain cultural caché. Ordinary viewers would for the most part not have read works of literature like *Wuthering Heights* and so would view the experience of viewing the film as educative and culturally uplifting. However, to the degree that the films were not faithful adaptations of the novel, this shaded into kitsch, as viewing the film became a substitute for the experience of reading. The audience participated in a fantasy of acquiring cultural sophistication through viewing that was known as "snob appeal."

The particular appeal of British literature, as opposed to American, derived from its power to create a sense of shared Anglo-American culture, which began with the American experience of the First World War and seemed to many to be becoming increasingly urgent as the Second World War loomed in early 1939. World War I was also important to the social construction of *Wuthering Heights* in a quite different way. English-language literature had not been seriously studied by academics or considered *classic* in a culturally vital sense before the Great War. In the nineteenth century, higher education largely consisted of the study of Greek and Latin language and literature, a discipline that is indeed called "the classics." Then the massive and senseless loss of life in the Great War caused a reaction against the traditional culture that had produced it. Although abstract art and atonal music had existed before the war, only after 1918 did these become dominant forms of expression among cultural elites, precisely because they were seen to repudiate tradition. In the same way, the study of vernacular literature, as opposed to literature in the dead languages, took on a new vitality and a new prestige. English literature became an expression of shared Western culture that could stand as a bulwark against the barbarism that was rising in the fascist states. It took on a transcendent value that it had never had before.

The central image of the film is one that never occurs in the novel. After they are reunited as adults in the novel, Heathcliff and Cathy are never alone together. They never roam through the untamed nature of the moors as they had as children. But in the film this is precisely what they do. They climb together to the top of a mountain (a symbol hinting at a physical union) called Penistone Crag. There they sit and gaze up at the eternal transcendence of the sky—of heaven—in a state of rapture. They enter into a unity not only with each other but with the whole world around them. The unity of the world becomes a symbol of their shared love. The camera assumes a more stately gait to underline the sublimity of the scene, composing the scene of long still shots in contrast to its roving eye in much of the rest of the film. While the subtle romanticism of the scene indeed serves as a reasonable visual and climatic expression of the superhuman, or at least inhuman, love that exists between Heathcliff and Catherine, it also serves quite another purpose.

The mountaintop scene is not only the visual and dramatic climax of the film, it was also the most important image used in the publicity for the film and has attracted the most attention from critics and academics. It takes place in a decidedly British landscape, the heather-covered moors of Yorkshire, which the MGM studio spared no expense to recreate in Southern California, just as it imported British actors to act in the film. Heathcliff comes there only after his self-imposed exile, presented as a kind of pilgrimage in the film. In the novel, Brontë takes great pains never to reveal where Heathcliff went when he left Wuthering Heights or how he made his fortune. This uncertainty allows her to hint darkly at the illicit ways in which Heathcliff might have bettered himself. In the film, however, the mystery is dispelled. Heathcliff went to America and became a self-made man, living through his own version of the American dream. Heathcliff is made to encapsulate the American experience as a nation of immigrants who made good. He then returns to his homeland to be with his other self, his distinctly British self, in the form of Cathy.

In the climactic moment of Heathcliff's and Catherine's ecstatic union on the mountaintop, *Wuthering Heights* becomes a metaphor for Anglo-American cultural unity. The film reveals itself as an argument for American support for the United States joining in Britain's struggle in the war that was already seen as inevitable in 1939 and that became a reality shortly after the film's release. Hollywood was already preparing for its role as the partner of the federal government in preparing American opinion for the sacrifices the public would soon be called upon to make to support its British ally.

Source: Bradley Skeen, Critical Essay on *Wuthering Heights*, in *Novels for Students*, Gale, Cengage Learning, 2014.

Liora Brosh

In the following excerpt, Brosh points out the importance of clothes, appearance, and material wealth in Wyler's Wuthering Heights.

... Like the adaptation of *Pride and Prejudice*, Wyler's *Wuthering Heights* is situated within a Depression-era consumer culture and uses conventions of Hollywood glamour that the novel predates. Brontë's Cathy desires to embrace culture in a broad sense, in terms of genteel refinement, education, social propriety, and taste, while Wyler confines Cathy's desires to the wish

> LIKE THE WOMEN IN THE FALLEN WOMAN FILMS, CATHY USES A MAN FOR FINANCIAL GAIN, AND FOR THIS SHE IS PUNISHED."

for pretty dresses bought by an equally well-dressed man.

The novel uses clothing to symbolize Cathy's entry into the world of culture and civilization. In Brontë's novel, clothes are not only literal; Cathy's clothes function as a metaphor for the changes she undergoes. Not only does Brontë's Cathy never express a desire for clothes, but as soon as she is dressed as a "lady" she feels constricted. Dressed in the way her culture requires of women, when she returns from Thrushcross Grange, she has to hold up her skirts as she enters the house, cannot approach the dogs freely, and must keep a distance from Nelly because she is covered in flour. Brontë describes Cathy as frustrated by the cultural restrictions that the dress represents. She breaks these bonds when she runs to embrace Heathcliff despite his being dirty. Like Austen, Brontë uses clothing to represent her heroine's resistance to cultural definitions of appropriate feminine behavior. In contrast, in the same scene in 1939, Cathy refuses to embrace Heathcliff because she does not want to dirty her dress. The Hollywood convention of constructing femininity in terms of glamour is unshaken.

Although in one scene in the film Cathy tears off her elegant dress in frustration and runs to the Crag in an old shabby dress to meet Heathcliff, this scene is followed by another in which she admires herself in a mirror in a vain and excessive way. In the midst of Cathy's self-admiring reflective gaze, Nelly says to her, "You are lovely Miss Cathy." Cathy replies, "That's a very silly lie. I'm not lovely. What I am is very brilliant. I have a wonderful brain. . . . It enables me to be superior to myself. There's nothing to be gained by just looking pretty—like Isabella." As she recites the speech, she admires herself in the mirror from every angle, performing a narcissistic dance. Her actions belie the words she speaks, making her seem even more vain. Her shiny white dress with its silver decorations indicates that her brilliance resides far more in her looks and sparkling dress than in her mind.

In the same scene, when Heathcliff comes to ask Cathy why she is wearing the dress and is dismissed by her and forbidden to touch her, he retorts,

> Tell the dirty stable-boy to let go of you—he soils your pretty dress. But who soils your heart? Not Heathcliff. Who turns you into a vain cheap worldly fool... Linton does. You'll let yourself be loved by him because it pleases your stupid greedy vanity to be loved by that milksop.

The film supports Heathcliff's assessment that Linton brings out Cathy's greed and vanity.

Wuthering Heights prefigures the Depression-era paradox seen in *Pride and Prejudice* and also represents the desire to look glamorous as both a natural feminine ideal and a moral flaw that threatens men and marriage. While the camera lingers on Cathy's brilliant dress, encouraging audiences to admire its splendor, Cathy is depicted as vain for admiring it. The producers were so intent on having glamorous costumes that they decided to set the film in the last decades of the eighteenth century because "the Georgian period was marked by fancier dresses for women and Goldwyn was eager to show off Oberon in beautiful costumes." The type of vanity the film criticizes is also what enabled Hollywood to make a profit from its representations of glamour and the attendant marketing of clothes and cosmetics.

Mary Ann Doane discusses the relationship of women to fetishized representations of themselves on the screen and, relying on Freud, describes it as narcissistic: "Having and appearing are closely intertwined in the woman's purportedly narcissistic relation to the commodity.... The cinematic image for the woman is both shop window and mirror, the one simply a means of access to the other." Women want to buy cosmetics and clothes so that they can become the image they see in the mirror/screen. In Wyler's film, Cathy is made to replicate the female audience's purportedly narcissistic relationship to its own image. Both Cathy and Isabella often stare intently at themselves in mirrors. Even in *Pride and Prejudice*, where there is less emphasis on female narcissism, in the first scene of the film Jane sketches a picture of herself as she will look in her new dress and admires the image. Cathy's consumer-oriented narcissism threatens both Linton and Heathcliff.

Cathy constantly goads Heathcliff to be a "man" and make the money that will enable her to satisfy what he calls her "vain and greedy" desires. Cathy's dialogue with Heathcliff continues:

> *Cathy*: You had your chance to be something else....
>
> *Cathy*: Thief or servant were all you were born to be—or beggar beside a road. Begging for favors. Not earning them, but whimpering for them with your dirty hands.
>
> *Heathcliff*: That's all I have become to you—a pair of dirty hands... Well—have them. Then... (*he slaps her face*) Have them where they belong.

In the novel Heathcliff's violence is never directed toward Cathy, but in the film Cathy is represented as deserving of men's ire. Not only is Cathy excessively hungry for pretty things, but she also goads the man she loves for failing to be enough of a "man" to earn the wealth she desires.

At a time when men's sense of self-worth was often derived from their ability to earn wages to support their families, and when the Depression made this no longer possible or certain, Cathy's castigation of Heathcliff for not being a "man" because he is a bad wage earner has tremendous resonance. It represents the nightmare underlying the Depression-era crisis of masculinity: a beautiful woman refuses the devoted love of a man because he is unable to support her financially.

The film deflects the blame here from the man who cannot make a living to the woman who makes excessive demands of him. Although the film shows Cathy running desperately after Heathcliff on the night he runs away, and close-ups reveal that her acceptance of Linton's offer of marriage is partly reluctant, Cathy is presented as marrying Linton so that she can buy what she desires. Unlike Elizabeth in *Pride and Prejudice*, Cathy does not renounce her consumer desires and does marry for money. Like the women in the fallen woman films, Cathy uses a man for financial gain, and for this she is punished. Because of Brontë's plot, the producers choose the other form of self-censorship not used in *Pride and Prejudice*: the heroine does not renounce wealth but, instead, marries for it and then suffers for her actions.

Blaming Cathy alone for her demise, the adaptation departs from the usual reading of the novel, in which Cathy is interpreted as a character destroyed by her tragic inability to reconcile conflicting polarities. Cathy is seen as torn between storm and calm, between wild passions and tamer emotions, between natural energies and the habits, codes, and manners of civilization, or as split between the spirit and the body. All of these binaries can fall into the nature/culture divide that the film retains, but the adaptation, unlike the novel, represents culture narrowly, in economic terms, as a commodity culture. The adaptation does not represent Cathy as inescapably torn between broader and more profound irreconcilable forces.

Terry Eagleton has described Cathy as torn between the yeoman class of the Earnshaws and Heathcliff (before he becomes a capitalist) and the agrarian capitalists at the Grange. Eagleton claims that Cathy's mistaken decision to marry Linton destroys her as well as Edgar and Heathcliff. If Wyler's critique of consumerism were less gendered and he dealt as severely with Heathcliff once he was a capitalist as he does with Cathy, one could assume that his interpretation of *Wuthering Heights* is as Marxist as Eagleton's. More than Eagleton, however, Wyler's interpretation of *Wuthering Heights* faults Cathy alone for the destruction of her own and all of the other main characters' lives....

Source: Liora Brosh, "Consuming Women: *Pride and Prejudice* and *Wuthering Heights*," in *Screening Novel Women: From British Domestic Fiction to Film*, Palgrave Macmillan, 2008, pp. 38–41.

Karl Kroeber

In the following excerpt, Kroeber discusses Wyler's film's depiction of Catherine and Heathcliff's romance as unhealthy from childhood.

...All of *Rashomon* takes place out of doors, but almost all of the action of *Wuthering Heights* occurs inside houses. The contrast is neatly if ironically dramatized by the movie adaptation of 1940 directed by William Wyler, which did much to establish Laurence Olivier as a star: on its first release it was seen by over 200 million people. Much of this movie emphasizes the moors—showing far more of them (and Catherine and Heathcliff on them) than the novel tells us. This "infidelity" is entirely appropriate for a translation of novel into movie, and much of the film's effectiveness derives from the transposition into the spectacularly visible of what is sparingly described in the novel. The movie also shows much of Heathcliff and Catherine as children. It softens the novel's violence and brutality (we don't see Hareton hanging

puppies), and it cleans up both Joseph's appearance and his Yorkshire dialect, part of the denaturing of Emily Brontë's Dostoyevskian religious critique of her society. It reduces the complexities of Catherine and Heathcliff's love to an unambiguous romance. But the extended depiction of the protagonists as children, while it subverts the novel's challenge to accepted conventions of gender, and even fears of incest, is not an unreasonable decision, if one grants the moviemakers' right to create a movie with mass popular appeal.

The key to the adaptation is Pennistone Crag, the scene of a famous promotional still of Olivier together with Merle Oberon. In the book, the crag is trivial. But the central movie scene of the childhood of Catherine and Heathcliff focuses on this outdoor site, where Catherine urges Heathcliff to play the part of a noble knight slaying a dangerous enemy to save her, casting herself in the role of a conventionally helpless princess (Stoneman, 1996, 132–133). The movie thus affirms the most traditional social gendering, whereas much of the fascination of the novel arises from its revelations of frightening ambiguities at the heart of such conventions—as in Catherine's "betraying" Heathcliff by marrying Linton. This rather selfish woman wants to have both men. She rejects the idea that marrying Linton needs to shut her off from Heathcliff. That is why she accuses *both* men of killing her. The movie's utter conventionality sets into bold relief how Brontë attacked fundamental social attitudes toward gender without reducing Catherine to a mere victim of a stereotypical oppressive masculinity. The question in the novel of why in fact Catherine marries Linton is not easily answered. When Heathcliff asks, "Why did you betray your own heart, Cathy?" (Chapter 15), he implies that she has truly loved only him, that no essential part of her could have been attracted to Linton. But Catherine is not that simple: she loves Heathcliff, but is also attracted to Linton. Heathcliff later accuses her of killing herself, and it is true that her death is in a significant fashion suicide. Yet she is not unjustified in accusing both Heathcliff and Linton of driving her to self-destruction. Like Lamia in Keats's poem (which Brontë knew), Catherine is destroyed by two men who insist on treating her protean dualities of feeling as stereotypical "female duplicity."

The movie weakens Catherine's poignant emotional uncertainty by portraying the foundation of

Catherine and Heathcliff's passion in their unam-
biguously joyous experience as children on the
moor. The movie displays explicitly and unambig-
uously what the novel carefully keeps obscure and
doubtful. The novel forces us to speculate on their
doings through hints and tangential references, as
when Catherine recalls Heathcliff building a cage
over a nest of young birds so their parents cannot
feed them and they will starve. Had the film shown
this pretty piece of playfulness, it would have
destroyed its representation of Heathcliff and Catherine's love as conventionally pure. Yet unless the
movie is radically to transform the novel by elimi-
nating the protagonists' early experiences together,
it must *display* Catherine and Heathcliff's childhood, for much the same reason that a movie of
Pride and Prejudice must show the wallpaper in the
room where Darcy first proposes to Elizabeth.
Buñels' adaptation of Brontë's novel, *Abyss of Passion*, does eliminate the childhood experiences, one
result being a film more melodramatically romantic
than Wyler's picture. But Wyler in *showing* inevitably falsifies the childhood experiences, because
the novel makes them obscure, offering only tanta-
lizing hints evocative of the mysteriousness of the
children's relations and thereby endowing them
with an aura of strange dangerousness.

When Heathcliff tells Nelly about his race
with Catherine to Thrushcross Grange, he reports
Catherine was beaten because she lost one of her
shoes. Beyond its implication of how they behaved
on the moors, the detail also suggests that Heathcliff regarded Catherine as nearly his equal as a
runner. More than posing a challenge to conventional gender distinctions, the casual reference supports the blunt diagnosis of Dr. Keith later in the
novel that only some psychological trauma can
explain the physical decline of such a "stout, hearty
lass" as Catherine. This arouses readers' suspicions
that her early relationship to Heathcliff was in
some way "unhealthy." Any moviemaker might
reasonably decide such subtle allusiveness to be
inappropriate for his medium and aim for an adaptation at the least true to the novel's impassioned
love story. *Honi y soit qui mal y pense . . . .*

Source: Karl Kroeber, "*Rashomon* and *Wuthering
Heights*," in *Make Believe in Film and Fiction: Visual vs.
Verbal Storytelling*, Palgrave Macmillan, 2006, pp. 113–15.

Lin Haire-Sargeant

*In the following excerpt, Haire-Sargeant dis-
cusses the difficulty of making Heathcliff a sympathetic character.*

> OUR COMPLICITY MUST GIVE US SYMPATHY
> FOR THE DEVIL—EXCEPT THAT UNDER WYLER'S
> GENTLEMANLY DIRECTION HEATHCLIFF IS NO DEVIL,
> BUT A GREAT HEART MORE SINNED AGAINST THAN
> SINNING."

When, in her 1847 novel *Wuthering Heights*,
Emily Brontë created the pivotal character
Heathcliff, she set herself a daunting challenge:
how to tell the story of a brutal, calculating sad-
ist, the bane of two families over two generations,
in such a way that by the end of the book the
reader's horror is overwhelmed by sympathy. At
first, critical reaction seemed to indicate that she
had failed: most reviewers attacked the brutality
of the book, saving their worst condemnation for
Heathcliff. The *North American Review*'s pro-
nouncement was typical: Heathcliff was a brute
"whom the Mephistopheles of Goethe would
have nothing to say to, whom the Satan of Milton would consider an object of simple disgust"
(Oct. 1848). But over the next decades attitudes
changed. Readers became fascinated with
Heathcliff's villainy, as imitation in lesser works
made him the prototypical hero of Gothic
Romance. Eventually the allure of his evil was
recognized as part of the power of Brontë's book.

In the next century, when a novel as famous
as *Wuthering Heights* was bound to be made into
a movie, the stakes for a favorable response to
Heathcliff grew higher. It was not only sympathy
for the devil that was required of us; it was love—
a necessary generic condition of the feature film,
where characters project as gods, the movie
screen irresistibly our Olympus, our Sinai.
There, even our darkest demons must show as
angels dancing bright. Historically, the films of
Wuthering Heights have met this challenge in two
ways: either by changing the story so that
Heathcliff's evil deeds are lessened or mitigated,
or straight on, as Emily Brontë does, directing the
reader/viewer to absorb the totality of Heathcliff's evil and good within his human situation.

Of course, there is much more to *Wuthering
Heights* than Heathcliff. This is, of novels,
among the elect, judged to be great by critics

and the reading public alike. For the latter, its greatness lies in the love story between Heathcliff and Cathy; critics are more likely to cite the structure: the elegant symmetry and precision of the plot (as in C. P. Sanger's 1926 "The Structure of *Wuthering Heights*") or the even more elegant patterns of repetition of phrases and tropes (as in J. Hillis Miller's chapter "*Wuthering Heights*: Repetition and the 'Uncanny'" in his 1982 *Fiction and Repetition*).

Brontë's means to greatness were linguistic; the filmmaker's must be visual. Inevitable differences follow. Where the novelist's words spark individual, intimate mind pictures in each reader, the filmmaker must define the image on the screen, the same for all viewers, and in doing so ground the story in time and space—the time and space in which the movie is filmed, not that in which the story is set. In these ways and others, the filmmaker creates a work of art separate from its "original" yet connected in an intimate way. So the question is not "does the movie replicate the book?" since that is an impossibility. More interesting questions: does the movie communicate something of the book's art? And how, by what means, is that art communicated, since it must be communicated by analog? Finally, the most important question of all: does the film succeed as a work of art in its own right? If it does, it creates its own sufficient reason for being. If it does not, it can be criticized not only as a failed film but as a failed adaptation: every departure from the novel becomes a fault. And even a great movie based on a novel has one irredeemable flaw: it is not the novel.

. . . In his adaptation, Wyler goes a long way towards solving the problem of Heathcliff with his casting: Laurence Olivier plays Heathcliff like Heathcliff playing Laurence Olivier. The young Olivier delivers a bravura turn as an anesthetized brute whose intelligence takes him on forays into psychologizing sympathy ("You're lonely," he comforts Isabella [Geraldine Fitzgerald]. "It's lonely sitting like an outsider in so happy a household as your brother's. . . . You won't be lonely any more"). On the page this is almost laughably far from Brontë's Heathcliff, but paradoxically, of all the Heathcliffs, the Wyler/Olivier version gives the strongest analog of Heathcliff's felt emotion, the injustices endured and absorbed, the repressed passion and rage.

This is accomplished partly through Olivier's performance (of which more later), and

partly through Wyler's brilliantly conceptualized and realized artistic direction. The film is holographic; every frame, in narrative content and composition, contains the whole story. Wyler controls a black-and-white palette of exquisitely shaded tonality; even on a TV screen the numinously glowing whites, the engulfing blacks, and the shimmering grays eloquently express emotional and spiritual nuance.

The story is considerably truncated in this 103-minute version. It begins with Lockwood's arrival: "A stranger lost in a storm." Lockwood (Leo G. Carroll) runs the gamut of snarling dogs and unanswered knocks to finally gain shelter in Wuthering Heights. The family he encounters is not second generation Earnshaws and Lintons—that story has been cut. Rather it is Isabella, Nelly Dean (Flora Robson), Joseph, and a softened Heathcliff—who, when, reminded of his manners, responds with urbane irony: "I hardly know how to treat a guest—I and my *dog*" and himself offers Lockwood lodging. After Heathcliff, galvanized by Lockwood's dream of Cathy (Merle Oberon), bursts out into the blizzard to seek her, Nelly tells Lockwood the tale of the first generation of Earnshaws and Lintons. The conventional voice-over ("It began forty years ago when I was young") along with the track into a tight close-up of Nelly's face anticipate the dissolve to the long-ago scene of the boy Heathcliff's arrival at Wuthering Heights. The story of the entanglements of Heathcliff, Cathy, Edgar (David Niven), and Isabella, with occasional voice-over commentary by Nelly, is followed through to Cathy's death. Then there is a return to the frame story. As Nelly concludes her tale, Dr. Kenneth comes in out of the blizzard. He has found Heathcliff's body by Pennistone Crag after first having seen a vision of him with Cathy. The film ends with a long shot of Heathcliff and Cathy ascending Pennistone Crag together.

Paradoxically, Wyler and cinematographer Gregg Toland tell this tale of tightly caged violence through visuals that emphasize open space. In contrast to the description of a disorderly, cramped household in the novel, Wyler's Heights interiors, filmed deep focus, open an airy palatial zone behind the viewing screen. When Lockwood arrives, the camera follows him across uneasy expanses of floor while the family, huddled at the fireside, stare. Eventually Joseph leads Lockwood to his lodging for the night, Cathy's old bedroom. To get from Joseph's presentation—"the bridal chamber"—to Lockwood's reaction, the camera pans across what seems an immense expanse of dingy, candle-lit wall. The meaning of this emphasis on space is not the claustrophobia of the interlocking narratives and the closed worlds of the Heights and the Grange that really exist in Brontë's pages, but rather an edgy agoraphobia that at once contains its opposite and suggests its transcendence.

Another paradox: in the novel, Heathcliff and Cathy are characterized by violent movement—motion equals emotion. In the film, Cathy and Heathcliff, most tempestuous of lovers, are portrayed through the poetics of immobility. Olivier moves through much of the film with his trunk and arms stiff, his eyes fixed and unfocused, like a somnambulist who does not dream. This of course makes his occasional outbreaks of movement—two slaps across faithless Cathy's face, a plunge of bare knuckles through window glass—the more violently emotive, though ultimately we are taught to experience Heathcliff's giant rage most intensely in its tethering. Similarly, Merle Oberon's snow-queen Cathy, herself motionless, with each unmoving second builds charged emotion like a dynamo. She sits frozen at table while Hindley abuses Heathcliff, then flies from the house, over a wall, and up Pennistone Crag to a tryst with Heathcliff impelled by a blast of primal desire usually confined by this Cathy's strong proprietary and propertarian good sense.

There is one scene in the film that brilliantly deploys the narrative's two lines of emotional symbolism, the agoraphobic use of space and the burning paralysis of the lovers. In a scene that does not appear in Brontë's book, Edgar and Cathy give a ball at Thrushcross Grange. The scene begins with dance music, then a fade to a moving shot as the camera pans up over a stone wall for an exterior view of Thrushcross Grange, recalling an earlier scene where prelapsarian Heathcliff and Cathy spied on just such a ball. With Cathy's marriage to Edgar she has become part of this world, while Heathcliff, though mysteriously transformed into a gentleman, remains shut out. Through brilliantly lit windows we can glimpse dancing couples. Then there is a fade to the interior scene shown through an ornate mirror. The restless camera pans rather jerkily away from the mirror, across expanses of mechanistically dancing couples, other mirrors, crystal chandeliers. The effect is of a giant music box; artifice, not humanity, is the key. The camera roves nervously above the dancers, a questing,

disembodied point of view. Lighting is high key, focus is deep. The camera fixes its gaze on the entrance door; the footmen admit Heathcliff, in impeccable evening dress, a tall black column against the hard white surfaces of the ballroom. A bit later he stands immobile behind a seated Isabella; a harpsichordist begins to play a Mozart sonata. A crane shot circles above the frenetically pounding harpsichordist, surveys the immobilized audience. There is an extended close-up of a somber Heathcliff; we know where his unswerving gaze is directed. Cut to a close-up of Cathy. She is a snow woman with her white bared shoulders, and her apparel might as well be ice. The dress is highly polished white satin; diamonds sparkle from necklace, earrings, and tiara. She is like an ice sculpture, especially when Heathcliff's gaze freezes her. Then, though she struggles against it, her eyes are drawn to him. Such is the force of his gaze that it draws not only Cathy's notice but the notice of the crowd. The resulting voyeuristic heat is extraordinary. Will Cathy melt? Cut to an extreme close-up of the harpsichordist's hands banging away at the coda like jackhammers, invoking the brutal mocking mechanism of the social trap caging the lovers.

In Wyler's rationale for fabricating this scene we see his genius as a filmmaker. In the book *Wuthering Heights*, writing and reading, inscription and its decoding—the carving of Cathy's name on the wooden shelf in her bedroom, her palimpsistic writings in the book of sermons—these are the channels into the text, for the inside reader Lockwood, then for us outside readers. Part of the peculiar power of this device is that the medium doubles the message. For the book, the act of reading is an act of power and connection. First Lockwood's reading, then ours, becomes a process of spying on these distant lives; we catch ourselves brushing Lockwood's shoulder as we lean over to make sense of the words, and the distant lives become not so distant. For the film, Wyler translates this participatory mechanism to the visual. Passion, for Wyler's Cathy and Heathcliff, is always ocular, their gaze a conduit for voyeuristically charged eroticism—as is our gaze when we watch theirs. Our complicity must give us sympathy for the devil—except that under Wyler's gentlemanly direction Heathcliff is no devil, but a great heart more sinned against than sinning.

After the dancing resumes, Heathcliff's continued gaze compels Cathy to turn to him. They walk out to the veranda, a zone halfway between the Grange's caging civilization and the freedom of the natural world. Cathy chides Heathcliff for his somber air. "Don't pretend life hasn't improved for you." "Life has ended for me," he replies. As he leans toward Cathy with words of love, she turns away, and the howl of a cold wind from the moors overtakes the waltz music. The camera retreats through the leaves of the trees into darkness. By freezing his actors within open, uneasily shifting space, Wyler has shown both the spiritual connection of Cathy and Heathcliff and the terrifying emptiness of the universe for the one without the other . . . .

Source: Lin Haire-Sargeant, "Sympathy for the Devil: The Problem of Heathcliff in Film Versions of *Wuthering Heights*," in *Nineteenth Century Women at the Movies: Adapting Classic Women's Fiction to Film*, edited by Barbara Tepa Lupack, Bowling State Green University Popular Press, 1999, pp. 167–68, 170–73.

SOURCES

Brontë, Charlotte, "Editor's Preface to the New Edition," reprinted in *Wuthering Heights*, edited by William M. Sale and Richard J. Dunn, 3rd ed., W. W. Norton, 1990, pp. 319–22.

Brontë, Emily, *Wuthering Heights*, edited by William M. Sale and Richard J. Dunn, 3rd ed., W. W. Norton, 1990.

———, *Gondal's Queen: A Novel in Verse*, edited by Fannie Elizabeth Ratchford, University of Texas Press, 1955, pp. 41–42.

Herman, Jan, *A Talent for Trouble: The Life of Hollywood's Most Acclaimed Director, William Wyler*, G. P. Putnam's Sons, 1995, pp. 194–99.

Madsen, Axel, *William Wyler: The Authorized Biography*, Thomas Y. Crowell, 1973, pp. 180–91.

Said, Edward, *Orientalism*, Vintage Books, 1979, pp. 1–31.

Shachar, Hila, *Cultural Afterlives and Screen Adaptations of Classic Literature: "Wuthering Heights" and Company*, Palgrave, 2012, pp. 39–60, 181–204.

Stoneman, Patsy, *Brontë Transformations: The Cultural Dissemination of "Jane Eyre" and "Wuthering Heights,"* Prentice Hall, 1996, pp. 126–33.

Thormählen, Marianne, ed., *The Brontës in Context*, Cambridge University Press, 2012, pp. 102–105, 145, 185–87, 289–90, 297–98, 323–24, 330–34, 348–49.

Visick, M., *The Genesis of "Wuthering Heights,"* Hong Kong University Press, 1948, pp. 10–32.

Wuthering Heights, directed by William Wyler, Warner Home Video, 2012, DVD.

FURTHER READING

Brontë, Charlotte, *An Edition of the Early Writings of Charlotte Brontë*, 2 vols., edited by Christine Alexander, Blackwell, 1987–1991.

> This comprehensive survey covers all texts relevant to the fantasy world of Angria with extensive discussion and commentary.

———, *Jane Eyre*, Smith, Elder, 1847.

> Kept continuously in print, this work competes with *Wuthering Heights* as the greatest literary achievement of the Brontës'. It is, if anything, more revolutionary than *Wuthering Heights* in the formation of the modern psychological novel and is equally indebted to the Brontës' early literary play.

Gezari, Janet, *Last Things: Emily Brontë's Poems*, Oxford University Press, 2007.

> Gezari's volume offers incisive analysis of Brontë's poems, which form an important link between Gondal and *Wuthering Heights*, as well as being the only other body of work published by Emily Brontë in her lifetime.

Winnifrith, Tom, and Edward Chitham, *Charlotte and Emily Brontë*, Macmillan, 1989.

> This book gives a brief overview of the entwined literary lives of the two sisters and, to a lesser degree, the other Brontë siblings.

SUGGESTED SEARCH TERMS

Emily Brontë

William Wyler

Samuel Goldwyn

Wuthering Heights

gothic novel

psychological novel

surrealism

Yorkshire dialect

Gondal

Glossary of Literary Terms

A

Abstract: As an adjective applied to writing or literary works, abstract refers to words or phrases that name things not knowable through the five senses.

Aestheticism: A literary and artistic movement of the nineteenth century. Followers of the movement believed that art should not be mixed with social, political, or moral teaching. The statement "art for art's sake" is a good summary of aestheticism. The movement had its roots in France, but it gained widespread importance in England in the last half of the nineteenth century, where it helped change the Victorian practice of including moral lessons in literature.

Allegory: A narrative technique in which characters representing things or abstract ideas are used to convey a message or teach a lesson. Allegory is typically used to teach moral, ethical, or religious lessons but is sometimes used for satiric or political purposes.

Allusion: A reference to a familiar literary or historical person or event, used to make an idea more easily understood.

Analogy: A comparison of two things made to explain something unfamiliar through its similarities to something familiar, or to prove one point based on the acceptedness of another. Similes and metaphors are types of analogies.

Antagonist: The major character in a narrative or drama who works against the hero or protagonist.

Anthropomorphism: The presentation of animals or objects in human shape or with human characteristics. The term is derived from the Greek word for "human form."

Anti-hero: A central character in a work of literature who lacks traditional heroic qualities such as courage, physical prowess, and fortitude. Anti-heroes typically distrust conventional values and are unable to commit themselves to any ideals. They generally feel helpless in a world over which they have no control. Anti-heroes usually accept, and often celebrate, their positions as social outcasts.

Apprenticeship Novel: See *Bildungsroman*

Archetype: The word archetype is commonly used to describe an original pattern or model from which all other things of the same kind are made. This term was introduced to literary criticism from the psychology of Carl Jung. It expresses Jung's theory that behind every person's "unconscious," or repressed memories of the past, lies the "collective unconscious" of the human race: memories of the countless typical experiences of our ancestors. These memories are said to prompt illogical associations that trigger powerful emotions in the reader. Often, the emotional process is primitive, even primordial. Archetypes are the literary images that grow out of the "collective unconscious." They appear in literature as incidents and plots that repeat basic patterns of life. They may also appear as stereotyped characters.

Avant-garde: French term meaning "vanguard." It is used in literary criticism to describe new writing that rejects traditional approaches to literature in favor of innovations in style or content.

B

Beat Movement: A period featuring a group of American poets and novelists of the 1950s and 1960s—including Jack Kerouac, Allen Ginsberg, Gregory Corso, William S. Burroughs, and Lawrence Ferlinghetti—who rejected established social and literary values. Using such techniques as stream of consciousness writing and jazz-influenced free verse and focusing on unusual or abnormal states of mind—generated by religious ecstasy or the use of drugs—the Beat writers aimed to create works that were unconventional in both form and subject matter.

Bildungsroman: A German word meaning "novel of development." The *bildungsroman* is a study of the maturation of a youthful character, typically brought about through a series of social or sexual encounters that lead to self-awareness. *Bildungsroman* is used interchangeably with *erziehungsroman*, a novel of initiation and education. When a *bildungsroman* is concerned with the development of an artist (as in James Joyce's *A Portrait of the Artist as a Young Man*), it is often termed a *kunstlerroman*.

Black Aesthetic Movement: A period of artistic and literary development among African Americans in the 1960s and early 1970s. This was the first major African-American artistic movement since the Harlem Renaissance and was closely paralleled by the civil rights and black power movements. The black aesthetic writers attempted to produce works of art that would be meaningful to the black masses. Key figures in black aesthetics included one of its founders, poet and playwright Amiri Baraka, formerly known as LeRoi Jones; poet and essayist Haki R. Madhubuti, formerly Don L. Lee; poet and playwright Sonia Sanchez; and dramatist Ed Bullins.

Black Humor: Writing that places grotesque elements side by side with humorous ones in an attempt to shock the reader, forcing him or her to laugh at the horrifying reality of a disordered world.

Burlesque: Any literary work that uses exaggeration to make its subject appear ridiculous, either by treating a trivial subject with profound seriousness or by treating a dignified subject frivolously. The word "burlesque" may also be used as an adjective, as in "burlesque show," to mean "striptease act."

C

Character: Broadly speaking, a person in a literary work. The actions of characters are what constitute the plot of a story, novel, or poem. There are numerous types of characters, ranging from simple, stereotypical figures to intricate, multifaceted ones. In the techniques of anthropomorphism and personification, animals—and even places or things—can assume aspects of character. "Characterization" is the process by which an author creates vivid, believable characters in a work of art. This may be done in a variety of ways, including (1) direct description of the character by the narrator; (2) the direct presentation of the speech, thoughts, or actions of the character; and (3) the responses of other characters to the character. The term "character" also refers to a form originated by the ancient Greek writer Theophrastus that later became popular in the seventeenth and eighteenth centuries. It is a short essay or sketch of a person who prominently displays a specific attribute or quality, such as miserliness or ambition.

Climax: The turning point in a narrative, the moment when the conflict is at its most intense. Typically, the structure of stories, novels, and plays is one of rising action, in which tension builds to the climax, followed by falling action, in which tension lessens as the story moves to its conclusion.

Colloquialism: A word, phrase, or form of pronunciation that is acceptable in casual conversation but not in formal, written communication. It is considered more acceptable than slang.

Coming of Age Novel: See *Bildungsroman*

Concrete: Concrete is the opposite of abstract, and refers to a thing that actually exists or a description that allows the reader to experience an object or concept with the senses.

Connotation: The impression that a word gives beyond its defined meaning. Connotations may be universally understood or may be significant only to a certain group.

Convention: Any widely accepted literary device, style, or form.

D

Denotation: The definition of a word, apart from the impressions or feelings it creates (connotations) in the reader.

Denouement: A French word meaning "the unknotting." In literary criticism, it denotes the resolution of conflict in fiction or drama. The *denouement* follows the climax and provides an outcome to the primary plot situation as well as an explanation of secondary plot complications. The *denouement* often involves a character's recognition of his or her state of mind or moral condition.

Description: Descriptive writing is intended to allow a reader to picture the scene or setting in which the action of a story takes place. The form this description takes often evokes an intended emotional response—a dark, spooky graveyard will evoke fear, and a peaceful, sunny meadow will evoke calmness.

Dialogue: In its widest sense, dialogue is simply conversation between people in a literary work; in its most restricted sense, it refers specifically to the speech of characters in a drama. As a specific literary genre, a "dialogue" is a composition in which characters debate an issue or idea.

Diction: The selection and arrangement of words in a literary work. Either or both may vary depending on the desired effect. There are four general types of diction: "formal," used in scholarly or lofty writing; "informal," used in relaxed but educated conversation; "colloquial," used in everyday speech; and "slang," containing newly coined words and other terms not accepted in formal usage.

Didactic: A term used to describe works of literature that aim to teach some moral, religious, political, or practical lesson. Although didactic elements are often found in artistically pleasing works, the term "didactic" usually refers to literature in which the message is more important than the form. The term

may also be used to criticize a work that the critic finds "overly didactic," that is, heavy-handed in its delivery of a lesson.

Doppelganger: A literary technique by which a character is duplicated (usually in the form of an alter ego, though sometimes as a ghostly counterpart) or divided into two distinct, usually opposite personalities. The use of this character device is widespread in nineteenth- and twentieth-century literature, and indicates a growing awareness among authors that the "self" is really a composite of many "selves."

Double Entendre: A corruption of a French phrase meaning "double meaning." The term is used to indicate a word or phrase that is deliberately ambiguous, especially when one of the meanings is risqué or improper.

Dramatic Irony: Occurs when the audience of a play or the reader of a work of literature knows something that a character in the work itself does not know. The irony is in the contrast between the intended meaning of the statements or actions of a character and the additional information understood by the audience.

Dystopia: An imaginary place in a work of fiction where the characters lead dehumanized, fearful lives.

E

Edwardian: Describes cultural conventions identified with the period of the reign of Edward VII of England (1901-1910). Writers of the Edwardian Age typically displayed a strong reaction against the propriety and conservatism of the Victorian Age. Their work often exhibits distrust of authority in religion, politics, and art and expresses strong doubts about the soundness of conventional values.

Empathy: A sense of shared experience, including emotional and physical feelings, with someone or something other than oneself. Empathy is often used to describe the response of a reader to a literary character.

Enlightenment, The: An eighteenth-century philosophical movement. It began in France but had a wide impact throughout Europe and America. Thinkers of the Enlightenment valued reason and believed that both the individual and society could achieve a state of perfection. Corresponding to this essentially humanist vision was a resistance to religious authority.

Epigram: A saying that makes the speaker's point quickly and concisely. Often used to preface a novel.

Epilogue: A concluding statement or section of a literary work. In dramas, particularly those of the seventeenth and eighteenth centuries, the epilogue is a closing speech, often in verse, delivered by an actor at the end of a play and spoken directly to the audience.

Epiphany: A sudden revelation of truth inspired by a seemingly trivial incident.

Episode: An incident that forms part of a story and is significantly related to it. Episodes may be either self-contained narratives or events that depend on a larger context for their sense and importance.

Epistolary Novel: A novel in the form of letters. The form was particularly popular in the eighteenth century.

Epithet: A word or phrase, often disparaging or abusive, that expresses a character trait of someone or something.

Existentialism: A predominantly twentieth-century philosophy concerned with the nature and perception of human existence. There are two major strains of existentialist thought: atheistic and Christian. Followers of atheistic existentialism believe that the individual is alone in a godless universe and that the basic human condition is one of suffering and loneliness. Nevertheless, because there are no fixed values, individuals can create their own characters—indeed, they can shape themselves—through the exercise of free will. The atheistic strain culminates in and is popularly associated with the works of Jean-Paul Sartre. The Christian existentialists, on the other hand, believe that only in God may people find freedom from life's anguish. The two strains hold certain beliefs in common: that existence cannot be fully understood or described through empirical effort; that anguish is a universal element of life; that individuals must bear responsibility for their actions; and that there is no common standard of behavior or perception for religious and ethical matters.

Expatriates: See *Expatriatism*

Expatriatism: The practice of leaving one's country to live for an extended period in another country.

Exposition: Writing intended to explain the nature of an idea, thing, or theme. Expository writing is often combined with description, narration, or argument. In dramatic writing, the exposition is the introductory material which presents the characters, setting, and tone of the play.

Expressionism: An indistinct literary term, originally used to describe an early twentieth-century school of German painting. The term applies to almost any mode of unconventional, highly subjective writing that distorts reality in some way.

F

Fable: A prose or verse narrative intended to convey a moral. Animals or inanimate objects with human characteristics often serve as characters in fables.

Falling Action: See *Denouement*

Fantasy: A literary form related to mythology and folklore. Fantasy literature is typically set in non-existent realms and features supernatural beings.

Farce: A type of comedy characterized by broad humor, outlandish incidents, and often vulgar subject matter.

Femme fatale: A French phrase with the literal translation "fatal woman." A *femme fatale* is a sensuous, alluring woman who often leads men into danger or trouble.

Fiction: Any story that is the product of imagination rather than a documentation of fact. Characters and events in such narratives may be based in real life but their ultimate form and configuration is a creation of the author.

Figurative Language: A technique in writing in which the author temporarily interrupts the order, construction, or meaning of the writing for a particular effect. This interruption takes the form of one or more figures of speech such as hyperbole, irony, or simile. Figurative language is the opposite of literal language, in which every word is truthful, accurate, and free of exaggeration or embellishment.

Figures of Speech: Writing that differs from customary conventions for construction, meaning, order, or significance for the purpose of a special meaning or effect. There are two major types of figures of speech: rhetorical figures, which do not make changes in the meaning of the words, and tropes, which do.

Fin de siecle: A French term meaning "end of the century." The term is used to denote the last decade of the nineteenth century, a transition period when writers and other artists abandoned old conventions and looked for new techniques and objectives.

First Person: See *Point of View*

Flashback: A device used in literature to present action that occurred before the beginning of the story. Flashbacks are often introduced as the dreams or recollections of one or more characters.

Foil: A character in a work of literature whose physical or psychological qualities contrast strongly with, and therefore highlight, the corresponding qualities of another character.

Folklore: Traditions and myths preserved in a culture or group of people. Typically, these are passed on by word of mouth in various forms—such as legends, songs, and proverbs—or preserved in customs and ceremonies. This term was first used by W. J. Thoms in 1846.

Folktale: A story originating in oral tradition. Folktales fall into a variety of categories, including legends, ghost stories, fairy tales, fables, and anecdotes based on historical figures and events.

Foreshadowing: A device used in literature to create expectation or to set up an explanation of later developments.

Form: The pattern or construction of a work which identifies its genre and distinguishes it from other genres.

G

Genre: A category of literary work. In critical theory, genre may refer to both the content of a given work—tragedy, comedy, pastoral—and to its form, such as poetry, novel, or drama.

Gilded Age: A period in American history during the 1870s characterized by political corruption and materialism. A number of important novels of social and political criticism were written during this time.

Gothicism: In literary criticism, works characterized by a taste for the medieval or morbidly attractive. A gothic novel prominently features elements of horror, the supernatural, gloom, and violence: clanking chains, terror, charnel houses, ghosts, medieval castles, and mysteriously slamming doors. The term "gothic novel" is also applied to novels that lack elements of the traditional Gothic setting but that create a similar atmosphere of terror or dread.

Grotesque: In literary criticism, the subject matter of a work or a style of expression characterized by exaggeration, deformity, freakishness, and disorder. The grotesque often includes an element of comic absurdity.

H

Harlem Renaissance: The Harlem Renaissance of the 1920s is generally considered the first significant movement of black writers and artists in the United States. During this period, new and established black writers published more fiction and poetry than ever before, the first influential black literary journals were established, and black authors and artists received their first widespread recognition and serious critical appraisal. Among the major writers associated with this period are Claude McKay, Jean Toomer, Countee Cullen, Langston Hughes, Arna Bontemps, Nella Larsen, and Zora Neale Hurston.

Hero/Heroine: The principal sympathetic character (male or female) in a literary work. Heroes and heroines typically exhibit admirable traits: idealism, courage, and integrity, for example.

Holocaust Literature: Literature influenced by or written about the Holocaust of World War II. Such literature includes true stories of survival in concentration camps, escape, and life after the war, as well as fictional works and poetry.

Humanism: A philosophy that places faith in the dignity of humankind and rejects the medieval perception of the individual as a weak, fallen creature. "Humanists" typically believe in the perfectibility of human nature and view reason and education as the means to that end.

Hyperbole: In literary criticism, deliberate exaggeration used to achieve an effect.

I

Idiom: A word construction or verbal expression closely associated with a given language.

Image: A concrete representation of an object or sensory experience. Typically, such a representation helps evoke the feelings associated with the object or experience itself. Images are either "literal" or "figurative." Literal images are especially concrete and involve little or no extension of the obvious meaning of the words used to express them. Figurative images do not follow the literal meaning of the words exactly. Images in literature are usually visual, but the term "image" can also refer to the representation of any sensory experience.

Imagery: The array of images in a literary work. Also, figurative language.

In medias res: A Latin term meaning "in the middle of things." It refers to the technique of beginning a story at its midpoint and then using various flashback devices to reveal previous action.

Interior Monologue: A narrative technique in which characters' thoughts are revealed in a way that appears to be uncontrolled by the author. The interior monologue typically aims to reveal the inner self of a character. It portrays emotional experiences as they occur at both a conscious and unconscious level. images are often used to represent sensations or emotions.

Irony: In literary criticism, the effect of language in which the intended meaning is the opposite of what is stated.

J

Jargon: Language that is used or understood only by a select group of people. Jargon may refer to terminology used in a certain profession, such as computer jargon, or it may refer to any nonsensical language that is not understood by most people.

L

Leitmotiv: See *Motif*

Literal Language: An author uses literal language when he or she writes without exaggerating or embellishing the subject matter and without any tools of figurative language.

Lost Generation: A term first used by Gertrude Stein to describe the post-World War I generation of American writers: men and women haunted by a sense of betrayal and emptiness brought about by the destructiveness of the war.

M

Mannerism: Exaggerated, artificial adherence to a literary manner or style. Also, a popular style of the visual arts of late sixteenth-century Europe that was marked by elongation of the human form and by intentional spatial distortion. Literary works that are self-consciously high-toned and artistic are often said to be "mannered."

Metaphor: A figure of speech that expresses an idea through the image of another object. Metaphors suggest the essence of the first object by identifying it with certain qualities of the second object.

Modernism: Modern literary practices. Also, the principles of a literary school that lasted from roughly the beginning of the twentieth century until the end of World War II. Modernism is defined by its rejection of the literary conventions of the nineteenth century and by its opposition to conventional morality, taste, traditions, and economic values.

Mood: The prevailing emotions of a work or of the author in his or her creation of the work. The mood of a work is not always what might be expected based on its subject matter.

Motif: A theme, character type, image, metaphor, or other verbal element that recurs throughout a single work of literature or occurs in a number of different works over a period of time.

Myth: An anonymous tale emerging from the traditional beliefs of a culture or social unit. Myths use supernatural explanations for natural phenomena. They may also explain cosmic issues like creation and death. Collections of myths, known as mythologies, are common to all cultures and nations, but the best-known myths belong to the Norse, Roman, and Greek mythologies.

N

Narration: The telling of a series of events, real or invented. A narration may be either a simple narrative, in which the events are recounted chronologically, or a narrative with a plot, in which the account is given in a style reflecting the author's artistic concept of the story. Narration is sometimes used as a synonym for "storyline."

Narrative: A verse or prose accounting of an event or sequence of events, real or invented. The term is also used as an adjective in the sense "method of narration." For example, in literary criticism, the expression "narrative technique" usually refers to the way the author structures and presents his or her story.

Narrator: The teller of a story. The narrator may be the author or a character in the story through whom the author speaks.

Naturalism: A literary movement of the late nineteenth and early twentieth centuries. The movement's major theorist, French novelist Emile Zola, envisioned a type of fiction that would examine human life with the objectivity of scientific inquiry. The Naturalists typically viewed human beings as either the products of "biological determinism," ruled by hereditary instincts and engaged in an endless struggle for survival, or as the products of "socioeconomic determinism," ruled by social and economic forces beyond their control. In their works, the Naturalists generally ignored the highest levels of society and focused on degradation: poverty, alcoholism, prostitution, insanity, and disease.

Noble Savage: The idea that primitive man is noble and good but becomes evil and corrupted as he becomes civilized. The concept of the noble savage originated in the Renaissance period but is more closely identified with such later writers as Jean-Jacques Rousseau and Aphra Behn.

Novel: A long fictional narrative written in prose, which developed from the novella and other early forms of narrative. A novel is usually organized under a plot or theme with a focus on character development and action.

Novel of Ideas: A novel in which the examination of intellectual issues and concepts takes precedence over characterization or a traditional storyline.

Novel of Manners: A novel that examines the customs and mores of a cultural group.

Novella: An Italian term meaning "story." This term has been especially used to describe fourteenth-century Italian tales, but it also refers to modern short novels.

O

Objective Correlative: An outward set of objects, a situation, or a chain of events corresponding to an inward experience and evoking this experience in the reader. The term frequently appears in modern criticism in discussions of authors' intended effects on the emotional responses of readers.

Objectivity: A quality in writing characterized by the absence of the author's opinion or feeling about the subject matter. Objectivity is an important factor in criticism.

Oedipus Complex: A son's amorous obsession with his mother. The phrase is derived from the story of the ancient Theban hero Oedipus, who unknowingly killed his father and married his mother.

Omniscience: See *Point of View*

Onomatopoeia: The use of words whose sounds express or suggest their meaning. In its simplest sense, onomatopoeia may be represented by words that mimic the sounds they denote such as "hiss" or "meow." At a more subtle level, the pattern and rhythm of sounds and rhymes of a line or poem may be onomatopoeic.

Oxymoron: A phrase combining two contradictory terms. Oxymorons may be intentional or unintentional.

P

Parable: A story intended to teach a moral lesson or answer an ethical question.

Paradox: A statement that appears illogical or contradictory at first, but may actually point to an underlying truth.

Parallelism: A method of comparison of two ideas in which each is developed in the same grammatical structure.

Parody: In literary criticism, this term refers to an imitation of a serious literary work or the signature style of a particular author in a ridiculous manner. A typical parody adopts the style of the original and applies it to an inappropriate subject for humorous effect. Parody is a form of satire and could be considered the literary equivalent of a caricature or cartoon.

Pastoral: A term derived from the Latin word "pastor," meaning shepherd. A pastoral is a literary composition on a rural theme. The conventions of the pastoral were originated by the third-century Greek poet Theocritus, who wrote about the experiences, love affairs, and pastimes of Sicilian shepherds. In a pastoral, characters and language of a courtly nature are often placed in a simple setting. The term pastoral is also used to classify dramas, elegies, and lyrics that exhibit the use of country settings and shepherd characters.

Pen Name: See *Pseudonym*

Persona: A Latin term meaning "mask." *Personae* are the characters in a fictional work of literature. The *persona* generally functions as a mask through which the author tells a story in a voice other than his or her own. A *persona* is usually either a character in a story who acts as a narrator or an "implied author," a voice created by the author to act as the narrator for himself or herself.

Personification: A figure of speech that gives human qualities to abstract ideas, animals, and inanimate objects.

Picaresque Novel: Episodic fiction depicting the adventures of a roguish central character ("picaro" is Spanish for "rogue"). The picaresque hero is commonly a low-born but clever individual who wanders into and out of various affairs of love, danger, and farcical intrigue. These involvements may take place at all social levels and typically present a humorous and wide-ranging satire of a given society.

Plagiarism: Claiming another person's written material as one's own. Plagiarism can take the form of direct, word-for-word copying or the theft of the substance or idea of the work.

Plot: In literary criticism, this term refers to the pattern of events in a narrative or drama. In its simplest sense, the plot guides the author in composing the work and helps the reader follow the work. Typically, plots exhibit causality and unity and have a beginning, a middle, and an end. Sometimes, however, a plot may consist of a series of disconnected events, in which case it is known as an "episodic plot."

Poetic Justice: An outcome in a literary work, not necessarily a poem, in which the good are rewarded and the evil are punished, especially in ways that particularly fit their virtues or crimes.

Poetic License: Distortions of fact and literary convention made by a writer—not always a poet—for the sake of the effect gained. Poetic license is closely related to the concept of "artistic freedom."

Poetics: This term has two closely related meanings. It denotes (1) an aesthetic theory in literary criticism about the essence of poetry or (2) rules prescribing the proper methods, content, style, or diction of poetry. The term poetics may also refer to theories about literature in general, not just poetry.

Point of View: The narrative perspective from which a literary work is presented to the reader. There are four traditional points of view. The "third person omniscient" gives the reader a "godlike" perspective, unrestricted by time or place, from which to see actions and look into the minds of characters. This allows the author to comment openly on characters and events in the work. The "third person" point of view presents the events of the story from outside of any single character's perception, much like the omniscient point of view, but the reader must understand the action as it takes place and without any special insight into characters' minds or motivations. The "first person" or "personal" point of view relates events as they are perceived by a single character. The main character "tells" the story and may offer opinions about the action and characters which differ from those of the author. Much less common than omniscient, third person, and first person is the "second person" point of view, wherein the author tells the story as if it is happening to the reader.

Polemic: A work in which the author takes a stand on a controversial subject, such as abortion or religion. Such works are often extremely argumentative or provocative.

Pornography: Writing intended to provoke feelings of lust in the reader. Such works are often condemned by critics and teachers, but those which can be shown to have literary value are viewed less harshly.

Post-Aesthetic Movement: An artistic response made by African Americans to the black aesthetic movement of the 1960s and early '70s. Writers since that time have adopted a somewhat different tone in their work, with less emphasis placed on the disparity between black and white in the United States. In the words of post-aesthetic authors such as Toni Morrison, John Edgar Wideman, and Kristin Hunter, African Americans are portrayed as looking inward for answers to their own questions, rather than always looking to the outside world.

Postmodernism: Writing from the 1960s forward characterized by experimentation and continuing to apply some of the fundamentals of modernism, which included existentialism and alienation. Postmodernists have gone a step further in the rejection of tradition begun with the modernists by also rejecting traditional forms, preferring the anti-novel over the novel and the anti-hero over the hero.

Primitivism: The belief that primitive peoples were nobler and less flawed than civilized peoples because they had not been subjected to the tainting influence of society.

Prologue: An introductory section of a literary work. It often contains information establishing the situation of the characters or presents information about the setting, time period, or action. In drama, the prologue is spoken by a chorus or by one of the principal characters.

Prose: A literary medium that attempts to mirror the language of everyday speech. It is distinguished from poetry by its use of unmetered, unrhymed language consisting of logically related sentences. Prose is usually grouped into paragraphs that form a cohesive whole such as an essay or a novel.

Prosopopoeia: See *Personification*

Protagonist: The central character of a story who serves as a focus for its themes and incidents and as the principal rationale for its development. The protagonist is sometimes referred to in discussions of modern literature as the hero or anti-hero.

Protest Fiction: Protest fiction has as its primary purpose the protesting of some social injustice, such as racism or discrimination.

Proverb: A brief, sage saying that expresses a truth about life in a striking manner.

Pseudonym: A name assumed by a writer, most often intended to prevent his or her identification as the author of a work. Two or more authors may work together under one pseudonym, or an author may use a different name for each genre he or she publishes in. Some publishing companies maintain "house pseudonyms," under which any number of authors may write installations in a series. Some authors also choose a pseudonym over their real names the way an actor may use a stage name.

Pun: A play on words that have similar sounds but different meanings.

R

Realism: A nineteenth-century European literary movement that sought to portray familiar characters, situations, and settings in a realistic manner. This was done primarily by using an objective narrative point of view and through the buildup of accurate detail. The standard for success of any realistic work depends on how faithfully it transfers common experience into fictional forms. The realistic method may be altered or extended, as in stream of consciousness writing, to record highly subjective experience.

Repartee: Conversation featuring snappy retorts and witticisms.

Resolution: The portion of a story following the climax, in which the conflict is resolved.

Rhetoric: In literary criticism, this term denotes the art of ethical persuasion. In its strictest sense, rhetoric adheres to various principles developed since classical times for arranging facts and ideas in a clear, persuasive, appealing manner. The term is also used to refer to effective prose in general and theories of or methods for composing effective prose.

Rhetorical Question: A question intended to provoke thought, but not an expressed answer, in the reader. It is most commonly used in oratory and other persuasive genres.

Rising Action: The part of a drama where the plot becomes increasingly complicated. Rising action leads up to the climax, or turning point, of a drama.

Roman à clef: A French phrase meaning "novel with a key." It refers to a narrative in which real persons are portrayed under fictitious names.

Romance: A broad term, usually denoting a narrative with exotic, exaggerated, often idealized characters, scenes, and themes.

Romanticism: This term has two widely accepted meanings. In historical criticism, it refers to a European intellectual and artistic movement of the late eighteenth and early nineteenth centuries that sought greater freedom of personal expression than that allowed by the strict rules of literary form and logic of the eighteenth-century neoclassicists. The Romantics preferred emotional and imaginative expression to rational analysis. They considered the individual to be at the center of all experience and so placed him or her at the center of their art. The Romantics believed that the creative imagination reveals nobler truths—unique feelings and attitudes—than those that could be discovered by logic or by scientific examination. Both the natural world and the state of childhood were important sources for revelations of "eternal truths." "Romanticism" is also used as a general term to refer to a type of sensibility found in all periods of literary history and usually considered to be in opposition to the principles of classicism. In this sense, Romanticism signifies any work or philosophy in which the exotic or dreamlike figure strongly, or that is devoted to individualistic expression, self-analysis, or a pursuit of a higher realm of knowledge than can be discovered by human reason.

Romantics: See *Romanticism*

S

Satire: A work that uses ridicule, humor, and wit to criticize and provoke change in human nature and institutions. There are two major types of satire: "formal" or "direct" satire speaks directly to the reader or to a character in the work; "indirect" satire relies upon the ridiculous behavior of its characters to make its point. Formal satire is further divided into two manners: the "Horatian," which ridicules gently, and the "Juvenalian," which derides its subjects harshly and bitterly.

Science Fiction: A type of narrative about or based upon real or imagined scientific theories and technology. Science fiction is often peopled with alien creatures and set on other planets or in different dimensions.

Second Person: See *Point of View*

Setting: The time, place, and culture in which the action of a narrative takes place. The elements of setting may include geographic location, characters' physical and mental environments, prevailing cultural attitudes, or the historical time in which the action takes place.

Simile: A comparison, usually using "like" or "as," of two essentially dissimilar things, as in "coffee as cold as ice" or "He sounded like a broken record."

Slang: A type of informal verbal communication that is generally unacceptable for formal writing. Slang words and phrases are often colorful exaggerations used to emphasize the speaker's point; they may also be shortened versions of an often-used word or phrase.

Slave Narrative: Autobiographical accounts of American slave life as told by escaped slaves. These works first appeared during the abolition movement of the 1830s through the 1850s.

Socialist Realism: The Socialist Realism school of literary theory was proposed by Maxim Gorky and established as a dogma by the first Soviet Congress of Writers. It demanded adherence to a communist worldview in works of literature. Its doctrines required an objective viewpoint comprehensible to the working classes and themes of social struggle featuring strong proletarian heroes.

Stereotype: A stereotype was originally the name for a duplication made during the printing process; this led to its modern definition as a person or thing that is (or is assumed to be) the same as all others of its type.

Stream of Consciousness: A narrative technique for rendering the inward experience of a character. This technique is designed to give the impression of an ever-changing series of thoughts, emotions, images, and memories in the spontaneous and seemingly illogical order that they occur in life.

Structure: The form taken by a piece of literature. The structure may be made obvious for ease of understanding, as in nonfiction works, or may obscured for artistic purposes, as in some poetry or seemingly "unstructured" prose.

Sturm und Drang: A German term meaning "storm and stress." It refers to a German literary movement of the 1770s and 1780s that reacted against the order and rationalism of the enlightenment, focusing instead on the intense experience of extraordinary individuals.

Style: A writer's distinctive manner of arranging words to suit his or her ideas and purpose in writing. The unique imprint of the author's personality upon his or her writing, style is the product of an author's way of arranging ideas and his or her use of diction, different sentence structures, rhythm, figures of speech, rhetorical principles, and other elements of composition.

Subjectivity: Writing that expresses the author's personal feelings about his subject, and which may or may not include factual information about the subject.

Subplot: A secondary story in a narrative. A subplot may serve as a motivating or complicating force for the main plot of the work, or it may provide emphasis for, or relief from, the main plot.

Surrealism: A term introduced to criticism by Guillaume Apollinaire and later adopted by Andre Breton. It refers to a French literary and artistic movement founded in the 1920s. The Surrealists sought to express unconscious thoughts and feelings in their works. The best-known technique used for achieving this aim was automatic writing—transcriptions of spontaneous outpourings from the unconscious. The Surrealists proposed to unify the contrary levels of conscious and unconscious, dream and reality, objectivity and subjectivity into a new level of "super-realism."

Suspense: A literary device in which the author maintains the audience's attention through the buildup of events, the outcome of which will soon be revealed.

Symbol: Something that suggests or stands for something else without losing its original identity. In literature, symbols combine their literal meaning with the suggestion of an abstract concept. Literary symbols are of two types: those that carry complex associations of

meaning no matter what their contexts, and those that derive their suggestive meaning from their functions in specific literary works.

Symbolism: This term has two widely accepted meanings. In historical criticism, it denotes an early modernist literary movement initiated in France during the nineteenth century that reacted against the prevailing standards of realism. Writers in this movement aimed to evoke, indirectly and symbolically, an order of being beyond the material world of the five senses. Poetic expression of personal emotion figured strongly in the movement, typically by means of a private set of symbols uniquely identifiable with the individual poet. The principal aim of the Symbolists was to express in words the highly complex feelings that grew out of everyday contact with the world. In a broader sense, the term "symbolism" refers to the use of one object to represent another.

T

Tall Tale: A humorous tale told in a straightforward, credible tone but relating absolutely impossible events or feats of the characters. Such tales were commonly told of frontier adventures during the settlement of the west in the United States.

Theme: The main point of a work of literature. The term is used interchangeably with thesis.

Thesis: A thesis is both an essay and the point argued in the essay. Thesis novels and thesis plays share the quality of containing a thesis which is supported through the action of the story.

Third Person: See *Point of View*

Tone: The author's attitude toward his or her audience may be deduced from the tone of the work. A formal tone may create distance or convey politeness, while an informal tone may encourage a friendly, intimate, or intrusive feeling in the reader. The author's attitude toward his or her subject matter may also be deduced from the tone of the words he or she uses in discussing it.

Transcendentalism: An American philosophical and religious movement, based in New England from around 1835 until the Civil War. Transcendentalism was a form of American romanticism that had its roots abroad in the works of Thomas Carlyle, Samuel Coleridge, and Johann Wolfgang von Goethe. The Transcendentalists stressed the importance of intuition and subjective experience in communication with God. They rejected religious dogma and texts in favor of mysticism and scientific naturalism. They pursued truths that lie beyond the "colorless" realms perceived by reason and the senses and were active social reformers in public education, women's rights, and the abolition of slavery.

U

Urban Realism: A branch of realist writing that attempts to accurately reflect the often harsh facts of modern urban existence.

Utopia: A fictional perfect place, such as "paradise" or "heaven."

V

Verisimilitude: Literally, the appearance of truth. In literary criticism, the term refers to aspects of a work of literature that seem true to the reader.

Victorian: Refers broadly to the reign of Queen Victoria of England (1837-1901) and to anything with qualities typical of that era. For example, the qualities of smug narrowmindedness, bourgeois materialism, faith in social progress, and priggish morality are often considered Victorian. This stereotype is contradicted by such dramatic intellectual developments as the theories of Charles Darwin, Karl Marx, and Sigmund Freud (which stirred strong debates in England) and the critical attitudes of serious Victorian writers like Charles Dickens and George Eliot. In literature, the Victorian Period was the great age of the English novel, and the latter part of the era saw the rise of movements such as decadence and symbolism.

W

Weltanschauung: A German term referring to a person's worldview or philosophy.

Weltschmerz: A German term meaning "world pain." It describes a sense of anguish about the nature of existence, usually associated with a melancholy, pessimistic attitude.

Z

Zeitgeist: A German term meaning "spirit of the time." It refers to the moral and intellectual trends of a given era.

Cumulative Author/Title Index

Cumulative Nationality/ Ethnicity Index

Alvarez, Julia
  How the Garcia Girls Lost Their Accents: V5
  In the Time of Butterflies: V9
  Return to Sender: V42
Anaya, Rudolfo
  Bless Me, Ultima: V12
Anderson, Laurie Halse
  Fever 1793: V35
  Speak: V31
Anderson, M. T.
  Feed: V41
Anderson, Sherwood
  Winesburg, Ohio: V4
Angelou, Maya
  I Know Why the Caged Bird Sings: V2
Asimov, Isaac
  I, Robot: V29
Auel, Jean
  The Clan of the Cave Bear: V11
Avi
  Nothing But the Truth: A Documentary Novel: V34
Bambara, Toni Cade
  The Salt Eaters: V44
Banks, Russell
  The Sweet Hereafter: V13
Barrows, Annie
  The Guernsey Literary and Potato Peel Society: V43
Baskin, Nora Raleigh
  Anything but Typical: V43
Baum, L. Frank
  The Wizard of Oz (Motion picture): V43
  The Wonderful Wizard of Oz: V13
Bellamy, Edward
  Looking Backward: 2000–1887: V15
Bellow, Saul
  The Adventures of Augie March: V33
  Herzog: V14
  Humboldt's Gift: V26
  Seize the Day: V4
Benitez, Sandra
  A Place Where the Sea Remembers: V32
Bloor, Edward
  Tangerine: V33
Blume, Judy
  Forever...: V24
Borland, Hal
  When the Legends Die: V18
Boyle, T. C.
  The Tortilla Curtain: V41
Bradbury, Ray
  Dandelion Wine: V22
  Fahrenheit 451: V1
  The Martian Chronicles: V42

Something Wicked This Way Comes: V29
Bradley, Marion Zimmer
  The Mists of Avalon: V40
Bridal, Tessa
  The Tree of Red Stars: V17
Brown, Rita Mae
  Rubyfruit Jungle: V9
Buck, Pearl S.
  The Good Earth: V25
Burdick, Eugene J.
  The Ugly American: V23
Burns, Olive Ann
  Cold Sassy Tree: V31
Butler, Octavia
  Kindred: V8
  Parable of the Sower: V21
  Patternmaster: V34
Card, Orson Scott
  Ender's Game: V5
Cather, Willa
  Death Comes for the Archbishop: V19
  A Lost Lady: V33
  My Ántonia: V2
  The Song of the Lark: V41
Chabon, Michael
  The Amazing Adventures of Kavalier & Clay: V25
Chandler, Raymond
  The Big Sleep: V17
Chesnutt, Charles Waddell
  The House behind the Cedars: V45
Chevalier, Tracy
  Girl with a Pearl Earring: V45
Chin, Frank
  Donald Duk: V41
Choi, Sook Nyul
  Year of Impossible Goodbyes: V29
Chopin, Kate
  The Awakening: V3
Cisneros, Sandra
  The House on Mango Street: V2
Clark, Walter Van Tilburg
  The Ox-Bow Incident: V40
Clavell, James du Maresq
  Shogun: A Novel of Japan: V10
Cleage, Pearl
  What Looks Like Crazy on an Ordinary Day: V17
Clemens, Samuel Langhorne
  The Adventures of Huckleberry Finn: V1
  The Adventures of Tom Sawyer: V6
  A Connecticut Yankee in King Arthur's Court: V20
  The Prince and the Pauper: V31
Collier, Christopher
  My Brother Sam is Dead: V38
Collier, James Lincoln
  My Brother Sam is Dead: V38

Conroy, Frank
  Body and Soul: V11
Cooper, James Fenimore
  The Deerslayer: V25
  The Last of the Mohicans: V9
  The Last of the Mohicans (Motion picture): V32
  The Pathfinder; or, The Inland Sea: V38
Cormier, Robert
  The Chocolate War: V2
  I Am the Cheese: V18
Crane, Stephen
  The Red Badge of Courage: V4
  Maggie: A Girl of the Streets: V20
Crichton, Michael
  The Great Train Robbery: V34
Crutcher, Chris
  The Crazy Horse Electric Game: V11
  Staying Fat for Sarah Byrnes: V32
Cunningham, Michael
  The Hours: V23
Danticat, Edwidge
  Breath, Eyes, Memory: V37
  The Dew Breaker: V28
Davis, Rebecca Harding
  Margret Howth: A Story of To-Day: V14
DeLillo, Don
  White Noise: V28
Desai, Kiran
  Hullabaloo in the Guava Orchard: V28
Diamant, Anita
  The Red Tent: V36
Dick, Philip K.
  Do Androids Dream of Electric Sheep?: V5
  Martian Time-Slip: V26
Dickey, James
  Deliverance: V9
Didion, Joan
  Democracy: V3
Doctorow, E. L.
  Ragtime: V6
  Ragtime (Motion picture): V44
Dorris, Michael
  A Yellow Raft in Blue Water: V3
Dos Passos, John
  U.S.A.: V14
Draper, Sharon
  Tears of a Tiger: V42
Dreiser, Theodore
  An American Tragedy: V17
  Sister Carrie: V8
Ellis, Bret Easton
  Less Than Zero: V11
Ellison, Ralph
  Invisible Man: V2
  Juneteenth: V21

The Joys of Motherhood: V41
The Wrestling Match: V14

Norwegian
Rölvaag, O. E.
 Giants in the Earth: V5

Polish
Conrad, Joseph
 Heart of Darkness: V2
 Lord Jim: V16
Kosinski, Jerzy
 The Painted Bird: V12

Portuguese
Saramago, José
 Blindness: V27

Romanian
Wiesel, Eliezer
 Night: V4

Russian
Asimov, Isaac
 I, Robot: V29
Bulgakov, Mikhail
 The Master and Margarita: V8
Dostoyevsky, Fyodor
 The Brothers Karamazov: V8
 Crime and Punishment: V3
 The Idiot: V40
 Notes from Underground: V28
Nabokov, Vladimir
 Lolita: V9
Pasternak, Boris
 Doctor Zhivago: V26
 Doctor Zhivago (Motion picture):
  V41
Rand, Ayn
 Anthem: V29
 Atlas Shrugged: V10
 The Fountainhead: V16

Solzhenitsyn, Aleksandr
 *One Day in the Life of Ivan
  Denisovich:* V6
Tolstoy, Leo
 Anna Karenina: V28
 War and Peace: V10
Turgenev, Ivan
 Fathers and Sons: V16
Yezierska, Anzia
 Bread Givers: V29

Scottish
Grahame, Kenneth
 The Wind in the Willows: V20
Scott, Walter
 Ivanhoe: V31
Spark, Muriel
 The Prime of Miss Jean Brodie:
  V22
Stevenson, Robert Louis
 Kidnapped: V33
 Treasure Island: V20

South African
Coetzee, J. M.
 Dusklands: V21
Courtenay, Bryce
 The Power of One: V32
Gordimer, Nadine
 July's People: V4
Gordon, Sheila
 Waiting for the Rain: V40
Head, Bessie
 When Rain Clouds Gather: V31
Magona, Sindiwe
 Mother to Mother: V43
Paton, Alan
 Cry, the Beloved Country: V3
 Too Late the Phalarope: V12

Spanish
de Cervantes Saavedra, Miguel
 Don Quixote: V8

Jiménez, Juan Ramón
 Platero and I: V36

Sri Lankan
Ondaatje, Michael
 The English Patient: V23

Swedish
Spiegelman, Art
 Maus: A Survivor's Tale: V35

Swiss
Hesse, Hermann
 Demian: V15
 Siddhartha: V6
 Steppenwolf: V24

Trinidad and Tobagoan
Naipaul, V. S.
 A Bend in the River: V37
 Half a Life: V39

Turkish
Pamuk, Orhan
 My Name is Red: V27

Uruguayan
Bridal, Tessa
 The Tree of Red Stars: V17

Vietnamese
Duong Thu Huong
 Paradise of the Blind: V23

West Indian
Kincaid, Jamaica
 Annie John: V3

Zimbabwean
Dangarembga, Tsitsi
 Nervous Conditions: V28

Subject/Theme Index

Coincidence
  The House behind the Cedars:
    120–121, 126
Coming of age
  Banner in the Sky: 8
  Sons and Lovers: 189
  Stargirl: 215
  Sunrise over Fallujah: 226, 234
Community
  Desirable Daughters: 65, 66
  Sunrise over Fallujah: 244
  The Way to Rainy Mountain: 274,
    275, 288, 289
Competition
  Banner in the Sky: 17
Confinement
  Wuthering Heights: 313–314
Conflict
  Never Let Me Go: 174
  Sons and Lovers: 197, 199–200
  Stargirl: 210, 213, 219
Conformity
  Desirable Daughters: 51
  Stargirl: 204, 206, 211, 213–217,
    221, 223–224
Confusion
  The House behind the Cedars: 132
  A Map of the World: 153–154
  Sons and Lovers: 195
  Sunrise over Fallujah: 226
Connectedness
  Desirable Daughters: 63, 64
  The House behind the Cedars: 133
  The Way to Rainy Mountain: 277,
    289
  Wuthering Heights: 314
Conscience. *See* Morality
Contradiction
  The House behind the Cedars: 132
  Wuthering Heights: 298
Contrast
  Girl with a Pearl Earring: 76, 80–82
  The Heart of the Matter: 108
  Stargirl: 211
  Wuthering Heights: 310, 312
Control (Psychology)
  Desirable Daughters: 56–58
  Girl with a Pearl Earring: 75–76
  Sons and Lovers: 199
Cooperation
  Banner in the Sky: 5, 6, 8–9
Corruption
  The Heart of the Matter: 105, 109
  A Map of the World: 148
Courage
  Sunrise over Fallujah: 33
Cowardice
  The Heart of the Matter: 109
Crime
  Desirable Daughters: 63
Cultural conflict
  Desirable Daughters: 43, 50–51, 56

Cultural identity
  Desirable Daughters: 43, 49, 52,
    56–58, 60–61, 63, 66
  The Way to Rainy Mountain: 275,
    277, 287
  Wuthering Heights: 308
Culture
  Wuthering Heights: 308

D

Daily living
  Sunrise over Fallujah: 244
Death
  The Heart of the Matter: 107
  The House behind the Cedars: 134
  Never Let Me Go: 171
  Sunrise over Fallujah: 233
  Swallowing Stones: 248, 250
Decay
  The Heart of the Matter: 109
  A Map of the World: 148
Deception
  Desirable Daughters: 43, 49, 50, 58
  A Map of the World: 153
  Sons and Lovers: 198
  Swallowing Stones: 267
Defiance
  The Heart of the Matter: 107
Delusions
  A Map of the World: 150
Denial
  The House behind the Cedars: 130
  A Map of the World: 138, 140–142,
    150
Dependence
  Sons and Lovers: 187, 193, 196
Depression (Psychology)
  Swallowing Stones: 260–261
Desire
  Girl with a Pearl Earring: 86
  Sons and Lovers: 194
Despair
  The Heart of the Matter: 105
  Swallowing Stones: 263
Destiny
  Banner in the Sky: 14–17
Destruction
  Wuthering Heights: 303
Detachment
  Never Let Me Go: 161
  Sons and Lovers: 199
Devotion
  The House behind the Cedars: 116
  Sons and Lovers: 186, 194
Dialect. *See* Language and
    languages
Difference
  Stargirl: 223, 224
Dishonesty
  The Heart of the Matter: 108
Disorder
  Girl with a Pearl Earring: 76

Distance
  Sons and Lovers: 199
Doubt
  A Map of the World: 140
Dreams
  Swallowing Stones: 264
Dualism
  Wuthering Heights: 310
Duty
  Banner in the Sky: 18
  Desirable Daughters: 66
Dystopias
  Never Let Me Go: 165, 175

E

Eastern philosophy
  Banner in the Sky: 14–17
  Stargirl: 220
Economics
  A Map of the World: 152
Embarrassment
  Stargirl: 207
Emotions
  Sons and Lovers: 195
  Swallowing Stones: 267
  Wuthering Heights: 300, 310,
    312, 313
Empathy
  Stargirl: 219
  Swallowing Stones: 263
Emptiness (Psychology)
  Wuthering Heights: 314
English history
  Sons and Lovers: 190–192
Enlightenment (Psychology). *See*
  Revelation
Epistolary novels
  Sunrise over Fallujah: 237
Eroticism. *See* Sexuality
Escape
  The House behind the Cedars:
    129–130
Ethics
  Banner in the Sky: 19
  Cimarron: 33
  Never Let Me Go: 168, 173–175
Ethnic identity
  The House behind the Cedars: 112,
    114, 119, 124–126, 129, 130,
    132–134
Evil
  Never Let Me Go: 161
  Wuthering Heights: 311
Exploitation
  Never Let Me Go: 173
Exposure
  Girl with a Pearl Earring: 85

F

Faith
  A Map of the World: 140

Family
  Desirable Daughters: 66
  Girl with a Pearl Earring: 74–75
  The House behind the Cedars: 133
  A Map of the World: 152–153
  Sons and Lovers: 179
  The Way to Rainy Mountain: 283, 288, 289
  Wuthering Heights: 303
Father-child relationships
  Sons and Lovers: 181
Fear
  Sons and Lovers: 181, 195
  Swallowing Stones: 267
Female identity
  Desirable Daughters: 64–67
Female-male relations
  Girl with a Pearl Earring: 81–84
  Sons and Lovers: 195–196, 199–202
  Wuthering Heights: 309
Femininity
  The House behind the Cedars: 130–131
  Wuthering Heights: 308–309
Feminism
  Cimarron: 28
  Desirable Daughters: 65
  Girl with a Pearl Earring: 82–84
Flashbacks
  Never Let Me Go: 166–167
Folk culture
  Wuthering Heights: 300
Forgiveness
  Swallowing Stones: 266
Freedom
  Banner in the Sky: 7–8
  Girl with a Pearl Earring: 84
  Wuthering Heights: 314
Frontier life
  Cimarron: 19, 23, 31, 38–41

G

Ghosts
  Banner in the Sky: 18
Global perspective
  Desirable Daughters: 63
God
  A Map of the World: 148–149
Good and evil
  A Map of the World: 148, 149
  Wuthering Heights: 311
Goodness
  Stargirl: 221
Gossip
  A Map of the World: 145, 152
Gothicism
  A Map of the World: 136, 148–151
  Wuthering Heights: 293, 300, 305
Grace (Theology)
  A Map of the World: 153–154
Greed
  Wuthering Heights: 309

Grief
  A Map of the World: 142
  Sons and Lovers: 197
  Sunrise over Fallujah: 234
  Swallowing Stones: 263
Group hysteria
  A Map of the World: 145–146
Guilt (Psychology)
  The Heart of the Matter: 107
  A Map of the World: 142, 152–154
  Swallowing Stones: 248, 253, 256–258, 263

H

Happiness
  The Heart of the Matter: 106
Hatred
  Sons and Lovers: 181, 186
  Stargirl: 223
Healing
  Swallowing Stones: 265
Helpfulness
  Banner in the Sky: 18
Helplessness
  Girl with a Pearl Earring: 82
Heritage
  Banner in the Sky: 18
  Cimarron: 36–37
  Desirable Daughters: 57, 58
  The House behind the Cedars: 116, 130
  The Way to Rainy Mountain: 289
Heroism
  The House behind the Cedars: 128
  Sunrise over Fallujah: 242
Hinduism
  Desirable Daughters: 43, 50–51, 53–54
Historical fiction
  Banner in the Sky: 9–10
  Cimarron: 30, 38–41
  Girl with a Pearl Earring: 86–87
  The Way to Rainy Mountain: 287
Homosexuality
  Desirable Daughters: 48, 49, 52
Honor
  Banner in the Sky: 17
Hope
  Never Let Me Go: 171, 173
Hopelessness
  Sunrise over Fallujah: 239–240
Human nature
  The Heart of the Matter: 105
  A Map of the World: 148
Humanity
  Never Let Me Go: 165, 172
Humiliation
  Stargirl: 208
  Wuthering Heights: 296, 297
Humor
  Sunrise over Fallujah: 237

Husband-wife relationships
  Cimarron: 28
  Sons and Lovers: 198, 202
Hysteria. *See* Group hysteria

I

Idealism
  Cimarron: 33
  A Map of the World: 151, 153
Identity
  Desirable Daughters: 43, 52, 64–67
  The House behind the Cedars: 119, 132–134
  Sons and Lovers: 179
  Stargirl: 217
  The Way to Rainy Mountain: 282–286, 288
Ideology
  The House behind the Cedars: 132, 133
Imagery (Literature)
  Girl with a Pearl Earring: 77
Imagination
  The Way to Rainy Mountain: 289
Immigrant life
  Desirable Daughters: 51–52, 56
Imprisonment
  The House behind the Cedars: 132
  Never Let Me Go: 172–173
Independence
  Banner in the Sky: 5
  Cimarron: 25
  Girl with a Pearl Earring: 84
  Sons and Lovers: 200, 201
Indian culture
  Desirable Daughters: 43, 53–54, 59–61
Indian history
  Desirable Daughters: 53
Individual *vs.* society
  Never Let Me Go: 156
  Stargirl: 210, 213, 222, 223–224
Individualism
  Stargirl: 212–214
Individuality. *See* Uniqueness
Industrialization
  The House behind the Cedars: 120
Injustice
  The Heart of the Matter: 105
  Wuthering Heights: 312
Intellectualism
  Sons and Lovers: 201–202
Intertextuality
  A Map of the World: 145
Intuition
  Swallowing Stones: 248, 258–259
Iraq War, 2003-2011
  Sunrise over Fallujah: 226, 228–232, 237–241
Irony
  The House behind the Cedars: 130
  A Map of the World: 152

P

Pain
Girl with a Pearl Earring: 86
Sons and Lovers: 195, 200
Stargirl: 222
Swallowing Stones: 264

Paradoxes
Wuthering Heights: 312–313

Parent-child relationships
Sons and Lovers: 187
Swallowing Stones: 266

Passion
Girl with a Pearl Earring: 76, 86
Sons and Lovers: 187, 195
Wuthering Heights: 312

Past
The Way to Rainy Mountain: 277,
288, 290

Patriarchy
Desirable Daughters: 65

Perception (Psychology)
Sons and Lovers: 198–199

Persecution
A Map of the World: 136

Pilgrimages
Wuthering Heights: 308

Pity
The Heart of the Matter: 91, 108, 109

Place
The Way to Rainy Mountain:
289–291

Point of view (Literature)
The Heart of the Matter: 99–100
The House behind the Cedars: 120
Sons and Lovers: 198–199
Swallowing Stones: 267

Politics
A Map of the World: 152

Popular culture
Girl with a Pearl Earring: 79

Postmodernism
The Way to Rainy Mountain: 278
Wuthering Heights: 305

Poverty
Sons and Lovers: 200

Power (Philosophy)
Girl with a Pearl Earring: 82, 86
Sons and Lovers: 200

Prejudice
Cimarron: 29, 34–35
The House behind the Cedars: 129

Pride
Banner in the Sky: 17, 19
Sons and Lovers: 201

Protectiveness
Sons and Lovers: 187, 194, 195

Psychology
Sons and Lovers: 193
Stargirl: 217–220
Swallowing Stones: 267
Wuthering Heights: 293, 300, 305

Q

Questing
Banner in the Sky: 1
The Way to Rainy Mountain: 289

R

Race relations
The House behind the Cedars: 112,
117–119, 124, 128–129

Racial identity. *See* Ethnic identity

Racism
Cimarron: 35
The Heart of the Matter: 105
The House behind the Cedars: 128,
133
Wuthering Heights: 298

Rage. *See* Anger

Rationality
The House behind the Cedars: 130

Redemption
A Map of the World: 152, 154

Religion
The Heart of the Matter: 98–99,
108–109
A Map of the World: 138, 140–144,
148–150
Sunrise over Fallujah: 243–244

Religious beliefs
The Heart of the Matter: 96, 98–99
A Map of the World: 140

Remorse
Swallowing Stones: 256–257

Rescue
Banner in the Sky: 6

Resentment
Girl with a Pearl Earring: 73
The Heart of the Matter:
106–107
A Map of the World: 141

Responsibility
Banner in the Sky: 19
The Heart of the Matter: 109
Sons and Lovers: 202

Revelation
The Way to Rainy Mountain: 284

Revenge
A Map of the World: 141
Wuthering Heights: 297

Reverence
The Way to Rainy Mountain: 274,
285

Right and wrong
Swallowing Stones: 266

Roman Catholicism
The Heart of the Matter: 95, 96,
98–99, 102–103, 105–107, 109

Romantic love
Desirable Daughters: 66
Sons and Lovers: 179, 189

Rural life
A Map of the World: 148, 151–153

S

Sacrifice
Banner in the Sky: 18
The House behind the Cedars: 130
Never Let Me Go: 177
Sons and Lovers: 185
Sunrise over Fallujah: 241

Sadism
Wuthering Heights: 295

Salvation
A Map of the World: 138

Satire
Cimarron: 33–37

Scapegoating
A Map of the World: 152

Secrecy
Desirable Daughters: 58
Girl with a Pearl Earring: 82
Swallowing Stones: 251, 259,
266

Security
Girl with a Pearl Earring: 73

Self deception
Never Let Me Go: 172

Self destruction
Wuthering Heights: 310

Self identity
The House behind the Cedars: 119
The Way to Rainy Mountain:
282–286, 289

Self image
Never Let Me Go: 165

Self improvement
Banner in the Sky: 8, 14–17

Self judgment
The House behind the Cedars:
124–126

Self knowledge
Sons and Lovers: 200
The Way to Rainy Mountain:
289

Selfishness
Girl with a Pearl Earring: 74
A Map of the World: 142
Sons and Lovers: 195
Swallowing Stones: 265
Wuthering Heights: 310

Sensitivity
Sons and Lovers: 194

Sentimentality
The House behind the Cedars:
130–131

Separation (Psychology)
Sons and Lovers: 199

Servitude
Girl with a Pearl Earring: 87–88

Setting (Literature)
Cimarron: 30–31
The Heart of the Matter: 100,
103–106
Sunrise over Fallujah: 244

Sex roles
 The House behind the Cedars:
  123–124
 Sons and Lovers: 179, 201–202
Sexuality
 Girl with a Pearl Earring: 86, 88
 A Map of the World: 150–151
 Sons and Lovers: 197, 199
Similes
 Girl with a Pearl Earring: 76
Simplicity
 A Map of the World: 147
Sin
 The Heart of the Matter: 105
Skepticism
 A Map of the World: 142
Social change
 The House behind the Cedars:
  124–126
Social class
 Desirable Daughters: 53–54, 65–67
 Girl with a Pearl Earring: 87, 88
 The House behind the Cedars:
  123–124, 129
 Sons and Lovers: 179, 180,
  190–191, 197–199
 Wuthering Heights: 296, 298, 310
Social conventions
 Girl with a Pearl Earring: 83
 The House behind the Cedars: 132
 Stargirl: 209
Social identity
 The House behind the Cedars: 134
Social realism
 Sons and Lovers: 190
Southern United States
 The House behind the Cedars:
  113–114, 120, 121–123, 132
Spaces
 Wuthering Heights: 312–314
Spirituality
 A Map of the World: 142–144, 150
 The Way to Rainy Mountain: 288,
  290
Stereotypes (Psychology)
 Cimarron: 29
 Stargirl: 223
 Wuthering Heights: 310
Storytelling
 Banner in the Sky: 10
 Cimarron: 23, 40–41
 The Way to Rainy Mountain: 273,
  287–290
Strength
 Sons and Lovers: 201
Structure (Literature)
 The Way to Rainy Mountain: 287
Suburban life
 Stargirl: 223
Success
 Cimarron: 28
 The House behind the Cedars: 126

Suffering
 Swallowing Stones: 248, 263, 264
Suicide
 The Heart of the Matter: 95, 96,
  98, 105, 107, 109
 Wuthering Heights: 310
Superiority
 The House behind the Cedars: 131
Supremacy. *See* Superiority
Survival
 The Way to Rainy Mountain: 289
Suspicion
 Girl with a Pearl Earring: 73
 The Heart of the Matter: 105
Swiss history
 Banner in the Sky: 10–13
Symbolism
 Banner in the Sky: 19
 Girl with a Pearl Earring: 77
 The Heart of the Matter: 100
 A Map of the World: 148
 Swallowing Stones: 259, 264
 Wuthering Heights: 305, 308, 313
Sympathy
 Never Let Me Go: 161

T

Taoism
 Banner in the Sky: 14–17
Teamwork. *See* Cooperation
Technology
 Never Let Me Go: 168, 174–175
Tension
 Desirable Daughters: 59–62
 Girl with a Pearl Earring: 88
 A Map of the World: 148
 Sons and Lovers: 179, 193, 195
Time
 Never Let Me Go: 166
Tone
 A Map of the World: 153
 Never Let Me Go: 156
 Sunrise over Fallujah: 242
Tradition
 Desirable Daughters: 43, 51,
  58–62, 64, 66
 The Way to Rainy Mountain: 273,
  276, 288
Tragedy (Calamities)
 Swallowing Stones: 263, 267
Transcendentalism
 Stargirl: 222–223
Transformation
 Desirable Daughters: 56, 59–60, 64
 A Map of the World: 142
 Sunrise over Fallujah: 234
 Swallowing Stones: 266
 Wuthering Heights: 308
Trauma
 Sunrise over Fallujah: 226, 234,
  235–236
 Swallowing Stones: 262

Travel
 The Way to Rainy Mountain: 271,
  275, 278, 288, 289–291
Triumph
 Banner in the Sky: 19
Truth
 A Map of the World: 152
 Sunrise over Fallujah: 240–241
 Swallowing Stones: 266

U

Understanding
 Sons and Lovers: 200
Unhappiness
 The Heart of the Matter: 93, 96,
  105
Uniqueness
 Stargirl: 204, 209, 217, 221, 222,
  296
United States history
 Cimarron: 28–30
Unity
 Wuthering Heights: 307, 308
Universality
 Stargirl: 210
 The Way to Rainy Mountain: 285,
  289
Urban life
 A Map of the World: 148

V

Vanity
 Wuthering Heights: 308–309
Victorian values
 Wuthering Heights: 298
Vietnam War, 1959-1975
 Sunrise over Fallujah: 237
Violence
 Girl with a Pearl Earring: 86
 Sons and Lovers: 186
 Sunrise over Fallujah: 226, 234,
  235–236
 Wuthering Heights: 312
Virtue
 Banner in the Sky: 14–17
 A Map of the World: 148
Vision
 The Way to Rainy Mountain: 277,
  284

W

Wars
 The Heart of the Matter: 91,
  105
 Sunrise over Fallujah: 226,
  229–230, 234, 235
Weakness
 The Heart of the Matter: 108
 Sons and Lovers: 201
 Swallowing Stones: 255